PEARSON CUSTOM
BUSINESS RESOURCES

Compiled by

Statistics for Managers
Fashion Institute of Technology

Pearson Learning Solutions

New York   Boston   San Francisco
London   Toronto   Sydney   Tokyo   Singapore   Madrid
Mexico City   Munich   Paris   Cape Town   Hong Kong   Montreal

Senior Vice President, Editorial and Marketing: Patrick F. Boles
Editor: Ana Díaz-Caneja
Development Editor: Abbey Lee Briggs
Operations Manager: Eric M. Kenney
Production Manager: Jennifer Berry
Art Director: Renée Sartell
Cover Designer: Renée Sartell

Cover Art: Courtesy of EyeWire/Getty Images and PhotoDisc/Getty Images. Photodisc, "Globe surrounded by business people on computer monitors," courtesy of Photodisc/Getty Images. Dave Cutler (Artist), "Man Dropping Coins Into Glass Jar," courtesy of David Cutler/Images.com. Dave Cutler (Artist), "Three Coins in Glass Jar," courtesy of David Cutler/Images.com. Dean Turner, "Stock Vector: Global Finance" Courtesy of Dean Turner/iStockphoto. Hal Bergman, "Refinery Silhouette" Courtesy of Hal Bergman/iStockphoto. Dan Barnes, "Cargo Container Ship Aerial View" Courtesy of Dan Barnes/iStockphoto. Franc Podgorsek, "Stock Numbers" Courtesy of Franc Podgorsek/iStockphoto. "Customer in Line at Grocery Store" Courtesy of Digital Vision Photography/Veer Inc. Owaki-Kulla, "Pumping Gas" Courtesy of Flirt Photography/Veer Inc. Lynn Johnson, "Yunnan Province, People's Republic of China" Courtesy of Lynn Johnson/Getty Images, Inc. Thomas Bendy, "Student Typing" Courtesy of Thomas Bendy/iStockphoto.

This special edition published in cooperation with Pearson Learning Solutions.

Printed in the United States of America.

Please visit our web site at *www.pearsoncustom.com.*

Attention bookstores: For permission to return any unsold stock, contact us at *pe-uscustomreturns@pearson.com.*

Pearson Learning Solutions, 501 Boylston Street, Suite 900, Boston, MA 02116
A Pearson Education Company
www.pearsoned.com

ISBN 10: 0-558-95335-2
ISBN 13: 978-0-558-95335-5

Contents

To access the media accompanying

Levine, *Statistics for Managers Using Microsoft Excel*, 5/e

Please go to the following URL:

http://www.pearsoncustom.com/us/pcbr

Enter access code:

DSWXSF-ABOIL-OKAYS-SOUGH-HAUNT-TIRES

Technical Support

Assistance is available at http://247.pearsoned.com/

Custom support number for educators: 888-Way-2-Go-CP
(888-929-2462)

Chapter 1

Analysis of Variance

USING STATISTICS @ Perfect Parachutes

LEARNING OBJECTIVES

In this chapter, you learn:

- The basic concepts of experimental design
- How to use the one-way analysis of variance to test for differences among the means of several groups
- How to use the two-way analysis of variance and interpret the interaction effect

Using Statistics @ Perfect Parachutes

You oversee production at the Perfect Parachutes Company. Parachutes are woven in your factory using a synthetic fiber purchased from one of four different suppliers. Strength of these fibers is an important characteristic that ensures quality parachutes. You need to decide whether the synthetic fibers from each of your four suppliers result in parachutes of equal strength. Furthermore, your factory uses two types of looms to produce parachutes, the *Jetta* and the *Turk*. You need to establish that the parachutes woven on both types of looms are equally strong. You also want to know if any differences in the strength of the parachute that can be attributed to the four suppliers are dependent on the type of loom used. How would you go about finding this information?

You may have previously used hypothesis testing to reach conclusions about possible differences between two populations. As a manager at Perfect Parachutes, you need to design an experiment to test the strength of parachutes woven from the synthetic fibers from the *four* suppliers. That is, you need to evaluate differences among *more than two* populations. Populations are referred to as *groups* in this chapter. This chapter begins by examining the *completely randomized design*, which has one *factor* (which supplier to use), with several groups (the four suppliers).

The completely randomized design is then extended to the *factorial design*, in which more than one factor at a time is simultaneously studied in a single experiment. For example, an experiment incorporating the four suppliers and the two types of looms would help you determine which supplier and type of loom to use in order to manufacture the strongest parachutes. Throughout the chapter, emphasis is placed on the assumptions behind the use of the various testing procedures.

1 THE COMPLETELY RANDOMIZED DESIGN: ONE-WAY ANALYSIS OF VARIANCE

In many situations, you need to examine differences among more than two **groups**. The groups involved can be classified according to **levels** of a **factor** of interest. For example, a factor such as baking temperature may have several groups defined by *numerical levels* such as 300°, 350°, 400°, 450°, and a factor such as preferred supplier for a parachute manufacturer may have several groups defined by *categorical levels* such as Supplier 1, Supplier 2, Supplier 3, Supplier 4. When there is a single factor, the experimental design is called a **completely randomized design**.

F Test for Differences Among More Than Two Means

When you are analyzing a numerical variable and certain assumptions are met, you use the **analysis of variance (ANOVA)** to compare the means of the groups. The ANOVA procedure used for the completely randomized design is referred to as the **one-way ANOVA**, and it is an extension of the *t* test for the difference between two means. Although ANOVA is an acronym for *analysis of variance*, the term is misleading because the objective is to analyze differences among the group means, *not* the variances. However, by analyzing the variation among and within the groups, you can make conclusions about possible differences in group means. In

ANOVA, the total variation is subdivided into variation that is due to differences *among* the groups and variation that is due to differences *within* the groups (see Figure 1). **Within-group variation** is considered **random error**. **Among-group variation** is due to differences from group to group. The symbol c is used to indicate the number of groups.

FIGURE 1

Partitioning the total variation in a completely randomized design

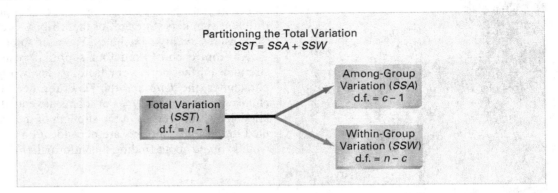

Assuming that the c groups represent populations whose values are randomly and independently selected, follow a normal distribution, and have equal variances, the null hypothesis of no differences in the population means:

$$H_0: \mu_1 = \mu_2 = \cdots = \mu_c$$

is tested against the alternative that not all the c population means are equal:

$$H_1: \text{Not all } \mu_j \text{ are equal (where } j = 1, 2, \ldots, c).$$

To perform an ANOVA test of equality of population means, you subdivide the total variation in the values into two parts—that which is due to variation among the groups and that which is due to variation within the groups. The **total variation** is represented by the **sum of squares total (SST)**. Because the population means of the c groups are assumed to be equal under the null hypothesis, you compute the total variation among all the values by summing the squared differences between each individual value and the **grand mean**, $\overline{\overline{X}}$. The grand mean is the mean of all the values in all the groups combined. Equation (1) shows the computation of the total variation.

TOTAL VARIATION IN ONE-WAY ANOVA

$$SST = \sum_{j=1}^{c} \sum_{i=1}^{n_j} (X_{ij} - \overline{\overline{X}})^2 \qquad (1)$$

where

$$\overline{\overline{X}} = \frac{\displaystyle\sum_{j=1}^{c} \sum_{i=1}^{n_j} X_{ij}}{n} = \text{Grand mean}$$

$X_{ij} = i$th value in group j

$n_j = $ number of values in group j

$n = $ total number of values in all groups combined
(that is, $n = n_1 + n_2 + \cdots + n_c$)

$c = $ number of groups

You compute the among-group variation, usually called the **sum of squares among groups (*SSA*)**, by summing the squared differences between the sample mean of each group, $\overline{X}_j$, and the grand mean, $\overline{\overline{X}}$, weighted by the sample size, n_j, in each group. Equation (2) shows the computation of the among-group variation.

AMONG-GROUP VARIATION IN ONE-WAY ANOVA

$$SSA = \sum_{j=1}^{c} n_j (\overline{X}_j - \overline{\overline{X}})^2 \qquad (2)$$

where

c = number of groups

n_j = number of values in group j

$\overline{X}_j$ = sample mean of group j

$\overline{\overline{X}}$ = grand mean

The within-group variation, usually called the **sum of squares within groups (*SSW*)**, measures the difference between each value and the mean of its own group and sums the squares of these differences over all groups. Equation (3) shows the computation of the within-group variation.

WITHIN-GROUP VARIATION IN ONE-WAY ANOVA

$$SSW = \sum_{j=1}^{c} \sum_{i=1}^{n_j} (X_{ij} - \overline{X}_j)^2 \qquad (3)$$

where

X_{ij} = ith value in group j

$\overline{X}_j$ = sample mean of group j

Because you are comparing c groups, there are $c - 1$ degrees of freedom associated with the sum of squares among groups. Because each of the c groups contributes $n_j - 1$ degrees of freedom, there are $n - c$ degrees of freedom associated with the sum of squares within groups. In addition, there are $n - 1$ degrees of freedom associated with the sum of squares total because you are comparing each value, X_{ij}, to the grand mean, $\overline{\overline{X}}$, based on all n values.

If you divide each of these sums of squares by its associated degrees of freedom, you have three variances or **mean square** terms—*MSA* (mean square among), *MSW* (mean square within), and *MST* (mean square total).

MEAN SQUARES IN ONE-WAY ANOVA

$$MSA = \frac{SSA}{c - 1} \qquad (4a)$$

$$MSW = \frac{SSW}{n - c} \qquad (4b)$$

$$MST = \frac{SST}{n - 1} \qquad (4c)$$

Although you want to compare the means of the c groups to determine whether a difference exists among them, the ANOVA procedure derives its name from the fact that you are comparing variances. If the null hypothesis is true and there are no real differences in the c group means, all three mean squares (which themselves are *variances*)—MSA, MSW, and MST—provide estimates of the overall variance in the data. Thus, to test the null hypothesis:

$$H_0: \mu_1 = \mu_2 = \cdots = \mu_c$$

against the alternative:

$$H_1: \text{Not all } \mu_j \text{ are equal (where } j = 1, 2, \ldots, c)$$

you compute the **one-way ANOVA F test statistic** as the ratio of MSA to MSW, as in Equation (5).

ONE-WAY ANOVA F TEST STATISTIC

$$F = \frac{MSA}{MSW} \tag{5}$$

The F test statistic follows an **F distribution**, with $c - 1$ degrees of freedom in the numerator and $n - c$ degrees of freedom in the denominator. For a given level of significance, α, you reject the null hypothesis if the F test statistic computed in Equation (5) is greater than the upper-tail critical value, F_U, from the F distribution having $c - 1$ degrees of freedom in the numerator and $n - c$ in the denominator (see the table of critical values of F). Thus, as shown in Figure 2, the decision rule is

Reject H_0 if $F > F_U$;
otherwise, do not reject H_0.

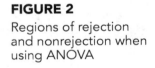

FIGURE 2

Regions of rejection and nonrejection when using ANOVA

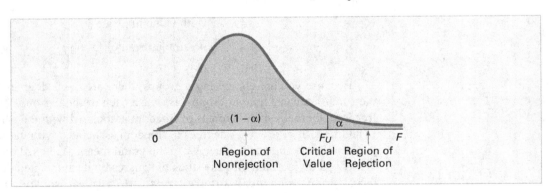

If the null hypothesis is true, the computed F statistic is expected to be approximately equal to 1 because both the numerator and denominator mean square terms are estimating the overall variance in the data. If H_0 is false (and there are real differences in the group means), the computed F statistic is expected to be substantially larger than 1 because the numerator, MSA, is estimating the differences among groups in addition to the overall variability in the values, while the denominator, MSW, is measuring only the overall variability. Thus, the ANOVA procedure provides an F test in which you reject the null hypothesis at a selected level of significance, α, only if the computed F statistic is greater than F_U, the upper-tail critical value of the F distribution having $c - 1$ and $n - c$ degrees of freedom, as illustrated in Figure 2.

The results of an analysis of variance are usually displayed in an **ANOVA summary table**, as shown in Table 1. The entries in this table include the sources of variation (that is, among-group, within-group, and total), the degrees of freedom, the sums of squares, the mean squares (that is, the variances), and the computed F statistic. In addition, Microsoft Excel includes the p-value (that is, the probability of having an F statistic as large as or larger than the one computed, given that the null hypothesis is true) in the ANOVA summary table. The p-value allows you to make direct conclusions about the null hypothesis without referring to a table of critical values of the F distribution. If the p-value is less than the chosen level of significance, α, you reject the null hypothesis.

TABLE 1

Analysis-of-Variance Summary Table

Source	Degrees of Freedom	Sum of Squares	Mean Square (Variance)	F
Among groups	$c - 1$	SSA	$MSA = \dfrac{SSA}{c - 1}$	$F = \dfrac{MSA}{MSW}$
Within groups	$n - c$	SSW	$MSW = \dfrac{SSW}{n - c}$	
Total	$n - 1$	SST		

To illustrate the one-way ANOVA F test, return to the Using Statistics scenario concerning Perfect Parachutes. An experiment was conducted to determine whether any significant differences exist in the strength of parachutes woven from synthetic fibers from the different suppliers. Five parachutes were woven for each group—Supplier 1, Supplier 2, Supplier 3, and Supplier 4. The strength of the parachutes is measured by placing them in a testing device that pulls on both ends of a parachute until it tears apart. The amount of force required to tear the parachute is measured on a tensile-strength scale, where the larger the value, the stronger the parachute. The data worksheet of the parachute.xls workbook contains the results of this experiment (in terms of tensile strength), along with the sample mean and the sample standard deviation for each group.

FIGURE 3

Data worksheet of the tensile strength for parachutes woven with synthetic fibers from four different suppliers along with the sample mean and sample standard deviation

	A	B	C	D	E
1		Supplier 1	Supplier 2	Supplier 3	Supplier 4
2		18.5	26.3	20.6	25.4
3		24.0	25.3	25.2	19.9
4		17.2	24.0	20.8	22.6
5		19.9	21.2	24.7	17.5
6		18.0	24.5	22.9	20.4
7					
8	Sample Mean	19.52	24.26	22.84	21.16
9	Sample Standard Deviation	2.69	1.92	2.13	2.98

In Figure 3, observe that there are differences in the sample means for the four suppliers. For Supplier 1, the mean tensile strength is 19.52. For Supplier 2, the mean tensile strength is 24.26. For Supplier 3, the mean tensile strength is 22.84, and for Supplier 4, the mean tensile strength is 21.16. What you need to determine is whether these sample results are sufficiently different to conclude that the *population* means are not all equal.

In the scatter plot shown in Figure 4, you can visually inspect the data and see how the measurements of tensile strength distribute. You can also observe differences among the groups as well as within groups. If the sample sizes in each group were larger, you could develop stem-and-leaf displays, box-and-whisker plots, and normal probability plots.

The null hypothesis states that there is no difference in mean tensile strength among the four suppliers:

$$H_0: \mu_1 = \mu_2 = \mu_3 = \mu_4$$

FIGURE 4

Microsoft Excel scatter plot of tensile strengths for four different suppliers

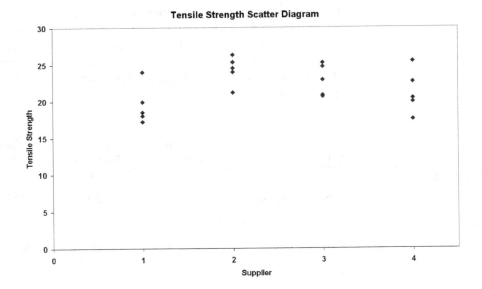

The alternative hypothesis states that at least one of the suppliers differs with respect to the mean tensile strength:

$$H_1: \text{Not all the means are equal.}$$

To construct the ANOVA summary table, you first compute the sample means in each group (see Figure 3). Then you compute the grand mean by summing all 20 values and dividing by the total number of values:

$$\overline{\overline{X}} = \frac{\displaystyle\sum_{j=1}^{c}\sum_{i=1}^{n_j} X_{ij}}{n} = \frac{438.9}{20} = 21.945$$

Then, using Equations (1) through (3), you compute the sum of squares:

$$SSA = \sum_{j=1}^{c} n_j (\overline{X}_j - \overline{\overline{X}})^2 = (5)(19.52 - 21.945)^2 + (5)(24.26 - 21.945)^2$$

$$+ (5)(22.84 - 21.945)^2 + (5)(21.16 - 21.945)^2$$

$$= 63.2855$$

$$SSW = \sum_{j=1}^{c}\sum_{i=1}^{n_j} (X_{ij} - \overline{X}_j)^2$$

$$= (18.5 - 19.52)^2 + \cdots + (18 - 19.52)^2 + (26.3 - 24.26)^2 + \cdots + (24.5 - 24.26)^2$$

$$+ (20.6 - 22.84)^2 + \cdots + (22.9 - 22.84)^2 + (25.4 - 21.16)^2 + \cdots + (20.4 - 21.16)^2$$

$$= 97.5040$$

$$SST = \sum_{j=1}^{c}\sum_{i=1}^{n_j} (X_{ij} - \overline{\overline{X}})^2$$

$$= (18.5 - 21.945)^2 + (24 - 21.945)^2 + \cdots + (20.4 - 21.945)^2$$

$$= 160.7895$$

You compute the mean square terms by dividing the sum of squares by the corresponding degrees of freedom [see Equation (4)]. Because $c = 4$ and $n = 20$,

$$MSA = \frac{SSA}{c - 1} = \frac{63.2855}{4 - 1} = 21.0952$$

$$MSW = \frac{SSW}{n - c} = \frac{97.5040}{20 - 4} = 6.0940$$

so that using Equation (5),

$$F = \frac{MSA}{MSW} = \frac{21.0952}{6.0940} = 3.4616$$

For a selected level of significance, α, you find the upper-tail critical value, F_U, from the F distribution using the table of critical values of F. A portion of the table is presented in Table 2. In the parachute supplier example, there are 3 degrees of freedom in the numerator and 16 degrees of freedom in the denominator. F_U, the upper-tail critical value at the 0.05 level of significance, is 3.24.

TABLE 2

Finding the Critical Value of F with 3 and 16 Degrees of Freedom at the 0.05 Level of Significance

Denominator, df_2	Numerator, df_1								
	1	2	3	4	5	6	7	8	9
⋮	⋮	⋮		⋮	⋮	⋮	⋮	⋮	⋮
⋮	⋮	⋮		⋮	⋮	⋮	⋮	⋮	⋮
11	4.84	3.98	3.59	3.36	3.20	3.09	3.01	2.95	2.90
12	4.75	3.89	3.49	3.26	3.11	3.00	2.91	2.85	2.80
13	4.67	3.81	3.41	3.18	3.03	2.92	2.83	2.77	2.71
14	4.60	3.74	3.34	3.11	2.96	2.85	2.76	2.70	2.65
15	4.54	3.68	3.29	3.06	2.90	2.79	2.71	2.64	2.59
16	4.49	3.63	3.24	3.01	2.85	2.74	2.66	2.59	2.54

Source: Extracted from table of Critical Values of F.

Because the computed test statistic $F = 3.4616$ is greater than $F_U = 3.24$, you reject the null hypothesis (see Figure 5). You conclude that there is a significant difference in the mean tensile strength among the four suppliers.

FIGURE 5

Regions of rejection and nonrejection for the one-way ANOVA at the 0.05 level of significance, with 3 and 16 degrees of freedom

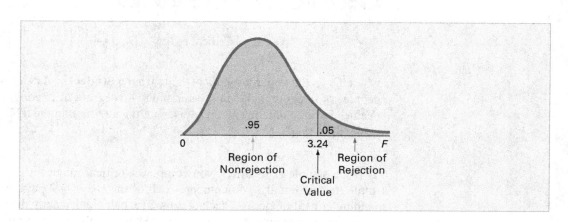

Figure 6 shows the Microsoft Excel ANOVA summary table and *p*-value.

FIGURE 6

Microsoft Excel ANOVA for the parachute example

See Section E1 to create this.

	A	B	C	D	E	F	G
1	Anova: Single Factor						
2							
3	SUMMARY						
4	*Groups*	*Count*	*Sum*	*Average*	*Variance*		
5	Supplier 1	5	97.6	19.52	7.237		
6	Supplier 2	5	121.3	24.26	3.683		
7	Supplier 3	5	114.2	22.84	4.553		
8	Supplier 4	5	105.8	21.16	8.903		
9							
10							
11	ANOVA						
12	*Source of Variation*	*SS*	*df*	*MS*	*F*	*P-value*	*F crit*
13	Between Groups	63.2855	3	21.0952	3.4616	0.0414	3.2389
14	Within Groups	97.5040	16	6.094			
15							
16	Total	160.7895	19				

The *p*-value, or probability of getting an *F* statistic of 3.4616 or larger when the null hypothesis is true, is 0.0414. Because this *p*-value is less than the specified α of 0.05, you reject the null hypothesis. The *p*-value of 0.0414 indicates that there is a 4.14% chance of observing differences this large or larger if the population means for the four suppliers are all equal.

After performing the one-way ANOVA and finding a significant difference among the suppliers, you still do not know *which* suppliers differ. All that you know is that there is sufficient evidence to state that the population means are not all the same. In other words, at least one or more population means are significantly different. To determine which suppliers differ, you can use a multiple comparison procedure such as the Tukey-Kramer procedure.

Multiple Comparisons: The Tukey-Kramer Procedure

In the Using Statistics scenario, you used the one-way ANOVA *F* test to determine that there was a difference among the suppliers. The next step is to make **multiple comparisons** to determine which suppliers are different.

Although many procedures are available (see references 5, 8, and 9), this text uses the **Tukey-Kramer multiple comparisons procedure** to determine which of the *c* means are significantly different. The Tukey-Kramer procedure enables you to simultaneously make comparisons between all pairs of groups. First, you compute the differences, $\bar{X}_j - \bar{X}_{j'}$ (where $j \neq j'$), among all $c(c-1)/2$ pairs of means. Then you compute the **critical range** for the Tukey-Kramer procedure using Equation (6).

CRITICAL RANGE FOR THE TUKEY-KRAMER PROCEDURE

$$\text{Critical range} = Q_U \sqrt{\frac{MSW}{2}\left(\frac{1}{n_j} + \frac{1}{n_{j'}}\right)} \tag{6}$$

where Q_U is the upper-tail critical value from a **Studentized range distribution** having *c* degrees of freedom in the numerator and $n - c$ degrees of freedom in the denominator. (Values for the Studentized range distribution are found in the table of critical values of the studentized range, *Q*.)

If the sample sizes differ, you compute a critical range for each pairwise comparison of sample means. Finally, you compare each of the $c(c-1)/2$ pairs of means against its corresponding critical range. You declare a specific pair significantly different if the absolute difference in the sample means $\left| \bar{X}_j - \bar{X}_{j'} \right|$ is greater than the critical range.

In the parachute example, there are four suppliers. Thus, there are $4(4 - 1)/2 = 6$ pairwise comparisons. To apply the Tukey-Kramer multiple comparison procedure, you first compute the absolute mean differences for all six pairwise comparisons. *Multiple comparison* refers to the fact that you are going to simultaneously make an inference about all six of these comparisons:

1. $\left| \overline{X}_1 - \overline{X}_2 \right| = \left| 19.52 - 24.26 \right| = 4.74$

2. $\left| \overline{X}_1 - \overline{X}_3 \right| = \left| 19.52 - 22.84 \right| = 3.32$

3. $\left| \overline{X}_1 - \overline{X}_4 \right| = \left| 19.52 - 21.16 \right| = 1.64$

4. $\left| \overline{X}_2 - \overline{X}_3 \right| = \left| 24.26 - 22.84 \right| = 1.42$

5. $\left| \overline{X}_2 - \overline{X}_4 \right| = \left| 24.26 - 21.16 \right| = 3.10$

6. $\left| \overline{X}_3 - \overline{X}_4 \right| = \left| 22.84 - 21.16 \right| = 1.68$

You need to compute only one critical range because the sample sizes in the four groups are equal. From the ANOVA summary table (Figure 6), $MSW = 6.094$ and $n_j = n_{j'} = 5$. From the table of critical values of the studentized range, Q for $\alpha = 0.05$, $c = 4$, and $n - c = 20 - 4 = 16$, Q_U, the upper-tail critical value of the test statistic, is 4.05 (see Table 3).

TABLE 3

Finding the Studentized Range Q_U Statistic for $\alpha = 0.05$, with 4 and 16 Degrees of Freedom

Denominator Degrees of Freedom	Numerator Degrees of Freedom							
	2	3	4	5	6	7	8	9
.	.	.		.	.	.	.	.
.	.	.		.	.	.	.	.
.	.	.		.	.	.	.	.
11	3.11	3.82	4.26	4.57	4.82	5.03	5.20	5.35
12	3.08	3.77	4.20	4.51	4.75	4.95	5.12	5.27
13	3.06	3.73	4.15	4.45	4.69	4.88	5.05	5.19
14	3.03	3.70	4.11	4.41	4.64	4.83	4.99	5.13
15	3.01	3.67	4.08	4.37	4.60	4.78	4.94	5.08
16	3.00	3.65	4.05	4.33	4.56	4.74	4.90	5.03

Source: Extracted from the table of Critical Values of the Studentized Range, Q.

From Equation (6),

$$\text{Critical range} = 4.05 \sqrt{\left(\frac{6.094}{2} \right) \left(\frac{1}{5} + \frac{1}{5} \right)} = 4.4712$$

Because $4.74 > 4.4712$, there is a significant difference between the means of Suppliers 1 and 2. All other pairwise differences are small enough that they may be due to chance. With 95% confidence, you can conclude that parachutes woven using fiber from Supplier 1 have a lower mean tensile strength than those from Supplier 2, but there are no statistically significant differences between Suppliers 1 and 3, Suppliers 1 and 4, Suppliers 2 and 3, Suppliers 2 and 4, and Suppliers 3 and 4. Note that by using $\alpha = 0.05$, you are able to make all six of the comparisons with an overall error rate of only 5%.

These results are summarized in the Microsoft Excel results presented in Figure 7.

FIGURE 7

Microsoft Excel worksheet of the Tukey-Kramer procedure for the parachute example

See Section E2 to create this.

	A	B	C	D	E	F	G	H	I
1	Parachute Tensile-Strength Analysis								
2									
3		Sample	Sample			Absolute	Std. Error	Critical	
4	Group	Mean	Size		Comparison	Difference	of Difference	Range	Results
5	1	19.52	5		Group 1 to Group 2	4.74	1.10399275	4.4712	Means are different
6	2	24.26	5		Group 1 to Group 3	3.32	1.10399275	4.4712	Means are not different
7	3	22.84	5		Group 1 to Group 4	1.64	1.10399275	4.4712	Means are not different
8	4	21.16	5		Group 2 to Group 3	1.42	1.10399275	4.4712	Means are not different
9					Group 2 to Group 4	3.1	1.10399275	4.4712	Means are not different
10	Other Data				Group 3 to Group 4	1.68	1.10399275	4.4712	Means are not different
11	Level of significance	0.05							
12	Numerator d.f.	4							
13	Denominator d.f.	16							
14	MSW	6.094							
15	Q Statistic	4.05							

ANOVA Assumptions

You may have previously learned about the assumptions made in the application of each hypothesis-testing procedure and the consequences of departures from these assumptions. To use the one-way ANOVA F test, you must also make certain assumptions about the data. These assumptions are

- Randomness and independence
- Normality
- Homogeneity of variance

The first assumption, **randomness and independence**, is critically important. The validity of any experiment depends on random sampling and/or the randomization process. To avoid biases in the outcomes, you need to select random samples from the c groups or randomly assign the items to the c levels of the factor. Selecting a random sample, or randomly assigning the levels, ensures that a value from one group is independent of any other value in the experiment. Departures from this assumption can seriously affect inferences from the ANOVA. These problems are discussed more thoroughly in references 5 and 8.

The second assumption, **normality**, states that the sample values in each group are from a normally distributed population. Just as in the case of the t test, the one-way ANOVA F test is fairly robust against departures from the normal distribution. As long as the distributions are not extremely different from a normal distribution, the level of significance of the ANOVA F test is usually not greatly affected, particularly for large samples. You can assess the normality of each of the c samples by constructing a normal probability plot or a box-and-whisker plot.

The third assumption, **homogeneity of variance**, states that the variances of the c groups are equal (that is, $\sigma_1^2 = \sigma_2^2 = \cdots = \sigma_c^2$). If you have equal sample sizes in each group, inferences based on the F distribution are not seriously affected by unequal variances. However, if you have unequal sample sizes, unequal variances can have a serious effect on inferences developed from the ANOVA procedure. Thus, when possible, you should have equal sample sizes in all groups. The Levene test for homogeneity of variance presented on the following page is one method to test whether the variances of the c groups are equal.

When only the normality assumption is violated, the Kruskal-Wallis rank test, a nonparametric procedure, is appropriate. When only the homogeneity-of-variance assumption is violated, procedures similar to those used in the separate-variance t test are available (see references 1 and 2). When both the normality and homogeneity-of-variance assumptions have been violated, you need to use an appropriate data transformation that both normalizes the data and reduces the differences in variances (see reference 9) or use a more general nonparametric procedure (see references 2 and 3).

Levene's Test for Homogeneity of Variance

Although the one-way ANOVA F test is relatively robust with respect to the assumption of equal group variances, large differences in the group variances can seriously affect the level of significance and the power of the F test. One procedure with high statistical power is the modified **Levene test** (see references 1, 4, 6, and 8). To test for the homogeneity of variance, you use the following null hypothesis:

$$H_0: \sigma_1^2 = \sigma_2^2 = \cdots = \sigma_c^2$$

against the alternative hypothesis:

$$H_1: \text{Not all } \sigma_j^2 \text{ are equal } (j = 1, 2, 3, \ldots, c).$$

To test the null hypothesis of equal variances, you first compute the absolute value of the difference between each value and the median of the group. Then you perform a one-way ANOVA on these *absolute differences*. To illustrate the modified Levene test, return to the Using Statistics scenario concerning the tensile strength of parachutes. Table 4 summarizes the absolute differences from the median of each supplier.

TABLE 4

Absolute Differences from the Median Tensile Strength for Four Suppliers

Supplier 1 (Median = 18.5)	Supplier 2 (Median = 24.5)	Supplier 3 (Median = 22.9)	Supplier 4 (Median = 20.4)
$\lvert 18.5 - 18.5 \rvert = 0.0$	$\lvert 26.3 - 24.5 \rvert = 1.8$	$\lvert 20.6 - 22.9 \rvert = 2.3$	$\lvert 25.4 - 20.4 \rvert = 5.0$
$\lvert 24.0 - 18.5 \rvert = 5.5$	$\lvert 25.3 - 24.5 \rvert = 0.8$	$\lvert 25.2 - 22.9 \rvert = 2.3$	$\lvert 19.9 - 20.4 \rvert = 0.5$
$\lvert 17.2 - 18.5 \rvert = 1.3$	$\lvert 24.0 - 24.5 \rvert = 0.5$	$\lvert 20.8 - 22.9 \rvert = 2.1$	$\lvert 22.6 - 20.4 \rvert = 2.2$
$\lvert 19.9 - 18.5 \rvert = 1.4$	$\lvert 21.2 - 24.5 \rvert = 3.3$	$\lvert 24.7 - 22.9 \rvert = 1.8$	$\lvert 17.5 - 20.4 \rvert = 2.9$
$\lvert 18.0 - 18.5 \rvert = 0.5$	$\lvert 24.5 - 24.5 \rvert = 0.0$	$\lvert 22.9 - 22.9 \rvert = 0.0$	$\lvert 20.4 - 20.4 \rvert = 0.0$

Using the absolute differences given in Table 4, you perform a one-way ANOVA (see Figure 8).

FIGURE 8

Microsoft Excel ANOVA of the absolute differences for the parachute data

See Section E3 to create this.

	A	B	C	D	E	F	G
1	Parachute Tensile-Strength Analysis						
2							
3	SUMMARY						
4	*Groups*	Count	Sum	Average	Variance		
5	Supplier 1	5	8.7	1.74	4.753		
6	Supplier 2	5	6.4	1.28	1.707		
7	Supplier 3	5	8.5	1.7	0.945		
8	Supplier 4	5	10.6	2.12	4.007		
9							
10							
11	ANOVA						
12	*Source of Variation*	SS	df	MS	F	P-value	F crit
13	Between Groups	1.77	3	0.59	0.2068	0.8902	3.2389
14	Within Groups	45.648	16	2.853			
15							
16	Total	47.418	19				

From Figure 8, observe that $F = 0.2068 < 3.2389$ (or the p-value $= 0.8902 > 0.05$). Thus, you do not reject H_0. There is no evidence of a significant difference among the four variances. In other words, it is reasonable to assume that the materials from the four suppliers produce parachutes with an equal amount of variability. Therefore, the homogeneity-of-variance assumption for the ANOVA procedure is justified.

EXAMPLE 1

ANOVA OF THE SPEED OF DRIVE-THROUGH SERVICE AT FAST-FOOD CHAINS

For fast-food restaurants, the drive-through window is an increasing source of revenue. The chain that offers the fastest service is likely to attract additional customers. In a study of drive-through times (from menu board to departure) at fast-food chains, the mean time was 150 seconds for Wendy's, 167 seconds for McDonald's, 169 seconds for Checkers, 171 seconds for Burger King, and 172 seconds for Long John Silver's (extracted from J. Ordonez, "An Efficiency Drive: Fast-Food Lanes Are Getting Even Faster," *The Wall Street Journal*, May 18, 2000, pp. A1, A10). Suppose the study was based on 20 customers for each fast-food chain and the ANOVA table given in Table 5 was developed.

TABLE 5

ANOVA Summary Table of the Speed of Drive-Through Service at Fast-Food Chains

Source	Degrees of Freedom	Sum of Squares	Mean Squares	F	p-Value
Among chains	4	6,536	1,634.0	12.51	0.0000
Within chains	95	12,407	130.6		

At the 0.05 level of significance, is there evidence of a difference in the mean drive-through times of the five chains?

SOLUTION

$H_0: \mu_1 = \mu_2 = \mu_3 = \mu_4 = \mu_5$ where 1 = Wendy's, 2 = McDonald's, 3 = Checkers, 4 = Burger King, 5 = Long John Silver's

$H_1:$ Not all μ_j are equal   where $j = 1, 2, 3, 4, 5$

Decision rule: If p-value < 0.05, reject H_0. Because the p-value is virtually 0, which is less than $\alpha = 0.05$, reject H_0. You have sufficient evidence to conclude that the mean drive-through times of the five chains are not all equal.

To determine which of the means are significantly different from one another, use the Tukey-Kramer procedure [Equation (6)] to establish the critical range:

$$Q_{U(c,n-c)} = Q_{U(5,95)} \cong 3.92$$

$$\text{Critical range} = Q_{U(c,n-c)}\sqrt{\left(\frac{MSW}{2}\right)\left(\frac{1}{n_j} + \frac{1}{n_{j'}}\right)} = (3.92)\sqrt{\left(\frac{130.6}{2}\right)\left(\frac{1}{20} + \frac{1}{20}\right)}$$

$$= 10.02$$

Any observed difference greater than 10.02 is considered significant. The mean drive-through times are different between Wendy's (mean of 150 seconds) and each of the other four chains. With 95% confidence, you can conclude that the mean drive-through time for Wendy's is faster than McDonald's, Burger King, Checkers, and Long John Silver's, but the mean drive-through times for McDonald's, Burger King, Checkers, and Long John Silver's are not statistically different.

PROBLEMS FOR SECTION 1

Learning the Basics

PH Grade ASSIST **1** An experiment has a single factor with five groups and seven values in each group.
a. How many degrees of freedom are there in determining the among-group variation?
b. How many degrees of freedom are there in determining the within-group variation?
c. How many degrees of freedom are there in determining the total variation?

PH Grade ASSIST **2** You are working with the same experiment as in Problem 1.
a. If $SSA = 60$ and $SST = 210$, what is SSW?
b. What is MSA?
c. What is MSW?
d. What is the value of the test statistic F?

PH Grade ASSIST **3** You are working with the same experiment as in Problems 1 and 2.
a. Construct the ANOVA summary table and fill in all values in the table.
b. At the 0.05 level of significance, what is the upper-tail critical value from the F distribution?
c. State the decision rule for testing the null hypothesis that all five groups have equal population means.
d. What is your statistical decision?

4 Consider an experiment with three groups, with seven values in each.
a. How many degrees of freedom are there in determining the among-group variation?
b. How many degrees of freedom are there in determining the within-group variation?
c. How many degrees of freedom are there in determining the total variation?

PH Grade ASSIST **5** Consider an experiment with four groups, with eight values in each. For the following ANOVA summary table, fill in all the missing results:

Source	Degrees of Freedom	Sum of Squares	Mean Square (Variance)	F
Among groups	$c - 1 = ?$	$SSA = ?$	$MSA = 80$	$F = ?$
Within groups	$n - c = ?$	$SSW = 560$	$MSW = ?$	
Total	$n - 1 = ?$	$SST = ?$		

6 You are working with the same experiment as in Problem 5.
a. At the 0.05 level of significance, state the decision rule for testing the null hypothesis that all four groups have equal population means.

b. What is your statistical decision?
c. At the 0.05 level of significance, what is the upper-tail critical value from the Studentized range distribution?
d. To perform the Tukey-Kramer procedure, what is the critical range?

Applying the Concepts

7 The Computer Anxiety Rating Scale (CARS) measures an individual's level of computer anxiety, on a scale from 20 (no anxiety) to 100 (highest level of anxiety). Researchers at Miami University administered CARS to 172 business students. One of the objectives of the study was to determine whether there are differences in the amount of computer anxiety experienced by students with different majors. They found the following:

Source	Degrees of Freedom	Sum of Squares	Mean Squares	F
Among majors	5	3,172		
Within majors	166	21,246		
Total	171	24,418		

Major	n	Mean
Marketing	19	44.37
Management	11	43.18
Other	14	42.21
Finance	45	41.80
Accountancy	36	37.56
MIS	47	32.21

Source: Extracted from T. Broome and D. Havelka, "Determinants of Computer Anxiety in Business Students," The Review of Business Information Systems, *Spring 2002, 6(2), pp. 9–16.*

a. Complete the ANOVA summary table.
b. At the 0.05 level of significance, is there evidence of a difference in the mean computer anxiety experienced by different majors?
c. If the results in (b) indicate that it is appropriate, use the Tukey-Kramer procedure to determine which majors differ in mean computer anxiety. Discuss your findings.

PH Grade ASSIST **8** Periodically, *The Wall Street Journal* has conducted a stock-picking contest. The last one was conducted in March 2001. In this experiment, three different methods were used to select stocks that were expected to perform well during the next five months. Four Wall Street professionals, considered experts on picking stocks, each selected one stock. Four randomly chosen readers of the *Wall Street Journal* each selected one stock. Finally, four stocks were selected by flinging darts at a table containing a list of stocks. The returns of the selected stocks for March 20, 2001, to August 31, 2001 (in percentage return), are given in the following table and stored in the file `contest2001.xls`. Note that during this period, the Dow Jones Industrial Average gained 2.4% (extracted from G. Jasen, "In Picking Stocks, Dartboard Beats the Pros," *The Wall Street Journal*, September 27, 2001, pp. C1, C10).

Experts	Readers	Darts
+39.5	−31.0	+39.0
−1.1	−20.7	+31.9
−4.5	−45.0	+14.1
−8.0	−73.3	+5.4

a. Is there evidence of a significant difference in the mean return for the three categories? (Use $\alpha = 0.05$.)
b. If appropriate, determine which categories differ in mean return.
c. Comment on the validity of the inference implied by the title of the article, which suggests that the dartboard was better than the professionals.
d. Is there evidence of a significant difference in the variation in the returns for the three categories? (Use $\alpha = 0.05$.)

9 A hospital conducted a study of the waiting time in its emergency room. The hospital has a main campus and three satellite locations. Management had a business objective of reducing waiting time for emergency room cases that did not require immediate attention. To study this, a random sample of 15 emergency room cases at each location were selected on a particular day, and the waiting time (measured from check-in to when the patient was called into the clinic area) was measured. The results are stored in the file `erwaiting.xls`.
a. At the 0.05 level of significance, is there evidence of a difference in the mean waiting times in the four locations?
b. If appropriate, determine which locations differ in mean waiting time.
c. At the 0.05 level of significance, is there evidence of a difference in the variation in waiting time among the four locations?

✓ SELF Test **10** Students in a business statistics course performed a completely randomized design to test the strength of four brands of trash bags. One-pound weights were placed into a bag, one at a time, until the bag broke. A total of 40 bags, 10 for each brand, were used. The data in the file `trashbags.xls` gives the weight (in pounds) required to break the trash bags.
a. At the 0.05 level of significance, is there evidence of a difference in the mean strength of the four brands of trash bags?

b. If appropriate, determine which brands differ in mean strength.
c. At the 0.05 level of significance, is there evidence of a difference in the variation in strength among the four brands of trash bags?
d. Which brand(s) should you buy and which brand(s) should you avoid? Explain.

11 The following data (stored in the file `cdyield.xls`) represent the nationwide highest yield of different types of accounts (extracted from Bankrate.com, January 24, 2006):

Money Market	6-Month CD	1-Yr CD	2.5-Yr CD	5-Yr CD
4.55	4.75	4.94	4.95	5.05
4.50	4.70	4.90	4.91	5.05
4.40	4.69	4.85	4.85	5.02
4.38	4.65	4.85	4.82	5.00
4.38	4.65	4.85	4.80	5.00

a. At the 0.05 level of significance, is there evidence of a difference in the mean yields of the different accounts?
b. If appropriate, determine which accounts differ in mean yields.
c. At the 0.05 level of significance, is there evidence of a difference in the variation in yields among the different accounts?
d. What effect does your result in (c) have on the validity of the results in (a) and (b)?

12 An advertising agency has been hired by a manufacturer of pens to develop an advertising campaign for the upcoming holiday season. To prepare for this project, the research director decides to initiate a study of the effect of advertising on product perception. An experiment is designed to compare five different advertisements. Advertisement *A* greatly undersells the pen's characteristics. Advertisement *B* slightly undersells the pen's characteristics. Advertisement *C* slightly oversells the pen's characteristics. Advertisement *D* greatly oversells the pen's characteristics. Advertisement *E* attempts to correctly state the pen's characteristics. A sample of 30 adult respondents, taken from a larger focus group, is randomly assigned to the five advertisements (so that there are six respondents to each). After reading the advertisement and developing a sense of "product expectation," all respondents unknowingly receive the same pen to evaluate. The respondents are permitted to test the pen and the plausibility of the advertising copy. The respondents are then asked to rate the pen from 1 to 7 on the product characteristic scales of appearance, durability, and writing performance. The *combined* scores of three ratings (appearance, durability, and writing performance) for the 30 respondents (stored in the file `pen.xls`) are as follows:

A	B	C	D	E
15	16	8	5	12
18	17	7	6	19
17	21	10	13	18
19	16	15	11	12
19	19	14	9	17
20	17	14	10	14

a. At the 0.05 level of significance, is there evidence of a difference in the mean rating of the five advertisements?

b. If appropriate, determine which advertisements differ in mean ratings.

c. At the 0.05 level of significance, is there evidence of a difference in the variation in ratings among the five advertisements?

d. Which advertisement(s) should you use and which advertisement(s) should you avoid? Explain.

13 The retailing manager of a supermarket chain wants to determine whether product location has any effect on the sale of pet toys. Three different aisle locations are considered: front, middle, and rear. A random sample of 18 stores is selected, with 6 stores randomly assigned to each aisle location. The size of the display area and price of the product are constant for all stores. At the end of a one-month trial period, the sales volumes (in thousands of dollars) of the product in each store were as follows (and are stored in the file locate.xls).

Aisle Location

Front	Middle	Rear
8.6	3.2	4.6
7.2	2.4	6.0
5.4	2.0	4.0
6.2	1.4	2.8
5.0	1.8	2.2
4.0	1.6	2.8

a. At the 0.05 level of significance, is there evidence of a significant difference in mean sales among the various aisle locations?

b. If appropriate, which aisle locations appear to differ significantly in mean sales?

c. At the 0.05 level of significance, is there evidence of a significant difference in the variation in sales among the various aisle locations?

d. What should the retailing manager conclude? Fully describe the retailing manager's options with respect to aisle locations.

14 A sporting goods manufacturing company wanted to compare the distance traveled by golf balls produced using each of four different designs. Ten balls were manufactured with each design and were brought to the local golf course for the club professional to test. The order in which the balls were hit with the same club from the first tee was randomized so that the pro did not know which type of ball was being hit. All 40 balls were hit in a short period of time, during which the environmental conditions were essentially the same. The results (distance traveled in yards) for the four designs were as follows (and are stored in the file golfball.xls):

Design

1	2	3	4
206.32	217.08	226.77	230.55
207.94	221.43	224.79	227.95
206.19	218.04	229.75	231.84
204.45	224.13	228.51	224.87
209.65	211.82	221.44	229.49
203.81	213.90	223.85	231.10
206.75	221.28	223.97	221.53
205.68	229.43	234.30	235.45
204.49	213.54	219.50	228.35
210.86	214.51	233.00	225.09

a. At the 0.05 level of significance, is there evidence of a difference in the mean distances traveled by the golf balls with different designs?

b. If the results in (a) indicate that it is appropriate, use the Tukey-Kramer procedure to determine which designs differ in mean distances.

c. What assumptions are necessary in (a)?

d. At the 0.05 level of significance, is there evidence of a difference in the variation of the distances traveled by the golf balls differing in design?

e. What golf ball design should the manufacturing manager choose? Explain.

2 THE FACTORIAL DESIGN: TWO-WAY ANALYSIS OF VARIANCE

In Section 1, you learned about the completely randomized design used for situations concerning one factor. In this section, the discussion is extended to the **two-factor factorial design**, in which two factors are simultaneously evaluated. Each factor is evaluated at two or more levels.

For example, in the Using Statistics scenario, Perfect Parachutes is interested in simultaneously evaluating four suppliers and two types of looms. While discussion here is limited to two factors, you can extend factorial designs to three or more factors (see references 4, 5, 6, and 8).

Data from a two-factor factorial design are analyzed using **two-way ANOVA**. Because of the complexity of the calculations involved, you should use software such as Microsoft Excel when conducting this analysis. However, for purposes of illustration and a better conceptual understanding of two-way ANOVA, the decomposition of the total variation is presented next. The following definitions are needed to develop the two-way ANOVA procedure:

r = number of levels of factor A

c = number of levels of factor B

n' = number of values (replicates) for each cell (combination of a particular level of factor A and a particular level of factor B)

n = number of values in the entire experiment (where $n = rcn'$)

X_{ijk} = value of the kth observation for level i of factor A and level j of factor B

$$\overline{\overline{X}} = \frac{\displaystyle\sum_{i=1}^{r}\sum_{j=1}^{c}\sum_{k=1}^{n'} X_{ijk}}{rcn'} = \text{grand mean}$$

$$\overline{X}_{i..} = \frac{\displaystyle\sum_{j=1}^{c}\sum_{k=1}^{n'} X_{ijk}}{cn'} = \text{mean of the } i\text{th level of factor } A \text{ (where } i = 1, 2, \ldots, r)$$

$$\overline{X}_{.j.} = \frac{\displaystyle\sum_{i=1}^{r}\sum_{k=1}^{n'} X_{ijk}}{rn'} = \text{mean of the } j\text{th level of factor } B \text{ (where } j = 1, 2, \ldots, c)$$

$$\overline{X}_{ij.} = \frac{\displaystyle\sum_{k=1}^{n'} X_{ijk}}{n'} = \text{mean of the cell } ij, \text{ the combination of the } i\text{th level of factor } A$$
$$\text{and the } j\text{th level of factor } B$$

This text deals only with situations in which there are an equal number of **replicates** (that is, sample sizes n') for each combination of the levels of factor A with those of factor B. (See references 1 and 9 for a discussion of two-factor factorial designs with unequal sample sizes.)

Testing for Factor and Interaction Effects

There is an **interaction** between factors A and B if the effect of factor A is dependent on the level of factor B. Thus, when dividing the total variation into different sources of variation, you need to account for a possible interaction effect, as well as for factor A, factor B, and random error. To accomplish this, the total variation (SST) is subdivided into sum of squares due to factor A (or SSA), sum of squares due to factor B (or SSB), sum of squares due to the interaction effect of A and B (or $SSAB$), and sum of squares due to random error (or SSE). This decomposition of the total variation (SST) is displayed in Figure 9.

FIGURE 9

Partitioning the total variation in a two-factor factorial design

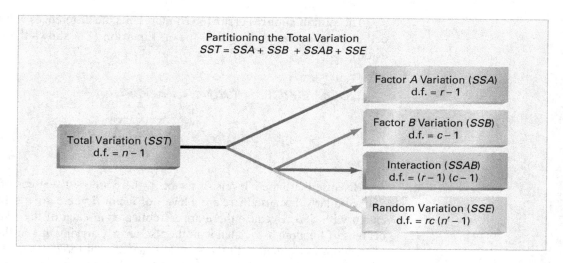

The sum of squares total (SST) represents the total variation among all the values around the grand mean. Equation (7) shows the computation for total variation.

TOTAL VARIATION IN TWO-WAY ANOVA

$$SST = \sum_{i=1}^{r} \sum_{j=1}^{c} \sum_{k=1}^{n'} (X_{ijk} - \overline{\overline{X}})^2 \tag{7}$$

The **sum of squares due to factor A (SSA)** represents the differences among the various levels of factor A and the grand mean. Equation (8) shows the computation for factor A variation.

FACTOR A VARIATION

$$SSA = cn' \sum_{i=1}^{r} (\overline{X}_{i..} - \overline{\overline{X}})^2 \tag{8}$$

The **sum of squares due to factor B (SSB)** represents the differences among the various levels of factor B and the grand mean. Equation (9) shows the computation for factor B variation.

FACTOR B VARIATION

$$SSB = rn' \sum_{j=1}^{c} (\overline{X}_{.j.} - \overline{\overline{X}})^2 \tag{9}$$

The **sum of squares due to interaction ($SSAB$)** represents the interacting effect of specific combinations of factor A and factor B. Equation (10) shows the computation for interaction variation.

INTERACTION VARIATION

$$SSAB = n' \sum_{i=1}^{r} \sum_{j=1}^{c} (\overline{X}_{ij.} - \overline{X}_{i..} - \overline{X}_{.j.} + \overline{\overline{X}})^2 \tag{10}$$

The **sum of squares error (SSE)** represents the differences among the values within each cell and the corresponding cell mean. Equation (11) shows the computation for random error.

RANDOM ERROR IN TWO-WAY ANOVA

$$SSE = \sum_{i=1}^{r} \sum_{j=1}^{c} \sum_{k=1}^{n'} (X_{ijk} - \overline{X}_{ij.})^2 \tag{11}$$

Because there are r levels of factor A, there are $r - 1$ degrees of freedom associated with SSA. Similarly, because there are c levels of factor B, there are $c - 1$ degrees of freedom associated with SSB. Because there are n' replicates in each of the rc cells, there are $rc(n' - 1)$ degrees of freedom associated with the SSE term. Carrying this further, there are $n - 1$ degrees of freedom associated with the sum of squares total (SST) because you are comparing each value, X_{ijk}, to the grand mean, $\overline{\overline{X}}$, based on all n values. Therefore, because the degrees of freedom for each of the sources of variation must add to the degrees of freedom for the total variation (SST), you calculate the degrees of freedom for the interaction component ($SSAB$) by subtraction. The degrees of freedom for interaction are $(r - 1)(c - 1)$.

If you divide each of the sums of squares by its associated degrees of freedom, you have the four variances or mean square terms (that is, MSA, MSB, $MSAB$, and MSE). Equations (12a–d) give the mean square terms needed for the two-way ANOVA table.

MEAN SQUARES IN TWO-WAY ANOVA

$$MSA = \frac{SSA}{r - 1} \tag{12a}$$

$$MSB = \frac{SSB}{c - 1} \tag{12b}$$

$$MSAB = \frac{SSAB}{(r - 1)(c - 1)} \tag{12c}$$

$$MSE = \frac{SSE}{rc(n' - 1)} \tag{12d}$$

There are three distinct tests to perform in a two-way ANOVA:

1. To test the hypothesis of no difference due to factor A:

$$H_0: \mu_{1..} = \mu_{2..} = \cdots = \mu_{r..}$$

against the alternative:

$$H_1: \text{Not all } \mu_{i..} \text{ are equal.}$$

you use the F statistic in Equation (13).

F TEST FOR FACTOR A EFFECT

$$F = \frac{MSA}{MSE} \tag{13}$$

You reject the null hypothesis at the α level of significance if

$$F = \frac{MSA}{MSE} > F_U$$

where F_U is the upper-tail critical value from an F distribution with $r - 1$ and $rc(n' - 1)$ degrees of freedom.

2. To test the hypothesis of no difference due to factor B:

$$H_0: \mu_{.1.} = \mu_{.2.} = \cdots = \mu_{.c.}$$

against the alternative:

$$H_1: \text{Not all } \mu_{.j.} \text{ are equal.}$$

you use the F statistic in Equation (14).

F TEST FOR FACTOR B EFFECT

$$F = \frac{MSB}{MSE} \tag{14}$$

You reject the null hypothesis at the α level of significance if

$$F = \frac{MSB}{MSE} > F_U$$

where F_U is the upper-tail critical value from an F distribution with $c - 1$ and $rc(n' - 1)$ degrees of freedom.

3. To test the hypothesis of no interaction of factors A and B:

$$H_0: \text{The interaction of } A \text{ and } B \text{ is equal to zero.}$$

against the alternative:

$$H_1: \text{The interaction of } A \text{ and } B \text{ is not equal to zero.}$$

you use the F statistic in Equation (15).

F TEST FOR INTERACTION EFFECT

$$F = \frac{MSAB}{MSE} \tag{15}$$

You reject the null hypothesis at the α level of significance if

$$F = \frac{MSAB}{MSE} > F_U$$

where F_U is the upper-tail critical value from an F distribution with $(r - 1)(c - 1)$ and $rc(n' - 1)$ degrees of freedom.

Table 6 presents the entire two-way ANOVA table.

TABLE 6

Analysis-of-Variance Table for the Two-Factor Factorial Design

Source	Degrees of Freedom	Sum of Squares	Mean Square (Variance)	F
A	$r-1$	SSA	$MSA = \dfrac{SSA}{r-1}$	$F = \dfrac{MSA}{MSE}$
B	$c-1$	SSB	$MSB = \dfrac{SSB}{c-1}$	$F = \dfrac{MSB}{MSE}$
AB	$(r-1)(c-1)$	$SSAB$	$MSAB = \dfrac{SSAB}{(r-1)(c-1)}$	$F = \dfrac{MSAB}{MSE}$
Error	$rc(n'-1)$	SSE	$MSE = \dfrac{SSE}{rc(n'-1)}$	
Total	$n-1$	SST		

To examine a two-way ANOVA, return to the Using Statistics scenario. As production manager at Perfect Parachutes, you have decided not only to evaluate the different suppliers but also to determine whether parachutes woven on the Jetta looms are as strong as those woven on the Turk looms. In addition, you need to determine whether any differences among the four suppliers in the strength of the parachutes are dependent on the type of loom being used. Thus, you have decided to perform an experiment in which five different parachutes from each supplier are manufactured on each of the two different looms. The results are given in Table 7 and stored in the parachute2.xls file.

TABLE 7

Tensile Strengths of Parachutes Woven by Two Types of Looms, Using Synthetic Fibers from Four Suppliers

LOOM	SUPPLIER			
	1	2	3	4
Jetta	20.6	22.6	27.7	21.5
	18.0	24.6	18.6	20.0
	19.0	19.6	20.8	21.1
	21.3	23.8	25.1	23.9
	13.2	27.1	17.7	16.0
Turk	18.5	26.3	20.6	25.4
	24.0	25.3	25.2	19.9
	17.2	24.0	20.8	22.6
	19.9	21.2	24.7	17.5
	18.0	24.5	22.9	20.4

Figure 10 presents Microsoft Excel results.

	A	B	C	D	E	F	G
1	Anova: Two-Factor With Replication						
2							
3	SUMMARY	Supplier 1	Supplier 2	Supplier 3	Supplier 4	Total	
4	Jetta						
5	Count	5	5	5	5	20	
6	Sum	92.1	117.7	109.9	102.5	422.2	
7	Average	18.42	23.54	21.98	20.5	21.11	
8	Variance	10.202	7.568	18.397	8.355	13.1283	
9							
10	Turk						
11	Count	5	5	5	5	20	
12	Sum	97.6	121.3	114.2	105.8	438.9	
13	Average	19.52	24.26	22.84	21.16	21.945	
14	Variance	7.237	3.683	4.553	8.903	8.4626	
15							
16	Total						
17	Count	10	10	10	10		
18	Sum	189.7	239	224.1	208.3		
19	Average	18.97	23.9	22.41	20.83		
20	Variance	8.0868	5.1444	10.4054	7.7912		
21							
22							
23	ANOVA						
24	Source of Variation	SS	df	MS	F	P-value	F crit
25	Sample	6.9723	1	6.9723	0.8096	0.3750	4.1491
26	Columns	134.3488	3	44.7829	5.1999	0.0049	2.9011
27	Interaction	0.2867	3	0.0956	0.0111	0.9984	2.9011
28	Within	275.5920	32	8.6123			
29							
30	Total	417.1998	39				

[1]Table "Critical Values of F"
does not provide the upper-
tail critical values from the F
distribution with 32 degrees
of freedom in the
denominator. The table
gives critical values either
for F distributions with 30
degrees of freedom in the
denominator or for F
distributions with 40
degrees of freedom in the
denominator. When the
desired degrees of freedom
are not provided in the
table, you can round to the
closest value that is given or
use the p-value approach.

In Figure 10, the summary tables provide the sample size, sum, mean, and variance for each combination of supplier and loom. The total columns in the first two tables provide these statistics for each loom, and the third table provides them for each supplier. In addition, in the ANOVA table, *df* represents degrees of freedom, *SS* refers to sum of squares, *MS* stands for mean squares, and *F* is the computed *F* test statistic.

To interpret the results, you start by testing whether there is an interaction effect between factor *A* (loom) and factor *B* (supplier). If the interaction effect is significant, further analysis will refer only to this interaction. If the interaction effect is not significant, you can focus on the **main effects**—potential differences in looms (factor *A*) and potential differences in suppliers (factor *B*).

Using the 0.05 level of significance, to determine whether there is evidence of an interaction effect, you reject the null hypothesis of no interaction between loom and supplier if the computed *F* value is greater than 2.92, the approximate upper-tail critical value from the *F* distribution, with 3 and 32 degrees of freedom (see Figure 11).[1]

Because $F = 0.0111 < F_U = 2.92$ or the *p*-value = 0.9984 > 0.05, you do not reject H_0. You conclude that there is insufficient evidence of an interaction effect between loom and supplier. You can now focus on the main effects.

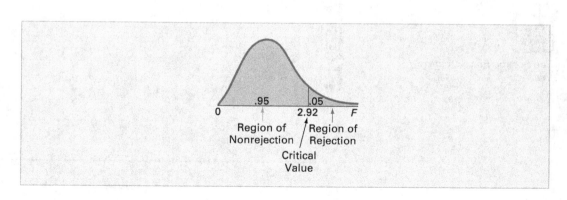

Using the 0.05 level of significance and testing for a difference between the two looms (factor A), you reject the null hypothesis if the calculated F value is greater than 4.17, the (approximate) upper-tail critical value from the F distribution with 1 and 32 degrees of freedom (see Figure 12). Because $F = 0.8096 < F_U = 4.17$ or the p-value = 0.3750 > 0.05, you do not reject H_0. You conclude that there is insufficient evidence of a difference between the two looms in terms of the mean tensile strengths of the parachutes manufactured.

FIGURE 12

Regions of rejection and nonrejection at the 0.05 level of significance, with 1 and 32 degrees of freedom

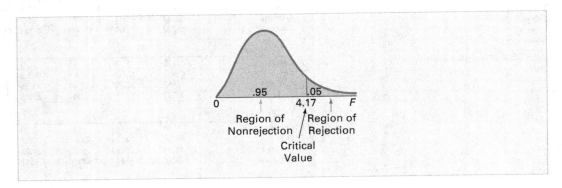

Using the 0.05 level of significance and testing for a difference among the suppliers (factor B), you reject the null hypothesis of no difference if the calculated F value exceeds 2.92, the approximate upper-tail critical value from the F, distribution with 3 degrees of freedom in the numerator and 32 degrees of freedom in the denominator (see Figure 11). Because $F = 5.1999 > F_U = 2.92$ or the p-value = 0.0049 < 0.05, reject H_0. You conclude that there is evidence of a difference among the suppliers in terms of the mean tensile strength of the parachutes.

Interpreting Interaction Effects

You can get a better understanding of the interpretation of the interaction by plotting the cell means (that is, the means of all possible factor level combinations), as shown in Figure 13. Figure 10 provides the cell means for the loom–supplier combinations. From the plot of the mean tensile strength for each combination of loom and supplier, observe that the two lines (representing the two looms) are roughly parallel. This indicates that the *difference* between the mean tensile strength of the two looms is virtually the same for the four suppliers. In other words, there is no *interaction* between these two factors, as was clearly substantiated from the F test.

FIGURE 13

Microsoft Excel cell means plot of tensile strength based on loom and supplier

See Section E5 to create this.

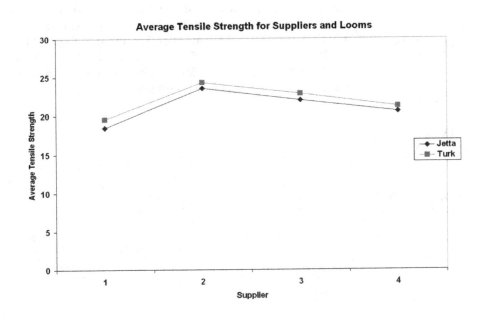

What is the interpretation if there is an interaction? In such a situation, some levels of factor A would respond better with certain levels of factor B. For example, with respect to tensile strength, suppose that some suppliers were better for the Jetta loom and other suppliers were better for the Turk loom. If this were true, the lines of Figure 13 would not be nearly as parallel, and the interaction effect might be statistically significant. In such a situation, the difference between the looms is no longer the same for all suppliers. Such an outcome would also complicate the interpretation of the *main effects* because differences in one factor (the loom) are not consistent across the other factor (the supplier).

Example 2 illustrates a situation with a significant interaction effect.

EXAMPLE 2

INTERPRETING SIGNIFICANT INTERACTION EFFECTS

A nationwide company specializing in preparing students for college entrance exams, such as the SAT, ACT, and LSAT, decided to conduct an experiment to investigate ways to improve its ACT Preparatory Course. Two factors of interest to the company are the length of the course (regular 30-day period or a condensed 10-day period) and the type of course (traditional classroom or online distance learning). The company randomly assigned 10 clients to each of the four cells. Table 8 lists the students' scores on the ACT for this two-factor design. The data are stored in the file act.xls.

What are the effects of the type of course and the length of the course on ACT scores?

TABLE 8

ACT Scores for Different Types and Lengths of Courses

TYPE OF COURSE	LENGTH OF COURSE			
	Condensed		Regular	
Traditional	26	18	34	28
	27	24	24	21
	25	29	35	23
	21	20	31	29
	21	28	28	26
Online	27	21	24	21
	29	32	26	19
	20	19	32	19
	24	28	20	24
	30	29	23	25

SOLUTION The cell means plot presented in Figure 14 illustrates a strong interaction between the type of course and the length of the course. The non-parallel lines indicate that the effect of condensing the course depends on whether the course is taught in the traditional classroom manner or via online distance learning. The online mean score is higher when the course is condensed to a 10-day period, whereas the traditional mean score is higher when the course takes place over the traditional 30-day period.

To verify the somewhat subjective analysis provided by interpreting the cell means plot, you begin by testing whether there is a statistically significant interaction between factor A (length of course) and factor B (type of course). Using a 0.05 level of significance, you reject the null hypothesis because the p-value equals $0.0184 < 0.05$ (see Figure 15). Thus, the hypothesis test confirms the interaction evident in the cell means plot. The existence of this significant interaction effect complicates the interpretation of the hypothesis tests concerning the two main effects. You cannot directly conclude that there is no effect with respect to length of course and type of course, even though both have p-values > 0.05. Whether condensing a course is a good

FIGURE 14

Microsoft Excel cell means plot of ACT scores

See Section E5 to create this.

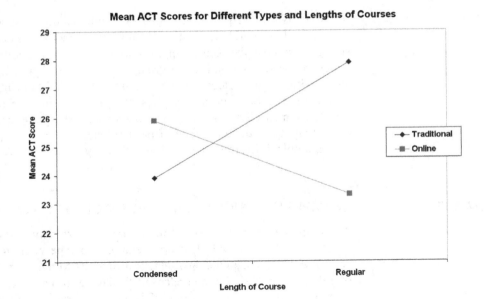

idea depends on whether the course is a traditional class or an online distance learning course. To ensure the highest mean ACT scores, the company should use the traditional approach when offering courses over a 30-day period but use the online approach when offering the condensed courses over a 10-day period.

FIGURE 15

Microsoft Excel two-way ANOVA for ACT scores

See Section E4 to create this.

	A	B	C	D	E	F	G
1	Anova: Two-Factor With Replication						
2							
3	SUMMARY	Condensed	Regular	Total			
4	Traditional						
5	Count	10	10	20			
6	Sum	239	279	518			
7	Average	23.9	27.9	25.9			
8	Variance	13.8778	20.9889	20.7263			
9							
10	Online						
11	Count	10	10	20			
12	Sum	259	233	492			
13	Average	25.9	23.3	24.6			
14	Variance	20.9889	15.5667	19.0947			
15							
16	Total						
17	Count	20	20				
18	Sum	498	512				
19	Average	24.9	25.6				
20	Variance	17.5684	22.8842				
21							
22							
23	ANOVA						
24	*Source of Variation*	*SS*	*df*	*MS*	*F*	*P-value*	*F crit*
25	Sample	16.9	1	16.9	0.9465	0.3371	4.1132
26	Columns	4.9	1	4.9	0.2744	0.6036	4.1132
27	Interaction	108.9	1	108.9	6.0989	0.0184	4.1132
28	Within	642.8	36	17.8556			
29							
30	Total	773.5	39				

Multiple Comparisons: The Tukey Procedure

If there is no significant interaction effect, you can determine the particular levels of the factors that are significantly different by using the **Tukey multiple comparions procedure** (see references 8 and 9). Equation (16) gives the critical range for factor A.

CRITICAL RANGE FOR FACTOR A

$$\text{Critical range} = Q_U \sqrt{\frac{MSE}{cn'}} \qquad (16)$$

where Q_U is the upper-tail critical value from a Studentized range distribution having r and $rc(n' - 1)$ degrees of freedom. (Values for the Studentized range distribution are found in the table of critical values of the studentized range, Q.)

Equation (17) gives the critical range for factor B.

CRITICAL RANGE FOR FACTOR B

$$\text{Critical range} = Q_U \sqrt{\frac{MSE}{rn'}} \qquad (17)$$

where Q_U is the upper-tail critical value from a Studentized range distribution having c and $rc(n' - 1)$ degrees of freedom. (Values for the Studentized range distribution are found in the table of cirtical values of the studentized range, Q.)

To use the Tukey procedure, return to the parachute manufacturing data of Table 7. In Figures 10 (the ANOVA summary table provided by Microsoft Excel), only one of the main effects is significant. Using $\alpha = 0.05$, there is no evidence of a significant difference between the two looms (Jetta and Turk) that comprise factor A, but there is evidence of a significant difference among the four suppliers that comprise factor B. Thus, you can use the Tukey multiple comparisons procedure to further analyze differences between the suppliers of factor B.

Because there are four levels of factor B, there are $4(4 - 1)/2 = 6$ pairwise comparisons. Using the calculations presented in Figures 10, the absolute mean differences are as follows:

1. $\left| \bar{X}_{.1.} - \bar{X}_{.2.} \right| = \left| 18.97 - 23.90 \right| = 4.93$

2. $\left| \bar{X}_{.1.} - \bar{X}_{.3.} \right| = \left| 18.97 - 22.41 \right| = 3.44$

3. $\left| \bar{X}_{.1.} - \bar{X}_{.4.} \right| = \left| 18.97 - 20.83 \right| = 1.86$

4. $\left| \bar{X}_{.2.} - \bar{X}_{.3.} \right| = \left| 23.90 - 22.41 \right| = 1.49$

5. $\left| \bar{X}_{.2.} - \bar{X}_{.4.} \right| = \left| 23.90 - 20.83 \right| = 3.07$

6. $\left| \bar{X}_{.3.} - \bar{X}_{.4.} \right| = \left| 22.41 - 20.83 \right| = 1.58$

To determine the critical range, refer to Figure 10 to find $MSE = 8.612$, $r = 2$, $c = 4$, and $n' = 5$. From the table of critical values of the studentized range, Q [for $\alpha = 0.05$, $c = 4$, and $rc(n' - 1) = 32$], Q_U, the upper-tail critical value of the test statistic with 4 and 32 degrees of freedom, is approximated as 3.84. Using Equation (17),

$$\text{Critical range} = 3.84 \sqrt{\frac{8.612}{10}} = 3.56$$

Because $4.93 > 3.56$, only the means of Suppliers 1 and 2 are different. You can conclude that the mean tensile strength is lower for Supplier 1 than for Supplier 2, but there are no statistically significant differences between Suppliers 1 and 3, Suppliers 1 and 4, Suppliers 2 and 3, Suppliers 2 and 4, and Suppliers 3 and 4. Note that by using $\alpha = 0.05$, you are able to make all six comparisons with an overall error rate of only 5%.

PROBLEMS FOR SECTION 2

Learning the Basics

 15 Consider a two-factor factorial design with three levels in factor A, three levels in factor B, and four replicates in each of the nine cells.
a. How many degrees of freedom are there in determining the factor A variation and the factor B variation?
b. How many degrees of freedom are there in determining the interaction variation?
c. How many degrees of freedom are there in determining the random error variation?
d. How many degrees of freedom are there in determining the total variation?

 16 Assume that you are working with the results from Problem 15.
a. If $SSA = 120$, $SSB = 110$, $SSE = 270$, and $SST = 540$, what is $SSAB$?
b. What are MSA and MSB?
c. What is $MSAB$?
d. What is MSE?

17 Assume that you are working with the results of Problems 15 and 16.
a. What is the value of the test statistic F for the interaction effect?
b. What is the value of the test statistic F for the factor A effect?
c. What is the value of the test statistic F for the factor B effect?
d. Form the ANOVA summary table and fill in all values in the body of the table.

 18 Given the results from Problems 15 through 17,
a. at the 0.05 level of significance, is there an effect due to factor A?
b. at the 0.05 level of significance, is there an effect due to factor B?
c. at the 0.05 level of significance, is there an interaction effect?

19 Given a two-way ANOVA with two levels for factor A, five levels for factor B, and four replicates in each of the 10 cells, with $SSA = 18$, $SSB = 64$, $SSE = 60$, and $SST = 150$,
a. form the ANOVA summary table and fill in all values in the body of the table.
b. at the 0.05 level of significance, is there an effect due to factor A?
c. at the 0.05 level of significance, is there an effect due to factor B?

d. at the 0.05 level of significance, is there an interaction effect?

 20 Given a two-factor factorial experiment and the ANOVA summary table that follows, fill in all the missing results:

Source	Degrees of Freedom	Sum of Squares	Mean Square (Variance)	F
Factor A	$r - 1 = 2$	$SSA = ?$	$MSA = 80$	$F = ?$
Factor B	$c - 1 = ?$	$SSB = 220$	$MSB = ?$	$F = 0$
AB interaction	$(r-1)(c-1) = 8$	$SSAB = ?$	$MSAB = 10$	$F = ?$
Error	$rc(n' - 1) = 30$	$SSE = ?$	$MSE = ?$	
Total	$n - 1 = ?$	$SST = ?$		

 21 From the results of Problem 20,
a. at the 0.05 level of significance, is there an effect due to factor A?
b. At the 0.05 level of significance, is there an effect due to factor B?
c. At the 0.05 level of significance, is there an interaction effect?

Applying the Concepts

22 The effects of developer strength (factor A) and development time (factor B) on the density of photographic plate film were being studied. Two strengths and two development times were used, and four replicates in each of the four cells were evaluated. The results (with larger being best) are stored in the file photo.xls and shown in the following table:

DEVELOPER STRENGTH	DEVELOPMENT TIME (MINUTES) 10	DEVELOPMENT TIME (MINUTES) 14
1	0	1
	5	4
	2	3
	4	2
2	4	6
	7	7
	6	8
	5	7

At the 0.05 level of significance,
a. is there an interaction between developer strength and development time?
b. is there an effect due to developer strength?
c. is there an effect due to development time?
d. Plot the mean density of each developer strength for each development time.
e. What can you conclude about the effect of developer strength and development time on density?

23 A chef in a restaurant that specializes in pasta dishes was experiencing difficulty in getting brands of pasta to be *al dente*—that is, cooked enough so as not to feel starchy or hard but still feel firm when bitten into. She decided to conduct an experiment in which two brands of pasta, one American and one Italian, were cooked for either 4 or 8 minutes. The variable of interest was weight of the pasta because cooking the pasta enables it to absorb water. A pasta with a faster rate of water absorption may provide a shorter interval in which the pasta is *al dente*, thereby increasing the chance that it might be overcooked. The experiment was conducted by using 150 grams of uncooked pasta. Each trial began by bringing a pot containing 6 quarts of cold, unsalted water to a moderate boil. The 150 grams of uncooked pasta was added and then weighed after a given period of time by lifting the pasta from the pot via a built-in strainer. The results (in terms of weight in grams) for two replicates of each type of pasta and cooking time are stored in the file pasta.xls and are as follows:

TYPE OF PASTA	COOKING TIME (MINUTES)	
	4	**8**
American	265	310
	270	320
Italian	250	300
	245	305

At the 0.05 level of significance,
a. is there an interaction between type of pasta and cooking time?
b. is there an effect due to type of pasta?
c. is there an effect due to cooking time?
d. Plot the mean weight for each type of pasta for each cooking time.
e. What conclusions can you reach concerning the importance of each of these two factors on the weight of the pasta?

24 A student team in a business statistics course performed a factorial experiment to investigate the time required for pain-relief tablets to dissolve in a glass of water. The two factors of interest were brand name (Equate, Kroger, or Alka-Seltzer) and temperature of the water (hot or cold). The experiment consisted of four replicates for each of the six factor combinations. The following data (stored in the file pain-relief.xls) show the time a tablet took to dissolve (in seconds) for the 24 tablets used in the experiment:

WATER	BRAND OF PAIN-RELIEF TABLET		
	Equate	**Kroger**	**Alka-Seltzer**
Cold	85.87	75.98	100.11
	78.69	87.66	99.65
	76.42	85.71	100.83
	74.43	86.31	94.16
Hot	21.53	24.10	23.80
	26.26	25.83	21.29
	24.95	26.32	20.82
	21.52	22.91	23.21

At the 0.05 level of significance,
a. is there an interaction between brand of pain reliever and temperature of water?
b. is there an effect due to brand?
c. is there an effect due to the temperature of the water?
d. Plot the mean dissolving time for each brand for the two temperatures.
e. Discuss the results of (a) through (d).

25 Integrated circuits are manufactured on silicon wafers through a process that involves a series of steps. An experiment was carried out to study the effect of the cleansing and etching steps on the yield (coded to maintain confidentiality). The results (stored in the file yield.xls) are as follows:

CLEANSING STEP	ETCHING STEP	
	New	**Standard**
New 1	38	34
	34	19
	38	28
New 2	29	20
	35	35
	34	37
Standard	31	29
	23	32
	38	30

Source: Extracted from J. Ramirez and W. Taam, "An Autologistic Model for Integrated Circuit Manufacturing," Journal of Quality Technology, *2000, 32, pp. 254–262.*

At the 0.05 level of significance,
a. is there an interaction between the cleansing step and the etching step?
b. is there an effect due to the cleansing step?
c. is there an effect due to the etching step?

d. Plot the mean yield for each cleansing step for the two etching steps.

e. Discuss the results of (a) through (d).

26 An experiment was conducted to study the distortion of drive gears in automobiles. Two factors were studied—the tooth size of the gear and the part positioning. The results (stored in the file `gear.xls`) are as follows: At the 0.05 level of significance,

a. is there an interaction between the tooth size and the part positioning?

b. is there an effect due to tooth size?

c. is there an effect due to the part positioning?

d. Plot the mean yield for each tooth size for the two part positions.

e. Discuss the results of (a) through (d).

TOOTH SIZE	PART POSITIONING Low	High
Low	18.0	13.5
	16.5	8.5
	26.0	11.5
	22.5	16.0
	21.5	~4.5
	21.0	4.0
	30.0	1.0
	24.5	9.0
High	27.5	17.5
	19.5	11.5
	31.0	10.0
	27.0	1.0
	17.0	14.5
	14.0	3.5
	18.0	7.5
	17.5	6.5

Source: Extracted from D. R. Bingham and R. R. Sitter, "Design Issues in Fractional Factorial Split-Plot Experiments," Journal of Quality Technology, *33, 2001, pp. 2–15.*

3 ● (*CD-ROM Topic*) THE RANDOMIZED BLOCK DESIGN

The randomized block design is an extension of the paired *t* test to more than two groups. For further discussion, see `section 3.pdf` on the Student CD-ROM that accompanies this text.

S U M M A R Y

In this chapter, various statistical procedures were used to analyze the effect of one or two factors of interest. You learned how the production manager of the Perfect Parachutes Company could use these procedures to identify the best suppliers and loom types in order to increase the strength of the parachutes. The assumptions required for using these procedures were discussed in detail. Remember that you need to critically investigate the validity of the assumptions underlying the hypothesis test procedures. Table 9 summarizes the topics covered in this chapter.

TABLE 9

Summary of Topics

Type of Analysis	Type of Data Numerical
Comparing more than two groups (one factor)	One-way analysis of variance (Section 1)
Factorial design	Two-way analysis of variance (Section 2)
Comparing more than two groups (one factor with repeated measurements or matched items)	Randomized block design (Section 11.3 on the Student CD-ROM)

KEY EQUATIONS

Total Variation in One-Way ANOVA

$$SST = \sum_{j=1}^{c} \sum_{i=1}^{n_j} (X_{ij} - \overline{\overline{X}})^2 \tag{1}$$

Among-Group Variation in One-Way ANOVA

$$SSA = \sum_{j=1}^{c} n_j (\overline{X}_j - \overline{\overline{X}})^2 \tag{2}$$

Within-Group Variation in One-Way ANOVA

$$SSW = \sum_{j=1}^{c} \sum_{i=1}^{n_j} (X_{ij} - \overline{X}_j)^2 \tag{3}$$

Mean Squares in One-Way ANOVA

$$MSA = \frac{SSA}{c-1} \tag{4a}$$

$$MSW = \frac{SSW}{n-c} \tag{4b}$$

$$MST = \frac{SST}{n-1} \tag{4c}$$

One-Way ANOVA F Test Statistic

$$F = \frac{MSA}{MSW} \tag{5}$$

Critical Range for the Tukey-Kramer Procedure

$$\text{Critical range} = Q_U \sqrt{\frac{MSW}{2} \left(\frac{1}{n_j} + \frac{1}{n_{j'}} \right)} \tag{6}$$

Total Variation in Two-Way ANOVA

$$SST = \sum_{i=1}^{r} \sum_{j=1}^{c} \sum_{k=1}^{n'} (X_{ijk} - \overline{\overline{X}})^2 \tag{7}$$

Factor A Variation

$$SSA = cn' \sum_{i=1}^{r} (\overline{X}_{i..} - \overline{\overline{X}})^2 \tag{8}$$

Factor B Variation

$$SSB = rn' \sum_{j=1}^{c} (\overline{X}_{.j.} - \overline{\overline{X}})^2 \tag{9}$$

Interaction Variation

$$SSAB = n' \sum_{i=1}^{r} \sum_{j=1}^{c} (\overline{X}_{ij.} - \overline{X}_{i..} - \overline{X}_{.j.} + \overline{\overline{X}})^2 \tag{10}$$

Random Error in Two-Way ANOVA

$$SSE = \sum_{i=1}^{r} \sum_{j=1}^{c} \sum_{k=1}^{n'} (X_{ijk} - \overline{X}_{ij.})^2 \tag{11}$$

Mean Squares in Two-Way ANOVA

$$MSA = \frac{SSA}{r-1} \tag{12a}$$

$$MSB = \frac{SSB}{c-1} \tag{12b}$$

$$MSAB = \frac{SSAB}{(r-1)(c-1)} \tag{12c}$$

$$MSE = \frac{SSE}{rc(n'-1)} \tag{12d}$$

F Test for Factor A Effect

$$F = \frac{MSA}{MSE} \tag{13}$$

F Test for Factor B Effect

$$F = \frac{MSB}{MSE} \tag{14}$$

F Test for Interaction Effect

$$F = \frac{MSAB}{MSE} \tag{15}$$

Critical Range for Factor A

$$\text{Critical range} = Q_U \sqrt{\frac{MSE}{cn'}} \tag{16}$$

Critical Range for Factor B

$$\text{Critical range} = Q_U \sqrt{\frac{MSE}{rn'}} \tag{17}$$

KEY TERMS

among-group variation
analysis of variance (ANOVA)
ANOVA summary table
completely randomized design
critical range
F distribution
factor
grand mean, $\overline{\overline{X}}$
group
homogeneity of variance
interaction
level
Levene test
main effect
mean square

multiple comparisons
normality
one-way ANOVA
one-way ANOVA F test statistic
random error
randomness and independence
replicate
Studentized range distribution
sum of squares among groups (SSA)
sum of squares due to factor A (SSA)
sum of squares due to factor B (SSB)

sum of squares due to interaction ($SSAB$)
sum of squares error (SSE)
sum of squares total (SST)
sum of squares within groups (SSW)
total variation
Tukey multiple comparisons procedure
Tukey-Kramer multiple comparisons procedure
two-factor factorial design
two-way ANOVA
within-group variation

CHAPTER REVIEW PROBLEMS

Checking Your Understanding

27 In a one-way ANOVA, what is the difference between among-group variation and within-group variation?

28 What are the distinguishing features of the completely randomized design and two-factor factorial designs?

29 What are the assumptions of ANOVA?

30 Under what conditions should you select the one-way ANOVA F test to examine possible differences among the means of c independent groups?

31 When and how should you use multiple comparisons procedures for evaluating pairwise combinations of the group means?

32 What is the difference between the one-way ANOVA F test and the Levene test?

33 Under what conditions should you use the two-way ANOVA F test to examine possible differences among the means of each factor in a factorial design?

34 What is meant by the concept of interaction in a two-factor factorial design?

35 How can you determine whether there is an interaction in the two-factor factorial design?

Applying the Concepts

36 The operations manager for an appliance manufacturer wants to determine the optimal length of time for the washing cycle of a household clothes washer. An experiment is designed to measure the effect of detergent brand and washing cycle time on the amount of dirt removed from standard household laundry loads. Four brands of detergent (A, B, C, D) and four levels of washing cycle (18, 20, 22, and 24 minutes) are specifically selected for analysis. In order to run the experiment, 32 standard household laundry loads (having equal weight and dirt) are randomly assigned, 2 each, to the 16 detergent-washing cycle time combinations. The results, in pounds of dirt removed (stored in the laundry.xls file), are as follows:

DETERGENT BRAND	WASHING CYCLE TIME (IN MINUTES)			
	18	20	22	24
A	0.11	0.13	0.17	0.17
	0.09	0.13	0.19	0.18
B	0.12	0.14	0.17	0.19
	0.10	0.15	0.18	0.17
C	0.08	0.16	0.18	0.20
	0.09	0.13	0.17	0.16
D	0.11	0.12	0.16	0.15
	0.13	0.13	0.17	0.17

At the 0.05 level of significance,
a. is there an interaction between detergent and washing cycle time?
b. is there an effect due to detergent brand?

c. is there an effect due to washing cycle time?

d. Plot the mean amount of dirt removed (in pounds) for each detergent brand for each washing cycle time.

e. If appropriate, use the Tukey procedure to determine differences between detergent brands and between washing cycle times.

f. What washing cycle should be used for this type of household clothes washer?

g. Repeat the analysis, using washing cycle time as the only factor. Compare your results to those of (c), (e), and (f).

37 The quality control director for a clothing manufacturer wants to study the effect of operators and machines on the breaking strength (in pounds) of wool serge material. A batch of the material is cut into square-yard pieces, and these are randomly assigned, 3 each, to all 12 combinations of 4 operators and 3 machines chosen specifically for the experiment. The results (stored in the file breakstw.xls) are as follows:

| | MACHINE | | |
OPERATOR	I	II	III
A	115	111	109
	115	108	110
	119	114	107
B	117	105	110
	114	102	113
	114	106	114
C	109	100	103
	110	103	102
	106	101	105
D	112	105	108
	115	107	111
	111	107	110

At the 0.05 level of significance,

a. is there an interaction between operator and machine?

b. is there an effect due to operator?

c. is there an effect due to machine?

d. Plot the mean breaking strength for each operator for each machine.

e. If appropriate, use the Tukey procedure to examine differences among operators and among machines.

f. What can you conclude about the effects of operators and machines on breaking strength? Explain.

g. Repeat the analysis, using machines as the only factor. Compare your results to those of (c), (e), and (f).

38 An operations manager wants to examine the effect of air-jet pressure (in psi) on the breaking strength of yarn. Three different levels of air-jet pressure are to be considered: 30 psi, 40 psi, and 50 psi. A random sample of 18 homogeneous filling yarns are selected from the same batch, and the yarns are randomly assigned, 6 each, to the 3 levels of air-jet pressure. The breaking strength scores are in the file yarn.xls.

a. Is there evidence of a significant difference in the variances of the breaking strengths for the three air-jet pressures? (Use $\alpha = 0.05$).

b. At the 0.05 level of significance, is there evidence of a difference among mean breaking strengths for the three air-jet pressures?

c. If appropriate, use the Tukey-Kramer procedure to determine which air-jet pressures significantly differ with respect to mean breaking strength. (Use $\alpha = 0.05$.)

d. What should the operations manager conclude?

39 Suppose that, when setting up his experiment in Problem 38, the operations manager is able to study the effect of side-to-side aspect in addition to air-jet pressure. Thus, instead of the one-factor completely randomized design in Problem 38, he used a two-factor factorial design, with the first factor, side-to-side aspects, having two levels (nozzle and opposite) and the second factor, air-jet pressure, having three levels (30 psi, 40 psi, and 50 psi). A sample of 18 yarns is randomly assigned, 3 to each of the 6 side-to-side aspect and pressure level combinations. The breaking-strength scores are as follows:

| SIDE-TO-SIDE ASPECT | AIR-JET PRESSURE | | |
	30 psi	40 psi	50 psi
Nozzle	25.5	24.8	23.2
	24.9	23.7	23.7
	26.1	24.4	22.7
Opposite	24.7	23.6	22.6
	24.2	23.3	22.8
	23.6	21.4	24.9

At the 0.05 level of significance,

a. is there an interaction between side-to-side aspect and air-jet pressure?

b. is there an effect due to side-to-side aspect?

c. is there an effect due to air-jet pressure?

d. Plot the mean yarn breaking strength for the two levels of side-to-side aspect for each level of air-jet pressure.

e. If appropriate, use the Tukey procedure to study differences among the air-jet pressures.

f. On the basis of the results of (a) through (c), what conclusions can you reach concerning yarn breaking strength? Discuss.

g. Compare your results in (a) through (f) with those from the completely randomized design in Problem 38 (a) through (d). Discuss fully.

40 A hotel wanted to develop a new system for delivering room service breakfasts. In the current system, an order form is left on the bed in each room. If the customer wishes to receive a room service breakfast, he or she places the order form on the doorknob before 11 p.m. The current system includes a delivery time that provides a 15-minute interval for desired delivery time (6:30–6:45 a.m., 6:45–7:00 a.m., and so on). The new system is designed to allow the customer to request a specific delivery time. The hotel wants to measure the difference between the actual delivery time and the requested delivery time of room service orders for breakfast. (A negative time means that the order was delivered before the requested time. A positive time means that the order was delivered after the requested time.) The factors included were the menu choice (American or Continental) and the desired time period in which the order was to be delivered (Early Time Period [6:30–8:00 a.m.] or Late Time Period [8:00–9:30 a.m.]). Ten orders for each combination of menu choice and desired time period were studied on a particular day. The data (stored in the file breakfast.xls) are as follows:

TYPE OF BREAKFAST	DESIRED TIME Early Time Period	Late Time Period
Continental	1.2	−2.5
	2.1	3.0
	3.3	−0.2
	4.4	1.2
	3.4	1.2
	5.3	0.7
	2.2	−1.3
	1.0	0.2
	5.4	−0.5
	1.4	3.8
American	4.4	6.0
	1.1	2.3
	4.8	4.2
	7.1	3.8
	6.7	5.5
	5.6	1.8
	9.5	5.1
	4.1	4.2
	7.9	4.9
	9.4	4.0

At the 0.05 level of significance,
a. is there an interaction between type of breakfast and desired time?
b. is there an effect due to type of breakfast?
c. is there an effect due to desired time?
d. Plot the mean delivery time difference for the two desired times for type of breakfast.
e. On the basis of the results of (a) through (d), what conclusions can you reach concerning delivery time difference? Discuss.

f. Suppose, instead, that the results are as shown below (and stored in the file breakfast2.xls). Repeat (a) through (e), using these data and compare the results to those of (a) through (e).

TYPE OF BREAKFAST	DESIRED TIME Early	Late
Continental	1.2	−0.5
	2.1	5.0
	3.3	1.8
	4.4	3.2
	3.4	3.2
	5.3	2.7
	2.2	0.7
	1.0	2.2
	5.4	1.5
	1.4	5.8
American	4.4	6.0
	1.1	2.3
	4.8	4.2
	7.1	3.8
	6.7	5.5
	5.6	1.8
	9.5	5.1
	4.1	4.2
	7.9	4.9
	9.4	4.0

41 Modern software applications require rapid data access capabilities. An experiment was conducted to test the effect of data file size on the ability to access the files (as measured by read time, in milliseconds). Three different levels of data file size were considered: small—50,000 characters; medium—75,000 characters; or large—100,000 characters. A sample of eight files of each size was evaluated. The access read times, in milliseconds, are in the data file access.xls.

a. Is there evidence of a significant difference in the variance of the access read times for the three file sizes? (Use $\alpha = 0.05$).
b. At the 0.05 level of significance, is there evidence of a difference among mean access read times for the three file sizes?
c. If appropriate, use the Tukey-Kramer multiple comparisons procedure to determine which file sizes significantly differ with respect to mean access read time. (Use $\alpha = 0.05$.)
d. What conclusions can you reach?

42 Suppose that in Problem 41, when setting up the experiment, the effects of the size of the input/output buffer was studied in addition to the effects of the data file size. Thus, instead of the one-factor completely randomized design given in Problem 41, the experiment used a two-factor factorial design, with the first factor, buffer size, having two levels (20 kilobytes and 40 kilobytes) and the second factor, data file size, having three levels (small, medium, and large). That is, there are two factors under consideration: buffer size and data file size. A sample of four programs (replicates) were evaluated for each buffer size and data file size combination. The access read times, in milliseconds, are in the data file access.xls.

At the 0.05 level of significance,

a. is there an interaction between buffer size and data file size?

b. is there an effect due to buffer size?

c. is there an effect due to data file size?

d. Plot the mean access read times (in milliseconds) for the two buffer size levels for each of the three data file size levels. Describe the interaction and discuss why you can or cannot interpret the main effects in (b) and (c).

e. On the basis of the results of (a) through (d), what conclusions can you reach concerning access read times? Discuss.

f. Compare and contrast your results in (a) through (e) with those from the completely randomized design in Problem 41(a) through (d). Discuss fully.

43 A student team in a business statistics course conducted an experiment to test the download times of the three different types of computers (MAC, iMAC, and Dell) available at the university library. The students randomly selected one computer of each type. The students went to the Microsoft game Web site and clicked on the download link for the NBA game. The time (in seconds) between clicking on the link and the completion of the download was recorded. After each download, the file was deleted, and the trash folder was emptied. A total of 30 downloads were completed, in random order. Completely analyze the data shown in the following table and stored in the file computers.xls.

Computer

MAC	iMAC	Dell
156	160	236
166	165	238
148	184	257
160	192	242
139	197	282
151	172	253
158	189	270
167	179	256
142	200	267
219	193	259

44 In a second experiment performed by the team in Problem 43, the browser (Netscape Communicator or Internet Explorer) was added as a second factor. In this experiment, only two of the types of computers were used (MAC and Dell). Eight downloads from each of the four factor combinations were completed. Completely analyze the data shown in the following table and stored in the file computers2.xls.

BROWSER	COMPUTER MAC	Dell
Netscape Communicator	142	284
	132	304
	125	273
	136	340
	127	326
	138	301
	147	291
	143	285
Internet Explorer	198	285
	210	292
	199	305
	202	325
	196	297
	213	301
	207	285
	201	290

Team Project

The data file Mutual Funds.xls contains information regarding nine variables from a sample of 838 mutual funds. The variables are

Category—Type of stocks comprising the mutual fund (small cap, mid cap, or large cap)

Objective—Objective of stocks comprising the mutual fund (growth or value)

Assets—In millions of dollars

Fees—Sales charges (no or yes)

Expense ratio—Ratio of expenses to net assets in percentage

2005 return—Twelve-month return in 2005

Three-year return—Annualized return, 2003–2005

Five-year return—Annualized return, 2001–2005

Risk—Risk-of-loss factor of the mutual fund (low, average, or high)

45 Completely analyze the difference between small cap, mid cap, and large cap mutual funds in terms of 2005 return, three-year return, five-year return, and expense ratio. Write a report summarizing your findings.

46 Completely analyze the difference between low-risk, average-risk, and high-risk mutual funds in terms of 2005 return, three-year return, five-year return, and expense ratio. Write a report summarizing your findings.

Managing the *Springville Herald*

Phase 1

In studying the home delivery solicitation process, the marketing department team determined that the so-called "later" calls made between 7:00 p.m. and 9:00 p.m. were significantly more conducive to lengthier calls than those made earlier in the evening (between 5:00 p.m. and 7:00 p.m.).

Knowing that the 7:00 p.m.-to-9:00 p.m. time period is superior, the team sought to investigate the effect of the type of presentation on the length of the call. A group of 24 female callers was randomly assigned, 8 each, to one of three presentation plans—structured, semistructured, and unstructured—and trained to make the telephone presentation. All calls were made between 7:00 p.m. and 9:00 p.m., the later time period, and the callers were to provide an introductory greeting that was personal but informal ("Hi, this is Mary Jones from the *Springville Herald*. May I speak to Bill Richards?"). The callers knew that the team was observing their efforts that evening but didn't know which particular calls were monitored. Measurements were taken on the length of call (defined as the difference, in seconds, between the time the person answers the phone and the time he or she hangs up). Table SH1 presents the results (which are stored in the file `sh11-1.xls`).

TABLE SH1 Length of Calls (in Seconds)
Based on Presentation Plan

PRESENTATION PLAN		
Structured	**Semistructured**	**Unstructured**
38.8	41.8	32.9
42.1	36.4	36.1
45.2	39.1	39.2
34.8	28.7	29.3
48.3	36.4	41.9
37.8	36.1	31.7
41.1	35.8	35.2
43.6	33.7	38.1

EXERCISE

SH1 Analyze these data and write a report to the team that indicates your findings. Be sure to include your recommendations based on your findings. Also, include an appendix in which you discuss the reason you selected a particular statistical test to compare the three independent groups of callers.

DO NOT CONTINUE UNTIL THE PHASE 1 EXERCISE HAS BEEN COMPLETED.

Phase 2

In analyzing the data of Table SH1, the marketing department team observed that the structured presentation plan resulted in a significantly longer call than either the semistructured or unstructured plans. The team decided to tentatively recommend that all solicitations be completely structured calls made later in the evening, from 7:00 p.m. to 9:00 p.m. The team also decided to study the effect of two additional factors on the length of call:

- Gender of the caller: male versus female.
- Type of greeting: personal but formal (for example, "Hello, my name is Mary Jones from the *Springville Herald*. May I speak to Mr. Richards?"), personal but informal (for example, "Hi, this is Mary Jones from the *Springville Herald*. May I speak to Bill Richards?"), or impersonal (for example, "I represent the *Springville Herald* . . .").

The team acknowledged that in its previous studies, it had controlled for these variables. Only female callers were selected to participate in the studies, and they were trained to use a personal but informal greeting style. However, the team wondered if this choice of gender and greeting type was, in fact, best.

The team designed a study in which a total of 30 callers, 15 males and 15 females, were chosen to participate. The callers were randomly assigned to one of the three greeting-style training groups so that there were five callers in each of the six combinations of the two factors, gender and greeting style (personal but formal—PF; personal but informal—PI; and impersonal). The callers knew that the team was observing their efforts that evening but didn't know which particular calls were monitored.

Measurements were taken on the length of call (defined as the difference, in seconds, between the time the person answers and the time he or she hangs up the phone). Table SH2 summarizes the results (which are stored in the file `sh11-2.xls`).

TABLE SH2 Length of Calls (in Seconds), Based on Gender and Type of Greeting

GENDER	GREETING		
	PF	**PI**	**Impersonal**
M	45.6	41.7	35.3
	49.0	42.8	37.7
	41.8	40.0	41.0
	35.6	39.6	28.7
	43.4	36.0	31.8
F	44.1	37.9	43.3
	40.8	41.1	40.0
	46.9	35.8	43.1
	51.8	45.3	39.6
	48.5	40.2	33.2

EXERCISES

SH2 Completely analyze these data and write a report to the team that indicates the importance of each of the two factors and/or the interaction between them on the length of the call. Include recommendations for future experiments to perform.

SH3 Do you believe the length of the telephone call is the most appropriate outcome to study? What other variables should be investigated next? Discuss.

Web Case

Apply your knowledge about ANOVA in this Web Case, on a cereal-fill packaging dispute.

After reviewing CCACC's latest posting, Oxford Cereals is complaining that the group is guilty of using selective data. Visit the company's response page at **www.prenhall.com/Springville/OC_DataSelective.htm**, or open this Web page file from the text CD's Web case folder and then answer the following:

1. Does Oxford Cereals have a legitimate argument? Why or why not?
2. Assuming that the samples the company has posted were randomly selected, perform the appropriate analysis to resolve the ongoing weight dispute.
3. What conclusions can you reach from your results? If you were called as an expert witness, would you support the claims of the CCACC or the claims of Oxford Cereals? Explain.

REFERENCES

1. Berenson, M. L., D. M. Levine, and M. Goldstein, *Intermediate Statistical Methods and Applications: A Computer Package Approach* (Upper Saddle River, NJ: Prentice Hall, 1983).
2. Conover, W. J., *Practical Nonparametric Statistics*, 3rd ed. (New York: Wiley, 2000).
3. Daniel, W. W., *Applied Nonparametric Statistics*, 2nd ed. (Boston: PWS Kent, 1990).
4. Gitlow, H. S., and D. M. Levine, *Six Sigma for Green Belts and Champions: Foundations, DMAIC, Tools, Cases, and Certification* (Upper Saddle River, NJ: Financial Times/Prentice Hall, 2005).
5. Hicks, C. R., and K. V. Turner, *Fundamental Concepts in the Design of Experiments*, 5th ed. (New York: Oxford University Press, 1999).
6. Levine, D. M., *Statistics for Six Sigma Green Belts* (Upper Saddle River, NJ: Financial Times/Prentice Hall, 2006).
7. *Microsoft Excel 2007* (Redmond, WA: Microsoft Corp., 2003).
8. Montgomery, D. M., *Design and Analysis of Experiments*, 6th ed. (New York: Wiley, 2005).
9. Neter, J., M. H. Kutner, C. Nachtsheim, and W. Wasserman, *Applied Linear Statistical Models*, 5th ed. (New York: McGraw-Hill-Irwin, 2005).

Excel Companion

E1 USING THE ONE-WAY ANOVA

You conduct the One-Way ANOVA by selecting the ToolPak Anova: Single Factor procedure.

Open to a worksheet that contains unstacked multiple group data to be analyzed. Select **Tools → Data Analysis**, select **Anova: Single Factor** from the **Data Analysis** list, and click **OK**. In the procedure's dialog box (shown below), enter the cell range of the data as the **Input Range**, click **Columns**, check **Labels in first row**, and click **OK**. Results appear on a new worksheet.

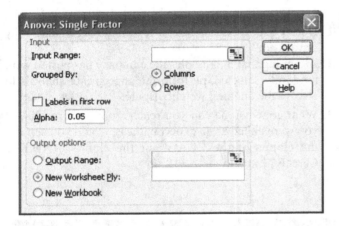

E2 USING THE TUKEY-KRAMER PROCEDURE

You conduct a Tukey-Kramer procedure for unstacked multiple group data by either selecting the PHStat2 Tukey-Kramer Procedure or by following a three-step process that includes making entries in the Tukey-Kramer.xls workbook.

Using PHStat2 Tukey-Kramer Procedure

Open to the worksheet that contains the unstacked multiple group data to be analyzed and select **PHStat → Multiple-Sample Tests → Tukey-Kramer Procedure**. In the Tukey-Kramer Procedure dialog box (shown at the top of the next column), enter the cell range of the data as the **Group Data Cell Range**, leave **First cells contains label** checked, enter a title as the **Title**, and click **OK**.

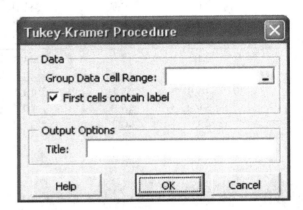

Complete the worksheet created by PHStat2 by looking up the value of Studentized Range Q statistic from the table for the desired level of significance and the numerator and denominator degrees of freedom values displayed in the worksheet.

Using Tukey-Kramer.xls

To use the Tukey-Kramer.xls workbook, first follow the instructions of Section E1 to create an ANOVA worksheet. Record the sample size and sample mean of each group (found in the Count and Average columns, respectively). Also record the *MSW* value, found in the cell that is the intersection of the MS column and the Within Groups row, and the denominator degrees of freedom, found in the cell that is the intersection of the df column and the Within Groups row.

Next, open the Tukey-Kramer.xls workbook and select the worksheet for your number of groups. If you have three groups, select the **TukeyKramer3** worksheet; for four groups, select the **TukeyKramer4** worksheet. (The workbook also has worksheets for five, six, and seven groups.) Enter the sample size, sample mean, denominator degrees of freedom, and *MSW* value you recorded earlier. Finally, look up the Studentized Range Q statistic from the table for the desired level of significance and the numerator and denominator degrees of freedom values displayed in the worksheet.

Figure E1 shows the formulas in column F, G, and H of the TukeyKramer4 worksheet shown in Figure 7. Figure E2 shows the formulas for column I of this worksheet. The IF comparison **B15 = ""**, in the cell I4 formula, holds if B15 is empty—that is, if you have not yet entered the Studentized

	E	F	G	H
1				
2				
3		Absolute	Std. Error	Critical
4	Comparison	Difference	of Difference	Range
5	Group 1 to Group 2	=ABS(B5 - B6)	=SQRT((B14/2) * ((1/C5) + (1/C6)))	=B15 * G5
6	Group 1 to Group 3	=ABS(B5 - B7)	=SQRT((B14/2) * ((1/C5) + (1/C7)))	=B15 * G6
7	Group 1 to Group 4	=ABS(B5 - B8)	=SQRT((B14/2) * ((1/C5) + (1/C8)))	=B15 * G7
8	Group 2 to Group 3	=ABS(B6 - B7)	=SQRT((B14/2) * ((1/C6) + (1/C7)))	=B15 * G8
9	Group 2 to Group 4	=ABS(B6 - B8)	=SQRT((B14/2) * ((1/C6) + (1/C8)))	=B15 * G9
10	Group 3 to Group 4	=ABS(B7 - B8)	=SQRT((B14/2) * ((1/C7) + (1/C8)))	=B15 * G10

FIGURE E1

TukeyKramer4 worksheet columns F, G, and H formulas

	I
1	
2	
3	
4	=IF(B15 = "", "Results are NOT valid until Q Statistic is entered into B15", "Results")
5	=IF(F5 > H5, "Means are different", "Means are not different")
6	=IF(F6 > H6, "Means are different", "Means are not different")
7	=IF(F7 > H7, "Means are different", "Means are not different")
8	=IF(F8 > H8, "Means are different", "Means are not different")
9	=IF(F9 > H9, "Means are different", "Means are not different")
10	=IF(F10 > H10, "Means are different", "Means are not different")

FIGURE E2

TukeyKramer4 worksheet column I formulas

Range Q statistic. If cell B15 is empty, a warning message is displayed; otherwise, the label "Results" is displayed.

E3 USING THE LEVENE TEST FOR HOMOGENEITY OF VARIANCE

You use the Levene test for unstacked multiple group data by either selecting the PHStat2 Levene Test procedure or by following a two-step manual process.

Using PHStat2 Levene Test

Open to the worksheet that contains the unstacked multiple group data to be analyzed and select **PHStat → Multiple-Sample Tests → Levene Test**. In the Levene Test dialog box (shown below), enter the **Level of Significance** and the cell range of the data to be analyzed as the **Sample Data Cell Range**. Leave **First cells contain label** checked, enter a title as the **Title**, and click **OK**.

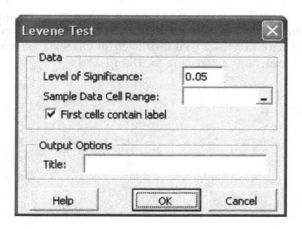

Using the Manual Process

Open to the worksheet that contains the unstacked multiple group data. Using Table 4 and the **Model** worksheet of the Absolute Differences.xls workbook as your guide, add a row of formulas to determine the median for each group and then add new columns that compute the absolute differences. (The **Formulas** worksheet of this workbook displays the formulas used in the **Model** worksheet.) After you create the new columns, perform a one-way ANOVA by following the instructions in Section E1, using the cell range of the new absolute difference columns as the **Input Range** cell range. For example, if you were using the **Model** worksheet of the Absolute Differences.xls workbook, you would enter **F1:I6** as the **Input Range**.

E4 USING THE TWO-WAY ANOVA

You conduct a two-way ANOVA for a two-factor factorial design by selecting the ToolPak Anova: Two Factor With Replication procedure.

To use this ToolPak procedure, factor A data must be placed in rows, starting with row 2, and factor B data must be placed in columns, starting with column B. Enter labels for factor A in column A, starting with cell A2, and enter labels for factor B in row 1, starting with cell B1. (Cell A1 is not used by the procedure, but as a placeholder, you should enter a label that identifies factor A.) The **Data** worksheet of the Parachute2.xls workbook (shown in Figure E3) illustrates these rules and is one that you can use as a model for your own two-factor worksheets.

	A	B	C	D	E
1	Loom	Supplier 1	Supplier 2	Supplier 3	Supplier 4
2	Jetta	20.6	22.6	27.7	21.5
3	Jetta	18.0	24.6	18.6	20.0
4	Jetta	19.0	19.6	20.8	21.1
5	Jetta	21.3	23.8	25.1	23.9
6	Jetta	13.2	27.1	17.7	16.0
7	Turk	18.5	26.3	20.6	25.4
8	Turk	24.0	25.3	25.2	19.9
9	Turk	17.2	24.0	20.8	22.6
10	Turk	19.9	21.2	24.7	17.5
11	Turk	18.0	24.5	22.9	20.4

FIGURE E3

Data worksheet of the Parachute2.xls workbook

With a two-factor factorial design data worksheet opened, select **Tools → Data Analysis**. Select **Anova: Two Factor With Replication** from the **Data Analysis** list and click **OK**. In the procedure's dialog box (shown on page 460), enter the cell range of the data (including all labels) as the **Input Range**. Enter the **Rows per sample** (if you were using the Figure E3 worksheet, you would enter **5**), enter the **Alpha** value, and then click **OK**. Results appear on a new worksheet.

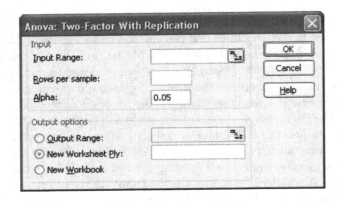

E5 CREATING PLOTS OF CELL MEANS

You create plots of cell means by using Excel charting features and the worksheet created by the ToolPak Anova: Two Factor With Replication procedure (see Section E4). Because this process differs for Excel 2007, this section includes passages specific to Excel 97-2003 and Excel 2007.

Creating a Plot (97-2003)

Open to the worksheet created by the ToolPak Anova: Two Factor With Replication procedure. Begin the Chart Wizard and make these entries:

Step 1 Click **Line** from the **Standard Types Chart type** box. Click the first choice of the second row in the **Chart sub-types** gallery, described as **Line with markers displayed at each value**.

Step 2 Click the **Data Range** tab. Enter the cell range of the means for each combination of factors (found in rows labeled "Average") as the **Data range** and select the **Rows** option. Because the means will appear in more than one area, enter the cell range using one or more commas. For example, to enter the cell means shown in Figure 10, enter **B7:E7,B13:E13** as the Data Range. Then click the **Series** tab. In the **Series** list box, select each generic Series*n* name and enter the appropriate factor *A* label in the **Name** box. For example, enter **Jetta** as the Series 1 name and **Turk** as the Series2 name if plotting the cell means from the Figure 10

worksheet. Finally, enter the cell range of the factor *B* labels as the **Category (X) axis labels** (**B3:E3** for the Figure 10 worksheet).

Step 3 Click the **Titles** tab. Enter values for the **Chart title**, the **Category (X) axis**, and the **Value (Y) axis** title. Click the **Legend** tab and click **Show legend**. Click, in turn, the **Axes, Gridlines, Data Labels**, and **Data Table** tabs and use the formatting settings given in the "Creating Charts (97-2003)" part of Section E2 of "Presenting Data in Tables and Charts" (consult your instructor for this text).

Creating a Plot (2007)

Open to the worksheet created by the ToolPak Anova: Two Factor With Replication procedure. Select the cell range of the means for each combination of factors (found in rows labeled "Average"). Because the means will appear in more than one area, select the first area, then hold down the **Ctrl** key while selecting the other areas. For example, to center the cell means shown in Figure 10, select the range **B7:E7**, hold down the **Ctrl** key, and continue by selecting **B13:E13**.

With the cell means selected, select **Insert → Line** and in the Line gallery select the choice labeled **Line with Markers**. Right-click the chart and click **Edit Data Source** on the shortcut menu. In the **Legend Entries (Series)** list box, do the following for each generic Series*n* name listed: (1) select the generic name, (2) click **Edit** [inside the Legend Entries (Series) dialog box], and (3) in the Edit Series dialog box that appears, enter the appropriate factor *A* label in the **Series name** box and click **OK**. For example, enter **Jetta** as the Series 1 name if plotting the cell means from the Figure 10 worksheet. When you are finished entering the Factor A labels, click **Edit** in the **Horizontal (Categories) Axis Labels** list box. In the Axis Labels dialog box, enter the cell range of the factor *B* labels as the **Axis Label Range** and click **OK**. Back in the Edit Data Source dialog box, click **OK**. For example, enter **Turk** as the Series2 name if plotting the cell means from the Figure 10 worksheet.

Finish by relocating your chart to a chart sheet. Customize your chart using the instructions in "Creating a Chart (2007)" in Section E2 of "Presenting Data in Tables and Charts" (consult your instructor for this text), skipping the instructions given there for **Data Labels**.

Self-Test Solutions and Answers to Selected Even-Numbered Problems

The following represent worked-out solutions to Self-Test Problems and brief answers to most of the even-numbered problems in the text.

2 (a) $SSW = 150$. **(b)** $MSA = 15$. **(c)** $MSW = 5$. **(d)** $F = 3$.

4 (a) 2. **(b)** 18. **(c)** 20.

6 (a) Reject H_0 if $F > 2.95$; otherwise, do not reject H_0. **(b)** Since $F = 4 > 2.95$, reject H_0. **(c)** The table does not have 28 degrees of freedom in the denominator, so use the next larger critical value, $Q_U = 3.90$. **(d)** Critical range = 6.166.

8 (a) Since $F = 10.99 > F = 4.26$, reject H_0. **(b)** Critical range = 40.39. The experts and darts are not different from each other, but they are both different from the readers. **(c)** It is not valid to infer that the dartboard is better than the professionals since their means are not significantly different. **(d)** Since $F = 0.101 < 4.26$, do not reject H_0. There is no evidence of a significant difference in the variation in the return for the three categories.

10 (a) H_0: $\mu_A = \mu_B = \mu_C = \mu_D$ and H_1: At least one mean is different.

$$MSA = \frac{SSA}{c-1} = \frac{1986.475}{3} = 662.1583$$

$$MSW = \frac{SSW}{n-c} = \frac{495.5}{36} = 13.76389$$

$$F = \frac{MSA}{MSW} = \frac{662.1583}{13.76389} = 48.1084$$

$$F_{\alpha, c-1, n-c} = F_{0.05, 3, 36} = 2.8663$$

Since the p-value is approximately zero and $F = 48.1084 > 2.8663$, reject H_0. There is sufficient evidence of a difference in the mean strength of the four brands of trash bags.

(b)
$$\text{Critical range} = Q_u \sqrt{\frac{MSW}{2}\left(\frac{1}{n_j} + \frac{1}{n_{j'}}\right)} = 3.79 \sqrt{\frac{13.7639}{2}\left(\frac{1}{10} + \frac{1}{10}\right)}$$
$$= 4.446$$

From the Tukey-Kramer procedure, there is a difference in mean strength between Kroger and Tuffstuff, Glad and Tuffstuff, and Hefty and Tuffstuff.
(c) ANOVA output for Levene's test for homogeneity of variance:

$$MSA = \frac{SSA}{c-1} = \frac{24.075}{3} = 8.025$$

$$MSW = \frac{SSW}{n-c} = \frac{198.2}{36} = 5.5056$$

$$F = \frac{MSA}{MSW} = \frac{8.025}{5.5056} = 1.4576$$

$$F_{\alpha, c-1, n-c} = F_{0.05, 3, 36} = 2.8663$$

Since the p-value = 0.2423 > 0.05 and $F = 1.458 < 2.866$, do not reject H_0. There is insufficient evidence to conclude that the variances in strength among the four brands of trash bags are different. **(d)** From the

results in (a) and (b), Tuffstuff has the lowest mean strength and should be avoided.

12 (a) Since $F = 12.56 > F_{0.05, 4, 25} = 2.76$, reject H_0. **(b)** Critical range = 4.67. Advertisements A and B are different from Advertisements C and D. Advertisement E is only different from Advertisement D. **(c)** Since $F = 1.927 < 2.76$, do not reject H_0. There is no evidence of a significant difference in the variation in the ratings among the five advertisements. **(d)** The advertisement underselling the pen's characteristics had the highest mean ratings, and the advertisements overselling the pen's characteristics had the lowest mean ratings. Therefore, use an advertisement that undersells the pen's characteristics and avoid advertisements that oversell the pen's characteristics.

14 (a) Since $F = 53.03 > F_{0.05, 3, 30} = 2.92$, reject H_0. **(b)** Critical range = 5.27 (using 30 degrees of freedom). Designs 3 and 4 are different from Designs 1 and 2. Designs 1 and 2 are different from each other. **(c)** The assumptions are that the samples are randomly and independently selected (or randomly assigned), the original populations of distances are approximately normally distributed, and the variances are equal. **(d)** Since $F = 2.093 < F_{3, 30} = 2.92$, do not reject H_0. There is no evidence of a significant difference in the variation in the distance among the four designs. **(e)** The manager should choose Design 3 or 4.

16 (a) 40. **(b)** 60 and 55. **(c)** 10. **(d)** 10.

18 (a) Since $F = 6.00 > 3.35$, reject H_0. **(b)** Since $F = 5.50 > F = 3.35$, reject H_0. **(c)** Since $F = 1.00 < F = 2.73$, do not reject H_0.

20 df B = 4, df total = 44, $SSA = 160$, $SSAB = 80$, $SSE = 150$, $SST = 610$, $MSB = 55$, $MSE = 5$, $F_A = 16$, $F_{AB} = 2$.

22 (a) Since $F = 1.37 < F = 4.75$, do not reject H_0. **(b)** Since $F = 23.58 > F_{0.05, 1, 12} = 4.75$, reject H_0. **(c)** Since $F = 0.70 < F_{0.05, 1, 12} = 4.75$, do not reject H_0. **(e)** Developer strength has a significant effect on density, but development time does not.

24 (a) H_0: There is no interaction between brand and water temperature. H_1: There is an interaction between brand and water temperature.

$$MSAB = \frac{SSAB}{(r-1)(c-1)} = \frac{506.3104}{(1)(2)} = 253.1552$$

$$F = \frac{MSAB}{MSE} = \frac{253.1552}{12.2199} = 20.7167$$

Since $F = 20.7167 > 3.555$ or the p-value = 0.0000214 < 0.05, reject H_0. There is evidence of interaction between brand of pain reliever and temperature of the water. **(b)** Since there is an interaction between brand and the temperature of the water, it is inappropriate to analyze the main effect due to brand. **(c)** Since there is an interaction between brand and the temperature of the water, it is an inappropriate to analyze the main effect due to water temperature. **(e)** The difference in the mean time a tablet took to dissolve in cold and hot water depends on the brand, with Alka-Seltzer having the largest difference and Equate with the smallest difference.

26 (a) Since $F = 0.43 < F_{0.05,1,28} = 4.20$, do not reject H_0. **(b)** Since $F = 0.02 < F_{0.05,1,28} = 4.20$, do not reject H_0. **(c)** Since $F = 45.47 > F_{0.05,1,28} = 4.20$, reject H_0. **(e)** Only part positioning has a significant effect on distortion.

36 (a) Since $F = 1.485 < F_{0.05,9,16} = 2.54$, do not reject H_0. **(b)** Since $F = 0.79 < F_{0.05,3,16} = 3.24$, do not reject H_0. **(c)** Since $F = 52.07 > F_{0.05,3,16} = 3.24$, reject H_0. **(e)** Critical range $= 0.0189$. Washing cycles for 22 and 24 minutes are not different with respect to dirt removal, but they are both different from 18- and 20-minute cycles. **(f)** 22 minutes. (24 minutes was not different, but 22 does just as well and would use less energy.) **(g)** The results are the same.

38 (a) Since $F = 0.075 < F_{0.05,2,15} = 3.68$, do not reject H_0. **(b)** Since $F = 4.09 > F_{0.05,2,15} = 3.68$, reject H_0. **(c)** Critical range $= 1.489$. Breaking strength is significantly different between 30 and 50 psi.

40 Since $F = 0.1899 < = 4.1132$, do not reject H_0. There is insufficient evidence to conclude that there is any interaction between type of breakfast and desired time. **(b)** Since $F = 30.4434 > 4.1132$, reject H_0. There is sufficient evidence to conclude that there is an effect that is due to type of breakfast. **(c)** Since $F = 12.4441 > 4.1132$, reject H_0. There is sufficient evidence to conclude that there is an effect that is due to desired time. **(e)** At the 5% level of significance, both the type of breakfast ordered and the desired time have an effect on delivery time difference. There is no interaction between the type of breakfast ordered and the desired time.
(f) (a) $F = 1.4611 < 4.1132$, do not reject H_0. There is insufficient evidence to conclude that there is any interaction between type of breakfast and desired time. **(b)** Since $F = 15.0000 > 4.1132$, reject H_0. There is sufficient evidence to conclude that there is an effect that is due to type of breakfast. **(c)** Since $F = 3.5458 < 4.1132$, do not reject H_0. There is insufficient evidence to conclude that there is an effect due to desired time. **(e)** At the 5% level of significance, only the type of breakfast ordered has an effect on delivery time difference. There is no interaction between the type of breakfast ordered and the desired time.

42 (a) Since $F = 4.0835 > 3.55$, reject H_0. There is sufficient evidence to conclude that there is an interaction between buffer size and data file size. **(b)** and **(c)** You cannot directly conclude that there is a significant difference in mean read times due to buffer size or file size (main effects) because the mean read times for different buffer sizes are different for different sizes of files. **(e)** Conclusions about the relative speed of the buffers or file sizes cannot be drawn because buffers and file sizes interact. **(f)** In the completely randomized design, there is not enough evidence of a difference between mean access read times for the three file sizes. In the two-factor factorial design, there is significant interaction between buffer size and data file size.

44

ANOVA

Source of Variation	SS	df	MS	F	p-value	F crit
Sample (Browser)	8192	1	8192	41.75787	5.33E-07	4.195982
Columns (Computer)	133644.5	1	133644.5	681.239	3.4E-21	4.195982
Interaction	9800	1	9800	49.95449	1.09E-07	4.195982
Within	5493	28	196.1786			
Total	157129.5	31				

Since the p-value for the interaction is virtually zero, reject H_0. There is sufficient evidence to conclude that there is an interaction between browser and the type of computer. The existence of an interaction effect complicates the interpretation of the main effects. You cannot directly conclude that there is a significant difference between the mean download times of different browsers because the difference is not the same over all the computers. Likewise, you cannot directly con clude that there is a significant difference between the mean download times of different computers because the difference is not the same over the two browsers. It appears that the Dell performs the same, regardless of browser type, and that the Mac performs faster with Netscape than it does with Internet Explorer.

Chapter 2

Chi-Square Tests and Nonparametric Tests

USING STATISTICS @ T.C. Resort Properties

1 **CHI-SQUARE TEST FOR THE DIFFERENCE BETWEEN TWO PROPORTIONS (INDEPENDENT SAMPLES)**

2 **CHI-SQUARE TEST FOR DIFFERENCES AMONG MORE THAN TWO PROPORTIONS**
The Marascuilo Procedure

3 **CHI-SQUARE TEST OF INDEPENDENCE**

4 **MCNEMAR TEST FOR THE DIFFERENCE BETWEEN TWO PROPORTIONS (RELATED SAMPLES)**

5 **WILCOXON RANK SUM TEST: NONPARAMETRIC ANALYSIS FOR TWO INDEPENDENT POPULATIONS**

6 **KRUSKAL-WALLIS RANK TEST: NONPARAMETRIC ANALYSIS FOR THE ONE-WAY ANOVA**

7 ● **(CD-ROM TOPIC) CHI-SQUARE TEST FOR A VARIANCE OR STANDARD DEVIATION**

EXCEL COMPANION

E1 Using the Chi-Square Test for the Difference Between Two Proportions
E2 Using the Chi-Square Test for the Differences Among More Than Two Proportions
E3 Using the Chi-Square Test of Independence
E4 Using the McNemar Test
E5 Using the Wilcoxon Rank Sum Test
E6 Using the Kruskal-Wallis Rank Test

LEARNING OBJECTIVES

In this chapter, you learn:
- How and when to use the chi-square test for contingency tables
- How to use the Marascuilo procedure for determining pairwise differences when evaluating more than two proportions
- How and when to use the McNemar test
- How and when to use nonparametric tests

Using Statistics @ T.C. Resort Properties

You are the manager of T.C. Resort Properties, a collection of five upscale hotels located on two resort islands. Guests who are satisfied with the quality of services during their stay are more likely to return on a future vacation and to recommend the hotel to friends and relatives. To assess the quality of services being provided by your hotels, guests are encouraged to complete a satisfaction survey when they check out. You need to analyze the data from these surveys to determine the overall satisfaction with the services provided, the likelihood that the guests will return to the hotel, and the reasons some guests indicate that they will not return. For example, on one island, T.C. Resort Properties operates the Beachcomber and Windsurfer hotels. Is the perceived quality at the Beachcomber Hotel the same as at the Windsurfer Hotel? If a difference is present, how can you use this information to improve the overall quality of service at T.C. Resort Properties? Furthermore, if guests indicate that they are not planning to return, what are the most common reasons given for this decision? Are the reasons given unique to a certain hotel or common to all hotels operated by T.C. Resort Properties?

This chapter uses hypothesis testing to analyze differences between population proportions based on two or more samples, as well as the hypothesis of *independence* in the joint responses to two categorical variables.

1 CHI-SQUARE TEST FOR THE DIFFERENCE BETWEEN TWO PROPORTIONS (INDEPENDENT SAMPLES)

You may have previously studied the Z test for the difference between two proportions. In this section, the data are examined from a different perspective. The hypothesis-testing procedure uses a test statistic that is approximated by a chi-square (χ^2) distribution. The results of this χ^2 test are equivalent to those` of the Z test.

If you are interested in comparing the counts of categorical responses between two independent groups, you can develop a two-way **contingency table** to display the frequency of occurrence of successes and failures for each group. Contingency tables are used to define and study probability.

To illustrate the contingency table, see the Using Statistics scenario concerning T.C. Resort Properties. On one of the islands, T.C. Resort Properties has two hotels (the Beachcomber and the Windsurfer). In tabulating the responses to the single question "Are you likely to choose this hotel again?" 163 of 227 guests at the Beachcomber responded yes, and 154 of 262 guests at the Windsurfer responded yes. At the 0.05 level of significance, is there evidence of a significant difference in guest satisfaction (as measured by likelihood to return to the hotel) between the two hotels?

The contingency table displayed in Table 1 has two rows and two columns and is called a **2 × 2 contingency table**. The cells in the table indicate the frequency for each row and column combination.

TABLE 1

Layout of a 2 × 2 Contingency Table

	COLUMN VARIABLE (GROUP)		
ROW VARIABLE	**1**	**2**	**Totals**
Successes	X_1	X_2	X
Failures	$n_1 - X_1$	$n_2 - X_2$	$n - X$
Totals	n_1	n_2	n

where

$$X_1 = \text{number of successes in group 1}$$

$$X_2 = \text{number of successes in group 2}$$

$$n_1 - X_1 = \text{number of failures in group 1}$$

$$n_2 - X_2 = \text{number of failures in group 2}$$

$$X = X_1 + X_2, \text{ the total number of successes}$$

$$n - X = (n_1 - X_1) + (n_2 - X_2), \text{ the total number of failures}$$

$$n_1 = \text{sample size in group 1}$$

$$n_2 = \text{sample size in group 2}$$

$$n = n_1 + n_2 = \text{total sample size}$$

Table 2 contains the contingency table for the hotel guest satisfaction study. The contingency table has two rows, indicating whether the guests would return to the hotel (that is, success) or would not return to the hotel (that is, failure), and two columns, one for each hotel. The cells in the table indicate the frequency of each row and column combination. The row totals indicate the number of guests who would return to the hotel and those who would not return to the hotel. The column totals are the sample sizes for each hotel location.

TABLE 2

2 × 2 Contingency Table for the Hotel Guest Satisfaction Survey

	HOTEL		
CHOOSE HOTEL AGAIN?	**Beachcomber**	**Windsurfer**	**Total**
Yes	163	154	317
No	64	108	172
Total	227	262	489

To test whether the population proportion of guests who would return to the Beachcomber, π_1, is equal to the population proportion of guests who would return to the Windsurfer, π_2, you can use the χ^2 test for equality of proportions. To test the null hypothesis that there is no difference between the two population proportions:

$$H_0: \pi_1 = \pi_2$$

against the alternative that the two population proportions are not the same:

$$H_1: \pi_1 \neq \pi_2$$

you use the χ^2 test statistic, shown in Equation (1).

χ^2 TEST FOR THE DIFFERENCE BETWEEN TWO PROPORTIONS

The χ^2 test statistic is equal to the squared difference between the observed and expected frequencies, divided by the expected frequency in each cell of the table, summed over all cells of the table.

$$\chi^2 = \sum_{all \text{ cells}} \frac{(f_o - f_e)^2}{f_e} \qquad (1)$$

where

f_o = **observed frequency** in a particular cell of a contingency table

f_e = **expected frequency** in a particular cell if the null hypothesis is true

The test statistic χ^2 approximately follows a chi-square distribution with 1 degree of freedom.[1]

[1]In general, in a contingency table, the degrees of freedom are equal to the (number of rows −1) times the (number of columns −1).

To compute the expected frequency, f_e, in any cell, you need to understand that if the null hypothesis is true, the proportion of successes in the two populations will be equal. Then the sample proportions you compute from each of the two groups would differ from each other only by chance. Each would provide an estimate of the common population parameter, π. A statistic that combines these two separate estimates together into one overall estimate of the population parameter provides more information than either of the two separate estimates could provide by itself. This statistic, given by the symbol $\bar{p}$ represents the estimated overall proportion of successes for the two groups combined (that is, the total number of successes divided by the total sample size). The complement of $\bar{p}$, $1 - \bar{p}$, represents the estimated overall proportion of failures in the two groups. Using the notation presented in Table 1, Equation (2) defines $\bar{p}$.

COMPUTING THE ESTIMATED OVERALL PROPORTION

$$\bar{p} = \frac{X_1 + X_2}{n_1 + n_2} = \frac{X}{n} \qquad (2)$$

To compute the expected frequency, f_e, for each cell pertaining to success (that is, the cells in the first row in the contingency table), you multiply the sample size (or column total) for a group by $\bar{p}$. To compute the expected frequency, f_e, for each cell pertaining to failure (that is, the cells in the second row in the contingency table), you multiply the sample size (or column total) for a group by $(1 - \bar{p})$.

The test statistic shown in Equation (1) approximately follows a **chi-square distribution** (see the table of critical values of χ^2) with 1 degree of freedom. Using a level of significance α, you reject the null hypothesis if the computed χ^2 test statistic is greater than χ_U^2, the upper-tail critical value from the χ^2 distribution having 1 degree of freedom. Thus, the decision rule is

Reject H_0 if $\chi^2 > \chi_U^2$;

otherwise, do not reject H_0.

Figure 1 illustrates the decision rule.

FIGURE 1

Regions of rejection and nonrejection when using the chi-square test for the difference between two proportions, with level of significance α

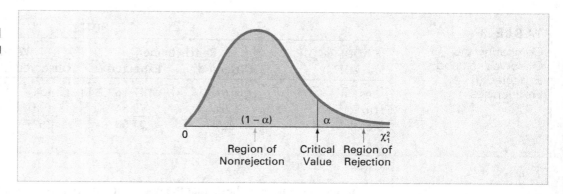

If the null hypothesis is true, the computed χ^2 statistic should be close to zero because the squared difference between what is actually observed in each cell, f_o, and what is theoretically expected, f_e, should be very small. If H_0 is false, then there are differences in the population proportions and the computed χ^2 statistic is expected to be large. However, what constitutes a large difference in a cell is relative. The same actual difference between f_o and f_e from a cell with a small number of expected frequencies contributes more to the χ^2 test statistic than a cell with a large number of expected frequencies.

To illustrate the use of the chi-square test for the difference between two proportions, return to the Using Statistics scenario concerning T.C. Resort Properties and the corresponding contingency table displayed in Table 2. The null hypothesis (H_0: $\pi_1 = \pi_2$) states that there is no difference between the proportion of guests who are likely to choose either of these hotels again. To begin,

$$\bar{p} = \frac{X_1 + X_2}{n_1 + n_2} = \frac{163 + 154}{227 + 262} = \frac{317}{489} = 0.6483$$

$\bar{p}$ is the estimate of the common parameter π, the population proportion of guests who are likely to choose either of these hotels again if the null hypothesis is true. The estimated proportion of guests who are *not* likely to choose these hotels again is the complement of $\bar{p}$, $1 - 0.6483 = 0.3517$. Multiplying these two proportions by the sample size for the Beachcomber Hotel gives the number of guests expected to choose the Beachcomber again and the number not expected to choose this hotel again. In a similar manner, multiplying the two respective proportions by the Windsurfer Hotel's sample size yields the corresponding expected frequencies for that group.

EXAMPLE 1

COMPUTING THE EXPECTED FREQUENCIES

Compute the expected frequencies for each of the four cells of Table 2.

SOLUTION

Yes—Beachcomber: $\bar{p} = 0.6483$ and $n_1 = 227$, so $f_e = 147.16$
Yes—Windsurfer: $\bar{p} = 0.6483$ and $n_2 = 262$, so $f_e = 169.84$
No—Beachcomber: $1 - \bar{p} = 0.3517$ and $n_1 = 227$, so $f_e = 79.84$
No—Windsurfer: $1 - \bar{p} = 0.3517$ and $n_2 = 262$, so $f_e = 92.16$

Table 3 presents these expected frequencies next to the corresponding observed frequencies.

TABLE 3

Comparing the Observed (f_o) and Expected (f_e) Frequencies

| CHOOSE HOTEL AGAIN? | HOTEL | | | | | |
| | Beachcomber | | Windsurfer | | | |
	Observed	Expected	Observed	Expected	Total
Yes	163	147.16	154	169.84	317
No	64	79.84	108	92.16	172
Total	227	227.00	262	262.00	489

To test the null hypothesis that the population proportions are equal:

$$H_0: \pi_1 = \pi_2$$

against the alternative that the population proportions are not equal:

$$H_1: \pi_1 \neq \pi_2$$

you use the observed and expected frequencies from Table 3 to compute the χ^2 test statistic given by Equation (1). Table 4 presents the calculations.

TABLE 4

Computation of χ^2 Test Statistic for the Hotel Guest Satisfaction Survey

f_o	f_e	$(f_o - f_e)$	$(f_o - f_e)^2$	$(f_o - f_e)^2/f_e$
163	147.16	15.84	250.91	1.71
154	169.84	−15.84	250.91	1.48
64	79.84	−15.84	250.91	3.14
108	92.16	15.84	250.91	2.72
				9.05

The **chi-square distribution** is a right-skewed distribution whose shape depends solely on the number of degrees of freedom. You find the critical value of the χ^2 test statistic from the table, a portion of which is presented as Table 5.

TABLE 5

Finding the χ^2 Critical Value from the Chi-Square Distribution with 1 Degree of Freedom, Using the 0.05 Level of Significance

| Degrees of Freedom | Upper-Tail Area | | | | | | |
	.995	.99	...	.05	.025	.01	.005
1			...	3.841	5.024	6.635	7.879
2	0.010	0.020	...	5.991	7.378	9.210	10.597
3	0.072	0.115	...	7.815	9.348	11.345	12.838
4	0.207	0.297	...	9.488	11.143	13.277	14.860
5	0.412	0.554	...	11.071	12.833	15.086	16.750

The values in Table 5 refer to selected upper-tail areas of the χ^2 distribution. A 2×2 contingency table has $(2 - 1)(2 - 1) = 1$ degree of freedom. Using $\alpha = 0.05$, with 1 degree of freedom, the critical value of χ^2 from Table 5 is 3.841. You reject H_0 if the computed χ^2 statistic is greater than 3.841 (see Figure 2). Because $9.05 > 3.841$, you reject H_0. You conclude that there is a difference in the proportion of guests who would return to the Beachcomber and the Windsurfer.

FIGURE 2

Regions of rejection and nonrejection when finding the χ^2 critical value with 1 degree of freedom, at the 0.05 level of significance

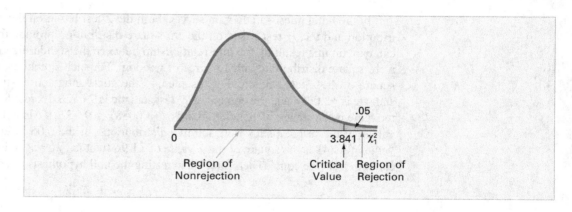

Figure 3 represents a Microsoft Excel worksheet for the guest satisfaction contingency table (Table 2).

FIGURE 3

Microsoft Excel worksheet for the hotel guest satisfaction data

See Section E1 to create this. Figure E1 in that section includes the formulas for the first 15 rows of the worksheet that are the basis for computing the chi-square statistic in cell B25.

	A	B	C	D
1	Guest Satisfaction Analysis			
2				
3		Observed Frequencies		
4		Hotel		
5	Choose Again?	Beachcomber	Windsurfer	Total
6	Yes	163	154	317
7	No	64	108	172
8	Total	227	262	489
9				
10		Expected Frequencies		
11		Hotel		
12	Choose Again?	Beachcomber	Windsurfer	Total
13	Yes	147.1554	169.8446	317
14	No	79.8446	92.1554	172
15	Total	227	262	489
16				
17	Data			
18	Level of Significance	0.05		
19	Number of Rows	2		
20	Number of Columns	2		
21	Degrees of Freedom	1		
22				
23	Results			
24	Critical Value	3.8415	=CHIINV(B18, B21)	
25	Chi-Square Test Statistic	9.0526	=SUM(F13:G14)	
26	p-Value	0.0026	=CHIDIST(B25, B21)	
27	Reject the null hypothesis		=IF(B26 < B18, "Reject the null hypothesis",	
28			"Do not reject the null hypothesis")	
29	Expected frequency assumption			
30	is met.		=IF(OR(B13 < 5, C13 < 5, B14 < 5, C14 < 5),	
			" is violated.", " is met.")	

This worksheet includes the expected frequencies, χ^2 test statistic, degrees of freedom, and p-value. The χ^2 test statistic is 9.0526, which is greater than the critical value of 3.8415 (or the p-value = 0.0026 < 0.05), so you reject the null hypothesis that there is no difference in guest satisfaction between the two hotels. The p-value of 0.0026 is the probability of observing sample proportions as different as or more different than the actual difference $(0.718 - 0.588 = 0.13$ observed in the sample data), if the population proportions for the Beachcomber and Windsurfer hotels are equal. Thus, there is strong evidence to conclude that the two hotels are significantly different with respect to guest satisfaction, as measured by whether the guest is likely to return to the hotel again. An examination of Table 3 indicates that a greater proportion of guests at the Beachcomber are likely to return than at the Windsurfer.

For the χ^2 test to give accurate results for a 2×2 table, you must assume that each expected frequency is at least 5. If this assumption is not satisfied, you can use alternative procedures such as Fisher's exact test (see references 1, 2, and 4).

In the hotel guest satisfaction survey, both the Z test based on the standardized normal distribution and the χ^2 test based on the chi-square distribution provide the same conclusion. You can explain this result by the interrelationship between the standardized normal distribution and a chi-square distribution with 1 degree of freedom. For such situations, the χ^2 test statistic is the square of the Z test statistic. For instance, in the guest satisfaction study, the computed Z test statistic is $+3.0088$ and the computed χ^2 test statistic is 9.0526. Except for rounding error, this latter value is the square of $+3.0088$ [that is, $(+3.0088)^2 \cong 9.0526$]. Also, if you compare the critical values of the test statistics from the two distributions, at the 0.05 level of significance, the χ_1^2 value of 3.841 is the square of the Z value of ± 1.96 (that is, $\chi_1^2 = Z^2$). Furthermore, the p-values for both tests are equal. Therefore, when testing the null hypothesis of equality of proportions:

$$H_0: \pi_1 = \pi_2$$

against the alternative that the population proportions are not equal:

$$H_1: \pi_1 \neq \pi_2$$

the Z test and the χ^2 test are equivalent methods. However, if you are interested in determining whether there is evidence of a *directional* difference, such as $\pi_1 > \pi_2$, you must use the Z test, with the entire rejection region located in one tail of the standardized normal distribution. In Section 2, the χ^2 test is extended to make comparisons and evaluate differences between the proportions among more than two groups. However, you cannot use the Z test if there are more than two groups.

PROBLEMS FOR SECTION 1

Learning the Basics

1 Determine the critical value of χ^2 with 1 degree of freedom in each of the following circumstances:
a. $\alpha = 0.01$, $n = 16$
b. $\alpha = 0.025$, $n = 11$
c. $\alpha = 0.05$, $n = 8$

2 Determine the critical value of χ^2 with 1 degree of freedom in each of the following circumstances:
a. $\alpha = 0.05$, $n = 28$
b. $\alpha = 0.025$, $n = 21$
c. $\alpha = 0.01$, $n = 5$

PH Grade
ASSIST
3 Use the following contingency table:

	A	B	Total
1	20	30	50
2	30	45	75
Total	50	75	125

a. Find the expected frequency for each cell.
b. Compare the observed and expected frequencies for each cell.
c. Compute the χ^2 statistic. Is it significant at $\alpha = 0.05$?

PH Grade
ASSIST
4 Use the following contingency table:

	A	B	Total
1	20	30	50
2	30	20	50
Total	50	50	100

a. Find the expected frequency for each cell.
b. Find the χ^2 statistic for this contingency table. Is it significant at $\alpha = 0.05$?

Applying the Concepts

5 A sample of 500 shoppers was selected in a large metropolitan area to determine various information concerning consumer behavior. Among the questions asked was, "Do you enjoy shopping for clothing?" The results are summarized in the following contingency table:

ENJOY SHOPPING FOR CLOTHING	GENDER Male	Female	Total
Yes	136	224	360
No	104	36	140
Total	240	260	500

a. Is there evidence of a significant difference between the proportion of males and females who enjoy shopping for clothing at the 0.01 level of significance?

b. Determine the *p*-value in (a) and interpret its meaning.

c. What are your answers to (a) and (b) if 206 males enjoyed shopping for clothing and 34 did not?

6 Is good gas mileage a priority for car shoppers? A survey conducted by Progressive Insurance asked this question of both men and women shopping for new cars. The data were reported as percentages, and no sample sizes were given:

	GENDER	
GAS MILEAGE A PRIORITY?	**Men**	**Women**
Yes	76%	84%
No	24%	16%

Source: Extracted from "Snapshots," **usatoday.com**, *June 21, 2004.*

a. Assume that 50 men and 50 women were included in the survey. At the 0.05 level of significance, is there a difference between males and females in the proportion who make gas mileage a priority?

b. Assume that 500 men and 500 women were included in the survey. At the 0.05 level of significance, is there a difference between males and females in the proportion who make gas mileage a priority?

c. Discuss the effect of sample size on the chi-square test.

7 The results of a yield improvement study at a semiconductor manufacturing facility provided defect data for a sample of 450 wafers. The following contingency table presents a summary of the responses to two questions: "Was a particle found on the die that produced the wafer?" and "Is the wafer good or bad?"

	QUALITY OF WAFER		
PARTICLES	**Good**	**Bad**	**Totals**
Yes	14	36	50
No	320	80	400
Totals	334	116	450

Source: Extracted from S. W. Hall, "Analysis of Defectivity of Semiconductor Wafers by Contingency Table," Proceedings Institute of Environmental Sciences, *Vol. 1 (1994), pp. 177–183.*

a. At the 0.05 level of significance, is there a difference between the proportion of good and bad wafers that have particles?

b. Determine the *p*-value in (a) and interpret its meaning.

c. What conclusions can you draw from this analysis?

 8 According to an Ipsos poll, the perception of unfairness in the U.S. tax code is spread fairly evenly across income groups, age groups, and education levels. In an April 2006 survey of 1,005 adults, Ipsos reported that almost 60% of all people said the code is unfair, while slightly more that 60% of those making more than $50,000 viewed the code as unfair (Extracted from "People Cry Unfairness," *The Cincinnati Enquirer*, April 16, 2006, p. A8). Suppose that the following contingency table represents the specific breakdown of responses:

	INCOME LEVEL		
U.S. TAX CODE	**Less Than $50,000**	**More Than $50,000**	**Total**
Fair	225	180	405
Unfair	280	320	600
Total	505	500	1,005

a. At the 0.05 level of significance, is there evidence of a difference in the proportion of adults who think the U.S. tax code is unfair between the two income groups?

b. Determine the *p*-value in (a) and interpret its meaning.

9 Where people turn to for news is different for various age groups. Suppose that a study conducted on this issue (extracted from P. Johnson, "Young People Turn to the Web for News," *USA Today*, March 23, 2006, p. 9D) was based on 200 respondents who were between the ages of 36 and 50 and 200 respondents who were above age 50. Of the 200 respondents who were between the ages of 36 and 50, 82 got their news primarily from newspapers. Of the 200 respondents who were above age 50, 104 got their news primarily from newspapers.

a. Construct a 2 × 2 contingency table.

b. Is there evidence of a significant difference in the proportion who get their news primarily from newspapers between those 36 to 50 years old and those above 50 years old? (Use α = 0.05.)

c. Determine the *p*-value in (a) and interpret its meaning.

10 An experiment was conducted to study the choices made in mutual fund selection. Undergraduate and MBA students were presented with different S&P 500 index funds that were identical except for fees. Suppose 100 undergraduate students and 100 MBA students were selected. Partial results are shown on the next page.

	STUDENT GROUP	
FUND	Undergraduate	MBA
Highest-cost fund	27	18
Not highest-cost fund	73	82

Source: *Extracted from J. Choi, D. Laibson, and B. Madrian, "Why Does the Law of One Practice Fail? An Experiment on Mutual Funds,"* **www.som.yale.edu/faculty/jjc83/fees.pdf**.

a. At the 0.05 level of significance, is there evidence of a difference between undergraduate and MBA students in the proportion who selected the highest-cost fund?

b. Determine the *p*-value in (a) and interpret its meaning.

2 CHI-SQUARE TEST FOR DIFFERENCES AMONG MORE THAN TWO PROPORTIONS

In this section, the χ^2 test is extended to compare more than two independent populations. The letter c is used to represent the number of independent populations under consideration. Thus, the contingency table now has two rows and c columns. To test the null hypothesis that there are no differences among the c population proportions:

$$H_0: \pi_1 = \pi_2 = \cdots = \pi_c$$

against the alternative that not all the c population proportions are equal:

$$H_1: \text{Not all } \pi_j \text{ are equal (where } j = 1, 2, \ldots, c)$$

you use Equation (1):

$$\chi^2 = \sum_{all \text{ cells}} \frac{(f_o - f_e)^2}{f_e}$$

where

f_o = observed frequency in a particular cell of a $2 \times c$ contingency table

f_e = expected frequency in a particular cell if the null hypothesis is true

If the null hypothesis is true and the proportions are equal across all c populations, the c sample proportions should differ only by chance. In such a situation, a statistic that combines these c separate estimates into one overall estimate of the population proportion, π, provides more information than any one of the c separate estimates alone. To expand on Equation (2), the statistic $\bar{p}$ in Equation (3) represents the estimated overall proportion for all c groups combined.

COMPUTING THE ESTIMATED OVERALL PROPORTION FOR c GROUPS

$$\bar{p} = \frac{X_1 + X_2 + \cdots + X_c}{n_1 + n_2 + \cdots + n_c} = \frac{X}{n} \qquad (3)$$

To compute the expected frequency, f_e, for each cell in the first row in the contingency table, multiply each sample size (or column total) by $\bar{p}$. To compute the expected frequency, f_e, for each cell in the second row in the contingency table, multiply each sample size (or column total) by $(1 - \bar{p})$. The test statistic shown in Equation (1) approximately follows a chi-square distribution, with degrees of freedom equal to the number of rows in the contingency table minus 1, times the number of columns in the table minus 1. For a **2 × c contingency table**, there are $c - 1$ degrees of freedom:

$$\text{Degrees of freedom} = (2 - 1)(c - 1) = c - 1$$

Using the level of significance α, you reject the null hypothesis if the computed χ^2 test statistic is greater than χ_U^2, the upper-tail critical value from a chi-square distribution having $c - 1$ degrees of freedom. Therefore, the decision rule is

$$\text{Reject H}_0 \text{ if } \chi^2 > \chi_U^2;$$

$$\text{otherwise, do not reject H}_0.$$

Figure 4 illustrates the decision rule.

FIGURE 4

Regions of rejection and nonrejection when testing for differences among c proportions using the χ^2 test

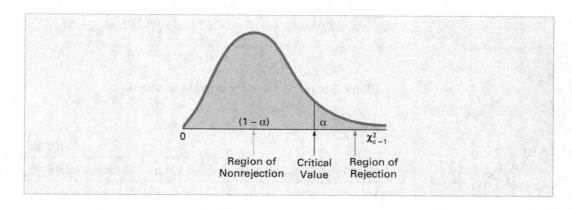

To illustrate the χ^2 test for equality of proportions when there are more than two groups, return to the Using Statistics scenario concerning T.C. Resort Properties. A similar survey was recently conducted on a different island on which T.C. Resort Properties has three different hotels. Table 6 presents the responses to a question concerning whether guests would be likely to choose this hotel again.

TABLE 6

2 × 3 Contingency Table for Guest Satisfaction Survey

			HOTEL	
CHOOSE HOTEL AGAIN	**Golden Palm**	**Palm Royale**	**Palm Princess**	**Total**
Yes	128	199	186	513
No	88	33	66	187
Total	216	232	252	700

Because the null hypothesis states that there are no differences among the three hotels in the proportion of guests who would likely return again, you use Equation (3) to calculate an estimate of π, the population proportion of guests who would likely return again:

$$\bar{p} = \frac{X_1 + X_2 + \cdots + X_c}{n_1 + n_2 + \cdots + n_c} = \frac{X}{n}$$

$$= \frac{(128 + 199 + 186)}{(216 + 232 + 252)} = \frac{513}{700}$$

$$= 0.733$$

The estimated overall proportion of guests who would *not* be likely to return again is the complement, $(1 - \bar{p})$, or 0.267. Multiplying these two proportions by the sample size taken at each hotel yields the expected number of guests who would and would not likely return.

EXAMPLE 2

COMPUTING THE EXPECTED FREQUENCIES

Compute the expected frequencies for each of the six cells in Table 6.

SOLUTION

Yes—Golden Palm: $\bar{p} = 0.733$ and $n_1 = 216$, so $f_e = 158.30$
Yes—Palm Royale: $\bar{p} = 0.733$ and $n_2 = 232$, so $f_e = 170.02$
Yes—Palm Princess: $\bar{p} = 0.733$ and $n_3 = 252$, so $f_e = 184.68$
No—Golden Palm: $1 - \bar{p} = 0.267$ and $n_1 = 216$, so $f_e = 57.70$
No—Palm Royale: $1 - \bar{p} = 0.267$ and $n_2 = 232$, so $f_e = 61.98$
No—Palm Princess: $1 - \bar{p} = 0.267$ and $n_3 = 252$, so $f_e = 67.32$

Table 7 presents these expected frequencies.

TABLE 7

Contingency Table of Expected Frequencies from a Guest Satisfaction Survey of Three Hotels

	HOTEL			
CHOOSE HOTEL AGAIN?	**Golden Palm**	**Palm Royale**	**Palm Princess**	**Total**
Yes	158.30	170.02	184.68	513
No	57.70	61.98	67.32	187
Total	216.00	232.00	252.00	700

To test the null hypothesis that the proportions are equal:

$$H_0: \pi_1 = \pi_2 = \pi_3$$

against the alternative that not all three proportions are equal:

$$H_1: \text{Not all } \pi_j \text{ are equal (where } j = 1, 2, 3).$$

You use the observed frequencies from Table 6 and the expected frequencies from Table 7 to compute the χ^2 test statistic (given by Equation (1)) displayed in Table 8.

TABLE 8

Computation of χ^2 Test Statistic for the Guest Satisfaction Survey of Three Hotels

f_o	f_e	$(f_o - f_e)$	$(f_o - f_e)^2$	$(f_o - f_e)^2/f_e$
128	158.30	−30.30	918.09	5.80
199	170.02	28.98	839.84	4.94
186	184.68	1.32	1.74	0.01
88	57.70	30.30	918.09	15.91
33	61.98	−28.98	839.84	13.55
66	67.32	−1.32	1.74	0.02
				40.23

You use the table of critical values of χ^2 to find the critical value of the χ^2 test statistic. In the guest satisfaction survey, because three hotels are evaluated, there are $(2 - 1)(3 - 1) = 2$ degrees of freedom. Using $\alpha = 0.05$, the χ^2 critical value with 2 degrees of freedom is 5.991. Because the computed test statistic ($\chi^2 = 40.23$) is greater than this critical value, you reject the null hypothesis (see Figure 5). Microsoft Excel (see Figure 6) also reports the p-value. Likewise, because the p-value is approximately 0.0000, which is less than $\alpha = 0.05$, you reject the null hypothesis. Further, this p-value indicates that there is virtually no chance to see differences this large or larger among the three sample proportions, if the population proportions for the three hotels are equal. Thus, there is sufficient evidence to conclude that the hotel properties are different with respect to the proportion of guests who are likely to return.

FIGURE 5

Regions of rejection and nonrejection when testing for differences in three proportions at the 0.05 level of significance, with 2 degrees of freedom

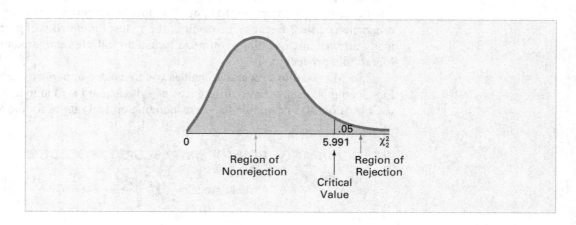

FIGURE 6

Microsoft Excel worksheet for the guest satisfaction data of Table 6

See Section E2 to create this.

For the χ^2 test to give accurate results when dealing with $2 \times c$ contingency tables, all expected frequencies must be large. There is much debate among statisticians about the definition of *large*. Some statisticians (see reference 5) have found that the test gives accurate results as long as all expected frequencies equal or exceed 0.5. Other statisticians, more conservative in their approach, require that no more than 20% of the cells contain expected frequencies less than 5 and no cells have expected frequencies less than 1 (see reference 3). A reasonable compromise between these points of view is to make sure that each expected frequency is at least 1. To accomplish this, you may need to collapse two or more low-expected-frequency categories into one category in the contingency table before performing the test. Such merging of categories usually results in expected frequencies sufficiently large to conduct the χ^2 test accurately. If combining categories is undesirable, alternative procedures are available (see references 1, 2 and 7).

The Marascuilo Procedure

Rejecting the null hypothesis in a χ^2 test of equality of proportions in a $2 \times c$ table only allows you to reach the conclusion that not all c population proportions are equal. But *which* of the proportions differ? Because the result of the χ^2 test for equality of proportions does not specifically answer this question, you need to use a multiple comparisons procedure such as the Marascuilo procedure.

The **Marascuilo procedure** enables you to make comparisons between all pairs of groups. First, compute the observed differences $p_j - p_{j'}$ (where $j \neq j'$) among all $c(c-1)/2$ pairs. Then, use Equation (4) to compute the corresponding critical ranges for the Marascuilo procedure.

CRITICAL RANGE FOR THE MARASCUILO PROCEDURE

$$\text{Critical range} = \sqrt{\chi_U^2} \sqrt{\frac{p_j(1-p_j)}{n_j} + \frac{p_{j'}(1-p_{j'})}{n_{j'}}} \qquad (4)$$

You need to compute a different critical range for each pairwise comparison of sample proportions. In the final step, you compare each of the $c(c-1)/2$ pairs of sample proportions against its corresponding critical range. You declare a specific pair significantly different if the absolute difference in the sample proportions $|p_j - p_{j'}|$ is greater than its critical range.

To apply the Marascuilo procedure, return to the guest satisfaction survey. Using the χ^2 test, you concluded that there was evidence of a significant difference among the population proportions. Because there are three hotels, there are $(3)(3-1)/2 = 3$ pairwise comparisons. From Table 6, the three sample proportions are

$$p_1 = \frac{X_1}{n_1} = \frac{128}{216} = 0.593$$

$$p_2 = \frac{X_2}{n_2} = \frac{199}{232} = 0.858$$

$$p_3 = \frac{X_3}{n_3} = \frac{186}{252} = 0.738$$

Using the table of critical values of χ^2 and an overall level of significance of 0.05, the upper-tail critical value of the χ^2 test statistic for a chi-square distribution having $(c-1) = 2$ degrees of freedom is 5.991. Thus,

$$\sqrt{\chi_U^2} = \sqrt{5.991} = 2.448$$

Next, you compute the three pairs of absolute differences in sample proportions and their corresponding critical ranges. If the absolute difference is greater than its critical range, the proportions are significantly different :

Absolute Difference in Proportions	Critical Range
$\|p_j - p_{j'}\|$	$2.448\sqrt{\dfrac{p_j(1-p_j)}{n_j} + \dfrac{p_{j'}(1-p_{j'})}{n_{j'}}}$
$\|p_1 - p_2\| = \|0.593 - 0.858\| = 0.265$	$2.448\sqrt{\dfrac{(0.593)(0.407)}{216} + \dfrac{(0.858)(0.142)}{232}} = 0.0992$
$\|p_1 - p_3\| = \|0.593 - 0.738\| = 0.145$	$2.448\sqrt{\dfrac{(0.593)(0.407)}{216} + \dfrac{(0.738)(0.262)}{252}} = 0.1063$
$\|p_2 - p_3\| = \|0.858 - 0.738\| = 0.120$	$2.448\sqrt{\dfrac{(0.858)(0.142)}{232} + \dfrac{(0.738)(0.262)}{252}} = 0.0880$

These computations are shown in worksheet format in Figure 7.

FIGURE 7

Microsoft Excel
Marascuilo procedure
worksheet

See the "Using the
Marascuilo Worksheets"
part of Section E2 to learn
more about this worksheet.

	A	B	C	D
1	**Marascuilo Procedure**			
2	**Guest Satisfaction (3-Hotels) Analysis**			
3	Level of Significance	0.05		
4	Square Root of Critical Value	2.4477		
5				
6	Sample Proportions			
7	Group 1	0.5926		
8	Group 2	0.8578		
9	Group 3	0.7381		
10				
11	MARASCUILO TABLE			
12	**Proportions**	**Absolute Differences**	**Critical Range**	
13	| Group 1 - Group 2 |	0.2652	0.0992	Significant
14	| Group 1 - Group 3 |	0.1455	0.1063	Significant
15				
16	| Group 2 - Group 3 |	0.1197	0.0880	Significant

With 95% confidence, you can conclude that guest satisfaction is higher at the Palm Royale ($p_2 = 0.858$) than at either the Golden Palm ($p_1 = 0.593$) or the Palm Princess ($p_3 = 0.738$) and that guest satisfaction is also higher at the Palm Princess than at the Golden Palm. These results clearly suggest that management should study the reasons for these differences and, in particular, should try to determine why satisfaction is significantly lower at the Golden Palm than at the other two hotels.

PROBLEMS FOR SECTION 2

Learning the Basics

 11 Consider a contingency table with two rows and five columns.
   a. Find the degrees of freedom.
b. Find the critical value for $\alpha = 0.05$.
c. Find the critical value for $\alpha = 0.01$.

12 Use the following contingency table:

	A	B	C	Total
1	10	30	50	90
2	40	45	50	135
Total	50	75	100	225

a. Compute the expected frequencies for each cell.
b. Compute the χ^2 statistic for this contingency table. Is it significant at $\alpha = 0.05$?
c. If appropriate, use the Marascuilo procedure and $\alpha = 0.05$ to determine which groups are different.

13 Use the following contingency table:

	A	B	C	Total
1	20	30	25	75
2	30	20	25	75
Total	50	50	50	150

a. Compute the expected frequencies for each cell.
b. Compute the χ^2 statistic for this contingency table. Is it significant at $\alpha = 0.05$?

c. If appropriate, use the Marascuilo procedure and $\alpha = 0.05$ to determine which groups are different.

Applying the Concepts

14 A survey was conducted in five countries. The percentages of respondents who said that they eat out once a week or more are as follows:

Germany	10%
France	12%
United Kingdom	28%
Greece	39%
United States	57%

Source: Adapted from M. Kissel, "Americans Are Keen on Cocooning," The Wall Street Journal, *July 22, 2003, p. D3.*

Suppose that the survey was based on 1,000 respondents in each country.

a. At the 0.05 level of significance, determine whether there is a significant difference in the proportion of people who eat out at least once a week in the various countries.

b. Find the p-value in (a) and interpret its meaning.

c. If appropriate, use the Marascuilo procedure and $\alpha = 0.05$ to determine which countries are different. Discuss your results.

15 Is the degree to which students withdraw from introductory business statistics courses the same for online courses and traditional courses taught in a classroom? Professor Constance McLaren at Indiana State University collected data for five semesters to investigate this question. The following table cross-classifies introductory business statistics students by the type of course (classroom or online) and student persistence (active, dropped, or vanished):

	STUDENT PERSISTENCE		
TYPE OF COURSE	**Active**	**Dropped**	**Vanished**
Classroom	127	8	4
Online	81	51	20

Source: Extracted from C. McLaren, "A Comparison of Student Persistence and Performance in Online and Classroom Business Statistics Experiences," Decision Sciences Journal of Innovative Education, *Spring 2004, 2(1), pp. 1–10. Published by the Decision Sciences Institute, headquartered at Georgia State University, Atlanta, GA.*

a. Is there evidence of a difference in student persistence (active, dropped, or vanished) based on type of course? (Use $\alpha = 0.05$.)

b. Compute the p-value and interpret its meaning.

c. If appropriate, use the Marascuilo procedure and $\alpha = 0.05$ to determine which groups are different.

 16 More shoppers do the majority of their grocery shopping on Saturday than any other day of the week. However, is the day of the week a person does the majority of grocery shopping dependent on age? A study cross-classified grocery shoppers by age and major shopping day ("Major Shopping by Day," *Progressive Grocer Annual Report*, April 30, 2002). The data were reported as percentages, and no sample sizes were given:

	AGE		
MAJOR SHOPPING DAY	**Under 35**	**35–54**	**Over 54**
Saturday	24%	28%	12%
A day other than Saturday	76%	72%	88%

Source: Extracted from "Major Shopping by Day," Progressive Grocer Annual Report, *April 30, 2002.*

Assume that 200 shoppers for each age category were surveyed.

a. Is there evidence of a significant difference among the age groups with respect to major grocery shopping day? (Use $\alpha = 0.05$.)

b. Determine the p-value in (a) and interpret its meaning.

c. If appropriate, use the Marascuilo procedure and $\alpha = 0.05$ to determine which age groups are different. Discuss your results.

d. Discuss the managerial implications of (a) and (c). How can grocery stores use this information to improve marketing and sales? Be specific.

17 Repeat (a) through (b) of Problem 16, assuming that only 50 shoppers for each age category were surveyed. Discuss the implications of sample size on the χ^2 test for differences among more than two populations.

18 An experiment was conducted by James Choi, David Laibson, and Brigitte Madrian to study the choices made in fund selection. When presented with four S&P 500 index funds that were identical except for their fees, undergraduate and MBA students chose the funds as follows (in percentages):

	FUND			
STUDENT GROUP	**Lowest Cost**	**Second-Lowest Cost**	**Third-Lowest Cost**	**Highest Cost**
Under-graduates	19	37	17	27
MBA	19	40	23	18

Source: Extracted from J. Choi, D. Laibson, and B. Madrian, "Why Does the Law of One Practice? An Experiment in Mutual Funds," **www.som.yale.edu/faculty/jjc83/fees.pdf.**

a. Determine whether there is a difference in the fund selection (lowest cost, second-lowest cost, third-lowest cost, highest cost) based on the student group. (Use $\alpha = 0.05$.)

b. Determine the p-value and interpret its meaning.

c. If appropriate, use the Marascuilo procedure and $\alpha = 0.05$ to determine which groups are different.

19 An article (Extracted from P. Kitchen, "Retirement Plan: To Keep Working," *Newsday*, September 24, 2003) discussed the results of a sample of 2,001 Americans ages 50 to 70 who were employed full time or part time. The results were as follows:

	PLANS					
GENDER	Not Work for Pay	Start Own Business	Work Full Time	Work Part Time	Don't Know	Other
Male	257	115	103	457	27	42
Female	359	87	49	436	34	35

a. Is there evidence of a significant difference among the plans for retirement with respect to gender? (Use $\alpha = 0.05$.)

b. Determine the p-value in (a) and interpret its meaning.

3   CHI-SQUARE TEST OF INDEPENDENCE

In Sections 1 and 2, you used the χ^2 test to evaluate potential differences among population proportions. For a contingency table that has r rows and c columns, you can generalize the χ^2 test as a *test of independence* for two categorical variables.

For a test of independence, the null and alternative hypotheses follow:

H_0: The two categorical variables are independent
(that is, there is no relationship between them).
H_1: The two categorical variables are dependent
(that is, there is a relationship between them).

Once again, you use Equation (1) to compute the test statistic:

$$\chi^2 = \sum_{all \text{ cells}} \frac{(f_o - f_e)^2}{f_e}$$

You reject the null hypothesis at the α level of significance if the computed value of the χ^2 test statistic is greater than χ_U^2, the upper-tail critical value from a chi-square distribution with $(r - 1)(c - 1)$ degrees of freedom (see Figure 8). Thus, the decision rule is

Reject H_0 if $\chi^2 > \chi_U^2$;

otherwise, do not reject H_0.

FIGURE 8

Regions of rejection and nonrejection when testing for independence in an $r \times c$ contingency table, using the χ^2 test

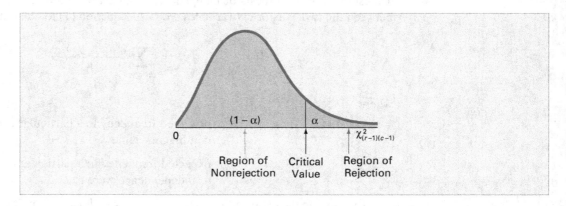

The χ^2 **test of independence** is similar to the χ^2 test for equality of proportions. The test statistics and the decision rules are the same, but the stated hypotheses and conclusions are different. For example, in the guest satisfaction survey of Sections 1 and 2, there is evidence of a significant difference between the hotels with respect to the proportion of guests who would return.

From a different viewpoint, you could conclude that there is a significant relationship between the hotels and the likelihood that a guest would return. Nevertheless, there is a fundamental difference between the two types of tests. The major difference is in how the samples are selected.

In a test for equality of proportions, there is one factor of interest, with two or more levels. These levels represent samples drawn from independent populations. The categorical responses in each sample group or level are classified into two categories, such as *success* and *failure*. The objective is to make comparisons and evaluate differences between the proportions of *success* among the various levels. However, in a test for independence, there are two factors of interest, each of which has two or more levels. You select one sample and tally the joint responses to the two categorical variables into the cells of a contingency table.

To illustrate the χ^2 test for independence, suppose that in the survey on hotel guest satisfaction, a second question was asked of all respondents who indicated that they were not likely to return. These guests were asked to indicate the primary reason for their response. Table 9 presents the resulting 4×3 contingency table.

TABLE 9

Contingency Table of Primary Reason for Not Returning and Hotel

PRIMARY REASON FOR NOT RETURNING	HOTEL			
	Golden Palm	Palm Royale	Palm Princess	Total
Price	23	7	37	67
Location	39	13	8	60
Room accommodation	13	5	13	31
Other	13	8	8	29
Total	88	33	66	187

In Table 9, observe that of the primary reasons for not planning to return to the hotel, 67 were due to price, 60 were due to location, 31 were due to room accommodation, and 29 were due to other reasons. As in Table 6, there were 88 guests in the Golden Palm, 33 guests in the Palm Royale, and 66 guests in the Palm Princess who were not planning to return. The observed frequencies in the cells of the 4×3 contingency table represent the joint tallies of the sampled guests with respect to primary reason for not returning and the hotel.

The null and alternative hypotheses are

H_0: There is no relationship between the primary reason for not returning and the hotel.
H_1: There is a relationship between the primary reason for not returning and the hotel.

To test this null hypothesis of independence against the alternative that there is a relationship between the two categorical variables, you use Equation (1) to compute the test statistic:

$$\chi^2 = \sum_{all\ cells} \frac{(f_o - f_e)^2}{f_e}$$

where

f_o = observed frequency in a particular cell of the $r \times c$ contingency table

f_e = expected frequency in a particular cell if the null hypothesis of independence were true

To compute the expected frequency, f_e, in any cell, use the multiplication rule for independent events.

$$P(A\ and\ B) = P(A)P(B)$$

For example, under the null hypothesis of independence, the probability of responses expected in the upper-left-corner cell representing primary reason of price for the Golden

Palm is the product of the two separate probabilities: P(Price) and P(Golden Palm). Here, the proportion of reasons that are due to price, P(Price), is $67/187 = 0.3583$, and the proportion of all responses from the Golden Palm, P(Golden Palm), is $88/187 = 0.4706$. If the null hypothesis is true, then the primary reason for not returning and the hotel are independent:

$$P(\text{Price } and \text{ Golden Palm}) = P(\text{Price}) \times P(\text{Golden Palm})$$
$$= (0.3583) \times (0.4706)$$
$$= 0.1686$$

The expected frequency is the product of the overall sample size, n, and this probability, $187 \times 0.1686 = 31.53$. The f_e values for the remaining cells are calculated in a similar manner (see Table 10).

Equation (5) presents a simpler way to compute the expected frequency.

COMPUTING THE EXPECTED FREQUENCY

The expected frequency in a cell is the product of its row total and column total, divided by the overall sample size.

$$f_e = \frac{\text{Row total} \times \text{Column total}}{n} \qquad (5)$$

where

$$\text{row total} = \text{sum of all the frequencies in the row}$$

$$\text{column total} = \text{sum of all the frequencies in the column}$$

$$n = \text{overall sample size}$$

For example, using Equation (5) for the upper-left-corner cell (price for the Golden Palm),

$$f_e = \frac{\text{Row total} \times \text{Column total}}{n} = \frac{(67)(88)}{187} = 31.53$$

and for the lower-right-corner cell (other reason for the Palm Princess),

$$f_e = \frac{\text{Row total} \times \text{Column total}}{n} = \frac{(29)(66)}{187} = 10.24$$

Table 10 lists the entire set of f_e values.

TABLE 10

Contingency Table of Expected Frequencies of Primary Reason for Not Returning with Hotel

PRIMARY REASON FOR NOT RETURNING	HOTEL			
	Golden Palm	Palm Royale	Palm Princess	Total
Price	31.53	11.82	23.65	67
Location	28.24	10.59	21.18	60
Room accommodation	14.59	5.47	10.94	31
Other	13.65	5.12	10.24	29
Total	88.00	33.00	66.00	187

To perform the test of independence, you use the χ^2 test statistic shown in Equation (1). Here, the test statistic approximately follows a chi-square distribution, with degrees of freedom equal to the number of rows in the contingency table minus 1, times the number of columns in the table minus 1:

$$\text{Degrees of freedom} = (r - 1)(c - 1)$$
$$= (4 - 1)(3 - 1) = 6$$

Table 11 illustrates the computations for the χ^2 test statistic.

TABLE 11

Computation of χ^2 Test Statistic for the Test of Independence

Cell	f_o	f_e	$(f_o - f_e)$	$(f_o - f_e)^2$	$(f_o - f_e)^2 / f_e$
Price/Golden Palm	23	31.53	−8.53	72.76	2.31
Price/Palm Royale	7	11.82	−4.82	23.23	1.97
Price/Palm Princess	37	23.65	13.35	178.22	7.54
Location/Golden Palm	39	28.24	10.76	115.78	4.10
Location/Palm Royale	13	10.59	2.41	5.81	0.55
Location/Palm Princess	8	21.18	−13.18	173.71	8.20
Room/Golden Palm	13	14.59	−1.59	2.53	0.17
Room/Palm Royale	5	5.47	−0.47	0.22	0.04
Room/Palm Princess	13	10.94	2.06	4.24	0.39
Other/Golden Palm	13	13.65	−0.65	0.42	0.03
Other/Palm Royale	8	5.12	2.88	8.29	1.62
Other/Palm Princess	8	10.24	−2.24	5.02	0.49
					27.41

Using the level of significance $\alpha = 0.05$, the upper-tail critical value from the chi-square distribution with 6 degrees of freedom is 12.592 (see the table of critical values of χ^2). Because the computed test statistic $\chi^2 = 27.41 > 12.592$, you reject the null hypothesis of independence (see Figure 9). Similarly, you can use the Microsoft Excel worksheet in Figure 10. Because the p-value = 0.0001 < 0.05, you reject the null hypothesis of independence. This p-value indicates that there is virtually no chance of having a relationship this large or larger between hotels and primary reasons for not returning in a sample, if the primary reasons for not returning are independent of the specific hotels in the entire population. Thus, there is strong evidence of a relationship between primary reason for not returning and the hotel.

FIGURE 9

Regions of rejection and nonrejection when testing for independence in the hotel guest satisfaction survey example at the 0.05 level of significance, with 6 degrees of freedom

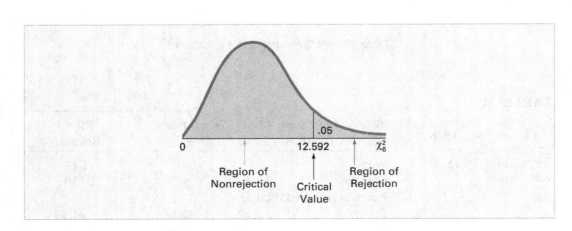

FIGURE 10

Microsoft Excel worksheet for the 4 × 3 contingency table for primary reason for not returning and hotel

See Section E3 to create this. Formulas not shown in Figure 10 (in rows 3 through 19) are similar to formulas shown in Figure E1.

	A	B	C	D	E
1	Cross-Classification Hotel Analysis				
2					
3		Observed Frequencies			
4		Hotel			
5	Reason for Not Returning	Golden Palm	Palm Royale	Palm Princess	Total
6	Price	23	7	37	67
7	Location	39	13	8	60
8	Room accommodation	13	5	13	31
9	Other	13	8	8	29
10	Total	88	33	66	187
11					
12		Expected Frequencies			
13		Hotel			
14	Reason for Not Returning	Golden Palm	Palm Royale	Palm Princess	Total
15	Price	31.5294	11.8235	23.6471	67
16	Location	28.2353	10.5882	21.1765	60
17	Room accommodation	14.5882	5.4706	10.9412	31
18	Other	13.6471	5.1176	10.2353	29
19	Total	88	33	66	187
20					
21	Data				
22	Level of Significance	0.05			
23	Number of Rows	4			
24	Number of Columns	3			
25	Degrees of Freedom	6	=(B23 - 1) * (B24 - 1)		
26					
27	Results				
28	Critical Value	12.5916	=CHIINV(B22, B25)		
29	Chi-Square Test Statistic	27.4104	=SUM(G15:I18)		
30	*p*-Value	0.0001	=CHIDIST(B29, B25)		
31	Reject the null hypothesis		=IF(B30 < B22, "Reject the null hypothesis", "Do not reject the null hypothesis")		
32					
33	Expected frequency assumption				
34	is met.		=IF(OR(B15 < 1, C15 < 1, D15 < 1, B16 < 1, C16 < 1 ,D16 < 1, B17 < 1, C17 < 1, D17 < 1, B18 < 1, C18 < 1, D18 < 1) " is violated."," is met.")		

Examination of the observed and expected frequencies (see Table 11) reveals that price is underrepresented as a reason for not returning to the Golden Palm (that is, $f_o = 23$ and $f_e = 31.53$) but is overrepresented at the Palm Princess. Guests are more satisfied with the price at the Golden Palm compared to the Palm Princess. Location is overrepresented as a reason for not returning to the Golden Palm but greatly underrepresented at the Palm Princess. Thus, guests are much more satisfied with the location of the Palm Princess than that of the Golden Palm.

To ensure accurate results, all expected frequencies need to be large in order to use the χ^2 test when dealing with $r \times c$ contingency tables. As in the case of $2 \times c$ contingency tables, all expected frequencies should be at least 1. For cases in which one or more expected frequencies are less than 1, you can use the test after collapsing two or more low-frequency rows into one row (or collapsing two or more low-frequency columns into one column). Merging of rows or columns usually results in expected frequencies sufficiently large to conduct the χ^2 test accurately.

PROBLEMS FOR SECTION 3

Learning the Basics

 20 If a contingency table has three rows and four columns, how many degrees of freedom are there for the χ^2 test for independence?

 21 When performing a χ^2 test for independence in a contingency table with r rows and c columns, determine the upper-tail critical value of the χ^2 test statistic in each of the following circumstances:

a. $\alpha = 0.05$, $r = 4$ rows, $c = 5$ columns

b. $\alpha = 0.01$, $r = 4$ rows, $c = 5$ columns

c. $\alpha = 0.01$, $r = 4$ rows, $c = 6$ columns

d. $\alpha = 0.01$, $r = 3$ rows, $c = 6$ columns

e. $\alpha = 0.01$, $r = 6$ rows, $c = 3$ columns

Applying the Concepts

22 During the Vietnam War, a lottery system was instituted to choose males to be drafted into the military. Numbers representing days of the year were "randomly" selected; men born on days of the year with low numbers were drafted first; those with high numbers were not drafted. The table on the next page shows how many low

(1–122), medium (123–244), and high (245–366) numbers were drawn for birth dates in each quarter of the year:

NUMBER SET	QUARTER OF YEAR				
	Jan.–Mar.	Apr.–Jun.	Jul.–Sep.	Oct.–Dec.	Total
Low	21	28	35	38	122
Medium	34	22	29	37	122
High	36	41	28	17	122
Total	91	91	92	92	366

a. Is there evidence that the numbers selected were significantly related to the time of year? (Use $\alpha = 0.05$.)
b. Would you conclude that the lottery drawing appears to have been random?
c. What are your answers to (a) and (b) if the frequencies are

    23 30 32 37
    27 30 34 31
    41 31 26 24

23 *USA Today* reported on preferred types of office communication by different age groups ("Talking Face to Face vs. Group Meetings," *USA Today*, October 13, 2003, p. A1). Suppose the results were based on a survey of 500 respondents in each age group. The results are cross-classified in the following table:

AGE GROUP	TYPE OF COMMUNICATION PREFERRED				
	Group Meetings	Face-to-face Meetings with Individuals	Emails	Other	Total
Generation Y	180	260	50	10	500
Generation X	210	190	65	35	500
Boomer	205	195	65	35	500
Mature	200	195	50	55	500
Total	795	840	230	135	2,000

Source: Extracted from "Talking Face to Face vs. Group Meetings," USA Today, October 13, 2003, p. A1.

At the 0.05 level of significance, is there evidence of a relationship between age group and type of communication preferred?

24 A large corporation is interested in determining whether a relationship exists between the commuting time of its employees and the level of stress-related problems observed on the job. A study of 116 assembly-line workers reveals the following:

COMMUTING TIME	STRESS LEVEL			
	High	Moderate	Low	Total
Under 15 min.	9	5	18	32
15–45 min.	17	8	28	53
Over 45 min.	18	6	7	31
Total	44	19	53	116

a. At the 0.01 level of significance, is there evidence of a significant relationship between commuting time and stress level?
b. What is your answer to (a) if you use the 0.05 level of significance?

25 Where people turn to for news is different for various age groups. A study indicated where different age groups primarily get their news:

MEDIA	AGE GROUP		
	Under 36	36–50	50+
Local TV	107	119	133
National TV	73	102	127
Radio	75	97	109
Local newspaper	52	79	107
Internet	95	83	76

At the 0.05 level of significance, is there evidence of a significant relationship between the age group and where people primarily get their news? If so, explain the relationship.

26 *USA Today* reported on when the decision of what to have for dinner is made. Suppose the results were based on a survey of 1,000 respondents and considered whether the household included any children under 18 years old. The results were cross-classified in the following table:

WHEN DECISION MADE	TYPE OF HOUSEHOLD		
	One Adult/No Children	Adult/Children	Two or More Adults/No Children
Just before eating	162	54	154
In the afternoon	73	38	69
In the morning	59	58	53
A few days before	21	64	45
The night before	15	50	45
Always eat the same thing on this night	2	16	2
Not sure	7	6	7

Source: Extracted from "What's for Dinner," USA Today, January 10, 2000.

At the 0.05 level of significance, is there evidence of a significant relationship between when the decision is made of what to have for dinner and the type of household?

4 McNEMAR TEST FOR THE DIFFERENCE BETWEEN TWO PROPORTIONS (RELATED SAMPLES)

You may have previously used the Z test, and in Section 1, you used the chi-square test to test for the difference between two proportions. These tests require that the samples are independent from one another. However, sometimes when you are testing differences between two proportions, the data are from repeated measurements or matched samples, and therefore the samples are related. Such situations arise often in marketing when you want to determine whether there has been a change in attitude, perception, or behavior from one time period to another.

To test whether there is evidence of a difference between the proportions of two related samples, you can use the **McNemar test**. If you are doing a two-tail test, you could use a test statistic that follows a chi-square distribution or one that approximately follows the normal distribution. However, if you are carrying out a one-tail test, you need to use the test statistic that approximately follows the normal distribution.

Table 12 presents the 2 × 2 table needed for the McNemar test.

TABLE 12

2 × 2 Contingency Table for the McNemar Test

CONDITION (GROUP) 1	CONDITION (GROUP) 2		
	Yes	No	Totals
Yes	A	B	$A + B$
No	C	D	$C + D$
Totals	$A + C$	$B + D$	n

where

A = number of respondents who answer yes to condition 1 and yes to condition 2

B = number of respondents who answer yes to condition 1 and no to condition 2

C = number of respondents who answer no to condition 1 and yes to condition 2

D = number of respondents who answer no to condition 1 and no to condition 2

n = number of respondents in the sample

The sample proportions are

$$p_1 = \frac{A + B}{n} = \text{proportion of respondents in the sample who answer yes to condition 1}$$

$$p_2 = \frac{A + C}{n} = \text{proportion of respondents in the sample who answer yes to condition 2}$$

The population proportions are

π_1 = proportion in the population who would answer yes to condition 1

π_2 = proportion in the population who would answer yes to condition 2

Equation (6) presents the McNemar test statistic used to test H_0: $\pi_1 = \pi_2$.

67

McNEMAR TEST

$$Z = \frac{B - C}{\sqrt{B + C}} \tag{6}$$

where the test statistic Z is approximately normally distributed.

To illustrate the McNemar test, suppose that a consumer panel of $n = 600$ participants is selected for a marketing study and the panel members are initially asked to state their preferences for two competing cell phone providers, Sprint and Verizon. Suppose that, initially, 282 panelists say they prefer Sprint and 318 say they prefer Verizon. After exposing the entire panel to an intensive marketing campaign strategy for Verizon, suppose the same 600 panelists are again asked to state their preferences, with the following results: Of the 282 panelists who previously preferred Sprint, 246 maintain their brand loyalty, but 36 switch to Verizon. Of the 318 panelists who initially preferred Verizon, 306 remain brand loyal, but 12 switch to Sprint. The results are displayed Table 13.

TABLE 13

Brand Loyalty for Cell Phone Providers

BEFORE MARKETING CAMPAIGN	AFTER MARKETING CAMPAIGN		
	Sprint	Verizon	Total
Sprint	246	36	282
Verizon	12	306	318
Total	258	342	600

You use the McNemar test for these data because you have repeated measurements from the same set of panelists. Each panelist gave a response about whether he or she preferred Sprint or Verizon before exposure to the intensive marketing campaign and then again after exposure to the campaign.

To determine whether the intensive marketing campaign was effective, you want to investigate whether there is a difference between the population proportion who favor Verizon before the campaign, π_1, versus the proportion who favor Verizon after the campaign, π_2. The null and alternative hypotheses are

$$H_0: \pi_1 = \pi_2$$
$$H_1: \pi_1 \neq \pi_2$$

Using a 0.05 level of significance, the critical values are -1.96 and $+1.96$ (see Figure 11), and the decision rule is

Reject H_0 if $Z < -1.96$ or if $Z > +1.96$;

otherwise, do not reject H_0.

FIGURE 11

Two-tail McNemar Test at the 0.05 level of significance

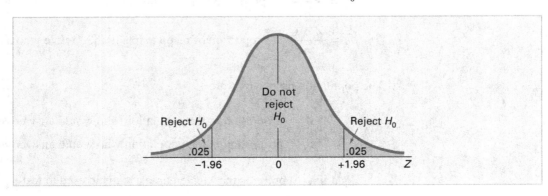

For the data in Table 13,

$$A = 246 \quad B = 36 \quad C = 12 \quad D = 306$$

so that

$$p_1 = \frac{A + B}{n} = \frac{246 + 36}{600} = \frac{282}{600} = 0.47 \text{ and } p_2 = \frac{A + C}{n} = \frac{246 + 12}{600} = \frac{258}{600} = 0.43$$

Using Equation (6),

$$Z = \frac{B - C}{\sqrt{B + C}} = \frac{36 - 12}{\sqrt{36 + 12}} = \frac{24}{\sqrt{48}} = 3.4641$$

Because $Z = 3.4641 > 1.96$, you reject H_0. Using the p-value approach (see Figure 12), the p-value is 0.0005. Because $0.0005 < 0.05$, you reject H_0. You can conclude that the proportion who preferred Verizon before the intensive marketing campaign is different from the proportion who prefer Verizon after exposure to the intensive marketing campaign. In fact, from Table 13, observe that more panelists actually preferred Verizon over Sprint after exposure to the intensive marketing campaign.

FIGURE 12

Microsoft Excel results for the McNemar test for brand loyalty of cell phone providers

See Section E4 to create this.

	A	B	C	D
1	McNemar Test			
2				
3	Observed Frequencies			
4		Column variable		
5	Row variable	Sprint	Verizon	Total
6	Sprint	246	36	282
7	Verizon	12	306	318
8	Total	258	342	600
9				
10	Data			
11	Level of Significance	0.05		
12				
13	Intermediate Calculations			
14	Numerator	24	=C6 - B7	
15	Denominator	6.9282	=SQRT(C6 + B7)	
16	Z Test Statistic	3.4641	=B14/B15	
17				
18	Two-Tail Test			
19	Lower Critical Value	-1.9600	=NORMSINV(B11/2)	
20	Upper Critical Value	1.9600	=NORMSINV(1 - B11/2)	
21	p-Value	0.0005	=2 * (1 - NORMSDIST(ABS(B16)))	
22	Reject the null hypothesis		=IF(B21 < B11, "Reject the null hypothesis", "Do not reject the null hypothesis")	

PROBLEMS FOR SECTION 4

Learning the Basics

27 Given the following table for two related samples:

	GROUP 2		
GROUP 1	Yes	No	Total
Yes	46	25	71
No	16	59	75
Total	62	84	146

a. Compute the McNemar test statistic.
b. At the 0.05 level of significance, is there evidence of a difference between group 1 and group 2?

Applying the Concepts

28 A market researcher wanted to determine whether the proportion of coffee drinkers who preferred Brand A increased as the result of an advertising campaign. A random sample of 200 coffee drinkers was selected. The results indicating preference for Brand A or Brand B prior to the beginning of the advertising campaign and after its completion are shown in the following table:

	PREFERENCE AFTER COMPLETION OF ADVERTISING CAMPAIGN		
PREFERENCE PRIOR TO ADVERTISING CAMPAIGN	Brand A	Brand B	Total
Brand A	101	9	110
Brand B	22	68	90
Total	123	77	200

a. At the 0.05 level of significance, is there evidence that the proportion of coffee drinkers who prefer Brand A is lower at the beginning of the advertising campaign than at the end of the advertising campaign?

b. Compute the p-value in (a) and interpret its meaning.

29 Two candidates for governor participated in a televised debate. A political pollster recorded the preferences of 500 registered voters in a random sample prior to and after the debate:

	PREFERENCE AFTER DEBATE		
PREFERENCE PRIOR TO DEBATE	Candidate A	Candidate B	Total
Candidate A	269	21	290
Candidate B	36	174	210
Total	305	195	500

a. At the 0.01 level of significance, is there evidence of a difference in the proportion of voters who favor Candidate A prior to and after the debate?

b. Compute the p-value in (a) and interpret its meaning.

30 A taste-testing experiment compared two brands of Chilean merlot wines. After the initial comparison, 60 preferred Brand A, and 40 preferred Brand B. The 100 respondents were then exposed to a very professional and powerful advertisement promoting Brand A. The 100 respondents were then asked to taste the two wines again and declare which brand they preferred. The results are shown in the following table.

	PREFERENCE AFTER COMPLETION OF ADVERTISING		
PREFERENCE PRIOR TO ADVERTISING	Brand A	Brand B	Total
Brand A	55	5	60
Brand B	15	25	40
Total	70	30	100

a. At the 0.05 level of significance, is there evidence that the proportion who prefer Brand A is lower before the advertising than after the advertising?

b. Compute the p-value in (a) and interpret its meaning.

31 The CEO of a large metropolitan health care facility would like to assess the effects of recent implementation of Six Sigma management on customer satisfaction. A random sample of 100 patients is selected from a list of thousands of patients who were at the facility the past week and also a year ago:

	SATISFIED NOW		
SATISFIED LAST YEAR	Yes	No	Total
Yes	67	5	72
No	20	8	28
Total	87	13	100

a. At the 0.05 level of significance, is there evidence that satisfaction was lower last year, prior to introduction of Six Sigma management?

b. Compute the p-value in (a) and interpret its meaning.

32 The personnel director of a large department store wants to reduce absenteeism among sales associates. She decides to institute an incentive plan that provides financial rewards for sales associates who are absent fewer than five days in a given calendar year. A sample of 100 sales associates selected at the end of the second year reveals the following:

	YEAR 2		
YEAR 1	<5 Days Absent	≥5 Days Absent	Total
<5 days absent	32	4	36
≥5 days absent	25	39	64
Total	57	43	100

a. At the 0.05 level of significance, is there evidence that the proportion of employees absent fewer than 5 days was lower in year 1 than in year 2?

b. Compute the p-value in (a) and interpret its meaning.

5 WILCOXON RANK SUM TEST: NONPARAMETRIC ANALYSIS FOR TWO INDEPENDENT POPULATIONS

"A nonparametric procedure is a statistical procedure that has (certain) desirable properties that hold under relatively mild assumptions regarding the underlying population(s) from which the data are obtained."

—Myles Hollander and Douglas A. Wolfe (reference 4, p. 1)

You may have previously used the t test for the difference between the means of two independent populations. If sample sizes are small and you cannot assume that the data in each sample are from normally distributed populations, you have two choices:

- Use the Wilcoxon rank sum test that does not depend on the assumption of normality for the two populations.
- Use the pooled-variance t test, following some *normalizing transformation* on the data (see reference 9).

This section introduces the **Wilcoxon rank sum test** for testing whether there is a difference between two medians. The Wilcoxon rank sum test is almost as powerful as the pooled-variance and separate-variance t tests under conditions appropriate to these tests and is likely to be more powerful when the assumptions of those t tests are not met. In addition, you can use the Wilcoxon rank sum test when you have only ordinal data, as often happens when dealing with studies in consumer behavior and marketing research.

To perform the Wilcoxon rank sum test, you replace the values in the two samples of size n_1 and n_2 with their combined ranks (unless the data contained the ranks initially). You begin by defining $n = n_1 + n_2$ as the total sample size. Next, you assign the ranks so that rank 1 is given to the smallest of the n combined values, rank 2 is given to the second smallest, and so on, until rank n is given to the largest. If several values are tied, you assign each the average of the ranks that otherwise would have been assigned had there been no ties.

For convenience, whenever the two sample sizes are unequal, n_1 represents the smaller sample and n_2 the larger sample. The Wilcoxon rank sum test statistic, T_1, is defined as the sum of the ranks assigned to the n_1 values in the smaller sample. (For equal samples, either sample may be selected for determining T_1.) For any integer value n, the sum of the first n consecutive integers is $n(n + 1)/2$. Therefore, the test statistic T_1 plus T_2, the sum of the ranks assigned to the n_2 items in the second sample, must equal $n(n + 1)/2$. You can use Equation (7) to check the accuracy of your rankings.

CHECKING THE RANKINGS

$$T_1 + T_2 = \frac{n(n + 1)}{2} \qquad (7)$$

The Wilcoxon rank sum test can be either a two-tail test or a one-tail test, depending on whether you are testing whether the two population medians are *different* or whether one median is *greater than* the other median:

Two-Tail Test	One-Tail Test	One-Tail Test
$H_0: M_1 = M_2$	$H_0: M_1 \geq M_2$	$H_0: M_1 \leq M_2$
$H_1: M_1 \neq M_2$	$H_1: M_1 < M_2$	$H_1: M_1 > M_2$

where

$$M_1 = \text{median of population 1}$$

$$M_2 = \text{median of population 2}$$

When both samples n_1 and n_2 are ≤ 10, you use the table of lower and upper critical values, T_l, of Wilcoxon sum rank test to find the critical values of the test statistic T_1. For a two-tail test, you reject the null hypothesis (see Panel A of Figure 13) if the computed value of T_1 equals or is greater than the upper critical value, or if T_1 is less than or equal to the lower critical value. For one-tail tests having the alternative hypothesis $H_1: M_1 < M_2$, you reject the null hypothesis if the observed value of T_1 is less than or equal to the lower critical value (see Panel B of Figure 13). For one-tail tests having the alternative hypothesis $H_1: M_1 > M_2$, you reject the null hypothesis if the observed value of T_1 equals or is greater than the upper critical value (see Panel C of Figure 13).

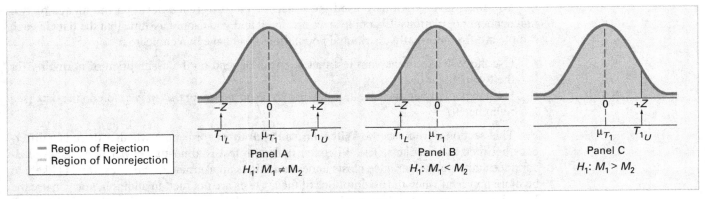

FIGURE 13 Regions of rejection and nonrejection using the Wilcoxon rank sum test

For large sample sizes, the test statistic T_1 is approximately normally distributed, with the mean, μ_{T_1}, equal to

$$\mu_{T_1} = \frac{n_1(n+1)}{2}$$

and the standard deviation, σ_{T_1}, equal to

$$\sigma_{T_1} = \sqrt{\frac{n_1 n_2 (n+1)}{12}}$$

Therefore, Equation (8) defines the standardized Z test statistic.

LARGE SAMPLE WILCOXON RANK SUM TEST

$$Z = \frac{T_1 - \dfrac{n_1(n+1)}{2}}{\sqrt{\dfrac{n_1 n_2(n+1)}{12}}} \qquad (8)$$

where the test statistic Z approximately follows a standardized normal distribution.

You use Equation (8) for testing the null hypothesis when the sample sizes are outside the range of the table of lower and upper critical values, T_1, of Wilcoxon rank sum test. Based on α, the level of significance selected, you reject the null hypothesis if the computed Z value falls in the rejection region.

To study an application of the Wilcoxon rank sum test, consider a scenario concerning sales of BLK cola for two locations: normal shelf display and end-aisle location. If you do not think that the populations are normally distributed, you can use the Wilcoxon rank sum test for evaluating possible differences in the median sales for the two display locations.[1] The data (stored in the file cola.xls) and the combined ranks are shown in Table 14.

Because you have not specified in advance which aisle location is likely to have a higher median, you use a two-tail test with the following null and alternative hypotheses:

$$H_0: M_1 = M_2 \text{ (the median sales are equal)}$$
$$H_1: M_1 \neq M_2 \text{ (the median sales are not equal)}$$

To perform the Wilcoxon rank sum test, you compute the rankings for the sales from the $n_1 = 10$ stores with a normal shelf display and the $n_2 = 10$ stores with an end-aisle display. Table 14 provides the combined rankings.

[1]To test for differences in the median sales between the two locations, you must assume that the distributions of sales in both populations are identical except for differences in location (that is, the medians).

TABLE 14

Forming the Combined Rankings

	Sales		
Normal Display $(n_1 = 10)$	**Combined Ranking**	**End-Aisle Display** $(n_2 = 10)$	**Combined Ranking**
22	1.0	52	5.5
34	3.0	71	14.0
52	5.5	76	15.0
62	10.0	54	7.0
30	2.0	67	13.0
40	4.0	83	17.0
64	11.0	66	12.0
84	18.5	90	20.0
56	8.0	77	16.0
59	9.0	84	18.5

The next step is to compute T_1, the sum of the ranks assigned to the *smaller* sample. When the sample sizes are equal, as in this example, you can identify either sample as the group from which to compute T_1. Choosing the normal display as the first sample,

$$T_1 = 1 + 3 + 5.5 + 10 + 2 + 4 + 11 + 18.5 + 8 + 9 = 72$$

As a check on the ranking procedure, you compute T_2 from

$$T_2 = 5.5 + 14 + 15 + 7 + 13 + 17 + 12 + 20 + 16 + 18.5 = 138$$

and then use Equation (7) to show that the sum of the first $n = 20$ integers in the combined ranking is equal to $T_1 + T_2$:

$$T_1 + T_2 = \frac{n(n + 1)}{2}$$

$$72 + 138 = \frac{20(21)}{2} = 210$$

$$210 = 210$$

To test the null hypothesis that there is no difference between the median sales of the two populations, you use the table of lower and upper critical values, T_1 of Wilcoxon rank sum test to determine the lower- and upper-tail critical values for the test statistic T_1. From Table 15, a portion of the larger table, observe that for a level of significance of 0.05, the critical values are 78 and 132. The decision rule is

Reject H_0 if $T_1 \leq 78$ or if $T_1 \geq 132$;

otherwise, do not reject H_0.

TABLE 15

Finding the Lower- and Upper-Tail Critical Values for the Wilcoxon Rank Sum Test Statistic, T_1, Where $n_1 = 10$, $n_2 = 10$, and $\alpha = 0.05$

	α					n_1			
n_2	One-Tail	Two-Tail	4	5	6	7	8	9	**10**
							(Lower, Upper)		
9	.05	.10	16,40	24,51	33,63	43,76	54,90	66,105	
	.025	.05	14,42	22,53	31,65	40,79	51,93	62,109	
	.01	.02	13,43	20,55	28,68	37,82	47,97	59,112	
	.005	.01	11,45	18,57	26,70	35,84	45,99	56,115	
	.05	.10	17,43	26,54	35,67	45,81	56,96	69,111	82,128
10	.025	.05	15,45	23,57	32,70	42,84	53,99	65,115	78,132
	.01	.02	13,47	21,59	29,73	39,87	49,103	61,119	74,136
	.005	.01	12,48	19,61	27,75	37,89	47,105	58,122	71,139

Source: Extracted from the Table of Lower and Upper Critical Values, T_1 of Wilcoxon Rank Sum Test.

Because the test statistic $T_1 = 72 < 78$, you reject H_0. There is evidence of a significant difference in the median sales for the two displays. Because the sum of the ranks is higher for the end-aisle display, you conclude that median sales are higher for the end-aisle display. From the Microsoft Excel worksheet in Figure 14, observe that the p-value is 0.0126, which is less than $\alpha = 0.05$. The p-value indicates that if the medians of the two populations are equal, the chance of finding a difference at least this large in the samples is only 0.0126.

FIGURE 14

Microsoft Excel
Wilcoxon rank sum test
worksheet for the BLK
cola sales example

See Section E5 to create this.

	A	B	
1	Display Location Analysis		
2			
3	Data		
4	Level of Significance	0.05	
5			
6	Population 1 Sample		
7	Sample Size	10	
8	Sum of Ranks	72	
9	Population 2 Sample		
10	Sample Size	10	
11	Sum of Ranks	138	
12			
13	Intermediate Calculations		
14	Total Sample Size n	20	=B7 + B10
15	T1 Test Statistic	72	=IF(B7 <= B10, B8, B11)
16	T1 Mean	105	=IF(B7 <= B10, B7 * (B14 + 1)/2, B10 * (B14 + 1)/2)
17	Standard Error of T1	13.2288	=SQRT(B7 * B10 * (B14 + 1)/12)
18	Z Test Statistic	-2.4946	=(B15 - B16)/B17
19			
20	Two-Tail Test		
21	Lower Critical Value	-1.9600	=NORMSINV(B4/2)
22	Upper Critical Value	1.9600	=NORMSINV(1 - B4/2)
23	p-Value	0.0126	=2 * (1 - NORMSDIST(ABS(B18)))
24	Reject the null hypothesis		=IF(B23 < B4, "Reject the null hypothesis", "Do not reject the null hypothesis")

The table shows the lower and upper critical values of the Wilcoxon rank sum test statistic, T_1, but only for situations in which both n_1 and n_2 are less than or equal to 10. If either one or both of the sample sizes are greater than 10, you *must* use the large-sample Z approximation formula [Equation (8)]. However, you can also use this approximation formula for small sample sizes. To demonstrate the large-sample Z approximation formula, consider the BLK cola sales data. Using Equation (8),

$$Z = \frac{T_1 - \dfrac{n_1(n+1)}{2}}{\sqrt{\dfrac{n_1 n_2 (n+1)}{12}}}$$

$$= \frac{72 - \dfrac{(10)(21)}{2}}{\sqrt{\dfrac{(10)(10)(21)}{12}}}$$

$$= \frac{72 - 105}{13.2288} = -2.4946$$

Because $Z = -2.4946 < -1.96$, the critical value of Z at the 0.05 level of significance, you reject H_0.

PROBLEMS FOR SECTION 5

Learning the Basics

33 Using the table, determine the lower- and upper-tail critical values for the Wilcoxon rank sum test statistic, T_1, in each of the following two-tail tests:

a. $\alpha = 0.10$, $n_1 = 6$, $n_2 = 8$
b. $\alpha = 0.05$, $n_1 = 6$, $n_2 = 8$
c. $\alpha = 0.01$, $n_1 = 6$, $n_2 = 8$
d. Given your results in (a) through (c), what do you conclude regarding the width of the region of nonrejection as the selected level of significance α gets smaller?

34 Using the table, determine the lower-tail critical value for the Wilcoxon rank sum test statistic, T_1, in each of the following one-tail tests:
a. $\alpha = 0.05$, $n_1 = 6$, $n_2 = 8$
b. $\alpha = 0.025$, $n_1 = 6$, $n_2 = 8$
c. $\alpha = 0.01$, $n_1 = 6$, $n_2 = 8$
d. $\alpha = 0.005$, $n_1 = 6$, $n_2 = 8$

35 The following information is available for two samples selected from independent populations:

Sample 1: $n_1 = 7$ Assigned ranks: 4 1 8 2 5 10 11

Sample 2: $n_2 = 9$ Assigned ranks: 7 16 12 9 3 14 13 6 15

What is the value of T_1 if you are testing the null hypothesis H_0: $M_1 = M_2$?

PH Grade **36** In Problem 35, what are the lower- and ASSIST upper-tail critical values for the test statistic T_1 from the table if you use a 0.05 level of significance and the alternative hypothesis is H_1: $M_1 \neq M_2$?

37 In Problems 35 and 36, what is your statistical decision?

38 The following information is available for two samples selected from independent and similarly shaped right-skewed populations:

Sample 1: $n_1 = 5$ 1.1 2.3 2.9 3.6 14.7

Sample 2: $n_2 = 6$ 2.8 4.4 4.4 5.2 6.0 18.5

a. Replace the observed values with the corresponding ranks (where 1 = smallest value; $n = n_1 + n_2 = 11$ = largest value) in the combined samples.
b. What is the value of the test statistic T_1?
c. Compute the value of T_2, the sum of the ranks in the larger sample.
d. To check the accuracy of your rankings, use Equation (7) to demonstrate that

$$T_1 + T_2 = \frac{n(n + 1)}{2}$$

PH Grade **39** From Problem 38, at the 0.05 level of signif-ASSIST icance, determine the lower-tail critical value for the Wilcoxon rank sum test statistic, T_1, if you want to test the null hypothesis, H_0: $M_1 \geq M_2$, against the one-tail alternative, H_1: $M_1 < M_2$.

40 In Problems 38 and 39, what is your statistical decision?

Applying the Concepts

41 A vice president for marketing recruits 20 college graduates for management training. The 20 individuals are randomly assigned, 10 each, to one of two groups. A "traditional" method of training (T) is used in one group, and an "experimental" method (E) is used in the other. After the graduates spend six months on the job, the vice president ranks them on the basis of their performance, from 1 (worst) to 20 (best), with the following results (stored in the file testrank.xls):

T	1	2	3	5	9	10	12	13	14	15
E	4	6	7	8	11	16	17	18	19	20

Is there evidence of a difference in the median performance between the two methods? (Use $\alpha = 0.05$.)

42 Wine experts Gaiter and Brecher use a six-category scale when rating wines: Yech, OK, Good, Very Good, Delicious, and Delicious! (D. Gaiter and J. Brecher, "A Good U.S. Cabernet Is Hard to Find," *The Wall Street Journal*, May 19, 2006, p. W7). Suppose Gaiter and Brecher tested a random sample of eight inexpensive California Cabernets and a random sample of eight inexpensive Washington Cabernets. *Inexpensive* is defined as a suggested retail value in the United States of under $20. The data, stored in the cabernet.xls file, are as follows:

California—Good, Delicious, Yech, OK, OK, Very Good, Yech, OK
Washington—Very Good, OK, Delicious!, Very Good, Delicious, Good, Delicious, Delicious!

a. Are the data collected by rating wines using this scale nominal, ordinal, interval, or ratio?
b. Why is the two-sample t test defined in Section 1 inappropriate to test the mean rating of California Cabernets versus Washington Cabernets?
c. Is there evidence of a significance difference in the median rating of California Cabernets and Washington Cabernets? (Use $\alpha = 0.05$.)

43 In intaglio printing, a design or figure is carved beneath the surface of hard metal or stone. Suppose that an experiment is designed to compare differences in surface hardness of steel plates used in intaglio printing (measured in indentation numbers), based on two different surface conditions—untreated and treated by lightly polishing with emery paper. In the experiment, 40 steel plates are randomly assigned—20 that are untreated, and 20 that are treated. The data are shown in the following table and are stored in the file intaglio.xls:

Untreated		Treated	
164.368	177.135	158.239	150.226
159.018	163.903	138.216	155.620
153.871	167.802	168.006	151.233
165.096	160.818	149.654	158.653
157.184	167.433	145.456	151.204
154.496	163.538	168.178	150.869
160.920	164.525	154.321	161.657
164.917	171.230	162.763	157.016
169.091	174.964	161.020	156.670
175.276	166.311	167.706	147.920

a. Is there evidence of a difference in the median surface hardness between untreated and treated steel plates? (Use $\alpha = 0.05$.)

b. What assumptions must you make in (a)?

 44 Management of a hotel was concerned with increasing the return rate for hotel guests. One aspect of first impressions by guests relates to the time it takes to deliver a guest's luggage to the room after check-in to the hotel. A random sample of 20 deliveries on a particular day were selected in Wing *A* of the hotel, and a random sample of 20 deliveries were selected in Wing *B*. The results are stored in the file luggage.xls.

a. Is there evidence of a difference in the median delivery time in the two wings of the hotel? (Use $\alpha = 0.05$.)

45 The director of training for an electronic equipment manufacturer wants to determine whether different training methods have an effect on the productivity of assembly-line employees. She randomly assigns 42 recently hired employees to two groups of 21. The first group receives a computer-assisted, individual-based training program, and the other group receives a team-based training program. Upon completion of the training, the employees are evaluated on the time (in seconds) it takes to assemble a part. The results are in the data file training.xls.

a. Using a 0.05 level of significance, is there evidence of a difference in the median assembly times (in seconds) between employees trained in a computer-assisted, individual-based program and those trained in a team-based program?

b. What assumptions must you make in order to do (a) of this problem?

46 Nondestructive evaluation is a method that is used to describe the properties of components or materials without causing any permanent physical change to the units. It includes the determination of properties of materials and the classification of flaws by size, shape, type, and location. This method is most effective for detecting surface flaws and characterizing surface properties of electrically conductive materials. Recently, data were collected that classified each component as having a flaw or not, based on manual inspection and operator judgment, and also reported the size of the crack in the material. Do the components classified as unflawed have a smaller median crack size than components classified as flawed? The results in terms of crack size (in inches) are in the data file crack.xls (extracted from B. D. Olin and W. Q. Meeker, "Applications of Statistical Methods to Nondestructive Evaluation," *Technometrics*, 38, 1996, p. 101.)

Unflawed

0.003 0.004 0.012 0.014 0.021 0.023 0.024 0.030 0.034
0.041 0.041 0.042 0.043 0.045 0.057 0.063 0.074 0.076

Flawed

0.022 0.026 0.026 0.030 0.031 0.034 0.042 0.043 0.044
0.046 0.046 0.052 0.055 0.058 0.060 0.060 0.070 0.071
0.073 0.073 0.078 0.079 0.079 0.083 0.090 0.095 0.095
0.096 0.100 0.102 0.103 0.105 0.114 0.119 0.120 0.130
0.160 0.306 0.328 0.440

a. Using a 0.05 level of significance, is there evidence that the median crack size is less for unflawed components than for flawed components?

b. What assumptions must you make in (a)?

47 A bank with a branch located in a commercial district of a city has developed an improved process for serving customers during the noon-to-1 p.m. lunch period. The waiting time (defined as the time elapsed from when the customer enters the line until he or she reaches the teller window) of all customers during this hour is recorded over a period of 1 week. A random sample of 15 customers is selected (and stored in the file bank1.xls), and the results (in minutes) are as follows:

4.21 5.55 3.02 5.13 4.77 2.34 3.54 3.20
4.50 6.10 0.38 5.12 6.46 6.19 3.79

Another branch, located in a residential area, is also concerned with the noon-to-1 p.m. lunch period. A random sample of 15 customers is selected (and stored in the file bank2.xls), and the results (in minutes) are as follows:

9.66 5.90 8.02 5.79 8.73 3.82 8.01 8.35
10.49 6.68 5.64 4.08 6.17 9.91 5.47

a. Is there evidence of a difference in the median waiting time between the two branches? (Use $\alpha = 0.05$.)

b. What assumptions must you make in (a)?

48 A problem with a telephone line that prevents a customer from receiving or making calls is upsetting to both the customer and the telephone company. The data in the file phone.xls represent samples of 20 problems reported to two different offices of a telephone company and the time to clear these problems (in minutes) from the customers' lines:

Central Office I Time to Clear Problems (Minutes)

1.48 1.75 0.78 2.85 0.52 1.60 4.15 3.97 1.48 3.10
1.02 0.53 0.93 1.60 0.80 1.05 6.32 3.93 5.45 0.97

Central Office II Time to Clear Problems (Minutes)

7.55	3.75	0.10	1.10	0.60	0.52	3.30	2.10	0.58	4.02
3.75	0.65	1.92	0.60	1.53	4.23	0.08	1.48	1.65	0.72

a. Is there evidence of a difference in the median time to clear these problems between the two offices? (Use $\alpha = 0.05$.)

b. What assumptions must you make in (a)?

6 KRUSKAL-WALLIS RANK TEST: NONPARAMETRIC ANALYSIS FOR THE ONE-WAY ANOVA

If the normality assumption of the one-way ANOVA F test is not met, you can use the Kruskal-Wallis rank test. The Kruskal-Wallis rank test for differences among c medians (where $c > 2$) is an extension of the Wilcoxon rank sum test for two independent populations, discussed in Section 5. Thus, the Kruskal-Wallis test has the same power relative to the one-way ANOVA F test that the Wilcoxon rank sum test has relative to the t test.

You use the **Kruskal-Wallis rank test** to test whether c independent groups have equal medians. The null hypothesis is

$$H_0: M_1 = M_2 = \cdots = M_c$$

and the alternative hypothesis is

$$H_1: \text{Not all } M_j \text{ are equal (where } j = 1, 2, \ldots, c).$$

To use the Kruskal-Wallis rank test, you first replace the values in the c samples with their combined ranks (if necessary). Rank 1 is given to the smallest of the combined values and rank n to the largest of the combined values (where $n = n_1 + n_2 + \cdots + n_c$). If any values are tied, you assign them the mean of the ranks they would have otherwise been assigned if ties had not been present in the data.

The Kruskal-Wallis test is an alternative to the one-way ANOVA F test. Instead of comparing each of the c group means, $\overline{X}_j$, against the grand mean, $\overline{\overline{X}}$, the Kruskal-Wallis test compares the mean rank in each of the c groups against the overall mean rank, based on all n combined values. If there is a significant difference among the c groups, the mean rank differs considerably from group to group. In the process of squaring these differences, the test statistic H becomes large. If there are no differences present, the test statistic H is small because the mean of the ranks assigned in each group should be very similar from group to group.

Equation (9) defines the Kruskal-Wallis test statistic, H.

KRUSKAL-WALLIS RANK TEST FOR DIFFERENCES AMONG c MEDIANS

$$H = \left[\frac{12}{n(n+1)} \sum_{j=1}^{c} \frac{T_j^2}{n_j} \right] - 3(n+1) \tag{9}$$

where

n = total number of values over the combined samples

n_j = number of values in the jth sample ($j = 1, 2, \ldots, c$)

T_j = sum of the ranks assigned to the jth sample

T_j^2 = square of the sum of the ranks assigned to the jth sample

c = number of groups

As the sample sizes in each group get large (that is, greater than 5), you can approximate the test statistic, H, by the chi-square distribution with $c - 1$ degrees of freedom. Thus, you reject the null hypothesis if the computed value of H is greater than the χ_U^2 upper-tail critical value (see Figure 15). Therefore, the decision rule is

$$\text{Reject } H_0 \text{ if } H > \chi_U^2;$$

$$\text{otherwise, do not reject } H_0.$$

FIGURE 15

Determining the rejection region for the Kruskal-Wallis test

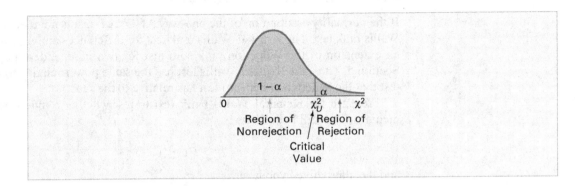

To illustrate the Kruskal-Wallis rank test for differences among c medians, consider a scenario concerning the strength of parachutes. If you cannot assume that the tensile strength is normally distributed in all c groups, you can use the Kruskal-Wallis rank test.

The null hypothesis is that the median tensile strengths of parachutes from four suppliers are equal. The alternative hypothesis is that at least one of the suppliers differs from the others.

$$H_0: M_1 = M_2 = M_3 = M_4$$
$$H_1: \text{Not all } M_j \text{ are equal (where } j = 1, 2, 3, 4).$$

Table 16 presents the data (stored in the file `parachute.xls`), along with the corresponding ranks.

TABLE 16

Tensile Strength and Ranks of Parachutes Woven from Synthetic Fibers from Four Suppliers

Supplier							
1		**2**		**3**		**4**	
Amount	**Rank**	**Amount**	**Rank**	**Amount**	**Rank**	**Amount**	**Rank**
18.5	4	26.3	20	20.6	8	25.4	19
24.0	13.5	25.3	18	25.2	17	19.9	5.5
17.2	1	24.0	13.5	20.8	9	22.6	11
19.9	5.5	21.2	10	24.7	16	17.5	2
18.0	3	24.5	15	22.9	12	20.4	7

In converting the 20 tensile strengths to ranks, observe in Table 16 that the third parachute for Supplier 1 has the lowest tensile strength, 17.2. It is given a rank of 1. The fourth value for Supplier 1 and the second value for Supplier 4 each have a value of 19.9. Because they are tied for ranks 5 and 6, they are assigned the rank 5.5. Finally, the first value for Supplier 2 is the largest value, 26.3, and is assigned a rank of 20.

After all the ranks are assigned, you compute the sum of the ranks for each group:

$$\text{Rank sums:} \quad T_1 = 27 \quad T_2 = 76.5 \quad T_3 = 62 \quad T_4 = 44.5$$

As a check on the rankings, recall from Equation (7) that for any integer n, the sum of the first n consecutive integers is $\dfrac{n(n+1)}{2}$. Therefore

$$T_1 + T_2 + T_3 + T_4 = \frac{n(n+1)}{2}$$

$$27 + 76.5 + 62 + 44.5 = \frac{(20)(21)}{2}$$

$$210 = 210$$

Using Equation (9) to test the null hypothesis of equal population medians,

$$H = \left[\frac{12}{n(n+1)} \sum_{j=1}^{c} \frac{T_j^2}{n_j} \right] - 3(n+1)$$

$$= \left\{ \frac{12}{(20)(21)} \left[\frac{(27)^2}{5} + \frac{(76.5)^2}{5} + \frac{(62)^2}{5} + \frac{(44.5)^2}{5} \right] \right\} - 3(21)$$

$$= \left(\frac{12}{420} \right)(2{,}481.1) - 63 = 7.8886$$

The statistic H approximately follows a chi-square distribution with $c-1$ degrees of freedom. Using a 0.05 level of significance, χ_U^2, the upper-tail critical value of the chi-square distribution with $c-1 = 3$ degrees of freedom is 7.815 (see Table 17). Because the computed value of the test statistic $H = 7.8886$ is greater than the critical value, you reject the null hypothesis and conclude that not all the suppliers are the same with respect to median tensile strength. The same conclusion is reached by using the p-value approach. In Figure 16, observe that the p-value $= 0.0484 < 0.05$.

TABLE 17

Finding χ_U^2, the Upper-Tail Critical Value for the Kruskal-Wallis Rank Test, at the 0.05 Level of Significance with 3 Degrees of Freedom

Degrees of Freedom	Upper-Tail Area									
	.995	.99	.975	.95	.90	.75	.25	.10	.05	.025
1	—	—	0.001	0.004	0.016	0.102	1.323	2.706	3.841	5.024
2	0.010	0.020	0.051	0.103	0.211	0.575	2.773	4.605	5.991	7.378
3	0.072	0.115	0.216	0.352	0.584	1.213	4.108	6.251	7.815	9.348
4	0.207	0.297	0.484	0.711	1.064	1.923	5.385	7.779	9.488	11.143
5	0.412	0.554	0.831	1.145	1.610	2.675	6.626	9.236	11.071	12.833

Source: Extracted from Table of Critical Value of χ^2.

FIGURE 16

Microsoft Excel worksheet for the Kruskal-Wallis rank test for differences among the four medians in the parachute example

See Section E6 to create this.

	A	B	C	D	E	F	G
1	Tensile-Strength Analysis						
2							
3	Data						
4	Level of Significance	0.05					
5					Group	Sample Size	Sum of Ranks	Mean Ranks
6	Intermediate Calculations				1	5	27	5.4
7	Sum of Squared Ranks/Sample Size	2481.1			2	5	76.5	15.3
8	Sum of Sample Sizes	20			3	5	62	12.4
9	Number of Groups	4			4	5	44.5	8.9
10							
11	Test Result						
12	H Test Statistic	7.8886		=(12/(B8 * (B8 + 1))) * B7 - (3 * (B8 + 1))			
13	Critical Value	7.8147		=CHIINV(B4, B9 - 1)			
14	p-Value	0.0484		=CHIDIST(B12, B9 - 1)			
15	Reject the null hypothesis			=IF(B14 < B4, "Reject the null hypothesis",			
16				"Do not reject the null hypothesis")			
17				Also			
18				Cell B7: =(G6 * F6) + (G7 * F7) + (G8 * F8) + (G9 * F9)			
19				Cell B8: =SUM(E6:E9)			

You reject the null hypothesis and conclude that there is evidence of a significant difference among the suppliers with respect to the median tensile strength. At this point, you could simultaneously compare all pairs of suppliers to determine which ones differ (see reference 2).

The following assumptions are needed to use the Kruskal-Wallis rank test:

- The c samples are randomly and independently selected from their respective populations.
- The underlying variable is continuous.
- The data provide at least a set of ranks, both within and among the c samples.
- The c populations have the same variability.
- The c populations have the same shape.

The Kruskal-Wallis procedure makes less stringent assumptions than does the F test. If you ignore the last two assumptions (variability and shape), you can still use the Kruskal-Wallis rank test to determine whether at least one of the populations differs from the other populations in some characteristic—such as central tendency, variation, or shape. However, to use the F test, you must assume that the c samples are from underlying normal populations that have equal variances.

When the more stringent assumptions of the F test hold, you should use the F test instead of the Kruskal-Wallis test because it has slightly more power to detect significant differences among groups. However, if the assumptions of the F test do not hold, you should use the Kruskal-Wallis test.

PROBLEMS FOR SECTION 6

Learning the Basics

49 What is the upper-tail critical value from the chi-square distribution if you use the Kruskal-Wallis rank test for comparing the medians in six populations at the 0.01 level of significance?

50 Using the results of Problem 49,
a. State the decision rule for testing the null hypothesis that all six groups have equal population medians.
b. What is your statistical decision if the computed value of the test statistic H is 13.77?

Applying the Concepts

51 Periodically, *The Wall Street Journal* has conducted a stock-picking contest. The last one was conducted in March 2001. In this experiment, three different methods were used to select stocks that were expected to perform well during the next five months. Four Wall Street professionals, considered experts on picking stocks, each selected one stock. Four randomly chosen readers of *The Wall Street Journal* each selected one stock. Finally, four stocks were selected by flinging darts at a table containing a list of stocks. The returns of the selected stocks for March 20, 2001, to August 31, 2001 (in percentage return), are given in the following table and stored in

the file `contest2001.xls`. Note that during this period, the Dow Jones Industrial Average gained 2.4% (extracted from G. Jasen, "In Picking Stocks, Dartboard Beats the Pros," *The Wall Street Journal*, September 27, 2001, pp. C1, C10).

Experts	Readers	Darts
+39.5	−31.0	+39.0
−1.1	−20.7	+31.9
−4.5	−45.0	+14.1
−8.0	−73.3	+5.4

a. Is there evidence of a significant difference in the median return for the three categories? (Use $\alpha = 0.05$.)

52 A hospital conducted a study of the waiting time in its emergency room. The hospital has a main campus, along with three satellite locations. Management had a business objective of reducing waiting time for emergency room cases that did not require immediate attention. To study this, a random sample of 15 emergency room cases at each location were selected on a particular day, and the waiting time (measured from check-in to when the patient was called into the clinic area) was measured. The results are stored in the file `erwaiting.xls`.
a. At the 0.05 level of significance, is there evidence of a difference in the median waiting times in the four locations?

53 The following data (stored in the file `cdyield.xls`) represent the nationwide highest yield of different types of accounts (extracted from Bankrate.com, January 24, 2006):

Money Market	6-Month CD	1-Yr CD	2.5-Yr CD	5-Yr CD
4.55	4.75	4.94	4.95	5.05
4.50	4.70	4.90	4.91	5.05
4.40	4.69	4.85	4.85	5.02
4.38	4.65	4.85	4.82	5.00
4.38	4.65	4.85	4.80	5.00

a. At the 0.05 level of significance, is there evidence of a difference in the median yields of the different accounts?

54 An advertising agency has been hired by a manufacturer of pens to develop an advertising campaign for the upcoming holiday season. To prepare for this project, the research director decides to initiate a study of the effect of advertising on product perception. An experiment is designed to compare five different advertisements. Advertisement *A* greatly undersells the pen's characteristics. Advertisement *B* slightly undersells the pen's characteristics. Advertisement *C* slightly oversells the pen's characteristics. Advertisement *D* greatly oversells the pen's characteristics. Advertisement *E* attempts to correctly state the pen's characteristics. A sample of 30 adult respondents, taken from a larger focus group, is randomly assigned to the five advertisements (so that there are six respondents to each). After reading the advertisement and developing a sense of product expectation, all respondents unknowingly receive the same pen to evaluate. The respondents are permitted to test the pen and the plausibility of the advertising copy. The respondents are then asked to rate the pen from 1 to 7 on the product characteristic scales of appearance, durability, and writing performance. The *combined* scores of three ratings (appearance, durability, and writing performance) for the 30 respondents (stored in the file `pen.xls`) are as follows:

A	B	C	D	E
15	16	8	5	12
18	17	7	6	19
17	21	10	13	18
19	16	15	11	12
19	19	14	9	17
20	17	14	10	14

a. At the 0.05 level of significance, is there evidence of a difference in the median ratings of the five advertisements?

55 A sporting goods manufacturing company wanted to compare the distance traveled by golf balls produced using each of four different designs. Ten balls were manufactured with each design and were brought to the local golf course for the club professional to test. The order in which the balls were hit with the same club from the first tee was randomized so that the pro did not know which type of ball was being hit. All 40 balls were hit in a short period of time, during which the environmental conditions were essentially the same. The results (distance traveled in yards) for the four designs are stored in the file `golfball.xls`:

a. At the 0.05 level of significance, is there evidence of a difference in the median distances traveled by the golf balls with different designs?

56 Students in a business statistics course performed an experiment to test the strength of four brands of trash bags. One-pound weights were placed into a bag, one at a time, until the bag broke. A total of 40 bags were used (10 for each brand). The data file `trashbags.xls` gives the weight (in pounds) required to break the trash bags.

a. At the 0.05 level of significance, is there evidence of a difference in the median strength of the four brands of trash bags?

7 ● (CD-ROM Topic) CHI-SQUARE TEST FOR A VARIANCE OR STANDARD DEVIATION

When analyzing numerical data, sometimes you need to make conclusions about a population variance or standard deviation. For further discussion, see Section 7 on the Student CD-ROM that accompanies this text.

SUMMARY

Figure 17 presents a roadmap for this chapter. First, you used hypothesis testing for analyzing categorical response data from two samples (independent and related) and from more than two independent samples. In addition, the rules of probability were extended to the hypothesis of independence in the joint responses to two categorical variables. You applied these methods to the surveys conducted by T.C. Resort Properties. You concluded that a greater proportion of guests are willing to return to the Beachcomber Hotel than to the Windsurfer; that the Golden Palm, Palm Royale, and Palm Princess hotels are different with respect

to the proportion of guests who are likely to return; and that the reasons given for not returning to a hotel are dependent on the hotel the guests visited. These inferences will allow T.C. Resort Properties to improve the quality of service it provides.

In addition to the chi-square tests, you also studied two nonparametric tests. You used the Wilcoxon rank sum test when the assumptions of the t test for two independent samples were violated and the Kruskal-Wallis test when the assumptions of the one-way ANOVA were violated.

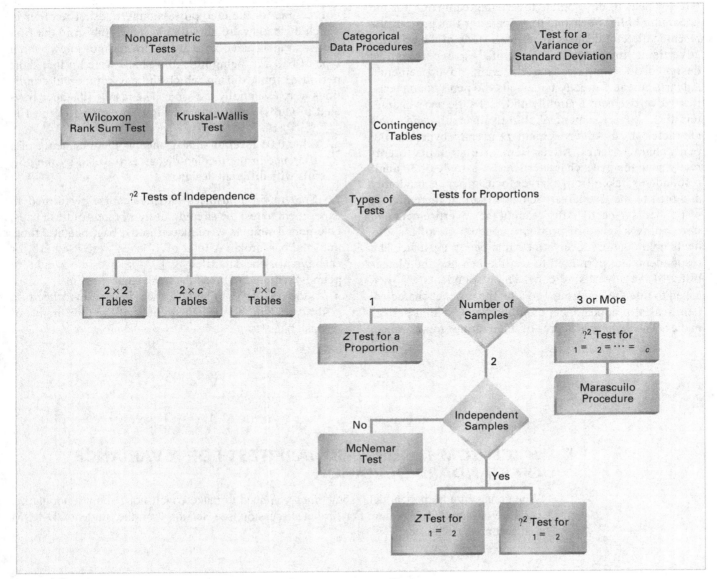

FIGURE 17 Roadmap of Chi-Square Tests and Nonparametric Tests

KEY EQUATIONS

χ^2 Test for the Difference Between Two Proportions

$$\chi^2 = \sum_{all\ cells} \frac{(f_o - f_e)^2}{f_e} \qquad (1)$$

Computing the Estimated Overall Proportion

$$\overline{p} = \frac{X_1 + X_2}{n_1 + n_2} = \frac{X}{n} \qquad (2)$$

Computing the Estimated Overall Proportion for c Groups

$$\overline{p} = \frac{X_1 + X_2 + \cdots + X_c}{n_1 + n_2 + \cdots + n_c} = \frac{X}{n} \qquad (3)$$

Critical Range for the Marascuilo Procedure

$$\text{Critical range} = \sqrt{\chi_U^2}\sqrt{\frac{p_j(1-p_j)}{n_j} + \frac{p_{j'}(1-p_{j'})}{n_{j'}}} \qquad (4)$$

Computing the Expected Frequency

$$f_e = \frac{\text{Row total} \times \text{Column total}}{n} \qquad (5)$$

McNemar Test

$$Z = \frac{B - C}{\sqrt{B + C}} \qquad (6)$$

Checking the Rankings

$$T_1 + T_2 = \frac{n(n + 1)}{2} \qquad (7)$$

Large-Sample Wilcoxon Rank Sum Test

$$Z = \frac{T_1 - \frac{n_1(n+1)}{2}}{\sqrt{\frac{n_1 n_2(n+1)}{12}}} \qquad (8)$$

Kruskal-Wallis Rank Test for Differences Among c Medians

$$H = \left[\frac{12}{n(n+1)} \sum_{j=1}^{c} \frac{T_j^2}{n_j}\right] - 3(n+1) \qquad (9)$$

KEY TERMS

chi-square (χ^2) distribution
chi-square (χ^2) test of independence
contingency table
expected frequency (f_e)

Kruskal-Wallis rank test
Marascuilo procedure
McNemar test
observed frequency (f_o)

$2 \times c$ contingency table
2×2 contingency table
Wilcoxon rank sum test

CHAPTER REVIEW PROBLEMS

Checking Your Understanding

57 Under what conditions should you use the χ^2 test to determine whether there is a difference between the proportions of two independent populations?

58 Under what conditions should you use the χ^2 test to determine whether there is a difference between the proportions of more than two independent populations?

59 Under what conditions should you use the χ^2 test of independence?

60 Under what conditions should you use the McNemar test?

61 What is a nonparametric procedure?

62 Under what conditions should you use the Wilcoxon rank sum test?

63 Under what conditions should you use the Kruskal-Wallis rank test?

Applying the Concepts

64 Undergraduate students at Miami University in Oxford, Ohio, were surveyed in order to evaluate the effect of gender and price on purchasing a pizza from Pizza Hut. Students were told to suppose that they were planning on having a large two-topping pizza delivered to their residence that evening. The students had to decide between ordering from Pizza Hut at a reduced price of $8.49 (the regular price for a large two-topping pizza from the Oxford Pizza Hut at this time was $11.49) and ordering a pizza from a different pizzeria. The results from this question are summarized in the following contingency table:

| | PIZZERIA | | |
GENDER	Pizza Hut	Other	Total
Female	4	13	17
Male	6	12	18
Total	10	25	35

The survey also evaluated purchase decisions at other prices. These results are summarized in the following contingency table:

| | PRICE | | | |
PIZZERIA	$8.49	$11.49	$14.49	Total
Pizza Hut	10	5	2	17
Other	25	23	27	75
Total	35	28	29	92

a. Using a 0.05 level of significance and using the data in the first contingency table, is there evidence of a significant relationship between a student's gender and his or her pizzeria selection?
b. What is your answer to (a) if nine of the male students selected Pizza Hut and nine selected other?
c. Using a 0.05 level of significance and using the data in the second contingency table, is there evidence of a difference in pizzeria selection based on price?
d. Determine the p-value in (c) and interpret its meaning.
e. If appropriate, use the Marascuilo procedure and $\alpha = 0.05$ to determine which prices are different in terms of pizzeria preference.

65 A 2004 study by the American Society for Quality investigated executives' views toward quality. Top executives were asked whether they view quality as a profession in the way law, medicine, engineering, and accounting are viewed, or whether they see practicing quality more as the ability to understand and use a variety of tools and techniques to produce a result. Table (1) provides the responses to this question, cross-classified by the type of industry with which the executive is involved. A second question asked whether the executives' companies actually measure the impact of process improvement initiatives designed to raise the quality of their products or services. Table (2) provides the results to this question.

(1) Do you believe that quality is a profession?

	Manufacturing	Service	Health Care
Yes	108	88	49
No	72	132	50

(2) Does your company measure the impact of process improvement initiatives?

	Manufacturing	Service	Health Care
Yes	132	129	54
No	48	91	46

Source: Adapted from G. Weiler, "What Do CEOs Think About Quality?" Quality Progress, May 2004, 37(5), pp. 52–56.

a. Is there a significant difference among the three industries with respect to the proportion of top executives who believe quality is a profession? (Use $\alpha = 0.05$.)
b. If appropriate, apply the Marascuilo procedure to (a), using $\alpha = 0.05$.
c. Is there a significant difference among the different industries with respect to the proportion of companies that measure the impact of process improvement initiatives? (Use $\alpha = 0.05$.)
d. If appropriate, apply the Marascuilo procedure to (c), using $\alpha = 0.05$.

66 A company is considering an organizational change by adopting the use of self-managed work teams. To assess the attitudes of employees of the company toward this change, a sample of 400 employees is selected and asked whether they favor the institution of self-managed work teams in the organization. Three responses are permitted: favor, neutral, or oppose. The results of the survey, cross-classified by type of job and attitude toward self-managed work teams, are summarized as follows:

| | SELF-MANAGED WORK TEAMS | | | |
TYPE OF JOB	Favor	Neutral	Oppose	Total
Hourly worker	108	46	71	225
Supervisor	18	12	30	60
Middle management	35	14	26	75
Upper management	24	7	9	40
Total	185	79	136	400

a. At the 0.05 level of significance, is there evidence of a relationship between attitude toward self-managed work teams and type of job?

The survey also asked respondents about their attitudes toward instituting a policy whereby an employee could take one additional vacation day per month without pay. The results, cross-classified by type of job, are shown on the next page.

TYPE OF JOB	VACATION TIME WITHOUT PAY			
	Favor	Neutral	Oppose	Total
Hourly worker	135	23	67	225
Supervisor	39	7	14	60
Middle management	47	6	22	75
Upper management	26	6	8	40
Total	247	42	111	400

b. At the 0.05 level of significance, is there evidence of a relationship between attitude toward vacation time without pay and type of job?

67 A company that produces and markets videotaped continuing education programs for the financial industry has traditionally mailed sample tapes that contain previews of the programs to prospective customers. Customers then agree to purchase the program tapes or return the sample tapes. A group of sales representatives studied how to increase sales and found that many prospective customers believed it was difficult to tell from a sample tape alone whether the educational programs would meet their needs. The sales representatives performed an experiment to test whether sending the complete program tapes for review by customers would increase sales. They selected 80 customers from the mailing list and randomly assigned 40 to receive the sample tapes and 40 to receive the full-program tapes for review. They then determined the number of tapes that were purchased and returned in each group. The results of the experiment are as follows:

ACTION	TYPE OF VIDEOTAPE RECEIVED		
	Sample	Full	Total
Purchased	6	14	20
Returned	34	26	60
Total	40	40	80

a. At the 0.05 level of significance, is there evidence of a difference in the proportion of tapes purchased on the basis of the type of tape sent to the customer?
b. On the basis of the results of (a), which tape do you think a representative should send in the future? Explain the rationale for your decision.

The sales representatives also wanted to determine which of three initial sales approaches result in the most sales: (1) a video sales-information tape mailed to prospective customers, (2) a personal sales call to prospective customers, and (3) a telephone call to prospective customers. A random sample of 300 prospective customers was selected, and 100 were randomly assigned to each of the three sales approaches. The results, in terms of purchases of the full-program tapes, are as follows:

ACTION	SALES APPROACH			
	Videotape	Personal Sales Call	Telephone	Total
Purchase	19	27	14	60
Don't purchase	81	73	86	240
Total	100	100	100	300

c. At the 0.05 level of significance, is there evidence of a difference in the proportion of tapes purchased on the basis of the sales strategy used?
d. If appropriate, use the Marascuilo procedure and $\alpha = 0.05$ to determine which sales approaches are different.
e. On the basis of the results of (c) and (d), which sales approach do you think a representative should use in the future? Explain the rationale for your decision.

68 A market researcher investigated consumer preferences for Coca-Cola and Pepsi before a taste test and after a taste test. The following table summarizes the results from a sample of 200 respondents:

PREFERENCE BEFORE TASTE TEST	PREFERENCE AFTER TASTE TEST		
	Coca-Cola	Pepsi	Total
Coca-Cola	104	6	110
Pepsi	14	76	90
Total	118	82	200

a. Is there evidence of a difference in the proportion of respondents who prefer Coca-Cola before and after the taste tests? (Use $\alpha = 0.10$.)
b. Compute the p-value and interpret its meaning.
c. Show how the following table was derived from the table above:

PREFERENCE	SOFT DRINK		
	Coca-Cola	Pepsi	Total
Before taste test	110	90	200
After taste test	118	82	200
Total	228	172	400

d. Using the second table, is there evidence of a difference in preference for Coca-Cola before and after the taste test? (Use $\alpha = 0.05$.)
e. Determine the p-value and interpret its meaning.
f. Explain the difference in the results of (a) and (d). Which method of analyzing the data should you use? Why?

69 A market researcher was interested in studying the effect of advertisements on brand preference of new car buyers. Prospective purchasers of new cars were first asked whether they preferred Toyota or GM and then watched video advertisements of comparable models of the two manufacturers. After viewing the ads, the prospective customers again indicated their preferences. The results are summarized in the following table:

PREFERENCE	PREFERENCE AFTER ADS		
BEFORE ADS	Toyota	GM	Total
Toyota	97	3	100
GM	11	89	100
Total	108	92	200

a. Is there evidence of a difference in the proportion of respondents who prefer Toyota before and after viewing the ads? (Use $\alpha = 0.05$.)
b. Compute the *p*-value and interpret its meaning.
c. Show how the following table was derived from the table above.

PREFERENCE	MANUFACTURER		
	Toyota	GM	Total
Before ad	100	100	200
After ad	108	92	200
Total	208	192	400

d. Using the second table, is there evidence of a difference in preference for Toyota before and after viewing the ads? (Use $\alpha = 0.05$.)
e. Determine the *p*-value and interpret its meaning.
f. Explain the difference in the results of (a) and (d). Which method of analyzing the data should you use? Why?

70 Researchers studied the goals and outcomes of 349 work teams from various manufacturing companies in Ohio. In the first table, teams are categorized as to whether they had specified environmental improvements as a goal and also according to one of four types of manufacturing processes that best described their workplace. The following three tables indicate different outcomes the teams accomplished, based on whether the team had specified cost cutting as one of the team goals.

TYPE OF MANUFACTURING	ENVIRONMENTAL GOAL		
PROCESS	Yes	No	Total
Job shop or batch	2	42	44
Repetitive batch	4	57	61
Discrete process	15	147	162
Continuous process	17	65	82
Total	38	311	349

	COST-CUTTING GOAL		
OUTCOME	Yes	No	Total
Improved environmental performance	77	52	129
Environmental performance not improved	91	129	220
Total	168	181	349

	COST-CUTTING GOAL		
OUTCOME	Yes	No	Total
Improved profitability	70	68	138
Profitability not improved	98	113	211
Total	168	181	349

	COST-CUTTING GOAL		
OUTCOME	Yes	No	Total
Improved morale	67	55	122
Morale not improved	101	126	227
Total	168	181	349

Source: Extracted from M. Hanna, W. Newman, and P. Johnson, "Linking Operational and Environmental Improvement Thru Employee Involvement," International Journal of Operations and Production Management, 2000, 20, pp. 148–165.

a. At the 0.05 level of significance, determine whether there is evidence of a significant relationship between the presence of environmental goals and the type of manufacturing process.
b. Determine the *p*-value in (a) and interpret its meaning.
c. At the 0.05 level of significance, is there evidence of a difference in improved environmental performance for teams with a specified goal of cutting costs?
d. Determine the *p*-value in (c) and interpret its meaning.
e. At the 0.05 level of significance, is there evidence of a difference in improved profitability for teams with a specified goal of cutting costs?
f. Determine the *p*-value in (e) and interpret its meaning.
g. At the 0.05 level of significance, is there evidence of a difference in improved morale for teams with a specified goal of cutting costs?
h. Determine the *p*-value in (g) and interpret its meaning.

Team Project

The data file Mutual Funds.xls contains information regarding nine variables from a sample of 838 mutual funds. The variables are:

Category—Type of stocks comprising the mutual fund (small cap, mid cap, or large cap)
Objective—Objective of stocks comprising the mutual fund (growth or value)
Assets—In millions of dollars
Fees—Sales charges (no or yes)

Expense ratio—Ratio of expenses to net assets in percentage

2005 return—Twelve-month return in 2005

Three-year return—Annualized return, 2003–2005

Five-year return—Annualized return, 2001–2005

Risk—Risk-of-loss factor of the mutual fund (low, average, or high)

71 a. Construct a 2×2 contingency table, using fees as the row variable and objective as the column variable.

b. At the 0.05 level of significance, is there evidence of a significant relationship between the objective of a mutual fund and whether there is a fee?

72 a. Construct a 2×3 contingency table, using fees as the row variable and risk as the column variable.

b. At the 0.05 level of significance, is there evidence of a significant relationship between the perceived risk of a mutual fund and whether there is a fee?

73 a. Construct a 3×2 contingency table, using risk as the row variable and objective as the column variable.

b. At the 0.05 level of significance, is there evidence of a significant relationship between the objective of a mutual fund and its perceived risk?

74 a. Construct a 3×3 contingency table, using risk as the row variable and category as the column variable.

b. At the 0.05 level of significance, is there evidence of a significant relationship between the category of a mutual fund and its perceived risk?

Managing the *Springville Herald*

Phase 1

Reviewing the results of its research, the marketing department concluded that a segment of Springville households might be interested in a discounted trial home subscription to the *Herald*. The team decided to test various discounts before determining the type of discount to offer during the trial period. It decided to conduct an experiment using three types of discounts plus a plan that offered no discount during the trial period:

1. No discount for the newspaper. Subscribers would pay $4.50 per week for the newspaper during the 90-day trial period.
2. Moderate discount for the newspaper. Subscribers would pay $4.00 per week for the newspaper during the 90-day trial period.

3. Substantial discount for the newspaper. Subscribers would pay $3.00 per week for the newspaper during the 90-day trial period.
4. Discount restaurant card. Subscribers would be given a card providing a discount of 15% at selected restaurants in Springville during the trial period.

Each participant in the experiment was randomly assigned to a discount plan. A random sample of 100 subscribers to each plan during the trial period was tracked to determine how many would continue to subscribe to the *Herald* after the trial period. Table SH1 summarizes the results.

TABLE SH1 Number of Subscribers Who Continue Subscriptions After Trial Period with Four Discount Plans

CONTINUE SUBSCRIPTIONS AFTER TRIAL PERIOD	DISCOUNT PLANS				
	No Discount	Moderate Discount	Substantial Discount	Restaurant Card	Total
Yes	34	37	38	61	170
No	66	63	62	39	230
Total	100	100	100	100	400

EXERCISE

SH1 Analyze the results of the experiment. Write a report to the team that includes your recommendation for which discount plan to use. Be prepared to discuss the limitations and assumptions of the experiment.

DO NOT CONTINUE UNTIL THE PHASE 1 EXERCISE HAS BEEN COMPLETED.

Phase 2

The marketing department team discussed the results of a survey. The team realized that the evaluation of individual questions was providing only limited information. In order to further understand the market for home-delivery subscriptions, the data were organized in the following cross-classification tables:

READ OTHER NEWSPAPER

HOME DELIVERY	Yes	No	Total
Yes	61	75	136
No	77	139	216
Total	138	214	352

RESTAURANT CARD

HOME DELIVERY	Yes	No	Total
Yes	26	110	136
No	40	176	216
Total	66	286	352

MONDAY–SATURDAY PURCHASE BEHAVIOR

INTEREST IN TRIAL SUBSCRIPTION	Every Day	Most Days	Occasionally or Never	Total
Yes	29	14	3	46
No	49	81	40	170
Total	78	95	43	216

SUNDAY PURCHASE BEHAVIOR

INTEREST IN TRIAL SUBSCRIPTION	Every Sunday	2–3 Times/ Month	No More Than Once/ Month	Total
Yes	35	10	1	46
No	103	44	23	170
Total	138	54	24	216

INTEREST IN TRIAL SUBSCRIPTION

WHERE PURCHASED	Yes	No	Total
Convenience store	12	62	74
Newsstand/candy store	15	80	95
Vending machine	10	11	21
Supermarket	5	8	13
Other locations	4	9	13
Total	46	170	216

MONDAY–SATURDAY PURCHASE BEHAVIOR

SUNDAY PURCHASE BEHAVIOR	Every Day	Most Days	Occasionally or Never	Total
Every Sunday	55	65	18	138
2–3 times/month	19	23	12	54
Once/month	4	7	13	24
Total	78	95	43	216

EXERCISE

SH2 Analyze the results of the cross-classification tables. Write a report for the marketing department team and discuss the marketing implications of the results for the *Springville Herald*.

Web Case

Apply your knowledge of testing for the difference between two proportions in this Web Case, which extends the T.C. Resort Properties Using Statistics scenario of this chapter.

As T.C. Resort Properties seeks to improve its customer service, the company faces new competition from SunLow Resorts. SunLow has recently opened resort hotels on the islands where T.C. Resort Properties has its five hotels. SunLow is currently advertising that a random survey of 300 customers revealed that about 60% percent of the customers preferred its "Concierge Class" travel reward program over the T.C. Resorts "TCPass Plus" program. Visit the SunLow Web site, **www.prenhall.com/ Springville/SunLowHome.htm** (or open the Web page file in the Web Case folder on the Student CD-ROM), and examine the survey data. Then answer the following:

1. Are the claims made by SunLow valid?

2. What analyses of the survey data would lead to a more favorable impression about T.C. Resort Properties?

3. Perform one of the analyses identified in your answer to step 2.

4. Review the data about the T.C. Resorts Properties customers presented in this chapter. Are there any other factors that you might include in a future survey of travel reward programs? Explain.

REFERENCES

1. Conover, W. J., *Practical Nonparametric Statistics*, 3rd ed. (New York: Wiley, 2000).

2. Daniel, W. W., *Applied Nonparametric Statistics*, 2nd ed. (Boston: PWS Kent, 1990).

3. Dixon, W. J., and F. J. Massey, Jr., *Introduction to Statistical Analysis*, 4th ed. (New York: McGraw-Hill, 1983).

4. Hollander, M., and D. A. Wolfe, *Nonparametric Statistical Methods* 2nd ed. (New York: Wiley, 1999).

5. Lewontin, R. C., and J. Felsenstein, "Robustness of Homogeneity Tests in $2 \times n$ Tables," *Biometrics* 21 (March 1965): 19–33.

6. Marascuilo, L. A., "Large-Sample Multiple Comparisons," *Psychological Bulletin* 65 (1966): 280–290.

7. Marascuilo, L. A., and M. McSweeney, *Nonparametric and Distribution-Free Methods for the Social Sciences* (Monterey, CA: Brooks/Cole, 1977).

8. *Microsoft Excel 2007* (Redmond, WA: Microsoft Corp., 2007).

9. Winer, B. J., D. R. Brown, and K. M. Michels, *Statistical Principles in Experimental Design*, 3rd ed. (New York: McGraw-Hill, 1989).

Excel Companion

E1 USING THE CHI-SQUARE TEST FOR THE DIFFERENCE BETWEEN TWO PROPORTIONS

You conduct a chi-square test for the difference between two proportions by either selecting the PHStat2 Chi-Square Test for Differences in Two Proportions procedure or by making entries in the Chi-Square.xls workbook.

Using PHStat2 Chi-Square Test for Differences in Two Proportions

Select **PHStat → Two-Sample Tests → Chi-Square Test for Differences in Two Proportions**. In the procedure's dialog box (shown below), enter the **Level of Significance**, enter a title as the **Title**, and click **OK**.

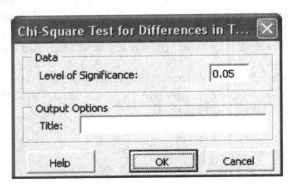

PHStat2 creates a worksheet in which you enter contingency table data, such as Table 2, into the rows 4 through 7 Observed Frequencies area. (You can also enter custom row and column labels for your data.) Before you enter contingency table data, many worksheet cells display the message #DIV/0!. This is not an error.

Using Chi-Square.xls

Open to the **ChiSquare2P** worksheet of the Chi-Square.xls workbook. This worksheet (see Figure 3) uses the function **CHIINV(*level of significance, degrees of freedom*)** to compute the critical value and the function **CHIDIST(χ^2 *test statistic, degrees of freedom*)** to compute the *p*-value for the Section 1 hotel guest satisfaction example. To adapt this worksheet to other problems, enter the problem's contingency table data into the rows 4 through 7 Observed Frequencies area, edit the title in cell A1, and change the level of significance in cell B18, if necessary.

Figure E1 shows the cell formulas for rows 6 through 15, not shown in Figure 3. Formulas in cells B11, A12, A13, A14, B12, and C12 display the row and column labels entered in the Observed Frequencies area. The results of the formulas in cells F13:G14 are summed in cell B25 to compute the χ^2 test statistic. (The other formulas shown compute row or column totals or the expected frequencies.)

Not shown in Figure E1 is the A30 formula. This formula uses an IF function to complete the phrase "Expected frequency assumption . . . ". The *comparison* part of this IF function **OR(B13 < 5, C13 < 5, B14 < 5, C14 < 5)**, uses the OR function to make sure that none of the expected frequencies is less than 5, an assumption that is necessary for the chi-square test to be accurate.

	A	B	C	D	E	F	G
3		Observed Frequencies					
4		Hotel				Calculations	
5	Choose Again?	Beachcomber	Windsurfer	Total		fo-fe	
6	Yes	163	154	=SUM(B6:C6)		=B6 - B13	=C6 - C13
7	No	64	108	=SUM(B7:C7)		=B7 - B14	=C7 - C14
8	Total	=SUM(B6:B7)	=SUM(C6:C7)	=SUM(B8:C8)			
9							
10		Expected Frequencies					
11		=B4					
12	=A5	=B5	=C5	Total		(fo-fe)^2/fe	
13	=A6	=D6 * B8/D8	=D6 * C8/D8	=SUM(B13:C13)		=F6^2/B13	=G6^2/C13
14	=A7	=D7 * B8/D8	=D7 * C8/D8	=SUM(B14:C14)		=F7^2/B14	=G7^2/C14
15		Total	=SUM(B13:B14)	=SUM(C13:C14)	=SUM(B15:C15)		

FIGURE E1 ChiSquare2P rows 3 through 15

E2 USING THE CHI-SQUARE TEST FOR THE DIFFERENCES AMONG MORE THAN TWO PROPORTIONS

You conduct a chi-square test for the differences among more than two proportions by either selecting the PHStat2 Chi-Square Test procedure or by making entries in the Chi-Square Worksheets.xls workbook.

Using PHStat2 Chi-Square Test

Select **PHStat → Multiple-Sample Tests → Chi-Square Test**. In the procedure's dialog box (shown below), enter the **Level of Significance**, enter **2** as the **Number of Rows**, and enter the **Number of Columns**. Enter a title as the **Title** and click **OK**. If you want to select the Marascuilo procedure, select **Marascuilo Procedure** before clicking **OK**.

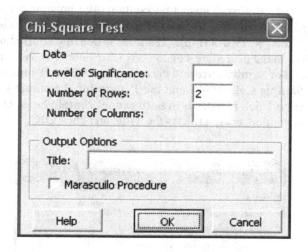

PHStat2 creates a worksheet in which you enter your $2 \times c$ contingency table data, such as Table 6, in the observed Frequencies area that begins in row 4. (You can also enter custom row and column labels for your data.) Before you enter contingency table data, many worksheet cells display the message #DIV/0!. This is not an error.

Using Chi-Square Worksheets.xls

Open the Chi-Square Worksheets.xls workbook to the worksheet that contains the appropriate $2 \times c$ observed frequency table for your problem. For example, for the guest satisfaction data in Table 6 that requires a 2×3 table, open to the **ChiSquare2x3** worksheet. Worksheets with empty observed frequencies tables display the message #DIV/0! in many cells. This is not an error, and these messages disappear when you enter your contingency table data.

All $2 \times c$ worksheets contain formulas similar to those in the ChiSquare2P worksheet discussed in Section E1. All worksheets have their level of significance set to 0.05, but you can change this value. The Chi-Square Worksheets.xls workbook includes the ChiSquare2x3Formulas worksheet, which allows you to examine the formulas of the ChiSquare2x3 worksheet in formatted, formulas view. You should note that the formula in cell A30 verifies whether all expected frequencies are at least 1, an assumption of the Chi-Square test.

Using the Marascuilo Worksheets

Each $2 \times c$ chi square worksheet is linked to a companion Marascuilo worksheet in the Chi-Square Worksheets.xls workbook. Marascuilo worksheet names echo the chi-square worksheet to which they are linked, so that **Marascuilo2x3** is linked to **ChiSquare2x3**. (The Marascuilo2x3 worksheet is shown in Figure 7.)

The **Marascuilo2x3Formulas** worksheet allows you to examine the formulas of the Marascuilo2x3 worksheet in formatted, formulas view. If you examine this worksheet, you see that the formulas for the level of significance, the square root of the critical value, the sample proportions, and the critical range all use one or more values from the ChiSquare2x3 worksheet.

All Marascuilo worksheets compare the absolute differences and critical range values for each pair of groups and display either Significant or Not Significant in column D.

E3 USING THE CHI-SQUARE TEST OF INDEPENDENCE

Adapt the instructions of the previous section to the chi-square test of independence. If you use PHStat2, enter your number of rows as the **Number of Rows**. If you use the Chi-Square Worksheets.xls workbook, open to either the chi-square worksheets for 3×4, 4×3, 7×3, or 8×3, or open one of the $2 \times c$ worksheets mentioned in Section E2.

E4 USING THE MCNEMAR TEST

You conduct a McNemar test by either selecting the PHStat2 McNemar Test procedure or by making entries in the McNemar.xls workbook.

Using PHStat2 McNemar Test

Select **PHStat → Two-Sample Tests → McNemar Test**. In the procedure's dialog box (see top of the next page), enter the **Level of Significance**, click a test option, enter a title as the **Title**, and click **OK**.

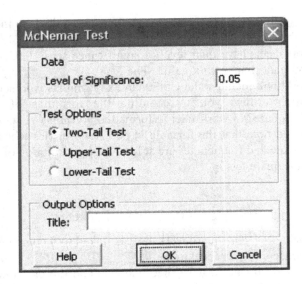

If you want the **McNemar_All** worksheet to show only one of the one-tail tests, first make a copy of that worksheet. For a lower-tail-test-only worksheet, select and delete rows 29 through 32 and then select and delete rows 18 through 23. For an upper-tail-test-only worksheet, select and delete rows 18 through 28.

E5   USING THE WILCOXON RANK SUM TEST

You conduct a Wilcoxon rank sum test by either selecting the PHStat2 Wilcoxon Rank Sum Test procedure or by making entries in the Wilcoxon.xls workbook. The PHStat2 procedure uses unsummarized, unstacked data, while the workbook uses summarized data. (See "Counting and Summing Ranks" on the next page if you have unsummarized, unstacked data and you wish to use the workbook.)

Using PHStat2 Wilcoxon Rank Sum Test

Open to the worksheet that contains the unsummarized, unstacked data for the two independent populations. Select **PHStat → Two-Sample Tests → Wilcoxon Rank Sum Test**. In the procedure's dialog box (shown below), enter the **Level of Significance** and the cell ranges for the **Population 1 Sample Cell Range** and the **Population 2 Sample Cell Range**. Click **First cells in both ranges contain label**, click a test option, enter a title as the **Title**, and click **OK**.

PHStat2 creates a worksheet in which you enter the observed frequencies, such as Table 13, in the Observed Frequencies area that begins in row 3. (You can also enter custom row and column labels for your data.) Before you enter data, many worksheet cells display the message #DIV/0!. This is not an error.

Using McNemar.xls

You open and use either the **McNemar_TT** or the **McNemar_All** worksheets of the McNemar.xls workbook to use the McNemar test. These worksheets use the **NORMSINV($P<X$)** function to determine the lower and upper critical values and use the **NORMSDIST(Z value)** function to compute the p-values from the Z value calculated in cell B16.

The **McNemar_TT** worksheet (see Figure 12) uses the two-tail test for the Section 4 consumer preference example. The **McNemar_All** worksheet also includes the one-tail tests (these additions are shown in Figure E2). To adapt these worksheets to other problems, change the observed frequency table data and labels in rows 4 through 7 and (if necessary) the level of significance in cell B11.

	A	B	
24	Lower-Tail Test		
25	Lower Critical Value	-1.6449	=NORMSINV(B11)
26	p-Value	0.9997	=NORMSDIST(B16)
27	Do not reject the null hypothesis		=IF(B26 < B11, "Reject the null hypothesis", "Do not reject the null hypothesis")
28			
29	Upper-Tail Test		
30	Upper Critical Value	1.6449	=NORMSINV(1-B11)
31	p-Value	0.0003	=1 - NORMSDIST(B16)
32	Reject the null hypothesis		=IF(B31 < B11, "Reject the null hypothesis", "Do not reject the null hypothesis")

FIGURE E2 McNemar_All worksheet one-tail tests

PHStat creates a worksheet similar to the Figure 14 worksheet. However, PHStat2 uses the functions **COUNTIF** and **SUMIF** in formulas in cells B7, B8, B10, and B11 to compute the sample size and sum of the ranks for each population. To learn more about these functions, read "Counting and Summing Ranks," later in this section.

Using Wilcoxon.xls

You open and use either the **Wilcoxon_TT** or the **Wilcoxon_All** worksheets of the Wilcoxon.xls workbook to use the Wilcoxon rank sum test. These worksheets use the **NORMSINV**(P<X) function to determine the lower and upper critical values and use the **NORMSDIST**(*Z value*) function to compute the p-values from the Z value calculated in cell B18.

The **Wilcoxon_TT** worksheet (see Figure 14) uses the two-tail test for the Section 5 BLK cola sales example. The **Wilcoxon_All** worksheet also includes the one-tail tests (these additions are shown in Figure E3). To adapt these worksheets to other problems, change the title in cell A1 and (if necessary) the level of significance, sample sizes, and rank sum values in the tinted cells B4, B7, B8, B10, and B11.

	A	B	
25			
26	**Lower-Tail Test**		
27	Lower Critical Value	-1.6449	=NORMSINV(B4)
28	*p*-Value	0.0063	=NORMSDIST(B18)
29	Reject the null hypothesis		=IF(B28 < B4, "Reject the null hypothesis",
30			"Do not reject the null hypothesis")
31	**Upper-Tail Test**		
32	Upper Critical Value	1.6449	=NORMSINV(1 - B4)
33	*p*-Value	0.9937	=1 - NORMSDIST(B18)
34	Do not reject the null hypothesis		=IF(B33 < B4, "Reject the null hypothesis",
			"Do not reject the null hypothesis")

FIGURE E3 Wilcoxon one-tail tests

If you want the Wilcoxon_All worksheet to show only one of the one-tail tests, first make a copy of that worksheet. For a lower-tail-test-only worksheet, select and delete rows 31 through 34 and then select and delete rows 20 through 25. For an upper-tail-test-only worksheet, select and delete rows 20 through 30.

Counting and Summing Ranks

If you want to use the Wilcoxon.xls workbook but have unsummarized, unstacked data, you can use the **COUNTIF**(*cell range for matching, value to be matched*) function to compute the sample size and the **SUMIF**(*cell range for matching, value to be matched, cell range for summing*) function to compute the sum of the ranks of each population.

To use these functions, first sort your unstacked data worksheet in ascending order, using the column containing the values (not the population labels). Then add a column of ranks, breaking ties by using the method stated earlier in the chapter. With your data so arranged, you can use the formula =**COUNTIF**(*cell range of all population labels,*

"population 1 name") to count the sample size of the population 1 sample and the formula =**SUMIF**(*cell range of all population labels, "population 1 name", cell range of all sorted values*) to sum the ranks of the population 1 sample. (The population 1 name must appear in a set of double quotation marks.) Create another pair of formulas and use the name of the second population as the *value to be matched* to count the sample size and sum the ranks of the population 2 sample.

For example, the formulas =**COUNTIF(A1:A21, "EndAisle")** and =**SUMIF(A1:A21, "EndAisle", C1:C21)** would compute the sample size and the sum of ranks for the BLK cola end-aisle sales if placed in empty cells of the **ColaSortedStacked** worksheet of the Cola.xls workbook. The formulas =**COUNTIF(A1:A21, "Normal")** and =**SUMIF(A1:A21, "Normal", C1:C21)** would do the same things for the normal display sample.

E6 USING THE KRUSKAL-WALLIS RANK TEST

You conduct a Kruskal-Wallis rank test by either selecting the PHStat2 Kruskal-Wallis Rank Test procedure or by making entries in the Kruskal-Wallis Worksheets.xls workbook. The PHStat2 procedure uses unsummarized, unstacked data, while the workbook uses summarized data.

Using PHStat2 Kruskal-Wallis Rank Test

Select **PHStat → Multiple-Sample Tests → Kruskal-Wallis Rank Test**. In the procedure's dialog box (shown below), enter the **Level of Significance** and enter the cell range of the unsummarized, unstacked data as the **Sample Data Cell Range**. Click **First cells contain label**, enter a title as the **Title**, and click **OK**.

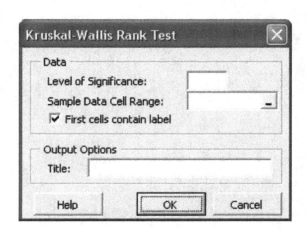

Using Kruskal-Wallis.xls

Open the `Kruskal-Wallis Worksheets.xls` workbook to the worksheet that contains the appropriate number of groups (populations) for your problem. For example, for the Section 6 parachute example that contains four different groups, open to the **Kruskal-Wallis4** worksheet (shown in Figure 16).

Kruskal-Wallis worksheets use the function **CHIINV**(*level of significance, degrees of freedom*) to compute the critical value and the function **CHIDIST**(χ^2 *test statistic, degrees of freedom*) to com-pute the *p*-value. When you open to a worksheet, enter the sample size, sum of ranks, and mean rank values in the tinted cells in columns E through G, the level of significance value in cell B4, and a title in cell A1 to complete the worksheet. #DIV/0! messages that may appear in several cells disappear after you enter data. This is not an error.

Forum Click on the ALTERNATIVE METHODS link to learn more about how the COUNTIF and SUMIF functions (see Section E4) could be used with Kruskal-Wallis worksheets.

Self-Test Solutions and Answers to Selected Even-Numbered Problems

The following represent worked-out solutions to Self-Test Problems and brief answers to most of the even-numbered problems in the text.

2 (a) For $df = 1$ and $\alpha = 0.05$, $\chi^2 = 3.841$. **(b)** For $df = 1$ and $\alpha = 0.025$, $\chi^2 = 5.024$. **(c)** For $df = 1$ and $\alpha = 0.01$, $\chi^2 = 6.635$.

4 (a) All $f_e = 25$. **(b)** Since $\chi^2 = 4.00 > 3.841$, reject H_0.

6 (a) Since $\chi^2 = 1.0 < 3.841$, do not reject H_0. There is not enough evidence to conclude that there is a significant difference between males and females in the proportion who make gas mileage a priority. **(b)** Since $\chi^2 = 10.0 > 3.841$, reject H_0. There is enough evidence to conclude that there is a significant difference between males and females in the proportion who make gas mileage a priority. **(c)** The larger sample size in (b) increases the difference between the observed and expected frequencies and, hence, results in a larger test statistic value.

8 (a) H_0: $\pi_1 = \pi_2$. H_1: $\pi_1 \neq \pi_2$.

Observed Frequencies

		Column variable		
		Less Than $50,000	More Than $50,000	Total
Row variable				
	Fair	225	180	405
	Unfair	280	320	600
	Total	505	500	1005

Expected Frequencies

		Column variable		
		Less Than $50,000	More Than $50,000	Total
Row variable				
	Fair	203.5075	201.4925	405
	Unfair	301.4925	298.5075	600
	Total	505	500	1005

Data	
Level of Significance	0.05
Number of Rows	2
Number of Columns	2
Degrees of Freedom	1
Results	
Critical Value	3.841459
Chi-Square Test Statistic	7.64198
p-Value	0.005703
Reject the null hypothesis	

Decision rule: $df = 1$. If $\chi^2 > 3.841$, reject H_0.

Test statistic: $\chi^2 = \sum_{\text{all cells}} \frac{(f_0 - f_e)^2}{f_e} = 7.642$.

Decision: Since $\chi^2 = 7.642 > 3.841$, reject H_0. There is enough evidence to conclude that there is a significant difference in the proportion of adults who think the U.S. tax code is unfair between the two income groups. **(b)** p-value is 0.0057. The probability of obtaining a test statistic of 7.642 or larger when the null hypothesis is true is 0.0057. **(c)** The results of (a) and (b) are exactly the same as those of Problem 10.36. The χ^2 in (a) and the Z in Problem 10.36 (a) satisfy the relationship that $\chi^2 = 7.642 = Z^2 = (-2.7644)^2$, and the p-value in Problem 10.36 (b) is exactly the same as the p-value obtained in (b).

10 (a) Since $\chi^2 = 2.3226 < 3.841$, do not reject H_0. There is not enough evidence to conclude that there is a significant difference between undergraduate and MBA students in the proportion who selected the highest-cost fund. **(b)** p-value = 0.1275. The probability of obtaining a test statistic of 2.3226 or larger when the null hypothesis is true is 0.1275.

12 (a) The expected frequencies for the first row are 20, 30, and 40. The expected frequencies for the second row are 30, 45, and 60. **(b)** Since $\chi^2 = 12.5 > 5.991$, reject H_0. **(c)** A vs. B: $0.20 > 0.196$; therefore, A and B are different. A vs. C: $0.30 > 0.185$; therefore, A and C are different. B vs. C: $0.10 < 0.185$; therefore, B and C are not different.

14 Since the calculated test statistic $742.3961 > 9.4877$, reject H_0 and conclude that there is a difference in the proportion of people who eat out at least once a week in the various countries. **(b)** p-value is virtually zero. The probability of a test statistic greater than 742.3961 or more is approximately zero if there is no difference in the proportion of people who eat out at least once a week in the various countries. **(c)** At the 5% level of significance, there is no significant difference between the proportions in Germany and France, while there is a significant difference between all the remaining pairs of countries.

16 (a) H_0: $\pi_1 = \pi_2 = \pi_3$. H_1: At least one proportion differs.

f_0	f_e	$(f_0 - f_e)$	$(f_0 - f_e)^2/f_e$
48	42.667	5.333	0.667
152	157.333	−5.333	0.181
56	42.667	13.333	4.167
144	157.333	−13.333	1.130
24	42.667	−18.667	8.167
176	157.333	18.667	2.215
			16.5254

Decision rule: $df = (c - 1) = (3 - 1) = 2$. If $\chi^2 > 5.9915$, reject H_0.

Test statistic: $\chi^2 = \sum_{\text{all cells}} \frac{(f_0 - f_e)^2}{f_e} = 16.5254$

Decision: Since $\chi^2 = 16.5254 > 5.9915$, reject H_0. There is a significant difference in the age groups with respect to major grocery shopping day. **(b)** p-value = 0.0003. The probability that the test statistic is greater than or equal to 16.5254 is 0.03%, if the null hypothesis is true.

(c)

Pairwise Comparisons	Critical Range	$\left|p_j - p_{j'}\right|$
1 to 2	0.1073	0.04
2 to 3	0.0959	0.16*
1 to 3	0.0929	0.12*

There is a significant difference between the 35–54 and over-54 groups, and between the under 35 and over 54 groups. **(d)** The stores can use this information to target their marketing on the specific groups of shoppers on Saturday and the days other than Saturday.

18 (a) Since $\chi^2 = 2.817 < 7.815$, do not reject H_0. There is no evidence of a difference in fund selection based on student group. **(b)** p-value = 0.4207 **(c)** The Marascuilo procedure is not appropriate since there is no evidence of a difference among the groups.

20 $df = (r-1)(c-1) = (3-1)(4-1) = 6$.

22 (a) and **(b)** Since $\chi^2 = 20.680 > 12.592$, reject H_0. There is evidence of a relationship between the quarter of the year in which draft-aged men were born and the numbers assigned. It appears that the results of the lottery drawing are different from what would be expected if the lottery were random. **(c)** Since $\chi^2 = 9.803 < 12.592$, do not reject H_0. There is not enough evidence to conclude there is any relationship between the quarter of the year in which draft-aged men were born and the numbers assigned as their draft eligibilities during the Vietnam War. It appears that the results of the lottery drawing are consistent with what would be expected if the lottery were random.

24 (a) H_0: There is no relationship between the commuting time of company employees and the level of stress-related problems observed on the job. H_1: There is a relationship between the commuting time of company employees and the level of stress-related problems observed on the job.

f_0	f_e	$(f_0 - f_e)$	$(f_0 - f_e)^2/f_e$
9	12.1379	−3.1379	0.8112
17	20.1034	−3.1034	0.4791
18	11.7586	6.2414	3.3129
5	5.2414	−0.2414	0.0111
8	8.6810	−0.6810	0.0534
6	5.0776	0.9224	0.1676
18	14.6207	3.3793	0.7811
28	24.2155	3.7845	0.5915
7	14.1638	−7.1638	3.6233
			9.8311

(a) Decision rule: If $\chi^2 > 13.277$, reject H_0.

Test statistic: $\chi^2 = \sum_{\text{all cells}} \dfrac{(f_0 - f_e)^2}{f_e} = 9.8311$.

Decision: Since the $\chi^2 = 9.8311 < 13.277$, do not reject H_0. There is not enough evidence to conclude that there is a relationship between the commuting time of company employees and the level of stress-related problems observed on the job. **(b)** Since $\chi^2 = 9.831 > 9.488$, reject H_0. There is enough evidence at the 0.05 level to conclude that there is a relationship.

26 Since $\chi^2 = 129.520 > 21.026$, reject H_0. There is a relationship between when the decision is made of what to have for dinner and the type of household.

28 (a) H_0: $\pi_1 \geq \pi_2$ and H_1: $\pi_1 < \pi_2$, where 1 = beginning, 2 = end. Decision rule: If $Z < -1.645$, reject H_0.

Test statistic: $Z = \dfrac{B - C}{\sqrt{B + C}} = \dfrac{9 - 22}{\sqrt{9 + 22}} = -2.3349$

Decision: Since $Z = -2.3349 < -1.645$, reject H_0. There is evidence that the proportion of coffee drinkers who prefer Brand A is lower at the beginning of the advertising campaign than at the end of the advertising campaign. **(b)** p-value = 0.0098. The probability of a test statistic smaller than −2.3349 is 0.98% if the proportion of coffee drinkers who prefer Brand A is not lower at the beginning of the advertising campaign than at the end of the advertising campaign.

30 (a) Since $Z = -2.2361 < -1.645$, reject H_0. There is evidence that the proportion who prefer Brand A is lower before the advertising than after the advertising. **(b)** p-value = 0.0127. The probability of a test statistic less than −2.2361 is 1.27% if the proportion who prefer Brand A is not lower before the advertising than after the advertising.

32 (a) Since $Z = -3.8996 < -1.645$, reject H_0. There is evidence that the proportion of employees absent fewer than five days was lower in Year 1 than in Year 2. **(b)** The p-value is virtually zero. The probability of a test statistic smaller than −3.8996 is essentially zero if the proportion of employees absent fewer than five days was not lower in Year 1 than in Year 2.

34 (a) 31. **(b)** 29. **(c)** 27. **(d)** 25.

36 40 and 79.

38 (a) The ranks for Sample 1 are 1, 2, 4, 5, and 10. The ranks for Sample 2 are 3, 6.5, 6.5, 8, 9, and 11. **(b)** 22. **(c)** 44.

40 Decision: Since $T_1 = 22 > 20$, do not reject H_0.

42 (a) The data are ordinal. **(b)** The two-sample t test is inappropriate because the data can only be placed in ranked order. **(c)** Since $Z = -2.2054 < -1.96$, reject H_0. There is evidence of a significance difference in the median rating of California Cabernets and Washington Cabernets.

44 (a) H_0: $M_1 = M_2$ where Populations: 1 = Wing A, 2 = Wing B H_1: $M_1 \neq M_2$

Data	
Level of Significance	0.05
Population 1 Sample	
Sample Size	20
Sum of Ranks	561
Population 2 Sample	
Sample Size	20
Sum of Ranks	259
Intermediate Calculations	
Total Sample Size n	40
T1 Test Statistic	561
T1 Mean	410
Standard Error of T1	36.96846
Z Test Statistic	4.084563

Two-Tailed Test	
Lower Critical Value	−1.95996
Upper Critical Value	1.959964
p-value	4.42E-05
Reject the null hypothesis	

$$\mu_{T_1} = \frac{n_1(n+1)}{2} = \frac{20(40+1)}{2} = 410$$

$$\sigma_{T_1} = \sqrt{\frac{n_1 n_2(n+1)}{12}} = \sqrt{\frac{20(20)(40+1)}{12}} = 36.9685$$

$$Z = \frac{T_1 - \mu_{T_1}}{\sigma_{T_1}} = \frac{561 - 410}{36.9685} = 4.0846$$

Decision: Since $Z = 4.0846 > 1.96$, reject H_0. There is enough evidence of a difference in the median delivery time in the two wings of the hotel.

46 (a) Since $Z = -4.118 < -1.645$, reject H_0. There is enough evidence to conclude that the median crack size is less for the unflawed sample than for the flawed sample. **(b)** You must assume approximately equal variability in the two populations.

48 (a) Since $-1.96 < Z = 0.6627 < 1.96$, do not reject H_0. There is not enough evidence to conclude that the median time to clear these problems between the two offices is different. **(b)** You must assume approximately equal variability in the two populations.

50 (a) Decision rule: If $H > \chi_U^2 = 15.086$, reject H_0. **(b)** Decision: Since $H = 13.77 < 15.086$, do not reject H_0.

52 (a) $H = 13.517 > 7.815$, p-value $= 0.0036 < 0.05$, reject H_0. There is sufficient evidence of a difference in the median waiting time in the four locations.

54 (a) $H = 19.3269 > 9.488$, reject H_0. There is evidence of a difference in the median ratings of the ads.

56 (a) Since $H = 22.26 > 7.815$ or the p-value is approximately zero, reject H_0. There is sufficient evidence of a difference in the median strength of the four brands of trash bags.

64 (a) Since $\chi^2 = 0.412 < 3.841$, do not reject H_0. There is not enough evidence to conclude that there is a relationship between a student's gender and pizzeria selection. **(b)** Since $\chi^2 = 2.624 < 3.841$, do not reject H_0. There is not enough evidence to conclude that there is a relationship between a student's gender and pizzeria selection. **(c)** Since $\chi^2 = 4.956 < 5.991$, do not reject H_0. There is not enough evidence to conclude that there is a relationship between price and pizzeria selection. **(d)** p-value $= 0.0839$. The probability of a sample that gives a test statistic equal to or greater than 4.956 is 8.39% if the null hypothesis of no relationship between price and pizzeria selection is true. **(e)** Since there is

no evidence that price and pizzeria selection are related, it is inappropriate to determine which prices are different in terms of pizzeria preference.

66 (a) Since $\chi^2 = 11.895 < 12.592$, do not reject H_0. There is not enough evidence to conclude that there is a relationship between the attitudes of employees toward the use of self-managed work teams and employee job classification. **(b)** Since $\chi^2 = 3.294 < 12.592$, do not reject H_0. There is not enough evidence to conclude that there is a relationship between the attitudes of employees toward vacation time without pay and employee job classification.

68 (a) Since $Z = -1.7889 < -1.645$, reject H_0. There is enough evidence of a difference in the proportion of respondents who prefer Coca-Cola before and after viewing the ads. **(b)** p-value $= 0.0736$. The probability of a test statistic that differs from 0 by 1.7889 or more in either direction is 7.36% if there is not a difference in the proportion of respondents who prefer Coca-Cola before and after viewing the ads. **(c)** The frequencies in the second table are computed from the row and column totals of the first table. **(d)** Since the calculated test statistic is $0.6528 < 3.8415$, do not reject H_0 and conclude that there is not a significant difference in preference for Coca-Cola before and after viewing the ads. **(e)** p-value $= 0.4191$. The probability of a test statistic larger than 0.6528 is 41.91% if there is not a significant difference in preference for Coca-Cola before and after viewing the ads. **(f)** The McNemar test performed using the information in the first table takes into consideration the fact that the same set of respondents are surveyed before and after viewing the ads while the chi-square test performed using the information in the second table ignores this fact. The McNemar test should be used because of the related samples (before–after comparison).

70 (a) Since $\chi^2 = 11.635 > 7.815$, reject H_0. There is enough evidence to conclude that there is a relationship between the presence of environmental goals and the type of manufacturing process. **(b)** p-value $= 0.00874$. The probability of obtaining a data set which gives rise to a test statistic of 11.635 or more is 0.00874 if there is no relationship between the presence of environmental goals and the type of manufacturing process. **(c)** Since $\chi^2 = 10.94 > 3.841$, reject H_0. There is enough evidence to conclude that there is a difference in improved environmental performance for teams with a specified goal of cutting costs. **(d)** p-value $= 0.000941$. The probability of obtaining a data set which gives rise to a test statistic of 10.94 or more is 0.000941 if there is no difference in improved environmental performance for teams with a specified goal of cutting costs. **(e)** Since $\chi^2 = 0.612 < 3.841$, do not reject H_0. There is not enough evidence to conclude that there is a difference in improved profitability for teams with a specified goal of cutting costs. **(f)** p-value $= 0.4341$. The probability of obtaining a data set which gives rise to a test statistic of 0.612 or more is 0.4341 if there is no difference in improved profitability for teams with a specified goal of cutting costs. **(g)** $\chi^2 = 3.454 < 3.841$, do not reject H_0. There is not enough evidence to conclude that there is a difference in improved morale for teams with a specified goal of cutting costs. **(h)** p-value $= 0.063$. The probability of obtaining a data set which gives rise to a test statistic of 3.454 or more is 0.063 if there is no difference in improved morale for teams with a specified goal of cutting costs.

Chapter 3

Simple Linear Regression

USING STATISTICS @ Sunflowers Apparel

LEARNING OBJECTIVES

In this chapter, you learn:

- To use regression analysis to predict the value of a dependent variable based on an independent variable
- The meaning of the regression coefficients b_0 and b_1
- To evaluate the assumptions of regression analysis and know what to do if the assumptions are violated
- To make inferences about the slope and correlation coefficient
- To estimate mean values and predict individual values

Using Statistics @ Sunflowers Apparel

The sales for Sunflowers Apparel, a chain of upscale clothing stores for women, have increased during the past 12 years as the chain has expanded the number of stores open. Until now, Sunflowers managers selected sites based on subjective factors, such as the availability of a good lease or the perception that a location seemed ideal for an apparel store. As the new director of planning, you need to develop a systematic approach that will lead to making better decisions during the site selection process. As a starting point, you believe that the size of the store significantly contributes to store sales, and you want to use this relationship in the decision-making process. How can you use statistics so that you can forecast the annual sales of a proposed store based on the size of that store?

In this chapter, you learn how **regression analysis** enables you to develop a model to predict the values of a numerical variable, based on the value of other variables.

In regression analysis, the variable you wish to predict is called the **dependent variable**. The variables used to make the prediction are called **independent variables**. In addition to predicting values of the dependent variable, regression analysis also allows you to identify the type of mathematical relationship that exists between a dependent and an independent variable, to quantify the effect that changes in the independent variable have on the dependent variable, and to identify unusual observations. For example, as the director of planning, you may wish to predict sales for a Sunflowers store, based on the size of the store. Other examples include predicting the monthly rent of an apartment, based on its size, and predicting the monthly sales of a product in a supermarket, based on the amount of shelf space devoted to the product.

This chapter discusses **simple linear regression**, in which a *single* numerical independent variable, X, is used to predict the numerical dependent variable Y, such as using the size of a store to predict the annual sales of the store. *Multiple regression models*, on the other hand, use several independent variables to predict a numerical dependent variable, Y. For example, you could use the amount of advertising expenditures, price, and the amount of shelf space devoted to a product to predict its monthly sales.

1   TYPES OF REGRESSION MODELS

You may have previously used a **scatter plot** (also known as a **scatter diagram**) to examine the relationship between an X variable on the horizontal axis and a Y variable on the vertical axis. The nature of the relationship between two variables can take many forms, ranging from simple to extremely complicated mathematical functions. The simplest relationship consists of a straight-line, or **linear relationship**. An example of this relationship is shown in Figure 1.

FIGURE 1

A positive straight-line relationship

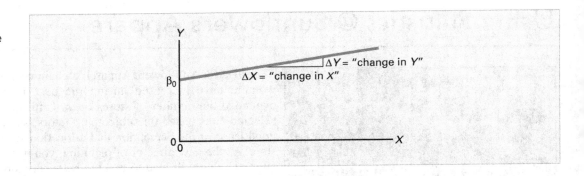

Equation (1) represents the straight-line (linear) model.

SIMPLE LINEAR REGRESSION MODEL

$$Y_i = \beta_0 + \beta_1 X_i + \varepsilon_i \qquad (1)$$

where

$\beta_0 = Y$ intercept for the population

$\beta_1 = $ slope for the population

$\varepsilon_i = $ random error in Y for observation i

$Y_i = $ dependent variable (sometimes referred to as the **response variable**) for observation i

$X_i = $ independent variable (sometimes referred to as the **explanatory variable**) for observation i

The portion $Y_i = \beta_0 + \beta_1 X_i$ of the simple linear regression model expressed in Equation (1) is a straight line. The **slope** of the line, β_1, represents the expected change in Y per unit change in X. It represents the mean amount that Y changes (either positively or negatively) for a one-unit change in X. The **Y intercept**, β_0, represents the mean value of Y when X equals 0. The last component of the model, ε_i, represents the random error in Y for each observation, i. In other words, ε_i is the vertical distance of the actual value of Y_i above or below the predicted value of Y_i on the line.

The selection of the proper mathematical model depends on the distribution of the X and Y values on the scatter plot. In Panel A of Figure 2, the values of Y are generally increasing linearly as X increases. This panel is similar to Figure 3, which illustrates the positive relationship between the square footage of the store and the annual sales at branches of the Sunflowers Apparel women's clothing store chain.

Panel B is an example of a negative linear relationship. As X increases, the values of Y are generally decreasing. An example of this type of relationship might be the price of a particular product and the amount of sales.

The data in Panel C show a positive curvilinear relationship between X and Y. The values of Y increase as X increases, but this increase tapers off beyond certain values of X. An example of a positive curvilinear relationship might be the age and maintenance cost of a machine. As a machine gets older, the maintenance cost may rise rapidly at first, but then level off beyond a certain number of years.

Panel D shows a U-shaped relationship between X and Y. As X increases, at first Y generally decreases; but as X continues to increase, Y not only stops decreasing but actually increases above its minimum value. An example of this type of relationship might be the number of errors per hour at a task and the number of hours worked. The number of errors per hour

FIGURE 2

Examples of types
of relationships found
in scatter plots

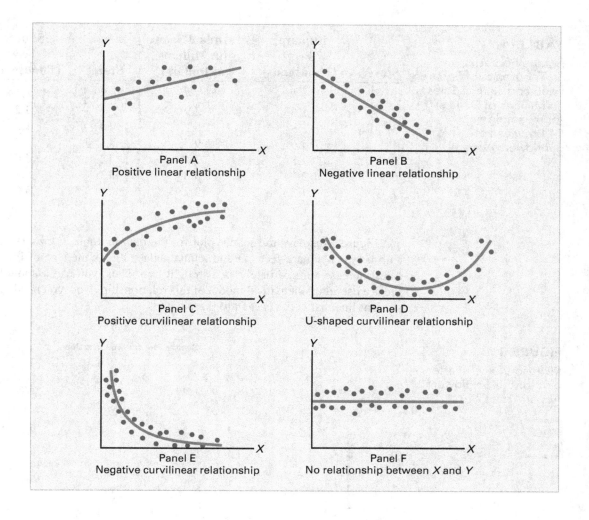

Panel A
Positive linear relationship

Panel B
Negative linear relationship

Panel C
Positive curvilinear relationship

Panel D
U-shaped curvilinear relationship

Panel E
Negative curvilinear relationship

Panel F
No relationship between X and Y

decreases as the individual becomes more proficient at the task, but then it increases beyond a certain point because of factors such as fatigue and boredom.

Panel E indicates an exponential relationship between X and Y. In this case, Y decreases very rapidly as X first increases, but then it decreases much less rapidly as X increases further. An example of an exponential relationship could be the resale value of an automobile and its age. In the first year, the resale value drops drastically from its original price; however, the resale value then decreases much less rapidly in subsequent years.

Finally, Panel F shows a set of data in which there is very little or no relationship between X and Y. High and low values of Y appear at each value of X.

In this section, a variety of different models that represent the relationship between two variables were briefly examined. Although scatter plots are useful in visually displaying the mathematical form of a relationship, more sophisticated statistical procedures are available to determine the most appropriate model for a set of variables. The rest of this chapter discusses the model used when there is a *linear* relationship between variables.

2 DETERMINING THE SIMPLE LINEAR REGRESSION EQUATION

In the Using Statistics scenario, the stated goal is to forecast annual sales for all new stores, based on store size. To examine the relationship between the store size in square feet and its annual sales, a sample of 14 stores was selected. Table 1 summarizes the results for these 14 stores, which are stored in the file site.xls.

TABLE 1

Square Footage
(in Thousands of Square
Feet) and Annual Sales
(in Millions of Dollars)
for a Sample of
14 Branches of
Sunflowers Apparel

Store	Square Feet (Thousands)	Annual Sales (in Millions of Dollars)	Store	Square Feet (Thousands)	Annual Sales (in Millions of Dollars)
1	1.7	3.7	8	1.1	2.7
2	1.6	3.9	9	3.2	5.5
3	2.8	6.7	10	1.5	2.9
4	5.6	9.5	11	5.2	10.7
5	1.3	3.4	12	4.6	7.6
6	2.2	5.6	13	5.8	11.8
7	1.3	3.7	14	3.0	4.1

Figure 3 displays the scatter plot for the data in Table 1. Observe the increasing relationship between square feet (X) and annual sales (Y). As the size of the store increases, annual sales increase approximately as a straight line. Thus, you can assume that a straight line provides a useful mathematical model of this relationship. Now you need to determine the specific straight line that is the *best* fit to these data.

FIGURE 3

Microsoft Excel scatter
plot for the Sunflowers
Apparel data

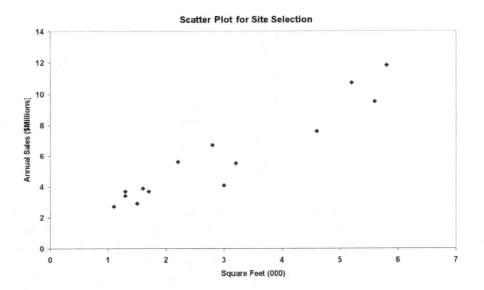

The Least-Squares Method

In the preceding section, a statistical model is hypothesized to represent the relationship between two variables, square footage and sales, in the entire population of Sunflowers Apparel stores. However, as shown in Table 1, the data are from only a random sample of stores. If certain assumptions are valid (see Section 4), you can use the sample Y intercept, b_0, and the sample slope, b_1, as estimates of the respective population parameters, β_0 and β_1. Equation (2) uses these estimates to form the **simple linear regression equation**. This straight line is often referred to as the **prediction line**.

SIMPLE LINEAR REGRESSION EQUATION: THE PREDICTION LINE

The predicted value of Y equals the Y intercept plus the slope times the value of X.

$$\hat{Y}_i = b_0 + b_1 X_i \qquad (2)$$

where

$$\hat{Y}_i = \text{predicted value of } Y \text{ for observation } i$$

$$X_i = \text{value of } X \text{ for observation } i$$

$$b_0 = \text{sample } Y \text{ intercept}$$

$$b_1 = \text{sample slope}$$

Equation (2) requires the determination of two **regression coefficients**—b_0 (the sample Y intercept) and b_1 (the sample slope). The most common approach to finding b_0 and b_1 is the method of least squares. This method minimizes the sum of the squared differences between the actual values (Y_i) and the predicted values ($\hat{Y}_i$) using the simple linear regression equation [that is, the prediction line; see Equation (2)]. This sum of squared differences is equal to

$$\sum_{i=1}^{n} (Y_i - \hat{Y}_i)^2$$

Because $\hat{Y}_i = b_0 + b_1 X_i$,

$$\sum_{i=1}^{n} (Y_i - \hat{Y}_i)^2 = \sum_{i=1}^{n} [Y_i - (b_0 + b_1 X_i)]^2$$

Because this equation has two unknowns, b_0 and b_1, the sum of squared differences depends on the sample Y intercept, b_0, and the sample slope, b_1. The **least-squares method** determines the values of b_0 and b_1 that minimize the sum of squared differences. Any values for b_0 and b_1 other than those determined by the least-squares method result in a greater sum of squared differences between the actual values (Y_i) and the predicted values $\hat{Y}_i$. In this text, Microsoft Excel is used to perform the computations involved in the least-squares method. For the data of Table 1, Figure 4 presents results from Microsoft Excel.

FIGURE 4

Microsoft Excel results for the Sunflowers Apparel data

See Section E1 to create this.

	A	B	C	D	E	F	G
1	**Site Selection Analysis**						
2							
3	**Regression Statistics**						
4	Multiple R	0.9509					
5	R Square	0.9042					
6	Adjusted R Square	0.8962					
7	Standard Error	0.9664 —S_{YX}					
8	Observations	14 —n					
9							
10	ANOVA						
11		*df*	*SS*	*MS*	*F*	*Significance F*	
12	Regression	1	SSR—105.7476	105.7476	113.2335	0.0000	
13	Residual	12	SSE—11.2067	0.9339		*p*-value	
14	Total	13	SST—116.9543				
15							
16		*Coefficients*	*Standard Error*	*t Stat*	*P-value*	*Lower 95%*	*Upper 95%*
17	Intercept	b_0—0.9645	0.5262	1.8329	0.0917	-0.1820	2.1110
18	Square Feet	b_1—1.6699	0.1569	10.6411	0.0000	1.3280	2.0118

To understand how the results are computed, many of the computations involved are illustrated in Examples 3 and 4. In Figure 4, observe that $b_0 = 0.9645$ and $b_1 = 1.6699$. Thus, the prediction line [see Equation (2)] for these data is

$$\hat{Y}_i = 0.9645 + 1.6699 X_i$$

The slope, b_1, is $+1.6699$. This means that for each increase of 1 unit in X, the mean value of Y is estimated to increase by 1.6699 units. In other words, for each increase of 1.0 thousand square feet in the size of the store, the mean annual sales are estimated to increase by 1.6699 millions of dollars. Thus, the slope represents the portion of the annual sales that are estimated to vary according to the size of the store.

The Y intercept, b_0, is $+0.9645$. The Y intercept represents the mean value of Y when X equals 0. Because the square footage of the store cannot be 0, this Y intercept has no practical interpretation. Also, the Y intercept for this example is outside the range of the observed values of the X variable, and therefore interpretations of the value of b_0 should be made cautiously. Figure 5 displays the actual observations and the prediction line. To illustrate a situation in which there is a direct interpretation for the Y intercept, b_0, see Example 1.

FIGURE 5

Microsoft Excel scatter plot and prediction line for Sunflowers Apparel data

See Section E2 to create this.

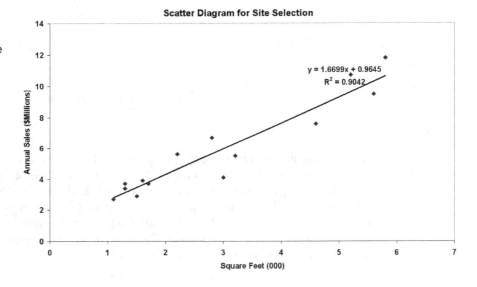

EXAMPLE 1

INTERPRETING THE Y INTERCEPT, b_0, AND THE SLOPE, b_1

A statistics professor wants to use the number of hours a student studies for a statistics final exam (X) to predict the final exam score (Y). A regression model was fit based on data collected for a class during the previous semester, with the following results:

$$\hat{Y}_i = 35.0 + 3X_i$$

What is the interpretation of the Y intercept, b_0, and the slope, b_1?

SOLUTION The Y intercept $b_0 = 35.0$ indicates that when the student does not study for the final exam, the mean final exam score is 35.0. The slope $b_1 = 3$ indicates that for each increase of one hour in studying time, the mean change in the final exam score is predicted to be $+3.0$. In other words, the final exam score is predicted to increase by 3 points for each one-hour increase in studying time.

VISUAL EXPLORATIONS Exploring Simple Linear Regression Coefficients

Use the Visual Explorations Simple Linear Regression procedure to produce a prediction line that is as close as possible to the prediction line defined by the least-squares solution. Open the `Visual Explorations.xla` add-in workbook and select **VisualExplorations → Simple Linear Regression** (Excel 97-2003) or **Add-ins → Visual Explorations → Simple Linear Regression** (Excel 2007).

When a scatter plot of the Sunflowers Apparel data of Table 1 with an initial prediction line appears (shown below), click the spinner buttons to change the values for b_1, the slope of the prediction line, and b_0, the Y intercept of the prediction line.

Try to produce a prediction line that is as close as possible to the prediction line defined by the least-squares estimates, using the chart display and the Difference from Target SSE value as feedback. Click **Finish** when you are done with this exploration.

At any time, click **Reset** to reset the b_1 and b_0 values, **Help** for more information, or **Solution** to reveal the prediction line defined by the least-squares method.

Using Your Own Regression Data

To use Visual Explorations to find a prediction line for your own data, open the `Visual Explorations.xla` add-in workbook and select **VisualExplorations → Simple**

Linear Regression with your worksheet data (97-2003) or **Add-ins → Visual Explorations → Simple Linear Regression with your worksheet data** (2007). In the procedure's dialog box (shown below), enter your Y variable cell range as the **Y Variable Cell Range** and your X variable cell range as the **X Variable Cell Range**. Click **First cells in both ranges contain a label**, enter a title as the **Title**, and click **OK**. When the scatter plot with an initial prediction line appears, use the instructions in the first part of this section to try to produce the prediction line defined by the least-squares method.

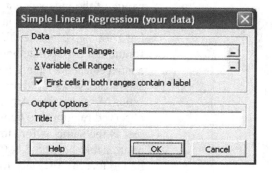

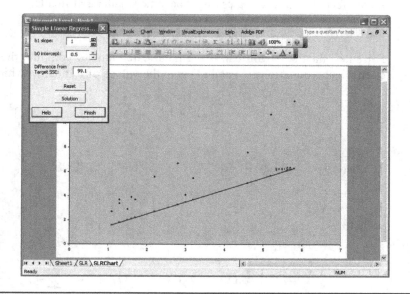

Return to the Using Statistics scenario concerning the Sunflowers Apparel stores. Example 2 illustrates how you use the prediction equation to predict the mean annual sales.

EXAMPLE 2

PREDICTING MEAN ANNUAL SALES, BASED ON SQUARE FOOTAGE

Use the prediction line to predict the mean annual sales for a store with 4,000 square feet.

SOLUTION You can determine the predicted value by substituting $X = 4$ (thousands of square feet) into the simple linear regression equation:

$$\hat{Y}_i = 0.9645 + 1.6699 X_i$$

$$\hat{Y}_i = 0.9645 + 1.6699(4) = 7.644 \text{ or } \$7,644,000$$

Thus, the predicted mean annual sales of a store with 4,000 square feet is \$7,644,000.

Predictions in Regression Analysis: Interpolation Versus Extrapolation

When using a regression model for prediction purposes, you need to consider only the **relevant range** of the independent variable in making predictions. This relevant range includes all values from the smallest to the largest X used in developing the regression model. Hence, when predicting Y for a given value of X, you can interpolate within this relevant range of the X values, but you should not extrapolate beyond the range of X values. When you use the square footage to predict annual sales, the square footage (in thousands of square feet) varies from 1.1 to 5.8 (see Table 1). Therefore, you should predict annual sales *only* for stores whose size is between 1.1 and 5.8 thousands of square feet. Any prediction of annual sales for stores outside this range assumes that the observed relationship between sales and store size for store sizes from 1.1 to 5.8 thousand square feet is the same as for stores outside this range. For example, you cannot extrapolate the linear relationship beyond 5,800 square feet in Example 2. It would be improper to use the prediction line to forecast the sales for a new store containing 8,000 square feet. It is quite possible that store size has a point of diminishing returns. If that is true, as square footage increases beyond 5,800 square feet, the effect on sales might become smaller and smaller.

Computing the Y Intercept, b_0, and the Slope, b_1

For small data sets, you can use a hand calculator to compute the least-squares regression coefficients. Equations (3) and (4) give the values of b_0 and b_1, which minimize

$$\sum_{i=1}^{n} (Y_i - \hat{Y}_i)^2 = \sum_{i=1}^{n} [Y_i - (b_0 + b_1 X_i)]^2$$

COMPUTATIONAL FORMULA FOR THE SLOPE, b_1

$$b_1 = \frac{SSXY}{SSX} \tag{3}$$

where

$$SSXY = \sum_{i=1}^{n} (X_i - \bar{X})(Y_i - \bar{Y}) = \sum_{i=1}^{n} X_i Y_i - \frac{\left(\sum_{i=1}^{n} X_i\right)\left(\sum_{i=1}^{n} Y_i\right)}{n}$$

$$SSX = \sum_{i=1}^{n} (X_i - \bar{X})^2 = \sum_{i=1}^{n} X_i^2 - \frac{\left(\sum_{i=1}^{n} X_i\right)^2}{n}$$

COMPUTATIONAL FORMULA FOR THE Y INTERCEPT, b_0

$$b_0 = \bar{Y} - b_1\bar{X} \tag{4}$$

where

$$\bar{Y} = \frac{\sum_{i=1}^{n} Y_i}{n}$$

$$\bar{X} = \frac{\sum_{i=1}^{n} X_i}{n}$$

EXAMPLE 3

COMPUTING THE Y INTERCEPT, b_0, AND THE SLOPE, b_1

Compute the Y intercept, b_0, and the slope, b_1, for the Sunflowers Apparel data.

SOLUTION Examining Equations (3) and (4), you see that five quantities must be calculated to determine b_1 and b_0. These are n, the sample size; $\sum_{i=1}^{n} X_i$, the sum of the X values; $\sum_{i=1}^{n} Y_i$, the sum of the Y values; $\sum_{i=1}^{n} X_i^2$, the sum of the squared X values; and $\sum_{i=1}^{n} X_iY_i$, the sum of the product of X and Y. For the Sunflowers Apparel data, the number of square feet is used to predict the annual sales in a store. Table 2 presents the computations of the various sums needed for the site selection problem, plus $\sum_{i=1}^{n} Y_i^2$, the sum of the squared Y values that will be used to compute SST in Section 3.

TABLE 2

Computations for the Sunflowers Apparel Data

Store	Square Feet (X)	Annual Sales (Y)	X^2	Y^2	XY
1	1.7	3.7	2.89	13.69	6.29
2	1.6	3.9	2.56	15.21	6.24
3	2.8	6.7	7.84	44.89	18.76
4	5.6	9.5	31.36	90.25	53.20
5	1.3	3.4	1.69	11.56	4.42
6	2.2	5.6	4.84	31.36	12.32
7	1.3	3.7	1.69	13.69	4.81
8	1.1	2.7	1.21	7.29	2.97
9	3.2	5.5	10.24	30.25	17.60
10	1.5	2.9	2.25	8.41	4.35
11	5.2	10.7	27.04	114.49	55.64
12	4.6	7.6	21.16	57.76	34.96
13	5.8	11.8	33.64	139.24	68.44
14	3.0	4.1	9.00	16.81	12.30
Totals	40.9	81.8	157.41	594.90	302.30

Using Equations (3) and (4), you can compute the values of b_0 and b_1:

$$b_1 = \frac{SSXY}{SSX}$$

$$SSXY = \sum_{i=1}^{n}(X_i - \overline{X})(Y_i - \overline{Y}) = \sum_{i=1}^{n} X_i Y_i - \frac{\left(\sum_{i=1}^{n} X_i\right)\left(\sum_{i=1}^{n} Y_i\right)}{n}$$

$$SSXY = 302.3 - \frac{(40.9)(81.8)}{14}$$
$$= 302.3 - 238.97285$$
$$= 63.32715$$

$$SSX = \sum_{i=1}^{n}(X_i - \overline{X})^2 = \sum_{i=1}^{n} X_i^2 - \frac{\left(\sum_{i=1}^{n} X_i\right)^2}{n}$$

$$= 157.41 - \frac{(40.9)^2}{14}$$
$$= 157.41 - 119.48642$$
$$= 37.92358$$

so that

$$b_1 = \frac{63.32715}{37.92358}$$
$$= 1.6699$$

and

$$b_0 = \overline{Y} - b_1\overline{X}$$

$$\overline{Y} = \frac{\sum_{i=1}^{n} Y_i}{n} = \frac{81.8}{14} = 5.842857$$

$$\overline{X} = \frac{\sum_{i=1}^{n} X_i}{n} = \frac{40.9}{14} = 2.92143$$

$$b_0 = 5.842857 - (1.6699)(2.92143)$$
$$= 0.9645$$

PROBLEMS FOR SECTION 2

Learning the Basics

 1 Fitting a straight line to a set of data yields the following prediction line:

$$\hat{Y}_i = 2 + 5X_i$$

a. Interpret the meaning of the Y intercept, b_0.
b. Interpret the meaning of the slope, b_1.
c. Predict the mean value of Y for $X = 3$.

2 If the values of X in Problem 1 range from 2 to 25, should you use this model to predict the mean value of Y when X equals
a. 3?
b. −3?
c. 0?
d. 24?

 3 Fitting a straight line to a set of data yields the following prediction line:

$$\hat{Y}_i = 16 - 0.5X_i$$

a. Interpret the meaning of the Y intercept, b_0.
b. Interpret the meaning of the slope, b_1.
c. Predict the mean value of Y for $X = 6$.

Applying the Concepts

 4 The marketing manager of a large supermarket chain would like to use shelf space to predict the sales of pet food. A random sample of 12 equal-sized stores is selected, with the following results (stored in the file petfood.xls):

Store	Shelf Space (X) (Feet)	Weekly Sales (Y) ($)
1	5	160
2	5	220
3	5	140
4	10	190
5	10	240
6	10	260
7	15	230
8	15	270
9	15	280
10	20	260
11	20	290
12	20	310

a. Construct a scatter plot.

For these data, $b_0 = 145$ and $b_1 = 7.4$.
b. Interpret the meaning of the slope, b_1, in this problem.
c. Predict the mean weekly sales (in hundreds of dollars) of pet food for stores with 8 feet of shelf space for pet food.

5 Circulation is the lifeblood of the publishing business. The larger the sales of a magazine, the more it can charge advertisers. Recently, a circulation gap has appeared between the publishers' reports of magazines' newsstand sales and subsequent audits by the Audit Bureau of Circulations. The data in the file circulation.xls represent the reported and audited newsstand sales (in thousands) in 2001 for the following 10 magazines:

Magazine	Reported (X)	Audited (Y)
YM	621.0	299.6
CosmoGirl	359.7	207.7
Rosie	530.0	325.0
Playboy	492.1	336.3
Esquire	70.5	48.6
TeenPeople	567.0	400.3
More	125.5	91.2
Spin	50.6	39.1
Vogue	353.3	268.6
Elle	263.6	214.3

Source: Extracted from M. Rose, "In Fight for Ads, Publishers Often Overstate Their Sales," The Wall Street Journal, August 6, 2003, pp. A1, A10.

a. Construct a scatter plot.

For these data $b_0 = 26.724$ and $b_1 = 0.5719$.
b. Interpret the meaning of the slope, b_1, in this problem.
c. Predict the mean audited newsstand sales for a magazine that reports newsstand sales of 400,000.

6 The owner of a moving company typically has his most experienced manager predict the total number of labor hours that will be required to complete an upcoming move. This approach has proved useful in the past, but he would like to be able to develop a more accurate method of predicting labor hours by using the number of cubic feet moved. In a preliminary effort to provide a more accurate method, he has collected data for 36 moves in which the origin and destination were within the borough of Manhattan in New York City and in which the travel time was an insignificant portion of the hours worked. The data are stored in the file moving.xls.

a. Construct a scatter plot.
b. Assuming a linear relationship, use the least-squares method to find the regression coefficients b_0 and b_1.
c. Interpret the meaning of the slope, b_1, in this problem.
d. Predict the mean labor hours for moving 500 cubic feet.

PH Grade ASSIST **7** A large mail-order house believes that there is a linear relationship between the weight of the mail it receives and the number of orders to be filled. It would like to investigate the relationship in order to predict the number of orders, based on the weight of the mail. From an operational perspective, knowledge of the number of orders will help in the planning of the order-fulfillment process. A sample of 25 mail shipments is selected that range from 200 to 700 pounds. The results (stored in the file **mail.xls**) are as follows:

Weight of Mail (Pounds)	Orders (Thousands)	Weight of Mail (Pounds)	Orders (Thousands)
216	6.1	432	13.6
283	9.1	409	12.8
237	7.2	553	16.5
203	7.5	572	17.1
259	6.9	506	15.0
374	11.5	528	16.2
342	10.3	501	15.8
301	9.5	628	19.0
365	9.2	677	19.4
384	10.6	602	19.1
404	12.5	630	18.0
426	12.9	652	20.2
482	14.5		

a. Construct a scatter plot.
b. Assuming a linear relationship, use the least-squares method to find the regression coefficients b_0 and b_1.
c. Interpret the meaning of the slope, b_1, in this problem.
d. Predict the mean number of orders when the weight of the mail is 500 pounds.

8 The value of a sports franchise is directly related to the amount of revenue that a franchise can generate. The data in the file **bbrevenue.xls** represent the value in 2005 (in millions of dollars) and the annual revenue (in millions of dollars) for 30 baseball franchises. Suppose you want to develop a simple linear regression model to predict franchise value based on annual revenue generated.
a. Construct a scatter plot.
b. Use the least-squares method to find the regression coefficients b_0 and b_1.
c. Interpret the meaning of b_0 and b_1 in this problem.
d. Predict the mean value of a baseball franchise that generates $150 million of annual revenue.

9 An agent for a residential real estate company in a large city would like to be able to predict the monthly rental cost for apartments, based on the size of the apartment, as defined by square footage. A sample of 25 apartments (stored in the file **rent.xls**) in a particular residential neighborhood was selected, and the information gathered revealed the following:

Apartment	Monthly Rent ($)	Size (Square Feet)	Apartment	Monthly Rent ($)	Size (Square Feet)
1	950	850	14	1,800	1,369
2	1,600	1,450	15	1,400	1,175
3	1,200	1,085	16	1,450	1,225
4	1,500	1,232	17	1,100	1,245
5	950	718	18	1,700	1,259
6	1,700	1,485	19	1,200	1,150
7	1,650	1,136	20	1,150	896
8	935	726	21	1,600	1,361
9	875	700	22	1,650	1,040
10	1,150	956	23	1,200	755
11	1,400	1,100	24	800	1,000
12	1,650	1,285	25	1,750	1,200
13	2,300	1,985			

a. Construct a scatter plot.
b. Use the least-squares method to find the regression coefficients b_0 and b_1.
c. Interpret the meaning of b_0 and b_1 in this problem.
d. Predict the mean monthly rent for an apartment that has 1,000 square feet.
e. Why would it not be appropriate to use the model to predict the monthly rent for apartments that have 500 square feet?
f. Your friends Jim and Jennifer are considering signing a lease for an apartment in this residential neighborhood. They are trying to decide between two apartments, one with 1,000 square feet for a monthly rent of $1,275 and the other with 1,200 square feet for a monthly rent of $1,425. What would you recommend to them based on (a) through (d)?

10 The data in the file **hardness.xls** provide measurements on the hardness and tensile strength for 35 specimens of die-cast aluminum. It is believed that hardness (measured in Rockwell E units) can be used to predict tensile strength (measured in thousands of pounds per square inch).
a. Construct a scatter plot.
b. Assuming a linear relationship, use the least-squares method to find the regression coefficients b_0 and b_1.
c. Interpret the meaning of the slope, b_1, in this problem.
d. Predict the mean tensile strength for die-cast aluminum that has a hardness of 30 Rockwell E units.

3   MEASURES OF VARIATION

When using the least-squares method to determine the regression coefficients for a set of data, you need to compute three important measures of variation. The first measure, the **total sum of squares (SST)**, is a measure of variation of the Y_i values around their mean, $\overline{Y}$. In a regression analysis, the **total variation** or total sum of squares is subdivided into **explained variation** and **unexplained variation**. The explained variation or **regression sum of squares (SSR)** is due to the relationship between X and Y, and the **unexplained variation**, or **error sum of squares (SSE)** is due to factors other than the relationship between X and Y. Figure 6 shows these different measures of variation.

FIGURE 6

Measures of variation

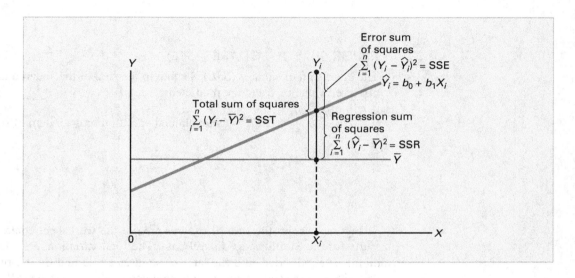

Computing the Sum of Squares

The regression sum of squares (SSR) is based on the difference between $\hat{Y}_i$ (the predicted value of Y from the prediction line) and $\overline{Y}$ (the mean value of Y). The error sum of squares (SSE) represents the part of the variation in Y that is not explained by the regression. It is based on the difference between Y_i and $\hat{Y}_i$. Equations (5), (6), (7), and (8) define these measures of variation.

MEASURES OF VARIATION IN REGRESSION

The total sum of squares is equal to the regression sum of squares plus the error sum of squares.

$$SST = SSR + SSE \qquad (5)$$

TOTAL SUM OF SQUARES (SST)

The total sum of squares (SST) is equal to the sum of the squared differences between each observed Y value and $\overline{Y}$, the mean value of Y.

$$SST = \text{Total sum of squares} \qquad (6)$$

$$= \sum_{i=1}^{n}(Y_i - \overline{Y})^2$$

REGRESSION SUM OF SQUARES (SSR)

The regression sum of squares (*SSR*) is equal to the sum of the squared differences between the predicted value of Y and $\overline{Y}$, the mean value of Y.

$$SSR = \text{Explained variation or regression of squares} \qquad (7)$$

$$= \sum_{i=1}^{n} (\hat{Y}_i - \overline{Y})^2$$

ERROR SUM OF SQUARES (SSE)

The error sum of squares (*SSE*) is equal to the sum of the squared differences between the observed value of Y and the predicted value of Y.

$$SSE = \text{Unexplained variation or error sum of squares} \qquad (8)$$

$$= \sum_{i=1}^{n} (Y_i - \hat{Y}_i)^2$$

Figure 7 shows the sum of squares area of the worksheet containing the Microsoft Excel results for the Sunflowers Apparel data. The total variation, *SST*, is equal to 116.9543. This amount is subdivided into the sum of squares explained by the regression (*SSR*), equal to 105.7476, and the sum of squares unexplained by the regression (*SSE*), equal to 11.2067. From Equation (5):

$$SST = SSR + SSE$$

$$116.9543 = 105.7476 + 11.2067$$

FIGURE 7

Microsoft Excel sum of squares for the Sunflowers Apparel data

See Section E1 to create the worksheet that contains this area.

	A	B	C	D	E	F	G
10	ANOVA						
11		*df*	*SS*	*MS*	*F*	*Significance F*	
12	Regression	1	105.7476	105.7476	113.2335	0.0000	
13	Residual	12	11.2067	0.9339			
14	Total	13	116.9543				
15							
16		Coefficients	Standard Error	t Stat	P-value	Lower 95%	Upper 95%
17	Intercept	0.9645	0.5262	1.8329	0.0917	-0.1820	2.1110
18	Square Feet	1.6699	0.1569	10.6411	0.0000	1.3280	2.0118

In a data set that has a large number of significant digits, the results of a regression analysis are sometimes displayed using a numerical format known as *scientific notation*. This type of format is used to display very small or very large values. The number after the letter E represents the number of digits that the decimal point needs to be moved to the left (for a negative number) or to the right (for a positive number). For example, the number 3.7431E+02 means that the decimal point should be moved two places to the right, producing the number 374.31. The number 3.7431E-02 means that the decimal point should be moved two places to the left, producing the number 0.037431. When scientific notation is used, fewer significant digits are usually displayed, and the numbers may appear to be rounded.

The Coefficient of Determination

By themselves, SSR, SSE, and SST provide little information. However, the ratio of the regression sum of squares (SSR) to the total sum of squares (SST) measures the proportion of variation in Y that is explained by the independent variable X in the regression model. This ratio is called the **coefficient of determination**, r^2, and is defined in Equation (9).

COEFFICIENT OF DETERMINATION

The coefficient of determination is equal to the regression sum of squares (that is, explained variation) divided by the total sum of squares (that is, total variation).

$$r^2 = \frac{\text{Regression sum of squares}}{\text{Total sum of squares}} = \frac{SSR}{SST} \tag{9}$$

The coefficient of determination measures the proportion of variation in Y that is explained by the independent variable X in the regression model. For the Sunflowers Apparel data, with $SSR = 105.7476$, $SSE = 11.2067$, and $SST = 116.9543$,

$$r^2 = \frac{105.7476}{116.9543} = 0.9042$$

Therefore, 90.42% of the variation in annual sales is explained by the variability in the size of the store, as measured by the square footage. This large r^2 indicates a strong positive linear relationship between two variables because the use of a regression model has reduced the variability in predicting annual sales by 90.42%. Only 9.58% of the sample variability in annual sales is due to factors other than what is accounted for by the linear regression model that uses square footage.

Figure 8 presents the coefficient of determination portion of the Microsoft Excel results for the Sunflowers Apparel data.

FIGURE 8

Partial Microsoft Excel regression results for the Sunflowers Apparel data

See Section E1 to create the worksheet that contains this area.

	A	B
3	**Regression Statistics**	
4	**Multiple R**	0.9509
5	**R Square**	0.9042
6	**Adjusted R Square**	0.8962
7	**Standard Error**	S_{YX}—0.9664
8	**Observations**	14

EXAMPLE 4

COMPUTING THE COEFFICIENT OF DETERMINATION

Compute the coefficient of determination, r^2, for the Sunflowers Apparel data.

SOLUTION You can compute SST, SSR, and SSE, that are defined in Equations (6), (7), and (8), by using Equations (10), (11), and (12).

COMPUTATIONAL FORMULA FOR SST

$$SST = \sum_{i=1}^{n} (Y_i - \bar{Y})^2 = \sum_{i=1}^{n} Y_i^2 - \frac{\left(\sum_{i=1}^{n} Y_i\right)^2}{n} \tag{10}$$

COMPUTATIONAL FORMULA FOR *SSR*

$$SSR = \sum_{i=1}^{n}(\hat{Y}_i - \bar{Y})^2 = b_0\sum_{i=1}^{n}Y_i + b_1\sum_{i=1}^{n}X_iY_i - \frac{\left(\sum_{i=1}^{n}Y_i\right)^2}{n} \qquad \textbf{(11)}$$

COMPUTATIONAL FORMULA FOR *SSE*

$$SSE = \sum_{i=1}^{n}(Y_i - \hat{Y})^2 = \sum_{i=1}^{n}Y_i^2 - b_0\sum_{i=1}^{n}Y_i - b_1\sum_{i=1}^{n}X_iY_i \qquad \textbf{(12)}$$

Using the summary results from Table 2,

$$SST = \sum_{i=1}^{n}(\hat{Y}_i - \bar{Y})^2 = \sum_{i=1}^{n}Y_i^2 - \frac{\left(\sum_{i=1}^{n}Y_i\right)^2}{n}$$

$$= 594.9 - \frac{(81.8)^2}{14}$$

$$= 594.9 - 477.94571$$

$$= 116.95429$$

$$SSR = \sum_{i=1}^{n}(\hat{Y}_i - \bar{Y})^2$$

$$= b_0\sum_{i=1}^{n}Y_i + b_1\sum_{i=1}^{n}X_iY_i - \frac{\left(\sum_{i=1}^{n}Y_i\right)^2}{n}$$

$$= (0.964478)(81.8) + (1.66986)(302.3) - \frac{(81.8)^2}{14}$$

$$= 105.74726$$

$$SSE = \sum_{i=1}^{n}(Y_i - \hat{Y}_i)^2$$

$$= \sum_{i=1}^{n}Y_i^2 - b_0\sum_{i=1}^{n}Y_i - b_1\sum_{i=1}^{n}X_iY_i$$

$$= 594.9 - (0.964478)(81.8) - (1.66986)(302.3)$$

$$= 11.2067$$

Therefore,

$$r^2 = \frac{105.74726}{116.95429} = 0.9042$$

Standard Error of the Estimate

Although the least-squares method results in the line that fits the data with the minimum amount of error, unless all the observed data points fall on a straight line, the prediction line is not a perfect predictor. Just as all data values cannot be expected to be exactly equal to their mean, neither can they be expected to fall exactly on the prediction line. An important statistic, called the **standard error of the estimate**, measures the variability of the actual Y values from the predicted Y values in the same way that the standard deviation (as you may have seen it previously) measures the variability of each value around the sample mean. In other words, the standard error of the estimate is the standard deviation *around* the prediction line, whereas the standard deviation (as you may have seen it previously) is the standard deviation *around* the sample mean.

Figure 5 illustrates the variability around the prediction line for the Sunflowers Apparel data. Observe that although many of the actual values of Y fall near the prediction line, none of the values are exactly on the line.

The standard error of the estimate, represented by the symbol S_{YX}, is defined in Equation (13).

STANDARD ERROR OF THE ESTIMATE

$$S_{YX} = \sqrt{\frac{SSE}{n-2}} = \sqrt{\frac{\sum_{i=1}^{n}(Y_i - \hat{Y}_i)^2}{n-2}} \tag{13}$$

where

Y_i = actual value of Y for a given X_i

$\hat{Y}_i$ = predicted value of Y for a given X_i

SSE = error sum of squares

From Equation (8) and Figure 4, $SSE = 11.2067$. Thus,

$$S_{YX} = \sqrt{\frac{11.2067}{14-2}} = 0.9664$$

This standard error of the estimate, equal to 0.9664 millions of dollars (that is, $966,400), is labeled Standard Error in the Microsoft Excel results shown in Figure 8. The standard error of the estimate represents a measure of the variation around the prediction line. It is measured in the same units as the dependent variable Y. The interpretation of the standard error of the estimate is similar to that of the standard deviation. Just as the standard deviation measures variability around the mean, the standard error of the estimate measures variability around the prediction line. For Sunflowers Apparel, the typical difference between actual annual sales at a store and the predicted annual sales using the regression equation is approximately $966,400.

PROBLEMS FOR SECTION 3

Learning the Basics

11 How do you interpret a coefficient of determination, r^2, equal to 0.80?

12 If $SSR = 36$ and $SSE = 4$, determine SST and then compute the coefficient of determination, r^2, and interpret its meaning.

13 If $SSR = 66$ and $SST = 88$, compute the coefficient of determination, r^2, and interpret its meaning.

14 If $SSE = 10$ and $SSR = 30$, compute the coefficient of determination, r^2, and interpret its meaning.

15 If $SSR = 120$, why is it impossible for SST to equal 110?

Applying the Concepts

16 In Problem 4, the marketing manager used shelf space for pet food to predict weekly sales (stored in the file petfood.xls). For that data, $SSR = 20,535$ and $SST = 30,025$.
a. Determine the coefficient of determination, r^2, and interpret its meaning.
b. Determine the standard error of the estimate.
c. How useful do you think this regression model is for predicting sales?

17 In Problem 5, you used reported magazine newsstand sales to predict audited sales (stored in the file circulation.xls). For that data, $SSR = 130,301.41$ and $SST = 144,538.64$.
a. Determine the coefficient of determination, r^2, and interpret its meaning.
b. Determine the standard error of the estimate.
c. How useful do you think this regression model is for predicting audited sales?

18 In Problem 6, an owner of a moving company wanted to predict labor hours, based on the cubic feet moved (stored in the file moving.xls). Using the results of that problem,
a. determine the coefficient of determination, r^2, and interpret its meaning.
b. determine the standard error of the estimate.
c. How useful do you think this regression model is for predicting labor hours?

19 In Problem 7, you used the weight of mail to predict the number of orders received (stored in the file mail.xls). Using the results of that problem,

a. determine the coefficient of determination, r^2, and interpret its meaning.
b. find the standard error of the estimate.
c. How useful do you think this regression model is for predicting the number of orders?

20 In Problem 8, you used annual revenues to predict the value of a baseball franchise (stored in the file bbrevenue.xls). Using the results of that problem,
a. determine the coefficient of determination, r^2, and interpret its meaning.
b. determine the standard error of the estimate.
c. How useful do you think this regression model is for predicting the value of a baseball franchise?

21 In Problem 9, an agent for a real estate company wanted to predict the monthly rent for apartments, based on the size of the apartment (stored in the file rent.xls). Using the results of that problem,
a. determine the coefficient of determination, r^2, and interpret its meaning.
b. determine the standard error of the estimate.
c. How useful do you think this regression model is for predicting the monthly rent?

22 In Problem 10, you used hardness to predict the tensile strength of die-cast aluminum (stored in the file hardness.xls). Using the results of that problem,
a. determine the coefficient of determination, r^2, and interpret its meaning.
b. find the standard error of the estimate.
c. How useful do you think this regression model is for predicting the tensile strength of die-cast aluminum?

4 ASSUMPTIONS

The discussion of hypothesis testing and the analysis of variance emphasized the importance of the assumptions to the validity of any conclusions reached. The assumptions necessary for regression are similar to those of the analysis of variance because both topics fall in the general category of *linear models* (reference 4).

The four **assumptions of regression** (known by the acronym LINE) are as follows:

- **L**inearity
- **I**ndependence of errors
- **N**ormality of error
- **E**qual variance

The first assumption, linearity, states that the relationship between variables is linear.

The second assumption, **independence of errors**, requires that the errors (ε_i) are independent of one another. This assumption is particularly important when data are collected over a period of time. In such situations, the errors for a specific time period are sometimes correlated with those of the previous time period.

The third assumption, **normality**, requires that the errors (ε_i) are normally distributed at each value of X. Like the t test and the ANOVA F test, regression analysis is fairly robust against departures from the normality assumption. As long as the distribution of the errors at each level of X is not extremely different from a normal distribution, inferences about β_0 and β_1 are not seriously affected.

The fourth assumption, **equal variance** or **homoscedasticity**, requires that the variance of the errors (ε_i) are constant for all values of X. In other words, the variability of Y values is the same when X is a low value as when X is a high value. The equal variance assumption is important when making inferences about β_0 and β_1. If there are serious departures from this assumption, you can use either data transformations or weighted least-squares methods (see reference 4).

5 RESIDUAL ANALYSIS

In Section 1, regression analysis was introduced. In Sections 2 and 3, a regression model was developed using the least-squares approach for the Sunflowers Apparel data. Is this the correct model for these data? Are the assumptions introduced in Section 4 valid? In this section, a graphical approach called **residual analysis** is used to evaluate the assumptions and determine whether the regression model selected is an appropriate model.

The **residual** or estimated error value, e_i, is the difference between the observed (Y_i) and predicted ($\hat{Y}_i$) values of the dependent variable for a given value of X_i. Graphically, a residual appears on a scatter plot as the vertical distance between an observed value of Y and the prediction line. Equation (14) defines the residual.

RESIDUAL

The residual is equal to the difference between the observed value of Y and the predicted value of Y.

$$e_i = Y_i - \hat{Y}_i \tag{14}$$

Evaluating the Assumptions

Recall from Section 4 that the four assumptions of regression (known by the acronym LINE) are linearity, independence, normality, and equal variance.

Linearity To evaluate linearity, you plot the residuals on the vertical axis against the corresponding X_i values of the independent variable on the horizontal axis. If the linear model is appropriate for the data, there is no apparent pattern in this plot. However, if the linear model is not appropriate, there is a relationship between the X_i values and the residuals, e_i. You can see such a pattern in Figure 9. Panel A shows a situation in which, although there is an increasing trend in Y as X increases, the relationship seems curvilinear because the upward trend decreases for increasing values of X. This quadratic effect is highlighted in Panel B, where there is a clear relationship between X_i and e_i. By plotting the residuals, the linear trend of X with Y has been removed, thereby exposing the lack of fit in the simple linear model. Thus, a quadratic model is a better fit and should be used in place of the simple linear model.

To determine whether the simple linear regression model is appropriate, return to the evaluation of the Sunflowers Apparel data. Figure 10 provides the predicted and residual values of the response variable (annual sales) computed by Microsoft Excel.

FIGURE 9

Studying the appropriateness of the simple linear regression model

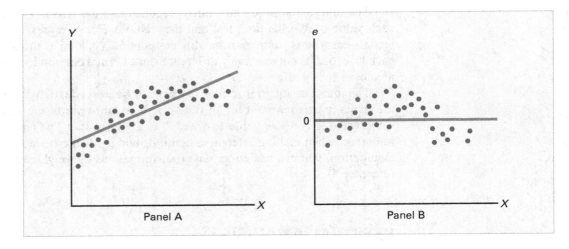

Panel A   Panel B

FIGURE 10

Microsoft Excel residual statistics for the Sunflowers Apparel data

See Section E3 to create the worksheet that contains this area.

	A	B	C
22	**RESIDUAL OUTPUT**		
23			
24	*Observation*	*Predicted Annual Sales*	*Residuals*
25	1	3.803239598	-0.103239598
26	2	3.636253367	0.263746633
27	3	5.640088147	1.059911853
28	4	10.31570263	-0.815702635
29	5	3.135294672	0.264705328
30	6	4.638170757	0.961829243
31	7	3.135294672	0.564705328
32	8	2.801322208	-0.101322208
33	9	6.308033074	-0.808033074
34	10	3.469267135	-0.569267135
35	11	9.647757708	1.052242292
36	12	8.645840318	-1.045840318
37	13	10.6496751	1.150324902
38	14	5.974060611	-1.874060611

To assess linearity, the residuals are plotted against the independent variable (store size, in thousands of square feet) in Figure 11. Although there is widespread scatter in the residual plot, there is no apparent pattern or relationship between the residuals and X_i. The residuals appear to be evenly spread above and below 0 for the differing values of X. You can conclude that the linear model is appropriate for the Sunflowers Apparel data.

FIGURE 11

Micosoft Excel plot of residuals against the square footage of a store for the Sunflowers Apparel data

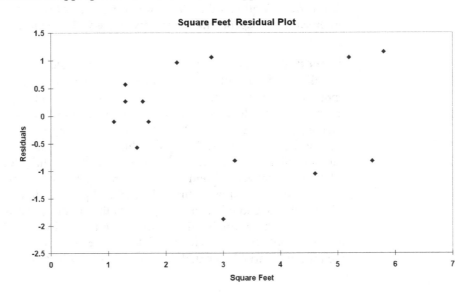

Independence You can evaluate the assumption of independence of the errors by plotting the residuals in the order or sequence in which the data were collected. Data collected over periods of time sometimes exhibit an autocorrelation effect among successive observations. In these instances, there is a relationship between consecutive residuals. If this relationship exists (which violates the assumption of independence), it is apparent in the plot of the residuals versus the time in which the data were collected. You can also test for autocorrelation by using the Durbin-Watson statistic, which is the subject of Section 6. Because the Sunflowers Apparel data were collected during the same time period, you do not need to evaluate the independence assumption.

Normality You can evaluate the assumption of normality in the errors by tallying the residuals into a frequency distribution and displaying the results in a histogram. For the Sunflowers Apparel data, the residuals have been tallied into a frequency distribution in Table 3. (There are an insufficient number of values, however, to construct a histogram.) You can also evaluate the normality assumption by comparing the actual versus theoretical values of the residuals or by constructing a normal probability plot of the residuals. Figure 12 is a normal probability plot of the residuals for the Sunflower Apparel data.

TABLE 3

Frequency Distribution of 14 Residual Values for the Sunflowers Apparel Data

Residuals	Frequency
−2.25 but less than −1.75	1
−1.75 but less than −1.25	0
−1.25 but less than −0.75	3
−0.75 but less than −0.25	1
−0.25 but less than +0.25	2
+0.25 but less than +0.75	3
+0.75 but less than +1.25	4
	14

FIGURE 12

Microsoft Excel normal probability plot of the residuals for the Sunflowers Apparel data

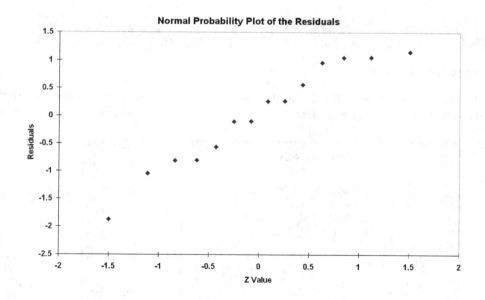

It is difficult to evaluate the normality assumption for a sample of only 14 values, regardless of whether you use a histogram, stem-and-leaf display, box-and-whisker plot, or normal probability plot. You can see from Figure 12 that the data do not appear to depart substantially from a normal distribution. The robustness of regression analysis with modest departures from normality enables you to conclude that you should not be overly concerned about departures from this normality assumption in the Sunflowers Apparel data.

Equal Variance You can evaluate the assumption of equal variance from a plot of the residuals with X_i. For the Sunflowers Apparel data of Figure 11, there do not appear to be major differences in the variability of the residuals for different X_i values. Thus, you can conclude that there is no apparent violation in the assumption of equal variance at each level of X.

To examine a case in which the equal variance assumption is violated, observe Figure 13, which is a plot of the residuals with X_i for a hypothetical set of data. In this plot, the variability of the residuals increases dramatically as X increases, demonstrating the lack of homogeneity in the variances of Y_i at each level of X. For these data, the equal variance assumption is invalid.

FIGURE 13

Violation of equal variance

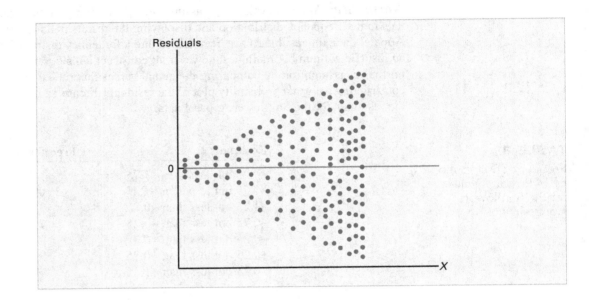

PROBLEMS FOR SECTION 5

Learning the Basics

23 The results below provide the X values, residuals, and a residual plot from a regression analysis:

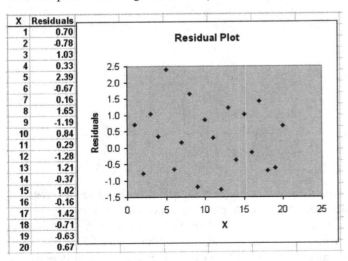

X	Residuals
1	0.70
2	-0.78
3	1.03
4	0.33
5	2.39
6	-0.67
7	0.16
8	1.65
9	-1.19
10	0.84
11	0.29
12	-1.28
13	1.21
14	-0.37
15	1.02
16	-0.16
17	1.42
18	-0.71
19	-0.63
20	0.67

Is there any evidence of a pattern in the residuals? Explain.

24 The results below show the X values, residuals, and a residual plot from a regression analysis:

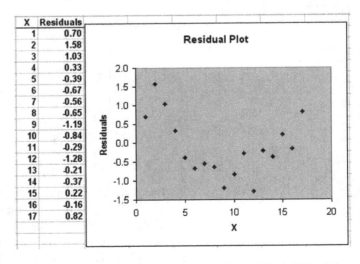

X	Residuals
1	0.70
2	1.58
3	1.03
4	0.33
5	-0.39
6	-0.67
7	-0.56
8	-0.65
9	-1.19
10	-0.84
11	-0.29
12	-1.28
13	-0.21
14	-0.37
15	0.22
16	-0.16
17	0.82

Is there any evidence of a pattern in the residuals? Explain.

Applying the Concepts

25 In Problem 5, you used reported magazine newsstand sales to predict audited sales. The data are stored in the file `circulation.xls`. Perform a residual analysis for these data.
a. Determine the adequacy of the fit of the model.
b. Evaluate whether the assumptions of regression have been seriously violated.

 26 In Problem 4, the marketing manager used shelf space for pet food to predict weekly sales. The data are stored in the file `petfood.xls`. Perform a residual analysis for these data.
a. Determine the adequacy of the fit of the model.
b. Evaluate whether the assumptions of regression have been seriously violated.

27 In Problem 7, you used the weight of mail to predict the number of orders received. Perform a residual analysis for these data. The data are stored in the file `mail.xls`. Based on these results,
a. determine the adequacy of the fit of the model.
b. evaluate whether the assumptions of regression have been seriously violated.

28 In Problem 6, the owner of a moving company wanted to predict labor hours based on the cubic feet moved. Perform a residual analysis for these data. The data are stored in the file `moving.xls`. Based on these results,

a. determine the adequacy of the fit of the model.
b. evaluate whether the assumptions of regression have been seriously violated.

29 In Problem 9, an agent for a real estate company wanted to predict the monthly rent for apartments, based on the size of the apartments. Perform a residual analysis for these data. The data are stored in the file `rent.xls`. Based on these results,
a. determine the adequacy of the fit of the model.
b. evaluate whether the assumptions of regression have been seriously violated.

30 In Problem 8, you used annual revenues to predict the value of a baseball franchise. The data are stored in the file `bbrevenue.xls`. Perform a residual analysis for these data. Based on these results,
a. determine the adequacy of the fit of the model.
b. evaluate whether the assumptions of regression have been seriously violated.

31 In Problem 10, you used hardness to predict the tensile strength of die-cast aluminum. The data are stored in the file `hardness.xls`. Perform a residual analysis for these data. Based on these results,
a. determine the adequacy of the fit of the model.
b. evaluate whether the assumptions of regression have been seriously violated.

6 MEASURING AUTOCORRELATION: THE DURBIN-WATSON STATISTIC

One of the basic assumptions of the regression model is the independence of the errors. This assumption is sometimes violated when data are collected over sequential time periods because a residual at any one time period may tend to be similar to residuals at adjacent time periods. This pattern in the residuals is called **autocorrelation**. When a set of data has substantial autocorrelation, the validity of a regression model can be in serious doubt.

Residual Plots to Detect Autocorrelation

As mentioned in Section 5, one way to detect autocorrelation is to plot the residuals in time order. If a positive autocorrelation effect is present, there will be clusters of residuals with the same sign, and you will readily detect an apparent pattern. If negative autocorrelation exists, residuals will tend to jump back and forth from positive to negative to positive, and so on. This type of pattern is very rarely seen in regression analysis. Thus, the focus of this section is on positive autocorrelation. To illustrate positive autocorrelation, consider the following example.

The manager of a package delivery store wants to predict weekly sales, based on the number of customers making purchases for a period of 15 weeks. In this situation, because data are collected over a period of 15 consecutive weeks at the same store, you need to determine whether autocorrelation is present. Table 4 presents the data (stored in the file `custsale.xls`). Figure 14 illustrates Microsoft Excel results for these data.

123

TABLE 4

Customers and
Sales for a Period of
15 Consecutive Weeks

Week	Customers	Sales (Thousands of Dollars)	Week	Customers	Sales (Thousands of Dollars)
1	794	9.33	9	880	12.07
2	799	8.26	10	905	12.55
3	837	7.48	11	886	11.92
4	855	9.08	12	843	10.27
5	845	9.83	13	904	11.80
6	844	10.09	14	950	12.15
7	863	11.01	15	841	9.64
8	875	11.49			

FIGURE 14

Microsoft Excel results
for the package delivery
store data of Table 4

*See Section E1 to create
this.*

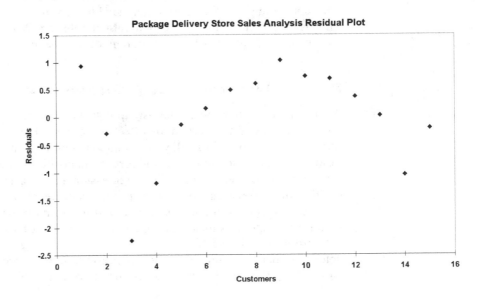

	A	B	C	D	E	F	G
1	Package Delivery Store Sales Analysis						
2							
3	*Regression Statistics*						
4	Multiple R	0.8108					
5	R Square	0.6574					
6	Adjusted R Square	0.6311					
7	Standard Error	0.9360					
8	Observations	15					
9							
10	ANOVA						
11		*df*	*SS*	*MS*	*F*	*Significance F*	
12	Regression	1	21.8604	21.8604	24.9501	0.0002	
13	Residual	13	11.3901	0.8762			
14	Total	14	33.2506				
15							
16		*Coefficients*	*Standard Error*	*t Stat*	*P-value*	*Lower 95%*	*Upper 95%*
17	Intercept	-16.0322	5.3102	-3.0192	0.0099	-27.5041	-4.5603
18	Customers	0.0308	0.0062	4.9950	0.0002	0.0175	0.0441

From Figure 14, observe that r^2 is 0.6574, indicating that 65.74% of the variation in sales is explained by variation in the number of customers. In addition, the Y intercept, b_0, is -16.0322, and the slope, b_1, is 0.0308. However, before using this model for prediction, you must undertake proper analyses of the residuals. Because the data have been collected over a consecutive period of 15 weeks, in addition to checking the linearity, normality, and equal-variance assumptions, you must investigate the independence-of-errors assumption. You can plot the residuals versus time to help you see whether a pattern exists. In Figure 15, you can see that the residuals tend to fluctuate up and down in a cyclical pattern. This cyclical pattern provides strong cause for concern about the autocorrelation of the residuals and, hence, a violation of the independence-of-errors assumption.

FIGURE 15

Microsoft Excel residual
plot for the package
delivery store data
of Table 4

*See Section E3 to create
this.*

The Durbin-Watson Statistic

The **Durbin-Watson statistic** is used to measure autocorrelation. This statistic measures the correlation between each residual and the residual for the time period immediately preceding the one of interest. Equation (15) defines the Durbin-Watson statistic.

DURBIN-WATSON STATISTIC

$$D = \frac{\sum_{i=2}^{n} (e_i - e_{i-1})^2}{\sum_{i=1}^{n} e_i^2} \tag{15}$$

where

$$e_i = \text{residual at the time period } i$$

To better understand the Durbin-Watson statistic, D, you can examine Equation (15). The numerator, $\sum_{i=2}^{n} (e_i - e_{i-1})^2$, represents the squared difference between two successive residuals, summed from the second value to the nth value. The denominator, $\sum_{i=1}^{n} e_i^2$, represents the sum of the squared residuals. When successive residuals are positively autocorrelated, the value of D approaches 0. If the residuals are not correlated, the value of D will be close to 2. (If there is negative autocorrelation, D will be greater than 2 and could even approach its maximum value of 4.) For the package delivery store data, as shown in the Microsoft Excel results of Figure 16, the Durbin-Watson statistic, D, is 0.8830.

FIGURE 16

Microsoft Excel results of the Durbin-Watson statistic for the package delivery store data

See Section E4 to create this.

	A	B
1	**Durbin-Watson Calculations**	
2		
3	Sum of Squared Difference of Residuals	10.0575
4	Sum of Squared Residuals	11.3901
5		
6	**Durbin-Watson Statistic**	0.8830 =B3/B4

You need to determine when the autocorrelation is large enough to make the Durbin-Watson statistic, D, fall sufficiently below 2 to conclude that there is significant positive autocorrelation. After computing D, you compare it to the critical values of the Durbin-Watson statistic found in the table of critical values d_L, and d_U of the Durbin-Watson statistic D, a portion of which is presented in Table 5. The critical values depend on α, the significance level chosen, n, the sample size, and k, the number of independent variables in the model (in simple linear regression, $k = 1$).

TABLE 5

Finding Critical Values of the Durbin-Watson Statistic

	$\alpha = .05$									
	$k=1$		$k=2$		$k=3$		$k=4$		$k=5$	
n	d_L	D_U	d_L	d_U	d_L	d_U	d_L	d_U	d_L	d_U
15	1.08	1.36	.95	1.54	.82	1.75	.69	1.97	.56	2.21
16	1.10	1.37	.98	1.54	.86	1.73	.74	1.93	.62	2.15
17	1.13	1.38	1.02	1.54	.90	1.71	.78	1.90	.67	2.10
18	1.16	1.39	1.05	1.53	.93	1.69	.82	1.87	.71	2.06

In Table 5, two values are shown for each combination of α (level of significance), n (sample size), and k (number of independent variables in the model). The first value, d_L, represents the lower critical value. If D is below d_L, you conclude that there is evidence of positive autocorrelation among the residuals. If this occurs, the least-squares method used in this chapter is inappropriate, and you should use alternative methods (see reference 4). The second value, d_U, represents the upper critical value of D, above which you would conclude that there is no evidence of positive autocorrelation among the residuals. If D is between d_L and d_U, you are unable to arrive at a definite conclusion.

For the package delivery store data, with one independent variable ($k = 1$) and 15 values ($n = 15$), $d_L = 1.08$ and $d_U = 1.36$. Because $D = 0.8830 < 1.08$, you conclude that there is positive autocorrelation among the residuals. The least-squares regression analysis of the data is inappropriate because of the presence of significant positive autocorrelation among the residuals. In other words, the independence-of-errors assumption is invalid. You need to use alternative approaches discussed in reference 4.

PROBLEMS FOR SECTION 6

Learning the Basics

 32 The residuals for 10 consecutive time periods are as follows:

Time Period	Residual	Time Period	Residual
1	−5	6	+1
2	−4	7	+2
3	−3	8	+3
4	−2	9	+4
5	−1	10	+5

a. Plot the residuals over time. What conclusion can you reach about the pattern of the residuals over time?
b. Based on (a), what conclusion can you reach about the autocorrelation of the residuals?

 33 The residuals for 15 consecutive time periods are as follows:

Time Period	Residual	Time Period	Residual
1	+4	9	+6
2	−6	10	−3
3	−1	11	+1
4	−5	12	+3
5	+2	13	0
6	+5	14	−4
7	−2	15	−7
8	+7		

a. Plot the residuals over time. What conclusion can you reach about the pattern of the residuals over time?

b. Compute the Durbin-Watson statistic. At the 0.05 level of significance, is there evidence of positive autocorrelation among the residuals?
c. Based on (a) and (b), what conclusion can you reach about the autocorrelation of the residuals?

Applying the Concepts

 34 In Problem 4 concerning pet food sales, the marketing manager used shelf space for pet food to predict weekly sales.
a. Is it necessary to compute the Durbin-Watson statistic in this case? Explain.
b. Under what circumstances is it necessary to compute the Durbin-Watson statistic before proceeding with the least-squares method of regression analysis?

35 The owner of a single-family home in a suburban county in the northeastern United States would like to develop a model to predict electricity consumption in his all-electric house (lights, fans, heat, appliances, and so on), based on average atmospheric temperature (in degrees Fahrenheit). Monthly kilowatt usage and temperature data are available for a period of 24 consecutive months in the file elecuse.xls.
a. Assuming a linear relationship, use the least-squares method to find the regression coefficients b_0 and b_1.
b. Predict the mean kilowatt usage when the average atmospheric temperature is 50° Fahrenheit.
c. Plot the residuals versus the time period.
d. Compute the Durbin-Watson statistic. At the 0.05 level of significance, is there evidence of positive autocorrelation among the residuals?
e. Based on the results of (c) and (d), is there reason to question the validity of the model?

36 A mail-order catalog business that sells personal computer supplies, software, and hardware maintains a centralized warehouse for the distribution of products ordered. Management is currently examining the process of distribution from the warehouse and is interested in studying the factors that affect warehouse distribution costs. Currently, a small handling fee is added to the order, regardless of the amount of the order. Data have been collected over the past 24 months, indicating the warehouse distribution costs and the number of orders received. They are stored in the file warecost.xls. The results are as follows:

Months	Distribution Cost (Thousands of Dollars)	Number of Orders
1	52.95	4,015
2	71.66	3,806
3	85.58	5,309
4	63.69	4,262
5	72.81	4,296
6	68.44	4,097
7	52.46	3,213
8	70.77	4,809
9	82.03	5,237
10	74.39	4,732
11	70.84	4,413
12	54.08	2,921
13	62.98	3,977
14	72.30	4,428
15	58.99	3,964
16	79.38	4,582
17	94.44	5,582
18	59.74	3,450
19	90.50	5,079
20	93.24	5,735
21	69.33	4,269
22	53.71	3,708
23	89.18	5,387
24	66.80	4,161

a. Assuming a linear relationship, use the least-squares method to find the regression coefficients b_0 and b_1.
b. Predict the monthly warehouse distribution costs when the number of orders is 4,500.
c. Plot the residuals versus the time period.
d. Compute the Durbin-Watson statistic. At the 0.05 level of significance, is there evidence of positive autocorrelation among the residuals?
e. Based on the results of (c) and (d), is there reason to question the validity of the model?

37 A freshly brewed shot of espresso has three distinct components: the heart, body, and crema. The separation of these three components typically lasts only 10 to 20 seconds.

To use the espresso shot in making a latte, cappuccino, or other drinks, the shot must be poured into the beverage during the separation of the heart, body, and crema. If the shot is used after the separation occurs, the drink becomes excessively bitter and acidic, ruining the final drink. Thus, a longer separation time allows the drink-maker more time to pour the shot and ensure that the beverage will meet expectations. An employee at a coffee shop hypothesized that the harder the espresso grounds were tamped down into the portafilter before brewing, the longer the separation time would be. An experiment using 24 observations was conducted to test this relationship. The independent variable Tamp measures the distance, in inches, between the espresso grounds and the top of the portafilter (that is, the harder the tamp, the larger the distance). The dependent variable Time is the number of seconds the heart, body, and crema are separated (that is, the amount of time after the shot is poured before it must be used for the customer's beverage). The data are stored in the file espresso.xls:

Shot	Tamp	Time	Shot	Tamp	Time
1	0.20	14	13	0.50	18
2	0.50	14	14	0.50	13
3	0.50	18	15	0.35	19
4	0.20	16	16	0.35	19
5	0.20	16	17	0.20	17
6	0.50	13	18	0.20	18
7	0.20	12	19	0.20	15
8	0.35	15	20	0.20	16
9	0.50	9	21	0.35	18
10	0.35	15	22	0.35	16
11	0.50	11	23	0.35	14
12	0.50	16	24	0.35	16

a. Determine the prediction line, using Time as the dependent variable and Tamp as the independent variable.
b. Predict the mean separation time for a Tamp distance of 0.50 inch.
c. Plot the residuals versus the time order of experimentation. Are there any noticeable patterns?
d. Compute the Durbin-Watson statistic. At the 0.05 level of significance, is there evidence of positive autocorrelation among the residuals?
e. Based on the results of (c) and (d), is there reason to question the validity of the model?

38 The owner of a chain of ice cream stores would like to study the effect of atmospheric temperature on sales during the summer season. A sample of 21 consecutive days is selected, with the results stored in the data file icecream.xls.

(**Hint:** Determine which are the independent and dependent variables.)

a. Assuming a linear relationship, use the least-squares method to find the regression coefficients b_0 and b_1.
b. Predict the sales per store for a day in which the temperature is 83°F.
c. Plot the residuals versus the time period.

d. Compute the Durbin-Watson statistic. At the 0.05 level of significance, is there evidence of positive autocorrelation among the residuals?
e. Based on the results of (c) and (d), is there reason to question the validity of the model?

7 INFERENCES ABOUT THE SLOPE AND CORRELATION COEFFICIENT

In Sections 1 through 3, regression was used solely for descriptive purposes. You learned how the least-squares method determines the regression coefficients and how to predict Y for a given value of X. In addition, you learned how to compute and interpret the standard error of the estimate and the coefficient of determination.

When residual analysis, as discussed in Section 5, indicates that the assumptions of a least-squares regression model are not seriously violated and that the straight-line model is appropriate, you can make inferences about the linear relationship between the variables in the population.

t Test for the Slope

To determine the existence of a significant linear relationship between the X and Y variables, you test whether β_1 (the population slope) is equal to 0. The null and alternative hypotheses are as follows:

$$H_0: \beta_1 = 0 \text{ (There is no linear relationship.)}$$
$$H_1: \beta_1 \neq 0 \text{ (There is a linear relationship.)}$$

If you reject the null hypothesis, you conclude that there is evidence of a linear relationship. Equation (16) defines the test statistic.

TESTING A HYPOTHESIS FOR A POPULATION SLOPE, β_1, USING THE t TEST

The t statistic equals the difference between the sample slope and hypothesized value of the population slope divided by the standard error of the slope.

$$t = \frac{b_1 - \beta_1}{S_{b_1}} \tag{16}$$

where

$$S_{b_1} = \frac{S_{YX}}{\sqrt{SSX}}$$

$$SSX = \sum_{i=1}^{n}(X_i - \bar{X})^2$$

The test statistic t follows a t distribution with $n - 2$ degrees of freedom.

Return to the Using Statistics scenario concerning Sunflowers Apparel. To test whether there is a significant linear relationship between the size of the store and the annual sales at the 0.05 level of significance, refer to the Microsoft Excel worksheet for the t test presented in Figure 17.

FIGURE 17

Microsoft Excel t test for the slope for the Sunflowers Apparel data

See Section E1 to create the worksheet that contains this area.

	A	B	C	D	E	F	G
15							
16		Coefficients	Standard Error	t Stat	P-value	Lower 95%	Upper 95%
17	Intercept	0.9645	0.5262	1.8329	0.0917	-0.1820	2.1110
18	Square Feet	1.6699	0.1569	10.6411	0.0000	1.3280	2.0118

From Figure 17,

$$b_1 = +1.6699 \qquad n = 14 \qquad S_{b_1} = 0.1569$$

and

$$t = \frac{b_1 - \beta_1}{S_{b_1}}$$

$$= \frac{1.6699 - 0}{0.1569} = 10.6411$$

Microsoft Excel labels this t statistic t Stat (see Figure 17). Using the 0.05 level of significance, the critical value of t with $n - 2 = 12$ degrees of freedom is 2.1788. Because $t = 10.6411 > 2.1788$, you reject H_0 (see Figure 18). Using the p-value, you reject H_0 because the p-value is approximately 0 which is less than $\alpha = 0.05$. Hence, you can conclude that there is a significant linear relationship between mean annual sales and the size of the store.

FIGURE 18

Testing a hypothesis about the population slope at the 0.05 level of significance, with 12 degrees of freedom

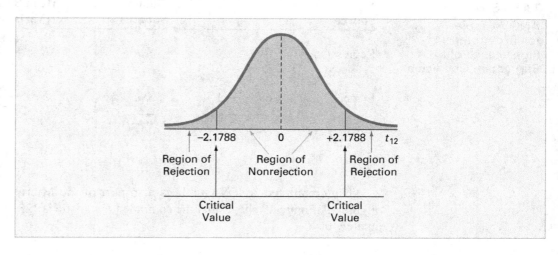

F Test for the Slope

As an alternative to the t test, you can use an F test to determine whether the slope in simple linear regression is statistically significant. You may have previously used the F distribution to test the ratio of two variances. Equation (17) defines the F test for the slope as the ratio of the variance that is due to the regression (MSR) divided by the error variance ($MSE = S_{YX}^2$).

TESTING A HYPOTHESIS FOR A POPULATION SLOPE, β_1, USING THE F TEST

The F statistic is equal to the regression mean square (MSR) divided by the error mean square (MSE).

$$F = \frac{MSR}{MSE} \qquad (17)$$

where

$$MSR = \frac{SSR}{k}$$

$$MSE = \frac{SSE}{n-k-1}$$

k = number of independent variables in the regression model

The test statistic F follows an F distribution with k and $n-k-1$ degrees of freedom.

Using a level of significance α, the decision rule is

Reject H_0 if $F > F_U$;

otherwise, do not reject H_0.

Table 6 organizes the complete set of results into an ANOVA table.

TABLE 6
ANOVA Table for Testing the Significance of a Regression Coefficient

Source	df	Sum of Squares	Mean Square (Variance)	F
Regression	k	SSR	$MSR = \dfrac{SSR}{k}$	$F = \dfrac{MSR}{MSE}$
Error	$n-k-1$	SSE	$MSE = \dfrac{SSE}{n-k-1}$	
Total	$n-1$	SST		

The completed ANOVA table is also part of the Microsoft Excel results shown in Figure 19. Figure 19 shows that the computed F statistic is 12335 and the p-value is approximately 0.

FIGURE 19
Microsoft Excel F test for the Sunflowers Apparel data

	A	B	C	D	E	F
10	ANOVA					
11		df	SS	MS	F	Significance F
12	Regression	1	105.7476	105.7476	113.2335	0.0000
13	Residual	12	11.2067	0.9339		
14	Total	13	116.9543			

See Section E1 to create the worksheet that contains this area.

Using a level of significance of 0.05, from the table of critical values of F the critical value of the F distribution, with 1 and 12 degrees of freedom, is 4.75 (see Figure 20). Because $F = 113.2335 > 4.75$ or because the p-value $= 0.0000 < 0.05$, you reject H_0 and conclude that the size of the store is significantly related to annual sales. Because the F test in Equation 17 is equivalent to the t test, you reach the same conclusion.

FIGURE 20

Regions of rejection and nonrejection when testing for significance of slope at the 0.05 level of significance, with 1 and 12 degrees of freedom

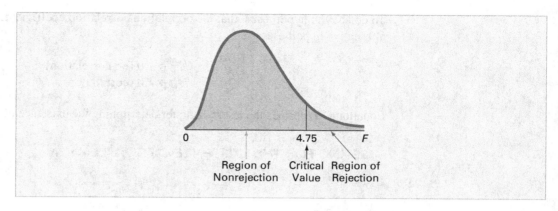

Confidence Interval Estimate of the Slope (β_1)

As an alternative to testing for the existence of a linear relationship between the variables, you can construct a confidence interval estimate of β_1 and determine whether the hypothesized value ($\beta_1 = 0$) is included in the interval. Equation (18) defines the confidence interval estimate of β_1.

CONFIDENCE INTERVAL ESTIMATE OF THE SLOPE, β_1

The confidence interval estimate for the slope can be constructed by taking the sample slope, b_1, and adding and subtracting the critical t value multiplied by the standard error of the slope.

$$b_1 \pm t_{n-2}S_{b_1} \tag{18}$$

From the Microsoft Excel results of Figure 17,

$$b_1 = 1.6699 \quad n = 14 \quad S_{b_1} = 0.1569$$

To construct a 95% confidence interval estimate, $\alpha/2 = 0.025$, and from the table of critical values of t, $t_{12} = 2.1788$. Thus,

$$b_1 \pm t_{n-2}S_{b_1} = 1.6699 \pm (2.1788)(0.1569)$$

$$= 1.6699 \pm 0.3419$$

$$1.3280 \le \beta_1 \le 2.0118$$

Therefore, you estimate with 95% confidence that the population slope is between 1.3280 and 2.0118. Because these values are above 0, you conclude that there is a significant linear relationship between annual sales and the size of the store. Had the interval included 0, you would have concluded that no significant relationship exists between the variables. The confidence interval indicates that for each increase of 1,000 square feet, mean annual sales are estimated to increase by at least $1,328,000 but no more than $2,011,800.

t Test for the Correlation Coefficient

You may have seen previously how the strength of the relationship between two numerical variables can be measured using the **correlation coefficient**, r. You can use the correlation coefficient to determine whether there is a statistically significant linear relationship between X and Y.

To do so, you hypothesize that the population correlation coefficient, ρ, is 0. Thus, the null and alternative hypotheses are

$$H_0: \rho = 0 \text{ (no correlation)}$$
$$H_1: \rho \neq 0 \text{ (correlation)}$$

Equation (19) defines the test statistic for determining the existence of a significant correlation.

TESTING FOR THE EXISTENCE OF CORRELATION

$$t = \frac{r - \rho}{\sqrt{\dfrac{1 - r^2}{n - 2}}} \tag{19}$$

where

$$r = +\sqrt{r^2} \text{ if } b_1 > 0$$
$$r = -\sqrt{r^2} \text{ if } b_1 < 0$$

The test statistic t follows a t distribution with $n - 2$ degrees of freedom.

In the Sunflowers Apparel problem, $r^2 = 0.9042$ and $b_1 = +1.6699$ (see Figure 4). Because $b_1 > 0$, the correlation coefficient for annual sales and store size is the positive square root of r^2, that is, $r^2 = +\sqrt{0.9042} = +0.9509$. Testing the null hypothesis that there is no correlation between these two variables results in the following observed t statistic:

$$t = \frac{r - 0}{\sqrt{\dfrac{1 - r^2}{n - 2}}}$$

$$= \frac{0.9509 - 0}{\sqrt{\dfrac{1 - (0.9509)^2}{14 - 2}}} = 10.6411$$

Using the 0.05 level of significance, because $t = 10.6411 > 2.1788$, you reject the null hypothesis. You conclude that there is evidence of an association between annual sales and store size. This t statistic is equivalent to the t statistic found when testing whether the population slope, β_1, is equal to zero (see Figure 17).

When inferences concerning the population slope were discussed, confidence intervals and tests of hypothesis were used interchangeably. However, developing a confidence interval for the correlation coefficient is more complicated because the shape of the sampling distribution of the statistic r varies for different values of the population correlation coefficient. Methods for developing a confidence interval estimate for the correlation coefficient are presented in reference 4.

PROBLEMS FOR SECTION 7

Learning the Basics

39 You are testing the null hypothesis that there is no linear relationship between two variables, X and Y. From your sample of $n = 10$, you determine that $r = 0.80$.

a. What is the value of the t test statistic?
b. At the $\alpha = 0.05$ level of significance, what are the critical values?
c. Based on your answers to (a) and (b), what statistical decision should you make?

40 You are testing the null hypothesis that there is no relationship between two variables, X and Y. From your sample of $n = 18$, you determine that $b_1 = +4.5$ and $S_{b_1} = 1.5$.

a. What is the value of the t test statistic?

b. At the $\alpha = 0.05$ level of significance, what are the critical values?

c. Based on your answers to (a) and (b), what statistical decision should you make?

d. Construct a 95% confidence interval estimate of the population slope, β_1.

 41 You are testing the null hypothesis that there is no relationship between two variables, X and Y. From your sample of $n = 20$, you determine that $SSR = 60$ and $SSE = 40$.

a. What is the value of the F test statistic?

b. At the $\alpha = 0.05$ level of significance, what is the critical value?

c. Based on your answers to (a) and (b), what statistical decision should you make?

d. Compute the correlation coefficient by first computing r^2 and assuming that b_1 is negative.

e. At the 0.05 level of significance, is there a significant correlation between X and Y?

Applying the Concepts

 42 In Problem 4, the marketing manager used shelf space for pet food to predict weekly sales. The data are stored in the file petfood.xls. From the results of that problem, $b_1 = 7.4$ and $S_{b_1} = 1.59$.

a. At the 0.05 level of significance, is there evidence of a linear relationship between shelf space and sales?

b. Construct a 95% confidence interval estimate of the population slope, β_1.

43 In Problem 5, you used reported magazine newsstand sales to predict audited sales. The data are stored in the file circulation.xls. Using the results of that problem, $b_1 = 0.5719$ and $S_{b_1} = 0.0668$.

a. At the 0.05 level of significance, is there evidence of a linear relationship between reported sales and audited sales?

b. Construct a 95% confidence interval estimate of the population slope, β_1.

44 In Problem 6, the owner of a moving company wanted to predict labor hours, based on the number of cubic feet moved. The data are stored in the file moving.xls. Using the results of that problem,

a. at the 0.05 level of significance, is there evidence of a linear relationship between the number of cubic feet moved and labor hours?

b. construct a 95% confidence interval estimate of the population slope, β_1.

 45 In Problem 7, you used the weight of mail to predict the number of orders received. The data are stored in the file mail.xls. Using the results of that problem,

a. at the 0.05 level of significance, is there evidence of a linear relationship between the weight of mail and the number of orders received?

b. construct a 95% confidence interval estimate of the population slope, β_1.

46 In Problem 8, you used annual revenues to predict the value of a baseball franchise. The data are stored in the file bbrevenue.xls. Using the results of that problem,

a. at the 0.05 level of significance, is there evidence of a linear relationship between annual revenue and franchise value?

b. construct a 95% confidence interval estimate of the population slope, β_1.

47 In Problem 9, an agent for a real estate company wanted to predict the monthly rent for apartments, based on the size of the apartment. The data are stored in the file rent.xls. Using the results of that problem,

a. at the 0.05 level of significance, is there evidence of a linear relationship between the size of the apartment and the monthly rent?

b. construct a 95% confidence interval estimate of the population slope, β_1.

48 In Problem 10, you used hardness to predict the tensile strength of die-cast aluminum. The data are stored in the file hardness.xls. Using the results of that problem,

a. at the 0.05 level of significance, is there evidence of a linear relationship between hardness and tensile strength?

b. construct a 95% confidence interval estimate of the population slope, β_1.

49 The volatility of a stock is often measured by its beta value. You can estimate the beta value of a stock by developing a simple linear regression model, using the percentage weekly change in the stock as the dependent variable and the percentage weekly change in a market index as the independent variable. The S&P 500 Index is a common index to use. For example, if you wanted to estimate the beta for IBM, you could use the following model, which is sometimes referred to as a *market model*:

$$(\% \text{ weekly change in IBM}) = \beta_0 + \beta_1 (\% \text{ weekly change in S \& P 500 index}) + \varepsilon$$

The least-squares regression estimate of the slope b_1 is the estimate of the beta value for IBM. A stock with a beta value of 1.0 tends to move the same as the overall market. A stock with a beta value of 1.5 tends to move 50% more than the overall market, and a stock with a beta value of 0.6 tends to move only 60% as much as the overall market. Stocks with negative beta values tend to move in a direction opposite that of the overall market. The following table gives some beta values for some widely held stocks:

Company	Ticker Symbol	Beta
AT&T	T	0.80
IBM	IBM	1.20
Disney Company	DIS	1.40
Alcoa	AA	2.26
LSI Logic	LSI	3.61

Source: Extracted from **finance.yahoo.com**, *May 31, 2006.*

a. For each of the five companies, interpret the beta value.
b. How can investors use the beta value as a guide for investing?

50 Index funds are mutual funds that try to mimic the movement of leading indexes, such as the S&P 500 Index, the NASDAQ 100 Index, or the Russell 2000 Index. The beta values for these funds (as described in Problem 49) are therefore approximately 1.0. The estimated market models for these funds are approximately

(% weekly change in index fund) = 0.0 + 1.0 (% weekly change in the index)

Leveraged index funds are designed to magnify the movement of major indexes. An article in *Mutual Funds* (L. O'Shaughnessy, "Reach for Higher Returns," *Mutual Funds*, July 1999, pp. 44–49) described some of the risks and rewards associated with these funds and gave details on some of the most popular leveraged funds, including those in the following table:

Name (Ticker Symbol)	Fund Description
Potomac Small Cap Plus (POSCX)	125% of Russell 2000 Index
Rydex "Inv" Nova (RYNVX)	150% of the S&P 500 Index
ProFund UltraOTC "Inv" (UOPIX)	Double (200%) the NASDAQ 100 Index

Thus, estimated market models for these funds are approximately

(% weekly change in POSCX) = 0.0 + 1.25 (% weekly change in the Russell 2000 Index)

(% weekly change in RYNVX) = 0.0 + 1.50 (% weekly change in the S&P 500 Index)

(% weekly change in UOPIX fund) = 0.0 + 2.0 (% weekly change in the NASDAQ 100 Index)

Thus, if the Russell 2000 Index gains 10% over a period of time, the leveraged mutual fund POSCX gains approximately

12.5%. On the downside, if the same index loses 20%, POSCX loses approximately 25%.

a. Consider the leveraged mutual fund ProFund UltraOTC "Inv" (UOPIX), whose description is 200% of the performance of the S&P 500 Index. What is its approximate market model?
b. If the NASDAQ gains 30% in a year, what return do you expect UOPIX to have?
c. If the NASDAQ loses 35% in a year, what return do you expect UOPIX to have?
d. What type of investors should be attracted to leveraged funds? What type of investors should stay away from these funds?

51 The data in the file coffeedrink.xls represent the calories and fat (in grams) of 16-ounce iced coffee drinks at Dunkin' Donuts and Starbucks:

Product	Calories	Fat
Dunkin' Donuts Iced Mocha Swirl latte (whole milk)	240	8.0
Starbucks Coffee Frappuccino blended coffee	260	3.5
Dunkin' Donuts Coffee Coolatta (cream)	350	22.0
Starbucks Iced Coffee Mocha Espresso (whole milk and whipped cream)	350	20.0
Starbucks Mocha Frappuccino blended coffee (whipped cream)	420	16.0
Starbucks Chocolate Brownie Frappuccino blended coffee (whipped cream)	510	22.0
Starbucks Chocolate Frappuccino Blended Crème (whipped cream)	530	19.0

Source: Extracted from "Coffee as Candy at Dunkin' Donuts and Starbucks," Consumer Reports, *June 2004, p. 9.*

a. Compute and interpret the coefficient of correlation, r.
b. At the 0.05 level of significance, is there a significant linear relationship between the calories and fat?

52 There are several methods for calculating fuel economy. The following table (contained in the file mileage.xls) indicates the mileage as calculated by owners and by current government standards:

Vehicle	Owner	Government Standards
2005 Ford F-150	14.3	16.8
2005 Chevrolet Silverado	15.0	17.8
2002 Honda Accord LX	27.8	26.2
2002 Honda Civic	27.9	34.2
2004 Honda Civic Hybrid	48.8	47.6
2002 Ford Explorer	16.8	18.3
2005 Toyota Camry	23.7	28.5
2003 Toyota Corolla	32.8	33.1
2005 Toyota Prius	37.3	56.0

a. Compute and interpret the coefficient of correlation, *r*.

b. At the 0.05 level of significance, is there a significant linear relationship between the mileage as calculated by owners and by current government standards?

53 College basketball is big business, with coaches' salaries, revenues, and expenses in millions of dollars. The data in the file colleges-basketball.xls represent the coaches' salaries and revenues for college basketball at selected schools in a recent year (extracted from R. Adams, "Pay for Playoffs," *The Wall Street Journal*, March 11–12, 2006, pp. P1, P8).

a. Compute and interpret the coefficient of correlation, *r*.

b. At the 0.05 level of significance, is there a significant linear relationship between a coach's salary and revenue?

54 College football players trying out for the NFL are given the Wonderlic standardized intelligence test. The data in the file wonderlic.xls represent the average Wonderlic scores of football players trying out for the NFL and the graduation rates for football players at selected schools (extracted from S. Walker, "The NFL's Smartest Team," *The Wall Street Journal*, September 30, 2005, pp. W1, W10).

a. Compute and interpret the coefficient of correlation, *r*.

b. At the 0.05 level of significance, is there a significant linear relationship between the average Wonderlic score of football players trying out for the NFL and the graduation rates for football players at selected schools?

c. What conclusions can you reach about the relationship between the average Wonderlic score of football players trying out for the NFL and the graduation rates for football players at selected schools?

8 ESTIMATION OF MEAN VALUES AND PREDICTION OF INDIVIDUAL VALUES

This section presents methods of making inferences about the mean of *Y* and predicting individual values of *Y*.

The Confidence Interval Estimate

In Example 2, you used the prediction line to predict the value of *Y* for a given *X*. The mean annual sales for stores with 4,000 square feet was predicted to be 7.644 millions of dollars ($7,644,000). This estimate, however, is a *point estimate* of the population mean. You may have previously studied the concept of the confidence interval as an estimate of the population mean. In a similar fashion, Equation (20) defines the **confidence interval estimate for the mean response** for a given *X*.

CONFIDENCE INTERVAL ESTIMATE FOR THE MEAN OF *Y*

$$\hat{Y}_i \pm t_{n-2} S_{YX} \sqrt{h_i}$$

$$\hat{Y}_i - t_{n-2} S_{YX} \sqrt{h_i} \leq \mu_{Y|X=X_i} \leq \hat{Y}_i + t_{n-2} S_{YX} \sqrt{h_i} \qquad (20)$$

$$h_i = \frac{1}{n} + \frac{(X_i - \overline{X})^2}{SSX}$$

where

$$\hat{Y}_i = \text{predicted value of } Y; \ \hat{Y}_i = b_0 + b_1 X_i$$

$$S_{YX} = \text{standard error of the estimate}$$

$$n = \text{sample size}$$

$$X_i = \text{given value of } X$$

$$\mu_{Y|X=X_i} = \text{mean value of } Y \text{ when } X = X_i$$

$$SSX = \sum_{i=1}^{n} (X_i - \overline{X})^2$$

The width of the confidence interval in Equation (20) depends on several factors. For a given level of confidence, increased variation around the prediction line, as measured by the standard error of the estimate, results in a wider interval. However, as you would expect, increased sample size reduces the width of the interval. In addition, the width of the interval also varies at different values of X. When you predict Y for values of X close to $\overline{X}$, the interval is narrower than for predictions for X values more distant from $\overline{X}$.

In the Sunflowers Apparel example, suppose you want to construct a 95% confidence interval estimate of the mean annual sales for the entire population of stores that contain 4,000 square feet ($X = 4$). Using the simple linear regression equation,

$$\hat{Y}_i = 0.9645 + 1.6699 X_i$$

$$= 0.9645 + 1.6699(4) = 7.6439 \text{ (millions of dollars)}$$

Also, given the following:

$$\overline{X} = 2.9214 \qquad S_{YX} = 0.9664$$

$$SSX = \sum_{i=1}^{n} (X_i - \overline{X})^2 = 37.9236$$

From the table of critical values of t, $t_{12} = 2.1788$. Thus,

$$\hat{Y}_i \pm t_{n-2} S_{YX} \sqrt{h_i}$$

where

$$h_i = \frac{1}{n} + \frac{(X_i - \overline{X})^2}{SSX}$$

so that

$$\hat{Y}_i \pm t_{n-2} S_{YX} \sqrt{\frac{1}{n} + \frac{(X_i - \overline{X})^2}{SSX}}$$

$$= 7.6439 \pm (2.1788)(0.9664) \sqrt{\frac{1}{14} + \frac{(4 - 2.9214)^2}{37.9236}}$$

$$= 7.6439 \pm 0.6728$$

so

$$6.9711 \le \mu_{Y|X=4} \le 8.3167$$

Therefore, the 95% confidence interval estimate is that the mean annual sales are between $6,971,100 and $8,316,700 for the population of stores with 4,000 square feet.

The Prediction Interval

In addition to the need for a confidence interval estimate for the mean value, you often want to predict the response for an individual value. Although the form of the prediction interval is similar to that of the confidence interval estimate of Equation (20), the prediction interval is predicting an individual value, not estimating a parameter. Equation (21) defines the **prediction interval for an individual response, Y,** at a particular value, X_i, denoted by $Y_{X=X_i}$.

PREDICTION INTERVAL FOR AN INDIVIDUAL RESPONSE, Y

$$\hat{Y}_i \pm t_{n-2} S_{YX} \sqrt{1 + h_i} \tag{21}$$

$$\hat{Y}_i - t_{n-2} S_{YX} \sqrt{1 + h_i} \leq Y_{X=X_i} \leq \hat{Y}_i + t_{n-2} S_{YX} \sqrt{1 + h_i}$$

where h_i, $\hat{Y}_i$, S_{YX}, n, and X_i are defined as in Equation (20) and $Y_{X=X_i}$ is a future value of Y when $X = X_i$.

To construct a 95% prediction interval of the annual sales for an individual store that contains 4,000 square feet ($X = 4$), you first compute $\hat{Y}_i$. Using the prediction line:

$$\hat{Y}_i = 0.9645 + 1.6699 X_i$$
$$= 0.9645 + 1.6699(4)$$
$$= 7.6439 \text{ (millions of dollars)}$$

Also, given the following:

$$\bar{X} = 2.9214 \quad S_{YX} = 0.9664$$

$$SSX = \sum_{i=1}^{n} (X_i - \bar{X})^2 = 37.9236$$

From the table of critical values of t, $t_{12} = 2.1788$. Thus,

$$\hat{Y}_i \pm t_{n-2} S_{YX} \sqrt{1 + h_i}$$

where

$$h_i = \frac{1}{n} + \frac{(X_i - \bar{X})^2}{\sum_{i=1}^{n} (X_i - \bar{X})^2}$$

so that

$$\hat{Y}_i \pm t_{n-2} S_{YX} \sqrt{1 + \frac{1}{n} + \frac{(X_i - \bar{X})^2}{SSX}}$$

$$= 7.6439 \pm (2.1788)(0.9664) \sqrt{1 + \frac{1}{14} + \frac{(4 - 2.9214)^2}{37.9236}}$$

$$= 7.6439 \pm 2.2104$$

so

$$5.4335 \leq Y_{X=4} \leq 9.8543$$

Therefore, with 95% confidence, you predict that the annual sales for an individual store with 4,000 square feet is between $5,433,500 and $9,854,300.

Figure 21 is a Microsoft Excel worksheet that illustrates the confidence interval estimate and the prediction interval for the Sunflowers Apparel problem. If you compare the results of the confidence interval estimate and the prediction interval, you see that the width of the prediction interval for an individual store is much wider than the confidence interval estimate for the mean. Remember that there is much more variation in predicting an individual value than in estimating a mean value.

FIGURE 21

Microsoft Excel confidence interval estimate and prediction interval for the Sunflowers Apparel data

See Section E5 to create this.

	A	B	
1	Site Selection Analysis		
2			
3	Data		
4	X Value	4	
5	Confidence Level	95%	
6			
7	Intermediate Calculations		
8	Sample Size	14	=DataCopy!F2
9	Degrees of Freedom	12	=B8 - 2
10	t Value	2.1788	=TINV(1 - B5, B9)
11	Sample Mean	2.9214	=DataCopy!F3
12	Sum of Squared Difference	37.9236	=DataCopy!F4
13	Standard Error of the Estimate	0.9664	from regression worksheet cell B7
14	h Statistic	0.1021	=1/B8 + (B4 - B11)^2/B12
15	Predicted Y (YHat)	7.6439	=DataCopy!F5
16			
17	For Average Y		
18	Interval Half Width	0.6728	=B10 * B13 * SQRT(B14)
19	Confidence Interval Lower Limit	6.9711	=B15 - B18
20	Confidence Interval Upper Limit	8.3167	=B15 + B18
21			
22	For Individual Response Y		
23	Interval Half Width	2.2104	=B10 * B13 * SQRT(1 + B14)
24	Prediction Interval Lower Limit	5.4335	=B15 - B23
25	Prediction Interval Upper Limit	9.8544	=B15 + B23

PROBLEMS FOR SECTION 8

Learning the Basics

55 Based on a sample of $n = 20$, the least-squares method was used to develop the following prediction line: $\hat{Y}_i = 5 + 3X_i$. In addition,

$$S_{YX} = 1.0 \quad \bar{X} = 2 \quad \sum_{i=1}^{n}(X_i - \bar{X})^2 = 20$$

a. Construct a 95% confidence interval estimate of the population mean response for $X = 2$.

b. Construct a 95% prediction interval of an individual response for $X = 2$.

56 Based on a sample of $n = 20$, the least-squares method was used to develop the following prediction line: $\hat{Y}_i = 5 + 3X_i$. In addition,

$$S_{YX} = 1.0 \quad \bar{X} = 2 \quad \sum_{i=1}^{n}(X_i - \bar{X})^2 = 20$$

a. Construct a 95% confidence interval estimate of the population mean response for $X = 4$.

b. Construct a 95% prediction interval of an individual response for $X = 4$.

c. Compare the results of (a) and (b) with those of Problem 55 (a) and (b). Which interval is wider? Why?

Applying the Concepts

57 In Problem 5, you used reported sales to predict audited sales of magazines. The data are stored in the file `circulation.xls`. For these data $S_{YX} = 42.186$ and $h_i = 0.108$ when $X = 400$.

a. Construct a 95% confidence interval estimate of the mean audited sales for magazines that report newsstand sales of 400,000.

b. Construct a 95% prediction interval of the audited sales for an individual magazine that reports newsstand sales of 400,000.

c. Explain the difference in the results in (a) and (b).

58 In Problem 4, the marketing manager used shelf space for pet food to predict weekly sales. The data are stored in the file `petfood.xls`. For these data $S_{YX} = 30.81$ and $h_i = 0.1373$ when $X = 8$.

a. Construct a 95% confidence interval estimate of the mean weekly sales for all stores that have 8 feet of shelf space for pet food.

b. Construct a 95% prediction interval of the weekly sales of an individual store that has 8 feet of shelf space for pet food.

c. Explain the difference in the results in (a) and (b).

59 In Problem 7, you used the weight of mail to predict the number of orders received. The data are stored in the file mail.xls.

a. Construct a 95% confidence interval estimate of the mean number of orders received for all packages with a weight of 500 pounds.

b. Construct a 95% prediction interval of the number of orders received for an individual package with a weight of 500 pounds.

c. Explain the difference in the results in (a) and (b).

60 In Problem 6, the owner of a moving company wanted to predict labor hours based on the number of cubic feet moved. The data are stored in the file moving.xls.

a. Construct a 95% confidence interval estimate of the mean labor hours for all moves of 500 cubic feet.

b. Construct a 95% prediction interval of the labor hours of an individual move that has 500 cubic feet.

c. Explain the difference in the results in (a) and (b).

61 In Problem 9, an agent for a real estate company wanted to predict the monthly rent for apartments, based on the size of the apartment. The data are stored in the file rent.xls.

a. Construct a 95% confidence interval estimate of the mean monthly rental for all apartments that are 1,000 square feet in size.

b. Construct a 95% prediction interval of the monthly rental of an individual apartment that is 1,000 square feet in size.

c. Explain the difference in the results in (a) and (b).

62 In Problem 8, you predicted the value of a baseball franchise, based on current revenue. The data are stored in the file bbrevenue.xls.

a. Construct a 95% confidence interval estimate of the mean value of all baseball franchises that generate $150 million of annual revenue.

b. Construct a 95% prediction interval of the value of an individual baseball franchise that generates $150 million of annual revenue.

c. Explain the difference in the results in (a) and (b).

63 In Problem 10, you used hardness to predict the tensile strength of die-cast aluminum. The data are stored in the file hardness.xls.

a. Construct a 95% confidence interval estimate of the mean tensile strength for all specimens with a hardness of 30 Rockwell E units.

b. Construct a 95% prediction interval of the tensile strength for an individual specimen that has a hardness of 30 Rockwell E units.

c. Explain the difference in the results in (a) and (b).

9 PITFALLS IN REGRESSION AND ETHICAL ISSUES

Some of the pitfalls involved in using regression analysis are as follows:

- Lacking an awareness of the assumptions of least-squares regression
- Not knowing how to evaluate the assumptions of least-squares regression
- Not knowing what the alternatives to least-squares regression are if a particular assumption is violated
- Using a regression model without knowledge of the subject matter
- Extrapolating outside the relevant range
- Concluding that a significant relationship identified in an observational study is due to a cause-and-effect relationship

The widespread availability of spreadsheet and statistical software has made regression analysis much more feasible. However, for many users, this enhanced availability of software has not been accompanied by an understanding of how to use regression analysis properly. Someone who is not familiar with either the assumptions of regression or how to evaluate the assumptions cannot be expected to know what the alternatives to least-squares regression are if a particular assumption is violated.

The data in Table 7 (stored in the file anscombe.xls) illustrate the importance of using scatter plots and residual analysis to go beyond the basic number crunching of computing the Y intercept, the slope, and r^2.

TABLE 7

Four Sets of Artificial Data

Data Set A		Data Set B		Data Set C		Data Set D	
X_i	Y_i	X_i	Y_i	X_i	Y_i	X_i	Y_i
10	8.04	10	9.14	10	7.46	8	6.58
14	9.96	14	8.10	14	8.84	8	5.76
5	5.68	5	4.74	5	5.73	8	7.71
8	6.95	8	8.14	8	6.77	8	8.84
9	8.81	9	8.77	9	7.11	8	8.47
12	10.84	12	9.13	12	8.15	8	7.04
4	4.26	4	3.10	4	5.39	8	5.25
7	4.82	7	7.26	7	6.42	19	12.50
11	8.33	11	9.26	11	7.81	8	5.56
13	7.58	13	8.74	13	12.74	8	7.91
6	7.24	6	6.13	6	6.08	8	6.89

Source: Extracted from F. J. Anscombe, "Graphs in Statistical Analysis," American Statistician, *Vol. 27 (1973), pp. 17–21.*

Anscombe (reference 1) showed that all four data sets given in Table 7 have the following identical results:

$$\hat{Y}_i = 3.0 + 0.5X_i$$

$$S_{YX} = 1.237$$

$$S_{b_1} = 0.118$$

$$r^2 = 0.667$$

$$SSR = \text{Explained variation} = \sum_{i=1}^{n}(\hat{Y}_i - \bar{Y})^2 = 27.51$$

$$SSE = \text{Unxplained variation} = \sum_{i=1}^{n}(Y_i - \hat{Y}_i)^2 = 13.76$$

$$SST = \text{Total variation} = \sum_{i=1}^{n}(Y_i - \bar{Y})^2 = 41.27$$

Thus, with respect to these statistics associated with a simple linear regression analysis, the four data sets are identical. Were you to stop the analysis at this point, you would fail to observe the important differences among the four data sets. By examining the scatter plots for the four data sets in Figure 22, and their residual plots in Figure 23, you can clearly see that each of the four data sets has a different relationship between X and Y.

From the scatter plots of Figure 22 and the residual plots of Figure 23, you see how different the data sets are. The only data set that seems to follow an approximate straight line is data set A. The residual plot for data set A does not show any obvious patterns or outlying residuals. This is certainly not true for data sets B, C, and D. The scatter plot for data set B shows that a quadratic regression model is more appropriate. This conclusion is reinforced by the residual plot for data set B. The scatter plot and the residual plot for data set C clearly show an outlying observation. If this is the case, you may want to remove the outlier and reestimate the regression model (see reference 4). Similarly, the scatter plot for data set D represents the situation in which the model is heavily dependent on the outcome of a single response ($X_8 = 19$ and $Y_8 = 12.50$). You would have to cautiously evaluate any regression model because its regression coefficients are heavily dependent on a single observation.

FIGURE 22

Scatter plots for four data sets

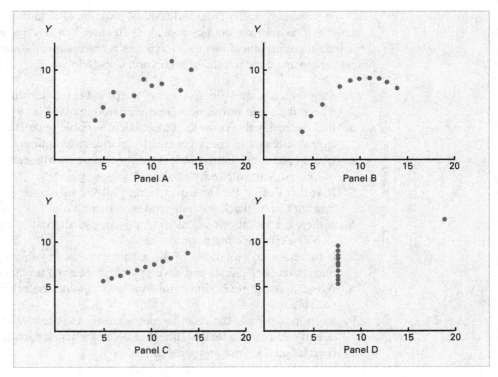

FIGURE 23

Residual plots for four data sets

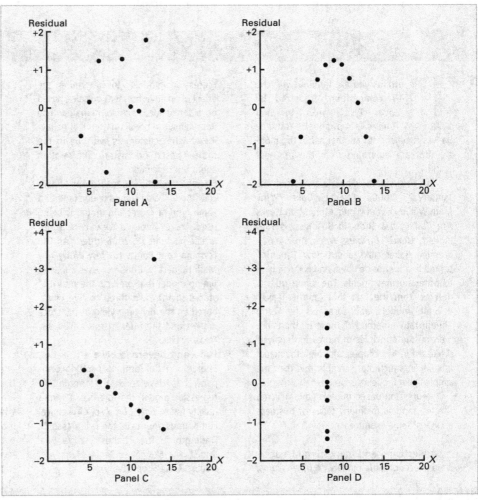

In summary, scatter plots and residual plots are of vital importance to a complete regression analysis. The information they provide is so basic to a credible analysis that you should always include these graphical methods as part of a regression analysis. Thus, a strategy that you can use to help avoid the pitfalls of regression is as follows:

1. Start with a scatter plot to observe the possible relationship between X and Y.
2. Check the assumptions of regression before moving on to using the results of the model.
3. Plot the residuals versus the independent variable to determine whether the linear model is appropriate and to check the equal-variance assumption.
4. Use a histogram, stem-and-leaf display, box-and-whisker plot, or normal probability plot of the residuals to check the normality assumption.
5. If you collected the data over time, plot the residuals versus time and use the Durbin-Watson test to check the independence assumption.
6. If there are violations of the assumptions, use alternative methods to least-squares regression or alternative least-squares models.
7. If there are no violations of the assumptions, carry out tests for the significance of the regression coefficients and develop confidence and prediction intervals.
8. Avoid making predictions and forecasts outside the relevant range of the independent variable.
9. Keep in mind that the relationships identified in observational studies may or may not be due to cause-and-effect relationships. Remember that while causation implies correlation, correlation does not imply causation.

America's Top Models

From the Author's Desktop

Perhaps you are familiar with the TV competition organized by model Tyra Banks to find "America's top model." You may be less familiar with another set of top models that are emerging from the business world.

In a *Business Week* article from its January 23, 2006, edition (S. Baker, "Why Math Will Rock Your World: More Math Geeks Are Calling the Shots in Business. Is Your Industry Next?" *Business Week*, pp. 54–62), Stephen Baker talks about how "quants" turned finance upside down and is moving on to other business fields. The name *quants* derives from the fact that "math geeks" develop models and forecasts by using "quantitative methods." These methods are built on the principles of regression analysis discussed in this chapter, although the actual models are much more complicated than the simple linear models discussed in this chapter.

Regression-based models have become the top models for many types of business analyses. Some examples include

- **Advertising and marketing** Managers use econometric models (in other words, regression models) to determine the effect of an advertisement on sales, based on a set of factors. Also, managers use data mining to predict patterns of behavior of what customers will buy in the future, based on historic information about the consumer.
- **Finance** Any time you read about a financial "model," you should understand that some type of regression model is being used. For example, a *New York Times* article on June 18, 2006, titled "An Old Formula That Points to New Worry" by Mark Hulbert (p. BU8) discusses a market timing model that predicts the return of stocks in the next three to five years, based on the dividend yield of the stock market and the interest rate of 90-day Treasury bills.
- **Food and beverage** Believe it or not, Enologix, a California consulting company, has developed a "formula" (a regression model) that predicts a wine's quality index, based on a set of chemical compounds found in the wine (see D. Darlington, "The Chemistry of a 90+ Wine," *The New York Times Magazine*, August 7, 2005, pp. 36–39).

- **Publishing** A study of the effect of price changes at Amazon.com and BN.com on sales (again, regression analysis) found that a 1% price change at BN.com pushed sales down 4%, but it pushed sales down only 0.5% at Amazon.com. (You can download the paper at **http://gsbadg. uchicago.edu/vitae.htm**.)
- **Transportation** Farecast.com uses data mining and predictive technologies to objectively predict airfare pricing (see D. Darlin, "Airfares Made Easy (Or Easier)," *The New York Times*, July 1, 2006, pp. C1, C6).
- **Real estate** Zillow.com uses information about the features contained in a home and its location to develop estimates about the market value of the home, using a "formula" built with a proprietary algorithm.

In the article, Baker stated that statistics and probability will become core skills for businesspeople and consumers. Those who are successful will know how to use statistics, whether they are building financial models or making marketing plans. He also strongly endorsed the need for everyone in business to have knowledge of Microsoft Excel to be able to produce statistical analysis and reports.

SUMMARY

As you can see from the chapter roadmap in Figure 24, this chapter develops the simple linear regression model and discusses the assumptions and how to evaluate them. Once you are assured that the model is appropriate, you can predict values by using the prediction line and test for the significance of the slope.

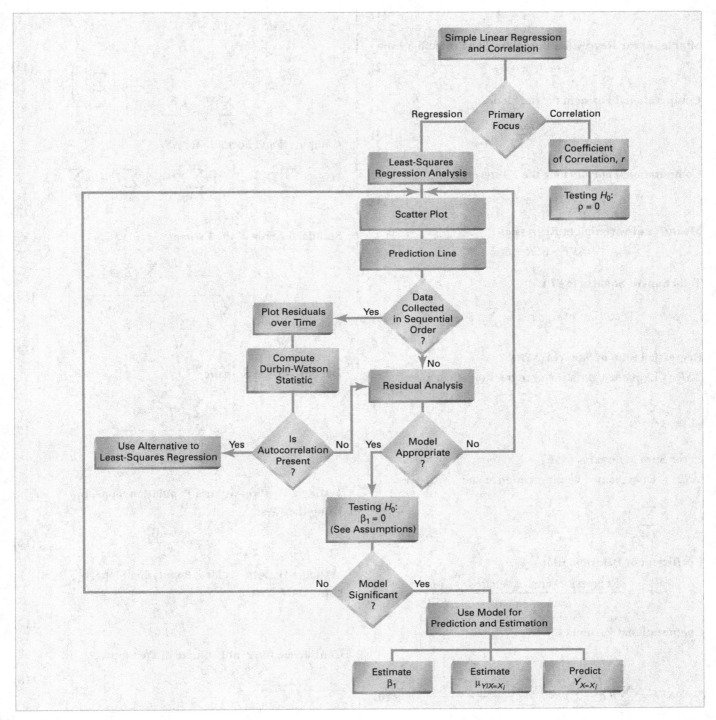

FIGURE 24 Roadmap for simple linear regression

You have learned how the director of planning for a chain of clothing stores can use regression analysis to investigate the relationship between the size of a store and its annual sales. You have used this analysis to make better decisions when selecting new sites for stores as well as to forecast sales for existing stores.

KEY EQUATIONS

Simple Linear Regression Model

$$Y_i = \beta_0 + \beta_1 X_i + \varepsilon_i \tag{1}$$

Simple Linear Regression Equation: The Prediction Line

$$\hat{Y}_i = b_0 + b_1 X_i \tag{2}$$

Computational Formula for the Slope, b_1

$$b_1 = \frac{SSXY}{SSX} \tag{3}$$

Computational Formula for the Y Intercept, b_0

$$b_0 = \bar{Y} - b_1 \bar{X} \tag{4}$$

Measures of Variation in Regression

$$SST = SSR + SSE \tag{5}$$

Total Sum of Squares (SST)

$$SST = \text{Total sum of squares} = \sum_{i=1}^{n}(Y_i - \bar{Y})^2 \tag{6}$$

Regression Sum of Squares (SSR)

SSR = Explained variation or regression of squares

$$= \sum_{i=1}^{n}(\hat{Y}_i - \bar{Y})^2 \tag{7}$$

Error Sum of Squares (SSE)

SSE = Unexplained variation or error sum of squares

$$= \sum_{i=1}^{n}(Y_i - \hat{Y}_i)^2 \tag{8}$$

Coefficient of Determination

$$r^2 = \frac{\text{Regression sum of squares}}{\text{Total sum of squares}} = \frac{SSR}{SST} \tag{9}$$

Computational Formula for SST

$$SST = \sum_{i=1}^{n}(Y_i - \bar{Y})^2 = \sum_{i=1}^{n}Y_i^2 - \frac{\left(\sum_{i=1}^{n}Y_i\right)^2}{n} \tag{10}$$

Computational Formula for SSR

$$SSR = \sum_{i=1}^{n}(\hat{Y}_i - \bar{Y})^2$$

$$= b_0\sum_{i=1}^{n}Y_i + b_1\sum_{i=1}^{n}X_iY_i - \frac{\left(\sum_{i=1}^{n}Y_i\right)^2}{n} \tag{11}$$

Computational Formula for SSE

$$SSE = \sum_{i=1}^{n}(Y_i - \hat{Y})^2 = \sum_{i=1}^{n}Y_i^2 - b_0\sum_{i=1}^{n}Y_i - b_1\sum_{i=1}^{n}X_iY_i \tag{12}$$

Standard Error of the Estimate

$$S_{YX} = \sqrt{\frac{SSE}{n-2}} = \sqrt{\frac{\sum_{i=1}^{n}(Y_i - \hat{Y}_i)^2}{n-2}} \tag{13}$$

Residual

$$e_i = Y_i - \hat{Y}_i \tag{14}$$

Durbin-Watson Statistic

$$D = \frac{\sum_{i=2}^{n}(e_i - e_{i-1})^2}{\sum_{i=1}^{n}e_i^2} \tag{15}$$

Testing a Hypothesis for a Population Slope, β_1, Using the t Test

$$t = \frac{b_1 - \beta_1}{S_{b_1}} \tag{16}$$

Testing a Hypothesis for a Population Slope, β_1, Using the F Test

$$F = \frac{MSR}{MSE} \tag{17}$$

Confidence Interval Estimate of the Slope, β_1

$$b_1 \pm t_{n-2}S_{b_1} \tag{18}$$

$$b_1 - t_{n-2}S_{b_1} \leq \beta_1 \leq b_1 + t_{n-2}S_{b_1}$$

Testing for the Existence of Correlation

$$t = \frac{r - \rho}{\sqrt{\dfrac{1 - r^2}{n - 2}}} \qquad (19)$$

Confidence Interval Estimate for the Mean of Y

$$\hat{Y}_i \pm t_{n-2} S_{YX} \sqrt{h_i} \qquad (20)$$

$$\hat{Y}_i - t_{n-2} S_{YX} \sqrt{h_i} \le \mu_{Y|X=X_i} \le \hat{Y}_i + t_{n-2} S_{YX} \sqrt{h_i}$$

Prediction Interval for an Individual Response, Y

$$\hat{Y}_i \pm t_{n-2} S_{YX} \sqrt{1 + h_i} \qquad (21)$$

$$\hat{Y}_i - t_{n-2} S_{YX} \sqrt{1 + h_i} \le Y_{X=X_i} \le \hat{Y}_i + t_{n-2} S_{YX} \sqrt{1 + h_i}$$

KEY TERMS

assumptions of regression
autocorrelation
coefficient of determination
confidence interval estimate for the
    mean response
correlation coefficient
dependent variable
Durbin-Watson statistic
error sum of squares (SSE)
equal variance
explained variation
explanatory variable
homoscedasticity

independence of errors
independent variable
least-squares method
linear relationship
normality
prediction interval for an individual
    response, Y
prediction line
regression analysis
regression coefficient
regression sum of squares (SSR)
relevant range
residual

residual analysis
response variable
scatter diagram
scatter plot
simple linear regression
simple linear regression equation
slope
standard error of the estimate
total sum of squares (SST)
total variation
unexplained variation
Y intercept

CHAPTER REVIEW PROBLEMS

Checking Your Understanding

64 What is the interpretation of the Y intercept and the slope in the simple linear regression equation?

65 What is the interpretation of the coefficient of determination?

66 When is the unexplained variation (that is, error sum of squares) equal to 0?

67 When is the explained variation (that is, regression sum of squares) equal to 0?

68 Why should you always carry out a residual analysis as part of a regression model?

69 What are the assumptions of regression analysis?

70 How do you evaluate the assumptions of regression analysis?

71 When and how do you use the Durbin-Watson statistic?

72 What is the difference between a confidence interval estimate of the mean response, $\mu_{Y|X=X_i}$, and a prediction interval of $Y_{X=X_i}$?

Applying the Concepts

73 Researchers from the Lubin School of Business at Pace University in New York City conducted a study on Internet-supported courses. In one part of the study, four numerical variables were collected on 108 students in an introductory management course that met once a week for an entire semester. One variable collected was *hit consistency*. To measure hit consistency, the researchers did the following: If a student did not visit the Internet site between classes, the student was given a 0 for that time period. If a student visited the Internet site one or more times between classes, the student was given a 1 for that time period. Because there were 13 time periods, a student's score on hit consistency could range from 0 to 13.

The other three variables included the student's course average, the student's cumulative grade point average

(GPA), and the total number of hits the student had on the Internet site supporting the course. The following table gives the correlation coefficient for all pairs of variables. Note that correlations marked with an * are statistically significant, using $\alpha = 0.001$:

Variable	Correlation
Course Average, Cumulative GPA	0.72*
Course Average, Total Hits	0.08
Course Average, Hit Consistency	0.37*
Cumulative GPA, Total Hits	0.12
Cumulative GPA, Hit Consistency	0.32*
Total Hits, Hit Consistency	0.64*

Source: Extracted from D. Baugher, A. Varanelli, and E. Weisbord, "Student Hits in an Internet-Supported Course: How Can Instructors Use Them and What Do They Mean?" Decision Sciences Journal of Innovative Education, Fall 2003, 1(2), pp. 159–179.

a. What conclusions can you reach from this correlation analysis?
b. Are you surprised by the results, or are they consistent with your own observations and experiences?

74 Management of a soft-drink bottling company wants to develop a method for allocating delivery costs to customers. Although one cost clearly relates to travel time within a particular route, another variable cost reflects the time required to unload the cases of soft drink at the delivery point. A sample of 20 deliveries within a territory was selected. The delivery times and the numbers of cases delivered were recorded in the delivery.xls file:

Customer	Number of Cases	Delivery Time (Minutes)	Customer	Number of Cases	Delivery Time (Minutes)
1	52	32.1	11	161	43.0
2	64	34.8	12	184	49.4
3	73	36.2	13	202	57.2
4	85	37.8	14	218	56.8
5	95	37.8	15	243	60.6
6	103	39.7	16	254	61.2
7	116	38.5	17	267	58.2
8	121	41.9	18	275	63.1
9	143	44.2	19	287	65.6
10	157	47.1	20	298	67.3

Develop a regression model to predict delivery time, based on the number of cases delivered.

a. Use the least-squares method to compute the regression coefficients b_0 and b_1.
b. Interpret the meaning of b_0 and b_1 in this problem.
c. Predict the delivery time for 150 cases of soft drink.
d. Should you use the model to predict the delivery time for a customer who is receiving 500 cases of soft drink? Why or why not?

e. Determine the coefficient of determination, r^2, and explain its meaning in this problem.
f. Perform a residual analysis. Is there any evidence of a pattern in the residuals? Explain.
g. At the 0.05 level of significance, is there evidence of a linear relationship between delivery time and the number of cases delivered?
h. Construct a 95% confidence interval estimate of the mean delivery time for 150 cases of soft drink.
i. Construct a 95% prediction interval of the delivery time for a single delivery of 150 cases of soft drink.
j. Construct a 95% confidence interval estimate of the population slope.
k. Explain how the results in (a) through (j) can help allocate delivery costs to customers.

75 A brokerage house wants to predict the number of trade executions per day, using the number of incoming phone calls as a predictor variable. Data were collected over a period of 35 days and are stored in the file trades.xls.
a. Use the least-squares method to compute the regression coefficients b_0 and b_1.
b. Interpret the meaning of b_0 and b_1 in this problem.
c. Predict the number of trades executed for a day in which the number of incoming calls is 2,000.
d. Should you use the model to predict the number of trades executed for a day in which the number of incoming calls is 5,000? Why or why not?
e. Determine the coefficient of determination, r^2, and explain its meaning in this problem.
f. Plot the residuals against the number of incoming calls and also against the days. Is there any evidence of a pattern in the residuals with either of these variables? Explain.
g. Determine the Durbin-Watson statistic for these data.
h. Based on the results of (f) and (g), is there reason to question the validity of the model? Explain.
i. At the 0.05 level of significance, is there evidence of a linear relationship between the volume of trade executions and the number of incoming calls?
j. Construct a 95% confidence interval estimate of the mean number of trades executed for days in which the number of incoming calls is 2,000.
k. Construct a 95% prediction interval of the number of trades executed for a particular day in which the number of incoming calls is 2,000.
l. Construct a 95% confidence interval estimate of the population slope.
m. Based on the results of (a) through (l), do you think the brokerage house should focus on a strategy of increasing the total number of incoming calls or on a strategy that relies on trading by a small number of heavy traders? Explain.

76 You want to develop a model to predict the selling price of homes based on assessed value. A sample of 30 recently sold single-family houses in a small city is selected to study the relationship between selling price (in thousands of dollars) and assessed value (in thousands of dollars). The houses in the city had been reassessed at full value one year prior to the study. The results are in the file house1.xls.

(**Hint:** First, determine which are the independent and dependent variables.)

a. Construct a scatter plot and, assuming a linear relationship, use the least-squares method to compute the regression coefficients b_0 and b_1.
b. Interpret the meaning of the Y intercept, b_0, and the slope, b_1, in this problem.
c. Use the prediction line developed in (a) to predict the selling price for a house whose assessed value is $170,000.
d. Determine the coefficient of determination, r^2, and interpret its meaning in this problem.
e. Perform a residual analysis on your results and determine the adequacy of the fit of the model.
f. At the 0.05 level of significance, is there evidence of a linear relationship between selling price and assessed value?
g. Construct a 95% confidence interval estimate of the mean selling price for houses with an assessed value of $170,000.
h. Construct a 95% prediction interval of the selling price of an individual house with an assessed value of $170,000.
i. Construct a 95% confidence interval estimate of the population slope.

77 You want to develop a model to predict the assessed value of houses, based on heating area. A sample of 15 single-family houses is selected in a city. The assessed value (in thousands of dollars) and the heating area of the houses (in thousands of square feet) are recorded, with the following results, stored in the file house2.xls:

House	Assessed Value ($000)	Heating Area of Dwelling (Thousands of Square Feet)
1	184.4	2.00
2	177.4	1.71
3	175.7	1.45
4	185.9	1.76
5	179.1	1.93
6	170.4	1.20
7	175.8	1.55
8	185.9	1.93
9	178.5	1.59
10	179.2	1.50
11	186.7	1.90
12	179.3	1.39
13	174.5	1.54
14	183.8	1.89
15	176.8	1.59

(**Hint:** First, determine which are the independent and dependent variables.)

a. Construct a scatter plot and, assuming a linear relationship, use the least-squares method to compute the regression coefficients b_0 and b_1.
b. Interpret the meaning of the Y intercept, b_0, and the slope, b_1, in this problem.
c. Use the prediction line developed in (a) to predict the assessed value for a house whose heating area is 1,750 square feet.
d. Determine the coefficient of determination, r^2, and interpret its meaning in this problem.
e. Perform a residual analysis on your results and determine the adequacy of the fit of the model.
f. At the 0.05 level of significance, is there evidence of a linear relationship between assessed value and heating area?
g. Construct a 95% confidence interval estimate of the mean assessed value for houses with a heating area of 1,750 square feet.
h. Construct a 95% prediction interval of the assessed value of an individual house with a heating area of 1,750 square feet.
i. Construct a 95% confidence interval estimate of the population slope.

78 The director of graduate studies at a large college of business would like to predict the grade point average (GPA) of students in an MBA program based on the Graduate Management Admission Test (GMAT) score. A sample of 20 students who had completed 2 years in the program is selected. The results are stored in the file gpigmat.xls:

Observation	GMAT Score	GPA	Observation	GMAT Score	GPA
1	688	3.72	11	567	3.07
2	647	3.44	12	542	2.86
3	652	3.21	13	551	2.91
4	608	3.29	14	573	2.79
5	680	3.91	15	536	3.00
6	617	3.28	16	639	3.55
7	557	3.02	17	619	3.47
8	599	3.13	18	694	3.60
9	616	3.45	19	718	3.88
10	594	3.33	20	759	3.76

(**Hint:** First, determine which are the independent and dependent variables.)

a. Construct a scatter plot and, assuming a linear relationship, use the least-squares method to compute the regression coefficients b_0 and b_1.
b. Interpret the meaning of the Y intercept, b_0, and the slope, b_1, in this problem.
c. Use the prediction line developed in (a) to predict the GPA for a student with a GMAT score of 600.
d. Determine the coefficient of determination, r^2, and interpret its meaning in this problem.
e. Perform a residual analysis on your results and determine the adequacy of the fit of the model.

f. At the 0.05 level of significance, is there evidence of a linear relationship between GMAT score and GPA?

g. Construct a 95% confidence interval estimate of the mean GPA of students with a GMAT score of 600.

h. Construct a 95% prediction interval of the GPA for a particular student with a GMAT score of 600.

i. Construct a 95% confidence interval estimate of the population slope.

79 The manager of the purchasing department of a large banking organization would like to develop a model to predict the amount of time it takes to process invoices. Data are collected from a sample of 30 days, and the number of invoices processed and completion time, in hours, is stored in the file invoice.xls.

(**Hint:** First, determine which are the independent and dependent variables.)

a. Assuming a linear relationship, use the least-squares method to compute the regression coefficients b_0 and b_1.

b. Interpret the meaning of the Y intercept, b_0, and the slope, b_1, in this problem.

c. Use the prediction line developed in (a) to predict the amount of time it would take to process 150 invoices.

d. Determine the coefficient of determination, r^2, and interpret its meaning.

e. Plot the residuals against the number of invoices processed and also against time.

f. Based on the plots in (e), does the model seem appropriate?

g. Compute the Durbin-Watson statistic and, at the 0.05 level of significance, determine whether there is any autocorrelation in the residuals.

h. Based on the results of (e) through (g), what conclusions can you reach concerning the validity of the model?

i. At the 0.05 level of significance, is there evidence of a linear relationship between the amount of time and the number of invoices processed?

j. Construct a 95% confidence interval estimate of the mean amount of time it would take to process 150 invoices.

k. Construct a 95% prediction interval of the amount of time it would take to process 150 invoices on a particular day.

80 On January 28, 1986, the space shuttle *Challenger* exploded, and seven astronauts were killed. Prior to the launch, the predicted atmospheric temperature was for freezing weather at the launch site. Engineers for Morton Thiokol (the manufacturer of the rocket motor) prepared charts to make the case that the launch should not take place due to the cold weather. These arguments were rejected, and the launch tragically took place. Upon investigation after the tragedy, experts agreed that the disaster occurred because of leaky rubber O-rings that did not seal properly due to the cold temperature. Data indicating the atmospheric temperature at the time of 23 previous launches and the O-ring damage index are stored in the file o-ring.xls:

Flight Number	Temperature (°F)	O-Ring Damage Index
1	66	0
2	70	4
3	69	0
5	68	0
6	67	0
7	72	0
8	73	0
9	70	0
41-B	57	4
41-C	63	2
41-D	70	4
41-G	78	0
51-A	67	0
51-B	75	0
51-C	53	11
51-D	67	0
51-F	81	0
51-G	70	0
51-I	67	0
51-J	79	0
61-A	75	4
61-B	76	0
61-C	58	4

Note: Data from flight 4 is omitted due to unknown O-ring condition.

Source: Extracted from Report of the Presidential Commission on the Space Shuttle Challenger Accident, *Washington, DC, 1986, Vol. II (H1–H3) and Vol. IV (664), and* Post Challenger Evaluation of Space Shuttle Risk Assessment and Management, *Washington, DC, 1988, pp. 135–136.*

a. Construct a scatter plot for the seven flights in which there was O-ring damage (O-ring damage index ≠ 0). What conclusions, if any, can you draw about the relationship between atmospheric temperature and O-ring damage?

b. Construct a scatter plot for all 23 flights.

c. Explain any differences in the interpretation of the relationship between atmospheric temperature and O-ring damage in (a) and (b).

d. Based on the scatter plot in (b), provide reasons why a prediction should not be made for an atmospheric temperature of 31°F, the temperature on the morning of the launch of the *Challenger*.

e. Although the assumption of a linear relationship may not be valid, fit a simple linear regression model to predict O-ring damage, based on atmospheric temperature.

f. Include the prediction line found in (e) on the scatter plot developed in (b).

g. Based on the results of (f), do you think a linear model is appropriate for these data? Explain.

h. Perform a residual analysis. What conclusions do you reach?

81 Crazy Dave, a well-known baseball analyst, would like to study various team statistics for the 2005 baseball season to determine which variables might be useful in predicting the number of wins achieved by teams during the season. He has decided to begin by using a team's earned run average (ERA), a measure of pitching performance, to predict the number of wins. The data for the 30 Major League Baseball teams are in the file **bb2005.xls**.

(**Hint:** First, determine which are the independent and dependent variables.)

a. Assuming a linear relationship, use the least-squares method to compute the regression coefficients b_0 and b_1.
b. Interpret the meaning of the Y intercept, b_0, and the slope, b_1, in this problem.
c. Use the prediction line developed in (a) to predict the number of wins for a team with an ERA of 4.50.
d. Compute the coefficient of determination, r^2, and interpret its meaning.
e. Perform a residual analysis on your results and determine the adequacy of the fit of the model.
f. At the 0.05 level of significance, is there evidence of a linear relationship between the number of wins and the ERA?
g. Construct a 95% confidence interval estimate of the mean number of wins expected for teams with an ERA of 4.50.
h. Construct a 95% prediction interval of the number of wins for an individual team that has an ERA of 4.50.
i. Construct a 95% confidence interval estimate of the slope.
j. The 30 teams constitute a population. In order to use statistical inference, as in (f) through (i), the data must be assumed to represent a random sample. What "population" would this sample be drawing conclusions about?
k. What other independent variables might you consider for inclusion in the model?

82 College football players trying out for the NFL are given the Wonderlic standardized intelligence test. The data in the file **wonderlic.xls** contains the average Wonderlic scores of football players trying out for the NFL and the graduation rates for football players at selected schools (extracted from S. Walker, "The NFL's Smartest Team," *The Wall Street Journal*, September 30, 2005, pp. W1, W10). You plan to develop a regression model to predict the Wonderlic scores for football players trying out for the NFL, based on the graduation rate of the school they attended.

a. Assuming a linear relationship, use the least-squares method to compute the regression coefficients b_0 and b_1.
b. Interpret the meaning of the Y intercept, b_0, and the slope, b_1, in this problem.
c. Use the prediction line developed in (a) to predict the Wonderlic score for football players trying out for the NFL from a school that has a graduation rate of 50%.

d. Compute the coefficient of determination, r^2, and interpret its meaning.
e. Perform a residual analysis on your results and determine the adequacy of the fit of the model.
f. At the 0.05 level of significance, is there evidence of a linear relationship between the Wonderlic score for a football player trying out for the NFL from a school and the school's graduation rate?
g. Construct a 95% confidence interval estimate of the mean Wonderlic score for football players trying out for the NFL from a school that has a graduation rate of 50%.
h. Construct a 95% prediction interval of the Wonderlic score for a football player trying out for the NFL from a school that has a graduation rate of 50%.
i. Construct a 95% confidence interval estimate of the slope.

83 College basketball is big business, with coaches' salaries, revenues, and expenses in millions of dollars. The data in the file **colleges-basketball.xls** contains the coaches' salaries and revenues for college basketball at selected schools in a recent year (extracted from R. Adams, "Pay for Playoffs," *The Wall Street Journal*, March 11–12, 2006, pp. P1, P8). You plan to develop a regression model to predict a coach's salary based on revenue.

a. Assuming a linear relationship, use the least-squares method to compute the regression coefficients b_0 and b_1.
b. Interpret the meaning of the Y intercept, b_0, and the slope, b_1, in this problem.
c. Use the prediction line developed in (a) to predict the coach's salary for a school that has revenue of $7 million.
d. Compute the coefficient of determination, r^2, and interpret its meaning.
e. Perform a residual analysis on your results and determine the adequacy of the fit of the model.
f. At the 0.05 level of significance, is there evidence of a linear relationship between the coach's salary for a school and revenue?
g. Construct a 95% confidence interval estimate of the mean salary of coaches at schools that have revenue of $7 million.
h. Construct a 95% prediction interval of the coach's salary for a school that has revenue of $7 million.
i. Construct a 95% confidence interval estimate of the slope.

84 During the fall harvest season in the United States, pumpkins are sold in large quantities at farm stands. Often, instead of weighing the pumpkins prior to sale, the farm stand operator will just place the pumpkin in the appropriate circular cutout on the counter. When asked why this was done, one farmer replied, "I can tell the weight of the pumpkin from its circumference." To determine whether this was really true, a sample of 23 pumpkins were measured for circumference and weighed, with the following results, stored in the file **pumpkin.xls**:

Circumference (cm)	Weight (Grams)	Circumference (cm)	Weight (Grams)
50	1,200	57	2,000
55	2,000	66	2,500
54	1,500	82	4,600
52	1,700	83	4,600
37	500	70	3,100
52	1,000	34	600
53	1,500	51	1,500
47	1,400	50	1,500
51	1,500	49	1,600
63	2,500	60	2,300
33	500	59	2,100
43	1,000		

a. Assuming a linear relationship, use the least-squares method to compute the regression coefficients b_0 and b_1.
b. Interpret the meaning of the slope, b_1, in this problem.
c. Predict the mean weight for a pumpkin that is 60 centimeters in circumference.
d. Do you think it is a good idea for the farmer to sell pumpkins by circumference instead of weight? Explain.
e. Determine the coefficient of determination, r^2, and interpret its meaning.
f. Perform a residual analysis for these data and determine the adequacy of the fit of the model.
g. At the 0.05 level of significance, is there evidence of a linear relationship between the circumference and the weight of a pumpkin?
h. Construct a 95% confidence interval estimate of the population slope, β_1.
i. Construct a 95% confidence interval estimate of the population mean weight for pumpkins that have a circumference of 60 centimeters.
j. Construct a 95% prediction interval of the weight for an individual pumpkin that has a circumference of 60 centimeters.

85 Can demographic information be helpful in predicting sales of sporting goods stores? The data stored in the file **sporting.xls** are the monthly sales totals from a random sample of 38 stores in a large chain of nationwide sporting goods stores. All stores in the franchise, and thus within the sample, are approximately the same size and carry the same merchandise. The county or, in some cases, counties in which the store draws the majority of its customers is referred to here as the customer base. For each of the 38 stores, demographic information about the customer base is provided. The data are real, but the name of the franchise is not used, at the request of the company. The variables in the data set are

Sales—Latest one-month sales total (dollars)
Age—Median age of customer base (years)
HS—Percentage of customer base with a high school diploma
College—Percentage of customer base with a college diploma
Growth—Annual population growth rate of customer base over the past 10 years
Income—Median family income of customer base (dollars)

a. Construct a scatter plot, using sales as the dependent variable and median family income as the independent variable. Discuss the scatter diagram.
b. Assuming a linear relationship, use the least-squares method to compute the regression coefficients b_0 and b_1.
c. Interpret the meaning of the Y intercept, b_0, and the slope, b_1, in this problem.
d. Compute the coefficient of determination, r^2, and interpret its meaning.
e. Perform a residual analysis on your results and determine the adequacy of the fit of the model.
f. At the 0.05 level of significance, is there evidence of a linear relationship between the independent variable and the dependent variable?
g. Construct a 95% confidence interval estimate of the slope and interpret its meaning.

86 For the data of Problem 85, repeat (a) through (g), using median age as the independent variable.

87 For the data of Problem 85, repeat (a) through (g), using high school graduation rate as the independent variable.

88 For the data of Problem 85, repeat (a) through (g), using college graduation rate as the independent variable.

89 For the data of Problem 85, repeat (a) through (g), using population growth as the independent variable.

90 Zagat's publishes restaurant ratings for various locations in the United States. The data file **restaurants.xls** contains the Zagat rating for food, decor, service, and the price per person for a sample of 50 restaurants located in an urban area (New York City) and 50 restaurants located in a suburb of New York City. Develop a regression model to predict the price per person, based on a variable that represents the sum of the ratings for food, decor, and service.

Source: Extracted from Zagat Survey 2002 New York City Restaurants *and* Zagat Survey 2001–2002, Long Island Restaurants.

a. Assuming a linear relationship, use the least-squares method to compute the regression coefficients b_0 and b_1.
b. Interpret the meaning of the Y intercept, b_0, and the slope, b_1, in this problem.
c. Use the prediction line developed in (a) to predict the price per person for a restaurant with a summated rating of 50.
d. Compute the coefficient of determination, r^2, and interpret its meaning.

e. Perform a residual analysis on your results and determine the adequacy of the fit of the model.

f. At the 0.05 level of significance, is there evidence of a linear relationship between the price per person and the summated rating?

g. Construct a 95% confidence interval estimate of the mean price per person for all restaurants with a summated rating of 50.

h. Construct a 95% prediction interval of the price per person for a restaurant with a summated rating of 50.

i. Construct a 95% confidence interval estimate of the slope.

j. How useful do you think the summated rating is as a predictor of price? Explain.

91 Refer to the discussion of beta values and market models in Problem 49. One hundred weeks of data, ending the week of May 22, 2006, for the S&P 500 and three individual stocks are included in the data file `sp500.xls`. Note that the *weekly percentage change* for both the S&P 500 and the individual stocks is measured as the percentage change from the previous week's closing value to the current week's closing value. The variables included are

    Week—Current week
    SP500—Weekly percentage change in the S&P 500 Index
    WALMART—Weekly percentage change in stock price of Wal-Mart Stores, Inc.
    TARGET—Weekly percentage change in stock price of the Target Corporation
    SARALEE—Weekly percentage change in stock price of the Sara Lee Corporation

Source: Extracted from **finance.yahoo.com**, *May 31, 2006.*

a. Estimate the market model for Wal-Mart Stores Inc. (*Hint:* Use the percentage change in the S&P 500 Index as the independent variable and the percentage change in Wal-Mart Stores, Inc.'s stock price as the dependent variable.)

b. Interpret the beta value for Wal-Mart Stores, Inc.

c. Repeat (a) and (b) for Target Corporation.

d. Repeat (a) and (b) for Sara Lee Corporation.

e. Write a brief summary of your findings.

92 The data file `returns.xls` contains the stock prices of four companies, collected weekly for 53 consecutive weeks, ending May 22, 2006. The variables are

    Week—Closing date for stock prices
    MSFT—Stock price of Microsoft, Inc.
    Ford—Stock price of Ford Motor Company
    GM—Stock price of General Motors, Inc.
    IAL—Stock price of International Aluminum, Inc.

Source: Extracted from **finance.yahoo.com**, *May 31, 2006.*

a. Calculate the correlation coefficient, r, for each pair of stocks. (There are six of them.)

b. Interpret the meaning of r for each pair.

c. Is it a good idea to have all the stocks in an individual's portfolio be strongly positively correlated among each other? Explain.

93 Is the daily performance of stocks and bonds correlated? The data file `stocks&bonds.xls` contains information concerning the closing value of the Dow Jones Industrial Average and the Vanguard Long-Term Bond Index Fund for 60 consecutive business days, ending May 30, 2006. The variables included are

    Date—Current day
    Bonds—Closing price of Vanguard Long-Term Bond Index Fund
    Stocks—Closing price of the Dow Jones Industrial Average

Source: Extracted from **finance.yahoo.com**, *May 31, 2006.*

a. Compute and interpret the correlation coefficient, r, for the variables Stocks and Bonds.

b. At the 0.05 level of significance, is there a relationship between these two variables? Explain.

Report Writing Exercises

94 In Problems 85–89, you developed regression models to predict monthly sales at a sporting goods store. Now, write a report based on the models you developed. Append to your report all appropriate charts and statistical information.

Managing the *Springville Herald*

To ensure that as many trial subscriptions as possible are converted to regular subscriptions, the *Herald* marketing department works closely with the distribution department to accomplish a smooth initial delivery process for the trial subscription customers. To assist in this effort, the marketing department needs to accurately forecast the number of new regular subscriptions for the coming months.

A team consisting of managers from the marketing and distribution departments was convened to develop a better method of forecasting new subscriptions. Previously, after

examining new subscription data for the prior three months, a group of three managers would develop a subjective forecast of the number of new subscriptions. Lauren Hall, who was recently hired by the company to provide special skills in quantitative forecasting methods, suggested that the department look for factors that might help in predicting new subscriptions.

Members of the team found that the forecasts in the past year had been particularly inaccurate because in some months, much more time was spent on telemarketing than in other months. In particular, in the past month, only 1,055 hours were completed because callers were busy during the first week of the month attending training sessions on the personal but formal greeting style and a new standard presentation guide. Lauren collected data (stored in the file **sh.xls**) for the number of new subscriptions and hours spent on telemarketing for each month for the past two years.

EXERCISES

SH1 What criticism can you make concerning the method of forecasting that involved taking the new subscriptions data for the prior three months as the basis for future projections?

SH2 What factors other than number of telemarketing hours spent might be useful in predicting the number of new subscriptions? Explain.

SH3 **a.** Analyze the data and develop a regression model to predict the mean number of new subscriptions for a month, based on the number of hours spent on telemarketing for new subscriptions.

b. If you expect to spend 1,200 hours on telemarketing per month, estimate the mean number of new subscriptions for the month. Indicate the assumptions on which this prediction is based. Do you think these assumptions are valid? Explain.

c. What would be the danger of predicting the number of new subscriptions for a month in which 2,000 hours were spent on telemarketing?

Web Case

Apply your knowledge of simple linear regression in this Web Case, which extends the Sunflowers Apparel Using Statistics scenario from this chapter.

Leasing agents from the Triangle Mall Management Corporation have suggested that Sunflowers consider several locations in some of Triangle's newly renovated lifestyle malls that cater to shoppers with higher-than-mean disposable income. Although the locations are smaller than the typical Sunflowers location, the leasing agents argue that higher-than-mean disposable income in the surrounding community is a better predictor of higher sales than store size. The leasing agents maintain that sample data from 14 Sunflowers stores prove that this is true.

Review the leasing agents' proposal and supporting documents that describe the data at the company's Web site,

www.prenhall.com/Springville/Triangle_Sunflower.htm, (or open this Web case file from the Student CD-ROM's Web Case folder), and then answer the following:

1. Should mean disposable income be used to predict sales based on the sample of 14 Sunflowers stores?

2. Should the management of Sunflowers accept the claims of Triangle's leasing agents? Why or why not?

3. Is it possible that the mean disposable income of the surrounding area is not an important factor in leasing new locations? Explain.

4. Are there any other factors not mentioned by the leasing agents that might be relevant to the store leasing decision?

REFERENCES

1. Anscombe, F. J., "Graphs in Statistical Analysis," *The American Statistician* 27 (1973): 17–21.
2. Hoaglin, D. C., and R. Welsch, "The Hat Matrix in Regression and ANOVA," *The American Statistician* 32 (1978): 17–22.
3. Hocking, R. R., "Developments in Linear Regression Methodology: 1959–1982," *Technometrics* 25 (1983): 219–250.
4. Kutner, M. H., C. J. Nachtsheim, J. Neter, and W. Li, *Applied Linear Statistical Models*, 5th ed. (New York: McGraw-Hill/Irwin, 2005).
5. *Microsoft Excel 2007* (Redmond, WA: Microsoft Corp., 2007).

Excel Companion

E1 PERFORMING SIMPLE LINEAR REGRESSION ANALYSES

You perform a simple linear regression analysis by either using the PHStat2 Simple Linear Regression procedure or by using the ToolPak Regression procedure.

Using PHStat2 Simple Linear Regression

Open to the worksheet that contains the data for the regression analysis. Select **PHStat → Regression → Simple Linear Regression**. In the procedure's dialog box (shown below), enter the cell range of the Y variable as the **Y Variable Cell Range** and the cell range of the X variable as the **X Variable Cell Range**. Click **First cells in both ranges contain label** and enter a value for the **Confidence level for regression coefficients**. Click the **Regression Statistics Table** and the **ANOVA and Coefficients Table** Regression Tool Output Options, enter a title as the **Title**, and click **OK**.

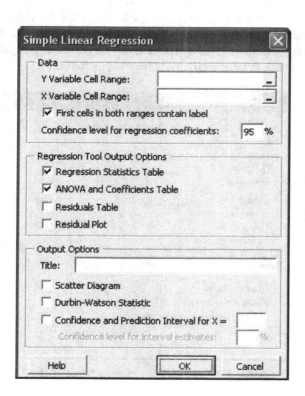

PHStat2 performs the regression analysis, using the ToolPak Regression procedure. Therefore, the worksheet produced does *not* dynamically change if you change your data. (Rerun the procedure to create revised results.) The three Output Options available in the PHStat2 dialog box enhance the ToolPak procedure and are explained in Sections E2, E4, and E5.

Using ToolPak Regression

Open to the worksheet that contains the data for the regression analysis. Select **Tools → Data Analysis**, select **Regression** from the Data Analysis list, and click **OK**. In the procedure's dialog box (shown below), enter the cell range of the Y variable data as the **Input Y Range** and enter the cell range of the X variable data as the **Input X Range**. Click **Labels**, click **Confidence Level** and enter a value in its box, and then click **OK**. Results appear on a new worksheet.

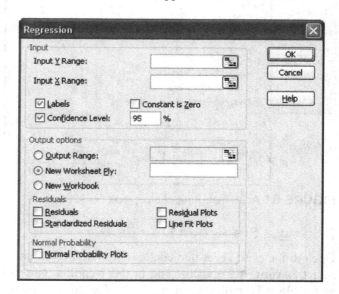

E2 CREATING SCATTER PLOTS AND ADDING A PREDICTION LINE

You use Excel charting features to create a scatter plot and add a prediction line to that plot. If you select the **Scatter Diagram** output option of the PHStat2 Simple Linear Regression procedure (see Section E1), you can skip to the "Adding a Prediction Line" section that applies to the Excel version you use.

Creating a Scatter Plot

Use the Section E1 instructions in "Using PHStat2 Simple Linear Regression", but clicking **Scatter Diagram** before you click **OK**.

Adding a Prediction Line (97–2003)

Open to the chart sheet that contains your scatter plot and select **Chart → Add Trendline**. In the Add Trendline dialog box (see Figure E1), click the **Type** tab and then click **Linear**. Click the **Options** tab and select the **Automatic** option. Click **Display equation on chart** and **Display R-squared value on chart** and then click **OK**. If you have included a label as part of your data range, you will see that label displayed in place of **Series1** in this dialog box.

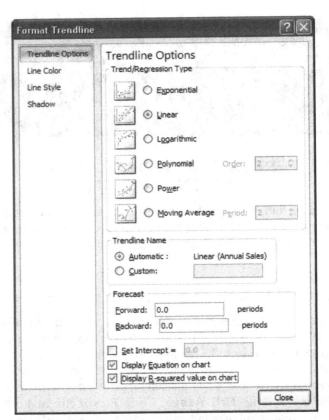

FIGURE E2 Format Trendline dialog box (2007)

relocate the X axis to the bottom of the chart, open to the chart, right-click the Y **axis** and select **Format Axis** from the shortcut menu.

If you use Excel 97–2003, select the **Scale** tab in the Format Axis dialog box (see Figure E3), and enter the value found in the **Minimum** box (-6 in Figure E3) as the **Value (X) axis Crosses at** value and click **OK**. (As you enter this value, the check box for this entry is cleared automatically.)

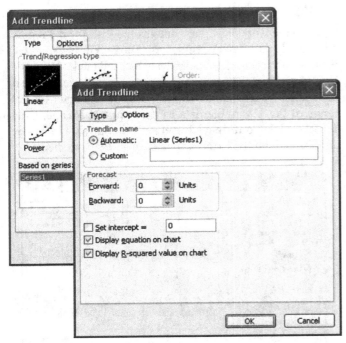

FIGURE E1 Add Trendline dialog box (97–2003)

Adding a Prediction Line (2007)

Open to the chart sheet that contains your scatter plot and select **Layout → Trendline** and in the Trendline gallery, select **More Trendline Options**. In the Trendline Options panel of the Format Trendline dialog box (see Figure E2), select the **Linear** option, click **Display equation on chart** and **Display R-squared value on chart**, and click **Close**.

Relocating an X Axis

If there are Y values on a residual plot or scatter plot that are less than zero, Microsoft Excel places the X axis at the point $Y = 0$, possibly obscuring some of the data points. To

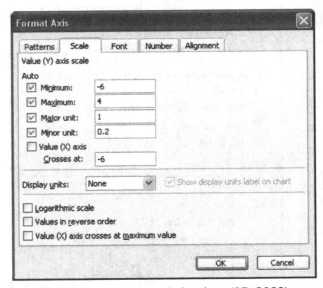

FIGURE E3 Format Axis dialog box (97–2003)

If you use Excel 2007, in the Axis Options panel of the Format Axis dialog box (see Figure E4), select the **Axis value** option, change its default value of 0.0 (shown in Figure E4) to a value less than the minimum *Y* value, and click **Close**.

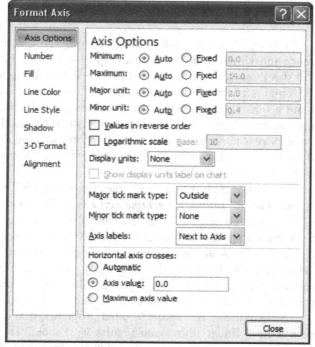

FIGURE E4 Format Axis dialog box (2007)

E3 PERFORMING RESIDUAL ANALYSES

You modify the procedures of Section E1 to perform a residual analysis. If you use the PHStat2 Simple Linear Regression procedure, click all the Regression Tool output options (**Regression Statistics Table, ANOVA and Coefficients Table, Residuals Table**, and **Residual Plot**). If you use the ToolPak Regression procedure, click **Residuals** and **Residual Plots** before clicking **OK**. If you need to relocate an *X* axis to the bottom of a residual plot, review the "Relocating an *X* Axis" part of Section E2.

E4 COMPUTING THE DURBIN-WATSON STATISTIC

You compute the Durbin-Watson Statistic by either using the PHStat2 Simple Linear Regression procedure or by using a several-step process that uses the Durbin-Watson.xls workbook.

Using PHStat2 Simple Linear Regression

Use the Section E1 instructions in "Using PHStat2 Simple Linear Regression," but clicking **Durbin-Watson Statistic** before you click **OK**. Choosing the Durbin-Watson

Statistic causes PHStat2 to create a residuals table, even if you did not check the **Residuals Table** Regression Tool output option.

The Durbin-Watson Statistic output option creates a new **Durbin-Watson** worksheet similar to the one shown in Figure 16. This worksheet references cells in the regression results worksheet that is also created by the procedure. If you delete the regression results worksheet, the DurbinWatson worksheet displays an error message.

Using Durbin-Watson.xls

Open to the **DurbinWatson** worksheet of the Durbin-Watson.xls workbook. This worksheet (see Figure 16) uses the **SUMXMY2 (*cell range 1, cell range 2*)** function in cell B3 to compute the sum of squared difference of the residuals, and the **SUMSQ (*residuals cell range*)** function in cell B4 to compute the sum of squared residuals for the Section 6 package delivery store example.

By setting *cell range 1* to the cell range of the first residual through the second-to-last residual and *cell range 2* to the cell range of the second residual through the last *residual*, you can get SUMXMY2 to compute the squared difference between two successive residuals, which is the numerator term of Equation (15). Because residuals appear in a regression results worksheet, cell references used in the SUMXMY2 function must refer to the regression results worksheet by name.

In the Durbin-Watson workbook, the **SLR** worksheet contains the simple linear regression analysis for the Section 6 package delivery example. The residuals appear in the cell range C25:C39. Therefore, cell range 1 is set to **SLR!C25:C38**, and cell range 2 is set to **SLR!C26:C39**. This makes the cell B3 formula **=SUMXMY2(SLR!C26:C39, SLR!C25:C38)**. The cell B4 formula, which also must refer to the SLR worksheet, is **=SUMSQ(SLR!C25:C39)**.

To adapt the Durbin-Watson workbook to other problems, first create a simple linear regression results worksheet that contains residual output and copy that worksheet to the Durbin-Watson workbook. Then open to the **Durbin-Watson** worksheet and edit the formulas in cells B3 and B4 so that they refer to the correct cell ranges on your regression worksheet. Finally, delete the no-longer-needed SLR worksheet.

E5 ESTIMATING THE MEAN OF Y AND PREDICTING Y VALUES

You compute a confidence interval estimate for the mean response and the prediction interval for an individual response either by selecting the PHStat2 Simple Linear Regression procedure or by making entries in the CIEandPIforSLR.xls workbook.

FIGURE E5

DataCopy worksheet
(first six rows)

	A	B	C	D	E	F	
1	Square Feet	Annual Sales	(X-XBar)^2				
2	1.7	3.7	1.4919		Sample Size	14	=COUNT(B:B)
3	1.6	3.9	1.7462		Sample Mean	2.9214	=AVERAGE(A:A)
4	2.8	6.7	0.0147		Sum of Squared Difference	37.9236	=SUM(C:C)
5	5.6	9.5	7.1747		Predicted Y (YHat)	7.6439	=TREND(B2:B15, A2:A15, CIEandPI!B4)
6	1.3	3.4	2.6290				
7	2.2	5.6	0.5205				

Using PHStat2 Simple Linear Regression

Use the Section E1 instructions in "Using PHStat2 Simple Linear Regression", but before you click **OK**, click **Confidence and Prediction Interval for X =** and enter an *X* value in its box (see below). Then enter a value for the **Confidence level for interval estimates** and click **OK**.

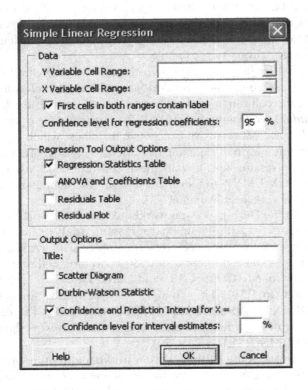

PHStat2 places the confidence interval estimate and prediction interval on a new worksheet similar to the one shown in Figure 21. (PHStat2 also creates a DataCopy worksheet that is discussed in the next part of this section.)

Using CIEandPIforSLR.xls

Open to the **CIEandPI** worksheet of the CIEandPIforSLR.xls workbook. This worksheet (shown in Figure 21) uses the function **TINV(1-*confidence level, degrees of freedom*)** to determine the *t* value and compute the confidence interval estimate and prediction interval for the Section 8 Sunflower's Apparel example.

Cells B8, B11, B12, and B15 contain formulas that reference individual cells on a **DataCopy** worksheet. This worksheet, the first six rows of which are shown in Figure E5, contains a copy of the regression data in columns A and B and a formula in column C that squares the difference between each *X* and $\bar{X}$. The worksheet also computes the sample size, the sample mean, the sum of the squared differences [*SSX* in Equation (20)], and the predicted *Y* value in cells F2, F3, F4, and F5.

The cell F5 formula uses the function **TREND (Y** *variable cell range*, **X** *variable cell range*, **X** *value*) to calculate the predicted *Y* value. Because the formula uses the *X* value that has been entered on the CIEandPI worksheet, the *X value* in the cell F5 formula is set to **CIEandPI!B4**. Because the DataCopy and CIEandPI worksheets reference each other, you should consider these worksheets a matched pair that should not be broken up.

To adapt these worksheets to other problems, first create a simple linear regression results worksheet. Then, transfer the standard error value, always found in the regression results worksheet cell B7, to cell **B13** of the CIEandPI worksheet. Change, as is necessary, the *X* Value and the confidence level in cells B4 and B5 of the CIEandPI worksheet. Next, open to the **DataCopy** worksheet, and if your sample size is not 14, follow the instructions found in the worksheet. Enter the problem's *X* values in column A and *Y* values in column B. Finally, return to the CIEandPI worksheet to examine its updated results.

E6   EXAMPLE: SUNFLOWERS APPAREL DATA

This section shows you how to use PHStat2 or Basic Excel to perform a regression analysis for Sunflowers Apparel using the square footage and annual sales data stored in the site.xls workbook.

Using PHStat2

Open to the **Data** worksheet of the SITE.xls workbook. Select **PHStat → Regression → Simple Linear Regression**. In the procedure's dialog box (see Figure E6), enter **C1:C15** as the **Y Variable Cell Range** and **B1:B15** as the **X Variable Cell Range**. Click **First cells in both ranges**

156

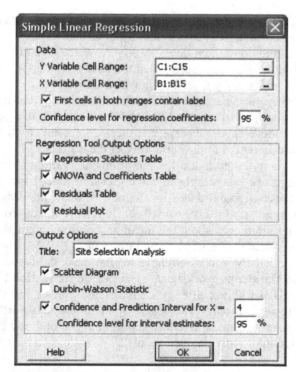

FIGURE E6 Completed Simple Linear Regression dialog box

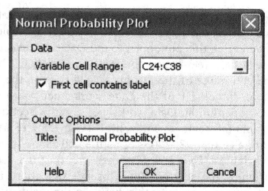

FIGURE E7 Completed Normal Probability Plot dialog box

You conclude that all assumptions are valid and that you can use this simple linear regression model for the Sunflowers Apparel data. You can now open to the **SLR** worksheet to view the details of the analysis or open to the **Estimate** worksheet to make inferences about the mean of *Y* and the prediction of individual values of *Y*.

Using Basic Excel

Open to the **Data** worksheet of the SITE.xls workbook. Select **Tools → Data Analysis** (97–2003) or **Data → Data Analysis** (2007). Select **Regression** from the Data Analysis list, and click **OK**. In the procedure's dialog box (see Figure E8), enter **C1:C15** as the **Input Y Range** and enter **B1:B15** as the **Input X Range**. Click **Labels**, click **Confidence Level** and enter **95** in its box, and click **Residuals**. Click **OK** to execute the procedure.

contain label and enter a value for the **Confidence level for regression coefficients**. Click the **Regression Statistics Table, ANOVA and Coefficients Table, Residuals Table**, and **Residual Plot** Regression Tool Output Options. Enter **Site Selection Analysis** as the **Title** and click **Scatter Diagram**. Click **Confidence and Prediction Interval for X=** and enter **4** in its box. Enter **95** in the **Confidence level for interval estimates** box. Click **OK** to execute the procedure.

To evaluate the assumption of linearity, you review the **Residual Plot for X1** chart sheet. Note that there is no apparent pattern or relationship between the residuals and *X* variable.

To evaluate the normality assumption, create a normal probability plot. With your workbook open to the **SLR** worksheet, select **PHStat → Probability & Prob. Distributions → Normal Probability Plot**. In the procedure's dialog box (see Figure E7), enter **C24:C38** as the **Variable Cell Range** and click **First cell contains label**. Enter **Normal Probability Plot** as the **Title** and click **OK**. In the **NormalPlot** chart sheet, observe that the data do not appear to depart substantially from a normal distribution.

To evaluate the assumption of equal variances, review the **Residual Plot for X1** chart sheet. Note that there do not appear to be major differences in the variability of the residuals.

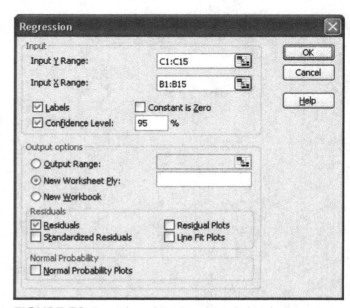

FIGURE E8 Completed Regression dialog box

To evaluate the assumption of linearity, you plot the residuals against the square feet (independent) variable. To simplify creating this plot, open to the Data worksheet and copy the square feet cell range B1:B15 to cell E1. Then copy the cell range of the residuals, C24:C38 on the SLR worksheet, to cell F1 of the Data worksheet. With your workbook open to the Data worksheet, use the Section E2 instructions to create a scatter plot. (Use **E1:F15** as the **Data range** (Excel 97–2003) or as the cell range of the X and Y variables (Excel 2007) when creating the scatter plot.) Review the scatter plot. Observe that there is no apparent pattern or relationship between the residuals and X variable. You conclude that the linearity assumption holds.

You now evaluate the normality assumption by creating a normal probability plot. Create a **Plot** worksheet, using the model worksheet in the NPP.xls workbook as your guide. In a new worksheet, enter **Rank** in cell A1 and then enter the series 1 through 14 in cells A2:A15. Enter **Proportion** in cell B1 and enter the formula **=A2/15** in cell B2. Next, enter **Z Value** in cell C1 and the formula **=NORMSINV(B2)** in cell C2. Copy the residuals (including their column heading) to the cell range D1:D15. Select the formulas in cell range B2:C2 and copy them down through row 15. Open to the probability plot and observe that the data do not appear to depart substantially from a normal distribution.

To evaluate the assumption of equal variance, return to the scatter plot of the residuals and the X variable that you already developed. Observe that there do not appear to be major differences in the variability of the residuals.

You conclude that all assumptions are valid and that you can use this simple linear regression model for the Sunflowers Apparel data. You can now evaluate the details of the regression results worksheet. If you are interested in making inferences about the mean of Y and the prediction of individual values of Y, open the CIEandPIforSLR.xls workbook. (Usually, you would have to first make adjustments to the **DataCopy** worksheet, as discussed in Section E5, but this workbook already contains the entries for the Sunflowers Apparel analysis.) Open to the **CIEandPI** worksheet to make inferences about the mean of Y and the prediction of individual values of Y.

Self-Test Solutions and Answers to Selected Even-Numbered Problems

The following represent worked-out solutions to Self-Test Problems and brief answers to most of the even-numbered problems in the text.

2 (a) Yes. **(b)** No. **(c)** No. **(d)** Yes.

4 (b)
$$b_1 = \frac{SSXY}{SSX} = \frac{2,775}{375} = 7.4$$

$$b_0 = \bar{Y} - b_1 \bar{X} = 237.5 - 7.4(12.5) = 145$$

For each increase in shelf space of an additional foot, weekly sales are estimated to increase by $7.40.
(c) $\hat{Y} = 145 + 7.4X = 145 + 7.4(8) = 204.2$, or $204.20.

6 (b) $b_0 = -2.37$, $b_1 = 0.0501$. **(c)** For every cubic foot increase in the amount moved, mean labor hours are estimated to increase by 0.0501. **(d)** 22.67 labor hours.

8 (b) $b_0 = -368.2846$, $b_1 = 4.7306$. **(c)** For each additional million-dollar increase in revenue, the mean annual value will increase by an estimated $4.7306 million. Literal interpretation of b_0 is not meaningful because an operating franchise cannot have zero revenue. **(d)** $341.3027 million.

10 (b) $b_0 = 6.048$, $b_1 = 2.019$. **(c)** For every one Rockwell E unit increase in hardness, the mean tensile strength is estimated to increase by 2,019 psi. **(d)** 66.62 or 66,620 psi.

12 $r^2 = 0.90$. 90% of the variation in the dependent variable can be explained by the variation in the independent variable.

14 $r^2 = 0.75$. 75% of the variation in the dependent variable can be explained by the variation in the independent variable.

16 (a) $r^2 = \dfrac{SSR}{SST} = \dfrac{20,535}{30,025} = 0.684$. 68.4% of the variation in sales can be explained by the variation in shelf space.

(b) $S_{YX} = \sqrt{\dfrac{SSE}{n-2}} = \sqrt{\dfrac{\sum\limits_{i-1}^{n}(Y_i - \hat{Y}_i)^2}{n-2}} = \sqrt{\dfrac{9490}{10}} = 30.8058$.

(c) Based on (a) and (b), the model should be very useful for predicting sales.

18 (a) $r^2 = 0.8892$. 88.92% of the variation in labor hours can be explained by the variation in cubic feet moved. **(b)** $S_{YX} = 5.0314$. **(c)** Based on (a) and (b), the model should be very useful for predicting the labor hours.

20 (a) $r^2 = 0.9334$. 93.34% of the variation in value of a baseball franchise can be explained by the variation in its annual revenue. **(b)** $S_{YX} = 42.4335$. **(c)** Based on (a) and (b), the model should be very useful for predicting the value of a baseball franchise.

22 (a) $r^2 = 0.4613$. 46.13% of the variation in the tensile strength can be explained by the variation in the hardness. **(b)** $S_{YX} = 9.0616$. **(c)** Based on (a) and (b), the model is only marginally useful for predicting tensile strength.

24 A residual analysis of the data indicates a pattern, with sizable clusters of consecutive residuals that are either all positive or all negative. This pattern indicates a violation of the assumption of linearity. A quadratic model should be investigated.

26 (a) There does not appear to be a pattern in the residual plot. **(b)** The assumptions of regression do not appear to be seriously violated.

28 (a) Based on the residual plot, there appears to be a nonlinear pattern in the residuals. A quadratic model should be investigated. **(b)** The assumptions of normality and equal variance do not appear to be seriously violated.

30 (a) Based on the residual plot, there appears to be a nonlinear pattern in the residuals. A quadratic model should be investigated. **(b)** There is some right-skewness in the residuals and some violation of the equal-variance assumption.

32 (a) An increasing linear relationship exists. **(b)** There is evidence of a strong positive autocorrelation among the residuals.

34 (a) No, because the data were not collected over time. **(b)** If a single store had been selected, then studied over a period of time, you would compute the Durbin-Watson statistic.

36 (a) $b_1 = \dfrac{SSXY}{SSX} = \dfrac{201399.05}{12495626} = 0.0161$.

$b_0 = \bar{Y} - b_1 \bar{X} = 71.2621 - 0.0161(4393) = 0.458$. **(b)** $\hat{Y} = 0.458 + 0.0161X = 0.458 + 0.0161(4500) = 72.908$, or $72,908. **(c)** There is no evidence of a pattern in the residuals over time.

(d) $D = \dfrac{\sum\limits_{i=2}^{n}(e_i - e_{i-1})^2}{\sum\limits_{i=1}^{n}e_i^2} = \dfrac{1243.2244}{599.0683} = 2.08 > 1.45$. There is no evidence of positive autocorrelation among the residuals. **(e)** Based on a residual analysis, the model appears to be adequate.

38 (a) $b_0 = -2.535$, $b_1 = .06073$. **(b)** $2,505.40. **(d)** $D = 1.64 > d_U = 1.42$, so there is no evidence of positive autocorrelation among the residuals. **(e)** The plot shows some nonlinear pattern, suggesting that a nonlinear model might be better. Otherwise, the model appears to be adequate.

40 (a) 3.00. **(b)** $t_{16} = \pm 2.1199$. **(c)** Reject H_0. There is evidence that the fitted linear regression model is useful. **(d)** $1.32 \leq \beta_1 \leq 7.68$.

42 (a) $t = \dfrac{b_1 - \beta_1}{S_{b_1}} = \dfrac{7.4}{1.59} = 4.65 > t_{10} = 2.2281$ with 10 degrees of freedom for $\alpha = 0.05$. Reject H_0. There is evidence that the fitted linear regression model is useful. **(b)** $b_1 \pm t_{n-2} S_{b_1} = 7.4 \pm 2.2281(1.59)$
$3.86 \leq \beta_1 \leq 10.94$

44 (a) $t = 16.52 > 2.0322$; reject H_0. **(b)** $0.0439 \leq \beta_1 \leq 0.0562$.

46 (a) Since the p-value is approximately zero, reject H_0 at the 5% level of significance. There is evidence of a linear relationship between annual revenue and franchise value. **(b)** $3.7888 \leq \beta_1 \leq 4.5906$.

48 (a) The p-value is virtually $0 < 0.05$; reject H_0. **(b)** $1.246 \leq \beta_1 \leq 2.792$.

50 (b) If the S&P gains 30% in a year, the UOPIX is expected to gain an estimated 60%. **(c)** If the S&P loses 35% in a year, the UOPIX is expected to lose an estimated 70%.

52 (a) $r = 0.8935$. There appears to be a strong positive linear relationship between the mileage as calculated by owners and by current government standards. **(b)** $t = 5.2639 > 2.3646$, p-value $= 0.0012 < 0.05$. Reject H_0. At the 0.05 level of significance, there is a significant linear relationship between the mileage as calculated by owners and by current government standards.

54 (a) $r = 0.5497$. There appears to be a moderate positive linear relationship between the average Wonderlic score of football players trying out for the NFL and the graduation rate for football players at selected schools. **(b)** $t = 3.9485$, p-value $= 0.0004 < 0.05$. Reject H_0. At the 0.05 level of significance, there is a significant linear relationship between the average Wonderlic score of football players trying out for the NFL and the graduation rate for football players at selected schools. **(c)** There is a significant linear relationship between the average Wonderlic score of football players trying out for the NFL and the graduation rate for football players at selected schools, but the positive linear relationship is only moderate.

56 (a) $15.95 \leq \mu_{Y|X=4} \leq 18.05$. **(b)** $14.651 \leq Y_{X=4} \leq 19.349$.

58 (a) $\hat{Y} \pm t_{n-2} S_{YX} \sqrt{h_i}$

$$= 204.2 \pm 2.2281 \, (30.81)\sqrt{0.1373}$$

$$178.76 \leq \mu_{Y|X=8} \leq 229.64$$

(b) $\hat{Y} \pm t_{n-2} S_{YX} \sqrt{1 + h_i}$

$$= 204.2 \pm 2.2281 \, (30.81)\sqrt{1 + 0.1373}$$

$$131.00 \leq Y_{X=8} \leq 277.40$$

(c) Part (b) provides a prediction interval for the individual response given a specific value of the independent variable, and part (a) provides an interval estimate for the mean value, given a specific value of the independent variable. Since there is much more variation in predicting an individual value than in estimating a mean value, a prediction interval is wider than a confidence interval estimate.

60 (a) $20.799 \leq \mu_{Y|X=500} \leq 24.542$. **(b)** $12.276 \leq Y_{X=500} \leq 33.065$.

62 (a) $367.0757 \leq \mu_{Y|X=150} \leq 397.3254$. **(b)** $311.3562 \leq Y_{X=150} \leq 453.0448$.

74 (a) $b_0 = 24.84$, $b_1 = 0.14$. **(b)** For each additional case, the predicted mean delivery time is estimated to increase by 0.14 minutes. **(c)** 45.84. **(d)** No, 500 is outside the relevant range of the data used to fit the regression equation. **(e)** $r^2 = 0.972$. **(f)** There is no obvious pattern in the residuals, so the assumptions of regression are met. The model appears to be adequate. **(g)** $t = 24.88 > 2.1009$; reject H_0. **(h)** $44.88 \leq \mu_{Y|X=150} \leq 46.80$. **(i)** $41.56 \leq Y_{X=150} \leq 50.12$. **(j)** $0.128 \leq \beta_1 \leq 0.152$.

76 (a) $b_0 = -122.3439$, $b_1 = 1.7817$. **(b)** For each additional thousand dollars in assessed value, the estimated mean selling price of a house increases by $1.7817 thousand. The estimated mean selling price of a house with a 0 assessed value is $-122.3439 thousand. However, this interpretation is not meaningful in the current setting since the assessed value is very unlikely to be 0 for a house. **(c)** $\hat{Y} = -122.3439 + 1.78171X = -122.3439 + 1.78171(170) = 180.5475$ thousand dollars.

(d) $r^2 = 0.9256$. So 92.56% of the variation in selling price can be explained by the variation in assessed value. **(e)** Neither the residual plot nor the normal probability plot reveal any potential violation of the linearity, equal variance and normality assumptions. **(f)** $t = 18.6648 > 2.0484$, p-value is virtually zero. Since p-value < 0.05, reject H_0. There is evidence of a linear relationship between selling price and assessed value. **(g)** $178.7066 \leq \mu_{Y|X=170} \leq 182.3884$. **(h)** $173.1953 \leq Y_{X=170} \leq 187.8998$. **(i)** $1.5862 \leq \beta_1 \leq 1.9773$.

78 (a) $b_0 = 0.30$, $b_1 = 0.00487$. **(b)** For each additional point on the GMAT score, the predicted mean GPI is estimated to increase by 0.00487. **(c)** 3.2225. **(d)** $r^2 = 0.798$. **(e)** There is no obvious pattern in the residuals, so the assumptions of regression are met. The model appears to be adequate. **(f)** $t = 8.43 > 2.1009$; reject H_0. **(g)** $3.144 \leq \mu_{Y|X=600} \leq 3.301$. **(h)** $2.886 \leq Y_{X=600} \leq 3.559$. **(i)** $.00366 \leq \beta_1 \leq .00608$.

80 (a) There is no clear relationship shown on the scatterplot. **(c)** Looking at all 23 flights, when the temperature is lower, there is likely to be some O-ring damage, particularly if the temperature is below 60 degrees. **(d)** 31 degrees is outside the relevant range, so a prediction should not be made. **(e)** Predicted $Y = 18.036 - 0.240X$, where X = temperature and Y = O-ring damage. **(g)** A nonlinear model would be more appropriate. **(h)** The appearance on the residual plot of a nonlinear pattern indicates a nonlinear model would be better.

82 (a) $b_0 = 14.6816$, $b_1 = 0.1135$. **(b)** For each additional percentage increase in graduation rate, the estimated mean average Wonderlic score increases by 0.1135. The estimated mean average Wonderlic score is 14.6816 for a school that has a 0% graduation rate. However, this interpretation is not meaningful in the current setting since graduation rate is very unlikely to be 0% for any school. **(c)** $\hat{Y} = 14.6816 + 0.11347X = 14.6816 + 0.11347(50) = 20.4$. **(d)** $r^2 = 0.3022$. So 30.22% of the variation in average Wonderlic score can be explained by the variation in graduation rate. **(e)** Neither the residual plot nor the normal probability plot reveal any potential violation of the linearity, equal variance, and normality assumptions. **(f)** $t = 3.9485 > 2.0281$, p-value $= 0.0004$. Since p-value < 0.05, reject H_0. There is evidence of a linear relationship between the average Wonderlic score for football players trying out for the NFL from a school and the graduation rate. **(g)** $19.6 \leq \mu_{Y|X=50} \leq 21.1$. **(h)** $15.9 \leq Y_{X=50} \leq 24.8$. **(i)** $0.0552 \leq \beta_1 \leq 0.1718$.

84 (a) $b_0 = -2629.222$, $b_1 = 82.472$. **(b)** For each additional centimeter in circumference, the mean weight is estimated to increase by 82.472 grams. **(c)** 2,319.08 grams. **(e)** $r^2 = 0.937$. **(f)** There appears to be a nonlinear relationship between circumference and weight. **(g)** p-value is virtually $0 < 0.05$; reject H_0. **(h)** $72.7875 \leq \beta_1 \leq 92.156$. **(i)** $2186.959 \leq \mu_{Y|X=60} \leq 2451.202$. **(j)** $1726.551 \leq Y_{X=60} \leq 2911.610$.

86 (b) $\hat{Y} = 931,626.16 + 21,782.76X$. **(c)** $b_1 = 21,782.76$ means that as the median age of the customer base increases by one year, the latest one-month mean sales total is estimated to increase by $21,782.76. **(d)** $r^2 = 0.0017$. Only 0.17% of the total variation in the franchise's latest one-month sales total can be explained by using the median age of customer base. **(e)** The residuals are very evenly spread out across different range of median age. **(f)** Since $-2.4926 < t = 0.2482 < 2.4926$, do not reject H_0. There is not enough evidence to conclude that there is a linear relationship between the one-month sales total and the median age of the customer base. **(g)** $-156,181.50 \leq \beta_1 \leq 199,747.02$.

88 (a) There is a positive linear relationship between total sales and the percentage of customer base with a college diploma. **(b)** $\hat{Y} = 789,847.38 + 35,854.15X$. **(c)** $b_1 = 35,854.15$ means that for each increase of one percent of the customer base having received a college diploma, the latest one-month mean sales total is estimated to increase by \$35,854.15. **(d)** $r^2 = 0.1036$. So 10.36% of the total variation in the franchise's latest one-month sales total can be explained by the percentage of the customer base with a college diploma. **(e)** The residuals are quite evenly spread out around zero. **(f)** Since $t = 2.0392 > 2.0281$, reject H_0. There is enough evidence to conclude that there is a linear relationship between one-month sales total and percentage of customer base with a college diploma. **(g)** $b_1 \pm t_{n-2} S_{b_1} = 35,854.15 \pm 2.0281(17,582.269)$ $195.75 \leq \beta_1 \leq 71,512.60$.

90 (a) $b_0 = -13.6561$, $b_1 = 0.8923$. **(b)** For each additional unit increase in summated rating, the mean price per person is estimated to increase by \$0.89. Since no restaurant will receive a summated rating of 0, it is inappropriate to interpret the Y intercept. **(c)** \$31.01. **(d)** $r^2 = 0.4246$. **(e)** There is no obvious pattern in the residuals so the assumptions of regression are met. The model appears to be adequate. **(f)** The p-value is virtually $0 < 0.05$; reject H_0. **(g)** $\$29.07 \leq \mu_{Y|X=50} \leq \$32.94$. **(h)** $\$16.95 \leq Y_{X=50} \leq \$45.06$. **(i)** $0.6848 \leq \beta_1 \leq 1.1017$.

92 (a) Correlation of Microsoft and Ford is -0.07176, Microsoft and GM is -0.39235, Microsoft and IAL is 0.06686, Ford and GM is 0.860418, Ford and IAL is -0.91585, and GM and IAL is -0.83584. **(b)** There is a strong negative linear relationship between the stock price of Ford Motor Company and International Aluminum, a strong negative linear relationship between the stock price of General Motors and International Aluminum, a strong positive linear relationship between Ford Motor Company and General Motors, Inc., a moderately weak negative linear relationship between the stock price of General Motors and Microsoft, Inc., and almost no linear relationship between the stock price of Microsoft and Ford Motor Company and between Microsoft and International Aluminum. **(c)** It is not a good idea to have all the stocks in an individual's portfolio be strongly positively correlated among each other because the portfolio risk can be reduced if some of the stocks are negatively correlated.

Chapter 4

Introduction to Multiple Regression

USING STATISTICS @ OmniFoods

LEARNING OBJECTIVES

In this chapter, you learn:

- How to develop a multiple regression model
- How to interpret the regression coefficients
- How to determine which independent variables to include in the regression model
- How to determine which independent variables are most important in predicting a dependent variable
- How to use categorical variables in a regression model

Using Statistics @ OmniFoods

You are the marketing manager for OmniFoods, a large food products company. The company is planning a nationwide introduction of OmniPower, a new high-energy bar. Although originally marketed to runners, mountain climbers, and other athletes, high-energy bars are now popular with the general public. OmniFoods is anxious to capture a share of this thriving market.

Because the marketplace already contains several successful energy bars, you want to maximize the effect of your marketing plans. In particular, you need to determine the effect that price and in-store promotions will have on the sales of OmniPower before marketing the bar nationwide. You plan to use a sample of 34 stores in a supermarket chain for a test-market study of OmniPower sales. How can you extend linear regression methods to incorporate the effects of price *and* promotion into the same model? How can you use this model to improve the success of the nationwide introduction of OmniPower?

You may already be familiar with simple linear regression models that use *one* numerical independent variable, X, to predict the value of a numerical dependent variable, Y. Often you can make better predictions by using *more than one* independent variable. This chapter introduces you to **multiple regression models** that use two or more independent variables to predict the value of a dependent variable.

1 DEVELOPING A MULTIPLE REGRESSION MODEL

A sample of 34 stores in a supermarket chain is selected for a test-market study of OmniPower. All the stores selected have approximately the same monthly sales volume. Two independent variables are considered here—the price of an OmniPower bar, as measured in cents (X_1), and the monthly budget for in-store promotional expenditures, measured in dollars (X_2). In-store promotional expenditures typically include signs and displays, in-store coupons, and free samples. The dependent variable Y is the number of OmniPower bars sold in a month. Table 1 presents the results (stored in the file omni.xls) of the test-market study.

TABLE 1

Monthly OmniPower Sales, Price, and Promotional Expenditures

Store	Sales	Price	Promotion	Store	Sales	Price	Promotion
1	4,141	59	200	18	2,730	79	400
2	3,842	59	200	19	2,618	79	400
3	3,056	59	200	20	4,421	79	400
4	3,519	59	200	21	4,113	79	600
5	4,226	59	400	22	3,746	79	600
6	4,630	59	400	23	3,532	79	600
7	3,507	59	400	24	3,825	79	600
8	3,754	59	400	25	1,096	99	200
9	5,000	59	600	26	761	99	200
10	5,120	59	600	27	2,088	99	200
11	4,011	59	600	28	820	99	200
12	5,015	59	600	29	2,114	99	400
13	1,916	79	200	30	1,882	99	400
14	675	79	200	31	2,159	99	400
15	3,636	79	200	32	1,602	99	400
16	3,224	79	200	33	3,354	99	600
17	2,295	79	400	34	2,927	99	600

Interpreting the Regression Coefficients

$$Y_i = \beta_0 + \beta_1 X_i + \varepsilon_i$$

When there are several independent variables, you can extend the simple linear regression model of the Equation above by assuming a linear relationship between each independent variable and the dependent variable. For example, with k independent variables, the multiple regression model is expressed in Equation (1).

MULTIPLE REGRESSION MODEL WITH k INDEPENDENT VARIABLES

$$Y_i = \beta_0 + \beta_1 X_{1i} + \beta_2 X_{2i} + \beta_3 X_{3i} + \cdots + \beta_k X_{ki} + \varepsilon_i \qquad (1)$$

where

$\beta_0 = Y$ intercept

$\beta_1 =$ slope of Y with variable X_1, holding variables $X_2, X_3, \ldots, X_k$ constant

$\beta_2 =$ slope of Y with variable X_2, holding variables $X_1, X_3, \ldots, X_k$ constant

$\beta_3 =$ slope of Y with variable X_3, holding variables $X_1, X_2, X_4, \ldots, X_k$ constant

.
.
.

$\beta_k =$ slope of Y with variable X_k, holding variables $X_1, X_2, X_3, \ldots, X_{k-1}$ constant

$\varepsilon_i =$ random error in Y for observation i

Equation (2) defines the multiple regression model with two independent variables.

MULTIPLE REGRESSION MODEL WITH TWO INDEPENDENT VARIABLES

$$Y_i = \beta_0 + \beta_1 X_{1i} + \beta_2 X_{2i} + \varepsilon_i \qquad (2)$$

where

$\beta_0 = Y$ intercept

$\beta_1 =$ slope of Y with variable X_1, holding variable X_2 constant

$\beta_2 =$ slope of Y with variable X_2, holding variable X_1 constant

$\varepsilon_i =$ random error in Y for observation i

Compare the multiple regression model to the simple linear regression model:

$$Y_i = \beta_0 + \beta_1 X_i + \varepsilon_i$$

In the simple linear regression model, the slope, β_1, represents the change in the mean of Y per unit change in X and does not take into account any other variables. In the multiple regression model with two independent variables [Equation (2)], the slope, β_1, represents the change in the mean of Y per unit change in X_1, taking into account the effect of X_2.

As in the case of simple linear regression, you use the sample regression coefficients (b_0, b_1, and b_2) as estimates of the population parameters (β_0, β_1, and β_2). Equation (3) defines the regression equation for a multiple regression model with two independent variables.

MULTIPLE REGRESSION EQUATION WITH TWO INDEPENDENT VARIABLES

$$\hat{Y}_i = b_0 + b_1 X_{1i} + b_2 X_{2i} \qquad (3)$$

You can use Microsoft Excel to compute the values of the three regression coefficients for the OmniPower sales data (see Figure 1).

FIGURE 1

Partial Microsoft Excel results for OmniPower sales data

See Section E1 to create this.

	A	B	C	D	E	F	G
1	OmniPower Sales Analysis						
2							
3	*Regression Statistics*						
4	Multiple R	0.8705					
5	R Square	0.7577					
6	Adjusted R Square	0.7421					
7	Standard Error	638.0653					
8	Observations	34					
9							
10	ANOVA						
11		*df*	*SS*	*MS*	*F*	*Significance F*	
12	Regression	2	39472730.77	19736365.387	48.4771	2.86258E-10	
13	Residual	31	12620946.67	407127.312			
14	Total	33	52093677.44				
15							
16		*Coefficients*	*Standard Error*	*t Stat*	*P-value*	*Lower 95%*	*Upper 95%*
17	Intercept	5837.5208	628.1502	9.2932	1.791E-10	4556.3992	7118.6423
18	Price	-53.2173	6.8522	-7.7664	9.200E-09	-67.1925	-39.2421
19	Promotion	3.6131	0.6852	5.2728	9.822E-06	2.2155	5.0106

From Figure 1, the computed values of the regression coefficients are

$$b_0 = 5{,}837.5208 \quad b_1 = -53.2173 \quad b_2 = 3.6131$$

Therefore, the multiple regression equation is

$$\hat{Y}_i = 5{,}837.5208 - 53.2173 X_{1i} + 3.6131 X_{2i}$$

where

$\hat{Y}_i$ = predicted monthly sales of OmniPower bars for store i

X_{1i} = price of OmniPower bar (in cents) for store i

X_{2i} = monthly in-store promotional expenditures (in dollars) for store i

The sample Y intercept ($b_0 = 5{,}837.5208$) estimates the number of OmniPower bars sold in a month if the price is \$0.00 and the total amount spent on promotional expenditures is also \$0.00. Because these values of price and promotion are outside the range of price and promotion used in the test-market study, and are nonsensical, the value of b_0 has no practical interpretation.

The slope of price with OmniPower sales ($b_1 = -53.2173$) indicates that, for a given amount of monthly promotional expenditures, the mean sales of OmniPower are estimated to decrease by 53.2173 bars per month for each 1-cent increase in the price. The slope of monthly promotional expenditures with OmniPower sales ($b_2 = 3.6131$) indicates that, for a given price, the mean sales of OmniPower are estimated to increase by 3.6131 bars for each additional \$1 spent on promotions. These estimates allow you to better understand the likely effect that price and promotion decisions will have in the marketplace. For example, a 10-cent decrease in price is estimated to increase mean sales by 532.173 bars, with a fixed amount of monthly promotional expenditures. A \$100 increase in promotional expenditures is estimated to increase mean sales by 361.31 bars, for a given price.

Regression coefficients in multiple regression are called **net regression coefficients**; they estimate the mean change in Y per unit change in a particular X, *holding constant the effect of the other X variables*. For example, in the study of OmniPower bar sales, for a store with a given amount of promotional expenditures, the mean sales are estimated to decrease by 53.2173 bars per month for each 1-cent increase in the price of an OmniPower bar. Another way to interpret this "net effect" is to think of two stores with an equal amount of promotional expenditures. If the first store charges 1 cent more than the other store, the net effect of this difference is that the first store is predicted to sell 53.2173 fewer bars per month than the second store. To interpret the net effect of promotional expenditures, you can consider two stores that are charging the same price. If the first store spends $1 more on promotional expenditures, the net effect of this difference is that the first store is predicted to sell 3.6131 more bars per month than the second store.

Predicting the Dependent Variable Y

You can use the multiple regression equation computed by Microsoft Excel to predict values of the dependent variable. For example, what is the predicted sales for a store charging 79 cents during a month in which promotional expenditures are $400? Using the multiple regression equation,

$$\hat{Y}_i = 5{,}837.5208 - 53.2173X_{1i} + 3.6131X_{2i}$$

with $X_{1i} = 79$ and $X_{2i} = 400$,

$$\hat{Y}_i = 5{,}837.5208 - 53.2173(79) + 3.6131(400)$$
$$= 3{,}078.57$$

Thus, your sales prediction for stores charging 79 cents and spending $400 in promotional expenditures is 3,078.57 OmniPower bars per month.

After you have predicted Y and done a residual analysis (see Section 3), the next step often involves a confidence interval estimate of the mean response and a prediction interval for an individual response. The computation of these intervals is too complex to do by hand, and you should use Microsoft Excel to perform the calculations. Figure 2 illustrates Microsoft Excel results.

FIGURE 2

Microsoft Excel confidence interval estimate and prediction interval for the OmniPower sales data

See Section E3 to create this.

	A	B	C	D
1	Confidence Interval Estimate and Prediction Interval			
2				
3	Data			
4	Confidence Level	95%		
5		1		
6	Price given value	79		
7	Promotion given value	400		
8				
9	XX	34	2646	13200
10		2646	214674	1018800
11		13200	1018800	6000000
12				
13	Inverse of XX	0.969163	-0.00941	-0.00053
14		-0.009408	0.000115	1.12E-06
15		-0.000535	1.12E-06	1.15E-06
16				
17	X'G times Inverse of XX	0.012054	0.000149	1.49E-05
18				
19	[X'G times Inverse of XX] times XG	0.029762	=MMULT(B17:D17, B5:B7)	
20	t Statistic	2.0395	=TINV(1 - B4, MR!B13)	
21	Predicted Y (YHat)	3078.57	{=MMULT(TRANSPOSE(B5:B7), MR!B17:B19)} 17:B19))	
22				
23	For Average Predicted Y (YHat)			
24	Interval Half Width	224.50	=B20 * SQRT(B19)* MR!B7	
25	Confidence Interval Lower Limit	2854.07	=B21 - B24	
26	Confidence Interval Upper Limit	3303.08	=B21 + B24	
27				
28	For Individual Response Y			
29	Interval Half Width	1320.57	=B20 * SQRT(1 + B19)* MR!B7	
30	Prediction Interval Lower Limit	1758.01	=B21 - B29	
31	Prediction Interval Upper Limit	4399.14	=B21 + B29	

The 95% confidence interval estimate of the mean OmniPower sales for all stores charging 79 cents and spending $400 in promotional expenditures is 2,854.07 to 3,303.08 bars. The prediction interval for an individual store is 1,758.01 to 4,399.14 bars.

PROBLEMS FOR SECTION 1

Learning the Basics

 1 For this problem, use the following multiple regression equation:

$$\hat{Y}_i = 10 + 5X_{1i} + 3X_{2i}$$

a. Interpret the meaning of the slopes.
b. Interpret the meaning of the Y intercept.

 2 For this problem, use the following multiple regression equation:

$$\hat{Y}_i = 50 + 2X_{1i} + 7X_{2i}$$

a. Interpret the meaning of the slopes.
b. Interpret the meaning of the Y intercept.

Appying the Concepts

3 A marketing analyst for a shoe manufacturer is considering the development of a new brand of running shoes. The marketing analyst wants to determine which variables to use in predicting durability (that is, the effect of long-term impact). Two independent variables under consideration are X_1 (FOREIMP), a measurement of the forefoot shock-absorbing capability, and X_2 (MIDSOLE), a measurement of the change in impact properties over time. The dependent variable Y is LTIMP, a measure of the shoe's durability after a repeated impact test. A random sample of 15 types of currently manufactured running shoes was selected for testing, with the following results:

ANOVA	df	SS	MS	F	Significance F
Regression	2	12.61020	6.30510	97.69	0.0001
Error	12	0.77453	0.06454		
Total	14	13.38473			

Variable	Coefficients	Standard Error	t Statistic	p-Value
INTERCEPT	−0.02686	0.06905	−0.39	0.7034
FOREIMP	0.79116	0.06295	12.57	0.0000
MIDSOLE	0.60484	0.07174	8.43	0.0000

a. State the multiple regression equation.
b. Interpret the meaning of the slopes in this problem.

 4 A mail-order catalog business selling personal computer supplies, software, and hardware maintains a centralized warehouse. Management is currently examining the process of distribution from the warehouse and wants to study the factors that affect warehouse distribution costs. Currently, a small handling fee is added to each order, regardless of the amount of the order. Data collected over the past 24 months (stored in the file **warecost.xls**) indicate the warehouse distribution costs (in thousands of dollars), the sales (in thousands of dollars), and the number of orders received.

a. State the multiple regression equation.
b. Interpret the meaning of the slopes, b_1 and b_2, in this problem.
c. Explain why the regression coefficient, b_0, has no practical meaning in the context of this problem.
d. Predict the mean monthly warehouse distribution cost when sales are $400,000 and the number of orders is 4,500.
e. Construct a 95% confidence interval estimate for the mean monthly warehouse distribution cost when sales are $400,000 and the number of orders is 4,500.
f. Construct a 95% prediction interval for the monthly warehouse distribution cost for a particular month when sales are $400,000 and the number of orders is 4,500.

 5 A consumer organization wants to develop a regression model to predict gasoline mileage (as measured by miles per gallon) based on the horsepower of the car's engine and the weight of the car, in pounds. A sample of 50 recent car models was selected, with the results recorded in the file **auto.xls**.

a. State the multiple regression equation.
b. Interpret the meaning of the slopes, b_1 and b_2, in this problem.
c. Explain why the regression coefficient, b_0, has no practical meaning in the context of this problem.
d. Predict the mean miles per gallon for cars that have 60 horsepower and weigh 2,000 pounds.
e. Construct a 95% confidence interval estimate for the mean miles per gallon for cars that have 60 horsepower and weigh 2,000 pounds.
f. Construct a 95% prediction interval for the miles per gallon for an individual car that has 60 horsepower and weighs 2,000 pounds.

 6 A consumer products company wants to measure the effectiveness of different types of advertising media in the promotion of its products. Specifically, the company is interested in the effectiveness of radio advertising and newspaper advertising (including the cost of discount coupons). A sample of 22 cities with approximately equal populations is selected for study during a test period of one month. Each city is allocated a specific expenditure level both for radio advertising and for newspaper advertising. The sales of the product (in thousands of dollars) and also the levels of media expenditure (in thousands of dollars) during the test month are recorded, with the following results stored in the file **advertise.xls**:

City	Sales ($000)	Radio Advertising ($000)	Newspaper Advertising $000)
1	973	0	40
2	1,119	0	40
3	875	25	25
4	625	25	25
5	910	30	30
6	971	30	30
7	931	35	35
8	1,177	35	35
9	882	40	25
10	982	40	25
11	1,628	45	45
12	1,577	45	45
13	1,044	50	0
14	914	50	0
15	1,329	55	25
16	1,330	55	25
17	1,405	60	30
18	1,436	60	30
19	1,521	65	35
20	1,741	65	35
21	1,866	70	40
22	1,717	70	40

a. State the multiple regression equation.
b. Interpret the meaning of the slopes, b_1 and b_2, in this problem.
c. Interpret the meaning of the regression coefficient, b_0.
d. Predict the mean sales for a city in which radio advertising is $20,000 and newspaper advertising is $20,000.
e. Construct a 95% confidence interval estimate for the mean sales for cities in which radio advertising is $20,000 and newspaper advertising is $20,000.
f. Construct a 95% prediction interval for the sales for an individual city in which radio advertising is $20,000 and newspaper advertising is $20,000.

7 The director of broadcasting operations for a television station wants to study the issue of standby hours (that is, hours in which unionized graphic artists at the station are paid but are not actually involved in any activity). The variables in the study include

Standby hours (Y)—Total number of standby hours in a week

Total staff present (X_1)—Weekly total of people-days
Remote hours (X_2)—Total number of hours worked by employees at locations away from the central plant
The results for a period of 26 weeks are in the data file standby.xls.
a. State the multiple regression equation.
b. Interpret the meaning of the slopes, b_1 and b_2, in this problem.
c. Explain why the regression coefficient, b_0, has no practical meaning in the context of this problem.
d. Predict the mean standby hours for a week in which the total staff present have 310 people-days and the remote hours are 400.
e. Construct a 95% confidence interval estimate for the mean standby hours for weeks in which the total staff present have 310 people-days and the remote hours are 400.
f. Construct a 95% prediction interval for the standby hours for a single week in which the total staff present have 310 people-days and the remote hours are 400.

8 Nassau County is located approximately 25 miles east of New York City. Until all residential property was recently reappraised, property taxes were assessed based on actual value in 1938 or when the property was built, if it was constructed after 1938. Data in the file glencove.xls include the appraised value, land area of the property in acres, and age, in years, for a sample of 30 single-family homes located in Glen Cove, a small city in Nassau County. Develop a multiple linear regression model to predict appraised value based on land area of the property and age, in years.
a. State the multiple regression equation.
b. Interpret the meaning of the slopes, b_1 and b_2, in this problem.
c. Explain why the regression coefficient, b_0, has no practical meaning in the context of this problem.
d. Predict the mean appraised value for a house that has a land area of 0.25 acres and is 45 years old.
e. Construct a 95% confidence interval estimate for the mean appraised value for houses that have a land area of 0.25 acres and are 45 years old.
f. Construct a 95% prediction interval estimate for the appraised value for an individual house that has a land area of 0.25 acres and is 45 years old.

2 r^2, ADJUSTED r^2, AND THE OVERALL F TEST

This section discusses three methods you can use to evaluate the overall usefulness of the multiple regression model: the coefficient of multiple determination r^2, the adjusted r^2, and the overall F test.

Coefficient of Multiple Determination

The coefficient of determination, r^2, measures the variation in Y that is explained by the independent variable X in the simple linear regression model. In multiple regression, the **coefficient of multiple determination** represents the proportion of the variation in Y that is explained by the set of independent variables. Equation (4) defines the coefficient of multiple determination for a multiple regression model with two or more independent variables.

COEFFICIENT OF MULTIPLE DETERMINATION

The coefficient of multiple determination is equal to the regression sum of squares (SSR) divided by the total sum of squares (SST).

$$r^2 = \frac{\text{Regression sum of squares}}{\text{Total sum of squares}} = \frac{SSR}{SST} \qquad (4)$$

where

$$SSR = \text{regression sum of squares}$$

$$SST = \text{total sum of squares}$$

In the OmniPower example, from Figure 1, $SSR = 39{,}472{,}730.77$ and $SST = 52{,}093{,}677.44$. Thus,

$$r^2 = \frac{SSR}{SST} = \frac{39{,}472{,}730.77}{52{,}093{,}677.44} = 0.7577$$

The coefficient of multiple determination ($r^2 = 0.7577$) indicates that 75.77% of the variation in sales is explained by the variation in the price and in the promotional expenditures.

Adjusted r^2

When considering multiple regression models, some statisticians suggest that you should use the **adjusted r^2** to reflect both the number of independent variables in the model and the sample size. Reporting the adjusted r^2 is extremely important when you are comparing two or more regression models that predict the same dependent variable but have a different number of independent variables. Equation (5) defines the adjusted r^2.

ADJUSTED r^2

$$r_{\text{adj}}^2 = 1 - \left[(1 - r^2) \frac{n-1}{n-k-1} \right] \qquad (5)$$

where k is the number of independent variables in the regression equation.

Thus, for the OmniPower data, because $r^2 = 0.7577$, $n = 34$, and $k = 2$,

$$r_{\text{adj}}^2 = 1 - \left[(1 - r^2) \frac{34-1}{(34-2-1)} \right]$$

$$= 1 - \left[(1 - 0.7577) \frac{33}{31} \right]$$

$$= 1 - 0.2579$$

$$= 0.7421$$

Hence, 74.21% of the variation in sales is explained by the multiple regression model—adjusted for number of independent variables and sample size.

Test for the Significance of the Overall Multiple Regression Model

You use the **overall F test** to test whether there is a significant relationship between the dependent variable and the entire set of independent variables (the overall multiple regression model). Because there is more than one independent variable, you use the following null and alternative hypotheses:

H_0: $\beta_1 = \beta_2 = \cdots = \beta_k = 0$ (There is no linear relationship between the dependent variable and the independent variables.)

H_1: At least one $\beta_j \neq 0$, $j = 1, 2, \ldots, k$ (There is a linear relationship between the dependent variable and at least one of the independent variables.)

Equation (6) defines the statistic for the overall F test. Table 2 presents the associated ANOVA summary table.

OVERALL F TEST STATISTIC

The F statistic is equal to the regression mean square (MSR) divided by the error mean square (MSE).

$$F = \frac{MSR}{MSE} \tag{6}$$

where

F = test statistic from an F distribution with k and $n - k - 1$ degrees of freedom

k = number of independent variables in the regression model

TABLE 2

ANOVA Summary Table for the Overall F Test

Source	Degrees of Freedom	Sum of Squares	Mean Square (Variance)	F
Regression	k	SSR	$MSR = \dfrac{SSR}{k}$	$F = \dfrac{MSR}{MSE}$
Error	$n - k - 1$	SSE	$MSE = \dfrac{SSE}{n - k - 1}$	
Total	$n - 1$	SST		

The decision rule is

Reject H_0 at the α level of significance if $F > F_{U(k,n-k-1)}$;

otherwise, do not reject H_0.

Using a 0.05 level of significance, the critical value of the F distribution with 2 and 31 degrees of freedom found from the table of critical values of F is approximately 3.32 (see Figure 3). From Figure 1, the F statistic given in the ANOVA summary table is 48.4771. Because $48.4771 > 3.32$, or because the p-value $= 0.000 < 0.05$, you reject H_0 and conclude that at least one of the independent variables (price and/or promotional expenditures) is related to sales.

FIGURE 3

Testing for the significance of a set of regression coefficients at the 0.05 level of significance, with 2 and 31 degrees of freedom

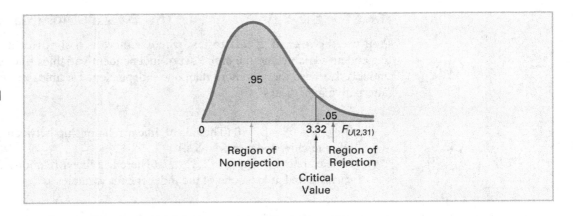

PROBLEMS FOR SECTION 2

Learning the Basics

9 The following ANOVA summary table is for a multiple regression model with two independent variables:

Source	Degrees of Freedom	Sum of Squares	Mean Squares	F
Regression	2	60		
Error	18	120		
Total	20	180		

a. Determine the regression mean square (MSR) and the mean square error (MSE).
b. Compute the F statistic.
c. Determine whether there is a significant relationship between Y and the two independent variables at the 0.05 level of significance.
d. Compute the coefficient of multiple determination, r^2, and interpret its meaning.
e. Compute the adjusted r^2.

10 The following ANOVA summary table is for a multiple regression model with two independent variables:

Source	Degrees of Freedom	Sum of Squares	Mean Squares	F
Regression	2	30		
Error	10	120		
Total	12	150		

a. Determine the regression mean square (MSR) and the mean square error (MSE).
b. Compute the F statistic.
c. Determine whether there is a significant relationship between Y and the two independent variables at the 0.05 level of significance.
d. Compute the coefficient of multiple determination, r^2, and interpret its meaning.
e. Compute the adjusted r^2.

Applying the Concepts

11 Eileen M. Van Aken and Brian M. Kleiner, professors at Virginia Polytechnic Institute and State University, investigated the factors that contribute to the effectiveness of teams ("Determinants of Effectiveness for Cross-Functional Organizational Design Teams," *Quality Management Journal*, 1997, 4, pp. 51–79). The researchers studied 34 independent variables, such as team skills, diversity, meeting frequency, and clarity in expectations. For each of the teams studied, each of the variables was given a value of 1 through 100, based on the results of interviews and survey data, where 100 represents the highest rating. The dependent variable, team performance, was also given a value of 1 through 100, with 100 representing the highest rating. Many different regression models were explored, including the following:

Model 1

$$\text{Team performance} = \beta_0 + \beta_1(\text{Team skills}) + \varepsilon,$$

$$r_{adj}^2 = 0.68$$

Model 2

$$\text{Team performance} = \beta_0 + \beta_1(\text{Clarity in expectations}) + \varepsilon,$$

$$r_{adj}^2 = 0.78$$

Model 3

$$\text{Team performance} = \beta_0 + \beta_1(\text{Team skills}) +$$
$$\beta_2(\text{Clarity in expectations}) + \varepsilon,$$

$$r_{adj}^2 = 0.97$$

a. Interpret the adjusted r^2 for each of the three models.
b. Which of these three models do you think is the best predictor of team performance?

12 In Problem 3, you predicted the durability of a brand of running shoe, based on the forefoot shock-absorbing capability and the change in impact properties over time. The regression analysis resulted in the following ANOVA summary table:

Source	Degrees of Freedom	Sum of Squares	Mean Squares	F	Significance
Regression	2	12.61020	6.30510	97.69	0.0001
Error	12	0.77453	0.06454		
Total	14	13.38473			

a. Determine whether there is a significant relationship between durability and the two independent variables at the 0.05 level of significance.
b. Interpret the meaning of the p-value.
c. Compute the coefficient of multiple determination, r^2, and interpret its meaning.
d. Compute the adjusted r^2.

 13 In Problem 5, you used horsepower and weight to predict gasoline mileage (see the auto.xls file). Using the results from that problem,
a. determine whether there is a significant relationship between gasoline mileage and the two independent variables (horsepower and weight) at the 0.05 level of significance.
b. interpret the meaning of the p-value.
c. compute the coefficient of multiple determination, r^2, and interpret its meaning.
d. compute the adjusted r^2.

 14 In Problem 4, you used sales and number of orders to predict distribution costs at a mail-order catalog business (see the warecost.xls file). Using the results from that problem,
a. determine whether there is a significant relationship between distribution costs and the two independent variables (sales and number of orders) at the 0.05 level of significance.

b. interpret the meaning of the p-value.
c. compute the coefficient of multiple determination, r^2, and interpret its meaning.
d. compute the adjusted r^2.

15 In Problem 7, you used the total staff present and remote hours to predict standby hours (see the file standby.xls). Using the results from that problem,
a. determine whether there is a significant relationship between standby hours and the two independent variables (total staff present and remote hours) at the 0.05 level of significance.
b. interpret the meaning of the p-value.
c. compute the coefficient of multiple determination, r^2, and interpret its meaning.
d. compute the adjusted r^2.

16 In Problem 6, you used radio advertising and newspaper advertising to predict sales (see the advertise.xls file). Using the results from that problem,
a. determine whether there is a significant relationship between sales and the two independent variables (radio advertising and newspaper advertising) at the 0.05 level of significance.
b. interpret the meaning of the p-value.
c. compute the coefficient of multiple determination, r^2, and interpret its meaning.
d. compute the adjusted r^2.

17 In Problem 8, you used the land area of a property and the age of a house to predict appraised value (see the glencove.xls file). Using the results from that problem,
a. determine whether there is a significant relationship between appraised value and the two independent variables (land area of a property and age of a house) at the 0.05 level of significance.
b. interpret the meaning of the p-value.
c. compute the coefficient of multiple determination, r^2, and interpret its meaning.
d. compute the adjusted r^2.

3 RESIDUAL ANALYSIS FOR THE MULTIPLE REGRESSION MODEL

You may have previously used residual analysis to evaluate the appropriateness of using the simple linear regression model for a set of data. For the multiple regression model with two independent variables, you need to construct and analyze the following residual plots:

1. Residuals versus $\hat{Y}_i$
2. Residuals versus X_{1i}
3. Residuals versus X_{2i}
4. Residuals versus time

The first residual plot examines the pattern of residuals versus the predicted values of Y. If the residuals show a pattern for different predicted values of Y, there is evidence of a possible quadratic effect in at least one independent variable, a possible violation of the assumption of equal variance, and/or the need to transform the Y variable.

173

The second and third residual plots involve the independent variables. Patterns in the plot of the residuals versus an independent variable may indicate the existence of a quadratic effect and, therefore, indicate the need to add a quadratic independent variable to the multiple regression model. The fourth plot is used to investigate patterns in the residuals in order to validate the independence assumption when the data are collected in time order. Associated with this residual plot, you can compute the Durbin-Watson statistic to determine the existence of positive autocorrelation among the residuals.

Figure 4 illustrates the Microsoft Excel residual plots for the OmniPower sales example. In Figure 4, there is very little or no pattern in the relationship between the residuals and the predicted value of Y, the value of X_1 (price), or the value of X_2 (promotional expenditures). Thus, you can conclude that the multiple regression model is appropriate for predicting sales.

FIGURE 4

Microsoft Excel residual plots for the OmniPower sales data: Panel *A*, residuals versus predicted *Y*; Panel *B*, residuals versus price; Panel *C*, residuals versus promotional expenditures

See Section E2 to create this.

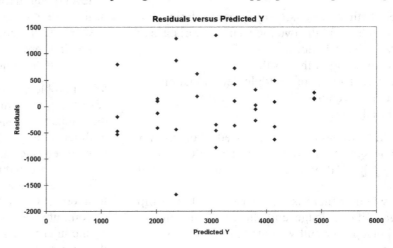

Panel A

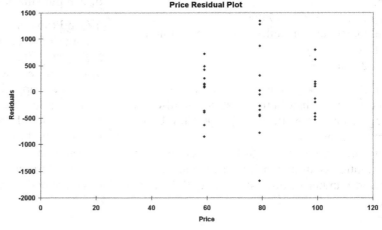

Panel B

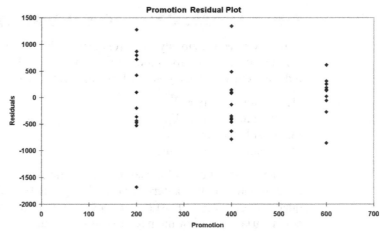

Panel C

PROBLEMS FOR SECTION 3

Applying the Concepts

 18 In Problem 4, you used sales and number of orders to predict distribution costs at a mail-order catalog business (see the `warecost.xls` file).
a. Perform a residual analysis on your results and determine the adequacy of the model.
b. Plot the residuals against the months. Is there any evidence of a pattern in the residuals? Explain.
c. Determine the Durbin-Watson statistic.
d. At the 0.05 level of significance, is there evidence of positive autocorrelation in the residuals?

 19 In Problem 5, you used horsepower and weight to predict gasoline mileage (see the `auto.xls` file). Perform a residual analysis on your results and determine the adequacy of the model.

20 In Problem 6, you used radio advertising and newspaper advertising to predict sales (see the `advertise.xls` file).

Perform a residual analysis on your results and determine the adequacy of the model.

21 In Problem 7, you used the total staff present and remote hours to predict standby hours (see the `standby.xls` file).
a. Perform a residual analysis on your results and determine the adequacy of the model.
b. Plot the residuals against the weeks. Is there evidence of a pattern in the residuals? Explain.
c. Determine the Durbin-Watson statistic.
d. At the 0.05 level of significance, is there evidence of positive autocorrelation in the residuals?

22 In Problem 8, you used the land area of a property and the age of a house to predict appraised value (see the `glencove.xls` file). Perform a residual analysis on your results and determine the adequacy of the model.

4 INFERENCES CONCERNING THE POPULATION REGRESSION COEFFICIENTS

You may have previously tested the slope in a simple linear regression model to determine the significance of the relationship between X and Y. In addition, you may have constructed a confidence interval estimate of the population slope. This section extends those procedures to multiple regression.

Tests of Hypothesis

In a simple linear regression model, to test a hypothesis concerning the population slope, β_1, you use this equation:

$$t = \frac{b_1 - \beta_1}{S_{b_1}}$$

Equation (7) generalizes this equation for multiple regression.

TESTING FOR THE SLOPE IN MULTIPLE REGRESSION

$$t = \frac{b_j - \beta_j}{S_{b_j}} \tag{7}$$

where

b_j = slope of variable j with Y, holding constant the effects of all other independent variables

S_{b_j} = standard error of the regression coefficient b_j

t = test statistic for a t distribution with $n - k - 1$ degrees of freedom

k = number of independent variables in the regression equation

β_j = hypothesized value of the population slope for variable j, holding constant the effects of all other independent variables

---

175

To determine whether variable X_2 (amount of promotional expenditures) has a significant effect on sales, taking into account the price of OmniPower bars, the null and alternative hypotheses are

$$H_0: \beta_2 = 0$$
$$H_1: \beta_2 \neq 0$$

From Equation (7) and Figure 1,

$$t = \frac{b_2 - \beta_2}{S_{b_2}}$$

$$= \frac{3.6131 - 0}{0.6852} = 5.2728$$

If you select a level of significance of 0.05, the critical values of t for 31 degrees of freedom from the table of critical values of t are -2.0395 and $+2.0395$ (see Figure 5).

FIGURE 5

Testing for significance of a regression coefficient at the 0.05 level of significance, with 31 degrees of freedom

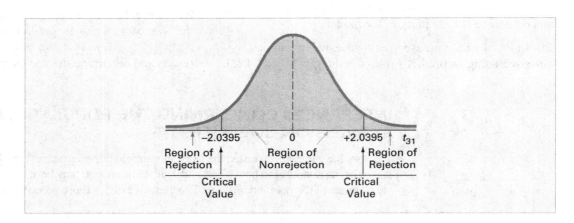

From Figure 1, the p-value is 0.000009822 (or 9.822E-06 in scientific notation). Because $t = 5.2728 > 2.0395$ or the p-value of $0.000009822 < 0.05$, you reject H_0 and conclude that there is a significant relationship between the variable X_2 (promotional expenditures) and sales, taking into account the price, X_1. This extremely small p-value allows you to strongly reject the null hypothesis that there is no linear relationship between sales and promotional expenditures. Example 1 presents the test for the significance of β_1, the slope of sales with price.

EXAMPLE 1

TESTING FOR THE SIGNIFICANCE OF THE SLOPE OF SALES WITH PRICE

At the 0.05 level of significance, is there evidence that the slope of sales with price is different from zero?

SOLUTION From Figure 1, $t = -7.7664 < -2.0395$ (the critical value for $\alpha = 0.05$) or the p-value $= 0.0000000092 < 0.05$. Thus, there is a significant relationship between price, X_1, and sales, taking into account the promotional expenditures, X_2.

As seen with each of the two X variables, the test of significance for a particular regression coefficient is actually a test for the significance of adding a particular variable into a regression model, given that the other variable is included. Therefore, the t test for the regression coefficient is equivalent to testing for the contribution of each independent variable.

Confidence Interval Estimation

Instead of testing the significance of a population slope, you may want to estimate the value of a population slope. Equation (8) defines the confidence interval estimate for a population slope in multiple regression.

CONFIDENCE INTERVAL ESTIMATE FOR THE SLOPE

$$b_j \pm t_{n-k-1} S_{b_j} \tag{8}$$

To construct a 95% confidence interval estimate of the population slope, β_1 (the effect of price, X_1, on sales, Y, holding constant the effect of promotional expenditures, X_2), the critical value of t at the 95% confidence level with 31 degrees of freedom is 2.0395 (see the table of critical values of t). Then, using Equation (8) and Figure 1.

$$b_1 \pm t_{n-k-1} S_{b_1}$$
$$-53.2173 \pm (2.0395)(6.8522)$$
$$-53.2173 \pm 13.9752$$
$$-67.1925 \le \beta_1 \le -39.2421$$

Taking into account the effect of promotional expenditures, the estimated effect of a 1-cent increase in price is to reduce mean sales by approximately 39.2 to 67.2 bars. You have 95% confidence that this interval correctly estimates the relationship between these variables. From a hypothesis-testing viewpoint, because this confidence interval does not include 0, you conclude that the regression coefficient, β_1, has a significant effect.

Example 2 constructs and interprets a confidence interval estimate for the slope of sales with promotional expenditures.

EXAMPLE 2

CONSTRUCTING A CONFIDENCE INTERVAL ESTIMATE FOR THE SLOPE OF SALES WITH PROMOTIONAL EXPENDITURES

Construct a 95% confidence interval estimate of the population slope of sales with promotional expenditures.

SOLUTION The critical value of t at the 95% confidence level, with 31 degrees of freedom, is 2.0395 (see the table of critical values of t). Using Equation (8) and Figure 1,

$$3.6131 \pm (2.0395)(0.6852)$$
$$3.6131 \pm 1.3975$$
$$2.2156 \le \beta_2 \le 5.0106$$

Thus, taking into account the effect of price, the estimated effect of each additional dollar of promotional expenditures is to increase mean sales by approximately 2.2 to 5.0 bars. You have 95% confidence that this interval correctly estimates the relationship between these variables. From a hypothesis-testing viewpoint, because this confidence interval does not include 0, you can conclude that the regression coefficient, β_2, has a significant effect.

PROBLEMS FOR SECTION 4

Learning the Basics

PH Grade ASSIST **23** Given the following information from a multiple regression analysis:

$$n = 25 \quad b_1 = 5 \quad b_2 = 10 \quad S_{b_1} = 2 \quad S_{b_2} = 8$$

a. Which variable has the largest slope, in units of a t statistic?
b. Construct a 95% confidence interval estimate of the population slope, β_1.
c. At the 0.05 level of significance, determine whether each independent variable makes a significant contribution to the regression model. On the basis of these results, indicate the independent variables to include in this model.

24 Given the following information from a multiple regression analysis:

$$n = 20 \quad b_1 = 4 \quad b_2 = 3 \quad S_{b_1} = 1.2 \quad S_{b_2} = 0.8$$

a. Which variable has the largest slope, in units of a t statistic?
b. Construct a 95% confidence interval estimate of the population slope, β_1.
c. At the 0.05 level of significance, determine whether each independent variable makes a significant contribution to the regression model. On the basis of these results, indicate the independent variables to include in this model.

Applying the Concepts

PH Grade ASSIST **25** In Problem 3, you predicted the durability of a brand of running shoe, based on the forefoot shock-absorbing capability (FOREIMP) and the change in impact properties over time (MIDSOLE) for a sample of 15 pairs of shoes. Use the following results:

Variable	Coefficient	Standard Error	t Statistic	p-Value
INTERCEPT	−0.02686	0.06905	−0.39	0.7034
FOREIMP	0.79116	0.06295	12.57	0.0000
MIDSOLE	0.60484	0.07174	8.43	0.0000

a. Construct a 95% confidence interval estimate of the population slope between durability and forefoot shock-absorbing capability.
b. At the 0.05 level of significance, determine whether each independent variable makes a significant contribution to the regression model. On the basis of these results, indicate the independent variables to include in this model.

PH Grade ASSIST **SELF Test** **26** In Problem 4, you used sales and number of orders to predict distribution costs at a mail-order catalog business (see the **warecost.xls** file). Using the results from that problem,

a. construct a 95% confidence interval estimate of the population slope between distribution cost and sales.
b. at the 0.05 level of significance, determine whether each independent variable makes a significant contribution to the regression model. On the basis of these results, indicate the independent variables to include in this model.

27 In Problem 5, you used horsepower and weight to predict gasoline mileage (see the **auto.xls** file). Using the results from that problem,

a. construct a 95% confidence interval estimate of the population slope between gasoline mileage and horsepower.
b. at the 0.05 level of significance, determine whether each independent variable makes a significant contribution to the regression model. On the basis of these results, indicate the independent variables to include in this model.

28 In Problem 6, you used radio advertising and newspaper advertising to predict sales (see the **advertise.xls** file). Using the results from that problem,

a. construct a 95% confidence interval estimate of the population slope between sales and radio advertising.
b. at the 0.05 level of significance, determine whether each independent variable makes a significant contribution to the regression model. On the basis of these results, indicate the independent variables to include in this model.

29 In Problem 7, you used the total number of staff present and remote hours to predict standby hours (see the **standby.xls** file). Using the results from that problem,

a. construct a 95% confidence interval estimate of the population slope between standby hours and total number of staff present.
b. at the 0.05 level of significance, determine whether each independent variable makes a significant contribution to the regression model. On the basis of these results, indicate the independent variables to include in this model.

30 In Problem 8, you used land area of a property and age of a house to predict appraised value (see the **glencove.xls** file). Using the results from that problem,

a. construct a 95% confidence interval estimate of the population slope between appraised value and land area of a property.
b. at the 0.05 level of significance, determine whether each independent variable makes a significant contribution to the regression model. On the basis of these results, indicate the independent variables to include in this model.

5 TESTING PORTIONS OF THE MULTIPLE REGRESSION MODEL

In developing a multiple regression model, you want to use only those independent variables that significantly reduce the error in predicting the value of a dependent variable. If an independent variable does not improve the prediction, you can delete it from the multiple regression model and use a model with fewer independent variables.

The **partial F test** is an alternative method to the t test discussed in Section 4 for determining the contribution of an independent variable. It involves determining the contribution to the regression sum of squares made by each independent variable after all the other independent variables have been included in the model. The new independent variable is included only if it significantly improves the model.

To conduct partial F tests for the OmniPower sales example, you need to evaluate the contribution of promotional expenditures (X_2) after price (X_1) has been included in the model, and also evaluate the contribution of price (X_1) after promotional expenditures (X_2) have been included in the model.

In general, if there are several independent variables, you determine the contribution of each independent variable by taking into account the regression sum of squares of a model that includes all independent variables except the one of interest, SSR (all variables except j). Equation (9) determines the contribution of variable j, assuming that all other variables are already included.

DETERMINING THE CONTRIBUTION OF AN INDEPENDENT VARIABLE TO THE REGRESSION MODEL

$SSR(X_j \mid$ All variables *except j*)
$$= SSR \text{ (All variables } \textit{including } j) - SSR \text{ (All variables } \textit{except } j) \qquad \textbf{(9)}$$

If there are two independent variables, you use Equations (10a) and (10b) to determine the contribution of each.

CONTRIBUTION OF VARIABLE X_1, GIVEN THAT X_2 HAS BEEN INCLUDED
$$SSR(X_1 \mid X_2) = SSR(X_1 \text{ and } X_2) - SSR(X_2) \qquad \textbf{(10a)}$$

CONTRIBUTION OF VARIABLE X_2, GIVEN THAT X_1 HAS BEEN INCLUDED
$$SSR(X_2 \mid X_1) = SSR(X_1 \text{ and } X_2) - SSR(X_1) \qquad \textbf{(10b)}$$

The term $SSR(X_2)$ represents the sum of squares that is due to regression for a model that includes only the independent variable X_2 (promotional expenditures). Similarly, $SSR(X_1)$ represents the sum of squares that is due to regression for a model that includes only the independent variable X_1 (price). Figures 6 and 7 present Microsoft Excel results for these two models.

FIGURE 6

Microsoft Excel results of a simple linear regression analysis for sales and promotional expenditures, $SSR(X_2)$

	A	B	C	D	E	F	G
1	Sales & Promotional Expenses Analysis						
2							
3	*Regression Statistics*						
4	Multiple R	0.5351					
5	R Square	0.2863					
6	Adjusted R Square	0.2640					
7	Standard Error	1077.8721					
8	Observations	34					
9							
10	ANOVA						
11		*df*	*SS*	*MS*	*F*	*Significance F*	
12	Regression	1	14915814.102	14915814.102	12.8384	0.0011	
13	Residual	32	37177863.339	1161808.229			
14	Total	33	52093677.441				
15							
16		*Coefficients*	*Standard Error*	*t Stat*	*P-value*	*Lower 95%*	*Upper 95%*
17	Intercept	1496.0161	483.9789	3.0911	0.0041	510.1843	2481.8480
18	Promotion	4.1281	1.1521	3.5831	0.0011	1.7813	6.4748

FIGURE 7

Microsoft Excel results of a simple linear regression model for sales and price, $SSR(X_1)$

	A	B	C	D	E	F	G
1	Sales & Price Analysis						
2							
3	Regression Statistics						
4	Multiple R	0.7351					
5	R Square	0.5404					
6	Adjusted R Square	0.5261					
7	Standard Error	864.9457					
8	Observations	34					
9							
10	ANOVA						
11		df	SS	MS	F	Significance F	
12	Regression	1	28153486.15	28153486.15	37.6318	7.35855E-07	
13	Residual	32	23940191.29	748130.98			
14	Total	33	52093677.44				
15							
16		Coefficients	Standard Error	t Stat	P-value	Lower 95%	Upper 95%
17	Intercept	7512.3480	734.6189	10.2262	1.30793E-11	6015.9796	9008.7164
18	Price	-56.7138	9.2451	-6.1345	7.35855E-07	-75.5455	-37.8822

From Figure 6, $SSR(X_2) = 14,915,8102$ and from Figure 1, $SSR(X_1 \text{ and } X_2) = 39,472,730.77$. Then, using Equation (10a),

$$SSR(X_1 \mid X_2) = SSR(X_1 \text{ and } X_2) - SSR(X_2)$$
$$= 39,472,730.77 - 14,915,814.102$$
$$= 24,556,916.67$$

To determine whether X_1 significantly improves the model after X_2 has been included, you divide the regression sum of squares into two component parts, as shown in Table 3.

TABLE 3

ANOVA Table Dividing the Regression Sum of Squares into Components to Determine the Contribution of Variable X_1

Source	Degrees of Freedom	Sum of Squares	Mean Square (Variance)	F
Regression	2	39,472,730.77	19,736,365.39	
$\left\{ \begin{array}{c} X_2 \\ X_1 \mid X_2 \end{array} \right\}$	$\left\{ \begin{array}{c} 1 \\ 1 \end{array} \right\}$	$\left\{ \begin{array}{c} 14,915,814.10 \\ 24,556,916.67 \end{array} \right\}$	24,556,916.67	60.32
Error	31	12,620,946.67	407,127.31	
Total	33	52,093,677.44		

The null and alternative hypotheses to test for the contribution of X_1 to the model are

H_0: Variable X_1 does not significantly improve the model after variable X_2 has been included.
H_1: Variable X_1 significantly improves the model after variable X_2 has been included.

Equation (11) defines the partial F test statistic for testing the contribution of an independent variable.

PARTIAL F TEST STATISTIC

$$F = \frac{SSR(X_j \mid \text{All variables } except\ j)}{MSE} \tag{11}$$

The partial F test statistic follows an F distribution with 1 and $n - k - 1$ degrees of freedom.

From Table 3,

$$F = \frac{24,556,916.67}{407,127.31} = 60.32$$

The partial F test statistic has 1 and $n - k - 1 = 34 - 2 - 1 = 31$ degrees of freedom. Using a level of significance of 0.05, the critical value from the table of critical values of F is approximately 4.17 (see Figure 8).

FIGURE 8

Testing for contribution of a regression coefficient to a multiple regression model at the 0.05 level of significance, with 1 and 31 degrees of freedom

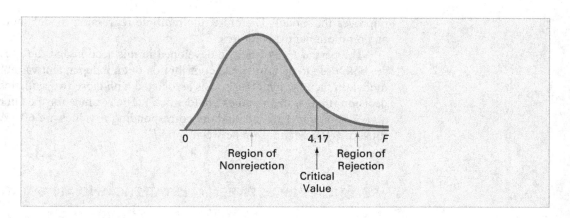

Because the partial F test statistic is greater than this critical F value ($60.32 > 4.17$), you reject H_0 and conclude that the addition of variable X_1 (price) significantly improves a regression model that already contains variable X_2 (promotional expenditures).

To evaluate the contribution of variable X_2 (promotional expenditures) to a model in which variable X_1 (price) has been included, you need to use Equation (10b). First, from Figure 7, observe that $SSR(X_1) = 28,153,486.15$. Second, from Table 3, observe that $SSR(X_1 \text{ and } X_2) = 39,472,730.77$. Then, using Equation (10b),

$$SSR(X_2 \mid X_1) = 39,472,730.77 - 28,153,486.15 = 11,319,244.62$$

To determine whether X_2 significantly improves a model after X_1 has been included, you can divide the regression sum of squares into two component parts, as shown in Table 4.

TABLE 4

ANOVA Table Dividing the Regression Sum of Squares into Components to Determine the Contribution of Variable X_2

Source	Degrees of Freedom	Sum of Squares	Mean Square (Variance)	F
Regression	2	39,472,730.77	19,736,365.39	
$\left\{\begin{array}{c} X_1 \\ X_2 \mid X_1 \end{array}\right.$	$\left[\begin{array}{c} 1 \\ 1 \end{array}\right]$	$\left[\begin{array}{c} 28,153,486.15 \\ 11,319,244.62 \end{array}\right]$	11,319,244.62	27.80
Error	31	12,620,946.67	407,127.31	
Total	33	52,093,677.44		

The null and alternative hypotheses to test for the contribution of X_2 to the model are

H_0: Variable X_2 does not significantly improve the model after variable X_1 has been included.
H_1: Variable X_2 significantly improves the model after variable X_1 has been included.

Using Equation (11) and Table 4,

$$F = \frac{11,319,244.62}{407,127.31} = 27.80$$

In Figure 8 above, you can see that, using a 0.05 level of significance, the critical value of F, with 1 and 31 degrees of freedom, is approximately 4.17. Because the partial F test statistic is greater than this critical value ($27.80 > 4.17$), you reject H_0 and conclude that the addition of variable X_2 (promotional expenditures) significantly improves the multiple regression model already containing X_1 (price).

Thus, by testing for the contribution of each independent variable after the other has been included in the model, you determine that each of the two independent variables significantly improves the model. Therefore, the multiple regression model should include both price, X_1, and promotional expenditures, X_2.

The partial F test statistic developed in this section and the t test statistic of Equation (7) are both used to determine the contribution of an independent variable to a multiple regression model. In fact, the hypothesis tests associated with these two statistics always result in the same decision (that is, the p-values are identical). The t values for the OmniPower regression model are -7.7664 and $+5.2728$, and the corresponding F values are 60.32 and 27.80. Equation (12) illustrates the relationship between t and F.

RELATIONSHIP BETWEEN A t STATISTIC AND AN F STATISTIC

$$t_a^2 = F_{1,a} \tag{12}$$

where

$$a = \text{degrees of freedom}$$

Coefficients of Partial Determination

Recall from Section 2 that the coefficient of multiple determination, r^2, measures the proportion of the variation in Y that is explained by variation in the independent variables. Now, the contribution of each independent variable to a multiple regression model, while holding constant the other variable, is examined. The **coefficients of partial determination** ($r_{Y1.2}^2$ and $r_{Y2.1}^2$) measure the proportion of the variation in the dependent variable that is explained by each independent variable while controlling for, or holding constant, the other independent variable. Equation (13) defines the coefficients of partial determination for a multiple regression model with two independent variables.

COEFFICIENTS OF PARTIAL DETERMINATION FOR A MULTIPLE REGRESSION MODEL CONTAINING TWO INDEPENDENT VARIABLES

$$r_{Y1.2}^2 = \frac{SSR(X_1 \mid X_2)}{SST - SSR(X_1 \, and \, X_2) + SSR(X_1 \mid X_2)} \tag{13a}$$

and

$$r_{Y2.1}^2 = \frac{SSR(X_2 \mid X_1)}{SST - SSR(X_1 \, and \, X_2) + SSR(X_2 \mid X_1)} \tag{13b}$$

where

$SSR(X_1 \mid X_2) =$ sum of squares of the contribution of variable X_1 to the regression model, given that variable X_2 has been included in the model

$SST =$ total sum of squares for Y

$SSR(X_1 \, and \, X_2) =$ regression sum of squares when variables X_1 and X_2 are both included in the multiple regression model

$SSR(X_2 \mid X_1) =$ sum of squares of the contribution of variable X_2 to the regression model, given that variable X_1 has been included in the model

For the OmniPower sales example,

$$r_{Y1.2}^2 = \frac{24{,}556{,}916.67}{52{,}093{,}677.44 - 39{,}472{,}730.77 + 24{,}556{,}916.67}$$

$$= 0.6605$$

$$r_{Y2.1}^2 = \frac{11{,}319{,}244.62}{52{,}093{,}677.44 - 39{,}472{,}730.77 + 11{,}319{,}244.62}$$

$$= 0.4728$$

The coefficient of partial determination of variable Y with X_1 while holding X_2 constant $(r_{Y1.2}^2)$ is 0.6605. Thus, for a given (constant) amount of promotional expenditures, 66.05% of the variation in OmniPower sales is explained by the variation in the price. The coefficient of partial determination of variable Y with X_2 while holding X_1 constant $(r_{Y2.1}^2)$ is 0.4728. Thus, for a given (constant) price, 47.28% of the variation in sales of OmniPower bars is explained by variation in the amount of promotional expenditures.

Equation (14) defines the coefficient of partial determination for the jth variable in a multiple regression model containing several (k) independent variables.

COEFFICIENT OF PARTIAL DETERMINATION FOR A MULTIPLE REGRESSION MODEL CONTAINING k INDEPENDENT VARIABLES

$$r_{Y_j.(\text{All variables } except\ j)}^2 = \frac{SSR(X_j|\text{All variables } except\ j)}{SST - SSR(\text{All variables } including\ j) + SSR(X_j|\text{All variables } except\ j)}$$

(14)

PROBLEMS FOR SECTION 5

Learning the Basics

 31 The following is the ANOVA summary table for a multiple regression model with two independent variables:

Source	Degrees of Freedom	Sum of Squares	Mean Squares	F
Regression	2	60		
Error	18	120		
Total	20	180		

If $SSR(X_1) = 45$ and $SSR(X_2) = 25$,
a. determine whether there is a significant relationship between Y and each of the independent variables at the 0.05 level of significance.
b. compute the coefficients of partial determination, $r_{Y1.2}^2$ and $r_{Y2.1}^2$, and interpret their meaning.

 32 The following is the ANOVA summary table for a multiple regression model with two independent variables:

Source	Degrees of Freedom	Sum of Squares	Mean Squares	F
Regression	2	30		
Error	10	120		
Total	12	150		

If $SSR(X_1) = 20$ and $SSR(X_2) = 15$,
a. determine whether there is a significant relationship between Y and each of the independent variables at the 0.05 level of significance.
b. compute the coefficients of partial determination, $r_{Y1.2}^2$ and $r_{Y2.1}^2$, and interpret their meaning.

Applying the Concepts

33 In Problem 5, you used horsepower and weight to predict gasoline mileage (see the auto.xls file). Using the results from that problem,
a. at the 0.05 level of significance, determine whether each independent variable makes a significant contribution to the regression model. On the basis of these results, indicate the most appropriate regression model for this set of data.

b. compute the coefficients of partial determination, $r_{Y1.2}^2$ and $r_{Y2.1}^2$, and interpret their meaning.

 34 In Problem 4, you used sales and number of orders to predict distribution costs at a mail-order catalog business (see the warecost.xls file). Using the results from that problem,

a. at the 0.05 level of significance, determine whether each independent variable makes a significant contribution to the regression model. On the basis of these results, indicate the most appropriate regression model for this set of data.

b. compute the coefficients of partial determination, $r_{Y1.2}^2$ and $r_{Y2.1}^2$, and interpret their meaning.

35 In Problem 7, you used the total staff present and remote hours to predict standby hours (see the standby.xls file). Using the results from that problem,

a. at the 0.05 level of significance, determine whether each independent variable makes a significant contribution to the regression model. On the basis of these results, indicate the most appropriate regression model for this set of data.

b. compute the coefficients of partial determination, $r_{Y1.2}^2$ and $r_{Y2.1}^2$, and interpret their meaning.

36 In Problem 6, you used radio advertising and newspaper advertising to predict sales (see the advertise.xls file). Using the results from that problem,

a. at the 0.05 level of significance, determine whether each independent variable makes a significant contribution to the regression model. On the basis of these results, indicate the most appropriate regression model for this set of data.

b. compute the coefficients of partial determination, $r_{Y1.2}^2$ and $r_{Y2.1}^2$, and interpret their meaning.

37 In Problem 8, you used land area of a property and age of a house to predict appraised value (see the glencove.xls file). Using the results from that problem,

a. at the 0.05 level of significance, determine whether each independent variable makes a significant contribution to the regression model. On the basis of these results, indicate the most appropriate regression model for this set of data.

b. compute the coefficients of partial determination, $r_{Y1.2}^2$ and $r_{Y2.1}^2$, and interpret their meaning.

6 USING DUMMY VARIABLES AND INTERACTION TERMS IN REGRESSION MODELS

The multiple regression models discussed in Sections 1 through 5 assumed that each independent variable is numerical. However, in some situations, you might want to include categorical variables as independent variables in the regression model. For example, in Section 1, you used price and promotional expenditures to predict the monthly sales of OmniPower high-energy bars. In addition to these numerical independent variables, you may want to include the effect of the shelf location in the store (for example, end-aisle display or no end-aisle display) when developing a model to predict OmniPower sales.

The use of **dummy variables** allows you to include categorical independent variables as part of the regression model. If a given categorical independent variable has two categories, then you need only one dummy variable to represent the two categories. A dummy variable, X_d, is defined as

$$X_d = 0 \text{ if the observation is in category 1}$$
$$X_d = 1 \text{ if the observation is in category 2}$$

To illustrate the application of dummy variables in regression, consider a model for predicting the assessed value from a sample of 15 houses, based on the size of the house (in thousands of square feet) and whether the house has a fireplace. To include the categorical variable concerning the presence of a fireplace, the dummy variable X_2 is defined as

$$X_2 = 0 \text{ if the house does not have a fireplace}$$
$$X_2 = 1 \text{ if the house has a fireplace}$$

Table 5 presents the data, which are also stored in the file house3.xls. In the last column of Table 5, you can see how the categorical data are converted to numerical values.

TABLE 5

Predicting Assessed Value, Based on Size of House and Presence of a Fireplace

House	Y = Assessed Value ($000)	X_1 = Size of House (Thousands of Square Feet)	Fireplace	X_2 = Fireplace
1	84.4	2.00	Yes	1
2	77.4	1.71	No	0
3	75.7	1.45	No	0
4	85.9	1.76	Yes	1
5	79.1	1.93	No	0
6	70.4	1.20	Yes	1
7	75.8	1.55	Yes	1
8	85.9	1.93	Yes	1
9	78.5	1.59	Yes	1
10	79.2	1.50	Yes	1
11	86.7	1.90	Yes	1
12	79.3	1.39	Yes	1
13	74.5	1.54	No	0
14	83.8	1.89	Yes	1
15	76.8	1.59	No	0

Assuming that the slope of assessed value with the size of the house is the same for houses that have and do not have a fireplace, the multiple regression model is

$$Y_i = \beta_0 + \beta_1 X_{1i} + \beta_2 X_{2i} + \varepsilon_i$$

where

Y_i = assessed value in thousands of dollars for house i

β_0 = Y intercept

X_{1i} = size of the house, in thousands of square feet, for house i

β_1 = slope of assessed value with size of the house, holding constant the presence or absence of a fireplace

X_{2i} = dummy variable representing the presence or absence of a fireplace for house i

β_2 = incremental effect of the presence of a fireplace on assessed value, holding constant the size of the house

ε_i = random error in Y for house i

Figure 9 illustrates the Microsoft Excel results for this model.

FIGURE 9

Microsoft Excel results for the regression model that includes size of the house and presence of fireplace

See Section E1 to create this.

	A	B	C	D	E	F	G
1	Assessed Value Analysis						
2							
3	Regression Statistics						
4	Multiple R	0.9006					
5	R Square	0.8111					
6	Adjusted R Square	0.7796					
7	Standard Error	2.2626					
8	Observations	15					
9							
10	ANOVA						
11		df	SS	MS	F	Significance F	
12	Regression	2	263.7039	131.8520	25.7557	4.54968E-05	
13	Residual	12	61.4321	5.1193			
14	Total	14	325.1360				
15							
16		Coefficients	Standard Error	t Stat	P-value	Lower 95%	Upper 95%
17	Intercept	50.0905	4.3517	11.5107	7.67943E-08	40.6090	59.5719
18	Size	16.1858	2.5744	6.2871	4.02437E-05	10.5766	21.7951
19	Fireplace	3.8530	1.2412	3.1042	0.0091	1.1486	6.5574

From Figure 9, the regression equation is

$$\hat{Y}_i = 50.0905 + 16.1858X_{1i} + 3.8530X_{2i}$$

For houses without a fireplace, you substitute $X_2 = 0$ into the regression equation:

$$\begin{aligned}
\hat{Y}_i &= 50.0905 + 16.1858X_{1i} + 3.8530X_{2i} \\
&= 50.0905 + 16.1858X_{1i} + 3.8530(0) \\
&= 50.0905 + 16.1858X_{1i}
\end{aligned}$$

For houses with a fireplace, you substitute $X_2 = 1$ into the regression equation:

$$\begin{aligned}
\hat{Y}_i &= 50.0905 + 16.1858X_{1i} + 3.8530X_{2i} \\
&= 50.0905 + 16.1858X_{1i} + 3.8530(1) \\
&= 53.9435 + 16.1858X_{1i}
\end{aligned}$$

In this model, the regression coefficients are interpreted as follows:

1. Holding constant whether a house has a fireplace, for each increase of 1.0 thousand square feet in the size of the house, the mean assessed value is estimated to increase by 16.1858 thousand dollars (that is, $16,185.80).
2. Holding constant the size of the house, the presence of a fireplace is estimated to increase the mean assessed value of the house by 3.8530 thousand dollars (or $3,853).

In Figure 9, the t statistic for the slope of the size of the house with assessed value is 6.2871, and the p-value is approximately 0.000; the t statistic for presence of a fireplace is 3.1042, and the p-value is 0.0091. Thus, each of the two variables makes a significant contribution to the model at a level of significance of 0.01. In addition, the coefficient of multiple determination indicates that 81.11% of the variation in assessed value is explained by variation in the size of the house and whether the house has a fireplace.

EXAMPLE 3	**MODELING A THREE-LEVEL CATEGORICAL VARIABLE**

Define a multiple regression model using sales as the dependent variable and package design and price as independent variables. Package design is a three-level categorical variable with designs A, B, or C.

SOLUTION To model a three-level categorical variable, two dummy variables are needed:

$$X_{1i} = 1 \text{ if package design A is used in observation } i; 0 \text{ otherwise}$$
$$X_{2i} = 1 \text{ if package design B is used in observation } i; 0 \text{ otherwise}$$

If observation i is for package design A, then $X_{1i} = 1$ and $X_{2i} = 0$; for package design B, then $X_{1i} = 0$ and $X_{2i} = 1$; and for package design C, then $X_{1i} = X_{2i} = 0$. A third independent variable is used for price:

$$X_{3i} = \text{price for observation } i$$

Thus, the regression model for this example is

$$Y_i = \beta_0 + \beta_1 X_{1i} + \beta_2 X_{2i} + \beta_3 X_{3i} + \varepsilon_i$$

where

$$Y_i = \text{sales for observation } i$$

$$\beta_0 = Y \text{ intercept}$$

$$\beta_1 = \text{difference between the mean sales of design A and the mean sales of design C, holding the price constant}$$

$$\beta_2 = \text{difference between the mean sales of design B and the mean sales of design C, holding the price constant}$$

$$\beta_3 = \text{slope of sales with price, holding the package design constant}$$

$$\varepsilon_i = \text{random error in } Y \text{ for observation } i$$

Interactions

In all the regression models discussed so far, the *effect* an independent variable has on the dependent variable was assumed to be statistically independent of the other independent variables in the model. An **interaction** occurs if the effect of an independent variable on the dependent variable is affected by the *value* of a second independent variable. For example, it is possible for advertising to have a large effect on the sales of a product when the price of a product is low. However, if the price of the product is too high, increases in advertising will not dramatically change sales. In this case, price and advertising are said to interact. In other words, you cannot make general statements about the effect of advertising on sales. The effect that advertising has on sales is *dependent* on the price. You use an **interaction term** (sometimes referred to as a **cross-product term**) to model an interaction effect in a regression model.

To illustrate the concept of interaction and use of an interaction term, return to the example concerning the assessed values of homes. In the regression model, you assumed that the effect the size of the home has on the assessed value is independent of whether the house has a fireplace. In other words, you assumed that the slope of assessed value with size is the same for houses with fireplaces as it is for houses without fireplaces. If these two slopes are different, an interaction between size of the home and fireplace exists.

To evaluate the possibility of an interaction, you first define an interaction term that consists of the product of the independent variable X_1 (size of house) and the dummy variable X_2 (fireplace). You then test whether this interaction variable makes a significant contribution to the regression model. If the interaction is significant, you cannot use the original model for prediction. For the data of Table 5, let

$$X_3 = X_1 \times X_2$$

Figure 10 illustrates Microsoft Excel results for this regression model, which includes the size of the house, X_1, the presence of a fireplace, X_2, and the interaction of X_1 and X_2 (which is defined as X_3).

FIGURE 10

Microsoft Excel results for a regression model that includes size, presence of fireplace, and interaction of size and fireplace

See Sections E1 and E6 to create this.

	A	B	C	D	E	F	G
1	Assessed Value Analysis						
2							
3	*Regression Statistics*						
4	Multiple R	0.9179					
5	R Square	0.8426					
6	Adjusted R Square	0.7996					
7	Standard Error	2.1573					
8	Observations	15					
9							
10	ANOVA						
11		*df*	*SS*	*MS*	*F*	*Significance F*	
12	Regression	3	273.9441	91.3147	19.6215	0.0001	
13	Residual	11	51.1919	4.6538			
14	Total	14	325.1360				
15							
16		*Coefficients*	*Standard Error*	*t Stat*	*P-value*	*Lower 95%*	*Upper 95%*
17	Intercept	62.9522	9.6122	6.5492	4.13993E-05	41.7959	84.1085
18	Size	8.3624	5.8173	1.4375	0.1784	-4.4414	21.1662
19	Fireplace	-11.8404	10.6455	-1.1122	0.2898	-35.2710	11.5902
20	Size * Fireplace	9.5180	6.4165	1.4834	0.1661	-4.6046	23.6406

To test for the existence of an interaction, you use the null hypothesis $H_0: \beta_3 = 0$ versus the alternative hypothesis $H_1: \beta_3 \neq 0$. In Figure 10, the t statistic for the interaction of size and fireplace is 1.4834. Because the p-value $= 0.1661 > 0.05$, you do not reject the null hypothesis. Therefore, the interaction does not make a significant contribution to the model, given that size and presence of a fireplace are already included.

Regression models can have several numerical independent variables. Example 4 illustrates a regression model in which there are two numerical independent variables as well as a categorical independent variable.

EXAMPLE 4

STUDYING A REGRESSION MODEL THAT CONTAINS A DUMMY VARIABLE

A real estate developer wants to predict heating oil consumption in single-family houses, based on atmospheric temperature, X_1, and the amount of attic insulation, X_2. Suppose that, of 15 houses selected, houses 1, 4, 6, 7, 8, 10, and 12 are ranch-style houses. The data are stored in the file htngoil.xls. Develop and analyze an appropriate regression model, using these three independent variables, X_1, X_2, and X_3 (the dummy variable for ranch-style houses).

SOLUTION Define X_3, a dummy variable for ranch-style house, as follows:

$$X_3 = 0 \text{ if the style is not ranch}$$
$$X_3 = 1 \text{ if the style is ranch}$$

Assuming that the slope between home heating oil consumption and atmospheric temperature, X_1, and between home heating oil consumption and the amount of attic insulation, X_2, is the same for both styles of houses, the regression model is

$$Y_i = \beta_0 + \beta_1 X_{1i} + \beta_2 X_{2i} + \beta_3 X_{3i} + \varepsilon_i$$

where

$Y_i =$ monthly heating oil consumption, in gallons, for house i

$\beta_0 = Y$ intercept

$\beta_1 =$ slope of heating oil consumption with atmospheric temperature, holding constant the effect of attic insulation and the style of the house

$\beta_2 =$ slope of heating oil consumption with attic insulation, holding constant the effect of atmospheric temperature and the style of the house

$\beta_3 =$ incremental effect of the presence of a ranch-style house, holding constant the effect of atmospheric temperature and attic insulation

$\varepsilon_i =$ random error in Y for house i

Figure 11 displays Microsoft Excel results.

FIGURE 11

Microsoft Excel results for a regression model that includes temperature, insulation, and style for the heating oil data

	A	B	C	D	E	F	G
1	Heating Oil Consumption Analysis						
2							
3	Regression Statistics						
4	Multiple R	0.9942					
5	R Square	0.9884					
6	Adjusted R Square	0.9853					
7	Standard Error	15.7489					
8	Observations	15					
9							
10	ANOVA						
11		df	SS	MS	F	Significance F	
12	Regression	3	233406.9094	77802.3031	313.6822	6.21548E-11	
13	Residual	11	2728.3200	248.0291			
14	Total	14	236135.2293				
15							
16		Coefficients	Standard Error	t Stat	P-value	Lower 95%	Upper 95%
17	Intercept	592.5401	14.3370	41.3295	2.02317E-13	560.9846	624.0956
18	Temperature	-5.5251	0.2044	-27.0267	2.07188E-11	-5.9751	-5.0752
19	Insulation	-21.3761	1.4480	-14.7623	1.34816E-08	-24.5632	-18.1891
20	Ranch-style	-38.9727	8.3584	-4.6627	0.0007	-57.3695	-20.5759

From the results in Figure 11, the regression equation is

$$\hat{Y}_i = 592.5401 - 5.5251X_{1i} - 21.3761X_{2i} - 38.9727X_{3i}$$

For houses that are not ranch style, because $X_3 = 0$, this reduces to

$$\hat{Y}_i = 592.5401 - 5.5251X_{1i} - 21.3761X_{2i}$$

For houses that are ranch style, because $X_3 = 1$, this reduces to

$$\hat{Y}_i = 553.5674 - 5.5251X_{1i} - 21.3761X_{2i}$$

The regression coefficients are interpreted as follows:

1. Holding constant the attic insulation and the house style, for each additional 1°F increase in atmospheric temperature, you estimate that the mean oil consumption decreases by 5.5251 gallons.
2. Holding constant the atmospheric temperature and the house style, for each additional 1-inch increase in attic insulation, you estimate that the mean oil consumption decreases by 21.3761 gallons.
3. b_3 measures the effect on oil consumption of having a ranch-style house ($X_3 = 1$) compared with having a house that is not ranch style ($X_3 = 0$). Thus, with atmospheric temperature and attic insulation held constant, you estimate that the mean oil consumption is 38.9727 gallons less for a ranch-style house than for a house that is not ranch style.

The three t statistics representing the slopes for temperature, insulation, and ranch style are −27.0267, −7623, and −4.6627. Each of the corresponding p-values is extremely small, all being less than 0.001. Thus, each of the three variables makes a significant contribution to the model. In addition, the coefficient of multiple determination indicates that 98.84% of the variation in oil usage is explained by variation in the temperature, insulation, and whether the house is ranch style.

Before you can use the model in Example 4, you need to determine whether the independent variables interact with each other. In Example 5, three interaction terms are added to the model.

EXAMPLE 5

EVALUATING A REGRESSION MODEL WITH SEVERAL INTERACTIONS

For the data of Example 4, determine whether adding the interaction terms make a significant contribution to the regression model.

SOLUTION To evaluate possible interactions between the independent variables, three interaction terms are constructed. Let $X_4 = X_1 \times X_2$, $X_5 = X_1 \times X_3$, and $X_6 = X_2 \times X_3$. The regression model is now

$$Y_i = \beta_0 + \beta_1 X_{1i} + \beta_2 X_{2i} + \beta_3 X_{3i} + \beta_4 X_{4i} + \beta_5 X_{5i} + \beta_6 X_{6i} + \varepsilon_i$$

where X_1 is temperature, X_2 is insulation, X_3 is the dummy variable ranch style, X_4 is the interaction between temperature and insulation, X_5 is the interaction between temperature and ranch style, and X_6 is the interaction between insulation and ranch style.

To test whether the three interactions significantly improve the regression model, you use the partial F test. The null and alternative hypotheses are

H_0: $\beta_4 = \beta_5 = \beta_6 = 0$ (There are no interactions among X_1, X_2, and X_3.)
H_1: $\beta_4 \neq 0$ and/or $\beta_5 \neq 0$ and/or $\beta_6 \neq 0$ (X_1 interacts with X_2, and/or X_1 interacts with X_3, and/or X_2 interacts with X_3.)

From Figure 12,

$$SSR(X_1, X_2, X_3, X_4, X_5, X_6) = 234{,}510.582 \text{ with 6 degrees of freedom}$$

and from Figure 11, $SSR(X_1, X_2, X_3) = 233{,}406.9094$ with 3 degrees of freedom.

FIGURE 12

Microsoft Excel results for a regression model that includes temperature, X_1; insulation, X_2; the dummy variable ranch style, X_3; the interaction of temperature and insulation, X_4; the interaction of temperature and ranch style, X_5; and the interaction of insulation and ranch style, X_6

	A	B	C	D	E	F	G
1	Heating Oil Consumption Analysis						
2							
3	*Regression Statistics*						
4	Multiple R	0.9966					
5	R Square	0.9931					
6	Adjusted R Square	0.9880					
7	Standard Error	14.2506					
8	Observations	15					
9							
10	ANOVA						
11		df	SS	MS	F	Significance F	
12	Regression	6	234510.582	39085.097	192.4607	3.32423E-08	
13	Residual	8	1624.647	203.081			
14	Total	14	236135.229				
15							
16		Coefficients	Standard Error	t Stat	P-value	Lower 95%	Upper 95%
17	Intercept	642.8867	26.7059	24.0728	9.45284E-09	581.3027	704.4707
18	Temperature	-6.9263	0.7531	-9.1969	1.58014E-05	-8.6629	-5.1896
19	Insulation	-27.8825	3.5801	-7.7882	5.29456E-05	-36.1383	-19.6268
20	Style	-84.6088	29.9956	-2.8207	0.0225	-153.7788	-15.4389
21	Temperature * Insulation	0.1702	0.0886	1.9204	0.0911	-0.0342	0.3746
22	Temperature * Ranch-style	0.6596	0.4617	1.4286	0.1910	-0.4051	1.7242
23	Insulation * Ranch-style	4.9870	3.5137	1.4193	0.1936	-3.1156	13.0895

Thus, $SSR(X_1, X_2, X_3, X_4, X_5, X_6) - SSR(X_1, X_2, X_3) = 234{,}510.582 - 233{,}406.9094 = 1{,}103.67$. The difference in degrees of freedom is $6 - 3 = 3$.

To use the partial F test for the simultaneous contribution of three variables to a model, you use an extension of Equation (11).[1] The partial F test statistic is

$$F = \frac{[SSR(X_1, X_2, X_3, X_4, X_5, X_6) - SSR(X_1, X_2, X_3)] / 3}{MSE(X_1, X_2, X_3, X_4, X_5, X_6)} = \frac{1{,}103.67 / 3}{203.08} = 1.81$$

[1] In general, if a model has several independent variables and you want to test whether an additional set of independent variables contribute to the model, the numerator of the F test is [SSR (for all independent variables)] − SSR (for the initial set of variables) divided by the number of independent variables whose contribution is being tested.

You compare the F test statistic of 1.81 to the critical F value for 3 and 8 degrees of freedom. Using a level of significance of 0.05, the critical F value from the table of critical values of F is 4.07. Because $1.81 < 4.07$, you conclude that the interactions do not make a significant contribution to the model, given that the model already includes temperature, X_1; insulation, X_2; and whether the house is ranch style, X_3. Therefore, the multiple regression model using X_1, X_2, and X_3 but no interaction terms is the better model. If you rejected this null hypothesis, you would then test the contribution of each interaction separately in order to determine which interaction terms to include in the model.

PROBLEMS FOR SECTION 6

Learning the Basics

38 Suppose X_1 is a numerical variable and X_2 is a dummy variable and the regression equation for a sample of $n = 20$ is

$$\hat{Y}_i = 6 + 4X_{1i} + 2X_{2i}$$

a. Interpret the meaning of the slope for variable X_1.
b. Interpret the meaning of the slope for variable X_2.
c. Suppose that the t statistic for testing the contribution of variable X_2 is 3.27. At the 0.05 level of significance, is there evidence that variable X_2 makes a significant contribution to the model?

Applying the Concepts

39 The chair of the accounting department wants to develop a regression model to predict the grade point average in accounting for graduating accounting majors, based on the student's SAT score and whether the student received a grade of B or higher in the introductory statistics course (0 = no and 1 = yes).

a. Explain the steps involved in developing a regression model for these data. Be sure to indicate the particular models you need to evaluate and compare.
b. Suppose the regression coefficient for the variable of whether the student received a grade of B or higher in the introductory statistics course is +0.30. How do you interpret this result?

40 A real estate association in a suburban community would like to study the relationship between the size of a single-family house (as measured by the number of rooms) and the selling price of the house (in thousands of dollars). Two different neighborhoods are included in the study, one on the east side of the community (=0) and the other on the west side (=1). A random sample of 20 houses was selected, with the results given in the file **neighbor.xls**.

a. State the multiple regression equation.
b. Interpret the meaning of the slopes in this problem.
c. Predict the mean selling price for a house with nine rooms that is located in an east-side neighborhood. Construct a 95% confidence interval estimate and a 95% prediction interval.
d. Perform a residual analysis on the results and determine the adequacy of the model.
e. Is there a significant relationship between selling price and the two independent variables (rooms and neighborhood) at the 0.05 level of significance?
f. At the 0.05 level of significance, determine whether each independent variable makes a contribution to the

regression model. Indicate the most appropriate regression model for this set of data.

g. Construct 95% confidence interval estimates of the population slope for the relationship between selling price and number of rooms and between selling price and neighborhood.
h. Interpret the meaning of the coefficient of multiple determination.
i. Compute the adjusted r^2.
j. Compute the coefficients of partial determination and interpret their meaning.
k. What assumption do you need to make about the slope of selling price with number of rooms?
l. Add an interaction term to the model and, at the 0.05 level of significance, determine whether it makes a significant contribution to the model.
m. On the basis of the results of (f) and (l), which model is most appropriate? Explain.

41 The marketing manager of a large supermarket chain would like to determine the effect of shelf space and whether the product was placed at the front or back of the aisle on the sales of pet food. A random sample of 12 equal-sized stores is selected, with the following results (stored in the file **petfood.xls**):

Store	Shelf Space (Feet)	Location	Weekly Sales (Dollars)
1	5	Back	160
2	5	Front	220
3	5	Back	140
4	10	Back	190
5	10	Back	240
6	10	Front	260
7	15	Back	230
8	15	Back	270
9	15	Front	280
10	20	Back	260
11	20	Back	290
12	20	Front	310

a. State the multiple regression equation.
b. Interpret the meaning of the slopes in this problem.
c. Predict the mean weekly sales of pet food for a store with 8 feet of shelf space situated at the back of the aisle. Construct a 95% confidence interval estimate and a 95% prediction interval.
d. Perform a residual analysis on the results and determine the adequacy of the model.

e. Is there a significant relationship between sales and the two independent variables (shelf space and aisle position) at the 0.05 level of significance?

f. At the 0.05 level of significance, determine whether each independent variable makes a contribution to the regression model. Indicate the most appropriate regression model for this set of data.

g. Construct 95% confidence interval estimates of the population slope for the relationship between sales and shelf space and between sales and aisle location.

h. Interpret the meaning of the coefficient of multiple determination, r^2.

i. Compute the adjusted r^2.

j. Compute the coefficients of partial determination and interpret their meaning.

k. What assumption about the slope of shelf space with sales do you need to make in this problem?

l. Add an interaction term to the model and, at the 0.05 level of significance, determine whether it makes a significant contribution to the model.

m. On the basis of the results of (f) and (n), which model is most appropriate? Explain.

42 In mining engineering, holes are often drilled through rock, using drill bits. As the drill hole gets deeper, additional rods are added to the drill bit to enable additional drilling to take place. It is expected that drilling time increases with depth. This increased drilling time could be caused by several factors, including the mass of the drill rods that are strung together. A key question relates to whether drilling is faster using dry drilling holes or wet drilling holes. Using dry drilling holes involves forcing compressed air down the drill rods to flush the cuttings and drive the hammer. Using wet drilling holes involves forcing water rather than air down the hole. The data file drill.xls contains measurements for a sample of 50 drill holes of the time to drill each additional 5 feet (in minutes), the depth (in feet), and whether the hole was a dry drilling hole or a wet drilling hole. Develop a model to predict additional drilling time, based on depth and type of drilling hole (dry or wet).

Source: Extracted from R. Penner and D. G. Watts, "Mining Information," The American Statistician, *45, 1991, pp. 4–9.*

a. State the multiple regression equation.

b. Interpret the meaning of the slopes in this problem.

c. Predict the mean additional drilling time for a dry drilling hole at a depth of 100 feet. Construct a 95% confidence interval estimate and a 95% prediction interval.

d. Perform a residual analysis on the results and determine the adequacy of the model.

e. Is there a significant relationship between additional drilling time and the two independent variables (depth and type of drilling hole) at the 0.05 level of significance?

f. At the 0.05 level of significance, determine whether each independent variable makes a contribution to the regression model. Indicate the most appropriate regression model for this set of data.

g. Construct 95% confidence interval estimates of the population slope for the relationship between additional drilling time and depth and between additional drilling time and type of drilling hole.

h. Interpret the meaning of the coefficient of multiple determination.

i. Compute the adjusted r^2.

j. Compute the coefficients of partial determination and interpret their meaning.

k. What assumption do you need to make about the slope of additional drilling time with depth?

l. Add an interaction term to the model and, at the 0.05 level of significance, determine whether it makes a significant contribution to the model.

m. On the basis of the results of (f) and (l), which model is most appropriate? Explain.

43 The owner of a moving company typically has his most experienced manager predict the total number of labor hours that will be required to complete an upcoming move. This approach has proved useful in the past, but the owner would like to be able to develop a more accurate method of predicting the labor hours by using the number of cubic feet moved and whether there is an elevator in the apartment building. In a preliminary effort to provide a more accurate method, he has collected data for 36 moves in which the origin and destination were within the borough of Manhattan in New York City and the travel time was an insignificant portion of the hours worked. The data are stored in the file moving.xls.

a. State the multiple regression equation.

b. Interpret the meaning of the slopes in this problem.

c. Predict the mean labor hours for moving 500 cubic feet in an apartment building that has an elevator, and construct a 95% confidence interval estimate and a 95% prediction interval.

d. Perform a residual analysis on the results and determine the adequacy of the model.

e. Is there a significant relationship between labor hours and the two independent variables (cubic feet moved and whether there is an elevator in the apartment building) at the 0.05 level of significance?

f. At the 0.05 level of significance, determine whether each independent variable makes a contribution to the regression model. Indicate the most appropriate regression model for this set of data.

g. Construct a 95% confidence interval estimate of the population slope for the relationship between labor hours and cubic feet moved, and between labor hours and whether there is an elevator in the apartment building.

h. Interpret the meaning of the coefficient of multiple determination.

i. Compute the adjusted r^2.

j. Compute the coefficients of partial determination and interpret their meaning.

k. What assumption about the slope of labor hours with cubic feet moved do you need to make?

l. Add an interaction term to the model and, at the 0.05 level of significance, determine whether it makes a significant contribution to the model.

m. On the basis of the results of (f) and (l), which model is most appropriate? Explain.

 44 In Problem 4, you used sales and orders to predict distribution cost (see the file warecost.xls). Develop a regression model to predict distribution cost that includes the sales, orders, and the interaction of sales and orders.

a. At the 0.05 level of significance, is there evidence that the interaction term makes a significant contribution to the model?

b. Which regression model is more appropriate, the one used in (a) or the one used in Problem 4? Explain.

45 Zagat's publishes restaurant ratings for various locations in the United States. The data file restaurants.xls contains the Zagat rating for food, décor, service, and the price per person for a sample of 50 restaurants located in an urban area (New York City) and 50 restaurants located in a suburban area (Long Island). Develop a regression model to predict the price per person based on a variable that represents the sum of the ratings for food, décor, and service and a dummy variable concerning location (New York City or Long Island).

Source: Extracted from Zagat Survey 2002 New York City Restaurants *and* Zagat Survey 2001–2002 Long Island Restaurants.

a. State the multiple regression equation.

b. Interpret the meaning of the slopes in this problem.

c. Predict the mean price for a restaurant with a summated rating of 60 that is located in New York City and construct a 95% confidence interval estimate and a 95% prediction interval.

d. Perform a residual analysis on the results and determine the adequacy of the model.

e. Is there a significant relationship between price and the two independent variables (summated rating and location) at the 0.05 level of significance?

f. At the 0.05 level of significance, determine whether each independent variable makes a contribution to the

regression model. Indicate the most appropriate regression model for this set of data.

g. Construct a 95% confidence interval estimate of the population slope for the relationship between price and summated rating, and between price and location.

h. Interpret the meaning of the coefficient of multiple determination.

i. Compute the adjusted r^2.

j. Compute the coefficients of partial determination and interpret their meaning.

k. What assumption about the slope of price with summated rating do you need to make in this problem?

l. Add an interaction term to the model and, at the 0.05 level of significance, determine whether it makes a significant contribution to the model.

m. On the basis of the results of (f) and (n), which model is most appropriate? Explain.

46 In Problem 6, you used radio advertising and newspaper advertising to predict sales (see the file advertise.xls). Develop a regression model to predict sales that includes radio advertising, newspaper advertising, and the interaction of radio advertising and newspaper advertising.

a. At the 0.05 level of significance, is there evidence that the interaction term makes a significant contribution to the model?

b. Which regression model is more appropriate, the one used in this problem or the one used in Problem 6? Explain.

 47 In Problem 5, horsepower and weight were used to predict miles per gallon (see the file auto.xls). Develop a regression model that includes horsepower, weight, and the interaction of horsepower and weight to predict miles per gallon.

a. At the 0.05 level of significance, is there evidence that the interaction term makes a significant contribution to the model?

b. Which regression model is more appropriate, the one used in this problem or the one used in Problem 5? Explain.

48 In Problem 7, you used total staff present and remote hours to predict standby hours (see the file standby.xls). Develop a regression model to predict standby hours that includes total staff present, remote hours, and the interaction of total staff present and remote hours.

a. At the 0.05 level of significance, is there evidence that the interaction term makes a significant contribution to the model?

b. Which regression model is more appropriate, the one used in this problem or the one used in Problem 7? Explain.

49 The director of a training program for a large insurance company is evaluating three different methods of training underwriters. The three methods are traditional, CD-ROM based, and Web based. She divides 30 trainees into three randomly assigned groups of 10. Before the start of the training, each trainee is given a proficiency exam that measures mathematics and computer skills. At the end of the training, all students take the same end-of-training exam. The results, stored in the file underwriting.xls are as follows:

Proficiency Exam	End-of-Training Exam	Method
94	14	Traditional
96	19	Traditional
98	17	Traditional
100	38	Traditional
102	40	Traditional
105	26	Traditional
109	41	Traditional
110	28	Traditional
111	36	Traditional
130	66	Traditional
80	38	CD-ROM based
84	34	CD-ROM based
90	43	CD-ROM based
97	43	CD-ROM based
97	61	CD-ROM based
112	63	CD-ROM based
115	93	CD-ROM based
118	74	CD-ROM based
120	76	CD-ROM based
120	79	CD-ROM based
92	55	Web based
96	53	Web based
99	55	Web based
101	52	Web based
102	35	Web based
104	46	Web based
107	57	Web based
110	55	Web based
111	42	Web based
118	81	Web based

Develop a multiple regression model to predict the score on the end-of-training exam, based on the score on the proficiency exam and the method of training used.

a. State the multiple regression equation.

b. Interpret the meaning of the slopes in this problem.

c. Predict the mean end-of-training exam score for a student with a proficiency exam score of 100 who had Web-based training.

d. Perform a residual analysis on your results and determine the adequacy of the model.

e. Is there a significant relationship between the end-of-training exam score and the independent variables (proficiency score and training method) at the 0.05 level of significance?

f. At the 0.05 level of significance, determine whether each independent variable makes a contribution to the regression model. Indicate the most appropriate regression model for this set of data.

g. Construct 95% confidence interval estimates of the population slope for the relationship between end-of-training exam score and each independent variable.

h. Interpret the meaning of the coefficient of multiple determination.

i. Compute the adjusted r^2.

j. Compute the coefficients of partial determination and interpret their meaning.

k. What assumption about the slope of proficiency score with end-of-training exam score do you need to make in this problem?

l. Add interaction terms to the model and, at the 0.05 level of significance, determine whether any interaction terms make a significant contribution to the model.

m. On the basis of the results of (f) and (l), which model is most appropriate? Explain.

SUMMARY

In this chapter, you learned how a marketing manager can use multiple regression analysis to understand the effects of price and promotional expenses on the sales of a new product. You also learned how to include categorical independent variables and interaction terms in regression models. Figure 13 represents a roadmap of the chapter.

FIGURE 13
Roadmap for multiple
regression

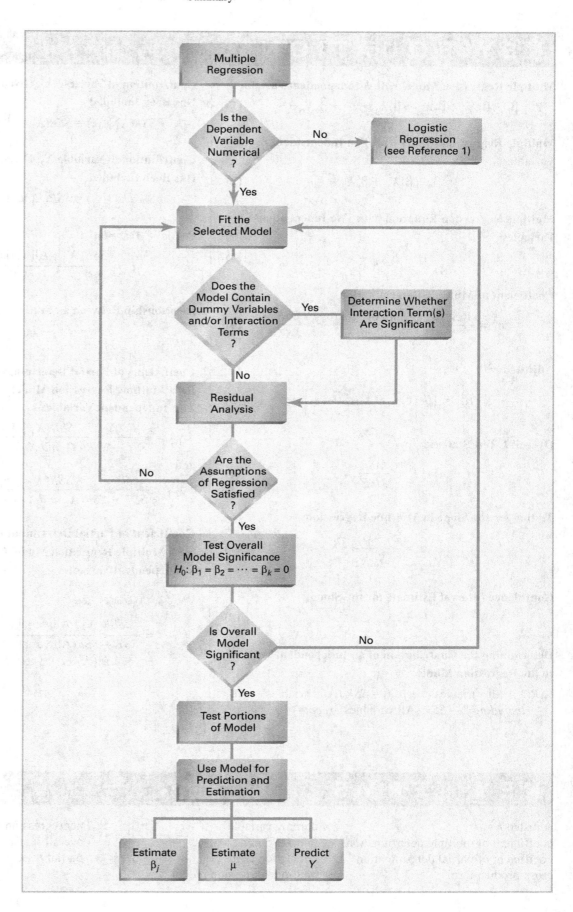

KEY EQUATIONS

Multiple Regression Model with *k* Independent Variables

$$Y_i = \beta_0 + \beta_1 X_{1i} + \beta_2 X_{2i} + \beta_3 X_{3i} + \cdots + \beta_k X_{ki} + \varepsilon_i \quad (1)$$

Multiple Regression Model with Two Independent Variables

$$Y_i = \beta_0 + \beta_1 X_{1i} + \beta_2 X_{2i} + \varepsilon_i \quad (2)$$

Multiple Regression Equation with Two Independent Variables

$$\hat{Y}_i = b_0 + b_1 X_{1i} + b_2 X_{2i} \quad (3)$$

Coefficient of Multiple Determination

$$r^2 = \frac{\text{Regression sum of squares}}{\text{Total sum of squares}} = \frac{SSR}{SST} \quad (4)$$

Adjusted r^2

$$r^2_{adj} = 1 - \left[(1 - r^2)\frac{n-1}{n-k-1}\right] \quad (5)$$

Overall *F* Test Statistic

$$F = \frac{MSR}{MSE} \quad (6)$$

Testing for the Slope in Multiple Regression

$$t = \frac{b_j - \beta_j}{S_{b_j}} \quad (7)$$

Confidence Interval Estimate for the Slope

$$b_j \pm t_{n-k-1} S_{b_j} \quad (8)$$

Determining the Contribution of an Independent Variable to the Regression Model

$$SSR(X_j \mid \text{All variables } except j) = SSR \text{ (All variables } including j) - SSR \text{ (All variables } except j) \quad (9)$$

Contribution of Variable X_1, Given That X_2 Has Been Included

$$SSR(X_1 \mid X_2) = SSR(X_1 \text{ and } X_2) - SSR(X_2) \quad (10a)$$

Contribution of Variable X_2, Given That X_1 Has Been Included

$$SSR(X_2 \mid X_1) = SSR(X_1 \text{ and } X_2) - SSR(X_1) \quad (10b)$$

Partial *F* Test Statistic

$$F = \frac{SSR(X_j \mid \text{All variables } except j)}{MSE} \quad (11)$$

Relationship Between a *t* Statistic and an *F* Statistic

$$t_a^2 = F_{1,a} \quad (12)$$

Coefficients of Partial Determination for a Multiple Regression Model Containing Two Independent Variables

$$r^2_{Y1.2} = \frac{SSR(X_1 \mid X_2)}{SST - SSR(X_1 \text{ and } X_2) + SSR(X_1 \mid X_2)} \quad (13a)$$

and

$$r^2_{Y2.1} = \frac{SSR(X_2 \mid X_1)}{SST - SSR(X_1 \text{ and } X_2) + SSR(X_2 \mid X_1)} \quad (13b)$$

Coefficient of Partial Determination for a Multiple Regression Model Containing *k* Independent Variables

$$r^2_{Y_j.(\text{All variables } except j)}$$
$$= \frac{SSR(X_j \mid \text{All variables } except j)}{SST - SSR(\text{All variables } including j) + SSR(X_j \mid \text{All variables } except j)} \quad (14)$$

KEY TERMS

adjusted r^2
coefficient of multiple determination
coefficient of partial determination
cross-product term

dummy variable
interaction
interaction term
multiple regression model

net regression coefficient
overall *F* test
partial *F* test

CHAPTER REVIEW PROBLEMS

Checking Your Understanding

50 How does the interpretation of the regression coefficients differ in multiple regression and simple regression?

51 How does testing the significance of the entire multiple regression model differ from testing the contribution of each independent variable?

52 How do the coefficients of partial determination differ from the coefficient of multiple determination?

53 Why and how do you use dummy variables?

54 How can you evaluate whether the slope of the response variable with an independent variable is the same for each level of the dummy variable?

55 Under what circumstances do you include an interaction in a regression model?

56 When a dummy variable is included in a regression model that has one numerical independent variable, what assumption do you need to make concerning the slope between the response variable, Y, and the numerical independent variable, X?

Applying the Concepts

57 Increasing customer satisfaction typically results in increased purchase behavior. For many products, there is more than one measure of customer satisfaction. In many of these instances, purchase behavior can increase dramatically with an increase in any one of the customer satisfaction measures, not necessarily all of them at the same time. Gunst and Barry ("One Way to Moderate Ceiling Effects," *Quality Progress*, October 2003, pp. 83–85) consider a product with two satisfaction measures, X_1 and X_2, that range from the lowest level of satisfaction, 1, to the highest level of satisfaction, 7. The dependent variable, Y, is a measure of purchase behavior, with the highest value generating the most sales. The following regression equation is presented:

$$\hat{Y}_i = -3.888 + 1.449X_{1i} + 1.462X_{2i} - 0.190X_{1i}X_{2i}$$

Suppose that X_1 is the perceived quality of the product and X_2 is the perceived value of the product. (*Note:* If the product is overpriced in the view of the customer, he or she perceives it to be of low value and vice versa.)

a. What is the predicted purchase behavior when $X_1 = 2$ and $X_2 = 2$?

b. What is the predicted purchase behavior when $X_1 = 2$ and $X_2 = 7$?

c. What is the predicted purchase behavior when $X_1 = 7$ and $X_2 = 2$?

d. What is the predicted purchase behavior when $X_1 = 7$ and $X_2 = 7$?

e. What is the regression equation when $X_2 = 2$? What is the slope for X_1 now?

f. What is the regression equation when $X_2 = 7$? What is the slope for X_1 now?

g. What is the regression equation when $X_1 = 2$? What is the slope for X_2 now?

h. What is the regression equation when $X_1 = 7$? What is the slope for X_2 now?

i. Discuss the implications of (a) through (h) within the context of increasing sales for this product with two customer satisfaction measures.

58 The owner of a moving company typically has his most experienced manager predict the total number of labor hours that will be required to complete an upcoming move. This approach has proved useful in the past, but the owner would like to be able to develop a more accurate method of predicting the labor hours by using the number of cubic feet moved and the number of pieces of large furniture. In a preliminary effort to provide a more accurate method, he has collected data for 36 moves in which the origin and destination were within the borough of Manhattan in New York City and the travel time was an insignificant portion of the hours worked. The data are stored in the file `moving.xls`.

a. State the multiple regression equation.

b. Interpret the meaning of the slopes in this equation.

c. Predict the mean labor hours for moving 500 cubic feet with two large pieces of furniture.

d. Perform a residual analysis on your results and determine the adequacy of the model.

e. Determine whether there is a significant relationship between labor hours and the two independent variables (the amount of cubic feet moved and the number of pieces of large furniture) at the 0.05 level of significance.

f. Determine the *p*-value in (e) and interpret its meaning.

g. Interpret the meaning of the coefficient of multiple determination in this problem.

h. Determine the adjusted r^2.

i. At the 0.05 level of significance, determine whether each independent variable makes a significant contribution to the regression model. Indicate the most appropriate regression model for this set of data.

j. Determine the *p*-values in (i) and interpret their meaning.

k. Compute and interpret the coefficients of partial determination.

59 Professional basketball has truly become a sport that generates interest among fans around the world. More and more players come from outside the United States to play in the National Basketball Association (NBA). You want to develop a regression model to predict the number of wins achieved by each NBA team, based on field goal (shots made) percentage for the team and for the opponent. The data are stored in the file nba2006.xls.

a. State the multiple regression equation.
b. Interpret the meaning of the slopes in this equation.
c. Predict the mean number of wins for a team that has a field goal percentage of 45% and an opponent field goal percentage of 44%.
d. Perform a residual analysis on your results and determine the adequacy of the fit of the model.
e. Is there a significant relationship between number of wins and the two independent variables (field goal percentage for the team and for the opponent) at the 0.05 level of significance?
f. Determine the p-value in (e) and interpret its meaning.
g. Interpret the meaning of the coefficient of multiple determination in this problem.
h. Determine the adjusted r^2.
i. At the 0.05 level of significance, determine whether each independent variable makes a significant contribution to the regression model. Indicate the most appropriate regression model for this set of data.
j. Determine the p-values in (i) and interpret their meaning.
k. Compute and interpret the coefficients of partial determination.

60 A sample of 30 recently sold single-family houses in a small city is selected. Develop a model to predict the selling price (in thousands of dollars), using the assessed value (in thousands of dollars) as well as time period (in months since reassessment). The houses in the city had been reassessed at full value one year prior to the study. The results are contained in the file house1.xls.

a. State the multiple regression equation.
b. Interpret the meaning of the slopes in this equation.
c. Predict the mean selling price for a house that has an assessed value of $170,000 and was sold in time period 12.
d. Perform a residual analysis on your results and determine the adequacy of the model.
e. Determine whether there is a significant relationship between selling price and the two independent variables (assessed value and time period) at the 0.05 level of significance.
f. Determine the p-value in (e) and interpret its meaning.
g. Interpret the meaning of the coefficient of multiple determination in this problem.

h. Determine the adjusted r^2.
i. At the 0.05 level of significance, determine whether each independent variable makes a significant contribution to the regression model. Indicate the most appropriate regression model for this set of data.
j. Determine the p-values in (i) and interpret their meaning.
k. Compute and interpret the coefficients of partial determination.

61 Measuring the height of a California redwood tree is a very difficult undertaking because these trees grow to heights of over 300 feet. People familiar with these trees understand that the height of a California redwood tree is related to other characteristics of the tree, including the diameter of the tree at the breast height of a person and the thickness of the bark of the tree. The data in the file redwood.xls represent the height, diameter at breast height of a person, and bark thickness for a sample of 21 California redwood trees.

a. State the multiple regression equation.
b. Interpret the meaning of the slopes in this equation.
c. Predict the mean height for a tree that has a breast diameter of 25 inches and a bark thickness of 2 inches.
d. Interpret the meaning of the coefficient of multiple determination in this problem.
e. Perform a residual analysis on the results and determine the adequacy of the model.
f. Determine whether there is a significant relationship between the height of redwood trees and the two independent variables (breast diameter and the bark thickness) at the 0.05 level of significance.
g. Construct a 95% confidence interval estimate of the population slope between the height of the redwood trees and breast diameter and between the height of redwood trees and the bark thickness.
h. At the 0.05 level of significance, determine whether each independent variable makes a significant contribution to the regression model. Indicate the independent variables to include in this model.
i. Construct a 95% confidence interval estimate of the mean height for trees that have a breast diameter of 25 inches and a bark thickness of 2 inches along with a prediction interval for an individual tree.
j. Compute and interpret the coefficients of partial determination.

62 Develop a model to predict the assessed value (in thousands of dollars), using the size of the houses (in thousands of square feet) and the age of the houses (in years) from the following table (whose data are stored in the file house2.xls):

House	Assessed Value ($000)	Size of House (Thousands of Square Feet)	Age (Years)
1	184.4	2.00	3.42
2	177.4	1.71	11.50
3	175.7	1.45	8.33
4	185.9	1.76	0.00
5	179.1	1.93	7.42
6	170.4	1.20	32.00
7	175.8	1.55	16.00
8	185.9	1.93	2.00
9	178.5	1.59	1.75
10	179.2	1.50	2.75
11	186.7	1.90	0.00
12	179.3	1.39	0.00
13	174.5	1.54	12.58
14	183.8	1.89	2.75
15	176.8	1.59	7.17

a. State the multiple regression equation.

b. Interpret the meaning of the slopes in this equation.

c. Predict the mean assessed value for a house that has a size of 1,750 square feet and is 10 years old.

d. Perform a residual analysis on the results and determine the adequacy of the model.

e. Determine whether there is a significant relationship between assessed value and the two independent variables (size and age) at the 0.05 level of significance.

f. Determine the p-value in (e) and interpret its meaning.

g. Interpret the meaning of the coefficient of multiple determination in this problem.

h. Determine the adjusted r^2.

i. At the 0.05 level of significance, determine whether each independent variable makes a significant contribution to the regression model. Indicate the most appropriate regression model for this set of data.

j. Determine the p-values in (i) and interpret their meaning.

k. Compute and interpret the coefficients of partial determination.

l. The real estate assessor's office has been publicly quoted as saying that the age of a house has no bearing on its assessed value. Based on your answers to (a) through (l), do you agree with this statement? Explain.

63 Crazy Dave, a well-known baseball analyst, wants to determine which variables are important in predicting a team's wins in a given season. He has collected data related to wins, earned run average (ERA), and runs scored for the 2005 season (stored in the file bb2005.xls). Develop a model to predict the number of wins based on ERA and runs scored.

a. State the multiple regression equation.

b. Interpret the meaning of the slopes in this equation.

c. Predict the mean number of wins for a team that has an ERA of 4.50 and has scored 750 runs.

d. Perform a residual analysis on the results and determine the adequacy of the model.

e. Is there a significant relationship between number of wins and the two independent variables (ERA and runs scored) at the 0.05 level of significance?

f. Determine the p-value in (e) and interpret its meaning.

g. Interpret the meaning of the coefficient of multiple determination in this problem.

h. Determine the adjusted r^2.

i. At the 0.05 level of significance, determine whether each independent variable makes a significant contribution to the regression model. Indicate the most appropriate regression model for this set of data.

j. Determine the p-values in (i) and interpret their meaning.

k. Construct a 95% confidence interval estimate of the population slope between wins and ERA.

l. Compute and interpret the coefficients of partial determination.

m. Which is more important in predicting wins—pitching, as measured by ERA, or offense, as measured by runs scored? Explain.

64 Referring to Problem 63, suppose that in addition to using ERA to predict the number of wins, Crazy Dave wants to include the league (American vs. National) as an independent variable. Develop a model to predict wins based on ERA and league.

a. State the multiple regression equation.

b. Interpret the meaning of the slopes in this problem.

c. Predict the mean number of wins for a team with an ERA of 4.50 in the American League. Construct a 95% confidence interval estimate for all teams and a 95% prediction interval for an individual team.

d. Perform a residual analysis on the results and determine the adequacy of the model.

e. Is there a significant relationship between wins and the two independent variables (ERA and league) at the 0.05 level of significance?

f. At the 0.05 level of significance, determine whether each independent variable makes a contribution to the regression model. Indicate the most appropriate regression model for this set of data.

g. Construct 95% confidence interval estimates of the population slope for the relationship between wins and ERA and between wins and league.

h. Interpret the meaning of the coefficient of multiple determination.

i. Determine the adjusted r^2.

j. Compute and interpret the coefficients of partial determination.

k. What assumption do you have to make about the slope of wins with ERA?

l. Add an interaction term to the model and, at the 0.05 level of significance, determine whether it makes a significant contribution to the model.

m. On the basis of the results of (f) and (l), which model is most appropriate? Explain.

65 You are a real estate broker who wants to compare property values in Glen Cove and Roslyn (which are located approximately 8 miles apart). In order to do so, you will analyze the data in the gcroslyn.xls file that includes samples for Glen Cove and Roslyn. Making sure to include the dummy variable for location (Glen Cove or Roslyn) in the regression model, develop a regression model to predict appraised value, based on the land area of a property, the age of a house, and location. Be sure to determine whether any interaction terms need to be included in the model.

Managing the *Springville Herald*

In its continuing study of the home-delivery subscription solicitation process, a marketing department team wants to test the effects of two types of structured sales presentations (personal formal and personal informal) and the number of hours spent on telemarketing on the number of new subscriptions. The staff has recorded these data in the file sh14.xls for the past 24 weeks. You can find this data set at **www.prenhall.com/HeraldCase/EffectsData.htm** and

in the **EffectsData.htm** file in the **HeraldCase** folder on the Student CD-ROM that accompanies this text.

Analyze these data and develop a multiple regression model to predict the number of new subscriptions for a week, based on the number of hours spent on telemarketing and the sales presentation type. Write a report, giving detailed findings concerning the regression model used.

Web Case

Apply your knowledge of multiple regression models in this Web Case, which extends the Using Statistics OmniFoods scenario from this chapter.

To ensure a successful test marketing of its OmniPower energy bars, the OmniFoods marketing department has contracted with In-Store Placements Group (ISPG), a merchandising consultancy. ISPG will work with the grocery store chain that is conducting the test market study. Using the same 34-store sample used in the test market study, ISPG claims that the choice of shelf location and the presence of in-store OmniPower coupon dispensers each increase sale of the energy bars.

Review the ISPG claims and supporting data at the OmniFoods internal Web page, **www.prenhall.com/Springville/Omni_ISPGMemo.htm**, (or open this Web

page file from the Student CD-ROM Web Case folder) and then answer the following:

1. Are the supporting data consistent with ISPG's claims? Perform an appropriate statistical analysis to confirm (or discredit) the stated relationship between sales and the two independent variables of product shelf location and the presence of in-store OmniPower coupon dispensers.

2. If you were advising OmniFoods, would you recommend using a specific shelf location and in-store coupon dispensers to sell OmniPower bars?

3. What additional data would you advise collecting in order to determine the effectiveness of the sales promotion techniques used by ISPG?

REFERENCES

1. Hosmer, D. W., and S. Lemeshow, *Applied Logistic Regression*, 2nd ed. (New York: Wiley, 2001).
2. Kutner, M., C. Nachtsheim, J. Neter, and W. Li, *Applied Linear Statistical Models*, 5th ed. (New York: McGraw-Hill/Irwin, 2005).
3. *Microsoft Excel 2007* (Redmond, WA: Microsoft Corp., 2007).

Excel Companion

E1 PERFORMING MULTIPLE REGRESSION ANALYSES

You perform a multiple regression analysis by either selecting the PHStat2 Multiple Regression procedure or the ToolPak Regression procedure.

Using PHStat2 Multiple Regression

Select **PHStat → Regression → Multiple Regression**. In the procedure's dialog box (shown below), enter the cell range of the *Y* variable as the **Y Variable Cell Range** and the cell range of the *X* variables as the **X Variables Cell Range**. Click **First cells in both ranges contain label** and enter a value for the **Confidence level for regression coefficients**. Click the **Regression Statistics Table** and the **ANOVA and Coefficients Table** Regression Tool Output Options, enter a title as the **Title**, and click **OK**.

PHStat2 uses the ToolPak Regression procedure to create the regression results worksheet. This worksheet does

not dynamically change, and you need to rerun the PHStat2 procedure if you change your data.

The four output options found in the PHStat2 dialog box enhance the ToolPak procedure. The Durbin-Watson statistic is one such option, and the other three options are explained in Sections E3 and E4 here, and in E3 of "Multiple Regression Model Building" (consult your instructor for this text).

Using ToolPak Regression

Open to the worksheet that contains the data for the regression analysis. Select **Tools → Data Analysis**, select **Regression** from the Data Analysis list, and click **OK**. In the procedure's dialog box (shown below), enter the cell range of the *Y* variable data as the **Input Y Range** and enter the cell range of the *X* variables data as the **Input X Range**. (The *X* variables cell range must be contiguous columns.) Click **Labels**. Click **Confidence Level**, and enter a value in its box, and then click **OK**. Results appear on a new worksheet.

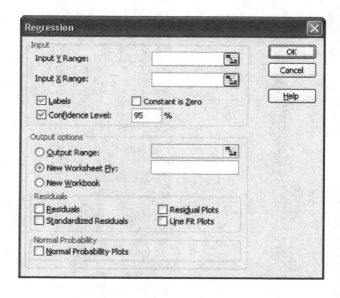

E2 CREATING MULTIPLE REGRESSION RESIDUAL PLOTS

You modify the instructions of Section E1 to create a table of residuals and then use Excel charting features to create the residual plots needed in multiple regression.

Creating a Table of Residuals

You create a table of residuals by clicking additional check boxes when you perform a multiple regression analysis. If you use the PHStat2 Multiple Regression procedure, click the **Regression Statistics Table, ANOVA and Coefficients Table, Residuals Table**, and **Residual Plots** check boxes before you click **OK**. If you use the ToolPak Regression procedure, click the **Residuals** check box before you click **OK**.

Using either one of these modifications creates a regression results worksheet that includes a residual output table that contains columns for observation number, predicted values, and residuals. Figure E1 shows the residual output area for the **MR** worksheet of the Chapter14 xls workbook that was used to create the residual plots in Figure 4 this table of residuals, you can use Excel charting features to create the four types of residual plots needed for a multiple regression residual analysis.

range of your residuals as the Y variable and the cell range of either $\hat{Y}_i$, X_{1i}, X_{2i}, or *Observation* as your X variable values. (If you use PHStat2, the **Residual Plots** option created the residuals versus X_{1i} plot and the residuals versus X_{2i} plot for you, so you do not need to manually create these two plots.)

Variables need to be arranged X variable first and then Y variable in order for the scatter plot to be correct. For the residuals versus $\hat{Y}_i$ (that is, the predicted values of Y) residual plot, this not a problem as the two exist in the proper order, in side-by-side columns, in the residual output table of the regression model worksheet. However, for the three other types of residual plots, the data for the plot is split between the regression model worksheet and the worksheet that contains the data for the model. You need to have all the data together on one worksheet (it does not matter which worksheet you use) and make sure that the column of residual values appears to the right of the column holding the X_{1i}, X_{2i} or *Observation* values.

	A	B	C
23	RESIDUAL OUTPUT		
24			
25	Observation	Predicted Sales	Residuals
26	1	3420.309524	720.6904762
27	2	3420.309524	421.6904762
28	3	3420.309524	-364.3095238
29	4	3420.309524	98.69047619
30	5	4142.921131	83.07886905
31	6	4142.921131	487.078869
32	7	4142.921131	-635.921131
33	8	4142.921131	-388.921131
34	9	4865.532738	134.4672619
35	10	4865.532738	254.4672619
36	11	4865.532738	-854.5327381
37	12	4865.532738	149.4672619
38	13	2355.962798	-439.9627976
39	14	2355.962798	-1680.962798
40	15	2355.962798	1280.037202
41	16	2355.962798	868.0372024
42	17	3078.574405	-783.5744048
43	18	3078.574405	-348.5744048
44	19	3078.574405	-460.5744048
45	20	3078.574405	1342.425595
46	21	3801.186012	311.8139881
47	22	3801.186012	-55.1860119
48	23	3801.186012	-269.1860119
49	24	3801.186012	23.8139881
50	25	1291.616071	-195.6160714
51	26	1291.616071	-530.6160714
52	27	1291.616071	796.3839286
53	28	1291.616071	-471.6160714
54	29	2014.227679	99.77232143
55	30	2014.227679	-132.2276786
56	31	2014.227679	144.7723214
57	32	2014.227679	-412.2276786
58	33	2736.839286	617.1607143
59	34	2736.839286	190.1607143

FIGURE E1 Creating residual plots

Use "Presenting Data in Tables and Charts," Section E12 instructions, "Creating Scatter Plots, to create residual plots. (Consult your instructor for this text.)" Use the cell

E3 COMPUTING THE CONFIDENCE INTERVAL ESTIMATE OF THE MEAN AND THE PREDICTION INTERVAL

You modify the instructions for using the PHStat2 Multiple Regression procedure in Section E1 to compute the confidence interval estimate of the mean response and prediction interval for an individual Y.

Click **Confidence Interval Estimate & Prediction Interval** and enter a value for the **Confidence level for interval estimates** (see Figure E2) before you click **OK** to create the confidence interval estimate and prediction interval estimate on a separate worksheet, similar to Figure 2.

Alternatives to using PHStat2 are complex and beyond the scope of this text. However, you can open to the **CIEandPI** worksheet of the CIEandPIforMR.xls workbook (shown in Figure 2) and review its contents. This worksheet uses the function **TINV(1-*confidence level, degrees of freedom*)** to compute the *t* statistic in cell B20. It uses the **TRANSPOSE(*cell range*), MMULT(*cell range 1, cell range 2*)**, and **MINVERSE(*cell range*)** functions to perform advanced matrix mathematics. Some formulas in the worksheet refer to cells on the **MR** regression model worksheet, while others, not shown in Figure 2, refer to a **DC** worksheet that contains a copy of the regression data and a column of all 1s.

Forum Click on the ADVANCED TECHNIQUES link to learn more about the techniques used in this worksheet.

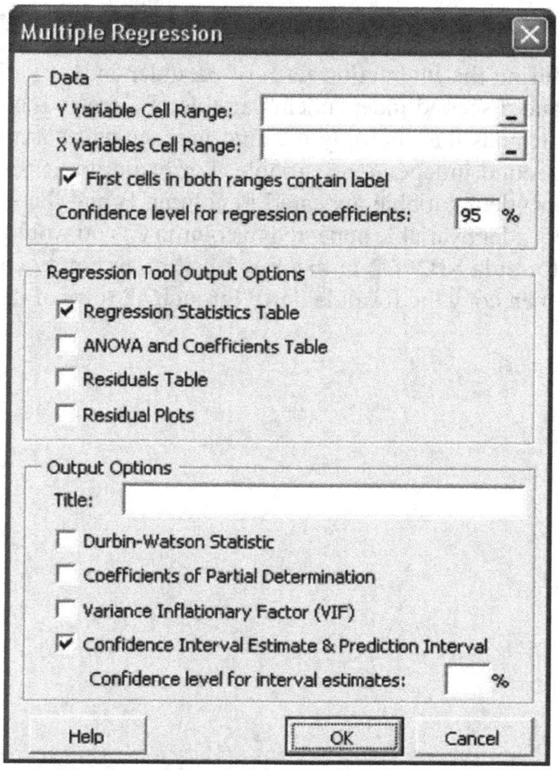

FIGURE E2 Dialog box after clicking the Confidence Interval Estimate & Prediction Interval output option

E4 COMPUTING THE COEFFICIENTS OF PARTIAL DETERMINATION

You modify the procedures of Section E1 to compute the coefficients of partial determination.

Using PHStat2 Multiple Regression

Use the Section E1 instructions in "Using PHStat2 Multiple Regression," but click the **Coefficients of Partial Determination** output option click **OK**. The coefficients of partial determination appear on a separate worksheet that is similar to Figure E3.

Using ToolPak Regression

If you use the ToolPak Regression procedure, use the Section E1 procedures to create all necessary regression results worksheets. (For example, if you have two independent variables, you need to perform a regression analysis using X_1 and X_2, X_1 alone, and X_2 alone.) Then open the

	A	B	C	D	E
1	**OmniPower Sales Analysis**				
2	**Coefficients of Partial Determination**				
3					
4	Intermediate Calculations			**Cell entries:**	
5	SSR(X1, X2)	39472730.7730		**Cell B5:**	**multiple regression worksheet cell C12 value**
6	SST	52093677.4412		**Cell B6:**	**multiple regression worksheet cell C14 value**
7	SSR(X2)	14915814.1025		**Cell B7:**	**exclude-first-X-regression worksheet cell C12 value**
8	SSR(X1)	28153486.1482		**Cell B8:**	**exclude-second-X-regression worksheet cell C12 value**
9	SSR(X1 | X2)	24556916.6706	**=B5 - B7**		
10	SSR(X2 | X1)	11319244.6249	**=B5 - B8**		
11					
12	**Coefficients**				
13	**r2 Y1.2**	**0.6605**	**=B9/(B6 - B5 + B9)**		
14	**r2 Y2.1**	**0.4728**	**=B10/(B6 - B5 + B10)**		

FIGURE E3 Completed CPD_2 worksheet for the Omni Power sales example

CPD.xls workbook. Copy the worksheets for all your regression models to this workbook and then open to the CPD worksheet that matches your model. (For example, if you have two independent variables, open the **CPD_2** worksheet.) Then follow the instructions on the worksheet to complete the worksheet. Some worksheet cells may display the #DIV/0! message until you are finished making your entries. This is not an error.

Figure E3 shows the CPD_2 worksheet completed for the OmniPower sales example.

E5 CREATING DUMMY VARIABLES

You use the Excel find-and-replace feature to create a dummy variable for a categorical variable. To do so, you find each categorical value and replace it with a number.

To use find-and-replace, first open the worksheet that contains your regression data. Select the (column) cell range of the categorical variable for which you are creating a dummy variable. Press **Crtl+C** to copy these values. Select the first cell of the first empty column in your worksheet and press **Crtl+V** to paste the values in this column.

Select all the newly pasted values and press **Crtl+H** to display the Find and Replace dialog box (shown below).

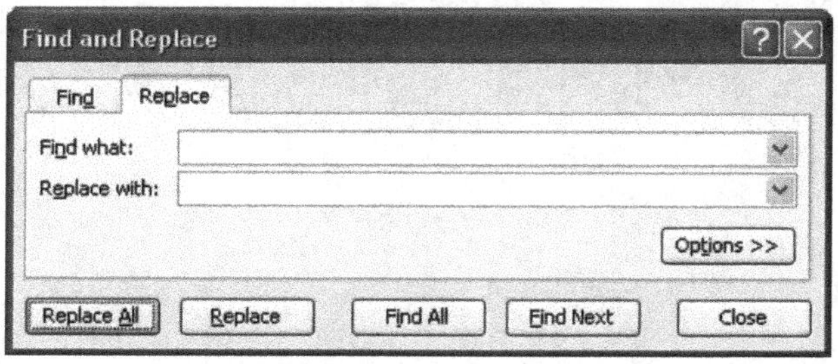

For each unique categorical value in the column,

- Enter the categorical value as the **Find what** value.
- Enter the number that will represent that categorical value as the **Replace with** value.
- Click **Replace All**.

If a message box to confirm the replacement appears, click **OK** to continue.

Click **Close** when you are finished making all replacements. If you inadvertently click the worksheet while using this dialog box, reselect all the newly pasted values before continuing to replace. When you finish, verify your work by comparing the original column of categorical values to your new column of numerical values.

E6 CREATING INTERACTION TERMS

To define the interaction term of an independent variable, X_1, and a second independent variable, X_2, create a column of formulas that multiply the first independent variable by the second independent variable. For example, if the first independent variable appeared in column B and the second independent variable appeared in column C, you would enter the formula **=B2*C2** in the row 2 cell of an empty column and then copy the formula down through all rows of data.

Self-Test Solutions and Answers to Selected Even-Numbered Problems

The following represent worked-out solutions to Self-Test Problems and brief answers to most of the even-numbered problems in the text.

2 (a) For each one-unit increase in X_1, you estimate that Y will decrease 2 units, holding X_2 constant. For each one-unit increase in X_2, you estimate that Y will increase 7 units, holding X_1 constant. **(b)** The Y-intercept equal to 50 estimates the predicted value of Y when both X_1 and X_2 are zero.

4 (a) $\hat{Y} = -2.72825 + 0.047114X_1 + 0.011947X_2$. **(b)** For a given number of orders, for each increase of $1,000 in sales, mean distribution cost is estimated to increase by $47.114. For a given amount of sales, for each increase of one order, mean distribution cost is estimated to increase by $11.95. **(c)** The interpretation of b_0 has no practical meaning here because it would represent the estimated distribution cost when there were no sales and no orders. **(d)** $\hat{Y} = -2.72825 + 0.047114(400) + 0.011947(4500) = 69.878$ or $69,878. **(e)** $66,419.93 \le \mu_{Y|X} \le$ $73,337.01. **(f)** $59,380.61 \le Y_X \le 80,376.33.

6 (a) $\hat{Y} = 156.4 + 13.081X_1 + 16.795X_2$. **(b)** For a given amount of newspaper advertising, each increase by $1,000 in radio advertising is estimated to result in a mean increase in sales of $13,081. For a given amount of radio advertising, each increase by $1,000 in newspaper advertising is estimated to result in a mean increase in sales of $16,795. **(c)** When there is no money spent on radio advertising and newspaper advertising, the estimated mean sales is $156,430.44. **(d)** $\hat{Y} = 156.4 + 13.081(20) + 16.795(20) = 753.95$ or $753,950. **(e)** $623,038.31 \le \mu_{Y|X} \le$ $884,860.93. **(f)** $396,522.63 \le Y_X \le 1,111,376.60.

8 (a) $\hat{Y} = 400.8057 + 456.4485X_1 - 2.4708X_2$, where $X_1 = $ land, $X_2 = $ age. **(b)** For a given age, each increase by one acre in land area is estimated to result in a mean increase in appraised value by $456.45 thousands. For a given acreage, each increase of one year in age is estimated to result in the mean decrease in appraised value by $2.47 thousands. **(c)** The interpretation of b_0 has no practical meaning here because it would represent the estimated appraised value of a new house that has no land area. **(d)** $\hat{Y} = 400.8057 + 456.4485(0.25) - 2.4708(45)$ = $403.73 thousands. **(e)** $372.7370 \le \mu_{Y|X} \le 434.7243$. **(f)** $235.1964 \le Y_X \le 572.2649$.

10 (a) $MSR = 15$, $MSE = 12$. **(b)** 1.25. **(c)** $F = 1.25 < 4.10$; do not reject H_0. **(d)** 0.20. **(e)** 0.04.

12 (a) $F = 97.69 > F_{U(2,15-2-1)} = 3.89$. Reject H_0. There is evidence of a significant linear relationship with at least one of the independent variables. **(b)** The p-value is 0.0001. **(c)** $r^2 = 0.9421$. 94.21% of the variation in the long-term ability to absorb shock can be explained by variation in forefoot absorbing capability and variation in midsole impact. **(d)** $r_{adj}^2 = 0.93245$.

14 (a) $F = 74.13 > 3.467$; reject H_0. **(b)** p-value = 0. **(c)** $r^2 = 0.8759$. 87.59% of the variation in distribution cost can be explained by variation in sales and variation in number of orders. **(d)** $r_{adj}^2 = 0.8641$.

16 (a) $F = 40.16 > F_{U(2,22-2-1)} = 3.522$. Reject H_0. There is evidence of a significant linear relationship. **(b)** The p-value is less than 0.001. **(c)** $r^2 = 0.8087$. 80.87% of the variation in sales can be explained by

variation in radio advertising and variation in newspaper advertising. **(d)** $r_{adj}^2 = 0.7886$.

18 (a) Based on a residual analysis, the model appears to be adequate. **(b)** There is no evidence of a pattern in the residuals versus time. **(c)** $D = \dfrac{1,077.0956}{477.0430} = 2.26$. **(d)** $D = 2.26 > 1.55$. There is no evidence of positive autocorrelation in the residuals.

20 There appears to be a quadratic relationship in the plot of the residuals against both radio and newspaper advertising. Thus, quadratic terms for each of these explanatory variables should be considered for inclusion in the model.

22 There is no particular pattern in the residual plots, and the model appears to be adequate.

24 (a) Variable X_2 has a larger slope in terms of the t statistic of 3.75 than variable X_1, which has a smaller slope in terms of the t statistic of 3.33. **(b)** $1.46824 \le \beta_1 \le 6.53176$. **(c)** For X_1: $t = 4/1.2 = 3.33 > 2.1098$, with 17 degrees of freedom for $\alpha = 0.05$. Reject H_0. There is evidence that X_1 contributes to a model already containing X_2. For X_2: $t = 3/0.8 = 3.75 > 2.1098$, with 17 degrees of freedom for $\alpha = 0.05$. Reject H_0. There is evidence that X_2 contributes to a model already containing X_1. Both X_1 and X_2 should be included in the model.

26 (a) 95% confidence interval on β_1: $b_1 \pm t_{n-k-1} S_{b_1}$, 0.0471 ± 2.0796 0.0203, $0.00488 \le \beta_1 \le 0.08932$. **(b)** For X_1: $t = b_1/S_{b_1} = 0.0471/0.0203 = 2.32 > 2.0796$. Reject H_0. There is evidence that X_1 contributes to a model already containing X_2. For X_2: $t = b_2/S_{b_2} = 0.01195/0.00225 = 5.31 > 2.0796$. Reject H_0. There is evidence that X_2 contributes to a model already containing X_1. Both X_1 (sales) and X_2 (orders) should be included in the model.

28 (a) $9.398 \le \beta_1 \le 16.763$. **(b)** For X_1: $t = 7.43 > 2.093$. Reject H_0. There is evidence that X_1 contributes to a model already containing X_2. For X_2: $t = 5.67 > 2.093$. Reject H_0. There is evidence that X_2 contributes to a model already containing X_1. Both X_1 (radio advertising) and X_2 (newspaper advertising) should be included in the model.

30 (a) $227.5865 \le \beta_1 \le 685.3104$. **(b)** For X_1: $t = 4.0922$ and p-value = 0.0003. Since p-value < 0.05, reject H_0. There is evidence that X_1 contributes to a model already containing X_2. For X_2: $t = -3.6295$ and p-value = 0.0012. Since p-value < 0.05, reject H_0. There is evidence that X_2 contributes to a model already containing X_1. Both X_1 (land area) and X_2 (age) should be included in the model.

32 (a) For X_1: $F = 1.25 < 4.96$; do not reject H_0. For X_2: $F = 0.833 < 4.96$; do not reject H_0. **(b)** 0.1111, 0.0769.

34 (a) For X_1: $SSR(X_1|X_2) = SSR(X_1 \text{ and } X_2) - SSR(X_2) = 3,368.087 - 3,246.062 = 122.025$,

$$F = \frac{SSR(X_2 \mid X_1)}{MSE} = \frac{122.025}{477.043 \, / \, 21} = 5.37 > 4.325.$$

Reject H_0. There is evidence that X_1 contributes to a model already containing X_2. For X_2: $SSR(X_2 \mid X_1) = SSR(X_1 \text{ and } X_2) - SSR(X_1) = 3{,}368.087 - 2{,}726.822 = 641.265$,

$$F = \frac{SSR(X_2 \mid X_1)}{MSE} = \frac{641.265}{477.043 \, / \, 21} = 28.23 > 4.325. \text{ Reject } H_0.$$

There is evidence that X_2 contributes to a model already containing X_1. Since both X_1 and X_2 make a significant contribution to the model in the presence of the other variable, both variables should be included in the model. **(b)** $r^2_{Y1.2} = \dfrac{SSR(X_1 \mid X_2)}{SST - SSR(X_1 \text{ and } X_2) + SSR(X_1 \mid X_2)}$

$$= \frac{122.025}{3{,}845.13 - 3{,}368.087 + 122.025} = 0.2037.$$

Holding constant the effect of the number of orders, 20.37% of the variation in distribution cost can be explained by the variation in sales.

$$r^2_{Y2.1} = \frac{SSR(X_2 \mid X_1)}{SST - SSR(X_1 \text{ and } X_2) + SSR(X_2 \mid X_1)}$$

$$= \frac{641.265}{3{,}845.13 - 3{,}368.087 + 641.265} = 0.5734$$

Holding constant the effect of sales, 57.34% of the variation in distribution cost can be explained by the variation in the number of orders.

36 (a) For X_1: $F = 55.28 > 4.381$. Reject H_0. There is evidence that X_1 contributes to a model already containing X_2. For X_2: $F = 32.12 > 4.381$. Reject H_0. There is evidence that X_2 contributes to a model already containing X_1. Since both X_1 and X_2 make a significant contribution to the model in the presence of the other variable, both variables should be included in the model. **(b)** $r^2_{Y1.2} = 0.7442$. Holding constant the effect of newspaper advertising, 74.42% of the variation in sales can be explained by the variation in radio advertising. $r^2_{Y2.1} = 0.6283$. Holding constant the effect of radio advertising, 62.83% of the variation in sales can be explained by the variation in newspaper advertising.

40 (a) $\hat{Y} = 243.7371 + 9.2189X_1 + 12.6967X_2$, where $X_1 = $ number of rooms and $X_2 = $ neighborhood (east = 0). **(b)** Holding constant the effect of neighborhood, for each additional room, the selling price is estimated to increase by a mean of 9.2189 thousands of dollars, or \$9218.9. For a given number of rooms, a west neighborhood is estimated to increase the mean selling price over an east neighborhood by 12.6967 thousands of dollars, or \$12,696.7. **(c)** $\hat{Y} = 243.7371 + 9.2189(9) + 12.6967(0) = 326.7076$, or \$326,707.6. \$309,560.04 $\leq Y_X \leq$ \$343,855.1. \$321,471.44 $\leq \mu_{Y\mid X} \leq$ \$331,943.71. **(d)** Based on a residual analysis, the model appears to be adequate. **(e)** $F = 55.39$, the p-value is virtually 0. Since p-value < 0.05, reject H_0. There is evidence of a significant relationship between selling price and the two independent variables (rooms and neighborhood). **(f)** For X_1: $t = 8.9537$, the p-value is virtually 0. Reject H_0. Number of rooms makes a significant contribution and should be included in the model. For X_2: $t = 3.5913$, p-value $= 0.0023 < 0.05$. Reject H_0. Neighborhood makes a significant contribution and should be included in the model. Based on these results, the regression model with the two independent variables should be used. **(g)** $7.0466 \leq \beta_1 \leq 11.3913$, $5.2378 \leq \beta_2 \leq 20.1557$.

(h) $r^2 = 0.867$. 86.7% of the variation in selling price can be explained by variation in number of rooms and variation in neighborhood. **(i)** $r^2_{adj} = 0.851$. **(j)** $r^2_{Y1.2} = 0.825$. Holding constant the effect of neighborhood, 82.5% of the variation in selling price can be explained by variation in number of rooms. $r^2_{Y2.1} = 0.431$. Holding constant the effect of number of rooms, 43.1% of the variation in selling price can be explained by variation in neighborhood. **(k)** The slope of selling price with number of rooms is the same, regardless of whether the house is located in an east or west neighborhood. **(l)** $\hat{Y} = 253.95 + 8.032X_1 - 5.90X_2 + 2.089X_1X_2$. For X_1X_2, p-value $= 0.330$. Do not reject H_0. There is no evidence that the interaction term makes a contribution to the model. **(m)** The model in (a) should be used.

42 (a) Predicted time $= 8.01 + 0.00523$ Depth $- 2.105$ Dry. **(b)** Holding constant the effect of type of drilling, for each foot increase in depth of the hole, the mean drilling time is estimated to increase by 0.0052 minutes. For a given depth, a dry drilling hole is estimated to reduce the mean drilling time over wet drilling by 2.1052 minutes. **(c)** 6.428 minutes, $6.210 \leq \mu_{Y\mid X} \leq 6.646$, $4.923 \leq Y_X \leq 7.932$. **(d)** The model appears to be adequate. **(e)** $F = 111.11 > 3.09$; reject H_0. **(f)** $t = 5.03 > 1.9847$; reject H_0. $t = -14.03 < -1.9847$; reject H_0. Include both variables. **(g)** $0.0032 \leq \beta_1 \leq 0.0073$, $-2.403 \leq \beta_2 \leq -1.808$. **(h)** 69.6% of the variation in drill time is explained by the variation of depth and variation in type of drilling. **(i)** 69.0%. **(j)** 0.207, 0.670. **(k)** The slope of the additional drilling time with the depth of the hole is the same, regardless of the type of drilling method used. **(l)** The p-value of the interaction term $= 0.462 > 0.05$, so the term is not significant and should not be included in the model. **(m)** The model in part (a) should be used.

44 (a) $\hat{Y} = 31.5594 + 0.0296X_1 + 0.0041X_2 + 0.000017159X_1X_2$, where $X_1 = $ sales, $X_2 = $ orders, p-value $= 0.3249 > 0.05$. Do not reject H_0. There is not enough evidence that the interaction term makes a contribution to the model. **(b)** Since there is not enough evidence of any interaction effect between sales and orders, the model in Problem 14.4 should be used.

46 (a) The p-value of the interaction term $= 0.002 < .05$, so the term is significant and should be included in the model. **(b)** Use the model developed in this problem.

48 (a) For X_1X_2, p-value $= 0.2353 > 0.05$. Do not reject H_0. There is not enough evidence that the interaction term makes a contribution to the model. **(b)** Since there is not enough evidence of an interaction effect between total staff present and remote hours, the model in Problem 14.7 should be used.

58 (a) $\hat{Y} = -3.9152 + 0.0319X_1 + 4.2228X_2$, where $X_1 = $ number of cubic feet moved and $X_2 = $ number of pieces of large furniture. **(b)** Holding constant the number of pieces of large furniture, for each additional cubic feet moved, the mean labor hours are estimated to increase by 0.0319. Holding constant the amount of cubic feet moved, for each additional piece of large furniture, the mean labor hours are estimated to increase by 4.2228. **(c)**

$$\hat{Y} = -3.9152 + 0.0319(500) + 4.2228(2) = 20.4926$$

(d) Based on a residual analysis, the errors appear to be normally distributed. The equal-variance assumption might be violated because the variances appear to be larger around the center region of both independent variables. There might also be violation of the linearity assumption. A model with quadratic terms for both independent variables might be fitted. **(e)** $F = 228.80$, p-value is virtually 0. Since p-value < 0.05, reject H_0. There is evidence of a significant relationship between labor hours and the two independent variables (the amount of cubic feet moved and the number of pieces of large furniture). **(f)** The p-value is virtually 0. The probability of obtaining a test statistic of 228.80 or greater is virtually 0 if there is no significant relationship between labor hours and the two independent variables (the amount of cubic feet moved and the number of pieces of large furniture). **(g)** $r^2 = 0.9327$. 93.27% of the variation in labor hours can be explained by variation in the amount of cubic feet moved and the number of pieces of large furniture. **(h)** $r^2_{adj} = 0.9287$. **(i)** For X_1: $t = 6.9339$, the p-value is virtually 0. Reject H_0. The amount of cubic feet moved makes a significant contribution and should be included in the model. For X_2: $t = 4.6192$, the p-value is virtually 0. Reject H_0. The number of pieces of large furniture makes a significant contribution and should be included in the model. Based on these results, the regression model with the two independent variables should be used. **(j)** For X_1: $t = 6.9339$, the p-value is virtually 0. The probability of obtaining a sample that will yield a test statistic farther away than 6.9339 is virtually 0 if the number of cubic feet moved does not make a significant contribution holding the effect of the number of pieces of large furniture constant. For X_2: $t = 4.6192$, the p-value is virtually 0. The probability of obtaining a sample that will yield a test statistic farther away than 4.6192 is virtually 0 if the number of pieces of large furniture does not make a significant contribution holding the effect of the amount of cubic feet moved constant. **(k)** $r^2_{Y1.2} = 0.5930$. Holding constant the effect of the number of pieces of large furniture, 59.3% of the variation in labor hours can be explained by variation in the amount of cubic feet moved. $r^2_{Y2.1} = 0.3927$. Holding constant the effect of the amount of cubic feet moved, 39.27% of the variation in labor hours can be explained by variation in the number of pieces of large furniture.

60 (a) $\hat{Y} = -120.0483 + 1.7506X_1 + 0.3680X_2$, where $X_1 =$ assessed value and $X_2 =$ time period. **(b)** Holding constant the time period, for each additional thousand dollars of assessed value, the mean selling price is estimated to increase by 1.7507 thousand dollars. Holding constant the assessed value, for each additional month since assessment, the mean selling price is estimated to increase by 0.3680 thousand dollars. **(c)** $\hat{Y} = -120.0483 + 1.7506(170) + 0.3680(12) = 181.9692$ thousand dollars. **(d)** Based on a residual analysis, the model appears to be adequate. **(e)** $F = 223.46$, the p-value is virtually 0. Since p-value < 0.05, reject H_0. There is evidence of a significant relationship between selling price and the two independent variables (assessed value and time period). **(f)** The p-value is virtually 0. The probability of obtaining a test statistic of 223.46 or greater is virtually 0 if there is no significant relationship between selling price and the two independent variables (assessed value and time period). **(g)** $r^2 = 0.9430$. 94.30% of the variation in selling price can be explained by variation in assessed value and time period. **(h)** $r^2_{adj} = 0.9388$. **(i)** For X_1: $t = 20.4137$, the p-value is virtually 0. Reject H_0. The assessed value makes a significant contribution and should be included in the model. For X_2: $t = 2.8734$, p-value $= 0.0078 < 0.05$. Reject H_0. The time period makes a significant contribution and should be included in the model. Based on these results, the regression model with the two independent variables should be used. **(j)** For X_1: $t = 20.4137$, the p-value is virtually 0. The probability of obtaining a sample that will yield a test statistic farther away than 20.4137 is virtually 0 if the assessed value does not make a significant contribution holding time period constant. For X_2: $t = 2.8734$, the p-value is virtually 0. The probability of obtaining a sample that will yield a test statistic farther away than 2.8734 is virtually 0 if the

time period does not make a significant contribution holding the effect of the assessed value constant. **(k)** $r^2_{Y1.2} = 0.9392$. Holding constant the effect of the time period, 93.92% of the variation in selling price can be explained by variation in the assessed value. $r^2_{Y2.1} = 0.2342$. Holding constant the effect of the assessed value, 23.42% of the variation in selling price can be explained by variation in the time period.

62 (a) $\hat{Y} = 163.7751 + 10.7252X_1 - 0.2843X_2$, where $X_1 =$ size and $X_2 =$ age. **(b)** Holding age constant for each additional thousand square feet, the mean assessed value is estimated to increase by \$10.7252 thousand. Holding constant the size, for each additional year, the mean assessed value is estimated to decrease by \$0.2843 thousand. **(c)** $\hat{Y} = 163.7751 + 10.7252(1.75) - 0.2843(10) = 179.7017$ thousand dollars. **(d)** Based on a residual analysis, the errors appear to be normally distributed. The equal-variance assumption appears to be valid. There might also be violation of the linearity assumption for age. You may want to include a quadratic term for age in the model. **(e)** $F = 28.58$, p-value $= 2.72776 \times 10^{-5}$. Since p-value < 0.05, reject H_0. There is evidence of a significant relationship between assessed value and the two independent variables (size and age). **(f)** p-value $= 0.0000272776$. The probability of obtaining a test statistic of 28.58 or greater is virtually 0 if there is no significant relationship between assessed value and the two independent variables (size and age). **(g)** $r^2 = 0.8265$. 82.65% of the variation in assessed value can be explained by variation in size and age. **(h)** $r^2_{adj} = 0.7976$. **(i)** For X_1: $t = 3.5581$, p-value $= 0.0039 < 0.05$. Reject H_0. The size of a house makes a significant contribution and should be included in the model. For X_2: $t = -3.4002$, p-value $= 0.0053 < 0.05$. Reject H_0. The age of a house makes a significant contribution and should be included in the model. Based on these results, the regression model with the two independent variables should be used. **(j)** For X_1: p-value $= 0.0039$. The probability of obtaining a sample that will yield a test statistic farther away than 3.5581 is 0.0039 if the size of a house does not make a significant contribution holding age constant. For X_2: p-value $= 0.0053$. The probability of obtaining a sample that will yield a test statistic farther away than -3.4002 is 0.0053 if the age of a house does not make a significant contribution, holding the effect of the size constant. **(k)** $r^2_{Y1.2} = 0.5134$. Holding constant the effect of age, 51.34% of the variation in assessed value can be explained by variation in the size. $r^2_{Y2.1} = 0.4907$. Holding constant the effect of the size, 49.07% of the variation in assessed value can be explained by variation in the age. **(m)** Based on your answers to (a) through (l), the age of a house does have an effect on its assessed value.

64 (a) $\hat{Y} = 146.0959 - 14.1276X_1 - 5.7491X_2$, where $X_1 =$ ERA and $X_2 =$ League (American $= 0$). **(b)** Holding constant the effect of the league, for each additional ERA, the mean number of wins is estimated to decrease by 14.1276. For a given ERA, a team in the National League is estimated to have a mean of 5.7491 fewer wins than a team in the American League. **(c)** $\hat{Y} = 146.0959 - 14.1276(4.5) - 5.7491(0) = 82.5216$ wins. **(d)** Based on a residual analysis, the errors appear to be right-skewed. The equal-variance and linearity assumptions appear to be valid. **(e)** $F = 26.37$, p-value $= 24.47667 \times 10^{-7}$. Since p-value < 0.05, reject H_0. There is evidence of a significant relationship between wins and the two independent variables (ERA and league). **(f)** For X_1: $t = -7.2404$, the p-value is virtually 0. Reject H_0. ERA makes a significant contribution and should be included in the model. For X_2: $t = -2.33$, p-value $= 0.0275 < 0.05$. Reject H_0. The league makes a significant contribution and should be included in the model. Based on these results, the regression model with the two independent variables should be used. **(g)** $-18.1312 \leq \beta_1 \leq -10.1241$. $-10.8119 \leq \beta_2 \leq -0.6863$.

(h) $r^2 = 0.6614$. So 66.14% of the variation in the number of wins can be explained by ERA and league. **(i)** $r^2_{adj} = 0.6363$. **(j)** $r^2_{Y1.2} = 0.6601$. Holding constant the effect of league, 66.01% of the variation in the number of wins can be explained by variation in ERA. $r^2_{Y2.1} = 0.1674$. Holding constant the effect of ERA, 16.74% of the variation in the number of wins can be explained by the league a team plays in. **(k)** The slope of the number of wins with ERA is the same, regardless of whether the team belongs to the American or the National League. **(l)** $\hat{Y} = 152.0064 - 15.4246X_1 - 19.1124X_2 + 3.0526X_1X_2$. For X_1X_2, the p-value is 0.4497. Do not reject H_0. There is no evidence that the interaction term makes a contribution to the model. **(m)** The model in (a) should be used.

Chapter 5

Multiple Regression Model Building

USING STATISTICS @ WTT-TV

1 THE QUADRATIC REGRESSION MODEL
Finding the Regression Coefficients
   and Predicting Y
Testing for the Significance of the Quadratic Model
Testing the Quadratic Effect
The Coefficient of Multiple Determination

2 USING TRANSFORMATIONS IN REGRESSION MODELS
The Square-Root Transformation
The Log Transformation

3 COLLINEARITY

4 MODEL BUILDING
The Stepwise Regression Approach
   to Model Building

The Best-Subsets Approach to Model Building
Model Validation

5 PITFALLS IN MULTIPLE REGRESSION AND ETHICAL ISSUES
Pitfalls in Multiple Regression
Ethical Issues

EXCEL COMPANION
E1 Creating a Quadratic Term
E2 Creating Transformations
E3 Computing Variance Inflationary Factors
E4 Using Stepwise Regression
E5 Using Best-Subsets Regression

LEARNING OBJECTIVES

In this chapter, you learn:
- To use quadratic terms in a regression model
- To use transformed variables in a regression model
- To measure the correlation among independent variables
- To build a regression model, using either the stepwise or best-subsets approach
- To avoid the pitfalls involved in developing a multiple regression model

From *Statistics for Managers Using Microsoft® Excel 5/e*, David M. Levine, David F. Stephan, Timothy C. Krehbiel, Mark L. Berenson. Copyright © 2008.
All rights reserved by Pearson Prentice Hall.

Using Statistics @ WTT-TV

As part of your job as the operations manager at WTT-TV, you look for ways to reduce labor expenses. Currently, the unionized graphic artists at the station receive hourly pay for a significant number of hours during which they are idle. These hours are called standby hours. You have collected data concerning standby hours and four factors that you suspect are related to the excessive number of standby hours the station is currently experiencing: the total number of staff present, remote hours, Dubner hours, and total labor hours.

You plan to build a multiple regression model to help determine which factors most heavily affect standby hours. You believe that an appropriate model will help you to predict the number of future standby hours, identify the root causes for excessive numbers of standby hours, and allow you to reduce the total number of future standby hours. How do you build the model with the most appropriate mix of independent variables? Are there statistical techniques to help you identify a "best" model without having to consider all possible models? How do you begin?

Y ou may have previously studied multiple regression models that contained two independent variables. In this chapter, regression analysis is extended to models containing more than two independent variables. In order to help you learn to develop the best model when confronted with a large set of data (such as the one described in the Using Statistics scenario), this chapter introduces you to various topics related to model building. These topics include quadratic independent variables, transformations of either the dependent or independent variables, stepwise regression, and best subsets regression.

1 THE QUADRATIC REGRESSION MODEL

The simple regression model and the multiple regression model assume that the relationship between Y and each independent variable is linear. However, several different types of nonlinear relationships between variables exist. One of the most common nonlinear relationships is a quadratic relationship between two variables in which Y increases (or decreases) at a changing rate for various values of X. You can use the quadratic regression model defined in Equation (1) to analyze this type of relationship between X and Y.

QUADRATIC REGRESSION MODEL

$$Y_i = \beta_0 + \beta_1 X_{1i} + \beta_2 X_{1i}^2 + \varepsilon_i \qquad (1)$$

where

$\beta_0 = Y$ intercept

$\beta_1 = $ coefficient of the linear effect on Y

$\beta_2 = $ coefficient of the quadratic effect on Y

$\varepsilon_i = $ random error in Y for observation i

This **quadratic regression model** is similar to the multiple regression model with two independent variables except that the second independent variable is the square of the first independent variable. Once again, you use the sample regression coefficients (b_0, b_1, and b_2) as estimates of the population parameters (β_0, β_1, and β_2). Equation (2) defines the regression equation for the quadratic model with one independent variable (X_1) and a dependent variable (Y).

QUADRATIC REGRESSION EQUATION

$$\hat{Y}_i = b_0 + b_1 X_{1i} + b_2 X_{1i}^2 \tag{2}$$

In Equation (2), the first regression coefficient, b_0, represents the Y intercept; the second regression coefficient, b_1, represents the linear effect; and the third regression coefficient, b_2, represents the quadratic effect.

Finding the Regression Coefficients and Predicting Y

To illustrate the quadratic regression model, consider the following experiment, conducted to study the effect of various amounts of an ingredient called fly ash on the strength of concrete. A sample of 18 specimens of 28-day-old concrete was collected, in which the percentage of fly ash in the concrete varies from 0 to 60%. Table 1 summarizes the data, which are stored in the file flyash.xls.

TABLE 1

Fly Ash Percentage and Strength of 18 Samples of 28-Day-Old Concrete

Fly Ash %	Strength (psi)	Fly Ash %	Strength (psi)
0	4,779	40	5,995
0	4,706	40	5,628
0	4,350	40	5,897
20	5,189	50	5,746
20	5,140	50	5,719
20	4,976	50	5,782
30	5,110	60	4,895
30	5,685	60	5,030
30	5,618	60	4,648

The scatter plot in Figure 1 can help you select the proper model for expressing the relationship between fly ash percentage and strength. Figure 1 indicates an initial increase in the

FIGURE 1

Microsoft Excel scatter plot of fly ash percentage (X) and strength (Y)

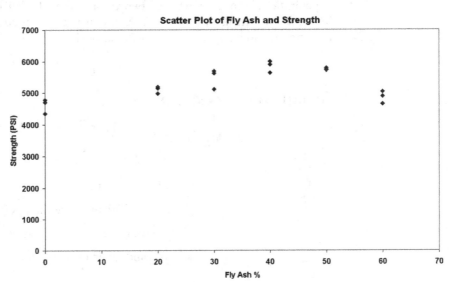

strength of the concrete as the percentage of fly ash increases. The strength appears to level off and then drop after achieving maximum strength at about 40% fly ash. Strength for 50% fly ash is slightly below strength at 40%, but strength at 60% is substantially below strength at 50%. Therefore, a quadratic model is a more appropriate choice than a linear model to estimate strength based on fly ash percentage.

Figure 2 shows the Excel worksheet for these data.

FIGURE 2

Microsoft Excel results for the concrete strength data

See Section E1 to create this.

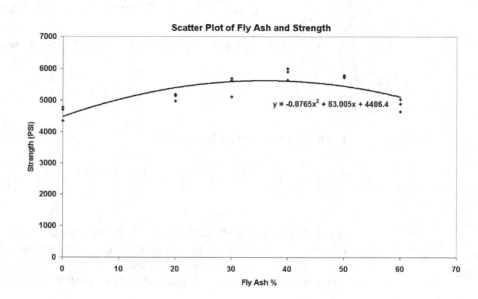

	A	B	C	D	E	F	G
1	Concrete Strength Analysis						
2							
3	*Regression Statistics*						
4	Multiple R	0.8053					
5	R Square	0.6485					
6	Adjusted R Square	0.6016					
7	Standard Error	312.1129					
8	Observations	18					
9							
10	ANOVA						
11		*df*	*SS*	*MS*	*F*	*Significance F*	
12	Regression	2	2695473.49	1347736.745	13.8351	0.0004	
13	Residual	15	1461217.01	97414.4674			
14	Total	17	4156690.5				
15							
16		*Coefficients*	*Standard Error*	*t Stat*	*P-value*	*Lower 95%*	*Upper 95%*
17	Intercept	4486.3611	174.7531	25.6726	8.24736E-14	4113.8834	4858.8389
18	Fly Ash%	63.0052	12.3725	5.0923	0.0001	36.6338	89.3767
19	Fly Ash% ^2	-0.8765	0.1966	-4.4578	0.0005	-1.2955	-0.4574

From Figure 2,

$$b_0 = 4{,}486.3611 \quad b_1 = 63.0052 \quad b_2 = -0.8765$$

Therefore, the quadratic regression equation is

$$\hat{Y}_i = 4{,}486.3611 + 63.0052 X_{1i} - 0.8765 X_{1i}^2$$

where

$$\hat{Y}_i = \text{predicted strength for sample } i$$

$$X_{1i} = \text{percentage of fly ash for sample } i$$

Figure 3 plots this quadratic regression equation on the scatter plot to show the fit of the quadratic regression model to the original data.

FIGURE 3

Microsoft Excel scatter plot expressing the quadratic relationship between fly ash percentage and strength for the concrete data

From the quadratic regression equation and Figure 3, the Y intercept ($b_0 = 4{,}486.3611$) is the predicted strength when the percentage of fly ash is 0. To interpret the coefficients b_1 and b_2, observe that after an initial increase, strength decreases as fly ash percentage increases. This nonlinear relationship is further demonstrated by predicting the strength for fly ash percentages of 20, 40, and 60. Using the quadratic regression equation,

$$\hat{Y}_i = 4{,}486.3611 + 63.0052X_{1i} - 0.8765X_{1i}^2$$

for $X_{1i} = 20$,

$$\hat{Y}_i = 4{,}486.3611 + 63.0052(20) - 0.8765(20)^2 = 5{,}395.865$$

for $X_{1i} = 40$,

$$\hat{Y}_i = 4{,}486.3611 + 63.0052(40) - 0.8765(40)^2 = 5{,}604.169$$

and for $X_{1i} = 60$,

$$\hat{Y}_i = 4{,}486.3611 + 63.0052(60) - 0.8765(60)^2 = 5{,}111.273$$

Thus, the predicted concrete strength for 40% fly ash is 208.304 psi above the predicted strength for 20% fly ash, but the predicted strength for 60% fly ash is 492.896 psi below the predicted strength for 40% fly ash.

Testing for the Significance of the Quadratic Model

After you calculate the quadratic regression equation, you can test whether there is a significant overall relationship between strength, Y, and fly ash percentage, X_1. The null and alternative hypotheses are as follows:

H_0: $\beta_1 = \beta_2 = 0$ (There is no overall relationship between X_1 and Y.)
H_1: β_1 and/or $\beta_2 \neq 0$ (There is an overall relationship between X_1 and Y.)

The following equation defines the overall F statistic used for this test:

$$F = \frac{MSR}{MSE}$$

From the Excel results in Figure 2,

$$F = \frac{MSR}{MSE} = \frac{1{,}347{,}736.745}{97{,}414.4674} = 13.8351$$

If you choose a level of significance of 0.05, from the table of critical values of F, the critical value of the F distribution, with 2 and 15 degrees of freedom, is 3.68 (see Figure 4). Because $F = 13.8351 > 3.68$, or because the p-value $= 0.0004 < 0.05$, you reject the null hypothesis (H_0) and conclude that there is a significant overall relationship between strength and fly ash percentage.

FIGURE 4

Testing for the existence of the overall relationship at the 0.05 level of significance, with 2 and 15 degrees of freedom

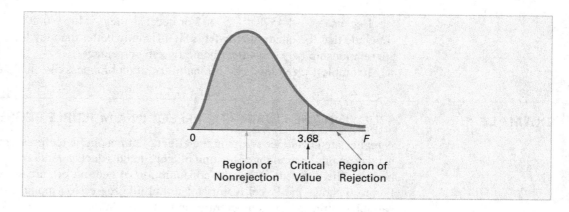

Testing the Quadratic Effect

In using a regression model to examine a relationship between two variables, you want to find not only the most accurate model but also the simplest model that expresses that relationship. Therefore, you need to examine whether there is a significant difference between the quadratic model:

$$Y_i = \beta_0 + \beta_1 X_{1i} + \beta_2 X_{1i}^2 + \varepsilon_i$$

and the linear model:

$$Y_i = \beta_0 + \beta_1 X_{1i} + \varepsilon_i$$

You may have previously used the t test to determine whether each independent variable makes a significant contribution to the regression model. To test the significance of the contribution of the quadratic effect, you use the following null and alternative hypotheses:

H_0: Including the quadratic effect does not significantly improve the model ($\beta_2 = 0$).
H_1: Including the quadratic effect significantly improves the model ($\beta_2 \neq 0$).

The standard error of each regression coefficient and its corresponding t statistic are part of the Excel results (see Figure 2). The following equation defines the t test statistic:

$$t = \frac{b_2 - \beta_2}{S_{b_2}}$$

$$= \frac{-0.8765 - 0}{0.1966} = -4.4578$$

If you select the 0.05 level of significance, then from the table of critical values of t, the critical values for the t distribution with 15 degrees of freedom are -2.1315 and $+2.1315$ (see Figure 5).

FIGURE 5

Testing for the contribution of the quadratic effect to a regression model at the 0.05 level of significance, with 15 degrees of freedom

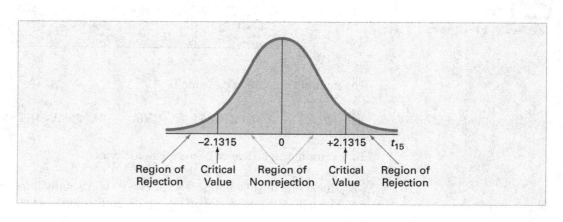

Because $t = -4.4578 < -2.1315$ or because the p-value $= 0.0005 < 0.05$, you reject H_0 and conclude that the quadratic model is significantly better than the linear model for representing the relationship between strength and fly ash percentage.

Example 1 provides an additional illustration of a possible quadratic effect.

EXAMPLE 1

STUDYING THE QUADRATIC EFFECT IN A MULTIPLE REGRESSION MODEL

A real estate developer studying the effect of atmospheric temperature and the amount of attic insulation on the amount of heating oil consumed selects a random sample of 15 single-family houses. The data, including the consumption of heating oil, are stored in the file htngoil.xls. Figure 6 shows the Excel results for a multiple regression model using the two independent variables, atmospheric temperature, and attic insulation.

FIGURE 6

Microsoft Excel results for the monthly consumption of heating oil

	A	B	C	D	E	F	G
1	Heating Oil Consumption Analysis						
2							
3	Regression Statistics						
4	Multiple R	0.9827					
5	R Square	0.9656					
6	Adjusted R Square	0.9599					
7	Standard Error	26.0138					
8	Observations	15					
9							
10	ANOVA						
11		df	SS	MS	F	Significance F	
12	Regression	2	228014.6263	114007.3132	168.4712	1.65411E-09	
13	Residual	12	8120.6030	676.7169			
14	Total	14	236135.2293				
15							
16		Coefficients	Standard Error	t Stat	P-value	Lower 95%	Upper 95%
17	Intercept	562.1510	21.0931	26.6509	4.77868E-12	516.1931	608.1089
18	Temperature	-5.4366	0.3362	-16.1699	1.64178E-09	-6.1691	-4.7040
19	Insulation	-20.0123	2.3425	-8.5431	1.90731E-06	-25.1162	-14.9084

The residual plot for attic insulation (not shown here) contained some evidence of a quadratic effect. Thus, the real estate developer reanalyzed the data by adding a quadratic term for attic insulation to the multiple regression model. At the 0.05 level of significance, is there evidence of a significant quadratic effect for attic insulation?

SOLUTION Figure 7 shows the Excel results for this regression model.

FIGURE 7

Microsoft Excel results for the multiple regression model with a quadratic term for attic insulation

See Section E1 to create this.

	A	B	C	D	E	F	G
1	Quadratic Effect for Insulation Variable?						
2							
3	Regression Statistics						
4	Multiple R	0.9862					
5	R Square	0.9725					
6	Adjusted R Square	0.9650					
7	Standard Error	24.2938					
8	Observations	15					
9							
10	ANOVA						
11		df	SS	MS	F	Significance F	
12	Regression	3	229643.2	76547.7215	129.7006	7.26403E-09	
13	Residual	11	6492.1	590.1877			
14	Total	14	236135.2				
15							
16		Coefficients	Standard Error	t Stat	P-value	Lower 95%	Upper 95%
17	Intercept	624.5864	42.4352	14.7186	1.39085E-08	531.1872	717.9856
18	Temperature	-5.3626	0.3171	-16.9099	3.20817E-09	-6.0606	-4.6646
19	Insulation	-44.5868	14.9547	-2.9815	0.0125	-77.5019	-11.6717
20	Insulation ^2	1.8667	1.1238	1.6611	0.1249	-0.6067	4.3401

The multiple regression equation is

$$\hat{Y}_i = 624.5864 - 5.3626X_{1i} - 44.5868X_{2i} + 1.8667X_{2i}^2$$

To test for the significance of the quadratic effect,

H_0: Including the quadratic effect does not significantly improve the model ($\beta_3 = 0$).
H_1: Including the quadratic effect significantly improves the model ($\beta_3 \neq 0$).

From Figure 7 and the table of critical values of t, $-2.2010 < t = 1.661 < 2.2010$ or the p value $= 0.1249 > 0.05$. Therefore, you do not reject the null hypothesis. You conclude that there is insufficient evidence that the quadratic effect for attic insulation is different from zero. In the interest of keeping the model as simple as possible, you should use the multiple regression equation computed in Figure 6:

$$\hat{Y}_i = 562.1510 - 5.4366X_{1i} - 20.0123X_{2i}$$

The Coefficient of Multiple Determination

In the multiple regression model, the coefficient of multiple determination, r^2, represents the proportion of variation in Y that is explained by variation in the independent variables. Consider the quadratic regression model you used to predict the strength of concrete using fly ash and fly ash squared. You compute r^2 by using the following equation:

$$r^2 = \frac{SSR}{SST}$$

From Figure 2,

$$SSR = 2{,}695{,}473.49 \quad SST = 4{,}156{,}690.5$$

Thus,

$$r^2 = \frac{SSR}{SST} = \frac{2{,}695{,}473.49}{4{,}156{,}690.5} = 0.6485$$

This coefficient of multiple determination indicates that 64.85% of the variation in strength is explained by the quadratic relationship between strength and the percentage of fly ash. You should also compute r^2_{adj} to account for the number of independent variables and the sample size. In the quadratic regression model, $k = 2$ because there are two independent variables, X_1 and X_1^2. Thus, using the following equation,

$$r^2_{adj} = 1 - \left[(1 - r^2)\frac{(n-1)}{(n-k-1)}\right]$$

$$= 1 - \left[(1 - 0.6485)\frac{17}{15}\right]$$

$$= 1 - 0.3984$$

$$= 0.6016$$

PROBLEMS FOR SECTION 1

Learning the Basics

 1 The following quadratic regression equation is for a sample of $n = 25$:

$$\hat{Y}_i = 5 + 3X_{1i} + 1.5X_{1i}^2$$

a. Predict the Y for $X_1 = 2$.
b. Suppose the t statistic for the quadratic regression coefficient is 2.35. At the 0.05 level of significance, is there evidence that the quadratic model is better than the linear model?

c. Suppose the t statistic for the quadratic regression coefficient is 1.17. At the 0.05 level of significance, is there evidence that the quadratic model is better than the linear model?
d. Suppose the regression coefficient for the linear effect is -3.0. Predict Y for $X_1 = 2$.

Applying the Concepts

2 Is the number of calories in a beer related to the number of carbohydrates and/or the percentage of alcohol in the beer? Data concerning 58 of the best-selling domestic beers in the United States are located in the file domesticbeer.xls. The values for three variables are included: the number of calories per 12 ounces, the percentage alcohol, and the number of carbohydrates (in grams) per 12 ounces (extracted from **www.Beer100.com**, March 31, 2006).

a. Perform a multiple regression analysis, using calories as the dependent variable and percentage alcohol and the number of carbohydrates as the independent variables.
b. Add quadratic terms for percentage alcohol and the number of carbohydrates.
c. Which model is better, the one in (a) or (b)?
d. Write a short summary concerning the relationship between the number of calories in a beer and the percentage alcohol and number of carbohydrates.

PH Grade
ASSIST **3** The marketing department of a large supermarket chain wants to study the effect of price on the sales of packages of disposable razors. A sample of 15 stores with equivalent store traffic and product placement (that is, at the checkout counter) is selected. Five stores are randomly assigned to each of three price levels (79, 99, and 119 cents) for the package of razors. The number of packages sold over a full week and the price at each store are in the following table (and in the file dispraz.xls):

Sales	Price (Cents)	Sales	Price (Cents)
142	79	115	99
151	79	126	99
163	79	77	119
168	79	86	119
176	79	95	119
91	99	100	119
100	99	106	119
107	99		

Assume a quadratic relationship between price and sales.
a. Construct a scatter plot for price and sales.
b. State the quadratic regression equation.
c. Predict the mean weekly sales for a price per package of 79 cents.
d. Perform a residual analysis on the results and determine the adequacy of the model.
e. At the 0.05 level of significance, is there a significant quadratic relationship between weekly sales and price?
f. At the 0.05 level of significance, determine whether the quadratic model is a better fit than the linear model.
g. Interpret the meaning of the coefficient of multiple determination.
h. Compute the adjusted r^2.

SELF
Test **4** An agronomist designed a study in which tomatoes were grown using six different amounts of fertilizer: 0, 20, 40, 60, 80, and 100 pounds per 1,000 square feet. These fertilizer application rates were then randomly assigned to plots of land. The results including the yield of tomatoes (in pounds) were as follows (see the file tomyld2.xls):

Plot	Fertilizer Application Rate	Yield	Plot	Fertilizer Application Rate	Yield
1	0	6	7	60	46
2	0	9	8	60	50
3	20	19	9	80	48
4	20	24	10	80	54
5	40	32	11	100	52
6	40	38	12	100	58

Assume a quadratic relationship between the fertilizer application rate and yield.
a. Construct a scatter plot for fertilizer application rate and yield.
b. State the quadratic regression equation.
c. Predict the mean yield for a plot of land fertilized with 70 pounds per 1,000 square feet.
d. Perform a residual analysis on the results and determine the adequacy of the model.
e. At the 0.05 level of significance, is there a significant overall relationship between the fertilizer application rate and tomato yield?
f. What is the p-value in (e)? Interpret its meaning.
g. At the 0.05 level of significance, determine whether there is a significant quadratic effect.
h. What is the p-value in (g)? Interpret its meaning.
i. Interpret the meaning of the coefficient of multiple determination.
j. Compute the adjusted r^2.

5 An auditor for a county government would like to develop a model to predict the county taxes, based on the age of single-family houses. She selects a random sample of 19 single-family houses, and the results are in the data file taxes.xls. Assume a quadratic relationship between age and county taxes.
a. Construct a scatter plot between age and county taxes.
b. State the quadratic regression equation.
c. Predict the mean county taxes for a house that is 20 years old.
d. Perform a residual analysis on the results and determine the adequacy of the model.
e. At the 0.05 level of significance, is there a significant overall relationship between age and county taxes?
f. What is the p-value in (e)? Interpret its meaning.
g. At the 0.05 level of significance, determine whether the quadratic model is superior to the linear model.
h. What is the p-value in (g)? Interpret its meaning.
i. Interpret the meaning of the coefficient of multiple determination.
j. Compute the adjusted r^2.

2 USING TRANSFORMATIONS IN REGRESSION MODELS

This section introduces regression models in which the independent variable, the dependent variable, or both are transformed in order to either overcome violations of the assumptions of regression or to make a model linear in form. Among the many transformations available (see reference 1) are the square-root transformation and transformations involving the common logarithm (base 10) and the natural logarithm (base e).[1]

[1]For more information on logarithms, see Appendix.

The Square-Root Transformation

The **square-root transformation** is often used to overcome violations of the equal-variance assumption as well as to transform a model that is not linear in form into one that is linear. Equation (3) shows a regression model that uses a square-root transformation of the independent variable.

REGRESSION MODEL WITH A SQUARE-ROOT TRANSFORMATION

$$Y_i = \beta_0 + \beta_1 \sqrt{X_{1i}} + \varepsilon_i \tag{3}$$

Example 2 illustrates the use of a square-root transformation.

EXAMPLE 2

USING THE SQUARE-ROOT TRANSFORMATION

Given the following values for Y and X, use a square-root transformation for the X variable:

Y	X	Y	X
42.7	1	100.4	3
50.4	1	104.7	4
69.1	2	112.3	4
79.8	2	113.6	5
90.0	3	123.9	5

Construct a scatter plot for X and Y and for the square root of X and Y.

SOLUTION Figure 8, Panel A, displays the scatter plot of X and Y; Panel B shows the square root of X versus Y.

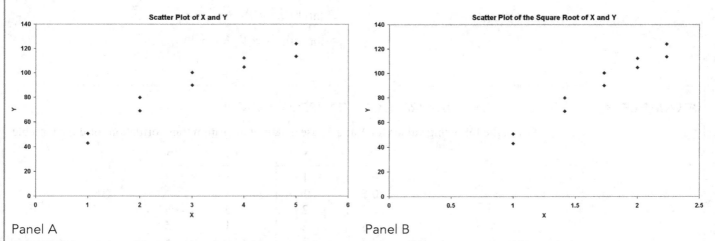

Panel A   Panel B

FIGURE 8 Panel A: Scatter plot of X and Y; Panel B: Scatter plot of the square root of X and Y

You can see that the square-root transformation has transformed a nonlinear relationship into a linear relationship.

The Log Transformation

The **logarithmic transformation** is often used to overcome violations to the equal-variance assumption. You can also use the logarithmic transformation to change a nonlinear model into a linear model. Equation (4) shows a multiplicative model.

ORIGINAL MULTIPLICATIVE MODEL

$$Y_i = \beta_0 X_{1i}^{\beta_1} X_{2i}^{\beta_2} \varepsilon_i \qquad (4)$$

By taking base 10 logarithms of both the dependent and independent variables, you can transform Equation (4) to the model shown in Equation (5).

TRANSFORMED MULTIPLICATIVE MODEL

$$
\begin{aligned}
\log Y_i &= \log(\beta_0 X_{1i}^{\beta_1} X_{2i}^{\beta_2} \varepsilon_i) \\
&= \log \beta_0 + \log(X_{1i}^{\beta_1}) + \log(X_{2i}^{\beta_2}) + \log \varepsilon_i \qquad (5) \\
&= \log \beta_0 + \beta_1 \log X_{1i} + \beta_2 \log X_{2i} + \log \varepsilon_i
\end{aligned}
$$

Hence, Equation (5) is linear in the logarithms. In a similar fashion, you can transform the exponential model shown in Equation (6) to linear form by taking the natural logarithm of both sides of the equation. Equation (7) is the transformed model.

ORIGINAL EXPONENTIAL MODEL

$$Y_i = e^{\beta_0 + \beta_1 X_{1i} + \beta_2 X_{2i}} \varepsilon_i \qquad (6)$$

TRANSFORMED EXPONENTIAL MODEL

$$
\begin{aligned}
\ln Y_i &= \ln(e^{\beta_0 + \beta_1 X_{1i} + \beta_2 X_{2i}} \varepsilon_i) \\
&= \ln(e^{\beta_0 + \beta_1 X_{1i} + \beta_2 X_{2i}}) + \ln \varepsilon_i \qquad (7) \\
&= \beta_0 + \beta_1 X_{1i} + \beta_2 X_{2i} + \ln \varepsilon_i
\end{aligned}
$$

EXAMPLE 3

USING THE NATURAL LOG TRANSFORMATION

Given the following values for Y and X, use a natural logarithm transformation for the Y variable:

Y	X	Y	X
0.7	1	4.8	3
0.5	1	12.9	4
1.6	2	11.5	4
1.8	2	32.1	5
4.2	3	33.9	5

Construct a scatter plot for X and Y and for X and the natural logarithm of Y.

SOLUTION As shown in Figure 9, the natural logarithm transformation has transformed a nonlinear relationship into a linear relationship.

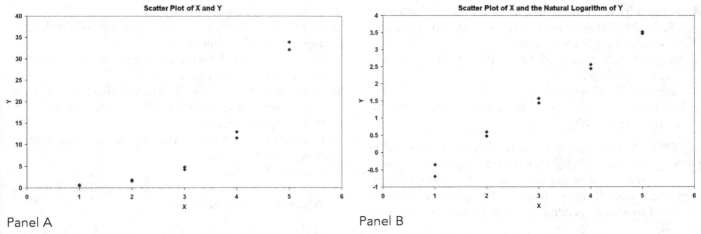

Panel A

Panel B

FIGURE 9 Panel *A*: Scatter plot of *X* and *Y*; Panel *B*: Scatter plot of *X* and the natural logarithm of *Y*

PROBLEMS FOR SECTION 2

Learning the Basics

 6 Consider the following regression equation:

$$\log \hat{Y}_i = \log 3.07 + 0.9 \log X_{1i} + 1.41 \log X_{2i}$$

a. Predict the value of *Y* when $X_1 = 8.5$ and $X_2 = 5.2$.
b. Interpret the meaning of the slopes.

 7 Consider the following regression equation:

$$\ln \hat{Y}_i = 4.62 + 0.5 X_{1i} + 0.7 X_{2i}$$

a. Predict the value of *Y* when $X_1 = 8.5$ and $X_2 = 5.2$.
b. Interpret the meaning of the slopes.

Applying the Concepts

 8 Referring to the data of Problem 2 and using the file **domesticbeer.xls**, perform a square-root transformation on each of the independent variables (percentage alcohol and the number of carbohydrates). Using calories as the dependent variable and the transformed independent variables, perform a multiple regression analysis.
a. State the regression equation.
b. Perform a residual analysis of the results and determine the adequacy of the model.
c. At the 0.05 level of significance, is there a significant relationship between calories and the square root of the percentage of alcohol and the square root of the number of carbohydrates?
d. Interpret the meaning of the coefficient of determination, r^2, in this problem.
e. Compute the adjusted r^2.

f. Compare your results with those in Problem 2. Which model is better? Why?

9 Referring to the data of Problem 2 and using the file **domesticbeer.xls**, perform a natural logarithmic transformation of the dependent variable (calories). Using the transformed dependent variable and the percentage of alcohol and the number of carbohydrates as the independent variables, perform a multiple regression analysis.
a. State the regression equation.
b. Perform a residual analysis of the results and determine the adequacy of the fit of the model.
c. At the 0.05 level of significance, is there a significant relationship between the natural logarithm of calories and the percentage of alcohol and the number of carbohydrates?
d. Interpret the meaning of the coefficient of determination, r^2, in this problem.
e. Compute the adjusted r^2.
f. Compare your results with those in Problems 2 and 8. Which model is best? Why?

 10 Referring to the data of Problem 4 and using the file **tomyld2.xls**, perform a natural logarithm transformation of the dependent variable (yield). Using the transformed dependent variable and the fertilizer application rate as the independent variable, perform a regression analysis.
a. State the regression equation.
b. Predict the mean yield when 55 pounds of fertilizer is applied per 1,000 square feet.
c. Perform a residual analysis of the results and determine the adequacy of the model.

d. At the 0.05 level of significance, is there a significant relationship between the natural logarithm of yield and the fertilizer application rate?

e. Interpret the meaning of the coefficient of determination, r^2, in this problem.

f. Compute the adjusted r^2.

g. Compare your results with those in Problem 4. Which model is better? Why?

PH Grade ASSIST **11** Referring to the data of Problem 4 and using the file **tomyld2.xls**, perform a square-root transformation of the independent variable (fertilizer application rate). Using yield as the dependent variable and the transformed independent variable, perform a regression analysis.

a. State the regression equation.

b. Predict the mean yield when 55 pounds of fertilizer is applied per 1,000 square feet.

c. Perform a residual analysis of the results and determine the adequacy of the model.

d. At the 0.05 level of significance, is there a significant relationship between yield and the square root of the fertilizer application rate?

e. Interpret the meaning of the coefficient of determination, r^2, in this problem.

f. Compute the adjusted r^2.

g. Compare your results with those of Problems 4 and 10. Which model is best? Why?

3 COLLINEARITY

One important problem in the application of multiple regression analysis involves the possible **collinearity** of the independent variables. This condition refers to situations in which one or more of the independent variables are highly correlated with each other. In such situations, collinear variables do not provide unique information, and it becomes difficult to separate the effect of such variables on the dependent variable. When collinearity exists, the values of the regression coefficients for the correlated variables may fluctuate drastically, depending on which independent variables are included in the model.

One method of measuring collinearity is the **variance inflationary factor (VIF)** for each independent variable. Equation (8) defines VIF_j, the variance inflationary factor for variable j.

VARIANCE INFLATIONARY FACTOR

$$VIF_j = \frac{1}{1 - R_j^2} \tag{8}$$

where R_j^2 is the coefficient of multiple determination of independent variable X_j with all other X variables.

If there are only two independent variables, R_1^2 is the coefficient of determination between X_1 and X_2. It is identical to R_2^2, which is the coefficient of determination between X_2 and X_1. If, for example, there are three independent variables, then R_1^2 is the coefficient of multiple determination of X_1 with X_2 and X_3; R_2^2 is the coefficient of multiple determination of X_2 with X_1 and X_3; and R_3^2 is the coefficient of multiple determination of X_3 with X_1 and X_2.

If a set of independent variables is uncorrelated, each VIF_j is equal to 1. If the set is highly correlated, then a VIF_j might even exceed 10. Marquardt (see reference 2) suggests that if VIF_j is greater than 10, there is too much correlation between the variable X_j and the other independent variables. However, other statisticians suggest a more conservative criterion. Snee (see reference 4) recommends using alternatives to least-squares regression if the maximum VIF_j exceeds 5.

You need to proceed with extreme caution when using a multiple regression model that has one or more large VIF values. You can use the model to predict values of the dependent variable *only* in the case where the values of the independent variables used in the prediction are in the relevant range of the values in the data set. However, you cannot extrapolate to values of the independent variables not observed in the sample data. And because the independent variables contain overlapping information, you should always avoid interpreting the regression coefficient estimates separately since there is no way to accurately estimate the individual effects of the independent variables. One solution to the problem is to delete the variable with the largest *VIF* value. The reduced model (that is, the model with the independent variable with the largest *VIF* value deleted) is often free of collinearity problems. If you determine that all the independent variables are needed in the model, you can use methods discussed in reference 1.

In OmniPower sales data, for instance, the correlation between two independent variables, price and promotional expenditure, is −0.0968. Because there are only two independent variables in the model, from Equation (8):

$$VIF_1 = VIF_2 = \frac{1}{1 - (-0.0968)^2}$$
$$= 1.009$$

Thus, you can conclude that there is no problem with collinearity for OmniPower sales data.

In models containing quadratic and interaction terms, collinearity is usually present. The linear and quadratic terms of an independent variable are usually highly correlated with each other, and an interaction term is often correlated with one or both of the independent variables making up the interaction. Thus, you cannot interpret individual parameter estimates separately. You need to interpret the linear and quadratic parameter estimates together in order to understand the nonlinear relationship. Likewise, you need to interpret an interaction parameter estimate in conjunction with the two parameter estimates associated with the variables comprising the interaction. In summary, large *VIF*s in quadratic or interaction models do not necessarily mean that the model is a poor one. They do, however, require you to carefully interpret the parameter estimates.

PROBLEMS FOR SECTION 3

Learning the Basics

12 If the coefficient of determination between two independent variables is 0.20, what is the *VIF*?

13 If the coefficient of determination between two independent variables is 0.50, what is the *VIF*?

4 MODEL BUILDING

This chapter has introduced you to many different topics in regression analysis, including quadratic terms, dummy variables, and interaction terms. In this section, you will learn a structured approach to building the most appropriate regression model. As you will see, successful model building incorporates many of the topics you have studied so far.

To begin, refer to the Using Statistics scenario, in which four independent variables (total staff present, remote hours, Dubner hours, and total labor hours) are considered in developing a regression model to predict standby hours of unionized graphic artists. Table 2 presents the data, which are contained in standby.xls.

TABLE 2

Predicting Standby Hours Based on Total Staff Present, Remote Hours, Dubner Hours, and Total Labor Hours

Week	Standby Hours	Total Staff Present	Remote Hours	Dubner Hours	Total Labor Hours
1	245	338	414	323	2,001
2	177	333	598	340	2,030
3	271	358	656	340	2,226
4	211	372	631	352	2,154
5	196	339	528	380	2,078
6	135	289	409	339	2,080
7	195	334	382	331	2,073
8	118	293	399	311	1,758
9	116	325	343	328	1,624
10	147	311	338	353	1,889
11	154	304	353	518	1,988
12	146	312	289	440	2,049
13	115	283	388	276	1,796
14	161	307	402	207	1,720
15	274	322	151	287	2,056
16	245	335	228	290	1,890
17	201	350	271	355	2,187
18	183	339	440	300	2,032
19	237	327	475	284	1,856
20	175	328	347	337	2,068
21	152	319	449	279	1,813
22	188	325	336	244	1,808
23	188	322	267	253	1,834
24	197	317	235	272	1,973
25	261	315	164	223	1,839
26	232	331	270	272	1,935

Before you develop a model to predict standby hours, you need to consider the principle of parsimony.

The principle of **parsimony** is the belief that you should select the simplest model that gets the job done adequately.

Regression models with fewer independent variables are simpler and easier to interpret, particularly because they are less likely to be affected by collinearity problems (described in Section 3).

The selection of an appropriate model when many independent variables are under consideration involves complexities that are not present with a model that has only two independent variables. The evaluation of all possible regression models is more computationally complex. Although you can quantitatively evaluate competing models, there may not be a *uniquely* best model but rather several *equally appropriate* models.

To begin analyzing the standby-hours data, you compute the variance inflationary factors [see Equation (8)] to measure the amount of collinearity among the independent variables. Figure 10 shows a worksheet that summarizes the *VIF* computations (Panel A), the multiple regression prediction equation worksheet using the four independent variables, and the Durbin-Watson statistic for this model (Panel B). Observe that all the *VIF* values are relatively small, ranging from a high of 1.99928 for the total labor hours to a low of 1.23325 for remote hours. Thus, on the basis of the criteria developed by Snee that all *VIF* values should be less than 5.0 (see reference 4), there is little evidence of collinearity among the set of independent variables.

Panel A

	A	B	C	D	E
1	**Standby Hours Analysis**				
2		*Regression Statistics*			
3		Total Staff and all other X	Remote and all other X	Dubner and all other X	Total Labor and all other X
4	**Multiple R**	0.64368	0.43490	0.56099	0.70698
5	**R Square**	0.41433	0.18914	0.31471	0.49982
6	**Adjusted R Square**	0.33446	0.07856	0.22126	0.43161
7	**Standard Error**	16.47151	124.93921	57.55254	114.41183
8	**Observations**	26	26	26	26
9	**VIF**	1.70743	1.23325	1.45924	1.99928

Panel B

	A	B	C	D	E	F	G
1	**Standby Hours Analysis**						
2							
3		*Regression Statistics*					
4	**Multiple R**	0.7894					
5	**R Square**	0.6231					
6	**Adjusted R Square**	0.5513					
7	**Standard Error**	31.8350					
8	**Observations**	26					
9							
10	**ANOVA**						
11			df	SS	MS	F	Significance F
12	**Regression**		4	35181.7937	8795.4484	8.6786	0.0003
13	**Residual**		21	21282.8217	1013.4677		
14	**Total**		25	56464.6154			
15							
16			Coefficients	Standard Error	t Stat	P-value	Lower 95%	Upper 95%
17	**Intercept**		-330.8318	110.8954	-2.9833	0.0071	-561.4514	-100.2123
18	**Total Staff**		1.2456	0.4121	3.0229	0.0065	0.3887	2.1026
19	**Remote**		-0.1184	0.0543	-2.1798	0.0408	-0.2314	-0.0054
20	**Dubner**		-0.2971	0.1179	-2.5189	0.0199	-0.5423	-0.0518
21	**Total Labor**		0.1305	0.0593	2.2004	0.0391	0.0072	0.2539

Durbin-Watson Calculations:

	A	B
1	**Durbin-Watson Calculations**	
2		
3	Sum of Squared Difference of Residuals	47241.6126
4	Sum of Squared Residuals	21282.8217
5		
6	**Durbin-Watson Statistic**	2.2197

FIGURE 10 Microsoft Excel regression results for predicting standby hours based on four independent variables

Panel A was created by copying and pasting results from four different regression results worksheets that were produced using instructions from Section 3.

The Stepwise Regression Approach to Model Building

You continue your analysis of the standby hours data by attempting to determine whether a subset of all independent variables yields an adequate and appropriate model. The first approach described here is **stepwise regression**, which attempts to find the "best" regression model without examining all possible models.

The first step of stepwise regression is to find the best model that uses one independent variable. The next step is to find the best of the remaining independent variables to add to the model selected in the first step. An important feature of the stepwise approach is that an independent variable that has entered into the model at an early stage may subsequently be removed after other independent variables are considered. Thus, in stepwise regression, variables are either added to or deleted from the regression model at each step of the model-building process. The partial *F*-test statistic is used to determine whether variables are added or deleted. The stepwise procedure terminates with the selection of a best-fitting model when no additional variables can be added to or deleted from the last model evaluated.

Figure 11 represents Microsoft Excel stepwise regression results for the standby-hours data. For this example, a significance level of 0.05 is used to enter a variable into the model or to delete a variable from the model. The first variable entered into the model is total staff, the variable that correlates most highly with the dependent variable standby hours. Because the *p*-value of 0.0011 is less than 0.05, total staff is included in the regression model.

The next step involves selecting a second independent variable for the model. The second variable chosen is one that makes the largest contribution to the model, given that the first variable has been selected. For this model, the second variable is remote hours. Because the *p*-value of 0.0269 for remote hours is less than 0.05, remote hours is included in the regression model.

FIGURE 11

Microsoft Excel stepwise regression results for the standby-hours data

See Section E4 to create this.

	A	B	C	D	E	F	G	H
1	Stepwise Analysis for Standby Hours							
2	Table of Results for General Stepwise							
3								
4	Total Staff entered.							
5								
6			df	SS	MS	F	Significance F	
7	Regression		1	20667.3980	20667.3980	13.8563	0.0011	
8	Residual		24	35797.2174	1491.5507			
9	Total		25	56464.6154				
10								
11			Coefficients	Standard Error	t Stat	P-value	Lower 95%	Upper 95%
12	Intercept		-272.3816	124.2402	-2.1924	0.0383	-528.8008	-15.9625
13	Total Staff		1.4241	0.3826	3.7224	0.0011	0.6345	2.2136
14								
15								
16	Remote entered.							
17								
18			df	SS	MS	F	Significance F	
19	Regression		2	27662.5429	13831.2714	11.0450	0.0004	
20	Residual		23	28802.0725	1252.2640			
21	Total		25	56464.6154				
22								
23			Coefficients	Standard Error	t Stat	P-value	Lower 95%	Upper 95%
24	Intercept		-330.6748	116.4802	-2.8389	0.0093	-571.6322	-89.7175
25	Total Staff		1.7649	0.3790	4.6562	0.0001	0.9808	2.5490
26	Remote		-0.1390	0.0588	-2.3635	0.0269	-0.2606	-0.0173
27								
28								
29	No other variables could be entered into the model. Stepwise ends.							

After remote hours is entered into the model, the stepwise procedure determines whether total staff is still an important contributing variable or whether it can be eliminated from the model. Because the *p*-value of 0.0001 for total staff is less than 0.05, total staff remains in the regression model.

The next step involves selecting a third independent variable for the model. Because none of the other variables meets the 0.05 criterion for entry into the model, the stepwise procedure terminates with a model that includes total staff present and the number of remote hours.

This stepwise regression approach to model building was originally developed more than four decades ago, in an era in which regression analysis on mainframe computers involved the costly use of large amounts of processing time. Under such conditions, stepwise regression became widely used, although it provides a limited evaluation of alternative models. With today's extremely fast personal computers, the evaluation of many different regression models is completed quickly, at a very small cost. Thus, a more general way of evaluating alternative regression models, in this era of fast computers, is the best-subsets approach discussed next. Stepwise regression is not obsolete, however. Today, many businesses use stepwise regression as part of a research technique called **data mining**, in which huge data sets are explored to discover significant statistical relationships among a large number of variables. These data sets are so large that the best-subsets approach is impractical.

The Best-Subsets Approach to Model Building

The **best-subsets approach** evaluates all possible regression models for a given set of independent variables. Figure 12 presents Microsoft Excel results of all possible regression models for the standby-hours data.

A criterion often used in model building is the adjusted r^2, which adjusts the r^2 of each model to account for the number of independent variables in the model as well as for the sample size. Because model building requires you to compare models with different numbers of independent variables, the adjusted r^2 is more appropriate than r^2.

Referring to Figure 12, you see that the adjusted r^2 reaches a maximum value of 0.5513 when all four independent variables plus the intercept term (for a total of five estimated parameters) are included in the model.

A second criterion often used in the evaluation of competing models is the C_p statistic developed by Mallows (see reference 1). The C_p **statistic**, defined in Equation (9), measures the differences between a fitted regression model and a *true* model, along with random error.

FIGURE 12

Microsoft Excel best-subsets regression results for the standby-hours data

See Section E5 to create this.

	A	B	C	D	E	F
1	**Best Subsets Analysis for Standby Hours**					
2						
3	**Intermediate Calculations**					
4	R2T	0.6231				
5	1 - R2T	0.3769				
6	n	26				
7	T	5				
8	n - T	21				
9						
10	**Model**	**Cp**	**k+1**	**R Square**	**Adj. R Square**	**Std. Error**
11	X1	13.3215	2	0.3660	0.3396	38.6206
12	X1X2	8.4193	3	0.4899	0.4456	35.3873
13	X1X2X3	7.8418	4	0.5362	0.4729	34.5029
14	X1X2X3X4	5.0000	5	0.6231	0.5513	31.8350
15	X1X2X4	9.3449	4	0.5092	0.4423	35.4921
16	X1X3	10.6486	3	0.4499	0.4021	36.7490
17	X1X3X4	7.7517	4	0.5378	0.4748	34.4426
18	X1X4	14.7982	3	0.3754	0.3211	39.1579
19	X2	33.2078	2	0.0091	-0.0322	48.2836
20	X2X3	32.3067	3	0.0612	-0.0205	48.0087
21	X2X3X4	12.1381	4	0.4591	0.3853	37.2608
22	X2X4	23.2481	3	0.2238	0.1563	43.6540
23	X3	30.3884	2	0.0597	0.0205	47.0345
24	X3X4	11.8231	3	0.4288	0.3791	37.4466
25	X4	24.1846	2	0.1710	0.1365	44.1619

C_p STATISTIC

$$C_p = \frac{(1 - R_k^2)(n - T)}{1 - R_T^2} - [n - 2(k + 1)] \tag{9}$$

where

k = number of independent variables included in a regression model

T = total number of parameters (including the intercept) to be estimated in the full regression model

R_k^2 = coefficient of multiple determination for a regression model that has k independent variables

R_T^2 = coefficient of multiple determination for a full regression model that contains all T estimated parameters

Using Equation (9) to compute C_p for the model containing total staff present and remote hours,

$$n = 26 \quad k = 2 \quad T = 4 + 1 = 5 \quad R_k^2 = 0.4899 \quad R_T^2 = 0.6231$$

so that

$$C_p = \frac{(1 - 0.4899)(26 - 5)}{1 - 0.6231} - [26 - 2(2 + 1)]$$

$$= 8.4193$$

When a regression model with k independent variables contains only random differences from a *true* model, the mean value of C_p is $k + 1$, the number of parameters. Thus, in evaluating many alternative regression models, the goal is to find models whose C_p is close to or less than $k + 1$.

In Figure 12, you see that only the model with all four independent variables considered contains a C_p value close to or below $k + 1$. Therefore, you should choose that model. Although it was not the case here, the C_p statistic often provides several alternative models for you to evaluate in greater depth, using other criteria, such as parsimony, interpretability, and departure from model assumptions (as evaluated by residual analysis). The model selected using stepwise regression has a C_p value of 8.4193, which is substantially above the suggested criterion of $k + 1 = 3$ for that model.

Because the data were collected in time order, you need to compute the Durbin-Watson statistic to determine whether there is autocorrelation in the residuals. From Panel B of Figure 10, you see that the Durbin-Watson statistic, D, is 2.2197. Because D is greater than 2.0, there is no indication of positive correlation in the residuals.

When you have finished selecting the independent variables to include in the model, you should perform a residual analysis to evaluate the regression assumptions. Figure 13 presents Microsoft Excel residual plots.

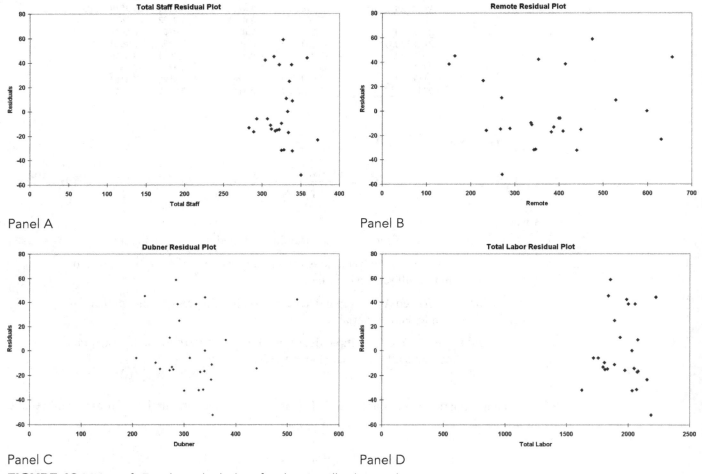

Panel A

Panel B

Panel C

Panel D

FIGURE 13 Microsoft Excel residual plots for the standby-hours data

None of the residual plots versus the total staff, the remote hours, the Dubner hours, and the total labor hours reveal apparent patterns. In addition, a histogram of the residuals (not shown here) indicates only moderate departure from normality, and a plot of the residuals versus the predicted values of Y ($\hat{Y}$) (also not shown here) does not show evidence of unequal variance. Thus, from Figure 10, the regression equation is

$$\hat{Y}_i = -330.8318 + 1.2456X_{1i} - 0.1184X_{2i} - 0.2971X_{3i} + 0.1305X_{4i}$$

Example 4 presents a situation in which there are several alternative models in which the C_p statistic is close to or less than $k + 1$.

EXAMPLE 4   CHOOSING AMONG ALTERNATIVE REGRESSION MODELS

Given the output in Table 3 from a best-subsets regression analysis of a regression model with seven independent variables, determine which regression model you would choose as the *best* model.

TABLE 3

Partial Output from Best-Subsets Regression

Number of Variables	r^2 (%)	Adjusted r^2 (%)	C_p	Variables Included
1	12.1	11.9	113.9	X_4
1	9.3	9.0	130.4	X_1
1	8.3	8.0	136.2	X_3
2	21.4	21.0	62.1	X_3, X_4
2	19.1	18.6	75.6	X_1, X_3
2	18.1	17.7	81.0	X_1, X_4
3	28.5	28.0	22.6	X_1, X_3, X_4
3	26.8	26.3	32.4	X_3, X_4, X_5
3	24.0	23.4	49.0	X_2, X_3, X_4
4	30.8	30.1	11.3	X_1, X_2, X_3, X_4
4	30.4	29.7	14.0	X_1, X_3, X_4, X_6
4	29.6	28.9	18.3	X_1, X_3, X_4, X_5
5	31.7	30.8	8.2	X_1, X_2, X_3, X_4, X_5
5	31.5	30.6	9.6	X_1, X_2, X_3, X_4, X_6
5	31.3	30.4	10.7	X_1, X_3, X_4, X_5, X_6
6	32.3	31.3	6.8	$X_1, X_2, X_3, X_4, X_5, X_6$
6	31.9	30.9	9.0	$X_1, X_2, X_3, X_4, X_5, X_7$
6	31.7	30.6	10.4	$X_1, X_2, X_3, X_4, X_6, X_7$
7	32.4	31.2	8.0	$X_1, X_2, X_3, X_4, X_5, X_6, X_7$

SOLUTION From Table 3, you need to determine which models have C_p values that are less than or close to $k + 1$. Two models meet this criterion. The model with six independent variables ($X_1, X_2, X_3, X_4, X_5, X_6$) has a C_p value of 6.8, which is less than $k + 1 = 6 + 1 = 7$, and the full model with seven independent variables ($X_1, X_2, X_3, X_4, X_5, X_6, X_7$) has a C_p value of 8.0. One way you can choose among models that meet this criterion is to determine whether the models contain a subset of variables that are common. Then you test whether the contribution of the additional variables is significant. In this case, because the models differ only by the inclusion of variable X_7 in the full model, you test whether variable X_7 makes a significant contribution to the regression model, given that the variables $X_1, X_2, X_3, X_4, X_5,$ and X_6 are already included in the model. If the contribution is statistically significant, then you should include variable X_7 in the regression model. If variable X_7 does not make a statistically significant contribution, you should not include it in the model.

Exhibit 1 summarizes the steps involved in model building.

EXHIBIT 1 STEPS INVOLVED IN MODEL BUILDING

1. Compile a listing of all independent variables under consideration.
2. Fit a regression model that includes all the independent variables under consideration and determine the *VIF* for each independent variable. Three possible results can occur:
   a. None of the independent variables have a *VIF* > 5; in this case, proceed to step 3.
   b. One of the independent variables has a *VIF* > 5; in this case, eliminate that independent variable and proceed to step 3.
   c. More than one of the independent variables has a *VIF* > 5; in this case, eliminate the independent variable that has the highest *VIF* and repeat step 2.

3. Perform a best-subsets regression with the remaining independent variables and determine the C_p statistic and/or the adjusted r^2 for each model.
4. List all models that have C_p close to or less than $k + 1$ and/or a high adjusted r^2.
5. From those models listed in step 4, choose a best model.
6. Perform a complete analysis of the model chosen, including a residual analysis.
7. Depending on the results of the residual analysis, add quadratic terms, transform variables, and reanalyze the data.
8. Use the selected model for prediction and inference.

Figure 14 represents a roadmap for the steps involved in model building.

FIGURE 14

Roadmap for model building

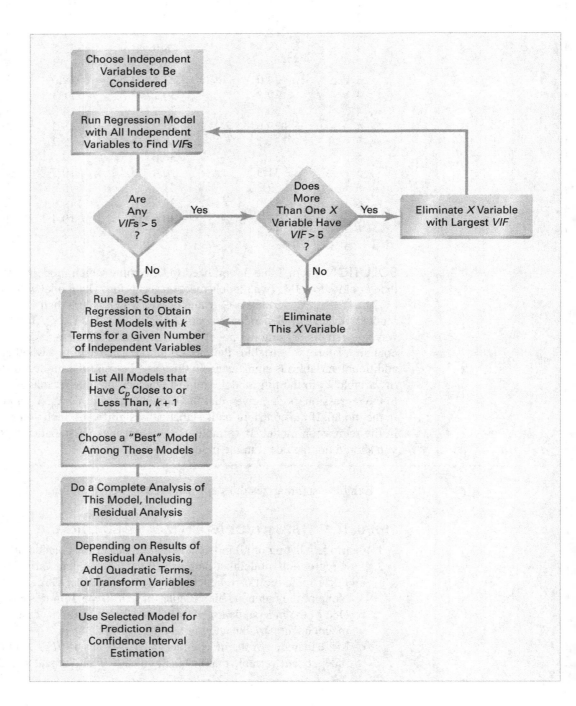

Model Validation

The final step in the model-building process is to validate the selected regression model. This step involves checking the model against data that were not part of the sample analyzed. Several ways of validating a regression model are

- Collect new data and compare the results.
- Compare the results of the regression model to previous results.
- If the data set is large, split the data into two parts and cross-validate the results.

Perhaps the best way of validating a regression model is by collecting new data. If the results with new data are consistent with the selected regression model, you have strong reason to believe that the fitted regression model is applicable in a wide set of circumstances.

If it is not possible to collect new data, you can use one of the two other approaches. In one approach, you compare your regression coefficients and predictions to previous results. If the data set is large, you can use **cross-validation**. First, you split the data into two parts. Then you use the first part of the data to develop the regression model. You then use the second part of the data to evaluate the predictive ability of the regression model.

PROBLEMS FOR SECTION 4

Learning the Basics

 14 You are considering four independent variables for inclusion in a regression model. You select a sample of 30 observations, with the following results:

1. The model that includes independent variables A and B has a C_p value equal to 4.6.
2. The model that includes independent variables A and C has a C_p value equal to 2.4.
3. The model that includes independent variables A, B, and C has a C_p value equal to 2.7.

a. Which models meet the criterion for further consideration? Explain.

b. How would you compare the model that contains independent variables A, B, and C to the model that contains independent variables A and B? Explain.

 15 You are considering six independent variables for inclusion in a regression model. You select a sample of 40 observations, with the following results:

$n = 40 \quad k = 2 \quad T = 6 + 1 = 7 \quad R_k^2 = 0.274 \quad R_T^2 = 0.653$

a. Compute the C_p value for this two-independent-variable model.

b. Based on your answer to (a), does this model meet the criterion for further consideration as the best model? Explain.

Applying the Concepts

 16 You need to develop a model to predict the selling price of houses, based on assessed value, time period in which a house is sold, and whether the house is new (0 = no; 1 = yes). A sample of 30 recently sold single-family houses in a small city is selected to study the relationship between selling price and assessed value. (The houses in the city were reassessed at full value one year prior to the study.) The results are in the data file **house1.xls**. Develop the most appropriate multiple regression model to predict selling price. Be sure to perform a thorough residual analysis. In addition, provide a detailed explanation of the results.

17 The human resources (HR) director for a large company that produces highly technical industrial instrumentation devices is interested in using regression modeling to help in making recruiting decisions concerning sales managers. The company has 45 sales regions, each headed by a sales manager. Many of the sales managers have degrees in electrical engineering, and due to the technical nature of the product line, several company officials believe that only applicants with degrees in electrical engineering should be considered. At the time of their application, candidates are asked to take the Strong-Campbell Interest Inventory Test and the Wonderlic Personnel Test. Due to the time and money involved with the testing, some discussion has taken place about dropping one or both of the tests. To start, the

HR director gathered information on each of the 45 current sales managers, including years of selling experience, electrical engineering background, and the scores from both the Wonderlic and Strong-Campbell tests. The dependent variable was "sales index" score, which is the ratio of the regions' actual sales divided by the target sales. The target values are constructed each year by upper management, in consultation with the sales managers, and are based on past performance and market potential within each region. The data file managers.xls contains information on the 45 current sales managers. The variables included are

Sales—Ratio of yearly sales divided by the target sales value for that region. The target values were mutually agreed-upon "realistic expectations."

Wonder—Score from the Wonderlic Personnel Test. The higher the score, the higher the applicant's perceived ability to manage.

SC—Score on the Strong-Campbell Interest Inventory Test. The higher the score, the higher the applicant's perceived interest in sales.

Experience—Number of years of selling experience prior to becoming a sales manager.

Engineer—Dummy variable that equals 1 if the sales manager has a degree in electrical engineering and 0 otherwise.

a. Develop the most appropriate regression model to predict sales.

b. Do you think that the company should continue administering the Wonderlic and Strong-Campbell tests? Explain.

c. Do the data support the argument that electrical engineers outperform the other sales managers? Would you support the idea to hire only electrical engineers? Explain.

d. How important is prior selling experience in this case? Explain.

e. Discuss in detail how the HR director should incorporate the regression model you developed into the recruiting process.

5 PITFALLS IN MULTIPLE REGRESSION AND ETHICAL ISSUES

Pitfalls in Multiple Regression

Model building is an art as well as a science. Different individuals may not always agree on the best multiple regression model. Nevertheless, you should use the process described in Exhibit 1. In doing so, you must avoid certain pitfalls that can interfere with the development of a useful model. You may already be familiar with the pitfalls in simple linear regression and the strategies for avoiding them. Now that you have studied a variety of multiple regression models, you need to take some additional precautions. To avoid pitfalls in multiple regression, you also need to

- Interpret the regression coefficient for a particular independent variable from a perspective in which the values of all other independent variables are held constant.
- Evaluate residual plots for each independent variable.
- Evaluate interaction and quadratic terms.
- Compute the *VIF* for each independent variable before determining which independent variables to include in the model.
- Examine several alternative models, using best-subsets regression.
- Validate the model before implementing it.

Ethical Issues

Ethical issues arise when a user who wants to make predictions manipulates the development process of the multiple regression model. The key here is intent. In addition to the situations you may have learned about previously, unethical behavior occurs when someone uses multiple regression analysis and *willfully fails* to remove from consideration variables that exhibit a high collinearity with other independent variables or *willfully fails* to use methods other than least-squares regression when the assumptions necessary for least-squares regression are seriously violated.

SUMMARY

In this chapter, various multiple regression topics were considered (see Figure 15), including quadratic regression models, transformations, collinearity, and model building.

You have learned how an operations manager for a television station can build a multiple regression model as an aid in reducing labor expenses.

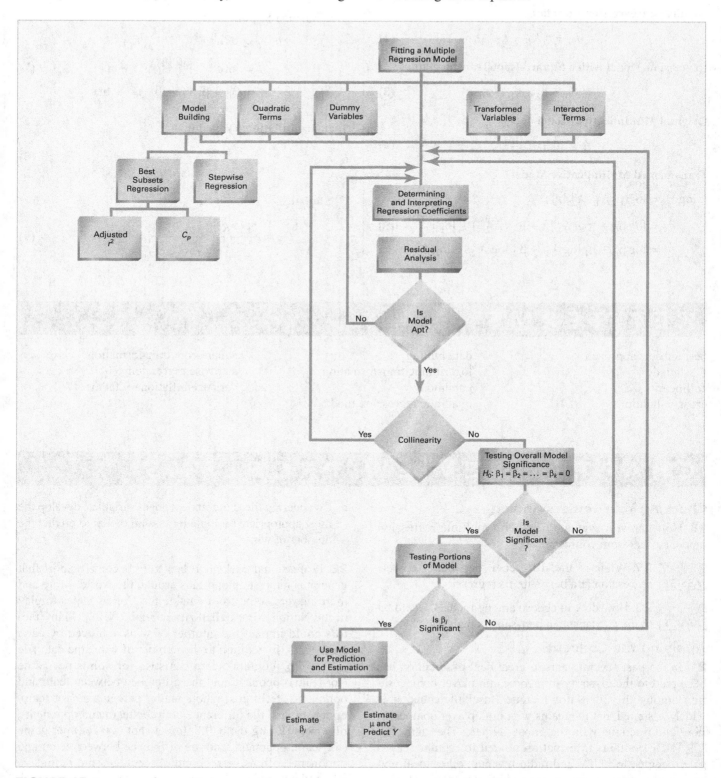

FIGURE 15 Roadmap for multiple regression

KEY EQUATIONS

Quadratic Regression Model

$$Y_i = \beta_0 + \beta_1 X_{1i} + \beta_2 X_{1i}^2 + \varepsilon_i \qquad (1)$$

Quadratic Regression Equation

$$\hat{Y}_i = b_0 + b_1 X_{1i} + b_2 X_{1i}^2 \qquad (2)$$

Regression Model with a Square-Root Transformation

$$Y_i = \beta_0 + \beta_1 \sqrt{X_{1i}} + \varepsilon_i \qquad (3)$$

Original Multiplicative Model

$$Y_i = \beta_0 X_{1i}^{\beta_1} X_{2i}^{\beta_2} \varepsilon_i \qquad (4)$$

Transformed Multiplicative Model

$$
\begin{aligned}
\log Y_i &= \log(\beta_0 X_{1i}^{\beta_1} X_{2i}^{\beta_2} \varepsilon_i) \\
&= \log \beta_0 + \log(X_{1i}^{\beta_1}) + \log(X_{2i}^{\beta_2}) + \log \varepsilon_i \qquad (5) \\
&= \log \beta_0 + \beta_1 \log X_{1i} + \beta_2 \log X_{2i} + \log \varepsilon_i
\end{aligned}
$$

Original Exponential Model

$$Y_i = e^{\beta_0 + \beta_1 X_{1i} + \beta_2 X_{2i}} \varepsilon_i \qquad (6)$$

Transformed Exponential Model

$$
\begin{aligned}
\ln Y_i &= \ln(e^{\beta_0 + \beta_1 X_{1i} + \beta_2 X_{2i}} \varepsilon_i) \\
&= \ln(e^{\beta_0 + \beta_1 X_{1i} + \beta_2 X_{2i}}) + \ln \varepsilon_i \qquad (7) \\
&= \beta_0 + \beta_1 X_{1i} + \beta_2 X_{2i} + \ln \varepsilon_i
\end{aligned}
$$

Variance Inflationary Factor

$$VIF_j = \frac{1}{1 - R_j^2} \qquad (8)$$

C_p Statistic

$$C_p = \frac{(1 - R_k^2)(n - T)}{1 - R_T^2} - [n - 2(k + 1)] \qquad (9)$$

KEY TERMS

best-subsets approach
C_p statistic
collinearity
cross-validation

data mining
logarithmic transformation
parsimony
quadratic regression model

square-root transformation
stepwise regression
variance inflationary factor (*VIF*)

CHAPTER REVIEW PROBLEMS

Checking Your Understanding

18 How can you evaluate whether a multiple regression model suffers from collinearity?

 19 What is the difference between stepwise regression and best-subsets regression?

 20 How do you choose among models according to the C_p statistic in best-subsets regression?

Applying the Concepts

21 In the past several years, a great deal of attention has been paid to the disparity in income and player compensation among the 30 Major League Baseball teams. It is widely assumed that the teams with high player compensation and income win the most games. The data file **bb2001.xls** contains information related to regular season gate receipts, local TV and radio revenue, other local revenue, and player compensation in addition to team statistics.

a. Considering these four independent variables, develop the most appropriate multiple regression model to predict the number of wins.

22 Professional basketball has truly become a sport that generates interest among fans around the world. More and more players come from outside the United States to play in the National Basketball Association (NBA). Many factors could impact the number of wins achieved by each NBA team. In addition to the number of wins, the data file **NBA2006.xls** contains team statistics for points per game (for team, opponent, and the difference between team and opponent), field goal (shots made) percentage (for team, opponent, and the difference between team and opponent), turnovers (losing the ball before a shot is taken) per game (for team, opponent, and the difference between team and opponent), offensive rebound percentage, and defensive rebound percentage.

a. Consider team points per game, opponent points per game, team field goal percentage, opponent field goal percentage, difference in team and opponent turnovers, offensive rebound percentage, and defensive rebound percentage as independent variables for possible inclusion in the multiple regression model. Develop the most appropriate multiple regression model to predict the number of wins.

b. Consider the difference between team points and opponent points per game, the difference between team field goal percentage and opponent field goal percentage, the difference in team and opponent turnovers, offensive rebound percentage, and defensive rebound percentage as independent variables for possible inclusion in the multiple regression model. Develop the most appropriate multiple regression model to predict the number of wins.

c. Compare the results of (a) and (b). Which model is better for predicting the number of wins? Explain.

23 Nassau County is located approximately 25 miles east of New York City. Until all residential property was reassessed in 2002, property taxes were assessed based on actual value in 1938 or when the property was built, if it was constructed after 1938. Data in the file glencove.xls are from a sample of 30 single-family homes located in Glen Cove. Variables included are the appraised value (in 2002), land area of the property (acres), interior size (square feet), age (years), number of rooms, number of bathrooms, and number of cars that can be parked in the garage.

a. Develop the most appropriate multiple regression model to predict appraised value.

b. Compare the results in (a) with those of Problems 24 (a) and 25 (a).

24 Data similar to those in Problem 23 are available for homes located in Roslyn and are stored in the file roslyn.xls.

a. Perform an analysis similar to that of Problem 23.

b. Compare the results in (a) with those of Problems 23 (a) and 25 (a).

25 Data similar to Problem 23 are available for homes located in Freeport and are stored in the file freeport.xls.

a. Perform an analysis similar to that of Problem 23.

b. Compare the results in (a) with those of Problems 23 (a) and 24 (a).

26 You are a real estate broker who wants to compare property values in Glen Cove and Roslyn (which are located approximately 8 miles apart). Use the data in the file gcroslyn.xls. Make sure to include the dummy variable for location (Glen Cove or Roslyn) in the regression model.

a. Develop the most appropriate multiple regression model to predict appraised value.

b. What conclusions can you reach concerning the differences in appraised value between Glen Cove and Roslyn?

27 You are a real estate broker who wants to compare property values in Glen Cove, Freeport, and Roslyn. Use the data in the file gcfreeroslyn.xls.

a. Develop the most appropriate multiple regression model to predict appraised value.

b. What conclusions can you reach concerning the differences in appraised value between Glen Cove, Freeport, and Roslyn?

PH Grade ASSIST **28** Over the past 30 years, public awareness and concern about air pollution have escalated dramatically. Venturi scrubbers are used for the removal of submicron particulate matter found in dust, fogs, fumes, odors, and smoke from gas streams. An experiment was conducted to determine the effect of air flow rate, water flow rate (liters/minute), recirculating water flow rate (liters/minute), and orifice size (mm) in the air side of the pneumatic nozzle on the performance of the scrubber, as measured by the number of transfer units. The results are provided in the file scrubber.xls.

Develop the most appropriate multiple regression model to predict the number of transfer units. Be sure to perform a thorough residual analysis. In addition, provide a detailed explanation of your results.

Source: Extracted from D. A. Marshall, R. J. Sumner, and C. A. Shook, "Removal of SiO$_2$ Particles with an Ejector Venturi Scrubber," Environmental Progress, *14, 1995, 28–32.*

29 A flux chamber is a Plexiglas dome about two feet in diameter that is placed over contaminated soil to sample soil gases. A study was carried out at a suspected radon hot spot to predict radon concentration (pCi/L) based on solar radiation (Ly/Day), soil temperature (°F), vapor pressure (mBar), wind speed (mph), relative humidity (%), dew point (°F), and ambient air temperature (°F). The data are contained in the radon.xls file.

Develop the most appropriate multiple regression model to predict radon concentration. Be sure to perform a thorough residual analysis. In addition, provide a detailed explanation of your results.

30 Oxford, Ohio, which is located 45 miles northwest of Cincinnati, is the home of Miami University. In addition to the 16,000 university students, the city has approximately 20,000 permanent residents. The data file homes.xls contains information on all the single-family houses sold in the city limits for one year. The variables included are

Price—Selling price of home, in dollars

Location—Rating of the location from 1 to 5, with 1 the worst and 5 the best

Condition—Rating of the condition of the home from 1 to 5, with 1 the worst and 5 the best

Bedrooms—Number of bedrooms in the home

Bathrooms—Number of bathrooms in the home

Other Rooms—Number of rooms in the home other than bedrooms and bathrooms

Perform a multiple regression analysis, using selling price as the dependent variable and the five remaining variables as independent variables.

a. State the multiple regression equation.

b. Interpret the meaning of the regression coefficients in this equation.

c. At the 0.05 level of significance, determine whether each independent variable makes a significant contribution to the regression model.

d. Determine the p-values in (c) and interpret their meaning.

e. Predict the price of a home with 3 bedrooms, 2.5 bathrooms, 4 other rooms, a location rating of 4, and a condition rating of 4. Construct a 95% confidence interval estimate and a 95% prediction interval.

f. Determine and interpret the coefficient of multiple determination.

g. Determine the adjusted r^2.

h. Do a residual analysis on the results and determine the adequacy of the model.

i. Delete any independent variables that are not making a significant contribution to the regression model, based on the best-subsets approach. Repeat (a) through (h), using this more parsimonious model. Which model do you think is better? Explain.

31 Many factors determine the attendance at Major League Baseball games. These factors can include when the game is played, the weather, the opponent, whether the team is having a good season, and whether a marketing promotion is held. Popular promotions during the 2002 season were the traditional hat days and poster days and the new craze, bobbleheads of star players (T. C. Boyd and T. C. Krehbiel, "An Analysis of the Effects of Specific Promotion Types on Attendance at Major League Baseball Games," *Mid-American Journal of Business*, 2006, 21, pp. 21–32). The data file baseball.xls includes the following variables for the 2002 Major League Baseball season:

TEAM—Kansas City Royals, Philadelphia Phillies, Chicago Cubs, or Cincinnati Reds

ATTENDANCE—Paid attendance for the game

TEMP—High temperature for the day

WIN%—Team's winning percentage at the time of the game

OPWIN%—Opponent team's winning percentage at the time of the game

WEEKEND—1 if game played on Friday, Saturday or Sunday; 0 otherwise

PROMOTION—1 if a promotion was held; 0 if no promotion was held

a. Construct a multiple regression model for the Kansas City Royals, using attendance as the dependent variable and the remaining five variables as the independent variables.

b. State the multiple regression equation.

c. Interpret the meaning of the regression coefficients.

d. At the 0.05 level of significance, determine whether each independent variable makes a significant contribution to the regression model.

e. Determine and interpret the adjusted r^2.

f. Do a residual analysis on the results and determine the adequacy of the model.

g. Based on the best-subsets approach, delete any independent variables that are not making a significant contribution to the regression model. Repeat (b) through (f), using this more parsimonious model. Which model do you think is better? Explain.

32 Repeat Problem 31 for the Philadelphia Phillies.

33 Repeat Problem 31 for the Chicago Cubs.

34 Repeat Problem 31 for the Cincinnati Reds.

35 Referring to Problems 31–34, in terms of increasing attendance, which team ran the most effective promotions in 2002?

36 Hemlock Farms is a community located in the Pocono Mountains area of eastern Pennsylvania. The data file hemlockfarms.xls contains information on homes that were for sale as of July 4, 2006. The variables included were

List Price—Asking price of the house

Hot Tub—Whether the house has a hot tub, with 0 = No and 1 = Yes

Rooms—Number of rooms in the house

Lake View—Whether the house has a lake view, with 0 = No and 1 = Yes

Bathrooms—Number of bathrooms

Bedrooms—Number of bedrooms

Loft/Den—Whether the house has a loft or den, with 0 = No and 1 = Yes

Finished basement—Whether the house has a finished basement, with 0 = No and 1 = Yes

Acres—Number of acres for the property

Develop the most appropriate multiple regression model to predict the asking price. Be sure to perform a thorough residual analysis. In addition, provide a detailed explanation of your results.

37 A headline on page 1 of *The New York Times* of March 4, 1990, read: "Wine equation puts some noses out of joint." The article explained that Professor Orley Ashenfelter, a Princeton University economist, had developed a multiple regression model to predict the quality of French Bordeaux, based on the amount of winter rain, the average temperature during the growing season, and the harvest rain. The sample multiple regression equation is

$$Q = -12.145 + 0.00117WR + 0.6164TMP - 0.00386HR$$

where

Q = logarithmic index of quality

WR = winter rain (October through March), in millimeters

TMP = average temperature during the growing season (April through September), in degrees Celsius

HR = harvest rain (August to September), in millimeters

You are at a cocktail party, sipping a glass of wine, when one of your friends mentions to you that she has read the article. She asks you to explain the meaning of the coefficients in the equation and also asks you about analyses that might have been done and were not included in the article. What is your reply?

Team Project

38 The data file **Mutual Funds.xls** contains information regarding nine variables from a sample of 838 mutual funds. The variables are

Category—Type of stocks comprising the mutual fund (small cap, mid cap, or large cap)

Objective—Objective of stocks comprising the mutual fund (growth or value)
Assets—In millions of dollars
Fees—Sales charges (no or yes)
Expense ratio—Ratio of expenses to net assets, in percentage
2005 return—Twelve-month return in 2005
Three-year return—Annualized return, 2003–2005
Five-year return—Annualized return, 2001–2005
Risk—Risk-of-loss factor of the mutual fund (low, average, or high)

Develop regression models to predict the 2005 return, the three-year return, and the five-year return, based on fees, expense ratio, objective, and risk. (For the purpose of this analysis, combine low risk and average risk into one category.) Be sure to perform a thorough residual analysis. In addition, provide a detailed explanation of your results. Append all appropriate charts and statistical information to your report.

The Mountain States Potato Company

Mountain States Potato Company sells a by-product of its potato-processing operation, called a filter cake, to area feedlots as cattle feed. Recently, the feedlot owners have noticed that the cattle are not gaining weight as quickly as they once were. They believe that the root cause of the problem is that the percentage of solids in the filter cake is too low.

Historically, the percentage of solids in the filter cakes ran slightly above 12%. Lately, however, the solids are running in the 11% range. What is actually affecting the solids is a mystery, but something has to be done quickly. Individuals involved in the process were asked to identify variables that might affect the percentage of solids. This review turned up the six variables (in addition to the percentage of solids) listed below in the following table. Data collected by monitoring the process several times daily for 20 days are stored in the **potato.xls** file.

Variable	Comments
SOLIDS	Percentage solids in the filter cake.
PH	Acidity. This measure of acidity indicates bacterial action in the clarifier and is controlled by

the amount of downtime in the system. As bacterial action progresses, organic acids are produced that can be measured using pH.

LOWER	Pressure of the vacuum line below the fluid line on the rotating drum.
UPPER	Pressure of the vacuum line above the fluid line on the rotating drum.
THICK	Filter cake thickness, measured on the drum.
VARIDRIV	Setting used to control the drum speed. May differ from DRUMSPD due to mechanical inefficiencies.
DRUMSPD	Speed at which the drum is rotating when collecting the filter cake. Measured with a stopwatch.

1. Thoroughly analyze the data and develop a regression model to predict the percentage of solids.
2. Write an executive summary concerning your findings to the president of the Mountain States Potato Company. Include specific recommendations on how to get the percentage of solids back above 12%.

Web Case

Apply your knowledge of multiple regression model building in this Web Case, on a scenario concerning OmniPower energy bars.

Still concerned about ensuring a successful test marketing of its OmniPower energy bars, the marketing department of OmniFoods has contacted Connect2Coupons

(C2C), another merchandising consultancy. C2C suggests that earlier analysis done by In-Store Placements Group (ISPG) was faulty because it did not use the correct type of data. C2C claims that its Internet-based viral marketing will have an even greater effect on OmniPower energy bar sales, as new data from the same 34-store sample will show. In response, ISPG says its earlier claims are valid and has reported to the OmniFoods marketing department that it can discern no simple relationship between C2C's viral marketing and increased OmniPower sales.

Review all these claims on the message board at the OmniFoods internal Web site, **www.prenhall.com/ Springville/Omni_OmniPowerMB.htm**, (or open this Web page file from the Student CD-ROM Web Case folder) and then answer the following:

1. Which of the claims are true? false? true but misleading? Support your answer by performing an appropriate statistical analysis.

2. If the grocery store chain allowed OmniFoods to use an unlimited number of sales techniques, which techniques should it use? Explain.

3. If the grocery store chain allowed OmniFoods to use only one sales technique, which technique should it use? Explain.

REFERENCES

1. Kutner, M., C. Nachtsheim, J. Neter, and W. Li, *Applied Linear Statistical Models*, 5th ed. (New York: McGraw-Hill/Irwin, 2005).

2. Marquardt, D. W., "You Should Standardize the Predictor Variables in Your Regression Models," discussion of "A Critique of Some Ridge Regression Methods," by G. Smith and F. Campbell, *Journal of the American Statistical Association* 75 (1980): 87–91.

3. *Microsoft Excel 2007* (Redmond, WA: Microsoft Corp., 2007).

4. Snee, R. D., "Some Aspects of Nonorthogonal Data Analysis, Part I. Developing Prediction Equations," *Journal of Quality Technology* 5 (1973): 67–79.

Excel Companion

E1 CREATING A QUADRATIC TERM

To create a quadratic term, open to the worksheet that contains your multiple regression data. Locate the column to the right of the column that contains the data for the linear term. If this column is not blank, select the column, right-click the column, and select **Insert** from the shortcut menu to create a (new) blank column.

In the row 1 cell of the (new or preexisting) blank column, enter a column heading. Then, starting in row 2, enter formulas in the form *=Previous Column'sCell ^2* down the column through all the data rows. For example, if column C contains the data for your linear term and column D is blank, enter the formula **=C2^2** in cell D2 and copy the formula down through all the data rows to create the data for the quadratic term.

With your expanded regression data worksheet, perform a multiple regression analysis that includes both the linear and quadratic terms.

E2 CREATING TRANSFORMATIONS

To create transformations, enter formulas in the form *=FUNCTION(Previous Column's Cell)* in a blank column to the right of the column that contains the data you want to transform. If the column to the right is not blank, select the column, right-click the column, and select **Insert** from the shortcut menu to create a (new) blank column.

FUNCTION could be the SQRT (square root), LOG (common logarithm), or LN (natural logarithm) functions. For example, to create a square-root transformation in a blank column D for an independent variable in column C, enter the formula **=SQRT(C2)** in cell D2 and copy the formula down through all data rows.

E3 COMPUTING VARIANCE INFLATIONARY FACTORS

You compute Variance Inflationary Factors by either selecting the PHStat2 Multiple Regression procedure or the ToolPak Regression procedure.

Using PHStat2 Multiple Regression

Use the "Introduction to Multiple Regression," Section E14.1 instructions in "Using PHStat2 Multiple Regression", but click **Variance Inflationary Factor**

(VIF) before you click **OK** in the Multiple Regression dialog box. (Consult your Instructor for this text.)

Using ToolPak Regression

Perform a regression analysis for every combination of X variables. Then, in each of the regression results worksheets, enter the label **VIF** in cell **A9** and enter the formula **=1/(1-B5)** in cell **B9**.

E4 USING STEPWISE REGRESSION

You use a stepwise regression approach to model building by selecting the PHStat2 Stepwise Regression procedure. (There are no basic Excel commands or features to perform stepwise regression.)

Open to the worksheet that contains your multiple regression data. Select **PHStat → Regression → Stepwise Regression**. In the procedure's dialog box (shown below), enter the cell range of the Y variable as the **Y Variable Cell**

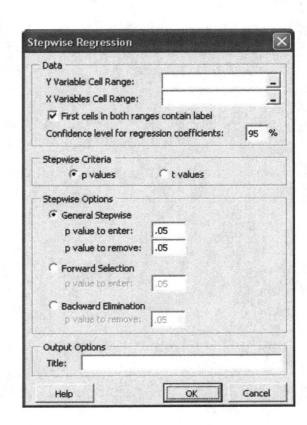

Range and the cell range of the X variables as the **X Variables Cell Range**. Click **First cells in both ranges contain label**, enter a value for the **Confidence level for regression coefficients**, and click the **p values** Stepwise Criteria option. Click the **General Stepwise** option and supply the necessary p-values. Enter a title as the **Title** and click **OK**. (The options and p-values shown in the figure on the previous page were used to create the stepwise regression worksheet shown in Figure 11.)

This procedure can take a noticeable amount of time (seconds) to complete. The procedure is finished when the stepwise model worksheet includes the statement "Stepwise ends" (seen in row 29 in Figure 11).

E5 USING BEST-SUBSETS REGRESSION

You use a best-subsets approach to model building by selecting the PHStat2 Best Subsets procedure. (There are no basic Excel commands or features to perform best-subsets regression.)

Open to the worksheet that contains your multiple regression data. Select **PHStat → Regression → Best Subsets**. In the procedure's dialog box (shown below), enter the cell range of the Y variable as the **Y Variable Cell Range** and the cell range of the X variables as the **X Variables Cell Range**. Click **First cells in both ranges contain label** and enter a value for the **Confidence level for regression coefficients**. Enter a title as the **Title** and click **OK**.

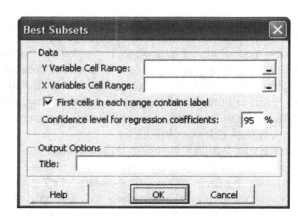

Self-Test Solutions and Answers to Selected Even-Numbered Problems

The following represent worked-out solutions to Self-Test Problems and brief answers to most of the even-numbered problems in the text.

2 (a) $\hat{Y} = -26.4007 + 3.7629X_1 + 26.5186X_2$, where X_1 = carbohydrates and X_2 = alcohol. **(b)** $\hat{Y} = 160.9443 + 5.7315X_1 - 0.0751X_1^2 - 53.4892X_2 + 7.9535X_2^2$, where X_1 = carbohydrates and X_2 = alcohol. **(c)** Carbohydrates: $t = -1.52$; p-value = 0.1332 > 0.05. Alcohol: $t = 2.0543$; p-value = 0.0449 < 0.05. The quadratic term for alcohol improves the model, but the quadratic term for carbohydrates does not.

4 (b) Predicted yield = 6.643 + 0.895 AmtFert − 0.00411 AmtFert^2. **(c)** 49.168 pounds. **(d)** The model appears to be adequate. **(e)** $F = 157.32$ > 4.26; reject H_0. **(f)** p-value = 0 < .05, so the model is significant. **(g)** $t = -4.27 < -2.2622$; reject H_0. There is a significant quadratic effect. **(h)** p-value = 0.002 < .05, so the quadratic term is significant. **(i)** 97.2% of the variation in yield can be explained by the quadratic model. **(j)** 96.6%.

6 (a) 215.37. **(b)** For each additional unit of the logarithm of X_1, the logarithm of Y is estimated to increase by 0.9 units, holding all other variables constant. For each additional unit of the logarithm of X_2, the logarithm of Y is estimated to increase by 1.41 units, holding all other variables constant.

8 (a) $\hat{Y} = -184.6439 + 115.5693\sqrt{X_1} + 22.8081\sqrt{X_2}$, where X_1 = alcohol and X_2 = carbohydrates. **(b)** The residual plot suggests that the errors are right-skewed. The residual plots from the square-root transformation of carbohydrates and alcohol suggest some violation of the equal-variance assumption. **(c)** $F = 288.0536$, the p-value is virtually 0. Reject H_0. There is evidence of a relationship between calories and the square root of alcohol and/or the square root of carbohydrates. $t = 10.0878$, the p-value is virtually 0. Since the p-value < 0.05, reject H_0. There is a significant relationship between calories and the square root of percent alcohol. $t = 11.7751$, the p-value is virtually 0. Since the p-value < 0.05, reject H_0. There is a significant relationship between calories and the square root of the number of carbohydrates. **(d)** $r^2 = 0.9129$. 91.29% of the variation in the number of calories can be explained by variation in the percent alcohol and the variation in the number of carbohydrates. **(e)** $r_{adj}^2 = 0.9097$. **(f)** The model in Problem 15.2 (b), which includes both the quadratic terms in alcohol and carbohydrates, is slightly better for prediction purpose since it has the highest adjusted r^2, of 0.92.

10 (a) Predicted ln(Yield) = 2.475 + 0.0185 AmtFert. **(b)** 32.95 pounds. **(c)** A quadratic pattern exists, so the model is not adequate. **(d)** $t = 6.11 > 2.2281$; reject H_0. **(e)** 78.9%. **(f)** 76.8%. **(g)** Choose the model from Problem 15.4. That model has a much higher adjusted r^2 of 96.6%.

12 1.25.

15 (a) 35.04. **(b)** $C_p > 3$. This does not meet the criterion for consideration of a good model.

16 Let Y = selling price, X_1 = assessed value, X_2 = time period, and X_3 = whether house was new (0 = no, 1 = yes). Based on a full regression model involving all of the variables, all the VIF values (1.3, 1.0, and 1.3, respectively) are less than 5. There is no reason to suspect the existence of collinearity.

Based on a best-subsets regression and examination of the resulting C_p values, the best models appear to be a model with variables X_1 and X_2, which has $C_p = 2.8$, and the full regression model, which has $C_p = 4.0$.

Based on a regression analysis with all the original variables, variable X_3 fails to make a significant contribution to the model at the 0.05 level. Thus, the best model is the model using the assessed value (X_1) and time (X_2) as the independent variables. A residual analysis shows no strong patterns.
The final model is $\hat{Y} = -44.9882 + 1.7506X_1 + 0.3680X_2$, $r^2 = 0.9430$, $r_{adj}^2 = 0.9388$. Overall significance of the model: $F = 223.4575$, $p < 0.001$. Each independent variable is significant at the 0.05 level.

21 (a) The most appropriate model includes only gate receipts as an independent variable. $\hat{Y} = 69.0198 + 0.2582X$; $r^2 = 0.202$.

23 (a) Best model: predicted Appraised Value = 136.794 + 276.0876 Land + 0.1288 House Size(sq ft) − 1.3989 Age.

25 (a) Predicted Appraised Value = 110.27 + 0.0821 House Size(sq ft).

27 Let Y = appraised value, X_1 = land area, X_2 = interior size, X_3 = age, X_4 = number of rooms, X_5 = number of bathrooms, X_6 = garage size, X_7 = 1 if Glen Cove and 0 otherwise, and X_8 = 1 if Roslyn and 0 otherwise. **(a)** All $VIFs$ are less than 5 in a full regression model involving all of the variables: There is no reason to suspect collinearity between any pair of variables. The following is the multiple regression model that has the smallest C_p (9.0) and the highest adjusted r^2 (0.891):

Appraised Value = 49.4 + 343 Land (acres) + 0.115 House Size (sq ft)

− 0.585 Age − 8.24 Rooms + 26.9 Baths + 5.0 Garage + 56.4 Glen Cove

+ 210 Roslyn

The individual t test for the significance of each independent variable at the 5% level of significance concludes that only X_1, X_2, X_5, X_7, and X_8 are significant individually. This subset, however, is not chosen when the C_p criterion is used. The following is the multiple regression output for the model chosen by stepwise regression:

Appraised Value = 23.4 + 347 Land (acres) + 0.106 House Size (sq ft)

− 0.792 Age + 26.4 Baths + 57.7 Glen Cove + 213 Roslyn

This model has a C_p value of 7.7 and an adjusted r^2 of 89.0. All the variables are significant individually at 5% level of significance. Combining the stepwise regression and the best subset regression results along with the individual t test results, the most appropriate multiple regression model for predicting the appraised value is

$$\hat{Y} = 23.40 + 347.02X_1 + 0.10614X_2 - 0.7921X_3$$
$$+26.38X_5 + 57.74X_7 + 213.46X_8$$

(b) The estimated mean appraised value in Glen Cove is 57.74 thousand dollars above Freeport for two otherwise identical properties. The estimated mean appraised value in Roslyn is 213.46 thousand dollars above Freeport for two otherwise identical properties.

29 Explanation: Remove vapor pressure, air temperature, soil radiation, and wind speed due to $VIF > 5$. After removing insignificant variables, the model has the single independent variable, dew point, and a coefficient of determination of only 10%.

31 (a) Let X_1 = Temp, X_2 = Win%, X_3 = OpWin%, X_4 = Weekend, X_5 = Promotion. (b) $\hat{Y} = -3,862.481 + 51.703X_1 + 21.108X_2 + 11.345X_3 + 367.538X_4 + 6,927.882X_5$. (c) Intercept: Since all the non-dummy independent variables cannot have zero values, the intercept cannot be interpreted. Temp: As the high temperature increases by 1 degree, the mean paid attendance is estimated to increase by 51.70, taking into consideration all the other independent variables included in the model. Win%: As the winning percentage of the team improves by 1%, the mean paid attendance is estimated to increase by 21.11, taking into consideration all the other independent variables included in the model. OpWin%: As the opponent team's winning percentage at the time of the game improves by 1%, the mean paid attendance is estimated to increase by 11.35, taking into consideration all the other independent variables included in the model. Weekend: The mean paid attendance of a game played on a weekend is estimated to be 367.54 higher than when the game is played on a weekday, taking into consideration all the other independent variables included in the model. Promotion: The mean paid attendance on a promotion day is estimated to be 6,927.88 higher than when there is no promotion, taking into consideration all the other independent variables included in the model. (d) At a 0.05 level of significance, the independent variable that makes a significant contribution to the regression model individually is the promotion dummy variable. (e) Adjusted $r^2 = 0.2538$. 25.38% of the variation in attendance can be explained by the 5 independent variables after adjusting for the number of independent variables and the sample size. (f) The residual plots of temperature, team's winning percentage, and opponent team's winning percentage reveal potential violation of the equal-variance assumption. The normal probability plot also reveals non-normality in the residuals. (g) With all the 5 independent variables in the model: None of the VIF is > 5. Based on the smallest C_p value and the highest adjusted r^2, the best model includes win percentage, opponent's win percentage, and promotion. Since only X_5 makes a significant contribution to the regression model at the 5% level of significance, the more parsimonious model includes only X_5. (b) $\hat{Y} = 13,935.703 + 6,813.228X_5$. (c) Intercept: The estimated mean paid attendance on non-promotion days is 13,935.70. Promotion: The estimated mean paid attendance on promotion days will be 6,813.23 higher than when there is no promotion. (d) At the 0.05 level of significance, promotion makes a significant contribution to the regression model. (e) $r^2 = 0.2101$. So 21.02% of the variation in attendance can be explained by promotion. (f) The residual plot reveals non-normality in the residuals.

33 (a) Let X_1 = Temp, X_2 = Win%, X_3 = OpWin%, X_4 = Weekend, X_5 = Promotion. (b) $\hat{Y} = 10,682.455 + 82.205X_1 + 26.263X_2 + 7.367X_3 + 3,369.908X_4 + 3,129.013X_5$. (c) Intercept: Since all the non-dummy independent variables cannot have zero values, the intercept cannot be interpreted. Temp: As the high temperature increases by one degree, the mean paid attendance is estimated to increase by 82.21, taking into consideration all the other independent variables included in the model. Win%: As the winning percentage of the team improves by 1%, the mean

paid attendance is estimated to increase by 26.26, taking into consideration all the other independent variables included in the model. OpWin%: As the opponent team's winning percentage at the time of the game increases by 1%, the mean paid attendance is estimated to increase by 7.37, taking into consideration all the other independent variables included in the model. Weekend: The mean paid attendance of a game played on a weekend is estimated to be 3,369.91 higher than when the game is played on a weekday, taking into consideration all the other independent variables included in the model. Promotion: The mean paid attendance on a promotion day is estimated to be 3,129.01 higher than when there is no promotion, taking into consideration all the other independent variables included in the model. (d) At the 0.05 level of significance, the independent variables that make a significant contribution to the regression model individually are temperature, team's winning percentage, and the weekend and promotion dummy variables. (e) Adjusted $r^2 = 0.3504$. So 35.04% of the variation in attendance can be explained by the five independent variables after adjusting for the number of independent variables and the sample size. (f) The residual plots of temperature, team's winning percentage, and opponent team's winning percentage do not show serious departure from the equal-variance assumption. The normal probability plot of the residuals does not show evidence of serious departure from normality. (g) With all the five independent variables in the model: None of the VIFs is > 5. Based on the smallest C_p value and the highest adjusted r^2, the best model is the full model that includes all the independent variables. Since only X_3 does not make significant contribution to the regression model at 5% level of significance, the more parsimonious model includes X_1, X_2, X_4, and X_5. (b) $\hat{Y} = 14,965.626 + 88.888X_1 + 23.269X_2 + 3,562.425X_4 + 3,029.087X_5$. (c) Intercept: Since all the non-dummy independent variables cannot have zero values, the intercept cannot be interpreted. Temp: As the high temperature increases by 1 degree, the mean paid attendance is estimated to increase by 88.89, taking into consideration all the other independent variables included in the model. Win%: As the winning percentage of the team increases by 1%, the mean paid attendance is estimated to increase by 23.27, taking into consideration all the other independent variables included in the model. Weekend: The mean paid attendance of a game played on a weekend is estimated to be 3,562.53 higher than when the game is played on a weekday, taking into consideration all the other independent variables included in the model. Promotion: The mean paid attendance on a promotion day is estimated to be 3,029.09 higher than when there is no promotion, taking into consideration all the other independent variables included in the model. (d) At the 0.05 level of significance, temperature and the weekend and promotion dummy variables make a significant contribution to the regression model individually. (e) Adjusted $r^2 = 0.3457$. So 34.57% of the variation in attendance can be explained by the four independent variables after adjusting for the number of independent variables and the sample size. (f) The residual plots of temperature and team's winning percentage do not show serious departure from the equal-variance assumption. The normal probability plot of the residuals also does not show evidence of serious departure from normality.

35 The Philadelphia Phillies ran the most effective promotions in 2002. An estimated additional 11,184.54 fans attended on days when a promotion was held.

Chapter 6

Time-Series Forecasting and Index Numbers

USING STATISTICS @ The Principled

LEARNING OBJECTIVES

In this chapter, you learn:

- About seven different time-series forecasting models: moving averages, exponential smoothing, the linear trend, the quadratic trend, the exponential trend, the autoregressive, and the least-squares models for seasonal data.
- To choose the most appropriate time-series forecasting model
- About price indexes and the difference between aggregated and unaggregated indexes

Using Statistics @ The Principled

You are a financial analyst for The Principled, a large financial services company. You need to forecast revenues for three companies in order to better evaluate investment opportunities for your clients. To assist in the forecasting, you have collected time-series data on three companies: Wm. Wrigley Jr. Company, Cabot Corporation, and Wal-Mart. Each time series has unique characteristics due to the different types of business activities and growth patterns experienced by the three companies. You understand that you can use several different types of forecasting models. How do you decide which type of forecasting model is best for each company? How do you use the information gained from the forecasting models to evaluate investment opportunities for your clients?

You may have previously used regression analysis as a tool for model building and prediction. In this chapter, regression analysis and other statistical methodologies are applied to time-series data. A **time series** is a set of numerical data collected over time. Due to differences in the features of data for various companies such as the three companies described in the Using Statistics scenario, you need to consider several different approaches to forecasting time-series data.

This chapter begins with an introduction to the importance of business forecasting (see Section 1) and a description of the classical multiplicative time-series model (see Section 2). The coverage of forecasting *models* begins with annual time-series data. Two techniques for smoothing a series are illustrated in Section 3: moving averages and exponential smoothing. The analysis of annual time series continues, with the use of least-squares trend fitting and forecasting (see Section 4) and other more sophisticated forecasting methods (see Section 5). These trend-fitting and forecasting models are then extended to monthly or quarterly time series (see Section 7). This chapter concludes with Section 8 that discusses several types of index numbers.

1 THE IMPORTANCE OF BUSINESS FORECASTING

Forecasting is done to monitor changes that occur over time. Forecasting is commonly used in both the for-profit and not-for-profit sectors of the economy. For example, officials in government forecast unemployment, inflation, industrial production, and revenues from income taxes in order to formulate policies. Marketing executives of a retailing corporation forecast product demand, sales revenues, consumer preferences, inventory, and so on in order to make timely decisions regarding promotions and strategic planning. And the administrators of a college or university forecast student enrollment in order to plan for the construction of dormitories and other academic facilities, plan for student and faculty recruitment, and make assessments of other needs.

There are two common approaches to forecasting: *qualitative* and *quantitative*. **Qualitative forecasting methods** are especially important when historical data are unavailable. Qualitative forecasting methods are considered to be highly subjective and judgmental.

Quantitative forecasting methods make use of historical data. The goal of these methods is to use past data to predict future values. Quantitative forecasting methods are subdivided into two types: *time series* and *causal*. **Time-series forecasting methods** involve forecasting future values based entirely on the past and present values of a variable. For example, the daily closing prices of a particular stock on the New York Stock Exchange constitute a time series. Other examples of economic or business time series are the monthly publication of the consumer price index (CPI), the quarterly gross domestic product (GDP), and the annual sales revenues of a particular company.

Causal forecasting methods involve the determination of factors that relate to the variable you are trying to forecast. These include multiple regression analysis with lagged variables, econometric modeling, leading indicator analysis, diffusion indexes, and other economic barometers that are beyond the scope of this text (see references 2–4). The primary emphasis in this chapter is on time-series forecasting methods.

2 COMPONENT FACTORS OF THE CLASSICAL MULTIPLICATIVE TIME-SERIES MODEL

The basic assumption of time-series forecasting is that the factors that have influenced activities in the past and present will continue to do so in approximately the same way in the future. Thus, the major goals of time-series forecasting are to identify and isolate these influencing factors in order to make predictions.

To achieve these goals, many mathematical models are available to measure the fluctuations among the component factors of a time series. Perhaps the most basic is the **classical multiplicative model** for annual, quarterly, or monthly data. To demonstrate the classical multiplicative time-series model, Figure 1 plots the actual gross revenues for the Wm. Wrigley Jr. Company from 1984 through 2005.

FIGURE 1

Microsoft Excel plot of actual gross revenues (in millions of current dollars) for the Wm. Wrigley Jr. Company (1984–2005)

See Section E2 to create this.

A **trend** is an overall long-term upward or downward movement in a time series. From Figure 1, you can see that actual gross revenues have increased over the 22-year period shown. Thus, actual gross revenues for the Wrigley Company exhibit an upward trend.

Trend is not the only component factor that influences data in an annual time series. Two other factors—the cyclical component and the irregular component—are also present in the data. The **cyclical component** depicts the up-and-down swings or movements through the series. Cyclical movements vary in length, usually lasting from 2 to 10 years. They differ in intensity and are often correlated with a business cycle. In some years, the values are higher than would be predicted by a trend line (that is, they are at or near the peak of a cycle). In other years, the values are lower than would be predicted by a trend line (that is, they are at or near the bottom of a cycle). Any data that do not follow the trend modified by the cyclical component are considered part of the **irregular**, or **random, component**. When you have monthly or quarterly data, an additional component, the **seasonal component**, is considered along with the trend, cyclical, and irregular components.

Table 1 summarizes the four component factors that can influence an economic or business time series.

TABLE 1 Factors Influencing Time-Series Data

Component	Classification of Component	Definition	Reason for Influence	Duration
Trend	Systematic	Overall or persistent, long-term upward or downward pattern of movement	Changes in technology, population, wealth, value	Several years
Seasonal	Systematic	Fairly regular periodic fluctuations that occur within each 12-month period year after year	Weather conditions, social customs, religious customs, school schedules	Within 12 months (or monthly or quarterly data)
Cyclical	Systematic	Repeating up-and-down swings or movements through four phases: from peak (prosperity) to contraction (recession) to trough (depression) to expansion (recovery or growth)	Interactions of numerous combinations of factors that influence the economy	Usually 2–10 years, with differing intensity for a complete cycle
Irregular	Unsystematic	The erratic, or "residual," fluctuations in a series that exist after taking into account the systematic effects	Random variations in data due to unforeseen events, such as strikes, natural disasters, and wars	Short duration and nonrepeating

The classical multiplicative time-series model states that any value in a time series is the product of these components. When forecasting an annual time series, you do not include the seasonal component. Equation (1) defines Y_i, the value of an annual time series recorded in year i, as the product of the trend, cyclical, and irregular components.

CLASSICAL MULTIPLICATIVE TIME-SERIES MODEL FOR ANNUAL DATA

$$Y_i = T_i \times C_i \times I_i \tag{1}$$

where

T_i = value of the trend component in year i

C_i = value of the cyclical component in year i

I_i = value of the irregular component in year i

When forecasting quarterly or monthly data, you include the seasonal component in the model. Equation (2) defines Y_i, a value recorded in time period i, as the product of all four components.

CLASSICAL MULTIPLICATIVE TIME-SERIES MODEL FOR DATA WITH A SEASONAL COMPONENT

$$Y_i = T_i \times S_i \times C_i \times I_i \tag{2}$$

where

T_i, C_i, I_i = value of the trend, cyclical, and irregular components in time period i

S_i = value of the seasonal component in time period i

Your first step in a time-series analysis is to plot the data and observe any patterns that occur over time. You must determine whether there is a long-term upward or downward movement in the series (that is, a trend). If there is no obvious long-term upward or downward trend, then you can use the method of moving averages or the method of exponential smoothing to smooth the series and provide an overall long-term impression (see Section 3). If a trend is present, you can consider several time-series forecasting methods (see Sections 4–5 for forecasting annual data and Section 7 for forecasting monthly or quarterly time series).

3 SMOOTHING AN ANNUAL TIME SERIES

One of the companies of interest in the Using Statistics scenario is the Cabot Corporation. Headquartered in Boston, Massachusetts, the Cabot Corporation is a global company with businesses specializing in the manufacture and distribution of chemicals, performance materials, specialty fluids, microelectronic materials, and liquefied natural gas. The company operates 36 manufacturing facilities in 21 countries. The Cabot Corporation, **w1.cabot-corp.com**, is traded on the New York Stock Exchange with ticker symbol CBT. Revenues in 2005 were approximately $2.1 billion. Table 2 gives the total revenues, in millions of dollars, for 1982 to 2005 (see the file cabot.xls). Figure 2 presents the time-series plot.

TABLE 2

Revenues (in Millions of Dollars) for the Cabot Corporation from 1982 to 2005

Year	Revenue	Year	Revenue	Year	Revenue
1982	1,588	1990	1,685	1998	1,653
1983	1,558	1991	1,488	1999	1,699
1984	1,753	1992	1,562	2000	1,698
1985	1,408	1993	1,619	2001	1,523
1986	1,310	1994	1,687	2002	1,557
1987	1,424	1995	1,841	2003	1,795
1988	1,677	1996	1,865	2004	1,934
1989	1,937	1997	1,637	2005	2,125

Source: Extracted from Moody's Handbook of Common Stocks, *1992, and* Mergent's Handbook of Common Stocks, *2006.*

FIGURE 2

Microsoft Excel plot of revenues (in millions of dollars) for the Cabot Corporation (1982–2005)

See Section E2 to create this.

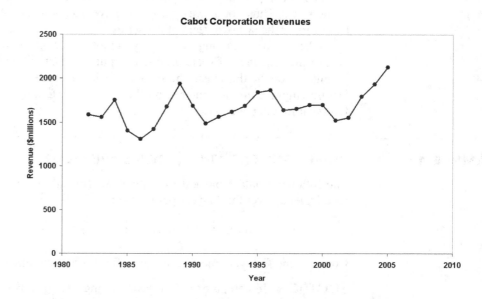

When you examine annual data, your visual impression of the long-term trend in the series is sometimes obscured by the amount of variation from year to year. Often, you cannot judge whether any long-term upward or downward trend exists in the series. To get a better overall impression of the pattern of movement in the data over time, you can use the methods of moving averages or exponential smoothing.

Moving Averages

Moving averages for a chosen period of length L consist of a series of means computed over time such that each mean is calculated for a sequence of L observed values. Moving averages are represented by the symbol $MA(L)$.

To illustrate, suppose you want to compute five-year moving averages from a series that has $n = 11$ years. Because $L = 5$, the five-year moving averages consist of a series of means computed by averaging consecutive sequences of five values. You compute the first five-year moving average by summing the values for the first five years in the series and dividing by 5:

$$MA(5) = \frac{Y_1 + Y_2 + Y_3 + Y_4 + Y_5}{5}$$

You compute the second five-year moving average by summing the values of years 2 through 6 in the series and then dividing by 5:

$$MA(5) = \frac{Y_2 + Y_3 + Y_4 + Y_5 + Y_6}{5}$$

You continue this process until you have computed the last of these five-year moving averages by summing the values of the last 5 years in the series (that is, years 7 through 11) and then dividing by 5:

$$MA(5) = \frac{Y_7 + Y_8 + Y_9 + Y_{10} + Y_{11}}{5}$$

When you are dealing with annual time-series data, L, the length of the period chosen for constructing the moving averages, should be an *odd* number of years. By following this rule, you are not able to compute any moving averages for the first $(L - 1)/2$ years or the last $(L - 1)/2$ years of the series. Thus, for a five-year moving average, you cannot make computations for the first two years or the last two years of the series.

When plotting moving averages, you plot each of the computed values against the middle year of the sequence of years used to compute it. If $n = 11$ and $L = 5$, the first moving average is centered on the third year, the second moving average is centered on the fourth year, and the last moving average is centered on the ninth year. Example 1 illustrates the computation of five-year moving averages.

EXAMPLE 1

COMPUTING FIVE-YEAR MOVING AVERAGES

The following data represent total revenues (in millions of constant 1995 dollars) for a car rental agency over the 11-year period 1996 to 2006:

| 4.0 | 5.0 | 7.0 | 6.0 | 8.0 | 9.0 | 5.0 | 2.0 | 3.5 | 5.5 | 6.5 |

Compute the five-year moving averages for this annual time series.

SOLUTION To compute the five-year moving averages, you first compute the five-year moving total and then divide this total by 5. The first of the five-year moving averages is

$$MA(5) = \frac{Y_1 + Y_2 + Y_3 + Y_4 + Y_5}{5} = \frac{4.0 + 5.0 + 7.0 + 6.0 + 8.0}{5} = \frac{30.0}{5} = 6.0$$

The moving average is then centered on the middle value—the third year of this time series. To compute the second of the five-year moving averages, you compute the moving total of the second through sixth years and divide this value by 5:

$$MA(5) = \frac{Y_2 + Y_3 + Y_4 + Y_5 + Y_6}{5} = \frac{5.0 + 7.0 + 6.0 + 8.0 + 9.0}{5} = \frac{35.0}{5} = 7.0$$

This moving average is centered on the new middle value—the fourth year of the time series. The remaining moving averages are

$$MA(5) = \frac{Y_3 + Y_4 + Y_5 + Y_6 + Y_7}{5} = \frac{7.0 + 6.0 + 8.0 + 9.0 + 5.0}{5} = \frac{35.0}{5} = 7.0$$

$$MA(5) = \frac{Y_4 + Y_5 + Y_6 + Y_7 + Y_8}{5} = \frac{6.0 + 8.0 + 9.0 + 5.0 + 2.0}{5} = \frac{30.0}{5} = 6.0$$

$$MA(5) = \frac{Y_5 + Y_6 + Y_7 + Y_8 + Y_9}{5} = \frac{8.0 + 9.0 + 5.0 + 2.0 + 3.5}{5} = \frac{27.5}{5} = 5.5$$

$$MA(5) = \frac{Y_6 + Y_7 + Y_8 + Y_9 + Y_{10}}{5} = \frac{9.0 + 5.0 + 2.0 + 3.5 + 5.5}{5} = \frac{25.0}{5} = 5.0$$

$$MA(5) = \frac{Y_7 + Y_8 + Y_9 + Y_{10} + Y_{11}}{5} = \frac{5.0 + 2.0 + 3.5 + 5.5 + 6.5}{5} = \frac{22.5}{5} = 4.5$$

These moving averages are then centered on their respective middle values—the fifth, sixth, seventh, eighth, and ninth years in the time series. By using the five-year moving averages, you are unable to compute a moving average for the first two or last two values in the time series.

In practice, you should use Microsoft Excel when computing moving averages to avoid the tedious computations. Figure 3 presents the annual Cabot Corporation revenue data for the 24-year period from 1982 through 2005, the computations for 3- and 7-year moving averages, and a plot of the original data and the moving averages.

FIGURE 3

Microsoft Excel three-year and seven-year moving averages for Cabot Corporation revenues

See Section E1 to create this.

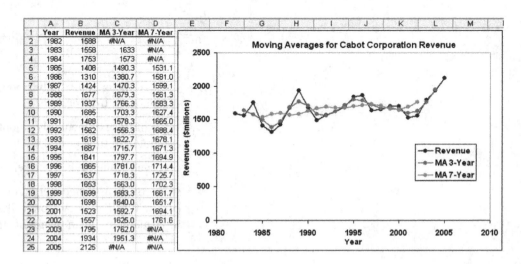

	A	B	C	D
1	Year	Revenue	MA 3-Year	MA 7-Year
2	1982	1588	#N/A	#N/A
3	1983	1558	1633	#N/A
4	1984	1753	1573	#N/A
5	1985	1408	1490.3	1531.1
6	1986	1310	1380.7	1581.0
7	1987	1424	1470.3	1599.1
8	1988	1677	1679.3	1561.3
9	1989	1937	1766.3	1583.3
10	1990	1685	1703.3	1627.4
11	1991	1488	1578.3	1665.0
12	1992	1562	1556.3	1688.4
13	1993	1619	1622.7	1678.1
14	1994	1687	1715.7	1671.3
15	1995	1841	1797.7	1694.9
16	1996	1865	1781.0	1714.4
17	1997	1637	1718.3	1725.7
18	1998	1653	1663.0	1702.3
19	1999	1699	1683.3	1661.7
20	2000	1698	1640.0	1651.7
21	2001	1523	1592.7	1694.1
22	2002	1557	1625.0	1761.6
23	2003	1795	1762.0	#N/A
24	2004	1934	1951.3	#N/A
25	2005	2125	#N/A	#N/A

In Figure 3, there is no three-year moving average for the first and the last year and no seven-year moving average for the first three years and last three years. You can see that the seven-year moving averages smooth the series a great deal more than the three-year moving averages because the period is longer. Unfortunately, the longer the period, the fewer the number of moving averages you can compute. Therefore, selecting moving averages that are longer than seven years is usually undesirable because too many moving average values are missing at the beginning and end of the series. This makes it more difficult to get an overall impression of the entire series.

The selection of L, the length of the period used for constructing the averages, is highly subjective. If cyclical fluctuations are present in the data, you should choose an integer value of L that corresponds to (or is a multiple of) the estimated length of a cycle in the series. If no obvious cyclical fluctuations are present, then the most common choices are three-year, five-year, or seven-year moving averages, depending on the amount of smoothing desired and the amount of data available.

Exponential Smoothing

Exponential smoothing is another method used to smooth a time series. In addition to smoothing, you can use exponential smoothing to compute short-term (that is, one period into the future) forecasts when the presence and type of long-term trend in a time series is questionable. In this respect, exponential smoothing has a clear advantage over the method of moving averages.

The name *exponential smoothing* comes from the fact that this method consists of a series of *exponentially weighted* moving averages. The weights assigned to the values decrease so that the most recent value receives the highest weight, the previous value receives the second-highest weight, and so on, with the first value receiving the lowest weight. Throughout the series, each exponentially smoothed value depends on all previous values, which is another advantage of exponential smoothing over the method of moving averages. Although the computations involved in exponential smoothing seem formidable, you can use Microsoft Excel to perform the computations.

The equation developed for exponentially smoothing a series in any time period, i, is based on only three terms—the current value in the time series, Y_i; the previously computed exponentially smoothed value, E_{i-1}; and an assigned weight or smoothing coefficient, W.[1] You use Equation (3) to exponentially smooth a time series.

[1]*The damping factor used by Microsoft Excel is equal to $1 - W$.*

COMPUTING AN EXPONENTIALLY SMOOTHED VALUE IN TIME PERIOD i

$$E_1 = Y_1 \qquad\qquad (3)$$

$$E_i = WY_i + (1-W)E_{i-1} \qquad i = 2, 3, 4, \ldots$$

where

E_i = value of the exponentially smoothed series being computed in time period i

E_{i-1} = value of the exponentially smoothed series already computed in time period $i - 1$

Y_i = observed value of the time series in period i

W = subjectively assigned weight or smoothing coefficient (where $0 < W < 1$). Although W can approach 1.0, in virtually all business applications, $W \leq 0.5$.

Choosing the smoothing coefficient (that is, weight) that you assign to the time series is critical. Unfortunately, this selection is somewhat subjective. If your goal is only to smooth a series by eliminating unwanted cyclical and irregular variations, you should select a small value for W (close to 0). If your goal is forecasting, you should choose a large value for W (close to 0.5). In the former case, the overall long-term tendencies of the series will be more apparent; in the latter case, future short-term directions may be more adequately predicted.

Figure 4 presents the Microsoft Excel exponentially smoothed values (with smoothing coefficients of $W = 0.50$ and $W = 0.25$) for annual revenue of the Cabot Corporation over the 24-year period 1982 to 2005, along with a plot of the original data and the two exponentially smoothed time series.

FIGURE 4

Microsoft Excel plot of exponentially smoothed series ($W = 0.50$ and $W = 0.25$) of the Cabot Corporation

See Section E3 to create this.

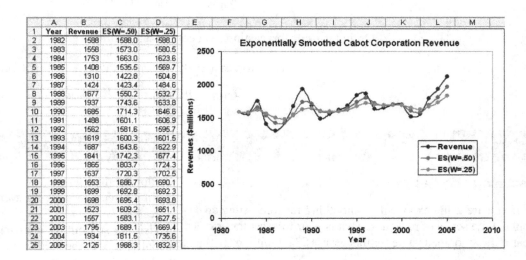

To illustrate these exponential smoothing computations for a smoothing coefficient of $W = 0.25$, you begin with the initial value $Y_{1982} = 1,588$ as the first smoothed value ($E_{1982} = 1,588$). Then, using the value of the time series for 1983 ($Y_{1983} = 1,558$), you smooth the series for 1983 by computing

$$E_{1983} = WY_{1983} + (1 - W)E_{1982}$$
$$= (0.25)(1,558) + (0.75)(1,588) = 1,580.5$$

To smooth the series for 1984:

$$E_{1984} = WY_{1984} + (1 - W)E_{1983}$$
$$= (0.25)(1,753) + (0.75)(1,580.5) = 1,623.6$$

To smooth the series for 1985:

$$E_{1985} = WY_{1985} + (1 - W)E_{1984}$$
$$= (0.25)(1,408) + (0.75)(1,623.6) = 1,569.7$$

You continue this process until you have computed the exponentially smoothed values for all 24 years in the series, as shown in Figure 4.

To use exponential smoothing for forecasting, you use the smoothed value in the current time period as the forecast of the value in the following period.

FORECASTING TIME PERIOD $i + 1$

$$\hat{Y}_{i+1} = E_i \qquad\qquad (4)$$

To forecast the revenue of Cabot Corporation during 2006, using a smoothing coefficient of $W = 0.25$, you use the smoothed value for 2005 as its estimate. Figure 4 shows that this value is $1,832.9 million. (How close is this forecast? Look up Cabot Corporation's revenue in a recent *Mergent's Handbook of Common Stocks* or search the World Wide Web to find out.)

When the value for 2006 becomes available, you can use Equation (3) to make a forecast for 2007 by computing the smoothed value for 2006, as follows:

Current smoothed value = (W)(Current value) + $(1 - W)$(previous smoothest value)

$$E_{2006} = WY_{2006} + (1 - W)E_{2005}$$

Or, in terms of forecasting, you compute the following:

New forecast = (W)(Current value) + $(1 - W)$(Current forecast)

$$\hat{Y}_{2007} = WY_{2006} + (1 - W)\hat{Y}_{2006}$$

PROBLEMS FOR SECTION 3

Learning the Basics

1 If you are using exponential smoothing for forecasting an annual time series of revenues, what is your forecast for next year if the smoothed value for this year is $32.4 million?

 2 Consider a nine-year moving average used to smooth a time series that was first recorded in 1955.

a. Which year serves as the first centered value in the smoothed series?

b. How many years of values in the series are lost when computing all the nine-year moving averages?

 3 You are using exponential smoothing on an annual time series concerning total revenues (in millions of constant 1995 dollars). You decide to use a smoothing coefficient of $W = 0.20$ and the exponentially smoothed value for 2006 is $E_{2006} = (0.20)(12.1) + (0.80)(9.4)$.

a. What is the smoothed value of this series in 2006?

b. What is the smoothed value of this series in 2007 if the value of the series in that year is 11.5 millions of constant 1995 dollars?

Applying the Concepts

 4 The following data (stored in the file movies.xls) represent the yearly movie attendance (in billions) from 1999 to 2005:

Year	Attendance
1999	1.47
2000	1.42
2001	1.49
2002	1.63
2003	1.57
2004	1.53
2005	1.41

Source: Extracted from C. Passy, "Good Night and Good Luck," Palm Beach Post, February 5, 2006, p. 1J).

a. Plot the time series.

b. Fit a three-year moving average to the data and plot the results.

c. Using a smoothing coefficient of $W = 0.50$, exponentially smooth the series and plot the results.

d. Repeat (c), using $W = 0.25$.

e. Compare the results of (c) and (d).

5 The following data, contained in the file deals.xls, provides the number of mergers and acquisitions made during January 1 through January 11 of each year from 1995 to 2006 (extracted from "Back of the Envelope," *The New York Times*, January 13, 2006, p. C7):

Year	Deals	Years	Deals
1995	715	2001	1,031
1996	865	2002	893
1997	708	2003	735
1998	861	2004	759
1999	931	2005	1,013
2000	939	2006	622

a. Plot the time series.

b. Fit a three-year moving average to the data and plot the results.

c. Using a smoothing coefficient of $W = 0.50$, exponentially smooth the series and plot the results.

d. Repeat (c), using $W = 0.25$.

e. Compare the results of (c) and (d).

6 The NASDAQ stock market includes small- and medium-sized companies, many of which are in high-tech industries. Because of the nature of these companies, the NASDAQ tends to be more volatile than the Dow Jones Industrial Average or the S&P 500. The weekly values for the NASDAQ during the first 20 weeks of 2006 are listed in the data file weeklyNASDAQ.xls (extracted from **finance.yahoo.com**):

Week	NASDAQ	Week	NASDAQ
3-Jan-06	2,305.62	13-Mar-06	2,306.48
9-Jan-06	2,317.04	20-Mar-06	2,312.82
17-Jan-06	2,247.70	27-Mar-06	2,339.79
23-Jan-06	2,304.23	3-Apr-06	2,339.02
30-Jan-06	2,262.58	10-Apr-06	2,326.11
6-Feb-06	2,261.88	17-Apr-06	2,342.86
13-Feb-06	2,282.36	24-Apr-06	2,322.57
21-Feb-06	2,287.04	1-May-06	2,342.57
27-Feb-06	2,302.60	8-May-06	2,243.78
6-Mar-06	2,262.04	15-May-06	2,193.88

a. Plot the time series.
b. Fit a three-period moving average to the data and plot the results.
c. Using a smoothing coefficient of $W = 0.50$, exponentially smooth the series and plot the results.
d. Repeat (c), using $W = 0.25$.
e. What conclusions can you reach concerning the presence or absence of trends during the first 20 weeks of 2006?

7 The following data (in the file treasury.xls) represent the three-month Treasury bill rates in the United States from 1991 to 2005:

Year	Rate	Year	Rate
1991	5.38	1999	4.64
1992	3.43	2000	5.82
1993	3.00	2001	3.40
1994	4.25	2002	1.61
1995	5.49	2003	1.01
1996	5.01	2004	2.17
1997	5.06	2005	3.89
1998	4.78		

Source: Board of Governors of the Federal Reserve System,
federalreserve.gov.

a. Plot the data.
b. Fit a three-year moving average to the data and plot the results.
c. Using a smoothing coefficient of $W = 0.50$, exponentially smooth the series and plot the results.
d. What is your exponentially smoothed forecast for 2006?
e. Repeat (c) and (d), using a smoothing coefficient of $W = 0.25$.
f. Compare the results of (d) and (e).

8 The following data (stored in the file electricity.xls) represent the average residential prices of electricity, in cost per kilowatt hour, in the October–March winter months from 1994–1995 to 2004–2005.

Year	Cost	Year	Cost
1994–1995	8.16	2000–2001	8.11
1995–1996	8.10	2001–2002	8.37
1996–1997	8.17	2002–2003	8.20
1997–1998	8.12	2003–2004	8.49
1998–1999	7.94	2004–2005	8.78
1999–2000	7.98		

Source: Energy Information Administration, Department of Energy,
www.eia.doe.gov.

a. Plot the data.
b. Fit a three-year moving average to the data and plot the results.
c. Using a smoothing coefficient of $W = 0.50$, exponentially smooth the series and plot the results.
d. What is your exponentially smoothed forecast for 2005–2006?
e. Repeat (c) and (d), using a smoothing coefficient of $W = 0.25$.
f. Compare the results of (d) and (e).

4 LEAST-SQUARES TREND FITTING AND FORECASTING

The component factor of a time series most often studied is trend. You study trend in order to make intermediate and long-range forecasts. To get a visual impression of the overall long-term movements in a time series, you construct a time-series plot (see Figure 1). If a straight-line trend adequately fits the data, the two most widely used methods of trend fitting are the methods of least squares [see Equation (5)] and *double exponential smoothing* (see reference 1). If the time-series data indicate some long-run downward or upward quadratic movement, the two most widely used trend-fitting methods are the method of least squares [see Equation (6)] and the method of *triple exponential smoothing* (see reference 1). When the time-series data increase at a rate such that the percentage difference from value to value is constant, an exponential trend model is appropriate [see Equation (7)]. The focus of this section is forecasting linear, quadratic, and exponential trends, using the method of least squares.

The Linear Trend Model

The **linear trend model**:

$$Y_i = \beta_0 + \beta_1 X_i + \varepsilon_i$$

is the simplest forecasting model. Equation (5) defines the linear trend forecasting equation.

LINEAR TREND FORECASTING EQUATION

$$\hat{Y}_i = b_0 + b_1 X_i \tag{5}$$

Recall that in linear regression analysis, you used the method of least squares to compute the sample slope, b_1, and the sample Y intercept, b_0. You then substitute the values for X into Equation (5) to predict Y.

When using the least-squares method for fitting trends in a time series, you can simplify the interpretation of the coefficients by coding the X values so that the first value is assigned a code value of $X = 0$. You then assign all successive values consecutively increasing integer codes: 1, 2, 3, . . . , so that the nth and last value in the series has code $n - 1$. For example, for time-series data recorded annually over 22 years, you assign the first year a coded value of 0, the second year a coded value of 1, the third year a coded value of 2, and so on, with the final (22nd) year assigned a coded value of 21.

In the Using Statistics scenario, one of the companies of interest is the Wm. Wrigley Jr. Company. Wrigley's is the world's largest manufacturer and marketer of chewing gum. Headquartered in Chicago, Illinois, Wrigley's operates factories in 12 countries and markets its products in more than 150 countries. Revenues in 2005 topped $4.1 billion (Wm. Wrigley Jr. Company, **www.wrigley.com**). Table 3 lists the actual gross revenues (in millions of current dollars) from 1984 to 2005 (see the file wrigley.xls). This time series is plotted in Figure 5. To adjust for inflation, you use the Bureau of Labor Statistics CPI to convert (and deflate) actual gross revenue dollars into real gross revenue dollars. This adjustment is achieved by multiplying each actual gross revenue value by the corresponding quantity $\left(\frac{100}{CPI}\right)$. The revised values are real gross revenues data in millions of constant 1982 to 1984 dollars. Figure 5 plots the real gross revenues along with the actual gross revenues, in millions of current dollars.

TABLE 3

Actual Gross Revenues (in Millions of Dollars) for the Wm. Wrigley Jr. Company (1984–2005)

Year	Actual Revenue	Year	Actual Revenue
1984	591	1995	1,770
1985	620	1996	1,851
1986	699	1997	1,954
1987	781	1998	2,023
1988	891	1999	2,079
1989	993	2000	2,146
1990	1,111	2001	2,430
1991	1,149	2002	2,746
1992	1,301	2003	3,069
1993	1,440	2004	3,649
1994	1,661	2005	4,159

Source: Extracted from Moody's Handbook of Common Stocks, *1992, and* Mergent's Handbook of Common Stocks, *2006.*

FIGURE 5

Microsoft Excel time-series plots of actual and real gross revenues at Wm. Wrigley Jr. Company (in millions of dollars), 1984–2005

See Section E2 to create this.

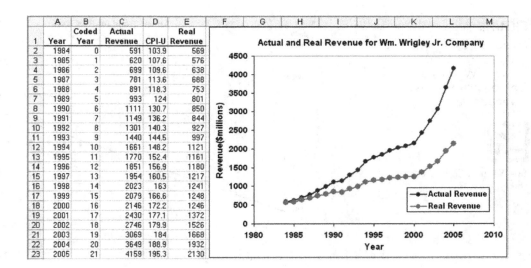

	A	B	C	D	E
1	Year	Coded Year	Actual Revenue	CPI-U	Real Revenue
2	1984	0	591	103.9	569
3	1985	1	620	107.6	576
4	1986	2	699	109.6	638
5	1987	3	781	113.6	688
6	1988	4	891	118.3	753
7	1989	5	993	124	801
8	1990	6	1111	130.7	850
9	1991	7	1149	136.2	844
10	1992	8	1301	140.3	927
11	1993	9	1440	144.5	997
12	1994	10	1661	148.2	1121
13	1995	11	1770	152.4	1161
14	1996	12	1851	156.9	1180
15	1997	13	1954	160.5	1217
16	1998	14	2023	163	1241
17	1999	15	2079	166.6	1248
18	2000	16	2146	172.2	1246
19	2001	17	2430	177.1	1372
20	2002	18	2746	179.9	1526
21	2003	19	3069	184	1668
22	2004	20	3649	188.9	1932
23	2005	21	4159	195.3	2130

Coding the consecutive X values from 0 through 21 and then using Microsoft Excel to perform a simple linear regression analysis on the adjusted time series (see Figure 6) results in the following linear trend forecasting equation:

$$\hat{Y}_i = 469.9158 + 62.1068X_i$$

where year zero is 1984.

FIGURE 6

Microsoft Excel results for a linear regression model to forecast real gross revenues (in millions of constant 1982–1984 dollars) at Wm. Wrigley Jr. Company

See Section E6 to create this.

	A	B	C	D	E	F	G
1	Linear Trend Model for Real Annual Gross Revenue for Wm. Wrigley Jr. Company						
2							
3	*Regression Statistics*						
4	Multiple R	0.9573					
5	R Square	0.9164					
6	Adjusted R Square	0.9122					
7	Standard Error	124.8304					
8	Observations	22					
9							
10	ANOVA						
11		df	SS	MS	F	Significance F	
12	Regression	1	3415597.1280	3415597.1280	219.1927	3.06194E-12	
13	Residual	20	311652.4806	15582.6240			
14	Total	21	3727249.6086				
15							
16		Coefficients	Standard Error	t Stat	P-value	Lower 95%	Upper 95%
17	Intercept	469.9158	51.4629	9.1312	1.42587E-08	362.5661	577.2655
18	Coded Year	62.1068	4.1949	14.8052	3.06194E-12	53.3563	70.8573

You interpret the regression coefficients as follows:

■ The Y intercept, $b_0 = 469.9158$, is the predicted real gross revenues (in millions of constant 1982–1984 dollars) at Wm. Wrigley Jr. during the origin or base year, 1984.

■ The slope, $b_1 = 62.1068$, indicates that real gross revenues are predicted to increase by 62.1068 million dollars per year.

To project the trend in the real gross revenues at Wm. Wrigley Jr. to 2006, you substitute $X_{23} = 22$, the code for 2006, into the linear trend forecasting equation:

$$\hat{Y}_i = 469.9158 + 62.1068(22) = 1,836.265 \text{ millions of constant 1982–1984 dollars}$$

The trend line is plotted in Figure 7, along with the observed values of the time series. There is a strong upward linear trend, and the adjusted r^2 is 0.9122, indicating that more than 90% of the variation in real gross revenues is explained by the linear trend over the time series. To investigate whether a different trend model might provide an even better fit, a *quadratic* trend model and an *exponential* trend model are presented next.

FIGURE 7

Microsoft Excel least-squares trend line for Wm. Wrigley Jr. Company real gross revenues data

See Section E6 to create this.

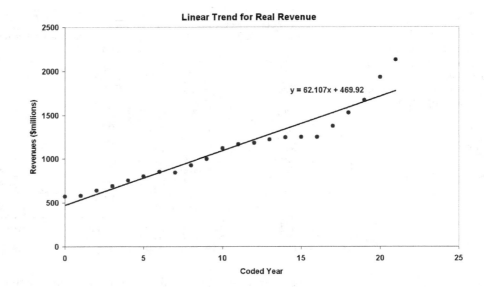

The Quadratic Trend Model

A **quadratic trend model**:

$$\hat{Y}_i = \beta_0 + \beta_1 X_i + \beta_2 X_i^2 + \varepsilon_i$$

is the simplest nonlinear model. Using the least-squares method, you can develop a quadratic trend forecasting equation, as presented in Equation (6).

QUADRATIC TREND FORECASTING EQUATION

$$\hat{Y}_i = b_0 + b_1 X_i + b_2 X_i^2 \qquad \textbf{(6)}$$

where

b_0 = estimated Y intercept

b_1 = estimated *linear* effect on Y

b_2 = estimated *quadratic* effect on Y

Once again, you use Microsoft Excel to compute the quadratic trend forecasting equation. Figure 8 provides the results for the quadratic trend model used to forecast real gross revenues at the Wm. Wrigley Jr. Company.

FIGURE 8

Microsoft Excel results for a quadratic regression model to forecast real gross revenues at Wm. Wrigley Jr. Company

See Section E7 to create this.

	A	B	C	D	E	F	G
1	Quadratic Trend Model for Real Annual Gross Revenue for Wm. Wrigley Jr. Company						
2							
3	*Regression Statistics*						
4	Multiple R	0.9750					
5	R Square	0.9506					
6	Adjusted R Square	0.9454					
7	Standard Error	98.4859					
8	Observations	22					
9							
10	ANOVA						
11		*df*	*SS*	*MS*	*F*	*Significance F*	
12	Regression	2	3542959.4693	1771479.7346	182.6365	3.9272E-13	
13	Residual	19	184290.1393	9699.4810			
14	Total	21	3727249.6086				
15							
16		*Coefficients*	*Standard Error*	*t Stat*	*P-value*	*Lower 95%*	*Upper 95%*
17	Intercept	618.3211	57.6698	10.7217	1.6933E-09	497.6167	739.0255
18	Coded Year	17.5852	12.7243	1.3820	0.1830	-9.0472	44.2176
19	Coded Year Squared	2.1201	0.5851	3.6237	0.0018	0.8955	3.3446

In Figure 8,

$$\hat{Y}_i = 618.3211 + 17.5852X_i + 2.1201X_i^2$$

where year zero is 1984.

To compute a forecast using the quadratic trend equation, you substitute the appropriate coded X values into this equation. For example, to forecast the trend in real gross revenues for 2006 (that is, $X_{23} = 22$),

$$\hat{Y}_i = 618.3211 + 17.5852(22) + 2.1201(22)^2 = 2,031.324 \text{ millions of dollars}$$

Figure 9 plots the quadratic trend forecasting equation along with the time series for the actual data. This quadratic trend model provides a better fit (adjusted $r^2 = 0.9454$) to the time series than does the linear trend model. The t statistic for the contribution of the quadratic term to the model is 3.6237 (p-value = 0.0018).

FIGURE 9

Microsoft Excel fitted quadratic trend forecasting equation for the Wm. Wrigley Jr. Company

See Section E7 to create this.

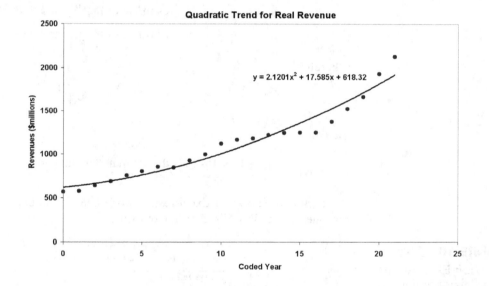

The Exponential Trend Model

When a time series increases at a rate such that the percentage difference from value to value is constant, an exponential trend is present. Equation (7) defines the **exponential trend model**.

EXPONENTIAL TREND MODEL

$$Y_i = \beta_0\beta_1^{X_i}\varepsilon_i \qquad (7)$$

where

$\beta_0 = Y$ intercept

$(\beta_1 - 1) \times 100\%$ is the annual compound growth rate (in %)

[2]*Alternatively, you can use base e logarithms. For more information on logarithms, see Appendix.*

The model in Equation (7) is not in the form of a linear regression model. To transform this nonlinear model to a linear model, you use a base 10 logarithm transformation.[2] Taking the logarithm of each side of Equation (7) results in Equation (8).

TRANSFORMED EXPONENTIAL TREND MODEL

$$\log(Y_i) = \log(\beta_0 \beta_1^{X_i} \varepsilon_i)$$
$$= \log(\beta_0) + \log(\beta_1^{X_i}) + \log(\varepsilon_i) \qquad \textbf{(8)}$$
$$= \log(\beta_0) + X_i \log(\beta_1) + \log(\varepsilon_i)$$

Equation (8) is a linear model you can estimate, using the least-squares method, with $\log(Y_i)$ as the dependent variable and X_i as the independent variable. This results in Equation (9).

EXPONENTIAL TREND FORECASTING EQUATION

$$\log(\hat{Y}_i) = b_0 + b_1 X_i \qquad \textbf{(9a)}$$

where

$$b_0 = \text{estimate of } \log(\beta_0) \text{ and thus } 10^{b_0} = \hat{\beta}_0$$
$$b_1 = \text{estimate of } \log(\beta_1) \text{ and thus } 10^{b_1} = \hat{\beta}_1$$

therefore,

$$\hat{Y}_i = \hat{\beta}_0 \hat{\beta}_1^{X_i} \qquad \textbf{(9b)}$$

where

$$(\hat{\beta}_1 - 1) \times 100\% \text{ is the estimated annual compound growth rate (in \%)}$$

Figure 10 shows an Excel results worksheet for an exponential trend model of real gross revenues at the Wm. Wrigley Jr. Company.

FIGURE 10

Microsoft Excel results for an exponential regression model to forecast real gross revenues at Wm. Wrigley Jr. Company

See Section E8 to create this.

	A	B	C	D	E	F	G
1	Exponential Trend Model for Real Annual Gross Revenues for Wm. Wrigley Jr. Company						
2							
3	*Regression Statistics*						
4	Multiple R	0.9853					
5	R Square	0.9709					
6	Adjusted R Square	0.9694					
7	Standard Error	0.0282					
8	Observations	22					
9							
10	ANOVA						
11		*df*	*SS*	*MS*	*F*	*Significance F*	
12	Regression	1	0.5298	0.5298	666.5416	7.8607E-17	
13	Residual	20	0.0159	0.0008			
14	Total	21	0.5457				
15							
16		*Coefficients*	*Standard Error*	*t Stat*	*P-value*	*Lower 95%*	*Upper 95%*
17	Intercept	2.7647	0.0116	237.8723	5.345E-36	2.7405	2.7890
18	Coded Year	0.0245	0.0009	25.8175	7.8607E-17	0.0225	0.0264

Using Equation (9a) and the results from Figure 10,

$$\log(\hat{Y}_i) = 2.7647 + 0.0245 X_i$$

where year zero is 1984.

You compute the values for $\hat{\beta}_0$ and $\hat{\beta}_1$ by taking the antilog of the regression coefficients (b_0 and b_1):

$$\hat{\beta}_0 = \text{antilog } b_0 = \text{antilog}(2.7647) = 10^{2.7647} = 581.701$$

$$\hat{\beta}_1 = \text{antilog } b_1 = \text{antilog}(0.0245) = 10^{0.0245} = 1.058$$

Thus, using Equation (9b), the exponential trend forecasting equation is

$$\hat{Y}_i = (581.701)(1.058)^{X_i}$$

where year zero is 1984.

The Y intercept, $\hat{\beta}_0 = 581.70$[1] millions of dollars, is the real gross revenues forecast for the base year 1984. The value $(\hat{\beta}_1 - 1) \times 100\% = 5.8\%$ is the annual compound growth rate in real gross revenues at the Wm. Wrigley Jr. Company.

For forecasting purposes, substitute the appropriate coded X values into either Equation (9a) or Equation (9b). For example, to forecast real gross revenues for 2006 (that is, $X_{23} = 22$) using Equation (9a),

$$\log(\hat{Y}_i) = 2.7647 + 0.0245(22) = 3.3037$$

$$\hat{Y}_i = \text{antilog}(3.3037) = 10^{3.3037} = 2{,}012.334 \text{ millions of dollars}$$

Figure 11 plots the exponential trend forecasting equation, along with the time series for the real revenue data. The adjusted r^2 for the exponential trend model (0.9694) is higher than the adjusted r^2 for the linear trend model (0.9122) or the quadratic model (0.9454).

FIGURE 11

Fitting an exponential trend equation using Microsoft Excel for the Wm. Wrigley Jr. Company real gross revenues data

See Section E8 to create this.

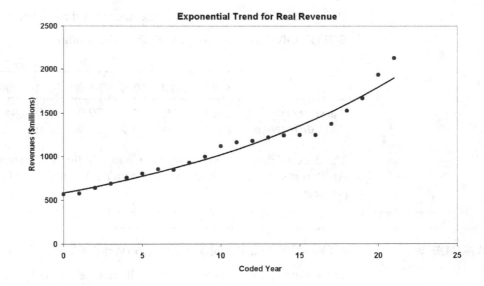

Model Selection Using First, Second, and Percentage Differences

You have used the linear, quadratic, and exponential models to forecast real gross revenues for the Wm. Wrigley Jr. Company. How can you determine which of these models is the most appropriate model? In addition to visually inspecting scatter plots and comparing adjusted r^2 values, you can compute and examine first, second, and percentage differences. The identifying features of linear, quadratic, and exponential trend models are as follows:

- If a linear trend model provides a perfect fit to a time series, then the first differences are constant. Thus, the differences between consecutive values in the series are the same throughout:

$$(Y_2 - Y_1) = (Y_3 - Y_2) = \cdots = (Y_n - Y_{n-1})$$

- If a quadratic trend model provides a perfect fit to a time series, then the second differences are constant. Thus,

$$[(Y_3 - Y_2) - (Y_2 - Y_1)] = [(Y_4 - Y_3) - (Y_3 - Y_2)] = \cdots = [(Y_n - Y_{n-1}) - (Y_{n-1} - Y_{n-2})]$$

- If an exponential trend model provides a perfect fit to a time series, then the percentage differences between consecutive values are constant. Thus,

$$\frac{Y_2 - Y_1}{Y_1} \times 100\% = \frac{Y_3 - Y_2}{Y_2} \times 100\% = \cdots = \frac{Y_n - Y_{n-1}}{Y_{n-1}} \times 100\%$$

Although you should not expect a perfectly fitting model for any particular set of time-series data, you can consider the first differences, second differences, and percentage differences for a given series as guides in choosing an appropriate model. Examples 2, 3, and 4 illustrate applications of linear, quadratic, and exponential trend models having perfect fits to their respective data sets.

EXAMPLE 2

A LINEAR TREND MODEL WITH A PERFECT FIT

The following time series represents the number of passengers per year (in millions) on ABC Airlines:

	Year									
	1997	1998	1999	2000	2001	2002	2003	2004	2005	2006
Passengers	30.0	33.0	36.0	39.0	42.0	45.0	48.0	51.0	54.0	57.0

Using first differences, show that the linear trend model provides a perfect fit to these data.

SOLUTION The following table shows the solution:

	Year									
	1997	1998	1999	2000	2001	2002	2003	2004	2005	2006
Passengers	30.0	33.0	36.0	39.0	42.0	45.0	48.0	51.0	54.0	57.0
First differences		3.0	3.0	3.0	3.0	3.0	3.0	3.0	3.0	3.0

The differences between consecutive values in the series are the same throughout. Thus, ABC Airlines is exhibiting a linear growth pattern. The number of passengers increases by 3 million per year.

EXAMPLE 3

A QUADRATIC TREND MODEL WITH A PERFECT FIT

The following time series represents the number of passengers per year (in millions) on XYZ Airlines:

	Year									
	1997	1998	1999	2000	2001	2002	2003	2004	2005	2006
Passengers	30.0	31.0	33.5	37.5	43.0	50.0	58.5	68.5	80.0	93.0

Using second differences, show that the quadratic trend model provides a perfect fit to these data.

SOLUTION The following table shows the solution:

	Year									
	1997	1998	1999	2000	2001	2002	2003	2004	2005	2006
Passengers	30.0	31.0	33.5	37.5	43.0	50.0	58.5	68.5	80.0	93.0
First differences		1.0	2.5	4.0	5.5	7.0	8.5	10.0	11.5	13.0
Second differences			1.5	1.5	1.5	1.5	1.5	1.5	1.5	1.5

The second differences between consecutive pairs of values in the series are the same throughout. Thus, XYZ airlines is exhibiting a quadratic growth pattern. Its rate of growth is accelerating over time.

EXAMPLE 4

AN EXPONENTIAL TREND MODEL WITH A PERFECT FIT

The following time series represents the number of passengers per year (in millions) for EXP Airlines:

	Year									
	1997	1998	1999	2000	2001	2002	2003	2004	2005	2006
Passengers	30.0	31.5	33.1	34.8	36.5	38.3	40.2	42.2	44.3	46.5

Using percentage differences, show that the exponential trend model provides almost a perfect fit to these data.

SOLUTION The following table shows the solution:

	Year									
	1997	1998	1999	2000	2001	2002	2003	2004	2005	2006
Passengers	30.0	31.5	33.1	34.8	36.5	38.3	40.2	42.2	44.3	46.5
First differences		1.5	1.6	1.7	1.7	1.8	1.9	2.0	2.1	2.2
Percentage differences		5.0	5.1	5.1	4.9	4.9	5.0	5.0	5.0	5.0

The percentage differences between consecutive values in the series are approximately the same throughout. Thus, EXP Airlines is exhibiting an exponential growth pattern. Its rate of growth is approximately 5% per year.

Figure 12 presents the first, second, and percentage differences for the real gross revenues data at Wm. Wrigley Jr. Company. Neither the first differences, second differences, nor percentage differences are constant across the series. Therefore, other models (including those considered in Section 5) may be more appropriate.

FIGURE 12

Comparing first, second, and percentage differences in real annual gross revenues (in millions of constant 1982–1984 dollars) for Wm. Wrigley Jr. Company (1984–2005)

	A	B	C	D	E
1	Year	Real Revenue	First Difference	Second Difference	Percentage Difference
2	1984	569	---	---	---
3	1985	576	7	---	1.23%
4	1986	638	62	55	10.76%
5	1987	688	50	-12	7.84%
6	1988	753	65	15	9.45%
7	1989	801	48	-17	6.37%
8	1990	850	49	1	6.12%
9	1991	844	-6	-55	-0.71%
10	1992	927	83	89	9.83%
11	1993	997	70	-13	7.55%
12	1994	1121	124	54	12.44%
13	1995	1161	40	-84	3.57%
14	1996	1180	19	-21	1.64%
15	1997	1217	37	18	3.14%
16	1998	1241	24	-13	1.97%
17	1999	1248	7	-17	0.56%
18	2000	1246	-2	-9	-0.16%
19	2001	1372	126	128	10.11%
20	2002	1526	154	28	11.22%
21	2003	1668	142	-12	9.31%
22	2004	1932	264	122	15.83%
23	2005	2130	198	-66	10.25%

PROBLEMS FOR SECTION 4

Learning the Basics

9 If using the method of least squares for fitting trends in an annual time series containing 25 consecutive yearly values,

a. what coded value do you assign to X for the first year in the series?

b. what coded value do you assign to X for the fifth year in the series?

c. what coded value do you assign to X for the most recent recorded year in the series?

d. what coded value do you assign to X if you want to project the trend and make a forecast five years beyond the last observed value?

 10 The linear trend forecasting equation for an annual time series containing 22 values (from 1985 to 2006) on total revenues (in millions of dollars) is

$$\hat{Y}_i = 4.0 + 1.5X_i$$

a. Interpret the Y intercept, b_0.

b. Interpret the slope, b_1.

c. What is the fitted trend value for the fifth year?

d. What is the fitted trend value for the most recent year?

e. What is the projected trend forecast three years after the last value?

11 The linear trend forecasting equation for an annual time series containing 42 values (from 1965 to 2006) on net sales (in billions of dollars) is

$$\hat{Y}_i = 1.2 + 0.5X_i$$

a. Interpret the Y intercept, b_0.

b. Interpret the slope, b_1.

c. What is the fitted trend value for the tenth year?

d. What is the fitted trend value for the most recent year?

e. What is the projected trend forecast two years after the last value?

Applying the Concepts

12 The following data (in the file **CPI-U.xls**) reflect the annual values of the CPI in the United States over the 41-year period 1965 through 2005, using 1982 through 1984 as the base period. This index measures the average change in prices over time in a fixed "market basket" of goods and services purchased by all urban consumers, including urban wage earners (that is, clerical, professional, managerial, and technical workers; self-employed individuals; and short-term workers), unemployed individuals, and retirees.

Year	CPI	Year	CPI	Year	CPI
1965	31.5	1979	72.6	1993	144.5
1966	32.4	1980	82.4	1994	148.2
1967	33.4	1981	90.9	1995	152.4
1968	34.8	1982	96.5	1996	156.9
1969	36.7	1983	99.6	1997	160.5
1970	38.8	1984	103.9	1998	163.0
1971	40.5	1985	107.6	1999	166.6
1972	41.8	1986	109.6	2000	172.2
1973	44.4	1987	113.6	2001	177.1
1974	49.3	1988	118.3	2002	179.9
1975	53.8	1989	124.0	2003	184.0
1976	56.9	1990	130.7	2004	188.9
1977	60.6	1991	136.2	2005	195.3
1978	65.2	1992	140.3		

Source: Bureau of Labor Statistics, U.S. Department of Labor, **www.bls.gov**.

a. Plot the data.

b. Describe the movement in this time series over the 41-year period.

13 Gross domestic product (GDP) is a major indicator of a nation's overall economic activity. It consists of personal consumption expenditures, gross domestic investment, net exports of goods and services, and government consumption expenditures. The GDP (in billions of current dollars) for the United States from 1980 to 2005 is in the data file **GDP.xls**.

Source: Bureau of Economic Analysis, U.S. Department of Commerce, **www.bea.gov**.

a. Plot the data.

b. Compute a linear trend forecasting equation and plot the trend line.

c. What are your forecasts for 2006 and 2007?

d. What conclusions can you reach concerning the trend in GDP?

14 The data in the file **fedrecpt.xls** represent federal receipts from 1978 through 2004, in billions of current dollars, from individual and corporate income tax, social insurance, excise tax, estate and gift tax, customs duties, and federal reserve deposits.

Source: Tax Policy Center, **www.taxpolicycenter.org**.

a. Plot the series of data.

b. Compute a linear trend forecasting equation and plot the trend line.

c. What are your forecasts of the federal receipts for 2005 and 2006?

d. What conclusions can you reach concerning the trend in federal receipts between 1978 and 2004?

15 The data in the file `strategic.xls` represent the amount of oil, in millions of barrels held in the U.S. strategic oil reserve, from 1981 through 2004.

Source: Energy Information Administration, U.S. Department of Energy, **www.eia.doe.gov.**

a. Plot the data.

b. Compute a linear trend forecasting equation and plot the trend line.

c. Compute a quadratic trend forecasting equation and plot the results.

d. Compute an exponential trend forecasting equation and plot the results.

e. Which model is the most appropriate?

f. Using the most appropriate model, forecast the number of barrels, in millions, for 2005. Check how accurate your forecast is by locating the true value on the Internet or in your library.

16 The data in the file `cocacola.xls` represent the annual net operating revenues (in billions of current dollars) at Coca-Cola Company from 1975 through 2005.

Source: Extracted from Moody's Handbook of Common Stocks, *1980, 1989, 1999, and* Mergent's Handbook of Common Stocks, *2005, and the Coca-Cola Company,* **www.cocacola.com.**

a. Plot the data.

b. Compute a linear trend forecasting equation and plot the trend line.

c. Compute a quadratic trend forecasting equation and plot the results.

d. Compute an exponential trend forecasting equation and plot the results.

e. Using the models in (b) through (d), what are your annual trend forecasts of net operating revenues for 2006 and 2007?

17 The data in the following table represent the closing values of the Dow Jones Industrial Average (DJIA) from 1979 through 2005 (see the file `djia.xls`):

Year	DJIA	Year	DJIA	Year	DJIA
1979	838.7	1988	2,168.6	1997	7,908.3
1980	964.0	1989	2,753.2	1998	9,181.4
1981	875.0	1990	2,633.7	1999	11,497.1
1982	1,046.5	1991	3,168.8	2000	10,788.0
1983	1,258.6	1992	3,301.1	2001	10,021.5
1984	1,211.6	1993	3,754.1	2002	8,341.6
1985	1,546.7	1994	3,834.4	2003	10,453.9
1986	1,896.0	1995	5,117.1	2004	10,788.0
1987	1,938.8	1996	6,448.3	2005	10,717.5

Source: Extracted from **finance.yahoo.com.**

a. Plot the data.

b. Compute a linear trend forecasting equation and plot the trend line.

c. Compute a quadratic trend forecasting equation and plot the results.

d. Compute an exponential trend forecasting equation and plot the results.

e. Which model is the most appropriate?

f. Using the most appropriate model, forecast the closing value for the DJIA in 2006. Discuss the accuracy of your forecast and try to explain the difference between the forecast and the actual value.

18 General Electric (GE) is one of the world's largest companies; it develops, manufactures, and markets a wide range of products, including medical diagnostic imaging devices, jet engines, lighting products, and chemicals. Through its affiliate NBC Universal, GE produces and delivers network television and motion pictures. The data in the file `GE.xls` represent the January 1 stock price for the 20-year period from 1987 to 2006.

Source: Extracted from **finance.yahoo.com.**

a. Plot the data.

b. Compute a linear trend forecasting equation and plot the trend line.

c. Compute a quadratic trend forecasting equation and plot the results.

d. Compute an exponential trend forecasting equation and plot the results.

e. Which model is the most appropriate?

f. Using the most appropriate model, forecast the stock price for January 1, 2007.

19 Although you should not expect a perfectly fitting model for any time-series data, you can consider the first differences, second differences, and percentage differences for a given series as guides in choosing an appropriate model. For this problem, use each of the time series presented in the following table and stored in the file `tsmodel1.xls`:

	Year				
	1997	1998	1999	2000	2001
Time series I	10.0	15.1	24.0	36.7	53.8
Time series II	30.0	33.1	36.4	39.9	43.9
Time series III	60.0	67.9	76.1	84.0	92.2

	Year				
	2002	2003	2004	2005	2006
Time series I	74.8	100.0	129.2	162.4	199.0
Time series II	48.2	53.2	58.2	64.5	70.7
Time series III	100.0	108.0	115.8	124.1	132.0

a. Determine the most appropriate model.

b. Compute the forecasting equation.

c. Forecast the value for 2007.

20 A time-series plot often helps you determine the appropriate model to use. For this problem, use each of the time-series presented in the following table and stored in the file tsmodel2.xls:

| | **Year** | | | | |
	1997	**1998**	**1999**	**2000**	**2001**
Time series I	100.0	115.2	130.1	144.9	160.0
Time series II	100.0	115.2	131.7	150.8	174.1

| | **Year** | | | | |
	2002	**2003**	**2004**	**2005**	**2006**
Time series I	175.0	189.8	204.9	219.8	235.0
Time series II	200.0	230.8	266.1	305.5	351.8

a. Plot the observed data (Y) over time (X) and plot the logarithm of the observed data (log Y) over time (X) to determine whether a linear trend model or an exponential trend model is more appropriate. (*Hint:* If the plot of log Y versus X appears to be linear, an exponential trend model provides an appropriate fit.)

b. Compute the appropriate forecasting equation.

c. Forecast the value for 2007.

21 The data in the file oysters.xls represent the bushels of oysters harvested in Chesapeake Bay for 1990–1991 through 2003–2004 (Source: Maryland Department of Natural Resources).

a. Compare the first differences, second differences, and percentage differences to determine the most appropriate model.

b. Compute the appropriate forecasting equation.

c. Forecast the number of bushels harvested for 2004–2005 and 2005–2006.

d. What would you say about your forecasting model if you knew that in 1980–1981, 2,532,321 bushels were harvested?

22 ✓SELF Test Bed Bath & Beyond Inc. is a nationwide chain of retail stores that sell a wide assortment of merchandise, principally including domestics merchandise and home furnishings, as well as food, giftware, and health and beauty care items. The following data (stored in the file bedbath.xls) show the number of stores open at the end of the fiscal year from 1993 to 2006:

Year	Stores Open	Year	Stores Open
1993	38	2000	241
1994	45	2001	311
1995	61	2002	396
1996	80	2003	519
1997	108	2004	629
1998	141	2005	721
1999	186	2006	809

Source: Extracted from Bed Bath & Beyond Annual Report, 2005, May 24, 2006.

a. Plot the data.

b. Compute a linear trend forecasting equation and plot the results.

c. Compute a quadratic trend forecasting equation and plot the results.

d. Compute an exponential trend forecasting equation and plot the results.

e. Using the forecasting equations in (b) through (d), what are your annual forecasts of the number of stores open for 2007 and 2008?

f. How can you explain the differences in the three forecasts in (e)? What forecast do you think you should use? Why?

5 AUTOREGRESSIVE MODELING FOR TREND FITTING AND FORECASTING

[3]*The exponential smoothing model described in Section 3 and the autoregressive models described in this section are special cases of autoregressive integrated moving average (ARIMA) models developed by Box and Jenkins (reference 2).*

Frequently, the values of a time series are highly correlated with the values that precede and succeed them. This type of correlation is called autocorrelation. **Autoregressive modeling**[3] is a technique used to forecast time series with autocorrelation. A **first-order autocorrelation** refers to the association between consecutive values in a time series. A **second-order autocorrelation** refers to the relationship between values that are two periods apart. A ***p*th-order autocorrelation** refers to the correlation between values in a time series that are p periods apart. You can take into account the autocorrelation in data by using autoregressive modeling methods.

Equations (10), (11), and (12) define first-order, second-order, and pth-order autoregressive models.

FIRST-ORDER AUTOREGRESSIVE MODEL

$$Y_i = A_0 + A_1 Y_{i-1} + \delta_i \tag{10}$$

SECOND-ORDER AUTOREGRESSIVE MODEL

$$Y_i = A_0 + A_1 Y_{i-1} + A_2 Y_{i-2} + \delta_i \tag{11}$$

pTH-ORDER AUTOREGRESSIVE MODELS

$$Y_i = A_0 + A_1 Y_{i-1} + A_2 Y_{i-2} + \cdots + A_p Y_{i-p} + \delta_i \tag{12}$$

where

Y_i = the observed value of the series at time i

Y_{i-1} = the observed value of the series at time $i - 1$

Y_{i-2} = the observed value of the series at time $i - 2$

Y_{i-p} = the observed value of the series at time $i - p$

$A_0, A_1, A_2, \ldots, A_p$ = autoregression parameters to be estimated from least-squares regression analysis

δ_i = a nonautocorrelated random error component (with mean = 0 and constant variance)

The **first-order autoregressive model** [Equation (10)] is similar in form to the simple linear regression model. The **second-order autoregressive model** [Equation (11)] is similar to the multiple regression model with two independent variables. The **pth-order autoregressive model** [Equation (12)] is similar to the multiple regression model. In the regression models, the regression parameters are given by the symbols $\beta_0, \beta_1, \ldots, \beta_k$, with corresponding estimates denoted by $b_0, b_1, \ldots, b_k$. In the autoregressive models, the parameters are given by the symbols $A_0, A_1, \ldots, A_p$, with corresponding estimates denoted by $a_0, a_1, \ldots, a_p$.

Selecting an appropriate autoregressive model is not easy. You must weigh the advantages that are due to simplicity against the concern of failing to take into account important autocorrelation in the data. You also must be concerned with selecting a higher-order model requiring the estimation of numerous, unnecessary parameters—especially if n, the number of values in the series, is small. The reason for this concern is that p out of n data values are lost in computing an estimate of A_p when comparing each data value with another data value, when they are p periods apart.

Examples 5 and 6 illustrate this loss of data values.

EXAMPLE 5

COMPARISON SCHEMA FOR A FIRST-ORDER AUTOREGRESSIVE MODEL

Consider the following series of $n = 7$ consecutive annual values:

			Year				
	1	**2**	**3**	**4**	**5**	**6**	**7**
Series	31	34	37	35	36	43	40

Show the comparisons needed for a first-order autoregressive model.

SOLUTION

Year	First-Order Autoregressive Model
i	$(Y_i$ vs. $Y_{i-1})$
1	$31 \leftrightarrow \ldots$
2	$34 \leftrightarrow 31$
3	$37 \leftrightarrow 34$
4	$35 \leftrightarrow 37$
5	$36 \leftrightarrow 35$
6	$43 \leftrightarrow 36$
7	$40 \leftrightarrow 43$

Because there is no value recorded prior to Y_1, this value is lost for regression analysis. Therefore, the first-order autoregressive model is based on six pairs of values.

EXAMPLE 6

COMPARISON SCHEMA FOR A SECOND-ORDER AUTOREGRESSIVE MODEL

Consider the following series of $n = 7$ consecutive annual values:

	Year						
	1	2	3	4	5	6	7
Series	31	34	37	35	36	43	40

Show the comparisons needed for a second-order autoregressive model.

SOLUTION

Year	Second-Order Autoregressive Model
i	$(Y_i$ vs. Y_{i-1} and Y_i vs. $Y_{i-2})$
1	$31 \leftrightarrow \ldots$ and $31 \leftrightarrow \ldots$
2	$34 \leftrightarrow 31$ and $34 \leftrightarrow \ldots$
3	$37 \leftrightarrow 34$ and $37 \leftrightarrow 31$
4	$35 \leftrightarrow 37$ and $35 \leftrightarrow 34$
5	$36 \leftrightarrow 35$ and $36 \leftrightarrow 37$
6	$43 \leftrightarrow 36$ and $43 \leftrightarrow 35$
7	$40 \leftrightarrow 43$ and $40 \leftrightarrow 36$

Because there is no value recorded prior to Y_1, two values are lost for regression analysis. Therefore, the second-order autoregressive model is based on five pairs of values.

After selecting a model and using the least-squares method to compute estimates of the parameters, you need to determine the appropriateness of the model. Either you can select a particular pth-order autoregressive model based on previous experiences with similar data or, as a starting point, you can choose a model with several parameters and then eliminate the parameters that do not significantly contribute to the model. In this latter approach, you use a t test for the significance of A_p, the highest-order autoregressive parameter in the current model under consideration. The null and alternative hypotheses are

$$H_0: A_p = 0$$
$$H_1: A_p \neq 0$$

Equation (13) defines the test statistic.

---

t TEST FOR SIGNIFICANCE OF THE HIGHEST-ORDER AUTOREGRESSIVE PARAMETER, A_p

$$t = \frac{a_p - A_p}{S_{a_p}}$$

(13)

where

A_p = hypothesized value of the highest-order parameter, A_p, in the regression model

a_p = the estimate of the highest-order parameter, A_p, in the autoregressive model

S_{a_p} = the standard deviation of a_p

The test statistic t follows a t distribution having $n - 2p - 1$ degrees of freedom.[4]

---

[4]In addition to the degrees of freedom lost for each of the p population parameters you are estimating, p additional degrees of freedom are lost because there are p fewer comparisons to be made out of the original n values in the time series.

For a given level of significance α, you reject the null hypothesis if the computed t-test statistic is greater than the upper-tail critical value from the t distribution or if the computed test statistic is less than the lower-tail critical value from the t distribution. Thus, the decision rule is

Reject H_0 if $t > t_{n-2p-1}$ or if $t < -t_{n-2p-1}$;

otherwise, do not reject H_0.

Figure 13 illustrates the decision rule and regions of rejection and nonrejection.

FIGURE 13

Rejection regions for a two-tail test for the significance of the highest-order autoregressive parameter, A_p

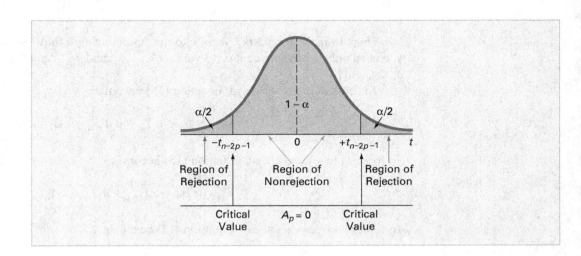

If you do not reject the null hypothesis that $A_p = 0$, you conclude that the selected model contains too many estimated parameters. You then discard the highest-order term and estimate an autoregressive model of order $p - 1$, using the least-squares method. You then repeat the test of the hypothesis that the new highest-order term is 0. This testing and modeling continues until you reject H_0. When this occurs, you know that the remaining highest-order parameter is significant, and you can use that model for forecasting purposes.

Equation (14) defines the fitted pth-order autoregressive equation.

FITTED pTH-ORDER AUTOREGRESSIVE EQUATION

$$\hat{Y}_i = a_0 + a_1 Y_{i-1} + a_2 Y_{i-2} + \cdots + a_p Y_{i-p} \tag{14}$$

where

$$\hat{Y}_i = \text{fitted values of the series at time } i$$

$$Y_{i-1} = \text{observed value of the series at time } i - 1$$

$$Y_{i-2} = \text{observed value of the series at time } i - 2$$

$$Y_{i-p} = \text{observed value of the series at time } i - p$$

$$a_0, a_1, a_2, \ldots, a_p = \text{regression estimates of the parameters } A_0, A_1, A_2, \ldots, A_p$$

You use Equation (15) to forecast j years into the future from the current nth time period.

---

pTH-ORDER AUTOREGRESSIVE FORECASTING EQUATION

$$\hat{Y}_{n+j} = a_0 + a_1 \hat{Y}_{n+j-1} + a_2 \hat{Y}_{n+j-2} + \cdots + a_p \hat{Y}_{n+j-p} \tag{15}$$

where

$$a_0, a_1, a_2, \ldots, a_p = \text{regression estimates of the parameters } A_0, A_1, A_2, \ldots, A_p$$

$$j = \text{number of years into the future}$$

$$\hat{Y}_{n+j-p} = \text{forecast of } Y_{n+j-p} \text{ from the current time period for } j - p > 0$$

$$\hat{Y}_{n+j-p} = \text{observed value for } Y_{n+j-p} \text{ for } j - p \leq 0$$

Thus, to make forecasts j years into the future, using a third-order autoregressive model, you need only the most recent $p = 3$ values (Y_n, Y_{n-1}, and Y_{n-2}) and the regression estimates a_0, a_1, a_2, and a_3.

To forecast one year ahead, Equation (15) becomes

$$\hat{Y}_{n+1} = a_0 + a_1 Y_n + a_2 Y_{n-1} + a_3 Y_{n-2}$$

To forecast two years ahead, Equation (15) becomes

$$\hat{Y}_{n+2} = a_0 + a_1 \hat{Y}_{n+1} + a_2 Y_n + a_3 Y_{n-1}$$

To forecast three years ahead, Equation (15) becomes

$$\hat{Y}_{n+3} = a_0 + a_1 \hat{Y}_{n+2} + a_2 \hat{Y}_{n+1} + a_3 Y_n$$

and so on.

Autoregressive modeling is a powerful forecasting technique for time series that have autocorrelation. Although slightly more complicated than other methods, the following step-by-step approach should guide you through the analysis:

1. Choose a value for p, the highest-order parameter in the autoregressive model to be evaluated, realizing that the t test for significance is based on $n - 2p - 1$ degrees of freedom.
2. Form a series of p "lagged predictor" variables such that the first variable lags by one time period, the second variable lags by two time periods, and so on and the last predictor variable lags by p time periods (see Figure 14).
3. Use Microsoft Excel to perform a least-squares analysis of the multiple regression model containing all p lagged predictor variables.
4. Test for the significance of A_p, the highest-order autoregressive parameter in the model.
   a. If you do not reject the null hypothesis, discard the pth variable and repeat steps 3 and 4. The test for the significance of the new highest-order parameter is based on a t distribution whose degrees of freedom are revised to correspond with the new number of predictors.
   b. If you reject the null hypothesis, select the autoregressive model with all p predictors for fitting [see Equation (14)] and forecasting [see Equation (15)].

FIGURE 14

Developing first-order, second-order, and third-order autoregressive models on real gross revenues for the Wm. Wrigley Jr. Company (1984–2005)

See Section E9 to create this.

	A	B	C	D	E
		Real			
1	Year	Revenue	Lag1	Lag2	Lag3
2	1984	569	#N/A	#N/A	#N/A
3	1985	576	569	#N/A	#N/A
4	1986	638	576	569	#N/A
5	1987	688	638	576	569
6	1988	753	688	638	576
7	1989	801	753	688	638
8	1990	850	801	753	688
9	1991	844	850	801	753
10	1992	927	844	850	801
11	1993	997	927	844	850
12	1994	1121	997	927	844
13	1995	1161	1121	997	927
14	1996	1180	1161	1121	997
15	1997	1217	1180	1161	1121
16	1998	1241	1217	1180	1161
17	1999	1248	1241	1217	1180
18	2000	1246	1248	1241	1217
19	2001	1372	1246	1248	1241
20	2002	1526	1372	1246	1248
21	2003	1668	1526	1372	1246
22	2004	1932	1668	1526	1372
23	2005	2130	1932	1668	1526

To demonstrate the autoregressive modeling approach, return to the time series concerning the real gross revenues (in millions of constant 1982 to 1984 dollars) for the Wm. Wrigley Jr. Company over the 22-year period 1984 through 2005. Figure 14 displays the real gross revenues and the setup for the first-order, second-order, and third-order autoregressive models. All the columns in this table are needed for fitting the third-order autoregressive model. The last column is omitted when fitting second-order autoregressive models, and the last two columns are omitted when fitting first-order autoregressive models. Thus, out of $n = 22$ values, $p = 1, 2,$ or 3 values out of $n = 22$ are lost in the comparisons needed for developing the first-order, second-order, and third-order autoregressive models.

Selecting an autoregressive model that best fits the annual time series begins with the third-order autoregressive model shown in Figure 15, using Microsoft Excel.

From Figure 15, the fitted third-order autoregressive equation is

$$\hat{Y}_i = -36.2995 + 1.5050Y_{i-1} - 0.2777Y_{i-2} - 0.1615Y_{i-3}$$

where the first year in the series is 1987.

FIGURE 15

Microsoft Excel results for the third-order autoregressive model for the Wm. Wrigley Jr. real gross revenues data

See Section E11 to create this.

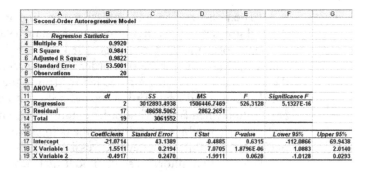

	A	B	C	D	E	F	G
1	Third-Order Autoregressive Model						
2							
3	*Regression Statistics*						
4	Multiple R	0.9917					
5	R Square	0.9835					
6	Adjusted R Square	0.9802					
7	Standard Error	55.0683					
8	Observations	19					
9							
10	ANOVA						
11		*df*	*SS*	*MS*	*F*	*Significance F*	
12	Regression	3	2710252.6157	903417.5386	297.9098	1.3804E-13	
13	Residual	15	45487.8054	3032.5204			
14	Total	18	2755740.4211				
15							
16		*Coefficients*	*Standard Error*	*t Stat*	*P-value*	*Lower 95%*	*Upper 95%*
17	Intercept	-36.2995	47.8528	-0.7586	0.4599	-138.2955	65.6965
18	X Variable 1	1.5050	0.2532	5.9432	2.6960E-05	0.9652	2.0447
19	X Variable 2	-0.2777	0.5066	-0.5481	0.5917	-1.3574	0.8021
20	X Variable 3	-0.1615	0.3362	-0.4803	0.6379	-0.8782	0.5552

Next, you test for the significance of A_3, the highest-order parameter. The highest-order parameter estimate, a_3, for the fitted third-order autoregressive model is -0.1615, with a standard error of 0.3362.

To test the null hypothesis:

$$H_0: A_3 = 0$$

against the alternative hypothesis:

$$H_1: A_3 \neq 0$$

Using Equation (13) and the Microsoft Excel output given in Figure 15,

$$t = \frac{a_3 - A_3}{S_{a_3}} = \frac{-0.1615 - 0}{0.3362} = -0.4803$$

Using a 0.05 level of significance, the two-tail t test with 15 degrees of freedom has critical values of t_{15} of ± 2.1315. Because $-2.1315 < t = -0.4803 < +2.1315$ or because the p-value = $0.6379 > 0.05$, you do not reject H_0. You conclude that the third-order parameter of the autoregressive model is not significant and can be deleted.

Using Microsoft Excel once again (see Figure 16), you fit a second-order autoregressive model.

FIGURE 16

Microsoft Excel results for the second-order autoregressive model for the Wm. Wrigley Jr. Company real gross revenues data

See Section E11 to create this.

	A	B	C	D	E	F	G
1	Second-Order Autoregressive Model						
2							
3	*Regression Statistics*						
4	Multiple R	0.9920					
5	R Square	0.9841					
6	Adjusted R Square	0.9822					
7	Standard Error	53.5001					
8	Observations	20					
9							
10	ANOVA						
11		*df*	*SS*	*MS*	*F*	*Significance F*	
12	Regression	2	3012893.4938	1506446.7469	526.3128	5.1327E-16	
13	Residual	17	48658.5062	2862.2651			
14	Total	19	3061552				
15							
16		*Coefficients*	*Standard Error*	*t Stat*	*P-value*	*Lower 95%*	*Upper 95%*
17	Intercept	-21.0714	43.1389	-0.4885	0.6315	-112.0866	69.9438
18	X Variable 1	1.5511	0.2194	7.0705	1.8796E-06	1.0883	2.0140
19	X Variable 2	-0.4917	0.2470	-1.9911	0.0628	-1.0128	0.0293

The fitted second-order autoregressive equation is

$$\hat{Y}_i = -21.0714 + 1.5511Y_{i-1} - 0.4917Y_{i-2}$$

where the first year of the series is 1986.

From Figure 16, the highest-order parameter estimate is $a_2 = -0.4917$, with a standard error of 0.247.

To test the null hypothesis:

$$H_0: A_2 = 0$$

against the alternative hypothesis:

$$H_1: A_2 \neq 0$$

using Equation (13),

$$t = \frac{a_2 - A_2}{S_{a_2}} = \frac{-0.4917 - 0}{0.2470} = -1.9911$$

Using the 0.05 level of significance, the two-tail t test with 17 degrees of freedom has critical values t_{17} of ± 2.1098. Because $-2.1098 < t = -1.9911 < +2.1098$ or because the p-value = 0.0628 > 0.05, you do not reject H_0. You conclude that the second-order parameter of the autoregressive model is not significant and should be deleted from the model.

Using Microsoft Excel once again (see Figure 17), you fit a first-order autoregressive model.

FIGURE 17

Microsoft Excel results for the first-order autoregressive model for the Wm. Wrigley Jr. Company real gross revenues data

See Section E10 to create this.

	A	B	C	D	E	F	G
1	First-Order Autoregressive Model						
2							
3	*Regression Statistics*						
4	Multiple R	0.9911					
5	R Square	0.9824					
6	Adjusted R Square	0.9814					
7	Standard Error	56.2185					
8	Observations	21					
9							
10	ANOVA						
11		*df*	*SS*	*MS*	*F*	*Significance F*	
12	Regression	1	3345503.1055	3345503.1055	1058.5299	3.9850E-18	
13	Residual	19	60049.8469	3160.5183			
14	Total	20	3405552.9524				
15							
16		*Coefficients*	*Standard Error*	*t Stat*	*P-value*	*Lower 95%*	*Upper 95%*
17	Intercept	-55.7697	38.9911	-1.4303	0.1689	-137.3790	25.8396
18	X Variable 1	1.1211	0.0345	32.5351	3.9850E-18	1.0490	1.1933

The first-order autoregressive equation is

$$\hat{Y}_i = -55.7697 + 1.1211 Y_{i-1}$$

where the first year of the series is 1985.

From the Microsoft Excel results, the highest-order parameter estimate is $a_1 = 1.1211$ and $S_{a_1} = 0.0345$.

To test the null hypothesis:

$$H_0: A_1 = 0$$

against the alternative hypothesis:

$$H_1: A_1 \neq 0$$

using Equation (13),

$$t = \frac{a_1 - A_1}{S_{a_1}} = \frac{1.1211 - 0}{0.0345} = 32.5351$$

Using the 0.05 level of significance, the two-tail t test with 19 degrees of freedom has critical values t_{19} of ± 2.0930. Because $t = 32.5351 > 2.0930$, or because the p-value $= 0.0000 < 0.05$, you reject H_0. You conclude that the first-order parameter of the autoregressive model is significant and should remain in the model. The model-building approach has led to the selection of the first-order autoregressive model as the most appropriate for the given data. Using the estimates $a_0 = -55.7697$ and $a_1 = 1.1211$, as well as the most recent data value $Y_{22} = 2,130$, the forecasts of real gross revenues at the Wm. Wrigley Jr. Company for 2006 and 2007 from Equation (15) are

$$\hat{Y}_{n+j} = -55.7697 + 1.1211\hat{Y}_{n+j-1}$$

Therefore,

2006: 1 year ahead, $\hat{Y}_{23} = -55.7697 + 1.1211(2,130) = 2,332.173$ millions of dollars

2007: 2 year ahead, $\hat{Y}_{24} = -55.9697 + 1.1211(2,332.173) = 2,558.630$ millions of dollars

Figure 18 displays the actual value and predicted Y values from the first-order autoregressive model.

FIGURE 18

Microsoft Excel plot of actual and predicted real gross revenues from a first-order autoregressive model at the Wm. Wrigley Jr. Company

See Section E2 to create this.

PROBLEMS FOR SECTION 5

Learning the Basics

23 You are given an annual time series with 40 consecutive values and asked to fit a fifth-order autoregressive model.

a. How many comparisons are lost in the development of the autoregressive model?

b. How many parameters do you need to estimate?

c. Which of the original 40 values do you need for forecasting?

d. State the model.

e. Write an equation to indicate how you would forecast j years into the future.

 24 A third-order autoregressive model is fitted to an annual time series with 17 values and has the following estimated parameters and standard deviations:

$$a_0 = 4.50 \qquad a_1 = 1.80 \qquad a_2 = 0.80 \qquad a_3 = 0.24$$
$$S_{a_1} = 0.50 \qquad S_{a_2} = 0.30 \qquad S_{a_3} = 0.10$$

At the 0.05 level of significance, test the appropriateness of the fitted model.

25 Refer to Problem 24. The three most recent values are

$$Y_{15} = 23 \quad Y_{16} = 28 \quad Y_{17} = 34$$

Forecast the values for the next year and the following year.

26 Refer to Problem 24. Suppose, when testing for the appropriateness of the fitted model, the standard deviations are

$$S_{a_1} = 0.45 \quad S_{a_2} = 0.35 \quad S_{a_3} = 0.15$$

a. What conclusions can you make?

b. Discuss how to proceed if forecasting is still your main objective.

Applying the Concepts

27 Refer to the data given in Problem 15 that represent the amount of oil (in millions of barrels) held in the U.S. strategic reserve from 1981 through 2004 (see the file strategic.xls).

a. Fit a third-order autoregressive model to the amount of oil and test for the significance of the third-order autoregressive parameter. (Use $\alpha = 0.05$.)

b. If necessary, fit a second-order autoregressive model to the amount of oil and test for the significance of the second-order autoregressive parameter. (Use $\alpha = 0.05$.)

c. If necessary, fit a first-order autoregressive model to the amount of oil and test for the significance of the first-order autoregressive parameter. (Use $\alpha = 0.05$.)

d. If appropriate, forecast the barrels held in 2005.

 28 Refer to the data introduced in Problem 16 (and stored in the file cocacola.xls) concerning annual net operating revenues (in billions of current dollars) at Coca-Cola Company over the 31-year period 1975 through 2005.

a. Fit a third-order autoregressive model to the annual net operating revenues and test for the significance of the third-order autoregressive parameter. (Use $\alpha = 0.05$.)

b. If necessary, fit a second-order autoregressive model to the annual net operating revenues and test for the significance of the second-order autoregressive parameter. (Use $\alpha = 0.05$.)

c. If necessary, fit a first-order autoregressive model to the annual net operating revenues and test for the significance of the first-order autoregressive parameter. (Use $\alpha = 0.05$.)

d. If appropriate, forecast net operating revenues for 2006 and 2007.

29 Refer to the data given in Problem 17 that represent the closing values of the DJIA from 1979 to 2005 (stored in the file djia.xls).

a. Fit a third-order autoregressive model to the DJIA and test for the significance of the third-order autoregressive parameter. (Use $\alpha = 0.05$.)

b. If necessary, fit a second-order autoregressive model to the DJIA and test for the significance of the second-order autoregressive parameter. (Use $\alpha = 0.05$.)

c. If necessary, fit a first-order autoregressive model to the DJIA and test for the significance of the first-order autoregressive parameter. (Use $\alpha = 0.05$.)

d. If appropriate, forecast the DJIA for 2006 and 2007.

30 Refer to the data given in Problem 18 (stored in the file GE.xls) that represent the stock prices for GE from 1987 through 2006.

a. Fit a third-order autoregressive model to the stock price and test for the significance of the third-order autoregressive parameter. (Use $\alpha = 0.05$.)

b. If necessary, fit a second-order autoregressive model to the stock price and test for the significance of the second-order autoregressive parameter. (Use $\alpha = 0.05$.)

c. If necessary, fit a first-order autoregressive model to the stock price and test for the significance of the first-order autoregressive parameter. (Use $\alpha = 0.05$.)

d. If appropriate, forecast the stock price for January 1, 2007.

31 Refer to the data given in Problem 22 that represent the number of stores open for Bed Bath & Beyond over the 14-year period 1993 through 2006 (see the file bedbath.xls).

a. Fit a third-order autoregressive model to the number of stores and test for the significance of the third-order autoregressive parameter. (Use $\alpha = 0.05$.)

b. If necessary, fit a second-order autoregressive model to the number of stores and test for the significance of the second-order autoregressive parameter. (Use $\alpha = 0.05$.)

c. If necessary, fit a first-order autoregressive model to the number of stores and test for the significance of the first-order autoregressive parameter. (Use $\alpha = 0.05$.)

d. If appropriate, forecast the number of stores open in 2007 and 2008.

6 CHOOSING AN APPROPRIATE FORECASTING MODEL

In Sections 4 and 5, you studied six time-series forecasting methods: the linear trend model, the quadratic trend model, and the exponential trend model in Section 4; and the first-order, second-order, and pth-order autoregressive models in Section 5. Is there a *best* model? Among these models, which one should you select for forecasting? The following guidelines are provided for determining the adequacy of a particular forecasting model. These guidelines are based on a judgment of how well the model fits the past data of a given time series and assumes that future movements in the time series can be projected by a study of the past data:

- Perform a residual analysis.
- Measure the magnitude of the residual error through squared differences.
- Measure the magnitude of the residual error through absolute differences.
- Use the principle of parsimony.

A discussion of these guidelines follows.

Performing a Residual Analysis

Residuals are the differences between the observed and predicted values. After fitting a particular model to a time series, you plot the residuals over the n time periods. As shown in Panel A of Figure 19, if the particular model fits adequately, the residuals represent the irregular component of the time series. Therefore, they should be randomly distributed throughout the series. However, as illustrated in the three remaining panels of Figure 19, if the particular model does not fit adequately, the residuals may show a systematic pattern, such as a failure to account for trend (Panel B), a failure to account for cyclical variation (Panel C), or, with monthly or quarterly data, a failure to account for seasonal variation (Panel D).

FIGURE 19

Residual analysis for studying error patterns

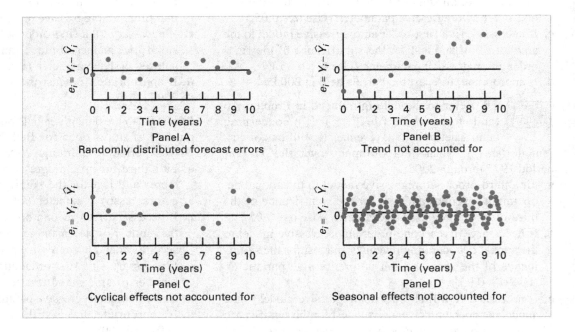

Measuring the Magnitude of the Residual Error Through Squared or Absolute Differences

If, after performing a residual analysis, you still believe that two or more models appear to fit the data adequately, you can use additional methods for model selection. Numerous measures based on the residual error are available (see references 1 and 4). However, there is no consensus among statisticians as to which particular measure is best for determining the most appropriate forecasting model.

Based on the principle of least squares, one measure that you have already used in regression analysis is the standard error of the estimate (S_{YX}). For a particular model, this measure is based on the sum of squared differences between the actual and predicted values in a time series. If a model fits the time-series data perfectly, then the standard error of the estimate is zero. If a model fits the time-series data poorly, then S_{YX} is large. Thus, when comparing the adequacy of two or more forecasting models, you can select the model with the minimum S_{YX} as most appropriate.

However, a major drawback to using S_{YX} when comparing forecasting models is that it penalizes a model too much for a large individual forecasting error. Thus, whenever there is a large difference between even a single Y_i and $\hat{Y}_i$, the value of S_{YX} becomes magnified through the squaring process. For this reason, many statisticians prefer the **mean absolute deviation (MAD)**. Equation (16) defines the *MAD* as the mean of the absolute differences between the actual and predicted values in a time series.

MEAN ABSOLUTE DEVIATION

$$MAD = \frac{\sum_{i=1}^{n} | Y_i - \hat{Y}_i |}{n} \qquad (16)$$

If a model fits the time-series data perfectly, the *MAD* is zero. If a model fits the time-series data poorly, the *MAD* is large. When comparing two or more forecasting models, you can select the one with the minimum *MAD* as the most appropriate model.

The Principle of Parsimony

If, after performing a residual analysis and comparing the S_{YX} and *MAD* measures, you still believe that two or more models appear to adequately fit the data, then you can use the principle of parsimony for model selection.

The principle of **parsimony** is the belief that you should select the simplest model that gets the job done adequately.

Among the six forecasting models studied in this chapter, the least-squares linear and quadratic models and the first-order autoregressive model are regarded by most statisticians as the simplest. The second- and *p*th-order autoregressive models and the least-squares exponential model are considered more complex.

A Comparison of Four Forecasting Methods

Consider once again the Wm. Wrigley Jr. Company's real gross revenues data. To illustrate the model selection process, you can compare four of the forecasting models used in Sections 4 and 5: the linear model, the quadratic model, the exponential model, and the first-order autoregressive model. (There is no need to further study the second-order or third-order autoregressive model for this time series because these models did not significantly improve the fit over the simpler first-order autoregressive model.)

Figure 20 displays the residual plots for the four models. In drawing conclusions from these residual plots, you must use caution because there are only 22 values.

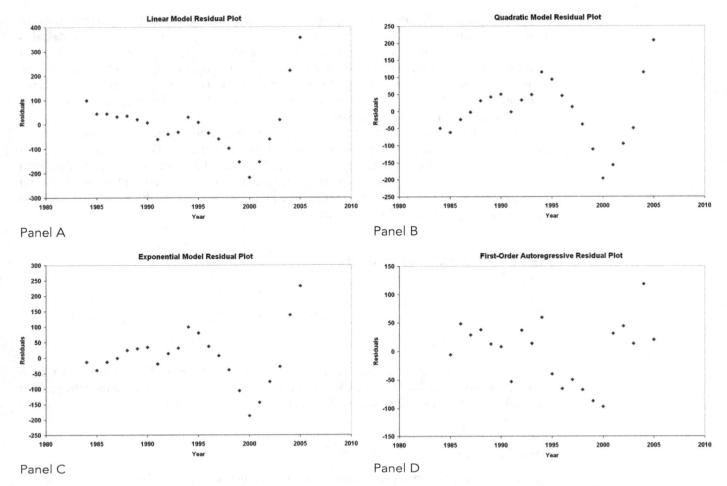

Panel A

Panel B

Panel C

Panel D

FIGURE 20 Microsoft Excel residual plots for four forecasting methods

See the Section E12 instructions to prepare the residual data.

In Figure 20, observe the systematic structure of the residuals in the linear model (Panel A), quadratic model (Panel B), and exponential model (Panel C). For the autoregressive model (Panel D), the residuals appear more random.

To summarize, on the basis of the residual analysis of all four forecasting models, it appears that the first-order autoregressive model is the most appropriate, and the linear, quadratic, and exponential models are less appropriate. For further verification, you can compare the four models with respect to the magnitude of their residuals. Figure 21 shows the actual values (Y_i) along with the predicted values ($\hat{Y_i}$), the residuals (e_i), the error sum of squares (*SSE*), the standard error of the estimate (S_{YX}), and the mean absolute deviation (*MAD*) for each of the four models.

For this time series, S_{YX} and *MAD* provide similar results. A comparison of the S_{YX} and *MAD* clearly indicates that the linear model provides the poorest fit. The first-order autoregressive model provides the best fit. Considering the results of the residual analysis and S_{YX} and *MAD*, the choice for the best model is the first-order autoregressive model.

After you select a particular forecasting model, you need to continually monitor your forecasts. If large errors occur between forecasted and actual values, the underlying structure of the time series may have changed. Remember that the forecasting methods presented in this chapter assume that the patterns inherent in the past will continue into the future. Large forecast errors are an indication that an assumption is no longer true.

FIGURE 21

Comparison of four forecasting methods, using S_{YX} and MAD

See Section E12 to create this.

	A	B	C	D	E	F	G	H	I	J	K	L	M	N
1				Linear			Quadratic			Exponential			Autoreg: First-Order	
2	Year	Actual		Predicted	Residual		Predicted	Residual		Predicted	Residual		Predicted	Residual
3	1984	569		469.916	98.900		618.321	-49.505		581.734	-12.734		#N/A	#N/A
4	1985	576		532.023	44.186		638.026	-61.818		615.438	-39.438		582.155	-6.155
5	1986	638		594.129	43.644		661.972	-24.198		651.095	-13.095		590.003	47.997
6	1987	688		656.236	31.264		690.157	-2.657		688.817	-0.817		659.513	28.487
7	1988	753		718.343	34.827		722.583	30.587		728.725	24.275		715.570	37.430
8	1989	801		780.450	20.357		759.249	41.557		770.945	30.055		788.444	12.556
9	1990	850		842.557	7.482		800.155	49.883		815.612	34.388		842.258	7.742
10	1991	844		904.663	-61.051		845.301	-1.689		862.866	-18.866		897.194	-53.194
11	1992	927		966.770	-39.471		894.688	32.611		912.858	14.142		890.467	36.533
12	1993	997		1028.877	-32.337		948.314	48.226		965.746	31.254		983.521	13.479
13	1994	1121		1090.984	29.799		1006.181	114.602		1021.698	99.302		1062.000	59.000
14	1995	1161		1153.090	8.327		1068.287	93.130		1080.892	80.108		1201.021	-40.021
15	1996	1180		1215.197	-35.465		1134.634	45.098		1143.516	36.484		1245.866	-65.866
16	1997	1217		1277.304	-59.859		1205.221	12.224		1209.768	7.232		1267.168	-50.168
17	1998	1241		1339.411	-98.306		1280.049	-38.944		1279.859	-38.859		1308.650	-67.650
18	1999	1248		1401.518	-153.618		1359.116	-111.217		1354.010	-106.010		1335.557	-87.557
19	2000	1246		1463.624	-217.399		1442.424	-196.198		1432.457	-186.457		1343.405	-97.405
20	2001	1372		1525.731	-153.625		1529.971	-157.865		1515.449	-143.449		1341.163	30.837
21	2002	1526		1587.838	-61.434		1621.759	-95.356		1603.250	-77.250		1482.425	43.575
22	2003	1668		1649.945	17.990		1717.787	-49.852		1696.138	-28.138		1655.080	12.920
23	2004	1932		1712.051	219.949		1818.055	113.945		1794.407	137.593		1814.281	117.719
24	2005	2130		1774.158	355.842		1922.564	207.436		1898.369	231.631		2110.260	19.740
25				SSE:	311652.481		SSE:	184290.139		SSE:	171194.826		SSE:	60049.847
26				S_{YX}:	124.830		S_{YX}:	98.486		S_{YX}:	92.519		S_{YX}:	56.218
27				MAD:	82.961		MAD:	71.755		MAD:	63.253		MAD:	44.573

PROBLEMS FOR SECTION 6

Learning the Basics

 32 The following residuals are from a linear trend model used to forecast sales:

2.0 −0.5 1.5 1.0 0.0 1.0 −3.0 1.5 −4.5 2.0 0.0 −1.0

a. Compute S_{YX} and interpret your findings.
b. Compute the MAD and interpret your findings.

 33 Refer to Problem 32. Suppose the first residual is 12.0 (instead of 2.0) and the last value is −11.0 (instead of −1.0).

a. Compute S_{YX} and interpret your findings
b. Compute the MAD and interpret your findings.

Applying the Concepts

34 Refer to the results in Problem 13 (see the file gdp.xls).
a. Perform a residual analysis.
b. Compute the standard error of the estimate (S_{YX}).
c. Compute the MAD.
d. On the basis of (a) through (c), are you satisfied with your linear trend forecasts in Problem 13? Discuss.

35 Refer to the results in Problem 15 and Problem 27 concerning the number of barrels of oil in the U.S. strategic oil reserve (see the file strategic.xls).
a. Perform a residual analysis for each model.
b. Compute the standard error of the estimate (S_{YX}) for each model.

c. Compute the MAD for each model.
d. On the basis of (a) through (c) and the principle of parsimony, which forecasting model would you select? Discuss.

36 Refer to the results in Problem 16 and Problem 28 concerning annual net operating revenues at Coca-Cola (see the file cocacola.xls).
a. Perform a residual analysis for each model.
b. Compute the standard error of the estimate (S_{YX}) for each model.
c. Compute the MAD for each model.
d. On the basis of (a) through (c) and the principle of parsimony, which forecasting model would you select? Discuss.

37 Refer to the results in Problem 17 and Problem 29 concerning the DJIA (see the file djia.xls).
a. Perform a residual analysis for each model.
b. Compute the standard error of the estimate (S_{YX}) for each model.
c. Compute the MAD for each model.
d. On the basis of (a) through (c) and the principle of parsimony, which forecasting model would you select? Discuss.

38 Refer to the results in Problem 18 and Problem 30 concerning the price per share for GE stock (see the file GE.xls).
a. Perform a residual analysis for each model.

b. Compute the standard error of the estimate (S_{YX}) for each model.

c. Compute the *MAD* for each model.

d. On the basis of (a) through (c) and the principle of parsimony, which forecasting model would you select? Discuss.

39 Refer to the results in Problem 22 and Problem 31 concerning the number of Bed Bath & Beyond stores open (see the data file bedbath.xls).

a. Perform a residual analysis for each model.

b. Compute the standard error of the estimate (S_{YX}) for each model.

c. Compute the *MAD* for each model.

d. On the basis of (a) through (c) and the principle of parsimony, which forecasting model would you select? Discuss.

7   TIME-SERIES FORECASTING OF SEASONAL DATA

So far, this chapter has focused on forecasting annual data. However, numerous time series are collected quarterly or monthly, and others are collected weekly, daily, and even hourly. When a time series is collected quarterly or monthly, you must consider the impact of seasonal effects (see Table 1). In this section, regression model building is used to forecast monthly or quarterly data.

One of the companies of interest in the Using Statistics scenario is Wal-Mart Stores, Inc. In 2006, Wal-Mart operated more than 6,500 Wal-Marts, Supercenters, Sam's Clubs, and Neighborhood Markets. Revenues in 2006 exceeded $312 billion (Wal-Mart Stores, Inc., **investor.walmartstores.com**). Sales for Wal-Mart are highly seasonal, and therefore you need to analyze quarterly revenue. The fiscal year for the company ends on January 31. Thus, the fourth quarter of 2006 includes November and December of 2005 and January of 2006. Table 4 lists the quarterly revenues, in billions of dollars, from 2000 to 2006 (see the file walmart.xls). Figure 22 displays the time series.

TABLE 4

Quarterly Revenues for Wal-Mart Stores, Inc., in Billions of Dollars (2000–2006)

Quarter	2000	2001	2002	2003	2004	2005	2006
1	34.7	43.0	48.6	55.0	56.7	64.8	71.6
2	38.2	46.1	53.3	59.7	62.6	69.7	76.8
3	40.4	45.7	51.8	58.8	62.4	68.5	75.4
4	51.4	56.6	64.2	71.1	74.5	82.2	88.6

Source: Extracted from Wal-Mart Stores, Inc., **investor.walmartstores.com.**

FIGURE 22

Microsoft Excel plot of quarterly revenues for Wal-Mart Stores, Inc., in billions of dollars (2000–2006)

See Section E13 to create this.

Least-Squares Forecasting with Monthly or Quarterly Data

To develop a least-squares regression model that includes trend, seasonal, cyclical, and irregular components, the approach to least-squares trend fitting in Section 4 is combined with the approach to model building using dummy variables to model the seasonal component.

Equation (17) defines the exponential trend model for quarterly data.

EXPONENTIAL MODEL WITH QUARTERLY DATA

$$Y_i = \beta_0 \beta_1^{X_i} \beta_2^{Q_1} \beta_3^{Q_2} \beta_4^{Q_3} \varepsilon_i \tag{17}$$

where

$$X_i = \text{coded quarterly value, } i = 0, 1, 2, \ldots$$
$$Q_1 = 1 \text{ if first quarter, 0 if not first quarter}$$
$$Q_2 = 1 \text{ if second quarter, 0 if not second quarter}$$
$$Q_3 = 1 \text{ if third quarter, 0 if not third quarter}$$
$$\beta_0 = Y \text{ intercept}$$
$$(\beta_1 - 1) \times 100\% = \text{quarterly compound growth rate (in \%)}$$
$$\beta_2 = \text{multiplier for first quarter relative to fourth quarter}$$
$$\beta_3 = \text{multiplier for second quarter relative to fourth quarter}$$
$$\beta_4 = \text{multiplier for third quarter relative to fourth quarter}$$
$$\varepsilon_i = \text{value of the irregular component for time period } i$$

The model in Equation (17) is not in the form of a linear regression model. To transform this nonlinear model to a linear model, you use a base 10 logarithmic transformation.[5] Taking the logarithm of each side of Equation (17) results in Equation (18).

[5]*Alternatively, you can use base e logarithms. For more information on logarithms, see Appendix.*

TRANSFORMED EXPONENTIAL MODEL WITH QUARTERLY DATA

$$\log(Y_i) = \log(\beta_0 \beta_1^{X_i} \beta_2^{Q_1} \beta_3^{Q_2} \beta_4^{Q_3} \varepsilon_i)$$
$$= \log(\beta_0) + \log(\beta_1^{X_i}) + \log(\beta_2^{Q_1}) + \log(\beta_3^{Q_2}) + \log(\beta_4^{Q_3}) + \log(\varepsilon_i)$$
$$= \log(\beta_0) + X_i \log(\beta_1) + Q_1 \log(\beta_2) + Q_2 \log(\beta_3) + Q_3 \log(\beta_4) + \log(\varepsilon_i) \tag{18}$$

Equation (18) is a linear model that you can estimate using least-squares regression. Performing the regression analysis using $\log(Y_i)$ as the dependent variable and X_i, Q_1, Q_2, and Q_3 as the independent variables results in Equation (19).

EXPONENTIAL GROWTH WITH QUARTERLY DATA FORECASTING EQUATION

$$\log(\hat{Y}_i) = b_0 + b_1 X_i + b_2 Q_1 + b_3 Q_2 + b_4 Q_3 \tag{19}$$

where

$$b_0 = \text{estimate of } \log(\beta_0) \text{ and thus } 10^{b_0} = \hat{\beta}_0$$
$$b_1 = \text{estimate of } \log(\beta_1) \text{ and thus } 10^{b_1} = \hat{\beta}_1$$
$$b_2 = \text{estimate of } \log(\beta_2) \text{ and thus } 10^{b_2} = \hat{\beta}_2$$
$$b_3 = \text{estimate of } \log(\beta_3) \text{ and thus } 10^{b_3} = \hat{\beta}_3$$
$$b_4 = \text{estimate of } \log(\beta_4) \text{ and thus } 10^{b_4} = \hat{\beta}_4$$

Equation (20) is used for monthly data.

EXPONENTIAL MODEL WITH MONTHLY DATA

$$Y_i = \beta_0 \beta_1^{X_i} \beta_2^{M_1} \beta_3^{M_2} \beta_4^{M_3} \beta_5^{M_4} \beta_6^{M_5} \beta_7^{M_6} \beta_8^{M_7} \beta_9^{M_8} \beta_{10}^{M_9} \beta_{11}^{M_{10}} \beta_{12}^{M_{11}} \varepsilon_i \qquad (20)$$

where

$$X_i = \text{coded monthly value, } i = 0, 1, 2, \ldots$$
$$M_1 = 1 \text{ if January, 0 if not January}$$
$$M_2 = 1 \text{ if February, 0 if not February}$$
$$M_3 = 1 \text{ if March, 0 if not March}$$
$$\vdots$$
$$M_{11} = 1 \text{ if November, 0 if not November}$$
$$\beta_0 = Y \text{ intercept}$$
$$(\beta_1 - 1) \times 100\% = \text{monthly compound growth rate (in \%)}$$
$$\beta_2 = \text{multiplier for January relative to December}$$
$$\beta_3 = \text{multiplier for February relative to December}$$
$$\beta_4 = \text{multiplier for March relative to December}$$
$$\vdots$$
$$\beta_{12} = \text{multiplier for November relative to December}$$
$$\varepsilon_i = \text{value of the irregular component for time period } i$$

The model in Equation (20) is not in the form of a linear regression model. To transform this nonlinear model to a linear model, you can use a base 10 logarithm transformation. Taking the logarithm of each side of Equation (20) results in Equation (21).

TRANSFORMED EXPONENTIAL MODEL WITH MONTHLY DATA

$$\log(Y_i) = \log(\beta_0 \beta_1^{X_i} \beta_2^{M_1} \beta_3^{M_2} \beta_4^{M_3} \beta_5^{M_4} \beta_6^{M_5} \beta_7^{M_6} \beta_8^{M_7} \beta_9^{M_8} \beta_{10}^{M_9} \beta_{11}^{M_{10}} \beta_{12}^{M_{11}} \varepsilon_i)$$
$$= \log(\beta_0) + X_i \log(\beta_1) + M_1 \log(\beta_2) + M_2 \log(\beta_3)$$
$$+ M_3 \log(\beta_4) + M_4 \log(\beta_5) + M_5 \log(\beta_6) + M_6 \log(\beta_7)$$
$$+ M_7 \log(\beta_8) + M_8 \log(\beta_9) + M_9 \log(\beta_{10}) + M_{10} \log(\beta_{11})$$
$$+ M_{11} \log(\beta_{12}) + \log(\varepsilon_i) \qquad (21)$$

Equation (21) is a linear model that you can estimate using the least-squares method. Performing the regression analysis using $\log(Y_i)$ as the dependent variable and $X_i, M_1, M_2, \ldots,$ and M_{11} as the independent variables results in Equation (22).

EXPONENTIAL GROWTH WITH MONTHLY DATA FORECASTING EQUATION

$$\log(\hat{Y}_i) = b_0 + b_1 X_i + b_2 M_1 + b_3 M_2 + b_4 M_3 + b_5 M_4 + b_6 M_5 + b_7 M_6$$
$$+ b_8 M_7 + b_9 M_8 + b_{10} M_9 + b_{11} M_{10} + b_{12} M_{11} \qquad \textbf{(22)}$$

where

$$b_0 = \text{estimate of } \log(\beta_0) \text{ and thus } 10^{b_0} = \hat{\beta}_0$$

$$b_1 = \text{estimate of } \log(\beta_1) \text{ and thus } 10^{b_1} = \hat{\beta}_1$$

$$b_2 = \text{estimate of } \log(\beta_2) \text{ and thus } 10^{b_2} = \hat{\beta}_2$$

$$b_3 = \text{estimate of } \log(\beta_3) \text{ and thus } 10^{b_3} = \hat{\beta}_3$$

$$\vdots$$

$$b_{12} = \text{estimate of } \log(\beta_{12}) \text{ and thus } 10^{b_{12}} = \hat{\beta}_{12}$$

Q_1, Q_2, and Q_3 are the three dummy variables needed to represent the four quarter periods in a quarterly time series. $M_1, M_2, M_3, \ldots, M_{11}$ are the 11 dummy variables needed to represent the 12 months in a monthly time series. In building the model, you use $\log(Y_i)$ instead of Y_i values and then find the regression coefficients by taking the antilog of the regression coefficients developed from Equations (19) and (22).

Although at first glance these regression models look imposing, when fitting or forecasting in any one time period, the values of all or all but one of the dummy variables in the model are set equal to zero, and the equations simplify dramatically. In establishing the dummy variables for quarterly time-series data, the fourth quarter is the base period and has a coded value of zero for each dummy variable. With a quarterly time series, Equation (19) reduces as follows:

For any first quarter: $\quad \log(\hat{Y}_i) = b_0 + b_1 X_i + b_2$

For any second quarter: $\quad \log(\hat{Y}_i) = b_0 + b_1 X_i + b_3$

For any third quarter: $\quad \log(\hat{Y}_i) = b_0 + b_1 X_i + b_4$

For any fourth quarter: $\quad \log(\hat{Y}_i) = b_0 + b_1 X_i$

When establishing the dummy variables for each month, December serves as the base period and has a coded value of zero for each dummy variable. For example, with a monthly time series, Equation (22) reduces as follows:

For any January: $\quad \log(\hat{Y}_i) = b_0 + b_1 X_i + b_2$

For any February: $\quad \log(\hat{Y}_i) = b_0 + b_1 X_i + b_3$

For any November: $\quad \log(\hat{Y}_i) = b_0 + b_1 X_i + b_{12}$

For any December: $\quad \log(\hat{Y}_i) = b_0 + b_1 X_i$

To demonstrate the process of model building and least-squares forecasting with a quarterly time series, return to the Wal-Mart revenue data (in billions of dollars) originally displayed in Table 4. The data are from each quarter from the first quarter of 2000 through the last quarter of 2006. Microsoft Excel results for the quarterly exponential trend model are displayed in Figure 23.

FIGURE 23

Microsoft Excel results for fitting and forecasting with the quarterly Wal-Mart revenue data

	A	B	C	D	E	F	G
1	Regression Analysis of Quarterly Revenue for Wal-Mart Stores 2000 - 2006						
2							
3	*Regression Statistics*						
4	Multiple R	0.9881					
5	R Square	0.9763					
6	Adjusted R Square	0.9722					
7	Standard Error	0.0172					
8	Observations	28					
9							
10	ANOVA						
11		*df*	*SS*	*MS*	*F*	*Significance F*	
12	Regression	4	0.2820	0.0705	236.8992	2.4904E-18	
13	Residual	23	0.0068	0.0003			
14	Total	27	0.2888				
15							
16		*Coefficients*	*Standard Error*	*t Stat*	*P-value*	*Lower 95%*	*Upper 95%*
17	Intercept	1.6677	0.0089	186.6163	4.3775E-38	1.6493	1.6862
18	Coded Quarter	0.0113	0.0004	27.6592	3.7316E-19	0.0104	0.0121
19	Q1	-0.0857	0.0093	-9.2171	3.4782E-09	-0.1050	-0.0665
20	Q2	-0.0609	0.0093	-6.5782	1.0343E-06	-0.0800	-0.0417
21	Q3	-0.0744	0.0092	-8.0567	3.7990E-08	-0.0934	-0.0553

From Figure 23, the model fits the data extremely well. The coefficient of determination $r^2 = 0.9763$ and the adjusted $r^2 = 0.9722$, and the overall F test results in an F statistic of 236.8992 (p-value = 0.000). Looking further, at the 0.05 level of significance, each regression coefficient is highly statistically significant and contributes to the classical multiplicative time-series model. Taking the antilogs of all the regression coefficients, you have the following summary:

Regression Coefficient	$b_i = \log \hat{\beta}_i$	$\hat{\beta}_i = \text{antilog}(b_i) = 10^{b_i}$
b_0: Y intercept	1.6677	46.52646
b_1: coded quarter	0.0113	1.02636
b_2: first quarter	−0.0857	0.82092
b_3: second quarter	−0.0609	0.86916
b_4: third quarter	−0.0744	0.84256

The interpretations for $\hat{\beta}_0$, $\hat{\beta}_1$, $\hat{\beta}_2$, $\hat{\beta}_3$, and $\hat{\beta}_4$ are as follows:

- The Y intercept, $\hat{\beta}_0 = 46.52646$ (in billions of dollars), is the *unadjusted* forecast for quarterly revenues in the first quarter of 2000, the initial quarter in the time series. *Unadjusted* means that the seasonal component is not incorporated in the forecast.
- The value $(\hat{\beta}_1 - 1) \times 100\% = 0.02636$, or 2.636%, is the estimated *quarterly compound growth rate* in revenues, after adjusting for the seasonal component.
- $\hat{\beta}_2 = 0.82092$ is the seasonal multiplier for the first quarter relative to the fourth quarter; it indicates that there is 17.908% less revenue for the first quarter as compared with the fourth quarter.
- $\hat{\beta}_3 = 0.86916$ is the seasonal multiplier for the second quarter relative to the fourth quarter; it indicates that there is 13.084% less revenue for the second quarter as compared with the fourth quarter.
- $\hat{\beta}_4 = 0.84256$ is the seasonal multiplier for the third quarter relative to the fourth quarter; it indicates that there is 15.744% less revenue for the third quarter than the fourth quarter. Thus, the fourth quarter, which includes the holiday shopping season, has the strongest sales.

Using the regression coefficients b_0, b_1, b_2, b_3, b_4, and Equation (19) you can make forecasts for selected quarters. As an example, to predict revenues for the fourth quarter of 2006 ($X_i = 27$):

$$\log(\hat{Y}_i) = b_0 + b_1 X_i$$
$$= 1.6677 + (0.0113)(27)$$
$$= 1.9728$$

Thus,

$$\hat{Y}_i = 10^{1.9728} = 93.929$$

The predicted revenue for the fourth quarter of fiscal 2006 is $93.929 billion. Observe that this forecast for the fourth quarter of fiscal 2006 differs markedly from the actual revenues of $88.6 billion. Special economic circumstances may have affected these sales during the 2005 holiday season.

To make a forecast for a future time period, such as the first quarter of fiscal 2007 ($X_i = 28$, $Q_1 = 1$):

$$\log(\hat{Y}_i) = b_0 + b_1 X_i + b_2 Q_1$$
$$= 1.6677 + (0.0113)(28) + (-0.0857)(1)$$
$$= 1.8984$$

Thus,

$$\hat{Y}_i = 10^{1.8984} = 79.1407$$

The predicted revenue for the first quarter of fiscal 2007 is $79.1407 billion.

PROBLEMS FOR SECTION 7

Learning the Basics

 40 In forecasting a monthly time series over a five-year period from January 2002 to December 2006, the exponential trend forecasting equation for January is

$$\log \hat{Y}_i = 2.0 + 0.01 X_i + 0.10 \text{ January}$$

Take the antilog of the appropriate coefficient from this equation and interpret the
a. Y intercept, $\hat{\beta}_0$.
b. monthly compound growth rate.
c. January multiplier.

41 In forecasting weekly time-series data, how many dummy variables are needed to account for the seasonal categorical variable week?

 42 In forecasting a quarterly time series over the five-year period from the first quarter of 2002 through the fourth quarter of 2006, the exponential trend forecasting equation is given by

$$\log \hat{Y}_i = 3.0 + 0.10 X_i - 0.25 Q_1 + 0.20 Q_2 + 0.15 Q_3$$

where quarter zero is first quarter of 2002. Take the antilog of the appropriate coefficient from this equation and interpret the
a. Y intercept, $\hat{\beta}_0$.
b. quarterly compound growth rate.
c. second-quarter multiplier.

PH Grade ASSIST **43** Refer to the exponential model given in Problem 42.
a. What is the fitted value of the series in the fourth quarter of 2004?
b. What is the fitted value of the series in the first quarter of 2005?
c. What is the forecast in the fourth quarter of 2007?
d. What is the forecast in the first quarter of 2008?

Applying the Concepts

44 The data given in the following table represent the S&P Composite Stock Price Index recorded at the end of each quarter from 1994 through 2005 (see the file **S&Pstkin.xls**).

			Year			
Quarter	1994	1995	1996	1997	1998	1999
1	445.77	500.71	645.50	757.12	1,101.75	1,286.37
2	444.27	544.75	670.63	885.14	1,133.84	1,372.71
3	462.69	584.41	687.31	947.28	1,017.01	1,282.71
4	459.27	615.93	740.74	970.43	1,229.23	1,469.25

			Year			
Quarter	2000	2001	2002	2003	2004	2005
1	1,498.58	1,160.33	1,147.38	848.18	1,126.21	1,180.95
2	1,454.60	1,224.38	989.81	974.51	1,140.81	1,191.33
3	1,436.51	1,040.94	815.28	995.97	1,114.58	1,228.81
4	1,320.28	1,148.08	879.28	1,111.92	1,211.92	1,248.29

Source: Extracted from **www.yahoo.com.**

a. Plot the data.
b. Develop an exponential trend forecasting equation with quarterly components.
c. What is the fitted value in the third quarter of 2005?
d. What is the fitted value in the fourth quarter of 2005?
e. What are the forecasts for all four quarters of 2006?
f. Interpret the quarterly compound growth rate.
g. Interpret the second-quarter multiplier.

45 Are gasoline prices higher during the height of the summer vacation season? The following table contains the mean monthly prices (in dollars per gallon) for unleaded gasoline in the United States from 2000 to 2005 (stored in the file `unleaded.xls`):

	Year					
Month	**2000**	**2001**	**2002**	**2003**	**2004**	**2005**
January	1.301	1.472	1.139	1.473	1.592	1.823
February	1.369	1.484	1.130	1.641	1.672	1.918
March	1.541	1.447	1.241	1.748	1.766	2.065
April	1.506	1.564	1.407	1.659	1.833	2.283
May	1.498	1.729	1.421	1.542	2.009	2.216
June	1.617	1.640	1.404	1.514	2.041	2.176
July	1.593	1.482	1.412	1.524	1.939	2.316
August	1.510	1.427	1.423	1.628	1.898	2.506
September	1.582	1.531	1.422	1.728	1.891	2.927
October	1.559	1.362	1.449	1.603	2.029	2.785
November	1.555	1.263	1.448	1.535	2.010	2.343
December	1.489	1.131	1.394	1.494	1.882	2.186

Source: Bureau of Labor Statistics, U.S. Department of Labor, **www.bls.gov**.

a. Construct a time-series plot.
b. Develop an exponential trend forecasting equation for monthly data.
c. Interpret the monthly compound growth rate.
d. Interpret the monthly multipliers.
e. Write a short summary of your findings.

 46 The U.S. Bureau of Labor Statistics compiles data on a wide variety of workforce issues. The data in the file `unemploy.xls` gives the monthly seasonally adjusted civilian unemployment rates for the United States from 2000 through 2005.

Source: Bureau of Labor Statistics, U.S. Department of Labor, **www.bls.gov**.

a. Plot the time-series data.
b. Develop an exponential trend forecasting equation with monthly components.
c. What is the fitted value in December 2005?
d. What are the forecasts for all 12 months of 2006?
e. Interpret the monthly compound growth rate.
f. Interpret the July multiplier.

g. Go to your library or the Internet and locate the actual unemployment rate in 2006. Discuss.

47 The following data (stored in the file `credit.xls`) are monthly credit card charges (in millions of dollars) for a popular credit card issued by a large bank (the name of which is not disclosed, at its request):

	Year		
Month	**2001**	**2002**	**2003**
January	31.9	39.4	45.0
February	27.0	36.2	39.6
March	31.3	40.5	
April	31.0	44.6	
May	39.4	46.8	
June	40.7	44.7	
July	42.3	52.2	
August	49.5	54.0	
September	45.0	48.8	
October	50.0	55.8	
November	50.9	58.7	
December	58.5	63.4	

a. Construct the time-series plot.
b. Describe the monthly pattern that is evident in the data.
c. In general, would you say that the overall dollar amounts charged on the bank's credit cards is increasing or decreasing? Explain.
d. Note that December 2002 charges were more than $63 million, but those for February 2003 were less than $40 million. Was February's total close to what you would have expected?
e. Develop an exponential trend forecasting equation with monthly components.
f. Interpret the monthly compound growth rate.
g. Interpret the January multiplier.
h. What is the predicted value for March 2003?
i. What is the predicted value for April 2003?
j. How can this type of time-series forecasting benefit the bank?

48 The data in the file `toys-rev.xls` are quarterly revenues (in millions of dollars) for Toys Я Us from 1996 through 2005.

Source: Extracted from Standard & Poor's Stock Reports, *November 1995, November 1998, and April 2002. New York: McGraw-Hill, Inc., and Toys Я Us, Inc.,* **www.toysrus.com**.

a. Do you think that the revenues for Toys Я Us are subject to seasonal variation? Explain.
b. Plot the data. Does this chart support your answer to (a)?
c. Develop an exponential trend forecasting equation with quarterly components.
d. Interpret the quarterly compound growth rate.

e. Interpret the quarter multipliers.

f. What are the forecasts for all four quarters of 2006?

49 The data in the file `ford-rev.xls` are quarterly revenues (in millions of dollars) for the Ford Motor Company, from 1996 through 2005.

Source: Standard & Poor's Stock Reports, *November 2000 and April 2002. New York: McGraw-Hill, Inc., and the Ford Motor Company,* **ford.com**.

a. Do you think that the revenues for the Ford Motor Company are subject to seasonal variation? Explain.

b. Plot the data. Does this chart support your answer to (a)?

c. Develop an exponential trend forecasting equation with quarterly components.

d. Interpret the quarterly compound growth rate.

e. Interpret the quarter multipliers.

f. What are the forecasts for all four quarters of 2006?

8 INDEX NUMBERS

This chapter has presented various methods for forecasting time-series data. In this section, index numbers are used to compare a value of a time series relative to another value of a time series. **Index numbers** measure the value of an item (or group of items) at a particular point in time, as a percentage of the value of an item (or group of items) at another point in time. They are commonly used in business and economics as indicators of changing business or economic activity. There are many kinds of index numbers, including price indexes, quantity indexes, value indexes, and sociological indexes. In this section, only the price index is considered. In addition to allowing comparison of prices at different points in time, price indexes are also used to deflate the effect of inflation on a time series in order to compare values in real dollars instead of actual dollars.

Price Indexes

A **price index** compares the price of a commodity in a given period of time to the price paid for that commodity at a particular point of time in the past. A **simple price index** tracks the price of a single commodity. An **aggregate price index** tracks the prices for a group of commodities (called a market basket) at a given period of time to the price paid for that group of commodities at a particular point of time in the past. The **base period** is the point of time in the past against which all comparisons are made. In selecting the base period for a particular index, if possible, you select a period of economic stability rather than one at or near the peak of an expanding economy or the bottom of a recession or declining economy. In addition, the base period should be relatively recent so that comparisons are not greatly affected by changing technology and consumer attitudes and habits. Equation (23) defines the simple price index.

SIMPLE PRICE INDEX

$$I_i = \frac{P_i}{P_{base}} \times 100 \tag{23}$$

where

$$I_i = \text{price index for year } i$$

$$P_i = \text{price for year } i$$

$$P_{base} = \text{price for the base year}$$

As an example of the simple price index, consider the price per gallon of unleaded gasoline in the United States from 1980 to 2005. Table 5 presents the prices plus two sets of index numbers (see the file gasoline.xls). To illustrate the computation of the simple price index for 2005, using 1980 as the base year, from Equation (23) and Table 5,

$$I_{2005} = \frac{P_{2005}}{P_{1980}} \times 100 = \frac{2.30}{1.25} \times 100 = 184.0$$

TABLE 5

Price per Gallon of Unleaded Gasoline in the United States and Simple Price Index, with 1980 and 1995 as the Base Years (1980–2005)

Year	Gasoline Price	Price Index, 1980	Price Index, 1995
1980	1.25	100.0	108.7
1981	1.38	110.4	120.0
1982	1.30	104.0	113.0
1983	1.24	99.2	107.8
1984	1.21	96.8	105.2
1985	1.20	96.0	104.3
1986	0.93	74.4	80.9
1987	0.95	76.0	82.6
1988	0.95	76.0	82.6
1989	1.02	81.6	88.7
1990	1.16	92.8	100.9
1991	1.14	91.2	99.1
1992	1.14	91.2	99.1
1993	1.11	88.8	96.5
1994	1.11	88.8	96.5
1995	1.15	92.0	100.0
1996	1.23	98.4	107.0
1997	1.23	98.4	107.0
1998	1.06	84.8	92.2
1999	1.17	93.6	101.7
2000	1.51	120.8	131.3
2001	1.46	116.8	127.0
2002	1.36	108.8	118.3
2003	1.59	127.2	138.3
2004	1.88	150.4	163.5
2005	2.30	184.0	200.0

Source: Bureau of Labor Statistics, U.S. Department of Labor, **www.bls.gov**.

Therefore, the price per gallon of unleaded gasoline in the United States in 2005 was 84.0% higher than in 1980. An examination of the price indexes for 1980 to 2005 in Table 5 indicates that the price of unleaded gasoline increased in 1981 and 1982 over the base year of 1980 but then was below the 1980 price every year until 2000. Because the base period for the index numbers in Table 5 is 1980, you should use a base year closer to the present. The price remained fairly constant from 1990 to 1995; thus, it is appropriate to use 1995 as a base year. Equation (24) is used to develop index numbers with a new base.

SHIFTING THE BASE FOR A SIMPLE PRICE INDEX

$$I_{new} = \frac{I_{old}}{I_{new\,base}} \times 100 \tag{24}$$

where

$$I_{new} = \text{new price index}$$

$$I_{old} = \text{old price index}$$

$$I_{new\,base} = \text{value of the old price index for the new base year}$$

To change the base year to 1995, $I_{new\,base} = 92.0$. Using Equation (24) to find the new price index for 2005,

$$I_{new} = \frac{I_{old}}{I_{new\,base}} \times 100 = \frac{184.0}{92.0} \times 100 = 200.0$$

Thus, the 2005 price for unleaded gasoline in the United States was twice the price that it was in 1995. See Table 5 for the complete set of price indexes.

Aggregate Price Indexes

An aggregate price index consists of a group of commodities taken together. The group of commodities under consideration is often called a *market basket*. There are two types of aggregate price indexes: unweighted aggregate price indexes and weighted aggregate price indexes. An **unweighted aggregate price index**, defined in Equation (25), places equal weight on all the items in the market basket.

UNWEIGHTED AGGREGATE PRICE INDEX

$$I_U^{(t)} = \frac{\sum_{i=1}^{n} P_i^{(t)}}{\sum_{i=1}^{n} P_i^{(0)}} \times 100 \qquad (25)$$

where

$$t = \text{time period } (0, 1, 2, \dots)$$

$$i = \text{item } (1, 2, \dots, n)$$

$$n = \text{total number of items under consideration}$$

$$\sum_{i=1}^{n} P_i^{(t)} = \text{sum of the prices paid for each of the } n \text{ commodities at time period } t$$

$$\sum_{i=1}^{n} P_i^{(0)} = \text{sum of the prices paid for each of the } n \text{ commodities at time period } 0$$

$$I_U^{(t)} = \text{value of the unweighted price index at time period } t$$

Table 6 presents the mean prices for three fruit items for selected periods from 1980 to 2005 (stored in the file `fruit.xls`).

TABLE 6

Prices (in Dollars per Pound) for Three Fruit Items

	Year					
Fruit	**1980** $P_i^{(0)}$	**1985** $P_i^{(1)}$	**1990** $P_i^{(2)}$	**1995** $P_i^{(3)}$	**2000** $P_i^{(4)}$	**2005** $P_i^{(5)}$
Apples	0.692	0.684	0.719	0.835	0.927	0.966
Bananas	0.342	0.367	0.463	0.490	0.509	0.838
Oranges	0.365	0.533	0.570	0.625	0.638	0.490

Source: Bureau of Labor Statistics, U.S. Department of Labor, **www.bls.gov**.

To calculate the unweighted aggregate price index for the various years, using Equation (25) and 1980 as the base period:

$$1980: I_U^{(0)} = \frac{\sum_{i=1}^{3} P_i^{(0)}}{\sum_{i=1}^{3} P_i^{(0)}} \times 100 = \frac{0.692 + 0.342 + 0.365}{0.692 + 0.342 + 0.365} \times 100 = \frac{1.399}{1.399} \times 100 = 100.0$$

$$1985: I_U^{(1)} = \frac{\sum_{i=1}^{3} P_i^{(1)}}{\sum_{i=1}^{3} P_i^{(0)}} \times 100 = \frac{0.684 + 0.367 + 0.533}{0.692 + 0.342 + 0.365} \times 100 = \frac{1.584}{1.399} \times 100 = 113.2$$

$$1990: I_U^{(2)} = \frac{\sum_{i=1}^{3} P_i^{(2)}}{\sum_{i=1}^{3} P_i^{(0)}} \times 100 = \frac{0.719 + 0.463 + 0.570}{0.692 + 0.342 + 0.365} \times 100 = \frac{1.752}{1.399} \times 100 = 125.2$$

$$1995: I_U^{(3)} = \frac{\sum_{i=1}^{3} P_i^{(3)}}{\sum_{i=1}^{3} P_i^{(0)}} \times 100 = \frac{0.835 + 0.490 + 0.625}{0.692 + 0.342 + 0.365} \times 100 = \frac{1.950}{1.399} \times 100 = 139.4$$

$$2000: I_U^{(4)} = \frac{\sum_{i=1}^{3} P_i^{(4)}}{\sum_{i=1}^{3} P_i^{(0)}} \times 100 = \frac{0.927 + 0.509 + 0.638}{0.692 + 0.342 + 0.365} \times 100 = \frac{2.074}{1.399} \times 100 = 148.2$$

$$2005: I_U^{(5)} = \frac{\sum_{i=1}^{3} P_i^{(5)}}{\sum_{i=1}^{3} P_i^{(0)}} \times 100 = \frac{0.966 + 0.838 + 0.490}{0.692 + 0.342 + 0.365} \times 100 = \frac{2.294}{1.399} \times 100 = 164.0$$

Thus, in 2005, the combined price of a pound of apples, a pound of bananas, and a pound of oranges was 64% more than it was in 1980.

An unweighted aggregate price index represents the changes in prices, over time, for an entire group of commodities. However, an unweighted aggregate price index has two shortcomings. First, this index considers each commodity in the group as equally important. Thus, the most expensive commodities per unit are overly influential. Second, not all the commodities are consumed at the same rate. In an unweighted index, changes in the price of the least-consumed commodities are overly influential.

Weighted Aggregate Price Indexes

Due to the shortcomings of unweighted aggregate price indexes, weighted aggregate price indexes are generally preferable. **Weighted aggregate price indexes** account for differences in the magnitude of prices per unit and differences in the consumption levels of the items in the market basket. Two types of weighted aggregate price indexes are commonly used in business and economics: the Laspeyres price index and the Paasche price index. Equation (26) defines the **Laspeyres price index**, which uses the consumption quantities associated with the base year in the calculation of all price indexes in the series.

LASPEYRES PRICE INDEX

$$I_L^{(t)} = \frac{\sum_{i=1}^{n} P_i^{(t)} Q_i^{(0)}}{\sum_{i=1}^{n} P_i^{(0)} Q_i^{(0)}} \times 100 \tag{26}$$

where

t = time period (0, 1, 2, . . .)

i = item (1, 2, . . . , n)

n = total number of items under consideration

$Q_i^{(0)}$ = quantity of item i at time period 0

$I_L^{(t)}$ = value of the Laspeyres price index at time t

$P_i^{(t)}$ = price paid for commodity i at time period t

$P_i^{(0)}$ = price paid for commodity i at time period 0

Table 7 gives the price and per capita consumption, in pounds, for the three fruit items comprising the market basket of interest (see the file fruit.xls).

TABLE 7

Prices (in Dollars per Pound) and Quantities (Annual per Capita Consumption, in Pounds) for Three Fruit Items*

	Year					
	1980	1985	1990	1995	2000	2005
Fruit	$P_i^{(0)}, Q_i^{(0)}$	$P_i^{(1)}, Q_i^{(1)}$	$P_i^{(2)}, Q_i^{(2)}$	$P_i^{(3)}, Q_i^{(3)}$	$P_i^{(4)}, Q_i^{(4)}$	$P_i^{(5)}, Q_i^{(5)}$
Apples	0.692, 19.2	0.684, 17.3	0.719, 19.6	0.835, 18.9	0.927, 17.5	0.966, 16.0
Bananas	0.342, 20.2	0.367, 23.5	0.463, 24.4	0.490, 27.4	0.509, 28.5	0.838, 26.8
Oranges	0.365, 14.3	0.533, 11.6	0.570, 12.4	0.625, 12.0	0.638, 11.7	0.490, 10.6

*Source: Bureau of Labor Statistics, U.S. Department of Labor, **www.bls.gov**, and Statistical Abstract of the United States, U.S. Census Bureau, **www.census.gov**.*
The 2005 consumption values are preliminary estimates. Actual values were not available at publication time.

Using 1980 as the base year, you calculate the Laspeyres price index for 2005 ($t = 5$) using Equation (26):

$$I_L^{(5)} = \frac{\sum_{i=1}^{3} P_i^{(5)} Q_i^{(0)}}{\sum_{i=1}^{3} P_i^{(0)} Q_i^{(0)}} \times 100 = \frac{(0.966 \times 19.2) + (0.838 \times 20.2) + (0.490 \times 14.3)}{(0.692 \times 19.2) + (0.342 \times 20.2) + (0.365 \times 14.3)} \times 100$$

$$= \frac{42.4818}{25.4143} \times 100 = 167.2$$

Thus, the Laspeyres price index is 167.2, indicating that the cost of purchasing these three items in 2005 was 67.2% more than in 1980. This index is more than the unweighted index, 164.0, because the least-purchased item, oranges, decreased in price over the time span while apples and bananas increased in price. In other words, in the unweighted index, the least-consumed commodity (oranges) is overly influential.

The **Paasche price index** uses the consumption quantities in the year of interest instead of using the initial quantities. Thus, the Paasche index is a more accurate reflection of total consumption costs at that point in time. However, there are two major drawbacks of the Paasche index. First, accurate consumption values for current purchases are often hard to obtain. Thus, many important indexes, such as the CPI, use the Laspeyres method. Second, if a particular product increases greatly in price compared to the other items in the market basket, consumers will avoid the high-priced item out of necessity, not because of changes in what they might prefer to purchase. Equation (27) defines the Paasche price index.

PAASCHE PRICE INDEX

$$I_P^{(t)} = \frac{\sum_{i=1}^{n} P_i^{(t)} Q_i^{(t)}}{\sum_{i=1}^{n} P_i^{(0)} Q_i^{(t)}} \times 100 \tag{27}$$

where

t = time period (0, 1, 2, . . .)

i = item (1, 2, . . . , n)

n = total number of items under consideration

$Q_i^{(t)}$ = quantity of item i at time period t

$I_P^{(t)}$ = value of the Paasche price index at time period t

$P_i^{(t)}$ = price paid for commodity i at time period t

$P_i^{(0)}$ = price paid for commodity i at time period 0

To calculate the Paasche price index in 2005, using 1980 as a base year, you use $t = 5$ in Equation (29):

$$I_P^{(5)} = \frac{\sum_{i=1}^{3} P_i^{(5)} Q_i^{(5)}}{\sum_{i=1}^{3} P_i^{(0)} Q_i^{(5)}} \times 100 = \frac{(0.966 \times 16.0) + (0.838 \times 26.8) + (0.490 \times 10.6)}{(0.692 \times 16.0) + (0.342 \times 26.8) + (0.365 \times 10.6)} \times 100$$

$$= \frac{43.1084}{24.1066} \times 100 = 178.8$$

The Paasche price index for this market basket is 178.8. Thus, the cost of these three fruit items in 2000 was 78.8% higher in 2005 than in 1980, when using 2005 quantities.

Some Common Price Indexes

Various price indexes are commonly used in business and economics. The CPI is the most familiar index in the United States. This index is officially referred to as the CPI-U to reflect that it measures the prices "urban" residents are subject to, but it is commonly referred to as the CPI. The CPI, published monthly by the U.S. Bureau of Labor Statistics, is the primary measure of changes in the cost of living in the United States. The CPI is a weighted aggregate price index, using the Laspeyres method, for 400 commonly purchased food, clothing, transportation, medical, and housing items. Currently computed using 1982–1984 averages as a base year, the CPI was 195.3 in 2005. (See data file **CPI-U.xls** for a listing of the CPI-U for 1965–2005.)

An important use of the CPI is as a price deflator. The CPI is used to convert (and deflate) actual dollars into real dollars by multiplying each dollar value in a time series by the quantity (100/CPI). For example, the gross revenues of the Wm. Wrigley Jr. Company were transformed from actual revenues to real gross revenues in Figure 5. This transformation allowed you to see that the increase in revenues for Wrigley's were actually *real* increases, not simply increases that could be explained by an increase in the cost of living.

Another important price index published by the U.S. Bureau of Labor Statistics is the producer price index (PPI). The PPI is a weighted aggregate price index that also uses the Laspeyres method, for prices of commodities sold by wholesalers. The PPI is considered a leading indicator of the CPI. In other words, increases in the PPI tend to precede increases in the CPI, and, similarly, decreases in the PPI tend to precede decreases in the CPI.

Financial indexes such as the DJIA Index, the S&P 500 Index, and the NASDAQ Index are price indexes for different sets of stocks in the United States. Many indexes measure the performance of international stock markets, including the Nikkei Index for Japan, the Dax 30 for Germany, and the SSE Composite for China.

PROBLEMS FOR SECTION 8

Learning the Basics

50 The simple price index for a commodity in 2006, using 1995 as the base year, is 175. Interpret this index number.

51 The following are prices for a commodity from 2004 to 2006:

2004: $5
2005: $8
2006: $7

a. Calculate the simple price indexes for 2004–2006, using 2004 as the base year.

b. Calculate the simple price indexes for 2004–2006, using 2005 as the base year.

 52 The following are prices and consumption quantities for three commodities in 1995 and 2006:

	Year	
Commodity	1995 Price, Quantity	2006 Price, Quantity
A	$2, 20	$3, 21
B	$18, 3	$36, 2
C	$3, 18	$4, 23

a. Calculate the unweighted aggregate price index for 2006, using 1995 as the base year.

b. Calculate the Laspeyres aggregate price index for 2006, using 1995 as the base year.

c. Calculate the Paasche aggregate price index for 2006, using 1995 as the base year.

Applying the Concepts

53 The data in the file **djia.xls** represent the closing values of the DJIA from 1979 to 2005.

a. Calculate the price index for the DJIA with 1979 as the base year.

b. Shift the base of the DJIA to 1990 and recalculate the price index.

c. Compare the results of (a) and (b). Which price index do you think is more useful in understanding the changes in the DJIA? Explain.

 54 The data in the file **coffeeprice.xls** represent the mean price per pound of coffee in the United States from 1980 to 2006.

Source: Bureau of Labor Statistics, U.S. Department of Labor, **www.bls.gov**.

a. Calculate the simple price indexes for 1980 to 2006, using 1980 as the base year.

b. Interpret the simple price index for 2006, using 1980 as the base year.

c. Recalculate the simple price indexes found in (a), using Equation (24), with 1990 as the base year.

d. Interpret the simple price index for 2006, using 1990 as the base year.

e. Would it be a good idea to use 1995 as the base year? Explain.

f. Describe the trends in coffee costs from 1980 to 2006.

55 The following data represent the mean prices per pound of fresh tomatoes in the United States from 1980 to 2006 (see the file tomatoes.xls):

Year	Price	Year	Price	Year	Price
1980	0.703	1989	0.797	1998	1.452
1981	0.792	1990	1.735	1999	1.904
1982	0.763	1991	0.912	2000	1.443
1983	0.726	1992	0.936	2001	1.414
1984	0.854	1993	1.141	2002	1.451
1985	0.697	1994	1.604	2003	1.711
1986	1.104	1995	1.323	2004	1.472
1987	0.943	1996	1.103	2005	1.660
1988	0.871	1997	1.213	2006	2.162

Source: Bureau of Labor Statistics, U.S. Department of Labor, **www.bls.gov**.

a. Calculate the simple price indexes for 1980 to 2006, using 1980 as the base year.

b. Interpret the simple price index for 2006, using 1980 as the base year.

c. Recalculate the simple price indexes found in (a), using Equation (24), with 1990 as the base year.

d. Interpret the simple price index for 2006, using 1990 as the base year.

e. Describe the trends in the cost of fresh tomatoes from 1980 to 2006.

56 The data in the file energy2.xls represent the mean price for three types of energy products in the United States from 1992 to 2006. Included are electricity (dollars per 500 KWH), natural gas (dollars per 40 therms), and fuel oil (dollars per gallon).

Source: Bureau of Labor Statistics, U.S. Department of Labor, **www.bls.gov**.

a. Calculate the 1992–2006 simple price indexes for electricity, natural gas, and fuel oil, using 1992 as the base year.

b. Recalculate the price indexes in (a), using 1996 as the base year.

c. Calculate the 1992–2006 unweighted aggregate price indexes for the group of three energy items.

d. Calculate the 2006 Laspeyres price index for the group of three energy items for a family that consumed 5,000 KWH of electricity (10 units), 960 therms of natural gas (24 units), and 400 gallons of fuel oil (400 units) in 1992.

e. Calculate the 2006 Laspeyres price index for the group of three energy items for a family that consumed 6,500 KWH of electricity, 1,040 therms of natural gas, and 235 gallons of fuel oil in 1992.

9 PITFALLS CONCERNING TIME-SERIES FORECASTING

The value of time-series forecasting methodology, which uses past and present information as guides to the future, was recognized and most eloquently expressed more than two centuries ago by the U.S. statesman Patrick Henry, who said:

> I have but one lamp by which my feet are guided, and that is the lamp of experience. I know no way of judging the future but by the past. [Speech at Virginia Convention (Richmond), March 23, 1775]

However, critics of time-series forecasting argue that these techniques are overly naive and mechanical. They argue that a mathematical model based on the past should not be used to mechanically extrapolate trends into the future without considering personal judgments, business experiences, or changing technologies, habits, and needs (see Problem 69). Thus, in recent years, econometricians have developed highly sophisticated computerized models of economic activity, incorporating such factors for forecasting purposes. Such forecasting methods, however, are beyond the scope of this text (see references 1–3).

Nevertheless, as you have seen from the preceding sections of this chapter, time-series methods provide useful guides for projecting future trends (on long- and short-term bases). If used properly and in conjunction with other forecasting methods as well as with business judgment and experience, time-series methods will continue to be useful tools for forecasting.

SUMMARY

In this chapter, you used time-series methods to develop forecasts for the Wm. Wrigley Jr. Company, Cabot Corporation, and Wal-Mart. You studied smoothing techniques, least-squares trend fitting, autoregressive models, forecasting of seasonal data, and index numbers. Figure 24 provides a summary chart for the time-series and index number methods discussed in this chapter.

If you are using time-series forecasting, you need to ask the following question: Is there a trend in the data? If there is no trend, then you should use moving averages or exponential smoothing. If there is a trend, then you can use the linear, quadratic, and exponential trend models and the autoregressive model.

If you are developing index numbers, you need to ask the following question: Are you developing an aggregate index of more than one commodity? If the answer is no, then you can use a simple price index. If the answer is yes, then you need to determine whether you will develop a weighted price index. If not, you can develop an unweighted price index. If you are developing a weighted price index, you can use a Laspeyres price index or a Paasche price index.

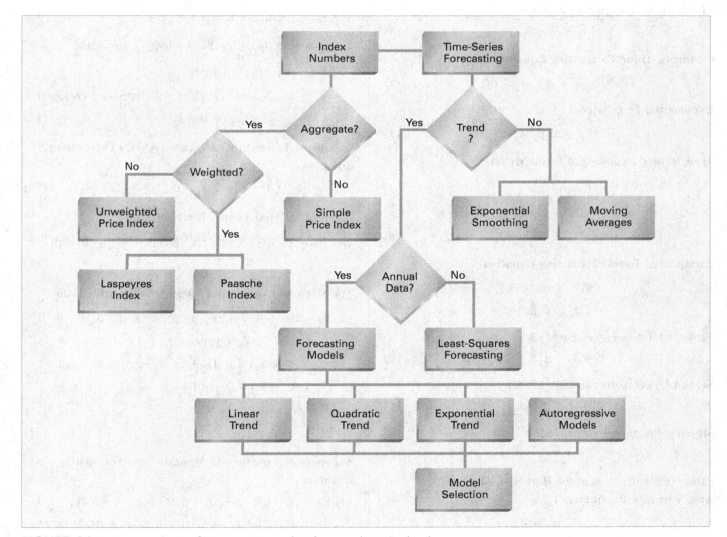

FIGURE 24 Summary chart of time series and index number methods

KEY EQUATIONS

Classical Multiplicative Time-Series Model for Annual Data

$$Y_i = T_i \times C_i \times I_i \qquad (1)$$

Classical Multiplicative Time-Series Model for Data with a Seasonal Component

$$Y_i = T_i \times S_i \times C_i \times I_i \qquad (2)$$

Computing an Exponentially Smoothed Value in Time Period i

$$E_1 = Y_1$$
$$E_i = WY_i + (1 - W)E_{i-1} \qquad i = 2, 3, 4, \dots \qquad (3)$$

Forecasting Time Period $i + 1$

$$\hat{Y}_{i+1} = E_i \qquad (4)$$

Linear Trend Forecasting Equation

$$\hat{Y}_i = b_0 + b_1 X_i \qquad (5)$$

Quadratic Trend Forecasting Equation

$$\hat{Y}_i = b_0 + b_1 X_i + b_2 X_i^2 \qquad (6)$$

Exponential Trend Model

$$Y_i = \beta_0 \beta_1^{X_i} \varepsilon_i \qquad (7)$$

Transformed Exponential Trend Model

$$\log(Y_i) = \log(\beta_0 \beta_1^{X_i} \varepsilon_i)$$
$$= \log(\beta_0) + \log(\beta_1^{X_i}) + \log(\varepsilon_i)$$
$$= \log(\beta_0) + X_i \log(\beta_1) + \log(\varepsilon_i) \qquad (8)$$

Exponential Trend Forecasting Equation

$$\log(\hat{Y}_i) = b_0 + b_1 X_i \qquad (9a)$$
$$\hat{Y}_i = \hat{\beta}_0 \hat{\beta}_1^{X_i} \qquad (9b)$$

First-Order Autoregressive Model

$$Y_i = A_0 + A_1 Y_{i-1} + \delta_i \qquad (10)$$

Second-Order Autoregressive Model

$$Y_i = A_0 + A_1 Y_{i-1} + A_2 Y_{i-2} + \delta_i \qquad (11)$$

pth-Order Autoregressive Models

$$Y_i = A_0 + A_1 Y_{i-1} + A_2 Y_{i-2} + \cdots + A_p Y_{i-p} + \delta_i \qquad (12)$$

t Test for Significance of the Highest-Order Autoregressive Parameter, A_p

$$t = \frac{a_p - A_p}{S_{a_p}} \qquad (13)$$

Fitted pth-Order Autoregressive Equation

$$\hat{Y}_i = a_0 + a_1 Y_{i-1} + a_2 Y_{i-2} + \cdots + a_p Y_{i-p} \qquad (14)$$

pth-Order Autoregressive Forecasting Equation

$$\hat{Y}_{n+j} = a_0 + a_1 \hat{Y}_{n+j-1} + a_2 \hat{Y}_{n+j-2} + \cdots + a_p \hat{Y}_{n+j-p} \qquad (15)$$

Mean Absolute Deviation

$$MAD = \frac{\sum_{i=1}^{n} |Y_i - \hat{Y}_i|}{n} \qquad (16)$$

Exponential Model with Quarterly Data

$$Y_i = \beta_0 \beta_1^{X_i} \beta_2^{Q_1} \beta_3^{Q_2} \beta_4^{Q_3} \varepsilon_i \qquad (17)$$

Transformed Exponential Model with Quarterly Data

$$\log(Y_i) = \log(\beta_0 \beta_1^{X_i} \beta_2^{Q_1} \beta_3^{Q_2} \beta_4^{Q_3} \varepsilon_i)$$
$$= \log(\beta_0) + \log(\beta_1^{X_i}) + \log(\beta_2^{Q_1}) + \log(\beta_3^{Q_2})$$
$$+ \log(\beta_4^{Q_3}) + \log(\varepsilon_i)$$
$$= \log(\beta_0) + X_i \log(\beta_1) + Q_1 \log(\beta_2) + Q_2 \log(\beta_3)$$
$$+ Q_3 \log(\beta_4) + \log(\varepsilon_i) \qquad (18)$$

Exponential Growth with Quarterly Data Forecasting Equation

$$\log(\hat{Y}_i) = b_0 + b_1 X_i + b_2 Q_1 + b_3 Q_2 + b_4 Q_3 \qquad (19)$$

Exponential Model with Monthly Data

$$Y_i = \beta_0 \beta_1^{X_i} \beta_2^{M_1} \beta_3^{M_2} \beta_4^{M_3} \beta_5^{M_4} \beta_6^{M_5} \beta_7^{M_6} \beta_8^{M_7} \beta_9^{M_8} \beta_{10}^{M_9} \beta_{11}^{M_{10}} \beta_{12}^{M_{11}} \varepsilon_i \qquad (20)$$

Transformed Exponential Model with Monthly Data

$$\log(Y_i) = \log(\beta_0 \beta_1^{X_i} \beta_2^{M_1} \beta_3^{M_2} \beta_4^{M_3} \beta_5^{M_4} \beta_6^{M_5} \beta_7^{M_6} \beta_8^{M_7} \beta_9^{M_8} \beta_{10}^{M_9} \beta_{11}^{M_{10}} \beta_{12}^{M_{11}} \varepsilon_i)$$
$$= \log(\beta_0) + X_i \log(\beta_1) + M_1 \log(\beta_2) + M_2 \log(\beta_3)$$
$$+ M_3 \log(\beta_4) + M_4 \log(\beta_5) + M_5 \log(\beta_6) + M_6 \log(\beta_7)$$
$$+ M_7 \log(\beta_8) + M_8 \log(\beta_9) + M_9 \log(\beta_{10}) + M_{10} \log(\beta_{11})$$
$$+ M_{11} \log(\beta_{12}) + \log(\varepsilon_i) \qquad (21)$$

Exponential Growth with Monthly Data Forecasting Equation

$$\log(\hat{Y}_i) = b_0 + b_1 X_i + b_2 M_1 + b_3 M_2 + b_4 M_3 + b_5 M_4 + b_6 M_5$$
$$+ b_7 M_6 + b_8 M_7 + b_9 M_8 + b_{10} M_9 + b_{11} M_{10} + b_{12} M_{11} \qquad (22)$$

Simple Price Index

$$I_i = \frac{P_i}{P_{base}} \times 100 \qquad (23)$$

Shifting the Base for a Simple Price Index

$$I_{new} = \frac{I_{old}}{I_{new\ base}} \times 100 \qquad (24)$$

Unweighted Aggregate Price Index

$$I_U^{(t)} = \frac{\sum\limits_{i=1}^{n} P_i^{(t)}}{\sum\limits_{i=1}^{n} P_i^{(0)}} \times 100 \qquad (25)$$

Laspeyres Price Index

$$I_L^{(t)} = \frac{\sum\limits_{i=1}^{n} P_i^{(t)} Q_i^{(0)}}{\sum\limits_{i=1}^{n} P_i^{(0)} Q_i^{(0)}} \times 100 \qquad (26)$$

Paasche Price Index

$$I_P^{(t)} = \frac{\sum\limits_{i=1}^{n} P_i^{(t)} Q_i^{(t)}}{\sum\limits_{i=1}^{n} P_i^{(0)} Q_i^{(t)}} \times 100 \qquad (27)$$

KEY TERMS

aggregate price index
autoregressive modeling
base period
causal forecasting method
classical multiplicative model
cyclical component
exponential smoothing
exponential trend model
first-order autocorrelation
first-order autoregressive model
forecasting
index numbers

irregular component
Laspeyres price index
linear trend model
mean absolute deviation (*MAD*)
moving averages
Paasche price index
parsimony
price index
*p*th-order autocorrelation
*p*th-order autoregressive model
quadratic trend model
qualitative forecasting methods

quantitative forecasting methods
random component
seasonal component
second-order autocorrelation
second-order autoregressive model
simple price index
time series
time-series forecasting methods
trend
unweighted aggregate price index
weighted aggregate price index

CHAPTER REVIEW PROBLEMS

Checking Your Understanding

57 What is a time series?

58 What are the distinguishing features among the various components of the classical multiplicative time-series model?

59 What is the difference between moving averages and exponential smoothing?

60 Under what circumstances is the exponential trend model most appropriate?

61 How does the least-squares linear trend forecasting model developed in this chapter differ from the least-squares linear regression model?

62 How does autoregressive modeling differ from the other approaches to forecasting?

63 What are the different approaches to choosing an appropriate forecasting model?

64 What is the major difference between using S_{YX} and *MAD* for evaluating how well a particular model fits the data?

65 How does forecasting for monthly or quarterly data differ from forecasting for annual data?

66 What is an index number?

67 What is the difference between a simple price index and an aggregate price index?

68 What is the difference between a Paasche price index and a Laspeyres price index?

Applying the Concepts

69 The following table (stored in the file polio.xls) represents the annual incidence rates (per 100,000 persons) of reported acute poliomyelitis recorded over five-year periods from 1915 to 1955:

YEAR	1915	1920	1925	1930	1935	1940	1945	1950	1955
RATE	3.1	2.2	5.3	7.5	8.5	7.4	10.3	22.1	17.6

Source: Extracted from B. Wattenberg, ed., The Statistical History of the United States: From Colonial Times to the Present, ser. B303 (New York: Basic Books, 1976).

a. Plot the data.
b. Compute the linear trend forecasting equation and plot the trend line.
c. What are your forecasts for 1960, 1965, and 1970?
d. Using a library or the Internet, find the actually reported incidence rates of acute poliomyelitis for 1960, 1965, and 1970. Record your results.
e. Why are the forecasts you made in (c) not useful? Discuss.

70 The U.S. Department of Labor gathers and publishes statistics concerning the labor market. The data file workforce.xls contains the U.S. civilian noninstitutional population of people 16 years and over (in thousands) and the U.S. civilian noninstitutional workforce of people 16 years and over (in thousands) for 1984–2005. The workforce variable reports the number of people in the population who have a job or are actively looking for a job.

Year	Population	Workforce	Year	Population	Workforce
1984	176,383	113,544	1995	198,584	132,304
1985	178,206	115,461	1996	200,591	133,943
1986	180,587	117,834	1997	203,133	136,297
1987	182,753	119,865	1998	205,220	137,673
1988	184,613	121,669	1999	207,753	139,368
1989	186,393	123,869	2000	212,577	142,583
1990	189,164	125,840	2001	215,092	143,734
1991	190,925	126,346	2002	217,570	144,863
1992	192,805	128,105	2003	221,168	146,510
1993	194,838	129,200	2004	223,351	146,817
1994	196,814	131,056	2005	226,082	147,956

Source: Bureau of Labor Statistics, U.S. Department of Labor, www.bls.gov.

a. Plot the time series for the U.S. civilian noninstitutional population of people 16 years and older.
b. Compute the linear trend forecasting equation.
c. Forecast the U.S. civilian noninstitutional population of people 16 years and older for 2006 and 2007.
d. Repeat (a) through (c) for the U.S. civilian noninstitutional workforce of people 16 years and older.

71 The quarterly price for natural gas (dollars per 40 therms) in the United States from 1994 through 2005 is given in the data file naturalgas.xls.
Source: Bureau of Labor Statistics, U.S. Department of Labor, www.bls.gov.

a. Do you think the price for natural gas has a seasonal component?
b. Plot the time series. Does this chart support your answer in (a)?
c. Compute an exponential trend forecasting equation for quarterly data.
d. Interpret the quarterly compound growth rate.
e. Interpret the quarter multipliers. Do the multipliers support your answers to (a) and (b)?

72 The data in the following table (stored in the file mcdonald.xls) represent the gross revenues (in billions of current dollars) of McDonald's Corporation over the 31-year period from 1975 through 2005:

Year	Revenues	Year	Revenues	Year	Revenues
1975	1.0	1986	4.2	1997	11.4
1976	1.2	1987	4.9	1998	12.4
1977	1.4	1988	5.6	1999	13.3
1978	1.7	1989	6.1	2000	14.2
1979	1.9	1990	6.8	2001	14.9
1980	2.2	1991	6.7	2002	15.4
1981	2.5	1992	7.1	2003	17.1
1982	2.8	1993	7.4	2004	19.0
1983	3.1	1994	8.3	2005	20.5
1984	3.4	1995	9.8		
1985	3.8	1996	10.7		

Source: Extracted from Moody's Handbook of Common Stocks, 1980, 1989, and 1999, and Mergent's Handbook of Common Stocks, Spring 2002 and Spring 2006.

a. Plot the data.
b. Compute the linear trend forecasting equation.
c. Compute the quadratic trend forecasting equation.
d. Compute the exponential trend forecasting equation.
e. Find the best-fitting autoregressive model, using $\alpha = 0.05$.
f. Perform a residual analysis for each of the models in (b) through (e).
g. Compute the standard error of the estimate (S_{YX}) and the MAD for each corresponding model in (f).
h. On the basis of your results in (f) and (g), along with a consideration of the principle of parsimony, which model would you select for purposes of forecasting? Discuss.
i. Using the selected model in (h), forecast gross revenues for 2006.

73 The data in the file sears.xls represent the gross revenues (in billions of current dollars) of Sears, Roebuck & Company over the 30-year period from 1975 through 2004.

Source: Extracted from Moody's Handbook of Common Stocks, *1980, 1989, and 1999, and* Mergent's Handbook of Common Stocks, *Spring 2002 and Spring 2006.*

a. Plot the data.
b. Compute the linear trend forecasting equation.
c. Compute the quadratic trend forecasting equation.
d. Compute the exponential trend forecasting equation.
e. Find the best-fitting autoregressive model, using $\alpha = 0.05$.
f. Perform a residual analysis for each of the models in (b) through (e).
g. Compute the standard error of the estimate (S_{YX}) and the *MAD* for each corresponding model in (f).
h. On the basis of your results in (f) and (g), along with a consideration of the principle of parsimony, which model would you select for purposes of forecasting? Discuss.
i. Using the selected model in (h), forecast gross revenues for 2005.

74 Teachers' Retirement System of the City of New York offers several types of investments for its members. Among the choices are investments with fixed and variable rates of return. There are currently two categories of variable-return investments. Variable *A* consists of investments that are primarily made in stocks, and variable *B* consists of investments in corporate bonds and other types of lower-risk instruments. The following data (stored in the file trsnyc.xls) represent the value of a unit of each type of variable return investment at the beginning of each year from 1984 to 2006:

Year	A	B	Year	A	B
1984	13.111	10.342	1996	39.644	17.682
1985	13.176	11.073	1997	45.389	18.004
1986	16.526	11.925	1998	54.882	18.341
1987	18.652	12.694	1999	64.790	18.678
1988	15.564	13.352	2000	74.220	18.962
1989	20.827	13.919	2001	67.534	19.320
1990	24.738	14.557	2002	57.709	19.673
1991	22.678	15.213	2003	44.843	19.735
1992	28.549	15.883	2004	55.993	19.609
1993	29.829	16.510	2005	60.909	19.520
1994	32.199	16.970	2006	63.038	19.452
1995	30.830	17.351			

Source: Teachers' Retirement System of the City of New York, **www.trs.nyc.ny.us**.

For each of the two time series,
a. plot the data.
b. compute the linear trend forecasting equation.
c. compute the quadratic trend forecasting equation.

d. compute the exponential trend forecasting equation.
e. find the best-fitting autoregressive model, using $\alpha = 0.05$.
f. Perform a residual analysis for each of the models in (b) through (e).
g. Compute the standard error of the estimate (S_{YX}) and the *MAD* for each corresponding model in (f).
h. On the basis of your results in (f) and (g), along with a consideration of the principle of parsimony, which model would you select for purposes of forecasting? Discuss.
i. Using the selected model in (h), forecast the unit values for 2007.
j. Based on the results of (a) through (i), what investment strategy would you recommend for a member of the Teachers' Retirement System of the City of New York? Explain.

75 The data file basket.xls contains the prices of a basket of food items from 1992 to 2006. Included are the prices (in dollars) for a one-pound loaf of white bread, a pound of beef (ground chuck), a dozen grade A large eggs, and one pound of iceberg lettuce:

Year	Bread	Beef	Eggs	Lettuce
1992	0.726	1.926	0.933	0.573
1993	0.748	1.970	0.898	0.625
1994	0.768	1.892	0.917	0.506
1995	0.767	1.847	0.882	0.821
1996	0.860	1.799	1.155	0.769
1997	0.862	1.850	1.148	0.651
1998	0.855	1.818	1.120	1.072
1999	0.872	1.834	1.053	0.649
2000	0.907	1.903	0.975	0.748
2001	0.982	2.037	1.011	0.736
2002	1.001	2.151	0.973	1.003
2003	1.042	2.131	1.175	0.734
2004	0.946	2.585	1.573	0.876
2005	0.997	2.478	1.211	0.817
2006	1.046	2.607	1.449	0.874

Source: Bureau of Labor Statistics, U.S. Department of Labor, **www.bls.gov**.

a. Compute the 1992–2006 simple price indexes for bread, beef, eggs, and lettuce, using 1992 as the base year.
b. Recalculate the price indexes in (a), using 1996 as the base year.
c. Compute the 1992–2006 unweighted aggregate price indexes for the basket of these four food items.
d. Compute the 2006 Laspeyres price index for the basket of these four food items for a family that consumed 50 loaves of bread, 22 pounds of beef, 24 dozen eggs, and 18 pounds of lettuce in 1992.
e. Compute the 2006 Paasche price index for the basket of these four food items for a family that consumed 55 loaves of bread, 17 pounds of beef, 20 dozen eggs, and 28 pounds of lettuce in 2006.

Report Writing Exercises

76 As a consultant to an investment company trading in various currencies, you have been assigned the task of studying the long-term trends in the exchange rates of the Canadian dollar, the Japanese yen, and the English pound. Data have been collected for the 39-year period from 1967 to 2005 and are contained in the file `currency.xls`, where the Canadian dollar, the Japanese yen, and the English pound are expressed in units per U.S. dollar.

Develop a forecasting model for the exchange rate of each of these three currencies and provide forecasts for 2006 and 2007 for each currency. Write an executive summary for a presentation to be given to the investment company. Append to this executive summary a discussion regarding possible limitations that may exist in these models.

Managing the *Springville Herald*

As part of the continuing strategic initiative to increase home-delivery subscriptions, the circulation department is closely monitoring the number of such subscriptions. The circulation department wants to forecast future home-delivery subscriptions. To accomplish this task, the circulation department compiled the number of home-delivery subscriptions for the most recent 24-month period in the file `sh.xls`.

EXERCISE

SH1 **a.** Analyze these data and develop a model to forecast home-delivery subscriptions. Present your findings in a report that includes the assumptions of the model and its limitations. Forecast home-delivery subscriptions for the next four months.

b. Would you be willing to use the model developed to forecast home-delivery subscriptions one year into the future? Explain.

c. Compare the trend in home-delivery subscriptions to the number of new subscriptions per month provided in the data file `sh.xls`. What explanation can you provide for any differences?

Web Case

Apply your knowledge about time-series forecasting in this Web Case on "Managing the Springville Herald."

The *Springville Herald* competes for readers in the Tri-Cities area with the newer *Oxford Glen Journal* (*OGJ*). Recently, the circulation staff at the *OGJ* claimed that their newspaper's circulation and subscription base is growing faster than that of the *Herald* and that local advertisers would do better transferring their advertisements from the *Herald* to the *OGJ*. The circulation department of the *Herald* has complained to the Springville Chamber of Commerce about *OGJ*'s claims and has asked the chamber to investigate, a request that was welcomed by *OGJ*'s circulation staff.

Review the circulation dispute information collected by the Springville Chamber of Commerce about the circulation dispute at the Web page, **www.prenhall.com/**

Springville/SCC_CirculationDispute.htm, (or open this Web page file from the Student CD-ROM's Web Case folder) and then answer the following:

1. Which newspaper would you say has the right to claim the fastest-growing circulation and subscription base? Support your answer by performing and summarizing an appropriate statistical analysis.

2. What is the single most positive fact about the *Herald*'s circulation and subscription base? What is the single most positive fact about the *OGJ*'s circulation and subscription base? Explain your answers.

3. What additional data would be helpful in investigating the circulation claims made by the staffs of each newspaper?

REFERENCES

1. Bowerman, B. L., R. T. O'Connell, and A. Koehler, *Forecasting, Time Series, and Regression*, 4th ed. (Belmont, CA: Duxbury Press, 2005).

2. Box, G. E. P., G. M. Jenkins, and G. C. Reinsel, *Time Series Analysis: Forecasting and Control*, 3rd ed. (Upper Saddle River, NJ: Prentice Hall, 1994).

3. Frees, E. W., *Data Analysis Using Regression Models: The Business Perspective* (Upper Saddle River, NJ: Prentice Hall, 1996).

4. Hanke, J. E., D. W. Wichern, and A. G. Reitsch, *Business Forecasting*, 7th ed. (Upper Saddle River, NJ: Prentice Hall, 2001).

5. *Microsoft Excel 2007* (Redmond, WA: Microsoft Corp., 2007).

Excel Companion

E1 COMPUTING MOVING AVERAGES

You compute moving averages by adding a column of formulas to your data worksheet. Open to the worksheet that contains time-series data. In a blank column, enter formulas that use the AVERAGE function to average values in the cell range that matches your chosen period of length L. Enter ranges such that each formula is located in the middle row of the cell range that the formula averages. Then enter the special value #N/A in the cells at the beginning and end of the column for which no moving average can be calculated.

For example, to create three-year and seven-year moving averages for the Cabot Corporation revenue data, open to the **Data** worksheet of the CABOT.xls workbook and make entries in the blank columns C and D. Figure E1 shows the entries for the first four and last four data rows of these columns and illustrates how the special value #N/A is used at the beginning and end of a moving average column.

	A	B	C	D
1	Year	Revenue	MA 3-Year	MA 7-Year
2	1982	1588	#N/A	#N/A
3	1983	1558	=AVERAGE(B2:B4)	#N/A
4	1984	1753	=AVERAGE(B3:B5)	#N/A
5	1985	1408	=AVERAGE(B4:B6)	=AVERAGE(B2:B8)
22	2002	1557	=AVERAGE(B21:B23)	=AVERAGE(B19:B25)
23	2003	1795	=AVERAGE(B22:B24)	#N/A
24	2004	1934	=AVERAGE(B23:B25)	#N/A
25	2005	2125	#N/A	#N/A

FIGURE E1 Moving averages columns (rows 6 through 21 not shown)

E2 CREATING TIME-SERIES PLOTS

You create time-series plots by using Excel charting features. Open to the worksheet that contains your time-series data. The column representing the time periods must be the first column of this worksheet. Then use Excel charting features to create the time-series plot.

Creating a Time-Series Plot (97–2003)

With your workbook open to the time-series data worksheet, begin the Chart Wizard and make the following entries and choices in the step dialog boxes:

Step 1 Click **XY (Scatter)** from the **Standard Types Chart type** box. Click the first choice of the third row in the **Chart sub-types** gallery, described as **Scatter with data points connected by lines**.

Step 2 Click the **Data range** tab. Enter the cell range of the data to be plotted as the **Data range** and select the **Columns** option. For example, for the modified Data worksheet shown in Figure E1, you would enter **A1:D25** as the **Data Range** to plot the revenues and the two moving averages on one chart.

Step 3 Click the **Titles** tab. Enter a title as the **Chart** title, and appropriate values for the **Value (Y) axis** title and **Year** as the **Value (X) axis** title. Click the **Legend** tab and click **Show legend**. Click, in turn, the **Axes, Gridlines**, and **Data Labels** tabs and use the formatting settings given in the "Creating Charts (97–2003)" part of Section E2 of "Presenting Data in Tables and Charts."

Creating a Time-Series Plot (2007)

With your workbook open to the time-series data worksheet, select the cell range of the original data and the moving-average data. If you were using the worksheet shown in Figure E1, you would select **A1:D25**. Then select **Insert → (Scatter)** and click the **Scatter with Straight Lines and Markers** gallery choice. Finish by relocating your chart to a chart sheet. Customize your chart by using the instructions in "Creating Charts (2007)" in Section E2 of "Presenting Data in Tables and Charts."

E3 CREATING EXPONENTIALLY SMOOTHED VALUES

You create exponentially smoothed values by using the ToolPak Exponential Smoothing procedure.

Open to the worksheet that contains your time-series data, with each row representing a time period. Select **Tools → Data Analysis** (97–2003) or **Data → Data Analysis** (2007) and then select **Exponential Smoothing** from the Data Analysis list and click **OK**. In the Exponential Smoothing dialog box (shown on page 703), enter the cell range of the time-series variable to be smoothed as the **Input Range**. Because the damping factor is $1 - W$, enter either **0.5** (for $W = 0.50$) or **0.75** (for $W = 0.25$) as the **damping factor**. Click **Labels**, enter the output column cell range to hold the smoothed values as the **Output Range**, and click **OK**. The column cell range should begin with row 2 so as to leave the row 1 cell blank. After the procedure creates the column, enter a column heading in the row 1 cell.

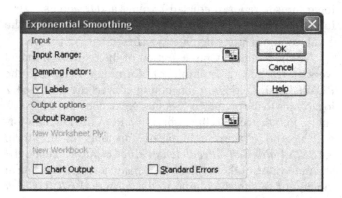

The new column contains exponentially smoothed values for each time period that are incorrectly displayed a row below their proper time periods. To adjust the column so that the exponentially smoothed values appear in the proper (same time period) rows, right-click the **row 2 cell** in that column and select **Delete** from the shortcut menu. In the Delete dialog box, select the **Shift cells up** option and click **OK**. Then copy the formula in the second-to-last cell of the column down to the last cell.

E4 CREATING CODED *X* VARIABLES

To create a coded *X* variable, add a new column that contains an integer series starting with zero to your time-series data. In a blank column, enter a column label in the row 1 cell and the first integer in the series in the row 2 cell. Automate the entry of the other integers by reselecting the row 2 cell and selecting **Edit → Fill → Series** (Excel 97–2003) or **Home → Fill → Series** (Excel 2007). In the Series dialog box (shown below), select the **Columns** and

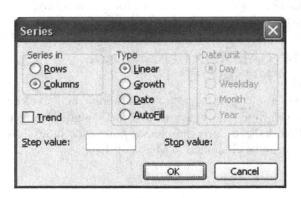

Linear options, enter the appropriate **Step value** and **Stop value**, and click **OK**. For example, enter **1** as the **Step value** and **23** as the **Stop value** to complete the 24-integer series 0 through 23.

E5 CREATING QUADRATIC AND EXPONENTIAL TERMS

See Sections E1 and E2 in the Excel Companion to "Multiple Regression Model Building" to review the methods for adding quadratic and exponential terms.

E6 USING LEAST-SQUARES LINEAR TREND FITTING

Use the "Simple Linear Regression," Section E1 instructions, but use the cell range of the coded variable as the *X* variable cell range.

E7 USING LEAST-SQUARES QUADRATIC TREND FITTING

Use the "Introduction to Multiple Regression," Section E1 instructions, but use the cell range of the coded variable and the squared coded variable as the *X* variable cell range. Use the "Multiple Regression Model Building," Section E1 instructions to create a column of squared coded variables.

E8 USING LEAST-SQUARES EXPONENTIAL TREND FITTING

Use the "Simple Linear Regression," Section E1 instructions, but use the cell range of the log *Y* values as the *Y* variable cell range and the cell range of the coded variable as the *X* variable cell range.

E9 CREATING LAGGED INDEPENDENT VARIABLES

To create lagged independent variables, open to the worksheet that contains your time-series data. For each lagged independent variable you want to add, use a blank column and enter formulas that refer to a previous row's (that is, previous time period's) *Y* value. Place the special value **#N/A** (not available) in the cells in the column for which lagged values do not apply.

For example, Figure E2 shows the first five rows and the last row of the worksheet shown in Figure 14 that contains lagged independent variables for the first-order, second-order, and third-order autoregressive models. Because

FIGURE E2 Lagged independent variables

cells C2, D2, D3, E2, E3, and E4, do not have lagged values, the value **#N/A** has been entered into those cells.

E10 CREATING FIRST-ORDER AUTOREGRESSIVE MODELS

Use the "Simple Linear Regression," Section E1 instructions but use the cell range of the first-order lagged variable as the X variable cell range. If using PHStat2, *do not* click **First cells in both ranges contain label**. If using the ToolPak procedure, *do not* click **Labels**.

E11 CREATING SECOND-ORDER OR THIRD-ORDER AUTOREGRESSIVE MODELS

Use the "Introduction to Multiple Regression," Section E1 instructions but use the cell range of the lagged variables as the X variable cell range. Use the cell range of the first-order and second-order lagged variables for a second-order model and use the cell range of the first-order, second-order, and third-order lagged variables for the third-order model. If using PHStat2, *do not* click **First cells in both ranges contain label**. If using the ToolPak procedure, *do not* click **Labels**.

E12 COMPUTING THE MEAN ABSOLUTE DEVIATION (MAD)

For a Linear, Quadratic, or Autoregressive Model

Begin by performing a regression analysis, making sure to select the residuals check box. Then, from the regression results worksheet, copy the residual values found in column C of the Residual Output section to a blank column on the worksheet that contains the regression data. Add a column of formulas in the form =*ABS(residual cell)* to calculate the absolute value of the residuals. Then

add a single formula in the form =*AVERAGE(cell range of residual absolute values)* to calculate the *MAD*.

For an Exponential Model

Begin by creating the exponential regression results worksheet with residuals. The model results will use base 10 logarithms to report predicted Y values and residuals. These logarithms will need to be converted to original units of the Y values in order to calculate the *MAD*.

To the Residual Output section of the regression model worksheet, add a column of formulas that use the **POWER(10, *LogValue*)** function to convert the predicted Y logarithms to the predicted Y values. Next, copy the original Y values into the cells to the right of the POWER function formulas. Add a third column of formulas in the form =*ABS(YValueCell - PredictedYValueCell)* to calculate the absolute value of the residuals. Then add a single formula at the end of this third column in the form =*AVERAGE(cell range of residual absolute values)* to calculate the *MAD*.

E13 CREATING DUMMY VARIABLES FOR QUARTERLY OR MONTHLY DATA

You create dummy variables for quarterly or monthly data by adding columns of formulas that use the **IF(*comparison, value if comparison is true, value to use if comparison is false*)** function.

Figure E3 shows the first four rows of columns F through K of a data worksheet that contains dummy variables. Columns F, G, and H contain the quarterly dummy variables Q1, Q2, and Q3 that are based on column B coded quarter values (not shown). Columns J and K contain the two monthly variables, M1 and M6, that are based on column C month values (also not shown).

FIGURE E3 Dummy variables for quarterly and monthly data

E14 CALCULATING INDEX NUMBERS

Open the **Index Numbers.xls** workbook and explore the **Unweighted Aggregate PI** and the **Weighted Aggregate PI** worksheets for examples of how price index calculations can be computed in Microsoft Excel.

Self-Test Solutions and Answers to Selected Even-Numbered Problems

The following represent worked-out solutions to Self-Test Problems and brief answers to most of the even-numbered problems in the text.

2 (a) 1959. **(b)** The first four years and the last four years.

4 (b), (c), and (d)

Year	Attendance	MA(3)	ES (W = 0.5)	ES (W = 0.25)
1999	1.47		1.4700	1.4700
2000	1.42	1.4600	1.4450	1.4575
2001	1.49	1.5133	1.4675	1.4656
2002	1.63	1.5633	1.5488	1.5067
2003	1.57	1.5767	1.5594	1.5225
2004	1.53	1.5033	1.5447	1.5244
2005	1.41		1.4773	1.4958

6 (b), (c), and (d)

Week	Nasdaq	MA (3)	ES(W = 0.50)	ES(W = 0.25)
3-Jan-06	2305.62	#N/A	2305.62	2305.62
9-Jan-06	2317.04	2290.12	2311.33	2308.48
17-Jan-06	2247.70	2289.66	2279.52	2293.28
23-Jan-06	2304.23	2271.50	2291.87	2296.02
30-Jan-06	2262.58	2276.23	2277.23	2287.66
6-Feb-06	2261.88	2268.94	2269.55	2281.21
13-Feb-06	2282.36	2277.09	2275.96	2281.50
21-Feb-06	2287.04	2290.67	2281.50	2282.89
27-Feb-06	2302.60	2283.89	2292.05	2287.81
6-Mar-06	2262.04	2290.37	2277.04	2281.37
13-Mar-06	2306.48	2293.78	2291.76	2287.65

Week	Nasdaq	MA (3)	ES(W = 0.50)	ES(W = 0.25)
20-Mar-06	2312.82	2319.70	2302.29	2293.94
27-Mar-06	2339.79	2330.54	2321.04	2305.40
3-Apr-06	2339.02	2334.97	2330.03	2313.81
10-Apr-06	2326.11	2336.00	2328.07	2316.88
17-Apr-06	2342.86	2330.51	2335.47	2323.38
24-Apr-06	2322.57	2336.00	2329.02	2323.18
1-May-06	2342.57	2302.97	2335.79	2328.02
8-May-06	2243.78	2260.08	2289.79	2306.96
15-May-06	2193.88	#N/A	2241.83	2278.69

(e) There appears to be very little trend in the first 20 weeks of 2006.

8 (b), (c), and (e)

Year	Cost	MA(3)	ES (W = 0.5)	ES (W = 0.25)
1994–1995	8.16		8.16	8.16
1995–1996	8.10	8.14	8.13	8.15
1996–1997	8.17	8.13	8.15	8.15

Year	Cost	MA(3)	ES (W = 0.5)	ES (W = 0.25)
1997–1998	8.12	8.08	8.14	8.14
1998–1999	7.94	8.01	8.04	8.09
1999–2000	7.98	8.01	8.01	8.06
2000–2001	8.11	8.15	8.06	8.08
2001–2002	8.37	8.23	8.21	8.15
2002–2003	8.20	8.35	8.21	8.16
2003–2004	8.49	8.49	8.35	8.24
2004–2005	8.78		8.56	8.38

(d) $W = 0.5$: $\hat{Y}_{2005-2006} = E_{2004-2005} = 8.56$. **(e)** $W = 0.25$ $Y_{2005-2006} = E_{2004-2005} = 8.38$. **(f)** The exponentially smoothed forecast for 2005–2006 with $W = 0.5$ is higher than that with $W = 0.25$.

10 (a) The Y intercept $b_0 = 4.0$ is the fitted trend value reflecting the real total revenues (in millions of dollars) during the origin or base year 1985. **(b)** The slope $b_1 = 1.5$ indicates that the real total revenues are increasing at an estimated rate of $1.5 million per year. **(c)** Year is 1989, $X = 1989 - 1985 = 4$ $\hat{Y}_5 = 4.0 + 1.5(4) = 10.0$ million dollars. **(d)** Year is 2006, $X = 2006 - 1985 = 21$, $\hat{Y}_{20} = 4.0 + 1.5(21) = 35.5$ million dollars. **(e)** Year is 2009, $X = 2009 - 1985 = 24$ $Y_{23} = 4.0 + 1.5(24) = 40$ million dollars.

12 (b) There was an upward trend in the CPI in the United States over the 41-year period. The rate of increase became faster in the late 1970s and mid-1980s, but the rate of increase tapered off in the early 1980s and early 1990s.

14 (b) $\hat{Y} = 317.7193 + 64.3897X$, where $X =$ years relative to 1978. **(c)** $2,056.2407 billion for 2005 and $2,120.6304 billion for 2006. **(d)** There was an upward trend in federal receipts between 1978 and 2004. The trend appears to be nonlinear. A quadratic trend or exponential trend model could be explored.

16 (b) Linear trend: $\hat{Y} = 1.1556 + 0.7273X$, where X is relative to 1975. **(c)** Quadratic trend: $\hat{Y} = 2.1731 + 0.5168X + 0.0070X^2$, where X is relative to 1975. **(d)** Exponential trend: $\log_{10} \hat{Y} = 0.5452 + 0.0304X$, where X is relative to 1975. **(e)** Linear trend: $23.7006 billion for 2006 and $24.4279 billion for 2007. Quadratic trend: $24.9356 billion for 2006 and $25.8944 billion for 2007. Exponential trend: $30.8320 billion for 2006 and $33.0711 billion for 2007.

18 (b) Linear trend: $\hat{Y} = -3.2919 + 2.2245X$, where X is relative to 1987. **(c)** Quadratic trend: $\hat{Y} = -2.8475 + 2.0764X + 0.0078X^2$, where X is relative to 1987. **(d)** Exponential trend: $\log_{10} \hat{Y} = 0.3318 + 0.0752X$, where X is relative to 1987. **(e)** Investigating the first, second, and percentage differences suggests that the linear and quadratic trend models have about the same fit, while the exponential trend model seems to fit the early years' data better. **(f)** Using the exponential trend model, the prediction for January 1, 2007, is 68.6460.

20 (a) For Time Series I, the graph of Y vs. X appears to be more linear than the graph of log Y vs. X, so a linear model appears to be more appropriate. For Time Series II, the graph of log Y vs. X appears to be more linear than the graph of Y vs. X, so an exponential model appears to be more appropriate. **(b)** Time Series I: $\hat{Y} = 100.082 + 14.9752X$, where X = years relative to 1997. Time Series II: $\hat{Y} = 99.704(1.1501)^X$, where X = years relative to 1997. **(c)** Forecasts for the year 2007: Time Series I: 249.834, Time Series II: 403.709.

22 (b) Linear trend: $\hat{Y} = -88.9143 + 60.7670X$, where X is relative to 1993. **(c)** Quadratic trend: $\hat{Y} = 44.2107 - 5.7955X + 5.1202X^2$, where X is relative to 1993. **(d)** Exponential trend: $\log_{10} \hat{Y} = 1.5906 + 0.1083X$, where X is relative to 1993. **(e)** Linear trend: $\hat{Y}_{2007} = -88.9143 + 60.7670(14) = 761.82 = 762$ stores, $\hat{Y}_{2008} = -88.9143 + 60.7670(15) = 822.59 = 822$ stores. Quadratic trend: $\hat{Y}_{2007} = 44.2107 - 5.7955(14) + 5.1202(14)^2 = 966.63 = 967$ stores, $\hat{Y}_{2008} = 44.2107 - 5.7955(15) + 5.1202(15)^2 = 1109.32 = 1109$ stores. Exponential trend: 2007: $\log_{10} \hat{Y} = 1.5906 + 0.1083(14) = 1{,}278.79$ stores. 2008: $\log_{10} \hat{Y} = 1.5906 + 0.1083(15) = 1{,}640.97$ stores. **(f)** Both the quadratic trend model and the exponential trend model are capable of capturing the increasing rate of growth of the number of stores open. The rate of growth estimated by the exponential trend model is the highest, followed by the quadratic trend model, and finally the linear trend model. The quadratic trend model appears to be tracking the growth rate of the real data more closely than the exponential trend model, so it should be used to forecast the number of stores open for 2007 and 2008.

24 $t = 2.40 > 2.2281$; reject H_0.

26 (a) $t = 1.60 < 2.2281$; do not reject H_0.

28 (a)

	Coefficients	Standard Error	t Stat	p-Value
Intercept	0.466403278	0.306356098	1.522422045	0.14097168
YLag1	1.317428641	0.20587346	6.399215533	1.28746E-06
YLag2	−0.332888609	0.332080298	−1.002434084	0.326134451
YLag3	0.017904368	0.206925767	0.086525562	0.931766483

Since the p-value = 0.9318 > 0.05 level of significance, the third order term can be dropped.
(b)

	Coefficients	Standard Error	t Stat	p-Value
Intercept	0.457509354	0.273531737	1.672600622	0.106398594
YLag1	1.312968152	0.18697971	7.02198195	1.86248E-07
YLag2	−0.310579599	0.189251728	−1.641092544	0.112821589

Since the p-value = 0.1128 > 0.05 level of significance, the second order term can be dropped.
(c)

	Coefficients	Standard Error	t Stat	p-Value
Intercept	0.548034694	0.252114387	2.173754149	0.038334876
YLag1	1.010712337	0.018891696	53.50034886	9.62708E-30

Since the p-value is virtually 0, the first-order term cannot be dropped. **(d)** The most appropriate model for forecasting is the first-order autoregressive model: $\hat{Y}_i = 0.5480 + 1.0107Y_{i=1}$. The forecasts are 23.8955 for 2006 and 24.6995 for 2007.

30 (a) Since the p-value = 0.4933 > 0.05 level of significance, the third-order term can be dropped. **(b)** Since the p-value = 0.1447 > 0.05 level of significance, the second-order term can be dropped. **(c)** Since the p-value is virtually 0, the first-order term cannot be dropped. **(d)** The most appropriate model for forecasting is the first-order autoregressive model. $\hat{Y}_i = 2.9753 + 0.9255 \hat{Y}_{i-1}$ The forecast is 35.1734 for 2007.

32 (a) 2.121. **(b)** 1.50.

34 (a) The residuals in the linear trend model show strings of consecutive positive and negative values. **(b)** $S_{YX} = 343.7342$. **(c)** $MAD = 267.1189$. **(d)** The residuals in the linear trend model show strings of consecutive positive and negative values. The linear trend model is inadequate in capturing the nonlinear trend.

36 (a) The residuals in the three trend models show strings of consecutive positive and negative values. The autoregressive model performs well for the historical data and has a fairly random pattern of residuals. The autoregressive model also has the smallest values in MAD and S_{YX}. **(b)** $S_{YX} = 1.3476$ for linear, 1.266 for quadratic, 2.181 for exponential, and 0.66 for first-order autoregressive. **(c)** $MAD = 1.073$ for linear, 0.95 for quadratic, 1.446 for exponential, and 0.468 for first-order autoregressive. **(d)** The autoregressive model would be the best model for forecasting.

38 (a) The residuals in the linear and quadratic trend models show strings of consecutive positive and negative values. The exponential trend model and the autoregressive model perform well for the historical data and have a fairly random pattern of residuals. **(b)** $S_{YX} = 7.6494$ for linear, 7.8672 for quadratic, 10.9752 for exponential, and 6.0344 for first-order autoregressive. **(c)** $MAD = 5.6777$ for linear, 5.6278 for quadratic, 6.7902 for exponential, and 4.3166 for first-order autoregressive. **(d)** Since the autoregressive model has the smallest values in MAD and S_{YX}, the autoregressive model would be the best model for forecasting.

40 (a) $\log \hat{\beta}_0 = 2$, $\hat{\beta}_0 = 10^2 = 100$. This is the fitted value for January 2000 prior to adjustment with the January multiplier. **(b)** $\log \hat{\beta}_1 = 0.01$, $\hat{\beta}_1 = 10^{0.01} = 1.0233$. The estimated average monthly compound growth rate is $(\hat{\beta}_1 - 1)100\% = 2.33\%$. **(c)** $\log \hat{\beta}_2 = 0.1$, $\hat{\beta}_2 = 10^{0.1} = 1.2589$. The January values in the time series are estimated to have a mean 25.89% higher than the December values.

16.42 (a) $\log \hat{\beta}_0 = 3.0$, $\hat{\beta}_0 = 10^{3.0} = 1{,}000$. This is the fitted value for January 2002 prior to adjustment by the quarterly multiplier. **(b)** $\log \hat{\beta}_1 = 0.1$, $\hat{\beta}_1 = 10^{0.1} = 1.2589$. The estimated average quarterly compound growth rate is $(\hat{\beta}_1 - 1)100\% = 25.89\%$. **(c)** $\log \hat{\beta}_3 = 0.2$, $\hat{\beta}_3 = 10^{0.2} = 1.5849$. The second-quarter values in the time series are estimated to have a mean 58.49% higher than the fourth-quarter values.

44 (b) $\log_{10} \hat{Y} = 2.8008 + 0.0077X - 0.0081Q_1 - 0.0011Q_2 - 0.0201Q_3$. **(c)** $\hat{Y}_{47} = 1362.3019$. **(d)** $\hat{Y}_{48} = 1452.4343$. **(e)** 2006: $\hat{Y}_{49} = 1450.9373$; $\hat{Y}_{50} = 1500.8344$; $\hat{Y}_{51} = 1462.2459$; $\hat{Y}_{52} = 1558.9907$. **(f)** The estimated quarterly compound growth rate is 1.79%. **(g)** The second-quarter values in the time series are estimated to have a mean 0.26% below the fourth-quarter values.

46 (b)

$$\log \hat{Y} = 0.6443 + 0.00178X + 0.00507M_1 + 0.00776M_2 + 0.00304M_3$$
$$+ 0.00034M_4 + 0.00187M_5 + 0.00429M_6 + 0.00164M_7$$
$$+ 0.00099M_8 - 5.20067 \times 10^{-5}M_9 - 0.00171M_{10} + 0.00194M_{11}$$

(c) $\hat{Y}_{72} = 5.90\%$. (d) Forecasts for all 12 months of 2006 are 5.991%, 6.053%, 6.012%, 6.0%, 6.046%, 6.104%, 6.092%, 6.108%, 6.118%, 6.12%, 6.197%, and 6.195%.
(e) $\log_{10} \hat{\beta}_1 = 0.00178$, $\hat{\beta}_1 = 10^{0.00178} = 1.0041$. The estimated quarterly compound growth rate is $(\hat{\beta}_1 - 1)100\% = 0.41\%$.
(f) $\log_{10} \hat{\beta}_8 = 0.00164$. $\hat{\beta}_8 = 10^{0.00164} = 1.0038$. $(\hat{\beta}_8 - 1)100\% = 0.38\%$. The July values in the time series are estimated to have a mean 0.38% above the December values.

48 (a) The retail industry is heavily subject to seasonal variation due to the holiday seasons, and so are the revenues for Toys Я Us.
(b) There is an obvious seasonal effect in the time series.
(c) $\log_{10} \hat{Y} = 3.6435 + 0.0020X - 0.3789Q_1 - 0.3846Q_2 - 0.3525Q_3$.
(d) The estimated quarterly compound growth rate is 0.46%
(e) $\log_{10} \hat{\beta}_2 = -0.3789$. $\hat{\beta}_2 = 10^{-0.3789} = 0.4179$. $(\hat{\beta}_2 - 1)100\% = -58.21\%$. The first-quarter values in the time series are estimated to have a mean 58.21% below the fourth-quarter values. $\log_{10} \hat{\beta}_3 = -0.3846$. $\hat{\beta}_3 = 10^{-0.3846} = 0.4124$. $(\hat{\beta}_3 - 1)100\% = -58.76\%$. The second-quarter values in the time series are estimated to have a mean 58.76% below the fourth-quarter values. $\log_{10} \hat{\beta}_4 = -0.3525$. $\hat{\beta}_4 = 10^{-0.3525} = 0.4441$. $(\hat{\beta}_4 - 1)100\% = -55.59\%$. The third-quarter values in the time series are estimated to have a mean 55.59% below the fourth-quarter values. (f) Forecasts for 2006: $\hat{Y}_{41} = \$2,209.4155$ millions; $\hat{Y}_{42} = \$2,190.6572$ millions; $\hat{Y}_{43} = \$2,369.9104$ millions; $\hat{Y}_{44} = \$5,360.4578$ millions.

50 The price of the commodity in 2006 was 75% higher than in 1995.

52 (a) 186.96. (b) 162.16. (c) 154.42.

54 (a) and (c)

Year	Price	Price Index (base = 1980)	Price Index (base = 1990)	Year	Price	Price Index (base = 1980)	Price Index (base = 1990)
1980	3.208	100.00	109.98	1994	2.53	78.87	86.73
1981	2.777	86.56	95.20	1995	4.398	137.09	150.77
1982	2.475	77.15	84.85	1996	3.577	111.50	122.63
1983	2.528	78.80	86.66	1997	3.3	102.87	113.13
1984	2.495	77.77	85.53	1998	4.025	125.47	137.98
1985	2.585	80.58	88.62	1999	3.435	107.08	117.76
1986	2.737	85.32	93.83	2000	3.54	110.35	121.36
1987	3.192	99.50	109.43	2001	3.224	100.50	110.52
1988	2.635	82.14	90.33	2002	2.936	91.52	100.65
1989	2.964	92.39	101.61	2003	2.999	93.49	102.81
1990	2.917	90.93	100.00	2004	2.892	90.15	99.14
1991	2.945	91.80	100.96	2005	3.049	95.04	104.53
1992	2.668	83.17	91.46	2006	3.232	100.75	110.80
1993	2.352	73.32	80.63				

(b) The price of coffee in 2006 was 0.75% higher than it was in 1980.
(d) The price of coffee in 2006 was 10.80% higher than it was in 1990.
(e) It would not be a good idea to use 1995 as the base year because that was when the coffee price was at its peak. (f) There was a slight upward trend in coffee costs from 1980 to 2006, with a prominent cyclical component.

56 (a)

Year	Electricity	Natural Gas	Fuel Oil	Electricity Price Index (base = 1992)	Natural Gas Price Index (base = 1992)	Fuel Oil Price Index (base = 1992)
1992	44.501	26.376	0.985	100.00	100.00	100.00
1993	16.959	28.749	0.969	38.11	109.00	98.38
1994	48.200	30.236	0.919	108.31	114.63	93.30
1995	48.874	29.872	0.913	109.83	113.25	92.69
1996	48.538	29.570	1.007	109.07	112.11	102.23
1997	49.245	32.904	1.136	110.66	124.75	115.33
1998	46.401	31.438	0.966	104.27	119.19	98.07
1999	45.061	30.699	0.834	101.26	116.39	84.67
2000	45.207	31.664	1.189	101.59	120.05	120.71
2001	47.472	49.734	1.509	106.68	188.56	153.20
2002	47.868	36.316	1.123	107.57	137.69	114.01
2003	47.663	40.227	1.396	107.11	152.51	141.73
2004	49.159	46.048	1.508	110.47	174.58	153.10
2005	50.847	50.932	1.859	114.26	193.10	188.73
2006	57.223	66.402	2.418	128.59	251.75	245.48

(b)

Year	Electricity	Natural Gas	Fuel Oil	Electricity Price Index (base = 1996)	Natural Gas Price Index (base = 1996)	Fuel Oil Price Index (base = 1996)
1992	44.501	26.376	0.985	91.68	89.20	97.82
1993	16.959	28.749	0.969	34.94	97.22	96.23
1994	48.200	30.236	0.919	99.30	102.25	91.26
1995	48.874	29.872	0.913	100.69	101.02	90.67
1996	48.538	29.570	1.007	100.00	100.00	100.00
1997	49.245	32.904	1.136	101.46	111.27	112.81
1998	46.401	31.438	0.966	95.60	106.32	95.93
1999	45.061	30.699	0.834	92.84	103.82	82.82
2000	45.207	31.664	1.189	93.14	107.08	118.07
2001	47.472	49.734	1.509	97.80	168.19	149.85
2002	47.868	36.316	1.123	98.62	122.81	111.52
2003	47.663	40.227	1.396	98.20	136.04	138.63
2004	49.159	46.048	1.508	101.28	155.73	149.75
2005	50.847	50.932	1.859	104.76	172.24	184.61
2006	57.223	66.402	2.418	117.89	224.56	240.12

(c)

Year	Electricity	Natural Gas	Fuel Oil	Unweighted
1992	44.501	26.376	0.985	100.00
1993	16.959	28.749	0.969	64.95
1994	48.200	30.236	0.919	110.43
1995	48.874	29.872	0.913	110.85
1996	48.538	29.570	1.007	110.09
1997	49.245	32.904	1.136	115.90
1998	46.401	31.438	0.966	109.66
1999	45.061	30.699	0.834	106.58
2000	45.207	31.664	1.189	108.62
2001	47.472	49.734	1.509	137.37
2002	47.868	36.316	1.123	118.71
2003	47.663	40.227	1.396	124.25
2004	49.159	46.048	1.508	134.58
2005	50.847	50.932	1.859	144.22
2006	57.223	66.402	2.418	175.40

(d) 212.84 **(e)** 203.15.

70 (b) Linear trend: $\hat{Y} = 174778.8261 + 2335.3845X$, where X is relative to 1984. **(c)** 2006: 226,157.2857 thousands. 2007: 228,492.6702 thousands. **(d) (b)** Linear trend: $\hat{Y} = 114660.249 + 1655.0282X$, where X is relative to 1984. **(c)** 2006: 151,070.8701 thousands. 2007: 152,725.8984 thousands.

72 (b) Linear trend: $\hat{Y} = -1.3448 + 0.6075X$, where X is relative to 1975. **(c)** Quadratic trend: $\hat{Y} = 1.3856 + 0.0426X + 0.0188X^2$, where X is relative to 1975. **(d)** Exponential trend: $\log_{10} \hat{Y} = 0.1305 + 0.0414X$, where X is relative to 1975. **(e)** AR(3): $\hat{Y}_i = 0.1545 + 1.3742Y_{i-1} - 0.6504Y_{i-2} + 0.3444Y_{i-3}$. Test of A_3: p-value = 0.1373 > 0.05. Do not reject H_0 that $A_3 = 0$. Third-order term can be deleted. AR(2): $\hat{Y}_i = 0.1096 + 1.3021Y_{i-1} - 0.2490Y_{i-2}$. Test of A_2: p-value = 0.2341 > 0.05. Do not reject H_0 that $A_2 = 0$. Second-order term can be deleted. AR(1): $\hat{Y}_i = 0.1349 + 1.0702Y_{i-1}$. Test of A_1: p-value is virtually 0. Reject H_0 that $A_1 = 0$. A first-order autoregressive model is appropriate. **(f)** The residuals in the first three models show strings of consecutive positive and negative values. The autoregressive model performs well for the historical data and has a fairly random pattern of residuals. **(g)** S_{YX} is 1.4471 for the linear model, 0.4064 for the quadratic model, 1.0848 for the exponential model, and 0.3149 for the first-order autoregressive model. MAD is 1.1324 for the linear model, 0.2868 for the quadratic model, 0.6795 for the exponential model, and 0.2013 for the first-order autoregressive model. **(h)** The autoregressive model is the best model for forecasting because it has the smallest values in the standard error of the estimate and MAD. **(i)** 22.0729 billions.

74 (b) Variable A: $\hat{Y} = 9.5933 + 2.6679X$, where X = years relative to 1984. Variable B: $\hat{Y} = 11.7531 + 0.4286X$, where X = years relative to 1984. **(c)** Variable A: $\hat{Y} = 7.2475 + 3.3381X - 0.0305X^2$, where X = years relative to 1984. Variable B: $\hat{Y} = 10.2405 + 0.8608X - 0.0196X^2$, where X = years relative to 1984. **(d)** Variable A: $\log_{10} \hat{Y} = 1.1535 + 0.0341X$, where X = years relative to 1984. Variable B: $\log_{10} \hat{Y} = 1.0762 + 0.0121X$, where X = years relative to 1984. **(e)** Variable A: AR(3): $\hat{Y}_i = 5.0878 + 1.2279Y_{i-1} - 0.4156Y_{i-2} + 0.1066Y_{i-3}$. Test of A_3: p-value = 0.6698 > 0.05. Do not reject H_0 that $A_3 = 0$. Third-order term can be deleted. AR(2): $\hat{Y}_i = 5.0802 + 1.2000Y_{i-1} - 0.2860Y_{i-2}$. Test of A_2: p-value = 0.2149 > 0.05. Do not reject H_0 that $A_2 = 0$. Second-order term can be deleted. AR(1): $\hat{Y}_i = 4.4815 + 0.9415Y_{i-1}$. Test of A_1: p-value is virtually 0. Reject H_0 that $A_1 = 0$. A first-order autoregressive model is appropriate. Variable B: AR(3): $\hat{Y}_i = 0.6661 + 2.0036Y_{i-1} - 1.4453Y_{i-2} + 0.4099Y_{i-3}$. Test of A_3: p-value = 0.0814 > 0.05. Do not reject H_0 that $A_3 = 0$. Third-order term can be deleted. AR(2): $\hat{Y}_i = 0.6289 + 1.6647Y_{i-1} - 0.6968Y_{i-2}$. Test of A_2: p-value = 0.0002 < 0.05. Reject H_0 that $A_2 = 0$. A second-order autoregressive model is appropriate. **(f)** Variable A: The residuals in the linear and quadratic trend models show strings of consecutive positive and negative values. There is no apparent pattern in the residuals of the exponential trend and autoregressive AR(1) model. Variable B: The residuals in the linear and exponential trend models show strings of consecutive positive and negative values. There is no apparent pattern in the residuals of the quadratic trend and autoregressive AR(2) model. **(g)** Variable A: S_{YX} is 8.3169 for the linear model, 8.4253 for the quadratic model, 10.4911 for the exponential model, and 6.4149 for the first-order autoregressive model. MAD is 5.7332 for the linear model, 5.9146 for the quadratic model, 6.8875 for the exponential model, and 4.9098 for the first-order autoregressive model. Variable B: S_{YX} is 0.8166 for the linear model, 0.1296 for the quadratic model, 1.0870 for the exponential model, and 0.0898 for the second-order autoregressive model. MAD is 0.6530 for the linear model, 0.0947 for the quadratic model, 0.8556 for the exponential model, and 0.0679 for the second-order autoregressive model. **(h)** The autoregressive model, AR(1), has the smallest values in the standard error of the estimate and MAD. Thus, the autoregressive model would probably be the best model for forecasting Variable A. The autoregressive model, AR(2), has the smallest values in the standard error of the estimate and MAD. Thus, the autoregressive model would probably be the best model for forecasting Variable B. **(i)** Variable A: 63.8349, Variable B: 19.4091. **(j)** You would recommend Variable A, which consists of investments that are primarily made in stocks, for a member of Teachers Retirement System of New York City because it had a higher return than Variable B over the past 23-year period.

STUDENT CD-ROM CONTENTS

1 CD-ROM OVERVIEW

The Student CD-ROM that is packaged with this book includes five folders that contain files that support your learning of statistics (each described separately below). For your convenience, the Student CD-ROM includes a small program that will copy the contents of folders to your system. (If you choose, you can manually explore and copy files from these folders as well.) Be sure to review the **Readme.txt** file in the root folder of the Student CD-ROM for any late-breaking changes to the contents of the CD.

Excel Data Files

Located in the **Browse** folder, the Excel Data Files folder contains the Microsoft Excel workbook files (with the extension.xls) used in the examples and problems in this text. A detailed list of the files appears in Section 2.

Herald Case

Located in the **Browse** folder, the Herald Case folder contains the files for the "Managing the *Springville Herald*" case. (These files are also available online at the URLs listed in the case.)

Web Case

Located in the **Browse** folder, the Web Case folder contains the files for all the Web Cases that appear at the end of chapters. (These files are also available online at the URLs listed in each case.)

PHStat2

Located in the **Install** folder, the PHStat2 folder contains the setup program to install PHStat2 version 2.7 on a Windows or Vista computer. You must run the setup program successfully before you can use PHStat2 inside Microsoft Excel. (Be sure to review Section 4 in Appendix on Excel and the PHStat2 readme file in the PHStat2 folder before you use the setup program.)

Excel Companion Workbooks

Located in the **Browse** folder, the Microsoft Excel Companion workbooks folder contains the workbooks described and used in the Excel Companion sections. Copies of these files also appear in the Excel Data Files folder.

Visual Explorations

Located in the **Browse** folder, Visual Explorations contains the files necessary to use the add-in workbook **Visual Explorations.xla**. Before using this workbook, you should review the "Macro Security Issues" part of Section E6 of the "Introduction" and you may also want to consult the Appendix FAQs.

You can open and use the **Visual Explorations.xla** file directly from the CD-ROM in Microsoft Excel. If you prefer to use Visual Explorations without the CD present, copy the files **Visual Explorations.xla** and **VEShelp.hlp** to the folder of your choice. (The Veshelp.hlp file contains the orientation and help files for this add-in.)

CD-ROM Topics

Located in the **Browse** folder, the CD-ROM Topics folder contains supplemental textbook sections in Adobe PDF files. You will need the Adobe Acrobat reader program installed on your system in order to read these sections. (In the Install folder is a version of the Adobe Reader that you can install on your system, if necessary.)

2 DATA FILE DESCRIPTIONS

The following presents in alphabetical order, a listing of the Excel data files that are in the Excel Data Files folder. These files are in .xls format, which can be opened in all Excel versions. Elsewhere in this book, these file names appear in this special typeface, and with the .xls extension for example as `Mutual Funds.xls`.

AAAMILEAGE Gasoline mileage from AAA members, and combined city-highway driving gasoline mileage according to current government standards
ACCESS Coded access read times (in msec), file size, programmer group, and buffer size
ACCRES Processing time, in seconds, and type of computer jobs (research = 0, accounting = 1)
ACT ACT scores for type of course (rows) and length of course (columns)
ADPAGES Magazine, ad pages in 2004, and ad pages in 2005
ADVERTISE Sales (in thousands of dollars), radio ads (in thousands of dollars), and newspaper ads (in thousands of dollars) for 22 cities
AMPHRS Capacity of batteries
ANGLE Subgroup number and angle

ANSCOMBE Data sets A, B, C, and D—each with 11 pairs of X and Y values

AUTO Miles per gallon, horsepower, and weight for a sample of 50 car models

BANKCOST1 Bank names and bounced check fees

BANKTIME Waiting times of bank customers

BANKYIELD Yield for money market account and yield for one-year CD

BANK1 Waiting time (in minutes) spent by a sample of 15 customers at a bank located in a commercial district

BANK2 Waiting time (in minutes) spent by a sample of 15 customers at a bank located in a residential area

BASEBALL Team, attendance, high temperature on game day, winning percentage of home team, opponents winning percentage, game played on Friday, Saturday, or Sunday (0 = no, 1 = yes), promotion held (0 = no, 1 = yes)

BASKET Year, price of bread, beef, eggs, and lettuce

BATTERYLIFE Life of a camera battery, in number of shots

BB2001 Team; league (0 = American, 1 = National); wins; earned run average; runs scored; hits allowed; walks allowed; saves; errors; average ticket prices; fan cost index; regular season gate receipts; local television, radio, and cable revenues; other local operating revenues; player compensation and benefits; national and other local expenses; and income from baseball operations

BB2005 Team, league (0 = American, 1 = National), wins, earned run average, runs scored, hits allowed, walks allowed, saves, and errors

BBREVENUE Team, value, and revenue

BEDBATH Year, coded year, and number of stores opened

BESTREST State, city, restaurant, hotel, cost (estimated price of dinner, including one drink and tip), and rating (1 to 100, with 1 the top-rated restaurant)

BREAKFAST Delivery time difference, menu choice, and desired time

BREAKFAST2 Delivery time difference, menu choice, and desired time

BREAKSTW Breaking strength for operators (rows) and machines (columns)

BUBBLEGUM Bubble diameters for four brands for six students

BULBS Length of life of 40 light bulbs from manufacturer A (= 1) and 40 light bulbs from manufacturer B (= 2)

CABERNET California and Washington ratings, California and Washington rankings

CABOT Year and revenue for Cabot Corporation

CANISTER Day and number of nonconforming film canisters

CATFOOD Time period and weight of cat food

CDYIELD Yield of money market account, 6-month CD, 1-year CD, 2.5-year CD, and 5-year CD

CEO Company and total compensation of CEOs

CHICKEN Sandwich, calories, fat (in grams), saturated fat (in grams), carbohydrates (in grams), and sodium (in milligrams)

CIRCUITS Thickness of semiconductor wafers, by batch and position

CIRCULATION Magazine, reported newsstand sales, and audited newsstand sales

CITYRESTAURANTS Location, food, décor, service, summated rating, coded location, and price

COCACOLA Year, coded year, and operating revenues (in billions of dollars) at Coca-Cola Company

COFFEE Rating of coffees, by expert and brand

COFFEEDRINK Product, calories, and fat in coffee drinks

COFFEEPRICE Year and price per pound of coffee in the United States

COLA Sales for normal and end-aisle locations

COLASPC Day, total number of cans filled, and number of unacceptable cans (over a 22-day period)

COLLEGES-BASKETBALL School, coach's salary for 2005–2006, expenses for 2004–2005, revenues for 2004–2005 (in millions of dollars), and winning percentage in 2005–2006

COMPUTERS Download time of three brands of computers

COMPUTERS2 Download time, brand, and browser

CONCRETE1 Compressive strength after two days and seven days

CONCRETE2 Compressive strength after 2 days, 7 days, and 28 days

CONTEST2001 Returns for experts, readers, and dart throwers

COST OF LIVING City, overall cost rating, apartment rent, and costs of a cup of coffee, a hamburger, dry cleaning a men's suit, toothpaste, and movie tickets

CPI-U Year, coded year, and value of CPI-U, the consumer price index

CRACK Type of crack and crack size

CREDIT Month, coded month, credit charges

CURRENCY Year, coded year, and mean annual exchange rates (against the U.S. dollar) for the Canadian dollar, Japanese yen, and English pound

CUSTSALE Week number, number of customers, and sales (in thousands of dollars) over a period of 15 consecutive weeks

DATING Year and number of subscribers

DEALS Year and number of mergers and acquisitions from January 1 to January 11

DELIVERY Customer number, number of cases, and delivery time

DENTAL Annual family dental expenses for 10 employees

DIFFTEST Differences in the sales invoices and actual amounts from a sample of 50 vouchers

DINNER Time to prepare and cook dinner

DISCOUNT The amount of discount taken from 150 invoices

DISPRAZ Price, price squared, and sales of disposable razors in 15 stores

DJIA Year, coded year, and Dow Jones Industrial Average at the end of the year

DOMESTICBEER Brand, alcohol percentage, calories, and carbohydrates in U.S. domestic beers

DOWMC Company, ticker symbol, and market capitalization, in billions of dollars

DRILL Time to drill additional 5 feet, depth, and type of hole

DRINK Amount of soft drink filled in a subgroup of 50 consecutive 2-liter bottles

ELECTRICITY Year and cost of electricity

ELECUSE Electricity consumption (in kilowatts) and mean temperature (in degrees Fahrenheit) over a consecutive 24-month period

ENERGY State and per capita kilowatt hour use

ENERGY2 Year, price of electricity, natural gas, and fuel oil

ERRORSPC Number of nonconforming items and number of accounts processed over 39 days

ERWAITING Emergency room waiting time (in minutes) at the main facility and at satellite 1, satellite 2, and satellite 3

ESPRESSO Tamp (the distance in inches between the espresso grounds and the top of the portafilter) and time (the number of seconds the heart, body, and crema are separated)

FEDRECPT Year, coded year, and federal receipts (in billions of current dollars)

FFCHAIN Raters and restaurant ratings

FIFO Historical cost (in dollars) and audited value (in dollars) for a sample of 120 inventory items

FLYASH Fly ash percentage, fly ash percentage squared, and strength

FORCE Force required to break an insulator

FORD-REV Quarter, coded quarter, revenue, and three dummy variables for quarters

FOULSPC Number of foul shots made and number taken over 40 days

FREEPORT Address, appraised value, property size (acres), house size, age, number of rooms, number of bathrooms, and number of cars that can be parked in the garage located in Freeport, New York

FRUIT Fruit and year, price, and quantity

FUNDTRAN Day, number of new investigations, and number of investigations closed over a 30-day period

FURNITURE Days between receipt and resolution of a sample of 50 complaints regarding purchased furniture

GAS Week and price per gallon, in cents

GASOLINE Year, gasoline price, 1980 price index, and 1995 price index

GCFREEROSLYN Address, appraised value, location, property size (acres), house size, age, number of rooms, number of bathrooms, and number of cars that can be parked in the garage in Glen Cove, Freeport, and Roslyn, New York

GCROSLYN Address, appraised value, location, property size (acres), house size, age, number of rooms, number of bathrooms, and number of cars that can be parked in the garage in Glen Cove and Roslyn, New York

GDP Year and real gross domestic product (in billions of constant 1996 dollars)

GE Year, coded year, and stock price

GEAR Tooth size, part positioning, and gear distortion

GLENCOVE Address, appraised value, property size (acres), house size, age, number of rooms, number of bathrooms, and number of cars that can be parked in the garage in Glen Cove, New York

GOLFBALL Distance for designs 1, 2, 3, and 4

GPIGMAT GMAT scores and GPI for 20 students

GRADSURVEY Gender, age (as of last birthday), height (in inches), major, current cumulative grade point average, undergraduate area of specialization, undergraduate cumulative grade point average, GMAT score, current employment status, number of different full-time jobs held in the past 10 years, expected salary upon completion of MBA (in thousands of dollars), anticipated salary after 5 years of experience after MBA (in thousands of dollars), satisfaction with student advisement services on campus, and amount spent for books and supplies this semester

GRANULE Granule loss in Boston and Vermont shingles

HARDNESS Tensile strength and hardness of aluminum specimens

HARNSWELL Day and diameter of cam rollers (in inches) for samples of five parts produced in each of 30 batches

HEMLOCKFARMS Asking price, hot tub, rooms, lake view, bathrooms, bedrooms, loft/den, finished basement, and number of acres

HOMES Price, location, condition, bedrooms, bathrooms, and other rooms

HOSPADM Day, number of admissions, mean processing time (in hours), range of processing times, and proportion of laboratory rework (over a 30-day period)

HOTEL1 Day, number of rooms, number of nonconforming rooms per day over a 28-day period, and proportion of nonconforming items

HOTEL2 Day and delivery time for subgroups of five luggage deliveries per day over a 28-day period

HOUSE1 Selling price (in thousands of dollars), assessed value (in thousands of dollars), type (new = 0, old = 1), and time period of sale for 30 houses

HOUSE2 Assessed value (in thousands of dollars), size (in thousands of square feet), and age (in years) for 15 houses

HOUSE3 Assessed value (in thousands of dollars), size (in thousands of square feet), and presence of a fireplace for 15 houses

HTNGOIL Monthly consumption of heating oil (in gallons), temperature (in degrees Fahrenheit), attic insulation (in inches), and style (0 = not ranch, 1 = ranch)

ICECREAM Daily temperature (in degrees Fahrenheit) and sales (in thousands of dollars) for 21 days

INDEXES Year and total rate of return (in percentage) for the Dow Jones Industrial Average (DJIA), the Standards &

Poor's 500 (S&P 500), and the technology-heavy NASDAQ Composite (NASDAQ)

INSURANCE Processing time for insurance policies

INTAGLIO Surface hardness of untreated and treated steel plates

INVOICE Number of invoices processed and amount of time (in hours) for 30 days

INVOICES Amount recorded (in dollars) from a sample of 12 sales invoices

ITEMERR Amount of error (in dollars) from a sample of 200 items

KEYBOARDDEFECTS Defect and frequency

LARGESTBONDS Five-year return of bond funds

LAUNDRY Dirt (in pounds) removed for detergent brands (rows) and cycle times (columns)

LOCATE Sales volume (in thousands of dollars) for front, middle, and rear locations

LUGGAGE Delivery time, in minutes, for luggage in Wing A and Wing B of a hotel

MAIL Weight of mail and orders

MANAGERS Sales (ratio of yearly sales divided by the target sales value for that region), score from the Wonderlic Personnel Test, score on the Strong-Campbell Interest Inventory Test, number of years of selling experience prior to becoming a sales manager, and whether the sales manager has a degree in electrical engineering (0 = no, 1 = yes)

MCDONALD Year, coded year, and annual total revenues (in billions of dollars) at McDonald's Corporation

MEASUREMENT Sample, in-line measurement, and analytical lab measurement

MEDICARE Difference in amount reimbursed and amount that should have been reimbursed for office visits

MEDREC Day, number of discharged patients, and number of records not processed for a 30-day period

METALS Year and the total rate of return (in percentage) for platinum, gold, and silver

MILEAGE Mileage of autos calculated by owner, currently, and forecasted according to government plans

MOISTURE Moisture content of Boston shingles and Vermont shingles

MOVIEPRICES Theatre chain and cost of two tickets, a large popcorn, and two sodas

MOVIES Year and movie attendance

MOVING Labor hours, cubic feet, number of large pieces of furniture, and availability of an elevator

MUSICONLINE Album/artist and prices at iTunes, Wal-Mart, MusicNow, Musicmatch, and Napster

MUTUALFUNDS Category, objective, assets, fees, expense ratio, 2005 return, three-year return, five-year return, and risk

MYELOMA Patient, measurement before transplant, and measurement after transplant

NATURALGAS Coded quarter, price, and three dummy variables for quarters

NBA2006 Team, number of wins, points per game (for team, opponent, and the difference between team and opponent), field goal (shots made), percentage (for team, opponent, and the difference between team and opponent), turnovers (losing the ball before a shot is taken) per game (for team, opponent, and the difference between team and opponent), offensive rebound percentage, and defensive rebound percentage

NEIGHBOR Selling price (in thousands of dollars), number of rooms, and neighborhood location (east = 0, west = 1) for 20 houses

OMNI Bars sold, price, and promotion expenses

O-RING Flight number, temperature, and O-ring damage index

OYSTERS Year, coded year, and number of bushels harvested

PAIN-RELIEF Temperature, brand of pain relief tablet, and time to dissolve

PALLET Weight of Boston and weight of Vermont shingles

PARACHUTE Tensile strength of parachutes from suppliers 1, 2, 3, and 4

PARACHUTE2 Tensile strength for looms and suppliers

PASTA Weight for type of pasta (rows) and cooking time (columns)

PEN Gender, ad, and product rating

PERFORM Performance rating before and after motivational training

PETFOOD Shelf space (in feet), weekly sales (in dollars), and aisle location (back = 0, front = 1)

PHONE Time (in minutes) to clear telephone line problems and location (I and II) for samples of 20 customer problems reported to each of the two office locations

PHOTO Density for developer strength (rows) and development time (columns)

PIZZATIME Time period, delivery time for local restaurant, delivery time for national chain

PLUMBINV Difference in dollars between actual amounts recorded on sales invoices and the amounts entered into the accounting system

POLIO Year and incidence rates per 100,000 persons of reported poliomyelitis

POTATO Percentage of solids content in filter cake, acidity (in pH), lower pressure, upper pressure, cake thickness, varidrive speed, and drum speed setting for 54 measurements

PRESCRIPTIONS Year and average prescription drug price

PROTEIN Calories (in grams), protein, percentage of calories from fat, percentage of calories from saturated fat, and cholesterol (in mg) for 25 popular protein foods

PUMPKIN Circumference and weight of pumpkins

RADON Solar radiation, soil temperature, vapor pressure, wind speed, relative humidity, dew point, ambient temperature, and radon concentration

RAISINS Weight of packages of raisins

REDWOOD Height, diameter, and bark thickness

RENT Monthly rental cost (in dollars) and apartment size (in square footage) for a sample of 25 apartments

RESTAURANTS Location, food rating, decor rating, service rating, summated rating, coded location (0 = urban, 1 = suburban), and price of restaurants

RETURNS Week and stock price of Microsoft, stock price of General Motors, stock price of Ford, and stock price of International Aluminum

ROSLYN Address, appraised value, property size (acres), house size, age, number of rooms, number of bathrooms, and number of cars that can be parked in the garage in Roslyn, New York

ROYALS Game, attendance, and whether there was a promotion at Kansas City Royals games

RUDYBIRD Day, total cases sold, and cases of Rudybird sold

S&PSTKIN Coded quarters, end-of-quarter values of the quarterly Standard & Poor's Composite Stock Price Index, and three quarterly dummy variables

SAVINGS Bank, money market rate, one-year CD rate, and five-year CD rate

SCRUBBER Airflow, water flow, recirculating water flow, orifice diameter, and NTU

SEALANT Sample number, sealant strength for Boston shingles, and sealant strength for Vermont shingles

SEARS Year, coded year, and annual total revenues (in billions of dollars) at Sears, Roebuck & Company

SH2 Day and number of calls received at the help desk

SH8 Rate ($) willing to pay for the newspaper

SH9 Blackness of newsprint

SH10 Length of early calls (in seconds), length of late calls (in seconds), and difference (in seconds)

SH11-1 Call, presentation plan (structured = 1, semi-structured = 2, unstructured = 3), and length of call (in seconds)

SH11-2 Gender of caller, type of greeting, and length of call

SH13 Hours per month spent telemarketing and number of new subscriptions per month over a 24-month period

SH14 Hours per week spent telemarketing, number of new subscriptions, and type of presentation

SH16 Month and number of home-delivery subscriptions over the most recent 24-month period

SH18-1 Day, number of ads with errors, number of ads, and number of errors over a 25-day period

SH18-2 Day and newsprint blackness measures for each of five spots made over 25 consecutive weekdays

SITE Store number, square footage (in thousands of square feet), and sales (in millions of dollars) in 14 Sunflowers Apparel stores

SP500 Week, weekly change in the S&P 500, weekly change in the price of Wal-Mart, weekly change in the price of Target, and weekly change in the price of Sara Lee

SPENDING State and per capita federal spending ($000) in 2004

SPONGE Day, number of sponges produced, number of nonconforming sponges, proportion of nonconforming sponges

SPORTING Sales, age, annual population growth, income, percentage with high school diploma, and percentage with college diploma

SPWATER Sample number and amount of magnesium

STANDBY Standby hours, staff, remote hours, Dubner hours, and labor hours for 26 weeks

STATES State, commuting time, percentage of homes with more than eight rooms, median income, and percentage of housing that costs more than 30% of family income

STEEL Error in actual length and specified length

STOCKS&BONDS Date, closing price of Vanguard Long-Term Bond Index Fund, and closing price of the Dow Jones Industrial Average

STOCKASSETS Fund and assets, in billions of dollars

STOCKS2005 Week and closing weekly stock price for S&P, Sears, Target, and Sara Lee

STRATEGIC Year and number of barrels in U.S. strategic oil reserve

TAX Quarterly sales tax receipts (in thousands of dollars) for 50 business establishments

TAXES County taxes (in dollars) and age of house (in years) for 19 single-family houses

TEA3 Sample number and weight of tea bags

TEABAGS Weight of tea bags

TELESPC Number of orders and number of corrections over 30 days

TENSILE Sample number and strength

TESTRANK Rank scores for 10 people trained using a "traditional" method (Method = 0) and 10 people trained using an "experimental" method (Method = 1)

TEXTBOOK Textbook, book store price, and Amazon price

THEMEPARKS Name of location and admission price for one-day tickets

TIMES Times to get ready

TOMATOES Year and price per pound in the United States

TOMYLD2 Amount of fertilizer (in pounds per 100 square feet) and yield (in pounds) for 12 plots of land

TOYS-REV Quarter, coded quarter, revenue, and three dummy variables for quarters

TRADE Days, number of undesirable trades, and number of total trades made over a 30-day period

TRADES Day, number of incoming calls, and number of trade executions per day over a 35-day period

TRAINING Assembly time and training program (team-based = 0, individual-based = 1)

TRANSMIT Day and number of errors in transmission

TRANSPORT Days and patient transport times (in minutes) for samples of four patients per day over a 30-day period

TRASHBAGS Weight required to break four brands of trash bags

TREASURY Year and interest rate

TROUGH Width of trough

TRSNYC Year, unit value of variable A, and unit value of variable B

TSMODEL1 Years, coded years, and three time series (I, II, III)

TSMODEL2 Years, coded years, and two time series (I, II)

TUITION2006 School, in-state tuition and fees, and out-of-state tuition and fees

UNDERGRADSURVEY Gender, age (*as of last birthday*), height (*in inches*), class designation, major, graduate school intention, cumulative grade point average, expected starting salary (in thousands of dollars), anticipated salary after five years of experience (in thousands of dollars), current employment status, number of campus club/group/organization/team affiliations, satisfaction with student advisement services on campus, and amount spent on books and supplies this semester

UNDERWRITING Score on proficiency exam, score on end of training exam, and training method

UNEMPLOY Year, month, and monthly unemployment rates

UNLEADED Year, month, and price

UTILITY Utilities charges for 50 one-bedroom apartments

VB Time (in minutes) for nine students to write and run a Visual Basic program

WAIT Waiting times and seating times, in minutes

WALMART Quarter and quarterly revenues

WARECOST Distribution cost (in thousands of dollars), sales (in thousands of dollars), and number of orders for 24 months

WAREHSE Number of units handled per day and employee number

WEEKLYNASDAQ Week and NASDAQ value

WHOLEFOODS1 Item, price at Whole Foods, and price at Fairway

WHOLEFOODS2 Item, price at Whole Foods, price at Gristede's, price at Fairway, and price at Stop & Shop

WIP Processing times at each of two plants (A = 1, B = 2)

WONDERLIC School, average Wonderlic score of football players trying out for the NFL, and graduation rate

WORKFORCE Year, population, and size of the workforce

WRIGLEY Year, coded year, actual revenue, consumer price index, and real revenue

YARN Breaking strength, pressure, yarn sample, and side-by-side aspect (nozzle = 1, opposite = 2)

YIELD Cleansing step, etching step, and yield

TABLES

TABLES

TABLE 1

Table of Random Numbers

Row	Column							
	00000 12345	00001 67890	11111 12345	11112 67890	22222 12345	22223 67890	33333 12345	33334 67890
01	49280	88924	35779	00283	81163	07275	89863	02348
02	61870	41657	07468	08612	98083	97349	20775	45091
03	43898	65923	25078	86129	78496	97653	91550	08078
04	62993	93912	30454	84598	56095	20664	12872	64647
05	33850	58555	51438	85507	71865	79488	76783	31708
06	97340	03364	88472	04334	63919	36394	11095	92470
07	70543	29776	10087	10072	55980	64688	68239	20461
08	89382	93809	00796	95945	34101	81277	66090	88872
09	37818	72142	67140	50785	22380	16703	53362	44940
10	60430	22834	14130	96593	23298	56203	92671	15925
11	82975	66158	84731	19436	55790	69229	28661	13675
12	30987	71938	40355	54324	08401	26299	49420	59208
13	55700	24586	93247	32596	11865	63397	44251	43189
14	14756	23997	78643	75912	83832	32768	18928	57070
15	32166	53251	70654	92827	63491	04233	33825	69662
16	23236	73751	31888	81718	06546	83246	47651	04877
17	45794	26926	15130	82455	78305	55058	52551	47182
18	09893	20505	14225	68514	47427	56788	96297	78822
19	54382	74598	91499	14523	68479	27686	46162	83554
20	94750	89923	37089	20048	80336	94598	26940	36858
21	70297	34135	53140	33340	42050	82341	44104	82949
22	85157	47954	32979	26575	57600	40881	12250	73742
23	11100	02340	12860	74697	96644	89439	28707	25815
24	36871	50775	30592	57143	17381	68856	25853	35041
25	23913	48357	63308	16090	51690	54607	72407	55538
26	79348	36085	27973	65157	07456	22255	25626	57054
27	92074	54641	53673	54421	18130	60103	69593	49464
28	06873	21440	75593	41373	49502	17972	82578	16364
29	12478	37622	99659	31065	83613	69889	58869	29571
30	57175	55564	65411	42547	70457	03426	72937	83792
31	91616	11075	80103	07831	59309	13276	26710	73000
32	78025	73539	14621	39044	47450	03197	12787	47709
33	27587	67228	80145	10175	12822	86687	65530	49325
34	16690	20427	04251	64477	73709	73945	92396	68263
35	70183	58065	65489	31833	82093	16747	10386	59293
36	90730	35385	15679	99742	50866	78028	75573	67257
37	10934	93242	13431	24590	02770	48582	00906	58595
38	82462	30166	79613	47416	13389	80268	05085	96666
39	27463	10433	07606	16285	93699	60912	94532	95632
40	02979	52997	09079	92709	90110	47506	53693	49892
41	46888	69929	75233	52507	32097	37594	10067	67327
42	53638	83161	08289	12639	08141	12640	28437	09268
43	82433	61427	17239	89160	19666	08814	37841	12847
44	35766	31672	50082	22795	66948	65581	84393	15890
45	10853	42581	08792	13257	61973	24450	52351	16602
46	20341	27398	72906	63955	17276	10646	74692	48438
47	54458	90542	77563	51839	52901	53355	83281	19177
48	26337	66530	16687	35179	46560	00123	44546	79896
49	34314	23729	85264	05575	96855	23820	11091	79821
50	28603	10708	68933	34189	92166	15181	66628	58599

continued

TABLE 1

Table of Random
Numbers (*Continued*)

	Column							
Row	**00000** **12345**	**00001** **67890**	**11111** **12345**	**11112** **67890**	**22222** **12345**	**22223** **67890**	**33333** **12345**	**33334** **67890**
51	66194	28926	99547	16625	45515	67953	12108	57846
52	78240	43195	24837	32511	70880	22070	52622	61881
53	00833	88000	67299	68215	11274	55624	32991	17436
54	12111	86683	61270	58036	64192	90611	15145	01748
55	47189	99951	05755	03834	43782	90599	40282	51417
56	76396	72486	62423	27618	84184	78922	73561	52818
57	46409	17469	32483	09083	76175	19985	26309	91536
58	74626	22111	87286	46772	42243	68046	44250	42439
59	34450	81974	93723	49023	58432	67083	36876	93391
60	36327	72135	33005	28701	34710	49359	50693	89311
61	74185	77536	84825	09934	99103	09325	67389	45869
62	12296	41623	62873	37943	25584	09609	63360	47270
63	90822	60280	88925	99610	42772	60561	76873	04117
64	72121	79152	96591	90305	10189	79778	68016	13747
65	95268	41377	25684	08151	61816	58555	54305	86189
66	92603	09091	75884	93424	72586	88903	30061	14457
67	18813	90291	05275	01223	79607	95426	34900	09778
68	38840	26903	28624	67157	51986	42865	14508	49315
69	05959	33836	53758	16562	41081	38012	41230	20528
70	85141	21155	99212	32685	51403	31926	69813	58781
71	75047	59643	31074	38172	03718	32119	69506	67143
72	30752	95260	68032	62871	58781	34143	68790	69766
73	22986	82575	42187	62295	84295	30634	66562	31442
74	99439	86692	90348	66036	48399	73451	26698	39437
75	20389	93029	11881	71685	65452	89047	63669	02656
76	39249	05173	68256	36359	20250	68686	05947	09335
77	96777	33605	29481	20063	09398	01843	35139	61344
78	04860	32918	10798	50492	52655	33359	94713	28393
79	41613	42375	00403	03656	77580	87772	86877	57085
80	17930	00794	53836	53692	67135	98102	61912	11246
81	24649	31845	25736	75231	83808	98917	93829	99430
82	79899	34061	54308	59358	56462	58166	97302	86828
83	76801	49594	81002	30397	52728	15101	72070	33706
84	36239	63636	38140	65731	39788	06872	38971	53363
85	07392	64449	17886	63632	53995	17574	22247	62607
86	67133	04181	33874	98835	67453	59734	76381	63455
87	77759	31504	32832	70861	15152	29733	75371	39174
88	85992	72268	42920	20810	29361	51423	90306	73574
89	79553	75952	54116	65553	47139	60579	09165	85490
90	41101	17336	48951	53674	17880	45260	08575	49321
91	36191	17095	32123	91576	84221	78902	82010	30847
92	62329	63898	23268	74283	26091	68409	69704	82267
93	14751	13151	93115	01437	56945	89661	67680	79790
94	48462	59278	44185	29616	76537	19589	83139	28454
95	29435	88105	59651	44391	74588	55114	80834	85686
96	28340	29285	12965	14821	80425	16602	44653	70467
97	02167	58940	27149	80242	10587	79786	34959	75339
98	17864	00991	39557	54981	23588	81914	37609	13128
99	79675	80605	60059	35862	00254	36546	21545	78179
100	72335	82037	92003	34100	29879	46613	89720	13274

Source: Partially extracted from the Rand Corporation, *A Million Random Digits with 100,000 Normal Deviates* (Glencoe, IL, The Free Press, 1955).

TABLE 2

The Cumulative Standardized Normal Distribution

Entry represents area under the cumulative standardized normal
distribution from $-\infty$ to Z

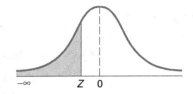

Z	0.00	0.01	0.02	0.03	0.04	0.05	0.06	0.07	0.08	0.09
−6.0	0.000000001									
−5.5	0.000000019									
−5.0	0.000000287									
−4.5	0.000003398									
−4.0	0.000031671									
−3.9	0.00005	0.00005	0.00004	0.00004	0.00004	0.00004	0.00004	0.00004	0.00003	0.00003
−3.8	0.00007	0.00007	0.00007	0.00006	0.00006	0.00006	0.00006	0.00005	0.00005	0.00005
−3.7	0.00011	0.00010	0.00010	0.00010	0.00009	0.00009	0.00008	0.00008	0.00008	0.00008
−3.6	0.00016	0.00015	0.00015	0.00014	0.00014	0.00013	0.00013	0.00012	0.00012	0.00011
−3.5	0.00023	0.00022	0.00022	0.00021	0.00020	0.00019	0.00019	0.00018	0.00017	0.00017
−3.4	0.00034	0.00032	0.00031	0.00030	0.00029	0.00028	0.00027	0.00026	0.00025	0.00024
−3.3	0.00048	0.00047	0.00045	0.00043	0.00042	0.00040	0.00039	0.00038	0.00036	0.00035
−3.2	0.00069	0.00066	0.00064	0.00062	0.00060	0.00058	0.00056	0.00054	0.00052	0.00050
−3.1	0.00097	0.00094	0.00090	0.00087	0.00084	0.00082	0.00079	0.00076	0.00074	0.00071
−3.0	0.00135	0.00131	0.00126	0.00122	0.00118	0.00114	0.00111	0.00107	0.00103	0.00100
−2.9	0.0019	0.0018	0.0018	0.0017	0.0016	0.0016	0.0015	0.0015	0.0014	0.0014
−2.8	0.0026	0.0025	0.0024	0.0023	0.0023	0.0022	0.0021	0.0021	0.0020	0.0019
−2.7	0.0035	0.0034	0.0033	0.0032	0.0031	0.0030	0.0029	0.0028	0.0027	0.0026
−2.6	0.0047	0.0045	0.0044	0.0043	0.0041	0.0040	0.0039	0.0038	0.0037	0.0036
−2.5	0.0062	0.0060	0.0059	0.0057	0.0055	0.0054	0.0052	0.0051	0.0049	0.0048
−2.4	0.0082	0.0080	0.0078	0.0075	0.0073	0.0071	0.0069	0.0068	0.0066	0.0064
−2.3	0.0107	0.0104	0.0102	0.0099	0.0096	0.0094	0.0091	0.0089	0.0087	0.0084
−2.2	0.0139	0.0136	0.0132	0.0129	0.0125	0.0122	0.0119	0.0116	0.0113	0.0110
−2.1	0.0179	0.0174	0.0170	0.0166	0.0162	0.0158	0.0154	0.0150	0.0146	0.0143
−2.0	0.0228	0.0222	0.0217	0.0212	0.0207	0.0202	0.0197	0.0192	0.0188	0.0183
−1.9	0.0287	0.0281	0.0274	0.0268	0.0262	0.0256	0.0250	0.0244	0.0239	0.0233
−1.8	0.0359	0.0351	0.0344	0.0336	0.0329	0.0322	0.0314	0.0307	0.0301	0.0294
−1.7	0.0446	0.0436	0.0427	0.0418	0.0409	0.0401	0.0392	0.0384	0.0375	0.0367
−1.6	0.0548	0.0537	0.0526	0.0516	0.0505	0.0495	0.0485	0.0475	0.0465	0.0455
−1.5	0.0668	0.0655	0.0643	0.0630	0.0618	0.0606	0.0594	0.0582	0.0571	0.0559
−1.4	0.0808	0.0793	0.0778	0.0764	0.0749	0.0735	0.0721	0.0708	0.0694	0.0681
−1.3	0.0968	0.0951	0.0934	0.0918	0.0901	0.0885	0.0869	0.0853	0.0838	0.0823
−1.2	0.1151	0.1131	0.1112	0.1093	0.1075	0.1056	0.1038	0.1020	0.1003	0.0985
−1.1	0.1357	0.1335	0.1314	0.1292	0.1271	0.1251	0.1230	0.1210	0.1190	0.1170
−1.0	0.1587	0.1562	0.1539	0.1515	0.1492	0.1469	0.1446	0.1423	0.1401	0.1379
−0.9	0.1841	0.1814	0.1788	0.1762	0.1736	0.1711	0.1685	0.1660	0.1635	0.1611
−0.8	0.2119	0.2090	0.2061	0.2033	0.2005	0.1977	0.1949	0.1922	0.1894	0.1867
−0.7	0.2420	0.2388	0.2358	0.2327	0.2296	0.2266	0.2236	0.2206	0.2177	0.2148
−0.6	0.2743	0.2709	0.2676	0.2643	0.2611	0.2578	0.2546	0.2514	0.2482	0.2451
−0.5	0.3085	0.3050	0.3015	0.2981	0.2946	0.2912	0.2877	0.2843	0.2810	0.2776
−0.4	0.3446	0.3409	0.3372	0.3336	0.3300	0.3264	0.3228	0.3192	0.3156	0.3121
−0.3	0.3821	0.3783	0.3745	0.3707	0.3669	0.3632	0.3594	0.3557	0.3520	0.3483
−0.2	0.4207	0.4168	0.4129	0.4090	0.4052	0.4013	0.3974	0.3936	0.3897	0.3859
−0.1	0.4602	0.4562	0.4522	0.4483	0.4443	0.4404	0.4364	0.4325	0.4286	0.4247
−0.0	0.5000	0.4960	0.4920	0.4880	0.4840	0.4801	0.4761	0.4721	0.4681	0.4641

continued

TABLE 2

The Cumulative Standardized Normal Distribution (*Continued*)

Entry represents area under the cumulative standardized normal distribution from $-\infty$ to Z

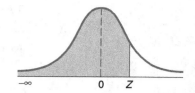

Z	0.00	0.01	0.02	0.03	0.04	0.05	0.06	0.07	0.08	0.09
0.0	0.5000	0.5040	0.5080	0.5120	0.5160	0.5199	0.5239	0.5279	0.5319	0.5359
0.1	0.5398	0.5438	0.5478	0.5517	0.5557	0.5596	0.5636	0.5675	0.5714	0.5753
0.2	0.5793	0.5832	0.5871	0.5910	0.5948	0.5987	0.6026	0.6064	0.6103	0.6141
0.3	0.6179	0.6217	0.6255	0.6293	0.6331	0.6368	0.6406	0.6443	0.6480	0.6517
0.4	0.6554	0.6591	0.6628	0.6664	0.6700	0.6736	0.6772	0.6808	0.6844	0.6879
0.5	0.6915	0.6950	0.6985	0.7019	0.7054	0.7088	0.7123	0.7157	0.7190	0.7224
0.6	0.7257	0.7291	0.7324	0.7357	0.7389	0.7422	0.7454	0.7486	0.7518	0.7549
0.7	0.7580	0.7612	0.7642	0.7673	0.7704	0.7734	0.7764	0.7794	0.7823	0.7852
0.8	0.7881	0.7910	0.7939	0.7967	0.7995	0.8023	0.8051	0.8078	0.8106	0.8133
0.9	0.8159	0.8186	0.8212	0.8238	0.8264	0.8289	0.8315	0.8340	0.8365	0.8389
1.0	0.8413	0.8438	0.8461	0.8485	0.8508	0.8531	0.8554	0.8577	0.8599	0.8621
1.1	0.8643	0.8665	0.8686	0.8708	0.8729	0.8749	0.8770	0.8790	0.8810	0.8830
1.2	0.8849	0.8869	0.8888	0.8907	0.8925	0.8944	0.8962	0.8980	0.8997	0.9015
1.3	0.9032	0.9049	0.9066	0.9082	0.9099	0.9115	0.9131	0.9147	0.9162	0.9177
1.4	0.9192	0.9207	0.9222	0.9236	0.9251	0.9265	0.9279	0.9292	0.9306	0.9319
1.5	0.9332	0.9345	0.9357	0.9370	0.9382	0.9394	0.9406	0.9418	0.9429	0.9441
1.6	0.9452	0.9463	0.9474	0.9484	0.9495	0.9505	0.9515	0.9525	0.9535	0.9545
1.7	0.9554	0.9564	0.9573	0.9582	0.9591	0.9599	0.9608	0.9616	0.9625	0.9633
1.8	0.9641	0.9649	0.9656	0.9664	0.9671	0.9678	0.9686	0.9693	0.9699	0.9706
1.9	0.9713	0.9719	0.9726	0.9732	0.9738	0.9744	0.9750	0.9756	0.9761	0.9767
2.0	0.9772	0.9778	0.9783	0.9788	0.9793	0.9798	0.9803	0.9808	0.9812	0.9817
2.1	0.9821	0.9826	0.9830	0.9834	0.9838	0.9842	0.9846	0.9850	0.9854	0.9857
2.2	0.9861	0.9864	0.9868	0.9871	0.9875	0.9878	0.9881	0.9884	0.9887	0.9890
2.3	0.9893	0.9896	0.9898	0.9901	0.9904	0.9906	0.9909	0.9911	0.9913	0.9916
2.4	0.9918	0.9920	0.9922	0.9925	0.9927	0.9929	0.9931	0.9932	0.9934	0.9936
2.5	0.9938	0.9940	0.9941	0.9943	0.9945	0.9946	0.9948	0.9949	0.9951	0.9952
2.6	0.9953	0.9955	0.9956	0.9957	0.9959	0.9960	0.9961	0.9962	0.9963	0.9964
2.7	0.9965	0.9966	0.9967	0.9968	0.9969	0.9970	0.9971	0.9972	0.9973	0.9974
2.8	0.9974	0.9975	0.9976	0.9977	0.9977	0.9978	0.9979	0.9979	0.9980	0.9981
2.9	0.9981	0.9982	0.9982	0.9983	0.9984	0.9984	0.9985	0.9985	0.9986	0.9986
3.0	0.99865	0.99869	0.99874	0.99878	0.99882	0.99886	0.99889	0.99893	0.99897	0.99900
3.1	0.99903	0.99906	0.99910	0.99913	0.99916	0.99918	0.99921	0.99924	0.99926	0.99929
3.2	0.99931	0.99934	0.99936	0.99938	0.99940	0.99942	0.99944	0.99946	0.99948	0.99950
3.3	0.99952	0.99953	0.99955	0.99957	0.99958	0.99960	0.99961	0.99962	0.99964	0.99965
3.4	0.99966	0.99968	0.99969	0.99970	0.99971	0.99972	0.99973	0.99974	0.99975	0.99976
3.5	0.99977	0.99978	0.99978	0.99979	0.99980	0.99981	0.99981	0.99982	0.99983	0.99983
3.6	0.99984	0.99985	0.99985	0.99986	0.99986	0.99987	0.99987	0.99988	0.99988	0.99989
3.7	0.99989	0.99990	0.99990	0.99990	0.99991	0.99991	0.99992	0.99992	0.99992	0.99992
3.8	0.99993	0.99993	0.99993	0.99994	0.99994	0.99994	0.99994	0.99995	0.99995	0.99995
3.9	0.99995	0.99995	0.99996	0.99996	0.99996	0.99996	0.99996	0.99996	0.99997	0.99997
4.0	0.999968329									
4.5	0.999996602									
5.0	0.999999713									
5.5	0.999999981									
6.0	0.999999999									

TABLE 3

Critical Values of *t*

For a particular number of degrees of freedom, entry represents the
critical value of *t* corresponding to a specified upper-tail area (α)

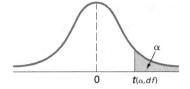

Degrees of Freedom	Upper-Tail Areas					
	0.25	0.10	0.05	0.025	0.01	0.005
1	1.0000	3.0777	6.3138	12.7062	31.8207	63.6574
2	0.8165	1.8856	2.9200	4.3027	6.9646	9.9248
3	0.7649	1.6377	2.3534	3.1824	4.5407	5.8409
4	0.7407	1.5332	2.1318	2.7764	3.7469	4.6041
5	0.7267	1.4759	2.0150	2.5706	3.3649	4.0322
6	0.7176	1.4398	1.9432	2.4469	3.1427	3.7074
7	0.7111	1.4149	1.8946	2.3646	2.9980	3.4995
8	0.7064	1.3968	1.8595	2.2060	2.8965	3.3554
9	0.7027	1.3830	1.8331	2.2622	2.8214	3.2498
10	0.6998	1.3722	1.8125	2.2281	2.7638	3.1693
11	0.6974	1.3634	1.7959	2.2010	2.7181	3.1058
12	0.6955	1.3562	1.7823	2.1788	2.6810	3.0545
13	0.6938	1.3502	1.7709	2.1604	2.6503	3.0123
14	0.6924	1.3450	1.7613	2.1448	2.6245	2.9768
15	0.6912	1.3406	1.7531	2.1315	2.6025	2.9467
16	0.6901	1.3368	1.7459	2.1199	2.5835	2.9208
17	0.6892	1.3334	1.7396	2.1098	2.5669	2.8982
18	0.6884	1.3304	1.7341	2.1009	2.5524	2.8784
19	0.6876	1.3277	1.7291	2.0930	2.5395	2.8609
20	0.6870	1.3253	1.7247	2.0860	2.5280	2.8453
21	0.6864	1.3232	1.7207	2.0796	2.5177	2.8314
22	0.6858	1.3212	1.7171	2.0739	2.5083	2.8188
23	0.6853	1.3195	1.7139	2.0687	2.4999	2.8073
24	0.6848	1.3178	1.7109	2.0639	2.4922	2.7969
25	0.6844	1.3163	1.7081	2.0595	2.4851	2.7874
26	0.6840	1.3150	1.7056	2.0555	2.4786	2.7787
27	0.6837	1.3137	1.7033	2.0518	2.4727	2.7707
28	0.6834	1.3125	1.7011	2.0484	2.4671	2.7633
29	0.6830	1.3114	1.6991	2.0452	2.4620	2.7564
30	0.6828	1.3104	1.6973	2.0423	2.4573	2.7500
31	0.6825	1.3095	1.6955	2.0395	2.4528	2.7440
32	0.6822	1.3086	1.6939	2.0369	2.4487	2.7385
33	0.6820	1.3077	1.6924	2.0345	2.4448	2.7333
34	0.6818	1.3070	1.6909	2.0322	2.4411	2.7284
35	0.6816	1.3062	1.6896	2.0301	2.4377	2.7238
36	0.6814	1.3055	1.6883	2.0281	2.4345	2.7195
37	0.6812	1.3049	1.6871	2.0262	2.4314	2.7154
38	0.6810	1.3042	1.6860	2.0244	2.4286	2.7116
39	0.6808	1.3036	1.6849	2.0227	2.4258	2.7079
40	0.6807	1.3031	1.6839	2.0211	2.4233	2.7045
41	0.6805	1.3025	1.6829	2.0195	2.4208	2.7012
42	0.6804	1.3020	1.6820	2.0181	2.4185	2.6981
43	0.6802	1.3016	1.6811	2.0167	2.4163	2.6951
44	0.6801	1.3011	1.6802	2.0154	2.4141	2.6923
45	0.6800	1.3006	1.6794	2.0141	2.4121	2.6896
46	0.6799	1.3022	1.6787	2.0129	2.4102	2.6870
47	0.6797	1.2998	1.6779	2.0117	2.4083	2.6846
48	0.6796	1.2994	1.6772	2.0106	2.4066	2.6822

continued

TABLE 3

Critical Values of *t*
(*Continued*)

Degrees of Freedom	Upper-Tail Areas					
	0.25	0.10	0.05	0.025	0.01	0.005
49	0.6795	1.2991	1.6766	2.0096	2.4049	2.6800
50	0.6794	1.2987	1.6759	2.0086	2.4033	2.6778
51	0.6793	1.2984	1.6753	2.0076	2.4017	2.6757
52	0.6792	1.2980	1.6747	2.0066	2.4002	2.6737
53	0.6791	1.2977	1.6741	2.0057	2.3988	2.6718
54	0.6791	1.2974	1.6736	2.0049	2.3974	2.6700
55	0.6790	1.2971	1.6730	2.0040	2.3961	2.6682
56	0.6789	1.2969	1.6725	2.0032	2.3948	2.6665
57	0.6788	1.2966	1.6720	2.0025	2.3936	2.6649
58	0.6787	1.2963	1.6716	2.0017	2.3924	2.6633
59	0.6787	1.2961	1.6711	2.0010	2.3912	2.6618
60	0.6786	1.2958	1.6706	2.0003	2.3901	2.6603
61	0.6785	1.2956	1.6702	1.9996	2.3890	2.6589
62	0.6785	1.2954	1.6698	1.9990	2.3880	2.6575
63	0.6784	1.2951	1.6694	1.9983	2.3870	2.6561
64	0.6783	1.2949	1.6690	1.9977	2.3860	2.6549
65	0.6783	1.2947	1.6686	1.9971	2.3851	2.6536
66	0.6782	1.2945	1.6683	1.9966	2.3842	2.6524
67	0.6782	1.2943	1.6679	1.9960	2.3833	2.6512
68	0.6781	1.2941	1.6676	1.9955	2.3824	2.6501
69	0.6781	1.2939	1.6672	1.9949	2.3816	2.6490
70	0.6780	1.2938	1.6669	1.9944	2.3808	2.6479
71	0.6780	1.2936	1.6666	1.9939	2.3800	2.6469
72	0.6779	1.2934	1.6663	1.9935	2.3793	2.6459
73	0.6779	1.2933	1.6660	1.9930	2.3785	2.6449
74	0.6778	1.2931	1.6657	1.9925	2.3778	2.6439
75	0.6778	1.2929	1.6654	1.9921	2.3771	2.6430
76	0.6777	1.2928	1.6652	1.9917	2.3764	2.6421
77	0.6777	1.2926	1.6649	1.9913	2.3758	2.6412
78	0.6776	1.2925	1.6646	1.9908	2.3751	2.6403
79	0.6776	1.2924	1.6644	1.9905	2.3745	2.6395
80	0.6776	1.2922	1.6641	1.9901	2.3739	2.6387
81	0.6775	1.2921	1.6639	1.9897	2.3733	2.6379
82	0.6775	1.2920	1.6636	1.9893	2.3727	2.6371
83	0.6775	1.2918	1.6634	1.9890	2.3721	2.6364
84	0.6774	1.2917	1.6632	1.9886	2.3716	2.6356
85	0.6774	1.2916	1.6630	1.9883	2.3710	2.6349
86	0.6774	1.2915	1.6628	1.9879	2.3705	2.6342
87	0.6773	1.2914	1.6626	1.9876	2.3700	2.6335
88	0.6773	1.2912	1.6624	1.9873	2.3695	2.6329
89	0.6773	1.2911	1.6622	1.9870	2.3690	2.6322
90	0.6772	1.2910	1.6620	1.9867	2.3685	2.6316
91	0.6772	1.2909	1.6618	1.9864	2.3680	2.6309
92	0.6772	1.2908	1.6616	1.9861	2.3676	2.6303
93	0.6771	1.2907	1.6614	1.9858	2.3671	2.6297
94	0.6771	1.2906	1.6612	1.9855	2.3667	2.6291
95	0.6771	1.2905	1.6611	1.9853	2.3662	2.6286
96	0.6771	1.2904	1.6609	1.9850	2.3658	2.6280
97	0.6770	1.2903	1.6607	1.9847	2.3654	2.6275
98	0.6770	1.2902	1.6606	1.9845	2.3650	2.6269
99	0.6770	1.2902	1.6604	1.9842	2.3646	2.6264
100	0.6770	1.2901	1.6602	1.9840	2.3642	2.6259
110	0.6767	1.2893	1.6588	1.9818	2.3607	2.6213
120	0.6765	1.2886	1.6577	1.9799	2.3578	2.6174
∞	0.6745	1.2816	1.6449	1.9600	2.3263	2.5758

TABLE 4

Critical Values of χ^2

For a particular number of degrees of freedom, entry represents the critical value of χ^2 corresponding to a specified upper-tail area (α).

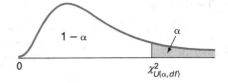

Degrees of Freedom	Upper-Tail Areas (α)											
	0.995	0.99	0.975	0.95	0.90	0.75	0.25	0.10	0.05	0.025	0.01	0.005
1			0.001	0.004	0.016	0.102	1.323	2.706	3.841	5.024	6.635	7.879
2	0.010	0.020	0.051	0.103	0.211	0.575	2.773	4.605	5.991	7.378	9.210	10.597
3	0.072	0.115	0.216	0.352	0.584	1.213	4.108	6.251	7.815	9.348	11.345	12.838
4	0.207	0.297	0.484	0.711	1.064	1.923	5.385	7.779	9.488	11.143	13.277	14.860
5	0.412	0.554	0.831	1.145	1.610	2.675	6.626	9.236	11.071	12.833	15.086	16.750
6	0.676	0.872	1.237	1.635	2.204	3.455	7.841	10.645	12.592	14.449	16.812	18.458
7	0.989	1.239	1.690	2.167	2.833	4.255	9.037	12.017	14.067	16.013	18.475	20.278
8	1.344	1.646	2.180	2.733	3.490	5.071	10.219	13.362	15.507	17.535	20.090	21.955
9	1.735	2.088	2.700	3.325	4.168	5.899	11.389	14.684	16.919	19.023	21.666	23.589
10	2.156	2.558	3.247	3.940	4.865	6.737	12.549	15.987	18.307	20.483	23.209	25.188
11	2.603	3.053	3.816	4.575	5.578	7.584	13.701	17.275	19.675	21.920	24.725	26.757
12	3.074	3.571	4.404	5.226	6.304	8.438	14.845	18.549	21.026	23.337	26.217	28.299
13	3.565	4.107	5.009	5.892	7.042	9.299	15.984	19.812	22.362	24.736	27.688	29.819
14	4.075	4.660	5.629	6.571	7.790	10.165	17.117	21.064	23.685	26.119	29.141	31.319
15	4.601	5.229	6.262	7.261	8.547	11.037	18.245	22.307	24.996	27.488	30.578	32.801
16	5.142	5.812	6.908	7.962	9.312	11.912	19.369	23.542	26.296	28.845	32.000	34.267
17	5.697	6.408	7.564	8.672	10.085	12.792	20.489	24.769	27.587	30.191	33.409	35.718
18	6.265	7.015	8.231	9.390	10.865	13.675	21.605	25.989	28.869	31.526	34.805	37.156
19	6.844	7.633	8.907	10.117	11.651	14.562	22.718	27.204	30.144	32.852	36.191	38.582
20	7.434	8.260	9.591	10.851	12.443	15.452	23.828	28.412	31.410	34.170	37.566	39.997
21	8.034	8.897	10.283	11.591	13.240	16.344	24.935	29.615	32.671	35.479	38.932	41.401
22	8.643	9.542	10.982	12.338	14.042	17.240	26.039	30.813	33.924	36.781	40.289	42.796
23	9.260	10.196	11.689	13.091	14.848	18.137	27.141	32.007	35.172	38.076	41.638	44.181
24	9.886	10.856	12.401	13.848	15.659	19.037	28.241	33.196	36.415	39.364	42.980	45.559
25	10.520	11.524	13.120	14.611	16.473	19.939	29.339	34.382	37.652	40.646	44.314	46.928
26	11.160	12.198	13.844	15.379	17.292	20.843	30.435	35.563	38.885	41.923	45.642	48.290
27	11.808	12.879	14.573	16.151	18.114	21.749	31.528	36.741	40.113	43.194	46.963	49.645
28	12.461	13.565	15.308	16.928	18.939	22.657	32.620	37.916	41.337	44.461	48.278	50.993
29	13.121	14.257	16.047	17.708	19.768	23.567	33.711	39.087	42.557	45.722	49.588	52.336
30	13.787	14.954	16.791	18.493	20.599	24.478	34.800	40.256	43.773	46.979	50.892	53.672

For larger values of degrees of freedom (df) the expression $Z = \sqrt{2\chi^2} - \sqrt{2(df) - 1}$ may be used and the resulting upper-tail area can be found from the cumulative standardized normal distribution (Table 2).

TABLE 5

Critical Values of F

For a particular combination of numerator and denominator degrees of freedom, entry represents the critical values of F corresponding to a specified upper-tail area (α).

$\alpha = 0.05$

$F_{U(\alpha, df_1, df_2)}$

	Numerator, df_1																		
Denominator, df_2	1	2	3	4	5	6	7	8	9	10	12	15	20	24	30	40	60	120	∞
1	161.40	199.50	215.70	224.60	230.20	234.00	236.80	238.90	240.50	241.90	243.90	245.90	248.00	249.10	250.10	251.10	252.20	253.30	254.30
2	18.51	19.00	19.16	19.25	19.30	19.33	19.35	19.37	19.38	19.40	19.41	19.43	19.45	19.45	19.46	19.47	19.48	19.49	19.50
3	10.13	9.55	9.28	9.12	9.01	8.94	8.89	8.85	8.81	8.79	8.74	8.70	8.66	8.64	8.62	8.59	8.57	8.55	8.53
4	7.71	6.94	6.59	6.39	6.26	6.16	6.09	6.04	6.00	5.96	5.91	5.86	5.80	5.77	5.75	5.72	5.69	5.66	5.63
5	6.61	5.79	5.41	5.19	5.05	4.95	4.88	4.82	4.77	4.74	4.68	4.62	4.56	4.53	4.50	4.46	4.43	4.40	4.36
6	5.99	5.14	4.76	4.53	4.39	4.28	4.21	4.15	4.10	4.06	4.00	3.94	3.87	3.84	3.81	3.77	3.74	3.70	3.67
7	5.59	4.74	4.35	4.12	3.97	3.87	3.79	3.73	3.68	3.64	3.57	3.51	3.44	3.41	3.38	3.34	3.30	3.27	3.23
8	5.32	4.46	4.07	3.84	3.69	3.58	3.50	3.44	3.39	3.35	3.28	3.22	3.15	3.12	3.08	3.04	3.01	2.97	2.93
9	5.12	4.26	3.86	3.63	3.48	3.37	3.29	3.23	3.18	3.14	3.07	3.01	2.94	2.90	2.86	2.83	2.79	2.75	2.71
10	4.96	4.10	3.71	3.48	3.33	3.22	3.14	3.07	3.02	2.98	2.91	2.85	2.77	2.74	2.70	2.66	2.62	2.58	2.54
11	4.84	3.98	3.59	3.36	3.20	3.09	3.01	2.95	2.90	2.85	2.79	2.72	2.65	2.61	2.57	2.53	2.49	2.45	2.40
12	4.75	3.89	3.49	3.26	3.11	3.00	2.91	2.85	2.80	2.75	2.69	2.62	2.54	2.51	2.47	2.43	2.38	2.34	2.30
13	4.67	3.81	3.41	3.18	3.03	2.92	2.83	2.77	2.71	2.67	2.60	2.53	2.46	2.42	2.38	2.34	2.30	2.25	2.21
14	4.60	3.74	3.34	3.11	2.96	2.85	2.76	2.70	2.65	2.60	2.53	2.46	2.39	2.35	2.31	2.27	2.22	2.18	2.13
15	4.54	3.68	3.29	3.06	2.90	2.79	2.71	2.64	2.59	2.54	2.48	2.40	2.33	2.29	2.25	2.20	2.16	2.11	2.07
16	4.49	3.63	3.24	3.01	2.85	2.74	2.66	2.59	2.54	2.49	2.42	2.35	2.28	2.24	2.19	2.15	2.11	2.06	2.01
17	4.45	3.59	3.20	2.96	2.81	2.70	2.61	2.55	2.49	2.45	2.38	2.31	2.23	2.19	2.15	2.10	2.06	2.01	1.96
18	4.41	3.55	3.16	2.93	2.77	2.66	2.58	2.51	2.46	2.41	2.34	2.27	2.19	2.15	2.11	2.06	2.02	1.97	1.92
19	4.38	3.52	3.13	2.90	2.74	2.63	2.54	2.48	2.42	2.38	2.31	2.23	2.16	2.11	2.07	2.03	1.98	1.93	1.88
20	4.35	3.49	3.10	2.87	2.71	2.60	2.51	2.45	2.39	2.35	2.28	2.20	2.12	2.08	2.04	1.99	1.95	1.90	1.84
21	4.32	3.47	3.07	2.84	2.68	2.57	2.49	2.42	2.37	2.32	2.25	2.18	2.10	2.05	2.01	1.96	1.92	1.87	1.81
22	4.30	3.44	3.05	2.82	2.66	2.55	2.46	2.40	2.34	2.30	2.23	2.15	2.07	2.03	1.98	1.94	1.89	1.84	1.78
23	4.28	3.42	3.03	2.80	2.64	2.53	2.44	2.37	2.32	2.27	2.20	2.13	2.05	2.01	1.96	1.91	1.86	1.81	1.76
24	4.26	3.40	3.01	2.78	2.62	2.51	2.42	2.36	2.30	2.25	2.18	2.11	2.03	1.98	1.94	1.89	1.84	1.79	1.73
25	4.24	3.39	2.99	2.76	2.60	2.49	2.40	2.34	2.28	2.24	2.16	2.09	2.01	1.96	1.92	1.87	1.82	1.77	1.71
26	4.23	3.37	2.98	2.74	2.59	2.47	2.39	2.32	2.27	2.22	2.15	2.07	1.99	1.95	1.90	1.85	1.80	1.75	1.69
27	4.21	3.35	2.96	2.73	2.57	2.46	2.37	2.31	2.25	2.20	2.13	2.06	1.97	1.93	1.88	1.84	1.79	1.73	1.67
28	4.20	3.34	2.95	2.71	2.56	2.45	2.36	2.29	2.24	2.19	2.12	2.04	1.96	1.91	1.87	1.82	1.77	1.71	1.65
29	4.18	3.33	2.93	2.70	2.55	2.43	2.35	2.28	2.22	2.18	2.10	2.03	1.94	1.90	1.85	1.81	1.75	1.70	1.64
30	4.17	3.32	2.92	2.69	2.53	2.42	2.33	2.27	2.21	2.16	2.09	2.01	1.93	1.89	1.84	1.79	1.74	1.68	1.62
40	4.08	3.23	2.84	2.61	2.45	2.34	2.25	2.18	2.12	2.08	2.00	1.92	1.84	1.79	1.74	1.69	1.64	1.58	1.51
60	4.00	3.15	2.76	2.53	2.37	2.25	2.17	2.10	2.04	1.99	1.92	1.84	1.75	1.70	1.65	1.59	1.53	1.47	1.39
120	3.92	3.07	2.68	2.45	2.29	2.17	2.09	2.02	1.96	1.91	1.83	1.75	1.66	1.61	1.55	1.50	1.43	1.35	1.25
∞	3.84	3.00	2.60	2.37	2.21	2.10	2.01	1.94	1.88	1.83	1.75	1.67	1.57	1.52	1.46	1.39	1.32	1.22	1.00

continued

TABLE 5

Critical Values of F (Continued)

$\alpha = 0.025$

$F_{U(\alpha, df_1, df_2)}$

Numerator, df_1

Denominator, df_2	1	2	3	4	5	6	7	8	9	10	12	15	20	24	30	40	60	120	∞
1	647.80	799.50	864.20	899.60	921.80	937.10	948.20	956.70	963.30	968.60	976.70	984.90	993.10	997.20	1,001.00	1,006.00	1,010.00	1,014.00	1,018.00
2	38.51	39.00	39.17	39.25	39.30	39.33	39.36	39.39	39.39	39.40	39.41	39.43	39.45	39.46	39.46	39.47	39.48	39.49	39.50
3	17.44	16.04	15.44	15.10	14.88	14.73	14.62	14.54	14.47	14.42	14.34	14.25	14.17	14.12	14.08	14.04	13.99	13.95	13.90
4	12.22	10.65	9.98	9.60	9.36	9.20	9.07	8.98	8.90	8.84	8.75	8.66	8.56	8.51	8.46	8.41	8.36	8.31	8.26
5	10.01	8.43	7.76	7.39	7.15	6.98	6.85	6.76	6.68	6.62	6.52	6.43	6.33	6.28	6.23	6.18	6.12	6.07	6.02
6	8.81	7.26	6.60	6.23	5.99	5.82	5.70	5.60	5.52	5.46	5.37	5.27	5.17	5.12	5.07	5.01	4.96	4.90	4.85
7	8.07	6.54	5.89	5.52	5.29	5.12	4.99	4.90	4.82	4.76	4.67	4.57	4.47	4.42	4.36	4.31	4.25	4.20	4.14
8	7.57	6.06	5.42	5.05	4.82	4.65	4.53	4.43	4.36	4.30	4.20	4.10	4.00	3.95	3.89	3.84	3.78	3.73	3.67
9	7.21	5.71	5.08	4.72	4.48	4.32	4.20	4.10	4.03	3.96	3.87	3.77	3.67	3.61	3.56	3.51	3.45	3.39	3.33
10	6.94	5.46	4.83	4.47	4.24	4.07	3.95	3.85	3.78	3.72	3.62	3.52	3.42	3.37	3.31	3.26	3.20	3.14	3.08
11	6.72	5.26	4.63	4.28	4.04	3.88	3.76	3.66	3.59	3.53	3.43	3.33	3.23	3.17	3.12	3.06	3.00	2.94	2.88
12	6.55	5.10	4.47	4.12	3.89	3.73	3.61	3.51	3.44	3.37	3.28	3.18	3.07	3.02	2.96	2.91	2.85	2.79	2.72
13	6.41	4.97	4.35	4.00	3.77	3.60	3.48	3.39	3.31	3.25	3.15	3.05	2.95	2.89	2.84	2.78	2.72	2.66	2.60
14	6.30	4.86	4.24	3.89	3.66	3.50	3.38	3.29	3.21	3.15	3.05	2.95	2.84	2.79	2.73	2.67	2.61	2.55	2.49
15	6.20	4.77	4.15	3.80	3.58	3.41	3.29	3.20	3.12	3.06	2.96	2.86	2.76	2.70	2.64	2.59	2.52	2.46	2.40
16	6.12	4.69	4.08	3.73	3.50	3.34	3.22	3.12	3.05	2.99	2.89	2.79	2.68	2.63	2.57	2.51	2.45	2.38	2.32
17	6.04	4.62	4.01	3.66	3.44	3.28	3.16	3.06	2.98	2.92	2.82	2.72	2.62	2.56	2.50	2.44	2.38	2.32	2.25
18	5.98	4.56	3.95	3.61	3.38	3.22	3.10	3.01	2.93	2.87	2.77	2.67	2.56	2.50	2.44	2.38	2.32	2.26	2.19
19	5.92	4.51	3.90	3.56	3.33	3.17	3.05	2.96	2.88	2.82	2.72	2.62	2.51	2.45	2.39	2.33	2.27	2.20	2.13
20	5.87	4.46	3.86	3.51	3.29	3.13	3.01	2.91	2.84	2.77	2.68	2.57	2.46	2.41	2.35	2.29	2.22	2.16	2.09
21	5.83	4.42	3.82	3.48	3.25	3.09	2.97	2.87	2.80	2.73	2.64	2.53	2.42	2.37	2.31	2.25	2.18	2.11	2.04
22	5.79	4.38	3.78	3.44	3.22	3.05	2.93	2.84	2.76	2.70	2.60	2.50	2.39	2.33	2.27	2.21	2.14	2.08	2.00
23	5.75	4.35	3.75	3.41	3.18	3.02	2.90	2.81	2.73	2.67	2.57	2.47	2.36	2.30	2.24	2.18	2.11	2.04	1.97
24	5.72	4.32	3.72	3.38	3.15	2.99	2.87	2.78	2.70	2.64	2.54	2.44	2.33	2.27	2.21	2.15	2.08	2.01	1.94
25	5.69	4.29	3.69	3.35	3.13	2.97	2.85	2.75	2.68	2.61	2.51	2.41	2.30	2.24	2.18	2.12	2.05	1.98	1.91
26	5.66	4.27	3.67	3.33	3.10	2.94	2.82	2.73	2.65	2.59	2.49	2.39	2.28	2.22	2.16	2.09	2.03	1.95	1.88
27	5.63	4.24	3.65	3.31	3.08	2.92	2.80	2.71	2.63	2.57	2.47	2.36	2.25	2.19	2.13	2.07	2.00	1.93	1.85
28	5.61	4.22	3.63	3.29	3.06	2.90	2.78	2.69	2.61	2.55	2.45	2.34	2.23	2.17	2.11	2.05	1.98	1.91	1.83
29	5.59	4.20	3.61	3.27	3.04	2.88	2.76	2.67	2.59	2.53	2.43	2.32	2.21	2.15	2.09	2.03	1.96	1.89	1.81
30	5.57	4.18	3.59	3.25	3.03	2.87	2.75	2.65	2.57	2.51	2.41	2.31	2.20	2.14	2.07	2.01	1.94	1.87	1.79
40	5.42	4.05	3.46	3.13	2.90	2.74	2.62	2.53	2.45	2.39	2.29	2.18	2.07	2.01	1.94	1.88	1.80	1.72	1.64
60	5.29	3.93	3.34	3.01	2.79	2.63	2.51	2.41	2.33	2.27	2.17	2.06	1.94	1.88	1.82	1.74	1.67	1.58	1.48
120	5.15	3.80	3.23	2.89	2.67	2.52	2.39	2.30	2.22	2.16	2.05	1.94	1.82	1.76	1.69	1.61	1.53	1.43	1.31
∞	5.02	3.69	3.12	2.79	2.57	2.41	2.29	2.19	2.11	2.05	1.94	1.83	1.71	1.64	1.57	1.48	1.39	1.27	1.00

continued

TABLE 5
Critical Values of F (Continued)

$\alpha = 0.01$

$F_{U(\alpha, df_1, df_2)}$

| Denominator, df_2 | \multicolumn{19}{c}{Numerator, df_1} |
	1	2	3	4	5	6	7	8	9	10	12	15	20	24	30	40	60	120	∞
1	4,052.00	4,999.50	5,403.00	5,625.00	5,764.00	5,859.00	5,928.00	5,982.00	6,022.00	6,056.00	6,106.00	6,157.00	6,209.00	6,235.00	6,261.00	6,287.00	6,313.00	6,339.00	6,366.00
2	98.50	99.00	99.17	99.25	99.30	99.33	99.36	99.37	99.39	99.40	99.42	99.43	44.45	99.46	99.47	99.47	99.48	99.49	99.50
3	34.12	30.82	29.46	28.71	28.24	27.91	27.67	27.49	27.35	27.23	27.05	26.87	26.69	26.60	26.50	26.41	26.32	26.22	26.13
4	21.20	18.00	16.69	15.98	15.52	15.21	14.98	14.80	14.66	14.55	14.37	14.20	14.02	13.93	13.84	13.75	13.65	13.56	13.46
5	16.26	13.27	12.06	11.39	10.97	10.67	10.46	10.29	10.16	10.05	9.89	9.72	9.55	9.47	9.38	9.29	9.20	9.11	9.02
6	13.75	10.92	9.78	9.15	8.75	8.47	8.26	8.10	7.98	7.87	7.72	7.56	7.40	7.31	7.23	7.14	7.06	6.97	6.88
7	12.25	9.55	8.45	7.85	7.46	7.19	6.99	6.84	6.72	6.62	6.47	6.31	6.16	6.07	5.99	5.91	5.82	5.74	5.65
8	11.26	8.65	7.59	7.01	6.63	6.37	6.18	6.03	5.91	5.81	5.67	5.52	5.36	5.28	5.20	5.12	5.03	4.95	4.86
9	10.56	8.02	6.99	6.42	6.06	5.80	5.61	5.47	5.35	5.26	5.11	4.96	4.81	4.73	4.65	4.57	4.48	4.40	4.31
10	10.04	7.56	6.55	5.99	5.64	5.39	5.20	5.06	4.94	4.85	4.71	4.56	4.41	4.33	4.25	4.17	4.08	4.00	3.91
11	9.65	7.21	6.22	5.67	5.32	5.07	4.89	4.74	4.63	4.54	4.40	4.25	4.10	4.02	3.94	3.86	3.78	3.69	3.60
12	9.33	6.93	5.95	5.41	5.06	4.82	4.64	4.50	4.39	4.30	4.16	4.01	3.86	3.78	3.70	3.62	3.54	3.45	3.36
13	9.07	6.70	5.74	5.21	4.86	4.62	4.44	4.30	4.19	4.10	3.96	3.82	3.66	3.59	3.51	3.43	3.34	3.25	3.17
14	8.86	6.51	5.56	5.04	4.69	4.46	4.28	4.14	4.03	3.94	3.80	3.66	3.51	3.43	3.35	3.27	3.18	3.09	3.00
15	8.68	6.36	5.42	4.89	4.56	4.32	4.14	4.00	3.89	3.80	3.67	3.52	3.37	3.29	3.21	3.13	3.05	2.96	2.87
16	8.53	6.23	5.29	4.77	4.44	4.20	4.03	3.89	3.78	3.69	3.55	3.41	3.26	3.18	3.10	3.02	2.93	2.81	2.75
17	8.40	6.11	5.18	4.67	4.34	4.10	3.93	3.79	3.68	3.59	3.46	3.31	3.16	3.08	3.00	2.92	2.83	2.75	2.65
18	8.29	6.01	5.09	4.58	4.25	4.01	3.84	3.71	3.60	3.51	3.37	3.23	3.08	3.00	2.92	2.84	2.75	2.66	2.57
19	8.18	5.93	5.01	4.50	4.17	3.94	3.77	3.63	3.52	3.43	3.30	3.15	3.00	2.92	2.84	2.76	2.67	2.58	2.49
20	8.10	5.85	4.94	4.43	4.10	3.87	3.70	3.56	3.46	3.37	3.23	3.09	2.94	2.86	2.78	2.69	2.61	2.52	2.42
21	8.02	5.78	4.87	4.37	4.04	3.81	3.64	3.51	3.40	3.31	3.17	3.03	2.88	2.80	2.72	2.64	2.55	2.46	2.36
22	7.95	5.72	4.82	4.31	3.99	3.76	3.59	3.45	3.35	3.26	3.12	2.98	2.83	2.75	2.67	2.58	2.50	2.40	2.31
23	7.88	5.66	4.76	4.26	3.94	3.71	3.54	3.41	3.30	3.21	3.07	2.93	2.78	2.70	2.62	2.54	2.45	2.35	2.26
24	7.82	5.61	4.72	4.22	3.90	3.67	3.50	3.36	3.26	3.17	3.03	2.89	2.74	2.66	2.58	2.49	2.40	2.31	2.21
25	7.77	5.57	4.68	4.18	3.85	3.63	3.46	3.32	3.22	3.13	2.99	2.85	2.70	2.62	2.54	2.45	2.36	2.27	2.17
26	7.72	5.53	4.64	4.14	3.82	3.59	3.42	3.29	3.18	3.09	2.96	2.81	2.66	2.58	2.50	2.42	2.33	2.23	2.13
27	7.68	5.49	4.60	4.11	3.78	3.56	3.39	3.26	3.15	3.06	2.93	2.78	2.63	2.55	2.47	2.38	2.29	2.20	2.10
28	7.64	5.45	4.57	4.07	3.75	3.53	3.36	3.23	3.12	3.03	2.90	2.75	2.60	2.52	2.44	2.35	2.26	2.17	2.06
29	7.60	5.42	4.54	4.04	3.73	3.50	3.33	3.20	3.09	3.00	2.87	2.73	2.57	2.49	2.41	2.33	2.23	2.14	2.03
30	7.56	5.39	4.51	4.02	3.70	3.47	3.30	3.17	3.07	2.98	2.84	2.70	2.55	2.47	2.39	2.30	2.21	2.11	2.01
40	7.31	5.18	4.31	3.83	3.51	3.29	3.12	2.99	2.89	2.80	2.66	2.52	2.37	2.29	2.20	2.11	2.02	1.92	1.80
60	7.08	4.98	4.13	3.65	3.34	3.12	2.95	2.82	2.72	2.63	2.50	2.35	2.20	2.12	2.03	1.94	1.84	1.73	1.60
120	6.85	4.79	3.95	3.48	3.17	2.96	2.79	2.66	2.56	2.47	2.34	2.19	2.03	1.95	1.86	1.76	1.66	1.53	1.38
∞	6.63	4.61	3.78	3.32	3.02	2.80	2.64	2.51	2.41	2.32	2.18	2.04	1.88	1.79	1.70	1.59	1.47	1.32	1.00

continued

TABLE 5

Critical Values of F (Continued)

| | | | | | Numerator, df_1 | | | | | | | | | | | | | | |
Denominator, df_2	1	2	3	4	5	6	7	8	9	10	12	15	20	24	30	40	60	120	∞
1	16,211.00	20,000.00	21,615.00	22,500.00	23,056.00	23,437.00	23,715.00	23,925.00	24,091.00	24,224.00	24,426.00	24,630.00	24,836.00	24,910.00	25,044.00	25,148.00	25,253.00	25,359.00	25,465.00
2	198.50	199.00	199.20	199.20	199.30	199.30	199.40	199.40	199.40	199.40	199.40	199.40	199.40	199.50	199.50	199.50	199.50	199.50	199.50
3	55.55	49.80	47.47	46.19	45.39	44.84	44.43	44.13	43.88	43.69	43.39	43.08	42.78	42.62	42.47	42.31	42.15	41.99	41.83
4	31.33	26.28	24.26	23.15	22.46	21.97	21.62	21.35	21.14	20.97	20.70	20.44	20.17	20.03	19.89	19.75	19.61	19.47	19.32
5	22.78	18.31	16.53	15.56	14.94	14.51	14.20	13.96	13.77	13.62	13.38	13.15	12.90	12.78	12.66	12.53	12.40	12.27	12.11
6	18.63	14.54	12.92	12.03	11.46	11.07	10.79	10.57	10.39	10.25	10.03	9.81	9.59	9.47	9.36	9.24	9.12	9.00	8.88
7	16.24	12.40	10.88	10.05	9.52	9.16	8.89	8.68	8.51	8.38	8.18	7.97	7.75	7.65	7.53	7.42	7.31	7.19	7.08
8	14.69	11.04	9.60	8.81	8.30	7.95	7.69	7.50	7.34	7.21	7.01	6.81	6.61	6.50	6.40	6.29	6.18	6.06	5.95
9	13.61	10.11	8.72	7.96	7.47	7.13	6.88	6.69	6.54	6.42	6.23	6.03	5.83	5.73	5.62	5.52	5.41	5.30	5.19
10	12.83	9.43	8.08	7.34	6.87	6.54	6.30	6.12	5.97	5.85	5.66	5.47	5.27	5.17	5.07	4.97	4.86	4.75	4.61
11	12.23	8.91	7.60	6.88	6.42	6.10	5.86	5.68	5.54	5.42	5.24	5.05	4.86	4.75	4.65	4.55	4.44	4.34	4.23
12	11.75	8.51	7.23	6.52	6.07	5.76	5.52	5.35	5.20	5.09	4.91	4.72	4.53	4.43	4.33	4.23	4.12	4.01	3.90
13	11.37	8.19	6.93	6.23	5.79	5.48	5.25	5.08	4.94	4.82	4.64	4.46	4.27	4.17	4.07	3.97	3.87	3.76	3.65
14	11.06	7.92	6.68	6.00	5.56	5.26	5.03	4.86	4.72	4.60	4.43	4.25	4.06	3.96	3.86	3.76	3.66	3.55	3.41
15	10.80	7.70	6.48	5.80	5.37	5.07	4.85	4.67	4.54	4.42	4.25	4.07	3.88	3.79	3.69	3.58	3.48	3.37	3.26
16	10.58	7.51	6.30	5.64	5.21	4.91	4.69	4.52	4.38	4.27	4.10	3.92	3.73	3.64	3.54	3.44	3.33	3.22	3.11
17	10.38	7.35	6.16	5.50	5.07	4.78	4.56	4.39	4.25	4.14	3.97	3.79	3.61	3.51	3.41	3.31	3.21	3.10	2.98
18	10.22	7.21	6.03	5.37	4.96	4.66	4.44	4.28	4.14	4.03	3.86	3.68	3.50	3.40	3.30	3.20	3.10	2.99	2.87
19	10.07	7.09	5.92	5.27	4.85	4.56	4.34	4.18	4.04	3.93	3.76	3.59	3.40	3.31	3.21	3.11	3.00	2.89	2.78
20	9.94	6.99	5.82	5.17	4.76	4.47	4.26	4.09	3.96	3.85	3.68	3.50	3.32	3.22	3.12	3.02	2.92	2.81	2.69
21	9.83	6.89	5.73	5.09	4.68	4.39	4.18	4.02	3.88	3.77	3.60	3.43	3.24	3.15	3.05	2.95	2.84	2.73	2.61
22	9.73	6.81	5.65	5.02	4.61	4.32	4.11	3.94	3.81	3.70	3.54	3.36	3.18	3.08	2.98	2.88	2.77	2.66	2.55
23	9.63	6.73	5.58	4.95	4.54	4.26	4.05	3.88	3.75	3.64	3.47	3.30	3.12	3.02	2.92	2.82	2.71	2.60	2.48
24	9.55	6.66	5.52	4.89	4.49	4.20	3.99	3.83	3.69	3.59	3.42	3.25	3.06	2.97	2.87	2.77	2.66	2.55	2.43
25	9.48	6.60	5.46	4.84	4.43	4.15	3.94	3.78	3.64	3.54	3.37	3.20	3.01	2.92	2.82	2.72	2.61	2.50	2.38
26	9.41	6.54	5.41	4.79	4.38	4.10	3.89	3.73	3.60	3.49	3.33	3.15	2.97	2.87	2.77	2.67	2.56	2.45	2.33
27	9.34	6.49	5.36	4.74	4.34	4.06	3.85	3.69	3.56	3.45	3.28	3.11	2.93	2.83	2.73	2.63	2.52	2.41	2.29
28	9.28	6.44	5.32	4.70	4.30	4.02	3.81	3.65	3.52	3.41	3.25	3.07	2.89	2.79	2.69	2.59	2.48	2.37	2.25
29	9.23	6.40	5.28	4.66	4.26	3.98	3.77	3.61	3.48	3.38	3.21	3.04	2.86	2.76	2.66	2.56	2.45	2.33	2.21
30	9.18	6.35	5.24	4.62	4.23	3.95	3.74	3.58	3.45	3.34	3.18	3.01	2.82	2.73	2.63	2.52	2.42	2.30	2.18
40	8.83	6.07	4.98	4.37	3.99	3.71	3.51	3.35	3.22	3.12	2.95	2.78	2.60	2.50	2.40	2.30	2.18	2.06	1.93
60	8.49	5.79	4.73	4.14	3.76	3.49	3.29	3.13	3.01	2.90	2.74	2.57	2.39	2.29	2.19	2.08	1.96	1.83	1.69
120	8.18	5.54	4.50	3.92	3.55	3.28	3.09	2.93	2.81	2.71	2.54	2.37	2.19	2.09	1.98	1.87	1.75	1.61	1.43
∞	7.88	5.30	4.28	3.72	3.35	3.09	2.90	2.74	2.62	2.52	2.36	2.19	2.00	1.90	1.79	1.67	1.53	1.36	1.00

TABLE 6

TABLE OF BINOMIAL PROBABILITIES
(BEGINS ON THE FOLLOWING PAGE)

TABLE 6

Table of Binomial Probabilities

For a given combination of n and p, entry indicates the probability of obtaining a specified value of X. To locate entry, **when $p \leq .50$**, read p across the top heading and both n and X down the left margin; **when $p \geq .50$**, read p across the bottom heading and both n and X up the right margin.

n	X	0.01	0.02	0.03	0.04	0.05	0.06	0.07	0.08	0.09	0.10	0.15	0.20	0.25	0.30	0.35	0.40	0.45	0.50	X	n
2	2	0.9801	0.9604	0.9409	0.9216	0.9025	0.8836	0.8649	0.8464	0.8281	0.8100	0.7225	0.6400	0.5625	0.4900	0.4225	0.3600	0.3025	0.2500	0	2
	1	0.0198	0.0392	0.0582	0.0768	0.0950	0.1128	0.1302	0.1472	0.1638	0.1800	0.2550	0.3200	0.3750	0.4200	0.4550	0.4800	0.4950	0.5000	1	
	0	0.0001	0.0004	0.0009	0.0016	0.0025	0.0036	0.0049	0.0064	0.0081	0.0100	0.0225	0.0400	0.0625	0.0900	0.1225	0.1600	0.2025	0.2500	2	2
3	3	0.9703	0.9412	0.9127	0.8847	0.8574	0.8306	0.8044	0.7787	0.7536	0.7290	0.6141	0.5120	0.4219	0.3430	0.2746	0.2160	0.1664	0.1250	0	3
	2	0.0294	0.0576	0.0847	0.1106	0.1354	0.1590	0.1816	0.2031	0.2236	0.2430	0.3251	0.3840	0.4219	0.4410	0.4436	0.4320	0.4084	0.3750	1	
	1	0.0003	0.0012	0.0026	0.0046	0.0071	0.0102	0.0137	0.0177	0.0221	0.0270	0.0574	0.0960	0.1406	0.1890	0.2389	0.2880	0.3341	0.3750	2	
	0	0.0000	0.0000	0.0000	0.0001	0.0001	0.0002	0.0003	0.0005	0.0007	0.0010	0.0034	0.0080	0.0156	0.0270	0.0429	0.0640	0.0911	0.1250	3	3
4	4	0.9606	0.9224	0.8853	0.8493	0.8145	0.7807	0.7481	0.7164	0.6857	0.6561	0.5220	0.4096	0.3164	0.2401	0.1785	0.1296	0.0915	0.0625	0	4
	3	0.0388	0.0753	0.1095	0.1416	0.1715	0.1993	0.2252	0.2492	0.2713	0.2916	0.3685	0.4096	0.4219	0.4116	0.3845	0.3456	0.2995	0.2500	1	
	2	0.0006	0.0023	0.0051	0.0088	0.0135	0.0191	0.0254	0.0325	0.0402	0.0486	0.0975	0.1536	0.2109	0.2646	0.3105	0.3456	0.3675	0.3750	2	
	1	0.0000	0.0000	0.0001	0.0002	0.0005	0.0008	0.0013	0.0019	0.0027	0.0036	0.0115	0.0256	0.0469	0.0756	0.1115	0.1536	0.2005	0.2500	3	
	0	0.0000	0.0000	0.0000	0.0000	0.0000	0.0000	0.0000	0.0000	0.0001	0.0001	0.0005	0.0016	0.0039	0.0081	0.0150	0.0256	0.0410	0.0625	4	4
5	5	0.9510	0.9039	0.8587	0.8154	0.7738	0.7339	0.6957	0.6591	0.6240	0.5905	0.4437	0.3277	0.2373	0.1681	0.1160	0.0778	0.0503	0.0312	0	5
	4	0.0480	0.0922	0.1328	0.1699	0.2036	0.2342	0.2618	0.2866	0.3086	0.3280	0.3915	0.4096	0.3955	0.3601	0.3124	0.2592	0.2059	0.1562	1	
	3	0.0010	0.0038	0.0082	0.0142	0.0214	0.0299	0.0394	0.0498	0.0610	0.0729	0.1382	0.2048	0.2637	0.3087	0.3364	0.3456	0.3369	0.3125	2	
	2	0.0000	0.0001	0.0003	0.0006	0.0011	0.0019	0.0030	0.0043	0.0060	0.0081	0.0244	0.0512	0.0879	0.1323	0.1811	0.2304	0.2757	0.3125	3	
	1	0.0000	0.0000	0.0000	0.0000	0.0000	0.0001	0.0001	0.0002	0.0003	0.0004	0.0022	0.0064	0.0146	0.0283	0.0488	0.0768	0.1128	0.1562	4	
	0	—	0.0000	0.0000	0.0000	0.0000	0.0000	0.0000	0.0000	0.0000	0.0000	0.0001	0.0003	0.0010	0.0024	0.0053	0.0102	0.0185	0.0312	5	5
6	6	0.9415	0.8858	0.8330	0.7828	0.7351	0.6899	0.6470	0.6064	0.5679	0.5314	0.3771	0.2621	0.1780	0.1176	0.0754	0.0467	0.0277	0.0156	0	6
	5	0.0571	0.1085	0.1546	0.1957	0.2321	0.2642	0.2922	0.3164	0.3370	0.3543	0.3993	0.3932	0.3560	0.3025	0.2437	0.1866	0.1359	0.0937	1	
	4	0.0014	0.0055	0.0120	0.0204	0.0305	0.0422	0.0550	0.0688	0.0833	0.0984	0.1762	0.2458	0.2966	0.3241	0.3280	0.3110	0.2780	0.2344	2	
	3	0.0000	0.0002	0.0005	0.0011	0.0021	0.0036	0.0055	0.0080	0.0110	0.0146	0.0415	0.0819	0.1318	0.1852	0.2355	0.2765	0.3032	0.3125	3	
	2	0.0000	0.0000	0.0000	0.0000	0.0001	0.0002	0.0003	0.0005	0.0008	0.0012	0.0055	0.0154	0.0330	0.0595	0.0951	0.1372	0.1861	0.2344	4	
	1	—	0.0000	0.0000	0.0000	0.0000	0.0000	0.0000	0.0000	0.0000	0.0001	0.0004	0.0015	0.0044	0.0102	0.0205	0.0369	0.0609	0.0937	5	
	0	—	—	—	—	0.0000	0.0000	0.0000	0.0000	0.0000	0.0000	0.0000	0.0001	0.0002	0.0007	0.0018	0.0041	0.0083	0.0156	6	6

n	X	0.50	0.55	0.60	0.65	0.70	0.75	0.80	0.85	0.90	0.91	0.92	0.93	0.94	0.95	0.96	0.97	0.98	0.99	X
7	0	0.0078	0.0152	0.0280	0.0490	0.0824	0.1335	0.2097	0.3206	0.4783	0.5168	0.5578	0.6017	0.6485	0.6983	0.7514	0.8080	0.8681	0.9321	7
	1	0.0547	0.0872	0.1306	0.1848	0.2471	0.3115	0.3670	0.3960	0.3720	0.3578	0.3396	0.3170	0.2897	0.2573	0.2192	0.1749	0.1240	0.0659	6
	2	0.1641	0.2140	0.2613	0.2985	0.3177	0.3115	0.2753	0.2097	0.1240	0.1061	0.0886	0.0716	0.0555	0.0406	0.0274	0.0162	0.0076	0.0020	5
	3	0.2734	0.2918	0.2903	0.2679	0.2269	0.1730	0.1147	0.0617	0.0230	0.0175	0.0128	0.0090	0.0059	0.0036	0.0019	0.0008	0.0003	0.0000	4
	4	0.2734	0.2388	0.1935	0.1442	0.0972	0.0577	0.0287	0.0109	0.0026	0.0017	0.0011	0.0007	0.0004	0.0002	0.0001	0.0000	0.0000	—	3
	5	0.1641	0.1172	0.0774	0.0466	0.0250	0.0115	0.0043	0.0012	0.0002	0.0001	0.0001	0.0000	0.0000	0.0000	0.0000	—	—	—	2
	6	0.0547	0.0320	0.0172	0.0084	0.0036	0.0013	0.0004	0.0001	0.0000	0.0000	0.0000	0.0000	—	—	—	—	—	—	1
	7	0.0078	0.0037	0.0016	0.0006	0.0002	0.0001	0.0000	0.0000	—	—	—	—	—	—	—	—	—	—	0
8	0	0.0039	0.0084	0.0168	0.0319	0.0576	0.1001	0.1678	0.2725	0.4305	0.4703	0.5132	0.5596	0.6096	0.6634	0.7214	0.7837	0.8508	0.9227	8
	1	0.0312	0.0548	0.0896	0.1373	0.1977	0.2670	0.3355	0.3847	0.3826	0.3721	0.3570	0.3370	0.3113	0.2793	0.2405	0.1939	0.1389	0.0746	7
	2	0.1094	0.1569	0.2090	0.2587	0.2965	0.3115	0.2936	0.2376	0.1488	0.1288	0.1087	0.0888	0.0695	0.0515	0.0351	0.0210	0.0099	0.0026	6
	3	0.2187	0.2568	0.2787	0.2786	0.2541	0.2076	0.1468	0.0839	0.0331	0.0255	0.0189	0.0134	0.0089	0.0054	0.0029	0.0013	0.0004	0.0001	5
	4	0.2734	0.2627	0.2322	0.1875	0.1361	0.0865	0.0459	0.0185	0.0046	0.0031	0.0021	0.0013	0.0007	0.0004	0.0002	0.0001	0.0000	0.0000	4
	5	0.2187	0.1719	0.1239	0.0808	0.0467	0.0231	0.0092	0.0026	0.0004	0.0002	0.0001	0.0001	0.0000	0.0000	0.0000	0.0000	—	—	3
	6	0.1094	0.0703	0.0413	0.0217	0.0100	0.0038	0.0011	0.0002	0.0000	0.0000	0.0000	0.0000	—	—	—	—	—	—	2
	7	0.0312	0.0164	0.0079	0.0033	0.0012	0.0004	0.0001	0.0000	—	—	—	—	—	—	—	—	—	—	1
	8	0.0039	0.0017	0.0007	0.0002	0.0001	0.0000	0.0000	0.0000	—	—	—	—	—	—	—	—	—	—	0
9	0	0.0020	0.0046	0.0101	0.0207	0.0404	0.0751	0.1342	0.2316	0.3874	0.4279	0.4722	0.5204	0.5730	0.6302	0.6925	0.7602	0.8337	0.9135	9
	1	0.0176	0.0339	0.0605	0.1004	0.1556	0.2253	0.3020	0.3679	0.3874	0.3809	0.3695	0.3525	0.3292	0.2985	0.2597	0.2116	0.1531	0.0830	8
	2	0.0703	0.1110	0.1612	0.2162	0.2668	0.3003	0.3020	0.2597	0.1722	0.1507	0.1285	0.1061	0.0840	0.0629	0.0433	0.0262	0.0125	0.0034	7
	3	0.1641	0.2119	0.2508	0.2716	0.2668	0.2336	0.1762	0.1069	0.0446	0.0348	0.0261	0.0186	0.0125	0.0077	0.0042	0.0019	0.0006	0.0001	6
	4	0.2461	0.2600	0.2508	0.2194	0.1715	0.1168	0.0661	0.0283	0.0074	0.0052	0.0034	0.0021	0.0012	0.0006	0.0003	0.0001	0.0000	0.0000	5
	5	0.2461	0.2128	0.1672	0.1181	0.0735	0.0390	0.0165	0.0050	0.0008	0.0005	0.0003	0.0002	0.0001	0.0000	0.0000	0.0000	—	—	4
	6	0.1641	0.1160	0.0743	0.0424	0.0210	0.0087	0.0028	0.0006	0.0001	0.0000	0.0000	0.0000	0.0000	—	—	—	—	—	3
	7	0.0703	0.0407	0.0212	0.0098	0.0039	0.0012	0.0003	0.0000	0.0000	—	—	—	—	—	—	—	—	—	2
	8	0.0176	0.0083	0.0035	0.0013	0.0004	0.0001	0.0000	0.0000	—	—	—	—	—	—	—	—	—	—	1
	9	0.0020	0.0008	0.0003	0.0001	0.0000	0.0000	0.0000	—	—	—	—	—	—	—	—	—	—	—	0
10	0	0.0010	0.0025	.0060	0.0135	0.0282	0.0563	0.1074	0.1969	0.3487	0.3894	0.4344	0.4840	0.5386	0.5987	0.6648	0.7374	0.8171	0.9044	10
	1	0.0098	0.0207	0.0403	0.0725	0.1211	0.1877	0.2684	0.3474	0.3874	0.3851	0.3777	0.3643	0.3438	0.3151	0.2770	0.2281	0.1667	0.0914	9
	2	0.0439	0.0763	0.1209	0.1757	0.2335	0.2816	0.3020	0.2759	0.1937	0.1714	0.1478	0.1234	0.0988	0.0746	0.0519	0.0317	0.0153	0.0042	8
	3	0.1172	0.1665	0.2150	0.2522	0.2668	0.2503	0.2013	0.1298	0.0574	0.0452	0.0343	0.0248	0.0168	0.0105	0.0058	0.0026	0.0008	0.0001	7
	4	0.2051	0.2384	0.2508	0.2377	0.2001	0.1460	0.0881	0.0401	0.0112	0.0078	0.0052	0.0033	0.0019	0.0010	0.0004	0.0001	0.0000	0.0000	6
	5	0.2461	0.2340	0.2007	0.1536	0.1029	0.0584	0.0264	0.0085	0.0015	0.0009	0.0005	0.0003	0.0001	0.0001	0.0000	0.0000	—	—	5
	6	0.2051	0.1596	0.1115	0.0689	0.0368	0.0162	0.0055	0.0012	0.0001	0.0001	0.0000	0.0000	0.0000	0.0000	—	—	—	—	4
	7	0.1172	0.0746	0.0425	0.0212	0.0090	0.0031	0.0008	0.0001	0.0000	0.0000	—	—	—	—	—	—	—	—	3
	8	0.0439	0.0229	0.0106	0.0043	0.0014	0.0004	0.0001	0.0000	0.0000	—	—	—	—	—	—	—	—	—	2
	9	0.0098	0.0042	0.0016	0.0005	0.0001	0.0000	0.0000	0.0000	—	—	—	—	—	—	—	—	—	—	1
	10	0.0010	0.0003	0.0001	0.0000	0.0000	0.0000	—	—	—	—	—	—	—	—	—	—	—	—	0
n	X	0.50	0.55	0.60	0.65	0.70	0.75	0.80	0.85	0.90	0.91	0.92	0.93	0.94	0.95	0.96	0.97	0.98	0.99	

continued

TABLE 6
Table of Binomial Probabilities (Continued)

n	X	0.01	0.02	0.03	0.04	0.05	0.06	0.07	0.08	0.09	0.10	0.15	0.20	0.25	0.30	0.35	0.40	0.45	0.50	X
20	0	0.8179	0.6676	0.5438	0.4420	0.3585	0.2901	0.2342	0.1887	0.1516	0.1216	0.0388	0.0115	0.0032	0.0008	0.0002	0.0000	0.0000	—	20
	1	0.1652	0.2725	0.3364	0.3683	0.3774	0.3703	0.3526	0.3282	0.3000	0.2702	0.1368	0.0576	0.0211	0.0068	0.0020	0.0005	0.0001	0.0000	19
	2	0.0159	0.0528	0.0988	0.1458	0.1887	0.2246	0.2521	0.2711	0.2818	0.2852	0.2293	0.1369	0.0699	0.0278	0.0100	0.0031	0.0008	0.0002	18
	3	0.0010	0.0065	0.0183	0.0364	0.0596	0.0860	0.1139	0.1414	0.1672	0.1901	0.2428	0.2054	0.1339	0.0716	0.0323	0.0123	0.0040	0.0011	17
	4	0.0000	0.0006	0.0024	0.0065	0.0133	0.0233	0.0364	0.0523	0.0703	0.0898	0.1821	0.2182	0.1897	0.1304	0.0738	0.0350	0.0139	0.0046	16
	5	—	0.0000	0.0002	0.0009	0.0022	0.0048	0.0088	0.0145	0.0222	0.0319	0.1028	0.1746	0.2023	0.1789	0.1272	0.0746	0.0365	0.0148	15
	6	—	—	0.0000	0.0001	0.0003	0.0008	0.0017	0.0032	0.0055	0.0089	0.0454	0.1091	0.1686	0.1916	0.1712	0.1244	0.0746	0.0370	14
	7	—	—	—	0.0000	0.0000	0.0001	0.0002	0.0005	0.0011	0.0020	0.0160	0.0545	0.1124	0.1643	0.1844	0.1659	0.1221	0.0739	13
	8	—	—	—	—	—	0.0000	0.0000	0.0001	0.0002	0.0004	0.0046	0.0222	0.0609	0.1144	0.1614	0.1797	0.1623	0.1201	12
	9	—	—	—	—	—	—	—	0.0000	0.0000	0.0001	0.0011	0.0074	0.0271	0.0654	0.1158	0.1597	0.1771	0.1762	11
	10	—	—	—	—	—	—	—	—	—	0.0000	0.0002	0.0020	0.0099	0.0308	0.0686	0.1171	0.1593	0.1762	10
	11	—	—	—	—	—	—	—	—	—	—	0.0000	0.0005	0.0030	0.0120	0.0336	0.0710	0.1185	0.1602	9
	12	—	—	—	—	—	—	—	—	—	—	—	0.0001	0.0008	0.0039	0.0136	0.0355	0.0727	0.1201	8
	13	—	—	—	—	—	—	—	—	—	—	—	0.0000	0.0002	0.0010	0.0045	0.0146	0.0366	0.0739	7
	14	—	—	—	—	—	—	—	—	—	—	—	—	0.0000	0.0002	0.0012	0.0049	0.0150	0.0370	6
	15	—	—	—	—	—	—	—	—	—	—	—	—	—	0.0000	0.0003	0.0013	0.0049	0.0148	5
	16	—	—	—	—	—	—	—	—	—	—	—	—	—	—	0.0000	0.0003	0.0013	0.0046	4
	17	—	—	—	—	—	—	—	—	—	—	—	—	—	—	—	0.0000	0.0002	0.0011	3
	18	—	—	—	—	—	—	—	—	—	—	—	—	—	—	—	—	0.0000	0.0002	2
	19	—	—	—	—	—	—	—	—	—	—	—	—	—	—	—	—	—	0.0000	1
	20	—	—	—	—	—	—	—	—	—	—	—	—	—	—	—	—	—	0.0000	0
n		0.99	0.98	0.97	0.96	0.95	0.94	0.93	0.92	0.91	0.90	0.85	0.80	0.75	0.70	0.65	0.60	0.55	0.50	20

p

TABLE 7

Table of Poisson Probabilities

For a given value of λ, entry indicates the probability of a specified value of X.

λ

X	0.1	0.2	0.3	0.4	0.5	0.6	0.7	0.8	0.9	1.0
0	0.9048	0.8187	0.7408	0.6703	0.6065	0.5488	0.4966	0.4493	0.4066	0.3679
1	0.0905	0.1637	0.2222	0.2681	0.3033	0.3293	0.3476	0.3595	0.3659	0.3679
2	0.0045	0.0164	0.0333	0.0536	0.0758	0.0988	0.1217	0.1438	0.1647	0.1839
3	0.0002	0.0011	0.0033	0.0072	0.0126	0.0198	0.0284	0.0383	0.0494	0.0613
4	0.0000	0.0001	0.0003	0.0007	0.0016	0.0030	0.0050	0.0077	0.0111	0.0153
5	0.0000	0.0000	0.0000	0.0001	0.0002	0.0004	0.0007	0.0012	0.0020	0.0031
6	0.0000	0.0000	0.0000	0.0000	0.0000	0.0000	0.0001	0.0002	0.0003	0.0005
7	0.0000	0.0000	0.0000	0.0000	0.0000	0.0000	0.0000	0.0000	0.0000	0.0001

λ

X	1.1	1.2	1.3	1.4	1.5	1.6	1.7	1.8	1.9	2.0
0	0.3329	0.3012	0.2725	0.2466	0.2231	0.2019	0.1827	0.1653	0.1496	0.1353
1	0.3662	0.3614	0.3543	0.3452	0.3347	0.3230	0.3106	0.2975	0.2842	0.2707
2	0.2014	0.2169	0.2303	0.2417	0.2510	0.2584	0.2640	0.2678	0.2700	0.2707
3	0.0738	0.0867	0.0998	0.1128	0.1255	0.1378	0.1496	0.1607	0.1710	0.1804
4	0.0203	0.0260	0.0324	0.0395	0.0471	0.0551	0.0636	0.0723	0.0812	0.0902
5	0.0045	0.0062	0.0084	0.0111	0.0141	0.0176	0.0216	0.0260	0.0309	0.0361
6	0.0008	0.0012	0.0018	0.0026	0.0035	0.0047	0.0061	0.0078	0.0098	0.0120
7	0.0001	0.0002	0.0003	0.0005	0.0008	0.0011	0.0015	0.0020	0.0027	0.0034
8	0.0000	0.0000	0.0001	0.0001	0.0001	0.0002	0.0003	0.0005	0.0006	0.0009
9	0.0000	0.0000	0.0000	0.0000	0.0000	0.0000	0.0001	0.0001	0.0001	0.0002

λ

X	2.1	2.2	2.3	2.4	2.5	2.6	2.7	2.8	2.9	3.0
0	0.1225	0.1108	0.1003	0.0907	0.0821	0.0743	0.0672	0.0608	0.0550	0.0498
1	0.2572	0.2438	0.2306	0.2177	0.2052	0.1931	0.1815	0.1703	0.1596	0.1494
2	0.2700	0.2681	0.2652	0.2613	0.2565	0.2510	0.2450	0.2384	0.2314	0.2240
3	0.1890	0.1966	0.2033	0.2090	0.2138	0.2176	0.2205	0.2225	0.2237	0.2240
4	0.0992	0.1082	0.1169	0.1254	0.1336	0.1414	0.1488	0.1557	0.1622	0.1680
5	0.0417	0.0476	0.0538	0.0602	0.0668	0.0735	0.0804	0.0872	0.0940	0.1008
6	0.0146	0.0174	0.0206	0.0241	0.0278	0.0319	0.0362	0.0407	0.0455	0.0504
7	0.0044	0.0055	0.0068	0.0083	0.0099	0.0118	0.0139	0.0163	0.0188	0.0216
8	0.0011	0.0015	0.0019	0.0025	0.0031	0.0038	0.0047	0.0057	0.0068	0.0081
9	0.0003	0.0004	0.0005	0.0007	0.0009	0.0011	0.0014	0.0018	0.0022	0.0027
10	0.0001	0.0001	0.0001	0.0002	0.0002	0.0003	0.0004	0.0005	0.0006	0.0008
11	0.0000	0.0000	0.0000	0.0000	0.0000	0.0001	0.0001	0.0001	0.0002	0.0002
12	0.0000	0.0000	0.0000	0.0000	0.0000	0.0000	0.0000	0.0000	0.0000	0.0001

λ

X	3.1	3.2	3.3	3.4	3.5	3.6	3.7	3.8	3.9	4.0
0	0.0450	0.0408	0.0369	0.0334	0.0302	0.0273	0.0247	0.0224	0.0202	0.0183
1	0.1397	0.1340	0.1217	0.1135	0.1057	0.0984	0.0915	0.0850	0.0789	0.0733
2	0.2165	0.2087	0.2008	0.1929	0.1850	0.1771	0.1692	0.1615	0.1539	0.1465
3	0.2237	0.2226	0.2209	0.2186	0.2158	0.2125	0.2087	0.2046	0.2001	0.1954
4	0.1734	0.1781	0.1823	0.1858	0.1888	0.1912	0.1931	0.1944	0.1951	0.1954
5	0.1075	0.1140	0.1203	0.1264	0.1322	0.1377	0.1429	0.1477	0.1522	0.1563
6	0.0555	0.0608	0.0662	0.0716	0.0771	0.0826	0.0881	0.0936	0.0989	0.1042
7	0.0246	0.0278	0.0312	0.0348	0.0385	0.0425	0.0466	0.0508	0.0551	0.0595
8	0.0095	0.0111	0.0129	0.0148	0.0169	0.0191	0.0215	0.0241	0.0269	0.0298
9	0.0033	0.0040	0.0047	0.0056	0.0066	0.0076	0.0089	0.0102	0.0116	0.0132
10	0.0010	0.0013	0.0016	0.0019	0.0023	0.0028	0.0033	0.0039	0.0045	0.0053
11	0.0003	0.0004	0.0005	0.0006	0.0007	0.0009	0.0011	0.0013	0.0016	0.0019
12	0.0001	0.0001	0.0001	0.0002	0.0002	0.0003	0.0003	0.0004	0.0005	0.0006
13	0.0000	0.0000	0.0000	0.0000	0.0001	0.0001	0.0001	0.0001	0.0002	0.0002
14	0.0000	0.0000	0.0000	0.0000	0.0000	0.0000	0.0000	0.0000	0.0000	0.0001

continued

TABLE 7

Table of Poisson
Probabilities
(*Continued*)

						λ				
X	4.1	4.2	4.3	4.4	4.5	4.6	4.7	4.8	4.9	5.0
0	0.0166	0.0150	0.0136	0.0123	0.0111	0.0101	0.0091	0.0082	0.0074	0.0067
1	0.0679	0.0630	0.0583	0.0540	0.0500	0.0462	0.0427	0.0395	0.0365	0.0337
2	0.1393	0.1323	0.1254	0.1188	0.1125	0.1063	0.1005	0.0948	0.0894	0.0842
3	0.1904	0.1852	0.1798	0.1743	0.1687	0.1631	0.1574	0.1517	0.1460	0.1404
4	0.1951	0.1944	0.1933	0.1917	0.1898	0.1875	0.1849	0.1820	0.1789	0.1755
5	0.1600	0.1633	0.1662	0.1687	0.1708	0.1725	0.1738	0.1747	0.1753	0.1755
6	0.1093	0.1143	0.1191	0.1237	0.1281	0.1323	0.1362	0.1398	0.1432	0.1462
7	0.0640	0.0686	0.0732	0.0778	0.0824	0.0869	0.0914	0.0959	0.1002	0.1044
8	0.0328	0.0360	0.0393	0.0428	0.0463	0.0500	0.0537	0.0575	0.0614	0.0653
9	0.0150	0.0168	0.0188	0.0209	0.0232	0.0255	0.0280	0.0307	0.0334	0.0363
10	0.0061	0.0071	0.0081	0.0092	0.0104	0.0118	0.0132	0.0147	0.0164	0.0181
11	0.0023	0.0027	0.0032	0.0037	0.0043	0.0049	0.0056	0.0064	0.0073	0.0082
12	0.0008	0.0009	0.0011	0.0014	0.0016	0.0019	0.0022	0.0026	0.0030	0.0034
13	0.0002	0.0003	0.0004	0.0005	0.0006	0.0007	0.0008	0.0009	0.0011	0.0013
14	0.0001	0.0001	0.0001	0.0001	0.0002	0.0002	0.0003	0.0003	0.0004	0.0005
15	0.0000	0.0000	0.0000	0.0000	0.0001	0.0001	0.0001	0.0001	0.0001	0.0002

						λ				
X	5.1	5.2	5.3	5.4	5.5	5.6	5.7	5.8	5.9	6.0
0	0.0061	0.0055	0.0050	0.0045	0.0041	0.0037	0.0033	0.0030	0.0027	0.0025
1	0.0311	0.0287	0.0265	0.0244	0.0225	0.0207	0.0191	0.0176	0.0162	0.0149
2	0.0793	0.0746	0.0701	0.0659	0.0618	0.0580	0.0544	0.0509	0.0477	0.0446
3	0.1348	0.1293	0.1239	0.1185	0.1133	0.1082	0.1033	0.0985	0.0938	0.0892
4	0.1719	0.1681	0.1641	0.1600	0.1558	0.1515	0.1472	0.1428	0.1383	0.1339
5	0.1753	0.1748	0.1740	0.1728	0.1714	0.1697	0.1678	0.1656	0.1632	0.1606
6	0.1490	0.1515	0.1537	0.1555	0.1571	0.1584	0.1594	0.1601	0.1605	0.1606
7	0.1086	0.1125	0.1163	0.1200	0.1234	0.1267	0.1298	0.1326	0.1353	0.1377
8	0.0692	0.0731	0.0771	0.0810	0.0849	0.0887	0.0925	0.0962	0.0998	0.1033
9	0.0392	0.0423	0.0454	0.0486	0.0519	0.0552	0.0586	0.0620	0.0654	0.0688
10	0.0200	0.0220	0.0241	0.0262	0.0285	0.0309	0.0334	0.0359	0.0386	0.0413
11	0.0093	0.0104	0.0116	0.0129	0.0143	0.0157	0.0173	0.0190	0.0207	0.0225
12	0.0039	0.0045	0.0051	0.0058	0.0065	0.0073	0.0082	0.0092	0.0102	0.0113
13	0.0015	0.0018	0.0021	0.0024	0.0028	0.0032	0.0036	0.0041	0.0046	0.0052
14	0.0006	0.0007	0.0008	0.0009	0.0011	0.0013	0.0015	0.0017	0.0019	0.0022
15	0.0002	0.0002	0.0003	0.0003	0.0004	0.0005	0.0006	0.0007	0.0008	0.0009
16	0.0001	0.0001	0.0001	0.0001	0.0001	0.0002	0.0002	0.0002	0.0003	0.0003
17	0.0000	0.0000	0.0000	0.0000	0.0000	0.0000	0.0001	0.0001	0.0001	0.0001

						λ				
X	6.1	6.2	6.3	6.4	6.5	6.6	6.7	6.8	6.9	7.0
0	0.0022	0.0020	0.0018	0.0017	0.0015	0.0014	0.0012	0.0011	0.0010	0.0009
1	0.0137	0.0126	0.0116	0.0106	0.0098	0.0090	0.0082	0.0076	0.0070	0.0064
2	0.0417	0.0390	0.0364	0.0340	0.0318	0.0296	0.0276	0.0258	0.0240	0.0223
3	0.0848	0.0806	0.0765	0.0726	0.0688	0.0652	0.0617	0.0584	0.0552	0.0521
4	0.1294	0.1249	0.1205	0.1162	0.1118	0.1076	0.1034	0.0992	0.0952	0.0912
5	0.1579	0.1549	0.1519	0.1487	0.1454	0.1420	0.1385	0.1349	0.1314	0.1277
6	0.1605	0.1601	0.1595	0.1586	0.1575	0.1562	0.1546	0.1529	0.1511	0.1490
7	0.1399	0.1418	0.1435	0.1450	0.1462	0.1472	0.1480	0.1486	0.1489	0.1490
8	0.1066	0.1099	0.1130	0.1160	0.1188	0.1215	0.1240	0.1263	0.1284	0.1304
9	0.0723	0.0757	0.0791	0.0825	0.0858	0.0891	0.0923	0.0954	0.0985	0.1014
10	0.0441	0.0469	0.0498	0.0528	0.0558	0.0588	0.0618	0.0649	0.0679	0.0710
11	0.0245	0.0265	0.0285	0.0307	0.0330	0.0353	0.0377	0.0401	0.0426	0.0452
12	0.0124	0.0137	0.0150	0.0164	0.0179	0.0194	0.0210	0.0277	0.0245	0.0264
13	0.0058	0.0065	0.0073	0.0081	0.0089	0.0098	0.0108	0.0119	0.0130	0.0142
14	0.0025	0.0029	0.0033	0.0037	0.0041	0.0046	0.0052	0.0058	0.0064	0.0071

continued

TABLE 7

Table of Poisson
Probabilities
(*Continued*)

					λ					
X	6.1	6.2	6.3	6.4	6.5	6.6	6.7	6.8	6.9	7.0
15	0.0010	0.0012	0.0014	0.0016	0.0018	0.0020	0.0023	0.0026	0.0029	0.0033
16	0.0004	0.0005	0.0005	0.0006	0.0007	0.0008	0.0010	0.0011	0.0013	0.0014
17	0.0001	0.0002	0.0002	0.0002	0.0003	0.0003	0.0004	0.0004	0.0005	0.0006
18	0.0000	0.0001	0.0001	0.0001	0.0001	0.0001	0.0001	0.0002	0.0002	0.0002
19	0.0000	0.0000	0.0000	0.0000	0.0000	0.0000	0.0000	0.0001	0.0001	0.0001

					λ					
X	7.1	7.2	7.3	7.4	7.5	7.6	7.7	7.8	7.9	8.0
0	0.0008	0.0007	0.0007	0.0006	0.0006	0.0005	0.0005	0.0004	0.0004	0.0003
1	0.0059	0.0054	0.0049	0.0045	0.0041	0.0038	0.0035	0.0032	0.0029	0.0027
2	0.0208	0.0194	0.0180	0.0167	0.0156	0.0145	0.0134	0.0125	0.0116	0.0107
3	0.0492	0.0464	0.0438	0.0413	0.0389	0.0366	0.0345	0.0324	0.0305	0.0286
4	0.0874	0.0836	0.0799	0.0764	0.0729	0.0696	0.0663	0.0632	0.0602	0.0573
5	0.1241	0.1204	0.1167	0.1130	0.1094	0.1057	0.1021	0.0986	0.0951	0.0916
6	0.1468	0.1445	0.1420	0.1394	0.1367	0.1339	0.1311	0.1282	0.1252	0.1221
7	0.1489	0.1486	0.1481	0.1474	0.1465	0.1454	0.1442	0.1428	0.1413	0.1396
8	0.1321	0.1337	0.1351	0.1363	0.1373	0.1382	0.1388	0.1392	0.1395	0.1396
9	0.1042	0.1070	0.1096	0.1121	0.1144	0.1167	0.1187	0.1207	0.1224	0.1241
10	0.0740	0.0770	0.0800	0.0829	0.0858	0.0887	0.0914	0.0941	0.0967	0.0993
11	0.0478	0.0504	0.0531	0.0558	0.0585	0.0613	0.0640	0.0667	0.0695	0.0722
12	0.0283	0.0303	0.0323	0.0344	0.0366	0.0388	0.0411	0.0434	0.0457	0.0481
13	0.0154	0.0168	0.0181	0.0196	0.0211	0.0227	0.0243	0.0260	0.0278	0.0296
14	0.0078	0.0086	0.0095	0.0104	0.0113	0.0123	0.0134	0.0145	0.0157	0.0169
15	0.0037	0.0041	0.0046	0.0051	0.0057	0.0062	0.0069	0.0075	0.0083	0.0090
16	0.0016	0.0019	0.0021	0.0024	0.0026	0.0030	0.0033	0.0037	0.0041	0.0045
17	0.0007	0.0008	0.0009	0.0010	0.0012	0.0013	0.0015	0.0017	0.0019	0.0021
18	0.0003	0.0003	0.0004	0.0004	0.0005	0.0006	0.0006	0.0007	0.0008	0.0009
19	0.0001	0.0001	0.0001	0.0002	0.0002	0.0002	0.0003	0.0003	0.0003	0.0004
20	0.0000	0.0000	0.0001	0.0001	0.0001	0.0001	0.0001	0.0001	0.0001	0.0002
21	0.0000	0.0000	0.0000	0.0000	0.0000	0.0000	0.0000	0.0000	0.0001	0.0001

					λ					
X	8.1	8.2	8.3	8.4	8.5	8.6	8.7	8.8	8.9	9.0
0	0.0003	0.0003	0.0002	0.0002	0.0002	0.0002	0.0002	0.0002	0.0001	0.0001
1	0.0025	0.0023	0.0021	0.0019	0.0017	0.0016	0.0014	0.0013	0.0012	0.0011
2	0.0100	0.0092	0.0086	0.0079	0.0074	0.0068	0.0063	0.0058	0.0054	0.0050
3	0.0269	0.0252	0.0237	0.0222	0.0208	0.0195	0.0183	0.0171	0.0160	0.0150
4	0.0544	0.0517	0.0491	0.0466	0.0443	0.0420	0.0398	0.0377	0.0357	0.0337
5	0.0882	0.0849	0.0816	0.0784	0.0752	0.0722	0.0692	0.0663	0.0635	0.0607
6	0.1191	0.1160	0.1128	0.1097	0.1066	0.1034	0.1003	0.0972	0.0941	0.0911
7	0.1378	0.1358	0.1338	0.1317	0.1294	0.1271	0.1247	0.1222	0.1197	0.1171
8	0.1395	0.1392	0.1388	0.1382	0.1375	0.1366	0.1356	0.1344	0.1332	0.1318
9	0.1256	0.1269	0.1280	0.1290	0.1299	0.1306	0.1311	0.1315	0.1317	0.1318
10	0.1017	0.1040	0.1063	0.1084	0.1104	0.1123	0.1140	0.1157	0.1172	0.1186
11	0.0749	0.0776	0.0802	0.0828	0.0853	0.0878	0.0902	0.0925	0.0948	0.0970
12	0.0505	0.0530	0.0555	0.0579	0.0604	0.0629	0.0654	0.0679	0.0703	0.0728
13	0.0315	0.0334	0.0354	0.0374	0.0395	0.0416	0.0438	0.0459	0.0481	0.0504
14	0.0182	0.0196	0.0210	0.0225	0.0240	0.0256	0.0272	0.0289	0.0306	0.0324
15	0.0098	0.0107	0.0116	0.0126	0.0136	0.0147	0.0158	0.0169	0.0182	0.0194
16	0.0050	0.0055	0.0060	0.0066	0.0072	0.0079	0.0086	0.0093	0.0101	0.0109
17	0.0024	0.0026	0.0029	0.0033	0.0036	0.0040	0.0044	0.0048	0.0053	0.0058
18	0.0011	0.0012	0.0014	0.0015	0.0017	0.0019	0.0021	0.0024	0.0026	0.0029
19	0.0005	0.0005	0.0006	0.0007	0.0008	0.0009	0.0010	0.0011	0.0012	0.0014
20	0.0002	0.0002	0.0002	0.0003	0.0003	0.0004	0.0004	0.0005	0.0005	0.0006
21	0.0001	0.0001	0.0001	0.0001	0.0001	0.0002	0.0002	0.0002	0.0002	0.0003
22	0.0000	0.0000	0.0000	0.0000	0.0001	0.0001	0.0001	0.0001	0.0001	0.0001

continued

TABLE 7

Table of Poisson
Probabilities
(*Continued*)

					λ					
X	9.1	9.2	9.3	9.4	9.5	9.6	9.7	9.8	9.9	10
0	0.0001	0.0001	0.0001	0.0001	0.0001	0.0001	0.0001	0.0001	0.0001	0.0000
1	0.0010	0.0009	0.0009	0.0008	0.0007	0.0007	0.0006	0.0005	0.0005	0.0005
2	0.0046	0.0043	0.0040	0.0037	0.0034	0.0031	0.0029	0.0027	0.0025	0.0023
3	0.0140	0.0131	0.0123	0.0115	0.0107	0.0100	0.0093	0.0087	0.0081	0.0076
4	0.0319	0.0302	0.0285	0.0269	0.0254	0.0240	0.0226	0.0213	0.0201	0.0189
5	0.0581	0.0555	0.0530	0.0506	0.0483	0.0460	0.0439	0.0418	0.0398	0.0378
6	0.0881	0.0851	0.0822	0.0793	0.0764	0.0736	0.0709	0.0682	0.0656	0.0631
7	0.1145	0.1118	0.1091	0.1064	0.1037	0.1010	0.0982	0.0955	0.0928	0.0901
8	0.1302	0.1286	0.1269	0.1251	0.1232	0.1212	0.1191	0.1170	0.1148	0.1126
9	0.1317	0.1315	0.1311	0.1306	0.1300	0.1293	0.1284	0.1274	0.1263	0.1251
10	0.1198	0.1210	0.1219	0.1228	0.1235	0.1241	0.1245	0.1249	0.1250	0.1251
11	0.0991	0.1012	0.1031	0.1049	0.1067	0.1083	0.1098	0.1112	0.1125	0.1137
12	0.0752	0.0776	0.0799	0.0822	0.0844	0.0866	0.0888	0.0908	0.0928	0.0948
13	0.0526	0.0549	0.0572	0.0594	0.0617	0.0640	0.0662	0.0685	0.0707	0.0729
14	0.0342	0.0361	0.0380	0.0399	0.0419	0.0439	0.0459	0.0479	0.0500	0.0521
15	0.0208	0.0221	0.0235	0.0250	0.0265	0.0281	0.0297	0.0313	0.0330	0.0347
16	0.0118	0.0127	0.0137	0.0147	0.0157	0.0168	0.0180	0.0192	0.0204	0.0217
17	0.0063	0.0069	0.0075	0.0081	0.0088	0.0095	0.0103	0.0111	0.0119	0.0128
18	0.0032	0.0035	0.0039	0.0042	0.0046	0.0051	0.0055	0.0060	0.0065	0.0071
19	0.0015	0.0017	0.0019	0.0021	0.0023	0.0026	0.0028	0.0031	0.0034	0.0037
20	0.0007	0.0008	0.0009	0.0010	0.0011	0.0012	0.0014	0.0015	0.0017	0.0019
21	0.0003	0.0003	0.0004	0.0004	0.0005	0.0006	0.0006	0.0007	0.0008	0.0009
22	0.0001	0.0001	0.0002	0.0002	0.0002	0.0002	0.0003	0.0003	0.0004	0.0004
23	0.0000	0.0001	0.0001	0.0001	0.0001	0.0001	0.0001	0.0001	0.0002	0.0002
24	0.0000	0.0000	0.0000	0.0000	0.0000	0.0000	0.0000	0.0001	0.0001	0.0001

X	$\lambda = 20$	X	$\lambda = 20$	X	$\lambda = 20$	X	$\lambda = 20$
0	0.0000	10	0.0058	20	0.0888	30	0.0083
1	0.0000	11	0.0106	21	0.0846	31	0.0054
2	0.0000	12	0.0176	22	0.0769	32	0.0034
3	0.0000	13	0.0271	23	0.0669	33	0.0020
4	0.0000	14	0.0387	24	0.0557	34	0.0012
5	0.0001	15	0.0516	25	0.0446	35	0.0007
6	0.0002	16	0.0646	26	0.0343	36	0.0004
7	0.0005	17	0.0760	27	0.0254	37	0.0002
8	0.0013	18	0.0844	28	0.0181	38	0.0001
9	0.0029	19	0.0888	29	0.0125	39	0.0001

TABLE 8

Lower and Upper Critical Values, T_1, of Wilcoxon Rank Sum Test

	α		n_1						
n_2	One-tail	Two-tail	4	5	6	7	8	9	10
4	0.05	0.10	11,25						
	0.025	0.05	10,26						
	0.01	0.02	—,—						
	0.005	0.01	—,—						
5	0.05	0.10	12,28	19,36					
	0.025	0.05	11,29	17,38					
	0.01	0.02	10,30	16,39					
	0.005	0.01	—,—	15,40					
6	0.05	0.10	13,31	20,40	28,50				
	0.025	0.05	12,32	18,42	26,52				
	0.01	0.02	11,33	17,43	24,54				
	0.005	0.01	10,34	16,44	23,55				
7	0.05	0.10	14,34	21,44	29,55	39,66			
	0.025	0.05	13,35	20,45	27,57	36,69			
	0.01	0.02	11,37	18,47	25,59	34,71			
	0.005	0.01	10,38	16,49	24,60	32,73			
8	0.05	0.10	15,37	23,47	31,59	41,71	51,85		
	0.025	0.05	14,38	21,49	29,61	38,74	49,87		
	0.01	0.02	12,40	19,51	27,63	35,77	45,91		
	0.005	0.01	11,41	17,53	25,65	34,78	43,93		
9	0.05	0.10	16,40	24,51	33,63	43,76	54,90	66,105	
	0.025	0.05	14,42	22,53	31,65	40,79	51,93	62,109	
	0.01	0.02	13,43	20,55	28,68	37,82	47,97	59,112	
	0.005	0.01	11,45	18,57	26,70	35,84	45,99	56,115	
10	0.05	0.10	17,43	26,54	35,67	45,81	56,96	69,111	82,128
	0.025	0.05	15,45	23,57	32,70	42,84	53,99	65,115	78,132
	0.01	0.02	13,47	21,59	29,73	39,87	49,103	61,119	74,136
	0.005	0.01	12,48	19,61	27,75	37,89	47,105	58,122	71,139

Source: Adapted from Table 1 of F. Wilcoxon and R. A. Wilcox, *Some Rapid Approximate Statistical Procedures* (Pearl River, NY: Lederle Laboratories, 1964), with permission of the American Cyanamid Company.

TABLE 9

Critical Values of the Studentized Range, Q

Upper 5% Points ($\alpha = 0.05$)

Denominator, df	\multicolumn{19}{c}{Numerator, df}
	2	3	4	5	6	7	8	9	10	11	12	13	14	15	16	17	18	19	20
1	18.00	27.00	32.80	37.10	40.40	43.10	45.40	47.40	49.10	50.60	52.00	53.20	54.30	55.40	56.30	57.20	58.00	58.80	59.60
2	6.09	8.30	9.80	10.90	11.70	12.40	13.00	13.50	14.00	14.40	14.70	15.10	15.40	15.70	15.90	16.10	16.40	16.60	16.80
3	4.50	5.91	6.82	7.50	8.04	8.48	8.85	9.18	9.46	9.72	9.95	10.15	10.35	10.52	10.69	10.84	10.98	11.11	11.24
4	3.93	5.04	5.76	6.29	6.71	7.05	7.35	7.60	7.83	8.03	8.21	8.37	8.52	8.66	8.79	8.91	9.03	9.13	9.23
5	3.64	4.60	5.22	5.67	6.03	6.33	6.58	6.80	6.99	7.17	7.32	7.47	7.60	7.72	7.83	7.93	8.03	8.12	8.21
6	3.46	4.34	4.90	5.31	5.63	5.89	6.12	6.32	6.49	6.65	6.79	6.92	7.03	7.14	7.24	7.34	7.43	7.51	7.59
7	3.34	4.16	4.68	5.06	5.36	5.61	5.82	6.00	6.16	6.30	6.43	6.55	6.66	6.76	6.85	6.94	7.02	7.09	7.17
8	3.26	4.04	4.53	4.89	5.17	5.40	5.60	5.77	5.92	6.05	6.18	6.29	6.39	6.48	6.57	6.65	6.73	6.80	6.87
9	3.20	3.95	4.42	4.76	5.02	5.24	5.43	5.60	5.74	5.87	5.98	6.09	6.19	6.28	6.36	6.44	6.51	6.58	6.64
10	3.15	3.88	4.33	4.65	4.91	5.12	5.30	5.46	5.60	5.72	5.83	5.93	6.03	6.11	6.20	6.27	6.34	6.40	6.47
11	3.11	3.82	4.26	4.57	4.82	5.03	5.20	5.35	5.49	5.61	5.71	5.81	5.90	5.99	6.06	6.14	6.20	6.26	6.33
12	3.08	3.77	4.20	4.51	4.75	4.95	5.12	5.27	5.40	5.51	5.62	5.71	5.80	5.88	5.95	6.03	6.09	6.15	6.21
13	3.06	3.73	4.15	4.45	4.69	4.88	5.05	5.19	5.32	5.43	5.53	5.63	5.71	5.79	5.86	5.93	6.00	6.05	6.11
14	3.03	3.70	4.11	4.41	4.64	4.83	4.99	5.13	5.25	5.36	5.46	5.55	5.64	5.72	5.79	5.85	5.92	5.97	6.03
15	3.01	3.67	4.08	4.37	4.60	4.78	4.94	5.08	5.20	5.31	5.40	5.49	5.58	5.65	5.72	5.79	5.85	5.90	5.96
16	3.00	3.65	4.05	4.33	4.56	4.74	4.90	5.03	5.15	5.26	5.35	5.44	5.52	5.59	5.66	5.72	5.79	5.84	5.90
17	2.98	3.63	4.02	4.30	4.52	4.71	4.86	4.99	5.11	5.21	5.31	5.39	5.47	5.55	5.61	5.68	5.74	5.79	5.84
18	2.97	3.61	4.00	4.28	4.49	4.67	4.82	4.96	5.07	5.17	5.27	5.35	5.43	5.50	5.57	5.63	5.69	5.74	5.79
19	2.96	3.59	3.98	4.25	4.47	4.65	4.79	4.92	5.04	5.14	5.23	5.32	5.39	5.46	5.53	5.59	5.65	5.70	5.75
20	2.95	3.58	3.96	4.23	4.45	4.62	4.77	4.90	5.01	5.11	5.20	5.28	5.36	5.43	5.49	5.55	5.61	5.66	5.71
24	2.92	3.53	3.90	4.17	4.37	4.54	4.68	4.81	4.92	5.01	5.10	5.18	5.25	5.32	5.38	5.44	5.50	5.54	5.59
30	2.89	3.49	3.84	4.10	4.30	4.46	4.60	4.72	4.83	4.92	5.00	5.08	5.15	5.21	5.27	5.33	5.38	5.43	5.48
40	2.86	3.44	3.79	4.04	4.23	4.39	4.52	4.63	4.74	4.82	4.91	4.98	5.05	5.11	5.16	5.22	5.27	5.31	5.36
60	2.83	3.40	3.74	3.98	4.16	4.31	4.44	4.55	4.65	4.73	4.81	4.88	4.94	5.00	5.06	5.11	5.16	5.20	5.24
120	2.80	3.36	3.69	3.92	4.10	4.24	4.36	4.48	4.56	4.64	4.72	4.78	4.84	4.90	4.95	5.00	5.05	5.09	5.13
∞	2.77	3.31	3.63	3.86	4.03	4.17	4.29	4.39	4.47	4.55	4.62	4.68	4.74	4.80	4.85	4.89	4.93	4.97	5.01

continued

Upper 1% Points ($\alpha = 0.01$)

Numerator, df

Denominator, df	2	3	4	5	6	7	8	9	10	11	12	13	14	15	16	17	18	19	20
1	90.00	135.00	164.00	186.00	202.00	216.00	227.00	237.00	246.00	253.00	260.00	266.00	272.00	277.00	282.00	286.00	290.00	294.00	298.00
2	14.00	19.00	22.30	24.70	26.60	28.20	29.50	30.70	31.70	32.60	33.40	34.10	34.80	35.40	36.00	36.50	37.00	37.50	37.90
3	8.26	10.60	12.20	13.30	14.20	15.00	15.60	16.20	16.70	17.10	17.50	17.90	18.20	18.50	18.80	19.10	19.30	19.50	19.80
4	6.51	8.12	9.17	9.96	10.60	11.10	11.50	11.90	12.30	12.60	12.80	13.10	13.30	13.50	13.70	13.90	14.10	14.20	14.40
5	5.70	6.97	7.80	8.42	8.91	9.32	9.67	9.97	10.24	10.48	10.70	10.89	11.08	11.24	11.40	11.55	11.68	11.81	11.93
6	5.24	6.33	7.03	7.56	7.97	8.32	8.61	8.87	9.10	9.30	9.49	9.65	9.81	9.95	10.08	10.21	10.32	10.43	10.54
7	4.95	5.92	6.54	7.01	7.37	7.68	7.94	8.17	8.37	8.55	8.71	8.86	9.00	9.12	9.24	9.35	9.46	9.55	9.65
8	4.74	5.63	6.20	6.63	6.96	7.24	7.47	7.68	7.87	8.03	8.18	8.31	8.44	8.55	8.66	8.76	8.85	8.94	9.03
9	4.60	5.43	5.96	6.35	6.66	6.91	7.13	7.32	7.49	7.65	7.78	7.91	8.03	8.13	8.23	8.32	8.41	8.49	8.57
10	4.48	5.27	5.77	6.14	6.43	6.67	6.87	7.05	7.21	7.36	7.48	7.60	7.71	7.81	7.91	7.99	8.07	8.15	8.22
11	4.39	5.14	5.62	5.97	6.26	6.48	6.67	6.84	6.99	7.13	7.25	7.36	7.46	7.56	7.65	7.73	7.81	7.88	7.95
12	4.32	5.04	5.50	5.84	6.10	6.32	6.51	6.67	6.81	6.94	7.06	7.17	7.26	7.36	7.44	7.52	7.59	7.66	7.73
13	4.26	4.96	5.40	5.73	5.98	6.19	6.37	6.53	6.67	6.79	6.90	7.01	7.10	7.19	7.27	7.34	7.42	7.48	7.55
14	4.21	4.89	5.32	5.63	5.88	6.08	6.26	6.41	6.54	6.66	6.77	6.87	6.96	7.05	7.12	7.20	7.27	7.33	7.39
15	4.17	4.83	5.25	5.56	5.80	5.99	6.16	6.31	6.44	6.55	6.66	6.76	6.84	6.93	7.00	7.07	7.14	7.20	7.26
16	4.13	4.78	5.19	5.49	5.72	5.92	6.08	6.22	6.35	6.46	6.56	6.66	6.74	6.82	6.90	6.97	7.03	7.09	7.15
17	4.10	4.74	5.14	5.43	5.66	5.85	6.01	6.15	6.27	6.38	6.48	6.57	6.66	6.73	6.80	6.87	6.94	7.00	7.05
18	4.07	4.70	5.09	5.38	5.60	5.79	5.94	6.08	6.20	6.31	6.41	6.50	6.58	6.65	6.72	6.79	6.85	6.91	6.96
19	4.05	4.67	5.05	5.33	5.55	5.73	5.89	6.02	6.14	6.25	6.34	6.43	6.51	6.58	6.65	6.72	6.78	6.84	6.89
20	4.02	4.64	5.02	5.29	5.51	5.69	5.84	5.97	6.09	6.19	6.29	6.37	6.45	6.52	6.59	6.65	6.71	6.76	6.82
24	3.96	4.54	4.91	5.17	5.37	5.54	5.69	5.81	5.92	6.02	6.11	6.19	6.26	6.33	6.39	6.45	6.51	6.56	6.61
30	3.89	4.45	4.80	5.05	5.24	5.40	5.54	5.65	5.76	5.85	5.93	6.01	6.08	6.14	6.20	6.26	6.31	6.36	6.41
40	3.82	4.37	4.70	4.93	5.11	5.27	5.39	5.50	5.60	5.69	5.77	5.84	5.90	5.96	6.02	6.07	6.12	6.17	6.21
60	3.76	4.28	4.60	4.82	4.99	5.13	5.25	5.36	5.45	5.53	5.60	5.67	5.73	5.79	5.84	5.89	5.93	5.98	6.02
120	3.70	4.20	4.50	4.71	4.87	5.01	5.12	5.21	5.30	5.38	5.44	5.51	5.56	5.61	5.66	5.71	5.75	5.79	5.83
∞	3.64	4.12	4.40	4.60	4.76	4.88	4.99	5.08	5.16	5.23	5.29	5.35	5.40	5.45	5.49	5.54	5.57	5.61	5.65

Source: Reprinted from E. S. Pearson and H. O. Hartley, eds., Table 29 of *Biometrika Tables for Statisticians, Vol. 1*, 3rd ed., 1966, by permission of the *Biometrika* Trustees, London.

TABLE 10
Critical Values d_L and d_U of the Durbin-Watson Statistic, D (Critical Values Are One Sided)[a]

	α = 0.05										α = 0.01									
	k = 1		k = 2		k = 3		k = 4		k = 5		k = 1		k = 2		k = 3		k = 4		k = 5	
n	d_L	d_U	d_L	d_U	d_L	d_U	d_L	d_U	d_L	d_U	d_L	d_U	d_L	d_U	d_L	d_U	d_L	d_U	d_L	d_U
15	1.08	1.36	.95	1.54	.82	1.75	.69	1.97	.56	2.21	.81	1.07	.70	1.25	.59	1.46	.49	1.70	.39	1.96
16	1.10	1.37	.98	1.54	.86	1.73	.74	1.93	.62	2.15	.84	1.09	.74	1.25	.63	1.44	.53	1.66	.44	1.90
17	1.13	1.38	1.02	1.54	.90	1.71	.78	1.90	.67	2.10	.87	1.10	.77	1.25	.67	1.43	.57	1.63	.48	1.85
18	1.16	1.39	1.05	1.53	.93	1.69	.82	1.87	.71	2.06	.90	1.12	.80	1.26	.71	1.42	.61	1.60	.52	1.80
19	1.18	1.40	1.08	1.53	.97	1.68	.86	1.85	.75	2.02	.93	1.13	.83	1.26	.74	1.41	.65	1.58	.56	1.77
20	1.20	1.41	1.10	1.54	1.00	1.68	.90	1.83	.79	1.99	.95	1.15	.86	1.27	.77	1.41	.68	1.57	.60	1.74
21	1.22	1.42	1.13	1.54	1.03	1.67	.93	1.81	.83	1.96	.97	1.16	.89	1.27	.80	1.41	.72	1.55	.63	1.71
22	1.24	1.43	1.15	1.54	1.05	1.66	.96	1.80	.86	1.94	1.00	1.17	.91	1.28	.83	1.40	.75	1.54	.66	1.69
23	1.26	1.44	1.17	1.54	1.08	1.66	.99	1.79	.90	1.92	1.02	1.19	.94	1.29	.86	1.40	.77	1.53	.70	1.67
24	1.27	1.45	1.19	1.55	1.10	1.66	1.01	1.78	.93	1.90	1.04	1.20	.96	1.30	.88	1.41	.80	1.53	.72	1.66
25	1.29	1.45	1.21	1.55	1.12	1.66	1.04	1.77	.95	1.89	1.05	1.21	.98	1.30	.90	1.41	.83	1.52	.75	1.65
26	1.30	1.46	1.22	1.55	1.14	1.65	1.06	1.76	.98	1.88	1.07	1.22	1.00	1.31	.93	1.41	.85	1.52	.78	1.64
27	1.32	1.47	1.24	1.56	1.16	1.65	1.08	1.76	1.01	1.86	1.09	1.23	1.02	1.32	.95	1.41	.88	1.51	.81	1.63
28	1.33	1.48	1.26	1.56	1.18	1.65	1.10	1.75	1.03	1.85	1.10	1.24	1.04	1.32	.97	1.41	.90	1.51	.83	1.62
29	1.34	1.48	1.27	1.56	1.20	1.65	1.12	1.74	1.05	1.84	1.12	1.25	1.05	1.33	.99	1.42	.92	1.51	.85	1.61
30	1.35	1.49	1.28	1.57	1.21	1.65	1.14	1.74	1.07	1.83	1.13	1.26	1.07	1.34	1.01	1.42	.94	1.51	.88	1.61
31	1.36	1.50	1.30	1.57	1.23	1.65	1.16	1.74	1.09	1.83	1.15	1.27	1.08	1.34	1.02	1.42	.96	1.51	.90	1.60
32	1.37	1.50	1.31	1.57	1.24	1.65	1.18	1.73	1.11	1.82	1.16	1.28	1.10	1.35	1.04	1.43	.98	1.51	.92	1.60
33	1.38	1.51	1.32	1.58	1.26	1.65	1.19	1.73	1.13	1.81	1.17	1.29	1.11	1.36	1.05	1.43	1.00	1.51	.94	1.59
34	1.39	1.51	1.33	1.58	1.27	1.65	1.21	1.73	1.15	1.81	1.18	1.30	1.13	1.36	1.07	1.43	1.01	1.51	.95	1.59
35	1.40	1.52	1.34	1.58	1.28	1.65	1.22	1.73	1.16	1.80	1.19	1.31	1.14	1.37	1.08	1.44	1.03	1.51	.97	1.59
36	1.41	1.52	1.35	1.59	1.29	1.65	1.24	1.73	1.18	1.80	1.21	1.32	1.15	1.38	1.10	1.44	1.04	1.51	.99	1.59
37	1.42	1.53	1.36	1.59	1.31	1.66	1.25	1.72	1.19	1.80	1.22	1.32	1.16	1.38	1.11	1.45	1.06	1.51	1.00	1.59
38	1.43	1.54	1.37	1.59	1.32	1.66	1.26	1.72	1.21	1.79	1.23	1.33	1.18	1.39	1.12	1.45	1.07	1.52	1.02	1.58
39	1.43	1.54	1.38	1.60	1.33	1.66	1.27	1.72	1.22	1.79	1.24	1.34	1.19	1.39	1.14	1.45	1.09	1.52	1.03	1.58
40	1.44	1.54	1.39	1.60	1.34	1.66	1.29	1.72	1.23	1.79	1.25	1.34	1.20	1.40	1.15	1.46	1.10	1.52	1.05	1.58
45	1.48	1.57	1.43	1.62	1.38	1.67	1.34	1.72	1.29	1.78	1.29	1.38	1.24	1.42	1.20	1.48	1.16	1.53	1.11	1.58
50	1.50	1.59	1.46	1.63	1.42	1.67	1.38	1.72	1.34	1.77	1.32	1.40	1.28	1.45	1.24	1.49	1.20	1.54	1.16	1.59
55	1.53	1.60	1.49	1.64	1.45	1.68	1.41	1.72	1.38	1.77	1.36	1.43	1.32	1.47	1.28	1.51	1.25	1.55	1.21	1.59
60	1.55	1.62	1.51	1.65	1.48	1.69	1.44	1.73	1.41	1.77	1.38	1.45	1.35	1.48	1.32	1.52	1.28	1.56	1.25	1.60
65	1.57	1.63	1.54	1.66	1.50	1.70	1.47	1.73	1.44	1.77	1.41	1.47	1.38	1.50	1.35	1.53	1.31	1.57	1.28	1.61
70	1.58	1.64	1.55	1.67	1.52	1.70	1.49	1.74	1.46	1.77	1.43	1.49	1.40	1.52	1.37	1.55	1.34	1.58	1.31	1.61
75	1.60	1.65	1.57	1.68	1.54	1.71	1.51	1.74	1.49	1.77	1.45	1.50	1.42	1.53	1.39	1.56	1.37	1.59	1.34	1.62
80	1.61	1.66	1.59	1.69	1.56	1.72	1.53	1.74	1.51	1.77	1.47	1.52	1.44	1.54	1.42	1.57	1.39	1.60	1.36	1.62
85	1.62	1.67	1.60	1.70	1.57	1.72	1.55	1.75	1.52	1.77	1.48	1.53	1.46	1.55	1.43	1.58	1.41	1.60	1.39	1.63
90	1.63	1.68	1.61	1.70	1.59	1.73	1.57	1.75	1.54	1.78	1.50	1.54	1.47	1.56	1.45	1.59	1.43	1.61	1.41	1.64
95	1.64	1.69	1.62	1.71	1.60	1.73	1.58	1.75	1.56	1.78	1.51	1.55	1.49	1.57	1.47	1.60	1.45	1.62	1.42	1.64
100	1.65	1.69	1.63	1.72	1.61	1.74	1.59	1.76	1.57	1.78	1.52	1.56	1.50	1.58	1.48	1.60	1.46	1.63	1.44	1.65

[a] n = number of observations; k = number of independent variables.

Source: This table is reproduced from *Biometrika*, 41 (1951): pp. 173 and 175, with the permission of the *Biometrika* Trustees.

TABLE 11

Control Chart Factors

Number of Observations in Sample	d_2	d_3	D_3	D_4	A_2
2	1.128	0.853	0	3.267	1.880
3	1.693	0.888	0	2.575	1.023
4	2.059	0.880	0	2.282	0.729
5	2.326	0.864	0	2.114	0.577
6	2.534	0.848	0	2.004	0.483
7	2.704	0.833	0.076	1.924	0.419
8	2.847	0.820	0.136	1.864	0.373
9	2.970	0.808	0.184	1.816	0.337
10	3.078	0.797	0.223	1.777	0.308
11	3.173	0.787	0.256	1.744	0.285
12	3.258	0.778	0.283	1.717	0.266
13	3.336	0.770	0.307	1.693	0.249
14	3.407	0.763	0.328	1.672	0.235
15	3.472	0.756	0.347	1.653	0.223
16	3.532	0.750	0.363	1.637	0.212
17	3.588	0.744	0.378	1.622	0.203
18	3.640	0.739	0.391	1.609	0.194
19	3.689	0.733	0.404	1.596	0.187
20	3.735	0.729	0.415	1.585	0.180
21	3.778	0.724	0.425	1.575	0.173
22	3.819	0.720	0.435	1.565	0.167
23	3.858	0.716	0.443	1.557	0.162
24	3.895	0.712	0.452	1.548	0.157
25	3.931	0.708	0.459	1.541	0.153

Source: Reprinted from ASTM-STP 15D by kind permission of the American Society for Testing and Materials.

MICROSOFT EXCEL AND PHSTAT2 FAQS

Use this appendix to find answers to the most frequently asked questions about using the resources on the Student CD-ROM and using Microsoft Excel and PHStat2.

1 STUDENT CD-ROM FAQS

What textbook materials will I find on the Student CD-ROM?

You will find the Excel workbooks (as .xls files) used in examples or named in problems, the CD-ROM sections (as .PDF files), several Excel add-in workbooks (as .xla files), and programs that set up and install the Adobe Reader and PHStat2 programs on Windows PCs.

Does the Student CD-ROM contain Microsoft Excel?

No, the Student CD-ROM does not contain Microsoft Excel. If your computer did not come with Microsoft Excel or Office, you can acquire a copy of Microsoft Office and install Excel on your computer.

Can I copy the Excel workbook files to my local hard disk or other storage device?

Yes, you can, and you are encouraged to do so. If you open and use a workbook file directly from the Student CD-ROM, Microsoft Excel labels that file as being a "read-only" file and will force you to save the file under a different name if you make changes to the file.

2 GENERAL COMPUTING FAQS

My computer came with Microsoft Works. Can I use that program instead of using Microsoft Excel?

No, the spreadsheet component of Microsoft Works does not contain the functionality of Microsoft Excel and cannot be used with this text.

Do I need the latest version of Microsoft Excel in order to use this text?

No, you can use this text with all Excel versions supported by Microsoft. This includes (as of the date of the printing of this book) Excel 97, Excel 2000, Excel 2002 (sometimes identified as Excel XP), Excel 2003, and Excel 2007.

How can I determine which version of Microsoft Excel is installed on my computer?

Open Microsoft Excel. Select **Help** → **About Microsoft Excel**. In the dialog box that appears, the first line states the version number and build number as well as the names of the service release (SR) or service pack (SP) updates that have been applied.

Should I update my copy of Excel using the security updates available on the Microsoft Web site?

Absolutely yes! You should visit the Microsoft Office Web site and apply any updates that are available for your version of Excel before you begin using this text. Then, you should periodically revisit the Web site to check for new updates that may have been added since your last visit.

Can I use an Apple Mac running Mac OS on which Microsoft Excel has been installed with the Excel data files on the Student CD-ROM?

Yes, you can. However, you will *not* be able to use PHStat2, which is designed for Microsoft Windows. (There is no Mac version of PHStat2 available.)

3 MICROSOFT EXCEL FAQS

Will I need access to my original Microsoft Office/Excel CDs or DVD?

Yes, you may need to use the original program discs if the Analysis ToolPak (referred to as the "ToolPak" in this book) has not been installed on your system.

How can I tell if the ToolPak has been installed? What Microsoft Office security settings should I use? How do I change Office security settings?

The answers to these related questions are discussed as part of Section E6, "Add-ins: Making Things Easier for You," in the introductory chapter.

Are there any special procedures for using the Visual Explorations add-in workbook (Visual Explorations.xla)?

No, you can open and immediately use this workbook, provided that you have adjusted your Office security settings using the Section E6 instructions in the introductory chapter. With the wrong security settings in effect, Visual Explorations (and PHStat2, also) will not open in Excel.

In Excel 97–2003, how can I turn toolbars such as the Standard and Formatting toolbars shown in Figure E1, on and off?

Select **View** → **Toolbars** and select the toolbars you want displayed.

For Excel 2007, how can I configure the Excel window to look similar to Figure E2?

Right-click the title bar of the Excel 2007 window and on the shortcut menu that appears, uncheck, if checked, **Minimize the Ribbon**. You can also review this setting by clicking the drop-down arrow to the immediate right of the Quick Access toolbar.

For Excel 97–2003, how can I specify the custom settings that you recommend?

First select **Tools → Customize**. In the Customize dialog box, clear (uncheck) the **Menus show recently used commands first** check box if it is checked and click the **Close** button. Then select **Tools → Options**. In the Options dialog box, click the **Calculation** tab and verify that the **Automatic** option button of the Calculation group has been selected. Click the **Edit** tab and verify that all check boxes *except* the **Fixed decimal, Provide feedback with Animation**, and **Enable automatic percent entry** have been selected. (Excel 97 does not contain an Automatic percent entry check box.) Click the **General** tab and verify that the **R1C1 reference style** check box is cleared (that is, unchecked) and, if using Excel 97, check the **Macro virus protection** check box. Enter **3** as the number of **Sheets in new workbook**, select **Arial** from the **Standard font** list box, and select **10** from the **Size** drop-down list box. Click **OK** to finish the customization.

For Excel 2007, how can I specify the custom settings that you recommend?

First, click **Office Button** and then click **Excel Options**. In the left panel of Excel Options, click **Formulas**. In the Formulas right pane, click **Automatic** under **Workbook Calculation** and verify that all check boxes are checked except **Enable iterative calculation, R1C1 reference style**, and **Formulas referring to cells**. Click **OK** to finish the customization.

4 PHSTAT2 FAQS

What is PHStat2?

PHStat2 is software that makes operating Microsoft Excel as distraction free as possible. As a student studying statistics, you can focus mainly on learning statistics and not worry about having to fully master Excel first. When PHStat2 is combined with the Analysis ToolPak add-in, just about all statistical methods taught in an introductory statistics course can be illustrated using Microsoft Excel.

I do not want to use an add-in that will not be available in my business environment. Any comments?

The introductory chapter talks about these issues in detail. To summarize those pages, PHStat2 helps you learn Microsoft Excel, and using PHStat2 will not leave you any less equipped to work with Microsoft Excel in a setting where it is not available.

What do I need to do in order to begin using PHStat2?

You need to run the PHStat2 setup program (setup.exe) that is on the Student CD-ROM. If you are using Windows 2000, Windows XP, or Windows Vista, you must have logged in to Windows using an account that has administrator or software-installing privileges. (Student and faculty accounts to log in to networked computers in academic settings typically do not have this privilege. If you have such an account, ask your network or lab technician for assistance.)

What are the technical requirements for setting up and adding PHStat2 to my system?

If your system can run Microsoft Excel, it can also run PHStat2. You need approximately 10 MB hard disk free space during the setup process and up to 3 MB hard disk space after program setup.

Are updates to PHStat2 available?

Yes, minor updates to resolve issues as they are identified are available for free download from the PHStat2 Web site (**www.prenhall.com/phstat**). When you visit that Web site, link to the page that applies to your version of PHStat2 (the Student CD-ROM contains Version 2.7).

How can I identify which version of PHStat2 I have?

Open Microsoft Excel with PHStat2 and select **Help for PHStat** from the PHStat menu. A dialog box will display your current XLA and DLL version numbers. The XLA version number identifies the version of PHStat2 you have.

Where can I get help setting up PHStat2?

First, carefully review the Student CD-ROM readme file for PHStat2. If your problem is unresolved, visit the PHStat2 Web site for further information. If your problem is still unresolved, contact Pearson Education technical support by following the appropriate link on the PHStat2 Web site.

5 EXCEL 2007 ISSUES FAQS

I do not see the menu for an add-in workbook that I opened, where is it?

Unlike earlier versions of Excel that allowed add-ins to add menus to the menu bar, Excel 2007 places all add-in menus under the Add-ins tab. If you click Add-ins, you find the menus of all properly loaded add-ins.

What does "Compatibility Mode" mean?

When you see "Compatibility Mode" in the title bar, Excel 2007 is telling you that you are using a workbook compatible with earlier Excel versions. When you save such a workbook, Excel 2007 will automatically use the .xls file format of earlier versions.

How can I update an older workbook to the Excel 2007 .xlsx format?

The simplest way is to open the workbook file and click **Office Button** ➔ **Convert**. Then save your file (click **Office Button** ➔ **Save**).

You can also open the workbook file and click **Office Button** ➔ **Save As** and select **Excel Workbook** (*.xlsx) from the **Save as type** list in the Save As dialog box.

Index